The XML Handbook™ Second Edition

©2000 The XML Handbook™

The Charles F. Goldfarb Series on Open Information Management

"Open Information Management" (OIM) means managing information so that it is open to processing by any program, not just the program that created it. That extends even to application programs not conceived of at the time the information was created.

OIM is based on the principle of data independence: data should be stored in computers in non-proprietary, genuinely standardized representations. And that applies even when the data is the content of a document. Its representation should distinguish the innate information from the proprietary codes of document processing programs and the artifacts of particular presentation styles.

Business data bases—which rigorously separate the real data from the input forms and output reports—achieved data independence decades ago. But documents, unlike business data, have historically been created in the context of a particular output presentation style. So for document data, independence was largely unachievable until recently.

That is doubly unfortunate. It is unfortunate because documents are a far more significant repository of humanity's information. And documents can contain significantly richer information structures than data bases.

It is also unfortunate because the need for OIM of documents is greater now than ever. The demands of "repurposing" require that information be deliverable in multiple formats: paper-based, online, multimedia, hypermedia. And information must now be delivered through multiple channels: traditional bookstores and libraries, the World Wide Web, corporate intranets and extranets. In the latter modes, what starts as data base data may become a document for browsing, but then may need to be reused by the reader as data.

Fortunately, in the past ten years a technology has emerged that extends to documents the data base's capacity for data independence. And it does so without the data base's restrictions on structural freedom. That technology is the "Standard Generalized Markup Language" (SGML), an official International Standard (ISO 8879) that has been adopted by the world's largest producers of documents and by the World Wide Web.

With SGML, organizations in government, aerospace, airlines, automotive, electronics, computers, and publishing (to name a few) have freed their documents from hostage relationships to processing software. SGML coexists with graphics, multimedia and other data standards needed for OIM and acts as the framework that relates objects in the other formats to one another and to SGML documents.

The World Wide Web's HTML and XML are both based on SGML. HTML is a particular, though very general, application of SGML, like those for the above industries. There is a limited set of markup tags that can be used with HTML. XML, in contrast, is a simplified subset of SGML facilities that, like full SGML, can be used with any set of tags. You can literally create your own markup language with XML.

As the enabling standard for OIM of documents, the SGML family of standards necessarily plays a leading role in this series. We provide tutorials on SGML, XML, and other key standards and the techniques for applying them. Our books vary in technical intensity from programming techniques for software developers to the business justification of OIM for enterprise executives. We share the practical experience of organizations and individuals who have applied the techniques of OIM in environments ranging from immense industrial publishing projects to websites of all sizes.

Our authors are expert practitioners in their subject matter, not writers hired to cover a "hot" topic. They bring insight and understanding that can only come from real-world experience. Moreover, they practice what they preach about standardization. Their books share a common standards-based vocabulary. In this way, knowledge gained from one book in the series is directly applicable when reading another, or the standards themselves. This is just one of the ways in

©2000 The XML Handbook™

which we strive for the utmost technical accuracy and consistency with the OIM standards.

And we also strive for a sense of excitement and fun. After all, the challenge of OIM—preserving information from the ravages of technology while exploiting its benefits—is one of the great intellectual adventures of our age. I'm sure you'll find this series to be a knowledgable and reliable guide on that adventure.

About the Series Editor

Dr. Charles F. Goldfarb invented the SGML language in 1974 and later led the team that developed it into the International Standard on which both HTML and XML are based. He serves as editor of the Standard (ISO 8879) and as a consultant to developers of SGML and XML applications and products. He is based in Saratoga, CA.

About the Series Logo

The rebus is an ancient literary tradition, dating from 16th century Picardy, and is especially appropriate to a series involving fine distinctions between things and the words that describe them. For the logo, Andrew Goldfarb incorporated a rebus of the series name within a stylized SGML/XML comment declaration.

The Charles F. Goldfarb Series on Open Information Management

As XML is a subset of SGML, the Series List is categorized to show the degree to which a title applies to XML. "XML Titles" are those that discuss XML explicitly and may also cover full SGML. "SGML Titles" do not mention XML per se, but the principles covered may apply to XML. A reader's guide to the complete series can be found beginning on page 986.

XML Titles

Goldfarb, Pepper, and Ensign
- SGML Buyer's Guide™: Choosing the Right XML and SGML Products and Services

Megginson
- Structuring XML Documents

Leventhal, Lewis, and Fuchs
- Designing XML Internet Applications

DuCharme
- XML: The Annotated Specification

Jelliffe
- The XML and SGML Cookbook: Recipes for Structured Information

McGrath
- XML by Example: Building E-commerce Applications

Goldfarb and Prescod
- The XML Handbook™ Second Edition

SGML Titles

Ensign
- $GML: The Billion Dollar Secret

Rubinsky and Maloney
- SGML on the Web: Small Steps Beyond HTML

McGrath
- ParseMe.1st: SGML for Software Developers

Ducharme
- SGML CD

General Titles

Martin
- TOP SECRET Intranet: How U.S. Intelligence Built Intelink—The World's Largest, Most Secure Network

©2000 The XML Handbook™

The XML Handbook™

Second Edition

Charles F. Goldfarb
Paul Prescod

Prentice Hall PTR, Upper Saddle River, NJ 07458
http://www.phptr.com

©2000 The XML Handbook™

Editorial/Production Supervision: *Camille Trentacoste*
Acquisitions Editor: *Mark L. Taub*
Editorial Assistant: *Michael Fredette*
Marketing Manager: *Dan Rush*
Manufacturing Manager: *Alexis R. Heydt*
Cover Design: *Anthony Gemmellaro*
Cover Design Direction: *Jerry Votta*
Series Design: *Gail Cocker-Bogusz*

© 2000 Charles F. Goldfarb
Published by Prentice Hall PTR
Prentice-Hall, Inc.
Upper Saddle River, NJ 07458

Prentice Hall books are widely used by corporations and government agencies for training, marketing, and resale.

The publisher offers discounts on this book when ordered in bulk quantities. For more information, contact: Corporate Sales Department, Phone: 800-382-3419; Fax: 201-236-7141; E-mail: corpsales@prenhall.com; or write: Prentice Hall PTR, Corp. Sales Dept., One Lake Street, Upper Saddle River, NJ 07458.

All rights reserved. No part of this book may be reproduced, in any form or by any means, without permission in writing from the publisher.

Printed in the United States of America

10 9 8 7 6 5 4 3

ISBN 0-13-014714-1

Prentice-Hall International (UK) Limited, London
Prentice-Hall of Australia Pty. Limited, Sydney
Prentice-Hall Canada Inc., Toronto
Prentice-Hall Hispanoamericana, S.A., Mexico
Prentice-Hall of India Private Limited, New Delhi
Prentice-Hall of Japan, Inc., Tokyo
Simon & Schuster Asia Pte. Ltd., Singapore
Editora Prentice-Hall do Brasil, Ltda., Rio de Janeiro

Adobe, the Adobe logo, Acrobat, FrameMaker, and PostScript are trademarks of Adobe Systems Incorporated. Microsoft and Windows are registered trademarks of Microsoft Corporation in the U.S. and other countries. DynaText, DynaBase, Inso, and the Inso Logo are trademarks or registered trademarks of Inso Corporation. Corel, WordPerfect, and the "Go further" logo are registered trademarks of Corel Corporation or Corel Corporation Limited. Oracle is a registered trademark, and Oracle8i is a trademark of Oracle Corporation. IBM and alphaWorks are registered trademarks of IBM Corporation in the U.S. and other countries.

Sun, Sun Microsystems, Java and all Java-based marks, Enterprise JavaBeans, JDBC, JavaServer Pages, and the Sun Logo are trademarks or registered trademarks of Sun Microsystems, Inc. in the U.S. and other countries. The authors and publisher of this book are independent of Sun Microsystems.

CSS, DOM, MathML, RDF, SMIL, SVG, W3C, WAI, XHTML, XML, and XSL are trademarks (one or more of which are registered in numerous countries) of the World Wide Web Consortium; marks of W3C are registered and held by its host institutions MIT, INRIA, and Keio.

The XML Handbook, XML Handbook Jargon Demystifier, HARP, and SGML Buyer's Guide are trademarks of Charles F. Goldfarb.

Names such as company names, trade names, font names, service names, and product names appearing in this book may be registered or unregistered trademarks or service marks, whether or not identified as such. All such names and all registered and unregistered trademarks, service marks, and logos appearing in this book or on its cover are used for identification purposes only and are the property of their respective owners.

Series logo by Andrew Goldfarb for EyeTech Graphics, copyright ©1996 Andrew Goldfarb.

Series foreword copyright ©1996, 1997, 1998, 1999 Charles F. Goldfarb.

This book and its accompanying CD-ROM contain statements regarding Wavo Corporation that constitute forward-looking statements, which may involve risks and uncertainties. Actual results could differ materially from such forward-looking statements as a result of a variety of factors, including, but not limited to, technology changes, competitive developments, industry and market acceptance of new products and services, and risk factors listed from time to time in Wavo Corporation's SEC filings.

The information in the sample news article entitled "Kansas gets $5.7 Million Relief" was taken from a White House press release dated May 6, 1999. The accuracy of the information in the sample has not been verified and is provided for illustrative purposes only.

Excerpts from International Standards are copyrighted by the International Organization for Standardization, and are included with the kind permission of the copyright owner. Complete copies of International Standards can be obtained from the national member body of ISO in your country, or contact ISO, case postale 56, CH-1211 Geneva 20, Switzerland.

Excerpts from World Wide Web Consortium documents, including but not limited to those listed below, are included in accordance with the W3C IPR Document Notice, http://www.w3.org/Consortium/Legal/copyright-documents.html. Copyright © World Wide Web Consortium, (Massachusetts Institute of Technology, Institut National de Recherche en Informatique et en Automatique, Keio University). All Rights Reserved.

Extensible Markup Language (XML) 1.0, http://www.w3.org/TR/REC-xml, W3C Recommendation 10-February-1998

Extensible Linking Language (XLink), http://www.w3.org/TR/WD-xlink, W3C Working Draft 26-July-1999

XML Pointer Language (XPointer), http://www.w3.org/TR/WD-xptr, W3C Working Draft 9-July-1999

The development of this book was partly subsidized by Sponsors, who provided both financial support and expert assistance in preparing the initial draft of the text identified with their names and in reviewing the edited version at varying stages of completion. However, as the Authors exercised final editorial control over the book, the Sponsors are not responsible for errors that may have been introduced during that process. Opinions expressed in this book are those of the Authors and are not necessarily those of the Series Editor, Sponsors, or Publisher.

This book, and the CD-ROM included with it, contain software and descriptive materials provided by (or adapted from materials made publicly available by) product developers, vendors, and service providers. Said software and materials have not been reviewed, edited, or tested, and neither the Authors, Contributors, Series Editor, Publisher, Sponsors, or other parties connected with this book are responsible for their accuracy or reliability. Readers are warned that they use said software and materials at their own risk, and are urged to test the software and confirm the validity of the information prior to use.

To Linda – With love, awe, and gratitude.

Charles F. Goldfarb

For Lilia – Your support makes it possible and your love makes it worthwhile.

Paul Prescod

©2000 THE XML HANDBOOK™

Overview

Contents

Preface

I wanted to call this the Millennium Edition of The XML Handbook.

Not because of the Year 2000, but because XML is ushering in a new millennium of wonderful services for Web users and amazing new opportunities for website developers and businesses.

HTML – the HyperText Markup Language – made the Web the world's library. Now its sibling, XML – the Extensible Markup Language – is making the Web the world's commercial and financial hub.

In the process, the Web is becoming much more than a static library. Increasingly, users are accessing the Web for "Web pages" that aren't actually on the shelves. Instead, the pages are generated dynamically from information available to the Web server. That information can come from databases on the Web server, from the site owner's enterprise databases, or even from other websites.

And that dynamic information needn't be served up raw. It can be analyzed, extracted, sorted, styled, and customized to create a personalized Web experience for the end-user. For this kind of power and flexibility, XML is the markup language of choice.

You can see why by comparing XML and HTML. Both are based on SGML – the International Standard for structured information – but look at the difference:

In HTML:

```
<p>P200 Laptop
<br>Friendly Computer Shop
<br>$1438
```

In XML:

```
<product>
<model>P200 Laptop</model>
<dealer>Friendly Computer Shop</dealer>
<price>$1438</price>
</product>
```

Both of these may appear the same in your browser, but the XML data is *smart* data. HTML tells how the data should *look*, but XML tells you what it *means.*

With XML, your browser knows there is a product, and it knows the model, dealer, and price. From a group of these it can show you the cheapest product or closest dealer without going back to the server.

Unlike HTML, with XML you create your own tags, so they describe exactly what you need to know. Because of that, your client-side applications can access data sources anywhere on the Web, in any format. New "middle-tier" servers sit between the data sources and the client, translating everything into your own task-specific XML.

But XML data isn't just smart data, it's also a smart document. That means when you display the information, the model name can be a different font from the dealer name, and the lowest price can be highlighted in green. Unlike HTML, where text is just text to be rendered in a uniform way, with XML text is smart, so it can control the rendition.

And you don't have to decide whether your information is data or documents; in XML, it is always both at once. You can do data processing or document processing or both at the same time.

With that kind of flexibility, it's no wonder that we're starting to see a Brave New Web of smart, structured information. Your broker sends your account data to Quicken using XML. Your "push" technology channel definitions are in XML. Everything from math to multimedia, chemistry to CommerceNet, is using XML or is preparing to start.

You should be too!

Welcome to the Brave New XML Web.

What about SGML?

This book is about XML. You won't find feature comparisons to SGML, or footnotes with nerdy observations like "the XML empty-element tag does not contradict the rule that every element has a start-tag and an end-tag because, in SGML terms, it is actually a start-tag followed immediately by a null end-tag".[1]

Nevertheless, for readers who use SGML, it is worth addressing the question of how XML and SGML relate. There has been a lot of speculation about this.

Some claim that XML will replace SGML because there will be so much free and low-cost software. Others assert that XML users, like HTML users before them, will discover that they need more of SGML and will eventually migrate to the full standard.

Both assertions are nonsense ... XML and SGML don't even compete.

XML is a simplified subset of SGML. The subsetting was optimized for the Web environment, which implies data-processing-oriented (rather than publishing-oriented), short life-span (in fact, usually dynamically-generated) information. The vast majority of XML documents will be created by computer programs and processed by other programs, then destroyed. Humans will never see them.

Eliot Kimber, who was a member of both the XML and SGML standards committees, says:

> There are certain use domains for which XML is simply not sufficient and where you need the additional features of SGML. These applications tend to be very large scale and of long term; e.g., aircraft maintenance information, government regulations, power plant documentation, etc.
>
> Any one of them might involve a larger volume of information than the entire use of XML on the Web. A single model of commercial aircraft, for example, requires some four million unique pages of documentation that must be revised and republished quarterly. Multiply that by the number of models produced by companies like Airbus and Boeing and you get a feel for the scale involved.

---

1. Well, yes, I did just make that nerdy observation, but it wasn't a footnote, was it?

I agree with Eliot. I invented SGML, I'm proud of it, and I'm awed that such a staggering volume of the world's mission-critical information is represented in it.

I'm thrilled that it has been such an enabler of the Web that the Society for Technical Communication awarded joint Honorary Fellowships to Tim Berners-Lee and myself in recognition of the synergy.

But I'm also proud of XML. I'm proud of my friend Jon Bosak who made it happen, and I'm excited that the World Wide Web is becoming XML-based.

If you are new to XML, don't worry about any of this. All you need to know is that the XML subset of SGML has been in use for a decade or more, so you can trust it.

SGML still keeps the airplanes flying, the nuclear plants operating safely, and the defense departments in a state of readiness. You should look into it if you produce documents on the scale of an Airbus or Boeing. For the rest of us, there's XML.

About our sponsors

With all the buzz surrounding a hot technology like XML, it can be tough for a newcomer to distinguish the solid projects and realistic applications from the fluff and the fantasies. It is tough for authors as well, to keep track of all that is happening in the brief time we can steal from our day jobs.

The solution to both problems was to seek support and expert help from our friends in the industry. We know the leading companies in the XML arena and knew they had experience with both proven and leading-edge applications and products.

In the usual way of doing things, had we years to write this book, we would have interviewed each company to learn about its products and/or application experiences, written the chapters, asked the companies to review them, etc., and gone on to the next company. To save time and improve accuracy, we engaged in parallel processing. I spoke with the sponsors, agreed on subject matter for their chapters, and asked them to write the first draft.

All sponsored chapters are identified with the name of the sponsor, and sometimes with the names of the experts who prepared the original text. I used their materials as though they were my own first drafts, editing, rewriting, deleting, and augmenting as necessary to achieve my objective for the chapter in the context of the book, with consistent terminology and an objective factual style. I'd like to take this opportunity to thank these experts publicly for being so generous with their time and knowledge.

The sponsorship program was directed by Linda Burman, the president of L. A. Burman Associates, a consulting company that provides marketing and business development services to the XML and SGML industries.

We are grateful to our sponsors just as we are grateful to you, our readers. Both of you together make it possible for the *XML Handbook* to exist. In the interests of everyone, we make our own editorial decisions and we don't recommend or endorse any product or service offerings over any others.

Our twenty-seven sponsors are:

- Adobe Systems Incorporated, `http://www.adobe.com`
- Arbortext, Inc., `http://www.arbortext.com`
- Bluestone Software, `http://www.bluestone.com`
- Corel, `http://www.corel.com`
- DataChannel, `http://www.datachannel.com`
- Data Conversion Laboratory, `http://www.dclab.com`
- the e-content company, `http://www.xmlecontent.com`
- Enigma, Inc., `http://www.enigma.com`
- Excosoft, `http://www.excosoft.com`
- Extensibility, `http://www.extensibility.com`
- Frank Russell Company, `http://www.russell.com`
- IBM Corporation, `http://www.ibm.com/xml`
- Inso Corporation, `http://www.inso.com`
- Microsoft, `http://msdn.microsoft.com/xml`
- Object Design, `http://www.objectdesign.com/excelon`
- Oracle Corporation, `http://www.oracle.com/xml`
- Reed Technology, `http://www.reedtech.com`
- RivCom, `http://www.rivcom.com`
- Sequoia Software Corporation, `http://www.sequoiasw.com`
- SGML Technologies Group, `http://www.sgmltech.com`
- STEP Electronic Publishing Solutions, `http://www.step.de`
- Sun Microsystems, `http://java.sun.com/xml`
- TANNER Dokuments, `http://www.tanner.de`
- Wavo, `http://www.wavo.com`
- webMethods, `http://www.webmethods.com`
- XMLSolutions Corporation, `http://www.xmls.com`
- Xyvision Enterprise Solutions, `http://www.xyenterprise.com`

How to use this book

The XML Handbook has thirteen parts, consisting of 66 chapters, that we intend for you to read in order.

Well, if authors didn't have dreams they wouldn't be authors.

In reality, we know that you, our readers, have diverse professional and technical backgrounds and won't all take the same route through a book this large and wide-ranging. Here are some hints for planning your trip.

In addition to the Table of Contents, you can get the best feel for the subject matter by reading the introductions to each part. They are less than a page and usually epitomize the subject area of the part in addition to introducing the chapters within it.

Part One contains introductory discussions and establishes the terminology used in the remainder of the book. Please read it first.

Parts Two through Ten cover different application domains. The chapters are application discussions, case studies, and tool discussions. You can read them with only the preceding parts (especially Part One) as background, although technical readers may want to complete the tutorials first.[1]

Parts Eleven and Twelve are the tutorials. We strove to keep them friendly and understandable for readers without a background in subjects not covered in this book. Chapters whose subject matter thwarted that goal are labeled as being a tad tougher so you will know what to expect, but not to discourage you from reading them.

Part Thirteen is a guide to the CD-ROM and to other XML-related books in this series.

Acknowledgments

The principal acknowledgment in a book of this nature has to be to the people who created the subject matter. In this case, I take special pleasure in the fact that all of them are friends and colleagues of long standing in the SGML community.

Tim Bray and C. Michael Sperberg-McQueen were the original editors of the XML specification, later joined by Jean Paoli. Dan Connolly put the

1. The chapters in these parts are illustrated by their sponsors' experiences and products. The organization into parts only classifies the subject matter of the chapters; there is no attempt to classify the products. A tool described in the content management part, for example, might also be an appropriate choice for publishing or information serving.

project on the W3C "todo list", got it started, and shepherded it through the approval process.

But all of them agree that, if a single person is to be thanked for XML, it is Jon Bosak. Jon not only sparked the original ideas and recruited the team, but organized and chaired the W3C XML Working Group.

As Tim put it: "Without Jon, XML wouldn't have happened. He was the prime mover."

Regarding the content of the book, Paul and I would like to thank Jean Paoli, Jon Bosak, G. Ken Holman, Bob DuCharme, Eliot Kimber, Andy Goldfarb, Lars Marius Garshol, and Steve Newcomb for contributing great material; Bryan Bell, inventor of MIDI and document system architect extraordinaire, for his advice and support; Steve Pepper and Bob DuCharme for talent-spotting; and John Bedunah for his insights into XSL.

We also thank Lilia Prescod, Thea Prescod, and Linda Goldfarb for serving as our useability test laboratory. That means they read lots of chapters and complained until we made them clear enough.

Prentice Hall PTR uses Adobe FrameMaker and other Adobe graphic arts and publishing software to produce the books in my series. We thank the late Lani Hajagos of Adobe for providing Paul and me with copies and, more importantly, for her encouraging support and suggestions when I first proposed this book. Her untimely passing was deeply felt by the markup language community, who greatly valued her friendship and counsel.

Paul and I designed, and Paul implemented, an SGML-based production system for the book. It uses James Clark's Jade DSSSL processor, FrameMaker+SGML, and some ingenious FrameMaker plug-ins designed and implemented by Doug Yagaloff of Caxton, Inc. We thank Doug, and also Randy Kelley, for their wizard-level FrameMaker consulting advice.

But a great production system is nothing without a great Production Editor. Camille Trentacoste meets that job description with a vengeance. Her rare combination of artistic sensibility and technical skill (meaning she could deal with Windows and Unix even though she prefers to work on a Mac) was perfect for bridging the gap between the technology-obsessed authors and the Prentice-Hall production team. Her 1000 kilowatt personality and wicked sense of humor didn't hurt one bit either![1]

This was my third project in which Linda Burman served as marketing consultant and Sponsorship Director. I thank her – again – for her sage counsel and always cheerful encouragement.

1. And she tought me to fish!

My personal thanks, also, to Mark Taub, now an Editor-in-Chief at Prentice Hall PTR, for his help, encouragement, and management of the project.

I'd also like to acknowledge a major debt to two people who have supported and encouraged my work for the last five years – since the very day in 1994 that I retired from IBM to become an independent consultant. Yasufumi Toyoshima and Charles Brauer, of Fujitsu Network Communications, epitomize vision and leadership in technical management. They saw the potential for a Web-friendly, grammatically simple SGML subset long before myself or anyone else I know.

As the senior author, I gave myself the preface to write. I'm senior because Paul's folks were conceiving him about the same time that I was conceiving SGML. (In return, Paul got to write the history chapter, because for him it really is history.)

This gives me the opportunity to thank Paul publicly for the tremendous reservoir of talent, energy, and good humor that he brought to the project. The book benefitted not just from his XML knowledge and fine writing skills, but from his expertise in SGML, Jade, and FrameMaker that enabled us to automate the production of the book (with the previously acknowledged help from our friends).

Thanks, Paul.

Charles F. Goldfarb
Saratoga, CA
September 7, 1999

Foreword

XML everywhere

By Jean Paoli
Product Unit Manager, XML Technologies
Microsoft Corporation
Co-editor of the XML Recommendation

When HTML came onto the scene it sparked a publishing phenomenon. Ordinary people everywhere began to publish documents on the Web. Presentation on the Web became a topic of conversation not just within the computer industry, but within coffeehouses. Overnight, it seemed as though everyone had a Web page.

I see the same phenomenon happening today with XML. Where data was once a mysterious binary blob, it has now become something ordinary people can read and author because it's text. With XML, ordinary people have the ability to craft their own data, the ability to shape and control data. The significance of this shift is difficult to overstate, for not only does it mean that more people can access data, but that there will undoubtedly be more data to access. We are on the verge of a data explosion. One ignited by XML.

By infusing the Web with data, XML makes the Web a better place for people to interact, to do business. XML allows us to do more precise searches, deliver software components, describe such things as collections of

Web pages and electronic commerce transactions, and much more. XML is changing not only the way we think about data, but the way we think about the Web.

And by doing so, it's changing the way we think about the traditional desktop application. I have already witnessed the impact of XML on all types of applications from word processors and spreadsheets to database managers and email. More and more, such applications are reaching out to the Web, tapping into the power of the Web, and it is XML that is enabling them to do so. Gone are the days of the isolated, incompatible application. Here are the days of universal access and shared data.

I joined Microsoft in the summer of 1996 with great faith in the Standard Generalized Markup Language (SGML) and a dream that its potential might one day be realized. As soon as I arrived at Microsoft, Jon Bosak of Sun Microsystems and I began discussing the possibility of creating an XML standard. Jon shared my enthusiasm for a markup language such as XML, understanding what it could mean to Web communication.

My goal in designing an XML standard was to produce a very simple markup language with as few abstractions as possible. Microsoft's success is due in no small part to its ability to develop products with mass-market appeal. It is this mass-market appeal that I wanted to bring to XML. Together with Jon and other long-time friends from the SGML world, C.M. Sperberg-McQueen, James Clark, Tim Bray, Steve DeRose, Eve Maler, Eliot Kimber, Dave Hollander, Makoto Murata, and Peter Sharpe, I co-designed the XML specification at the World Wide Web Consortium (W3C). This specification, I believe, reflects my original goals.

It was truly an exciting time. For years, we had all been part of a maverick band of text markup enthusiasts, singing its praises every chance we had, and before us was an opportunity to bring XML into the mainstream, maybe even into the operating system. At last, we were getting our chance to tell the World of the thing we had been so crazy about for all this time.

By the fall of 1996, many groups inside Microsoft, including Office, the Site Server Electronic Commerce Edition, the Data Access Group, to cite a few, were searching for an open format to enable interoperability on the Web. It was then that I began working with the managers of Internet Explorer 4, with the passionate Adam Bosworth, with Andrew Layman, with Thomas Reardon, to define the Channel Definition Format (CDF). CDF, the first major application of XML on the Web, became an immediate and incredible success, and XML started catching on like wildfire across the Web.

I remember those weeks and months that followed as a time where it seemed that every day another new group within Microsoft began coding applications using XML. Developers, left and right, were turning on to XML. They frenetically began to develop applications using XML, because XML gave them what they wanted: an easy-to-parse syntax for representing data. This flurry of activity was so great that by October of 1997, almost a year after my arrival at Microsoft, Chairman Bill Gates announced XML as "a breakthrough technology." Since that time we've never looked back.

This book is an excellent starting point where you can learn and experiment with XML. As the inventor of SGML, Dr. Charles F. Goldfarb is one of the most respected authorities on structured information. Charles has had a very direct influence on XML, as XML is a true subset of SGML, and he clearly understands the impact that XML will have on the world of data-driven, Web-based applications.

Charles and I share a common vision, that the most valuable asset for the user or for a corporation, namely the data, can be openly represented in a simple, flexible, and human-readable form. That it can easily travel from server to server, from server to client, and from application to application, fostering universal communication with anyone, anywhere. This vision can now be realized through XML.

Enjoy the book!

Redmond, April 24, 1998
Jean Paoli
Product Unit Manager, XML Technologies
Microsoft Corporation
Co-editor of the XML Recommendation

Prolog

XML: Looking back and looking forward

By Jon Bosak

XML Architect, Sun Microsystems

Chair, W3C XML Coordination Group

The World Wide Web is a medium that gained acceptance where earlier attempts had failed by providing the right combination of simplicity and fault tolerance. Now it faces the job of reinventing itself as a scalable, industrial-strength infrastructure strong enough to carry both human communication and electronic commerce into the new century. The story of XML and its companion standards is the story of that reinvention.

XML arose from the recognition that key components of the original Web – HTML tagging, simple hypertext linking, and hardcoded presentation – would not scale up to meet future needs. Those of us involved in industrial-strength SGML-based electronic publishing before the Web came into existence had learned the hard way that nothing substantially less powerful than SGML would work over the long run.

We also realized that any advanced solution not based on SGML – the only formal International Standard that addresses this problem – would likely employ a proprietary binary format that would require special proprietary tools. XML is the creation of a small group of SGML experts who were motivated in large part by a desire to ensure that the Web of the future would not be dominated by standards controlled by a single vendor or nation. Its adoption by the world's largest computer software and hardware companies marks a significant turning point in the struggle to keep data free.

XML is a tremendous victory for open standards. It is freely extensible, imposing no limits on the ability of users to define markup in any combination of the world's major natural languages; it is character-based and human-readable, which means that XML documents can be maintained using even the most primitive text processing tools; and it is relatively easy to implement, so users can look forward to an abundance of inexpensive commercial XML processing tools and an ever-growing number of free ones.

Most importantly, XML provides a standard framework for making agreements about communication. It allows people sharing a common data exchange problem to work out an open solution to that problem – without interference from third parties, without dependence on large software vendors, without bindings to specific tools, without language restrictions, and in a way that lets anyone with a similar problem use the same solution. While the task of defining such standards within each industry and user community still lies before us, the framework for doing so is now in place.

Nevertheless, we must not lose sight of the larger goal. True interoperability requires not just interoperable syntax, but interoperable semantics. This ultimate goal cannot be achieved with anything less than the standardization of meaning itself, at least in those areas in which we wish to achieve automatic interoperability.

The coming standardization of domain-specific element types and attributes will establish the semantically meaningful labeling of content in particular industries, but it cannot address the behavioral aspect. While interoperable behavior can always be specified using a platform-neutral programming language like Java, such a powerful tool is often disproportionate to simple tasks. Just as we cannot ask our airline pilots to be aircraft engineers, we cannot require every creator of meaning to also be a programmer.

In the areas of hypermedia linking and presentation of rendered data, we can and must establish standardized techniques for behavioral specification that are declarative enough to be usable by nonprogrammers and yet powerful enough to get the job done in industrial contexts of unlimited scale. In both areas we are being held back by early superficial successes with simple mechanisms that are easy to learn but place unacceptable limits on what can be done, just as the early success of HTML held back the adoption of extensible markup.

The parallels to be drawn among the recent histories of markup, linking, and presentation are striking.

- In all three cases, early visionaries went much farther than the majority of adopters were ready to follow.
- In all three cases, breakthroughs in public consciousness were made by relative newcomers whose major contribution was to radically simplify the early, more advanced techniques in a way that made them accessible to the first wave of implementors.
- In all three cases, the original work is now being reconsidered, as those who understand the essential coherence of the original, larger view labor patiently to reconstruct mechanisms adequate for the demands of the future.
- And in all three cases, the biggest roadblock to deployment of the more advanced solutions is the success of the limited ones that got the Web off the ground.

I have no doubt that we will eventually succeed in replacing today's anemic realization of hypertext with something closer to the ideal articulated by the visionaries of the 1960s and worked out in the research projects of the 1970s and 1980s. I also have no doubt that we will eventually achieve interoperability of formatting behavior in a way that preserves the delivery of textual semantics to Web clients while simultaneously enabling the level of typographic control associated with printed newspaper and magazine publishing. My certainty is based not on a logical analysis of the future but simply on the same from-the-trenches understanding of basic needs that motivated me to begin the XML project in the first place.

What is not clear is how long it will take for Web implementors to realize the limitations of their existing conceptions of hyperlinking and style specification in the way that the more advanced among them now understand the limitations of HTML markup. But whether it takes two years or ten, the next steps are as necessary as was the first step to XML.

The XML Handbook can help us take those steps.

Los Altos, August 1999
Jon Bosak
XML Architect, Sun Microsystems
Chair, W3C XML Coordination Group

The Who, What, and Why of XML

- Why XML?
- Just enough XML
- Where is XML going?
- XML in the real world
- The XML Jargon Demystifier

©2000 THE XML HANDBOOK™

Part One

This part is the essential introduction to everything else in the book, which is why we named it Part One! Please read it from beginning to end because each chapter builds on the preceding ones.

For example, the "Just enough XML" tutorial in Chapter 2 relies on important insights and markup fundamentals that are introduced in their historical and business contexts in Chapter 1. That knowledge in turn is the foundation for the survey of XML application domains and future directions in Chapter 3.

By Chapter 4 we are able to tackle the most fundamental real-world issue for XML: the relationship between documents and data and what that means for both applications and products.

Finally, in Chapter 5 we can apply what we have learned to an examination of the most important terms related to XML – the ones that people misuse the most! You'll learn what they really mean, and how to decipher the intended meaning when others get them wrong.

Reading this part will prepare you for the application and tool discussions in Parts Two through Ten. High-tech readers may want to complete the tutorials in Parts Eleven and Twelve first, but others can just dip into the tutorials on a need-to-know basis.

Why XML?

Introductory Discussion

- What is XML, really?
- Origins in document processing
- Abstraction vs. rendition
- Documents and data

©2000 THE XML HANDBOOK™

Chapter 1

Many of the most influential companies in the software industry are promoting XML as the next step in the Web's evolution. How can they be so confident about something so new? More important: how can you be sure that your time invested in learning and using XML will be profitable?

We can all safely bet on XML because the central ideas in this new technology are in fact very old and have been proven correct across several decades and thousands of projects. The easiest way to understand these ideas is to go back to their source, the *Standard Generalized Markup Language* (SGML).

XML is, in fact, a streamlined subset of SGML, so SGML's track record is XML's as well.

And if your interest is in moving data from Web sites to a browser or a spreadsheet, stay with us. All of this is interconnected and extremely relevant. For the amazing truth about XML is that with it, data processing and document processing are the same thing! If you understand where it all comes from, you'll understand where it – and the Web – are going.

1.1 | Text formatters and SGML

XML comes from a rich history of text processing systems. *Text processing* is the subdiscipline of *computer science* dedicated to creating computer systems that can automate parts of the document creation and publishing process. Text processing software includes simple word processors, advanced news item databases, hypertext document presentation systems and other publishing tools.

The first wave of automated text processing was computer typesetting. Authors would type in a document and describe how they would like it to be formatted. The computer would print out a document with the described text and formatting.

We call the file format that contained the mix of the actual data of the document, plus the description of the desired format, a *rendition*. Some well-known rendition notations include *troff*, *Rich Text Format* (*RTF*), and *LaTeX*.

The system would convert the rendition into something physically perceivable to a human being – a *presentation*. The presentation medium was historically paper, but eventually electronic display.

Typesetting systems sped up the process of publishing documents and evolved into what we now know as desktop publishing. Newer programs like *Microsoft Word* and *Adobe PageMaker* still work with renditions, but they give authors a nicer interface to manipulate them. The user interface to the rendition (the file with formatting codes in it) is designed to look like the presentation (the finished paper product). We call this *What You See Is What You Get* (*WYSIWYG*) publishing. Since a rendition merely describes a presentation, it makes sense for the user interface to reflect the end-product.

1.1.1 *Formatting markup*

The form of typesetting notation that predates WYSIWYG (and is still in use today) is called *formatting markup*. Consider an analogy: you might submit a manuscript to a human typesetter for publication. Imagine it had no formatting, not even paragraphs or different fonts, but rather was a single continuous paragraph that was "marked up" with written instructions for how it should be formatted. You could write very precise instructions for layout: "Move this word over two inches. Bold it. Move the next work beside it. Move the next word underneath it. Bold it. Start a new line here." and so forth. It might look like Figure 1-1.

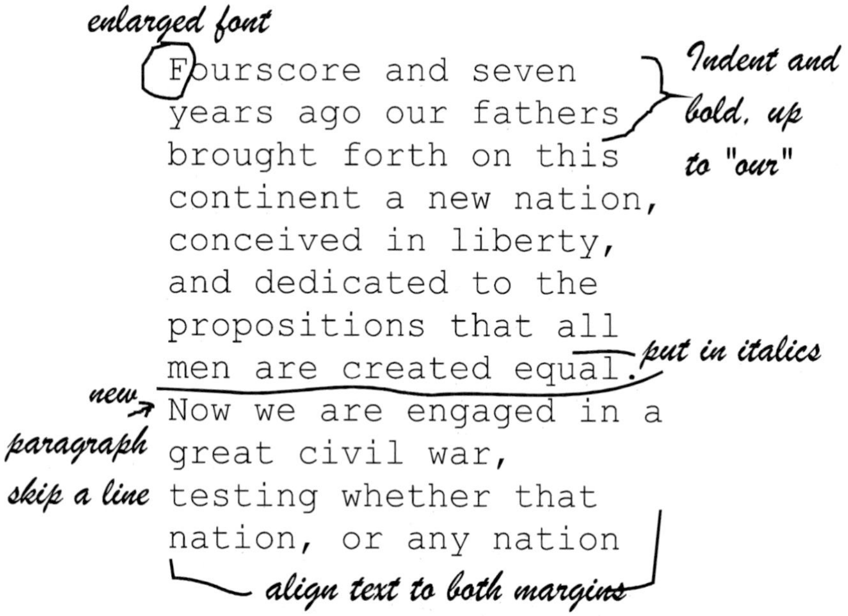

enlarged font

Fourscore and seven years ago our fathers brought forth on this continent a new nation, conceived in liberty, and dedicated to the propositions that all men are created equal.

Indent and bold, up to "our"

put in italics

new paragraph

Now we are engaged in a great civil war, testing whether that nation, or any nation

skip a line

align text to both margins

Figure 1-1 A manuscript "marked up" by hand

Formatting markup is very much the same. We "circle" text with instructions called *tags* or *codes* (depending on the particular formatting markup language). Here is an example of markup in one popular formatting markup language called LaTeX.

Example 1-1. A document with formatting markup

```
This is a marked up document. It contains words that are {\it italicized},
{\bf bold faced}, {\small small} and {\large large}.
```

In this markup language, the curly braces describe the extent of the formatting. So the italics started with the "\it" command extend until the end of the word "italicized". Because the markup uses only ordinary characters on typical keyboards, it can be created using existing text editors instead of special word processors (those came later).

1.1.2 *Generalized markup*

This process is adequate if your only goal is to type documents into the computer, describe a rendition and then print them. Around the late sixties, people started wanting to do more with their documents. In particular, IBM asked Charles Goldfarb (the name may sound familiar) to build a system for storing, finding, managing, and publishing legal documents.

Goldfarb found that there were many systems within IBM that could not communicate with each other. Each of them used a different command language. They could not read each other's files, just as you may have had trouble loading *WordPerfect* files into Word. The problem then, as now, was that they all had a different *representation* (sometimes also called a *file format*) for the information.

1.1.2.1 Common document representation

In the late sixties, Goldfarb and two other IBM researchers, Ed Mosher and Ray Lorie, set out to solve this problem. The team recognized three important facts. First, the programs needed to support a common document representation.

That part is easy to understand. Tools cannot work together if they do not speak the same language. As an analogy, consider the popularity of Latin terms in describing chemical and legal concepts and categories. To a certain extent, chemists and lawyers have chosen Latin as a common language for their fields. It made sense in the text processing context that the common language should be some form of markup language, because markup was well understood and very compatible with existing text editors and operating systems.

1.1.2.2 Customized document types

Second, the three realized that the common format should be *specific* to legal documents.

This is a little more subtle to grasp, but vital to understanding XML. The team could have invented a simple language, perhaps similar to the representation of a standard word processor, but that representation would not have allowed the sophisticated processing that was required. Lawyers and scientists both use Latin, but they do not use the same terminology. Rather they use Latin words as building blocks to create domain specific vocabularies (e.g. "habeas corpus", "ferruginous"). These domain specific vocabularies are even more important when we are describing documents to computers.

1.1.2.2.1 Computers are dumb

Usually we take for granted that computers are not very good at working with text and documents. We would never, for instance, ask a computer to search our hard disk and return a document that was a "letter" document, that was to "Martha" and that was about "John Smith's will". Even though this example seems much simpler than something a lawyer or chemist would run into, the fundamental problems are the same.

Most people recognize that the computer is completely incapable of understanding the concepts of "letter", "Martha" or "a will". Instead we might tell it to search for those words, and hope that we had included them all in the document. But what would happen if the system that we wanted to search was massive? It might turn up hundreds of unrelated documents. It might return documents that contained strings like "Martha, will you please write me a letter and tell me how John is doing?"

The fundamental problem is that the computer does not in any way understand the text. The solution is to teach the computer as much about the document as possible. Of course the computer will not understand the text in any real sense, but it can pretend to, in the same way that it pretends to understand simple data or decimal numbers.[1]. We can make this possible by reducing the complexity of the document to a few structural *elements* chosen from a common vocabulary.

1. We hope we haven't disillusioned anyone here. Computers may seem to know everything about math, but it is all a ruse. As far as they are concerned, they are only manipulating zeros and ones.

©2000 THE XML HANDBOOK™

1.1.2.2.2 But computers can be trained

Once we "teach" computers about documents, we can also program them to do things they would not have been able to otherwise. Using their new "understanding" they can help us to navigate through large documents, organize them, and automatically format the documents for publication in many different media, such as hypertext, print or tape.

In other words, we can get them to process text for us! The range of things we can get them to do with the documents is much wider than what we would get with WYSIWYG word processors or formatting markup.

Let us go back to the analogy of the typesetter working with a document marked up with a pen on paper to see why this is so powerful.

Imagine if we called her back the next day and told her to "change the formatting of the second chapter". She would have a lot of trouble mentally translating the codes for presentation back into high level constructs like sections and paragraphs.

To her, a title would only look like a line of text with a circle around it and instructions to make it italicized and 18 point. Making changes would be painful because recognizing the different logical constructs would be difficult. She probably could eventually accomplish the task by applying her human intuition and by reading the actual text. But computers do not have intuition, and cannot understand the text. That means that they cannot reliably recognize logical structure based totally on formatting. For instance they cannot reliably distinguish an italicized, 18 point title from an italicized, 18 point warning paragraph.

Even if human beings were consistent in formatting different types of documents (which we are not) computers would still have trouble. Even in a single document, the same formatting can mean two different things: italics could represent any kind of emphasis, foreign words, certain kinds of citations or other conventions.

1.1.2.2.3 Abstractions and renditions

Computers are not as smart as we are. If we want the computer to consider a piece of text to be written in a foreign language (for instance for spell checking purposes) then we must label it explicitly `foreign-language` and not just put it in italics! We call "foreign language" the *abstraction* that we are trying to represent, and we call the italics a particular rendition of the abstraction.

Formatting information has other problems. It is specific to a particular use of the information. Search engines cannot do very interesting searching on italics because they do not know what they mean. In contrast, the search engine could do something very interesting with `citation` elements: it could return a list of what documents are cited by other documents.

Italics are a form of markup specific to a particular application: formatting or printing. In contrast, the citation element is markup that can be used by a variety of applications. That is why we call this form of structural markup *generalized markup*. Generalized markup is the alternative to either formatting markup or WYSIWYG (lampooned by XML users as What You See is *All* You Get). Generalized markup is about getting more.

Because of the ambiguity of formatting, XML users typically do not bother to capture the document's presentational features at all, though XML would allow it. We are not interested, for instance, in fonts, page breaks and bullets. This formatting information would merely clutter up our abstract document's representation. Although typographic conventions allow the computer to print out or display the document properly, we want our markup to do more than that.

1.1.2.2.4 Stylesheets

Of course we must still be able to generate high quality print and online renditions of the document. Your readers do not want to read XML text directly. Instead of directly inserting the formatting commands in the XML document, we usually tell the computer how to generate formatted renditions *from* the XML abstraction.

For example in a print presentation, we can make the content of `TITLE` elements bold and large, insert page breaks before the beginning of chapters, and turn emphasis, citations and foreign words into italics. These rules are specified in a file called a *stylesheet*. The stylesheet is where human designers can express their creativity and understanding of formatting conventions. The stylesheet allows the computer to automatically convert the document from the abstraction to a formatted rendition.

We could use two different stylesheets to generate online and print renditions of the document. In the online rendition, there would be no page breaks, but cross-references would be represented as clickable hypertext links. Generalized markup allows us to easily produce high-quality print and online renditions of the same document.

©2000 THE XML HANDBOOK™

This may well turn out to be the feature of XML that will save organizations and individuals the most money in the near future. We can even use two different stylesheets in the same medium. For instance, the computer could format the same document into several different styles (e.g. "New York Times" style vs. "Wired Magazine") depending on the expressed preferences of a Web surfer, or even based on what Internet Service Provider they use.

We can also go beyond just print and online formatting and have our document be automatically rendered into braille or onto a text-to-speech machine. Generalized markup is highly endorsed by those who promote the *accessibility* of information to the visually impaired. XML should be similarly useful to those who want to widen the use of the Web.

Generalized markup documents are also "future-proof". They will not have to be redone to take advantage of future technologies. Instead, new stylesheets can be created to render existing documents in new ways.

Future renditions of documents might include three-dimensional virtual reality worlds where books are rendered as buildings, chapters as rooms and the text as wallpaper! Once again, the most important point is that these many different renditions will be possible without revising the document. There are millions of SGML documents that predate the Web, but many of them are now published on it.

Typically, they were republished in HTML without changing a single character of the SGML source's markup or data, or editing a single character of the generated HTML. The same will be true of the relationship between XML and all future representations.

The key is abstraction. SGML and XML can represent abstractions, and from abstractions you can easily create any number of renditions. This is a fact well-known to the world's database programmers, who constantly generate new renditions – reports and forms – from the same abstract data.

©2000 THE XML HANDBOOK™

1.1.2.2.5 Element types

Enough hype about generalized markup! You probably want to know what it looks like. To mark up a letter, we could identify the components of the letter like this:

Example 1-2. A simple memo

```
<to>Charles Goldfarb</to>
<from>Paul Prescod</from>
<re>John Smith's will</re>

<p>John Smith wants to update his will. Another wife left him.</p>
```

This text would be part of an XML document. The markup identifies components, called elements, of the document in ways that the computer can understand. The start-tag "<to>" marks the beginning of an element and the end-tag "</to>" marks the end of the element. Each element is an instance of an *element type*, such as `to`, `from`, `re` and `p`.

If you use an XML-aware word processor, you may never work with markup at the textual tag level, but you would still annotate sections of the document in this way (using the graphical interface that the tool provides).

Instead of each element type describing a formatting construct, each one instead describes the logical role of its elements – the *abstraction* it represents. The goal is for the abstraction to be descriptive enough and suitably chosen so that particular uses of the document (such as printing, searching and so forth) can be completely automated as computer processes acting on the elements.

For instance, we can search for a document that is "to" Martha, about ("re") John Smith's will. Of course the computer still does not understand the human interaction and concepts of sender and receiver, but it does know enough about the document to be able to tell me that in a "to" element of this particular document, the word "Martha" appears. If we expanded the letter a little to include addresses and so forth, we could also use an appropriate stylesheet to print it as a standard business letter.

1.1.2.2.6 Documents and databases

We can make our letter example even more precise and specific:

Example 1-3. Another letter

```
<to>Martha</to>
<from>Paul</from>
<re><customer-name>John Smith</customer-name>
    <customer-number>802-31348-5749</customer-number>
    <document-type-request>will</document-type-request>
</re>

<p>John Smith wants to update his will. Another wife left him.</p>
```

If you are familiar with databases, you might recognize that this looks database-ish in the sense that the customer number could be stored in a special index and you could easily search and sort this document based on customer numbers, document type requests and so forth.

But you can only do this sort of thing if your letter processing system understands your company's concepts of customer-numbers and your documents consistently provide the information. In other words, you must define your own set of element types just as the IBM team did.

In fact, many people have noticed that XML documents resemble traditional relational and object database data in many ways. Once you have a language for rigorously representing documents, those documents can be treated more like other forms of data.

But the converse is also true. As we have described, structured documents have many features in common with databases. They can preserve the abstract data and prevent it from being mingled with rendition information.

Furthermore, you can actually use this structured markup to represent data that is not what we would traditionally think of as documents, but too complex to be handled in conventional databases. In this brave new world, DNA patterns are data, and so are molecular diagrams and virtual reality worlds. In other words, generalized markup allows us to blow the doors off the word "document" and integrate diverse types of data. This database-ization of documents and document-ization of data is one of the major drivers of the XML excitement. Prior to XML, the Web had no standard data interchange format for even moderately complex data.

It may not have been obvious to its early, publishing-oriented adapters, that SGML would change the entire world of databases and *electronic data interchange* (EDI). But SGML's unique usefulness as a data interchange representation was a direct consequence of this second decision – to make SGML extensible through a customized vocabulary (set of element types).

1.1.2.3 Rule-based markup

The IBM team's third realization was that if computer systems were to work with these documents reliably, the documents would have to follow certain rules.

For instance a courtroom transcript might be required to have the name of the judge, defendant, both attorneys and (optionally) the names of members of the jury (if there is one). Since humans are prone to make mistakes, the computer would have to enforce the rules for us.

In other words the legal markup language should be specified in some formal way that would restrict elements appropriately. If the court stenographer tried to submit a transcript to the system without these elements being properly filled in, the system would check its *validity* and complain that it was *invalid.*

Of course, court transcripts have a different structure from wills, which in turn have a different structure from memos. So you would need to rigorously define what it means for each type of document to be valid. In SGML terminology, each of these is a *document type* and the formal definition that describes each type is called a *document type definition* (DTD).

Once again we can see why it is so important that the language provide us with the flexibility to choose our own vocabulary (our own set of element types). After all, the constraints that we apply must be described in terms of those element types. We use the word *document type* to refer both to a vocabulary and the constraints on its use.

Once again, this concept is very common in the database world. Database people typically have several layers of checking to guarantee that improper data cannot appear in their databases. For instance *syntactic* checks guarantee that phone numbers are composed of digits and that people's names are not. *Semantic* checks ensure that business rules are followed (such as "purchase order numbers must be unique"). The database world calls the set of constraints on the database structure a *schema*. In their termi-

©2000 The XML Handbook™

nology, document types are schemas for documents and DTDs are schema definitions.

Once you have a document type worked out, you can describe for the computer how to print or display documents that conform to it with a *stylesheet*. So you might say that the address line in memos would be bolded, or that there should be two lines between speeches in a court transcript. These processes can work reliably because documents are constrained by the document type definition.

For instance, a letter cannot have a postscript ("P.S.") at the beginning of the document nor an address at the end. Because there is no convention for formatting such a letter, a stylesheet would typically not do a good job with it. In fact, it might crash, as some word processors do when they try to load corrupted documents. The document type definition protects us from this.[1]

In 1969, the IBM team developed a language that could implement their vision of markup that was not specific to a particular system. They called it the *Generalized Markup Language* (which, not coincidentally, has the same initials as the names Goldfarb, Mosher and Lorie).[2]

However, it wasn't until 1974 that Goldfarb proved the concept of a "validating parser", one that could read a document type definition and check the accuracy of markup, without going to the expense of actually processing a document. As he recalls it: "At that point SGML was born – although it still had a lot of growing up to do."

Between 1978 and 1986, Goldfarb acted as technical leader of a team of users, programmers and academics that developed his nascent invention into the robust International Standard (ISO 8879) they called the *Standard Generalized Markup Language*.

That team, with many of the same players still involved, is now JTC1/SC34, which continues to develop SGML and related standards. Two of the most important are *HyTime*, which standardizes the representation of hyperlinking features, and DSSSL, which standarizes the creation of stylesheets.[3]

The SGML standard took a long time to develop, but arguably it was still ahead of the market when it was created. Over those years, the basic concepts of GML were broadened to support a very wide range of applica-

1. Of course, computer programmers will always invent new excuses for crashing software.
2. In fact, Goldfarb coined the term "markup language" for the purpose.

tions. Although GML was always extensible and generalized, the SGML standard added many features and options, many intended for niche markets. But the niches had to be catered for: some of the niche users have document collections that rival the Web in size!

By the time it was standardized in 1986, SGML had become large, intricate and powerful. In addition to being an official International Standard, SGML is the de facto standard for the interchange of large, complex documents and has been used in domains as diverse as programming language design and airplane maintenance.

1.2 | HTML and the Web

In 1989, a researcher named Tim Berners-Lee proposed that information could be shared within the CERN European Nuclear Research Facility using hyperlinked text documents. He was advised to use an SGML-ish syntax by a colleague named Anders Berglund, an early adopter of the new SGML standard. They started from a simple example document type in the SGML standard.[1] and developed a hypertext version called the *Hypertext Markup Language* (HTML).

Relative to the 20 year evolution of SGML, HTML was developed in a hurry, but it did the job. Tim called his hypertext system the *World Wide Web* and today it is the most diverse, popular hypertext information system in existence. Its simplicity is widely believed to be an important part of its success. The simplicity of HTML and the other Web specifications allowed programmers around the world to quickly build systems and tools to work with the Web.

HTML inherited some important strengths from SGML. With a few exceptions, its element types were generalized and descriptive, not formatting constructs as in languages like TeX and Microsoft Word. This meant

---

3. Knowing the full names probably won't help much, but just in case, HyTime is short for "Hypermedia/Time-based Structuring Language" and DSSSL (pronounced "dis-sal") is short for "Document Style Semantics and Specification Language". We warned you that it wouldn't help much.
1. That DTD was based on the very first published DTD, from a 1978 IBM manual written by Goldfarb, derived in turn from work that he and Mosher had done in the early 70's.

that HTML documents could be displayed on text screens, under graphical user interfaces, and even projected through speakers for the sight impaired.

HTML documents used SGML's simple angle bracket convention for markup. That meant that authors could create HTML documents in almost any text editor or word processor. The documents are also compatible with almost every computer system in existence.

On the other hand, HTML only uses a fixed set of element types. As we discussed before, no one document type can serve all purposes, so HTML only adopted the first of GML's revelations, that document representations must be standardized. It is not extensible and therefore cannot be tailored for particular document types, and it was not very rigorously defined until years after its invention. By the time HTML was given a formal DTD, there were already thousands of Web pages with erroneous HTML.[1]

1.2.1 *HTML gets extended – unofficially!*

As the Web grew in popularity many people started to chafe under HTML's fixed document type. Browser vendors saw an opportunity to gain market share by making incompatible extensions to HTML. Most of the extensions were formatting commands and thus damaged the Web's interoperability. The first golden rule, standardization was in serious danger.

For instance Netscape's popular `CENTER` element cannot be "pronounced" in a text to speech converter. A `BLINK` element cannot be rendered on some computers. Still, this was a fairly understandable reaction to HTML's limitations.

One argument for implementing formatting constructs instead of abstractions is that there are a fixed number of formatting constructs in wide use, but an ever growing number of abstractions. Let's say that next year biologists invent a new formatting notation for discussing a particular type of DNA. They might use italics to represent one kind of DNA construct and bold to represent another. In other words, as new abstractions are invented, we usually use existing formatting features to represent them. We

---

1. Today there are tens of thousands with misleading or downright erroneous informational content, so perhaps bad HTML markup is not that big a problem in the overall scheme of things.

have been doing this for thousands of years, and prior to computerization, it was essentially the only way.

We human readers can read a textual description of the meanings of the features ("in this book, we will use Roman text to represent...") and we can differentiate them from others using our reasoning and understanding of the text. But this system leaves computers more or less out of the loop.

For instance superscripts can be used for trademarks, footnotes and various mathematical constructs. Italics can be used for references to book titles, for emphasis and to represent foreign languages. Without generalized markup to differentiate, computers cannot do anything useful with that information. It would be impossible for them to translate foreign languages, convert emphasis to a louder voice for text to speech conversion, or do calculations on the mathematical formulae.

1.2.1 *The World Wide Web reacts*

As the interoperability and scalability of the Web became more and more endangered by proprietary formatting markup, the World Wide Web Consortium (headed by the same Tim Berners-Lee) decided to act. They attacked the problem in three ways. First, they decided to adopt the GML convention for attaching formatting to documents, the stylesheet.

They invented a simple HTML-specific stylesheet language called *Cascading Style Sheets* (CSS) that allowed people to attach formatting to HTML documents without filling the HTML itself with proprietary, rendition-oriented markup.

Second, they invented a simple mechanism for adding abstractions to HTML. We will not look at that mechanism here, because XML makes it obsolete. It allowed new abstractions to be invented but provided no mechanism for constraining their occurrence. In other words it addressed two of GML's revelations: it brought HTML back to being a single standard, more or less equally supported by the major vendors, and it allowed people to define arbitrary extensions (with many limitations).

But they knew that their stool would not stand long on two of its three legs. The (weakly) extensible HTML and CSS are only stopgaps. For the Web to move to a new level, it had to incorporate the third of GML's important ideas, that document types should be formally defined so that documents can be checked for validity against them.

Therefore, the World Wide Web Consortium decided to develop a subset of SGML that would retain SGML's major virtues but also embrace the Web ethic of minimalist simplicity. They decided to give the new language the catchy name *Extensible Markup Language* (XML). They also decided to make related standards for advanced hyperlinking and stylesheets.

The first, called the *Extensible Linking Language* (XLink), is inspired by HyTime, the ISO standard for linking SGML documents, and by the Text Encoding Initiative, the academic community's guidelines for applying SGML to scholarly applications.

The second, called the *Extensible Style Language* is a combination of ideas from the Web's Cascading Style Sheets and ISO's DSSSL standard.[1]

1.3 | Conclusion

Now we've seen the origins of XML, and some of its key ideas. Unlike lots of other "next great things" of the high-tech world, XML has solid roots and a proven track record. You can have confidence in XML because the particular subset of SGML that *is* XML has been in use for a dozen years.

---

1. This description necessarily presented as linear, straightforward, and obvious a process that was actually messy and at times confusing. It is fair to say that there were many people outside the World Wide Web Consortium who had a better grasp on the need for XML than many within it, and that various member corporations "caught on" to the importance of XML at different rates.

Just enough XML

Introductory Discussion

- Elements
- Character set
- Entities
- Markup
- Document types

©2000 THE XML HANDBOOK™

Chapter 2

In this chapter we will explore the fundamental concepts of XML documents and XML systems. If XML were a great work of literature then this chapter would be the Cliff notes. The chapter will introduce the ideas that define the language but will avoid the nitty-gritty details (the syntax) behind the constructs. As a result, some concepts may remain slightly fuzzy because you will not be able to work with them "hands on". Later chapters will provide that opportunity.

This early presentation of these ideas will allow you to see XML's "big picture". We will do this by walking through the design process for an XML-like language. Hopefully by the end of the process, you will understand each of the design decisions and XML's overall architecture.

Our objective is to equip you with "just enough" XML to appreciate the application scenarios and tool descriptions in the following parts of the book, but being over-achievers we may go a little too far. Feel free to leave at any time to read about XML in the real world.

2.1 | The goal

First we should summarize what we are trying to achieve. In short, "What is XML used for?" XML is for the *digital representation* of documents. You probably have an intuitive feel for what a document is. We will work from your intuition.

Documents can be large and small. Both a multi-volume encyclopedia and a memo can be thought of as documents. A particular volume of the encyclopedia can also be called a document. XML allows you to think of the encyclopedia whichever way will allow you to get your job done most efficiently. You'll notice that XML will give you these sorts of options in many places. XML also allows us to think of an email message as a document. XML can even represent the message from a police department's server to a police officer's handheld computer that reports that you have unpaid parking tickets.[1]

When we say that we want to *digitally represent* documents we mean that we want to put them in some kind of computer-readable notation so that a computer can help us store, process, search, transmit, display and print them. In order for a computer to do useful things with a document, we are going to have to tell it about the structure of the document. This is our simple goal: to represent the documents in a way that the computer can "understand", insofar as computers can understand anything.

XML documents can include pictures, movies and other multimedia, but we will not actually represent the multimedia components as XML. If you think of representation as a translation process, similar to language translation, then the multimedia components are the parts that we will leave in their "native language" because they have no simple translation into the "target language" (XML). We will just include them in their native formats as you might include a French or Latin phrase in an English text without explicit translation. Most pictures on the Web are files in formats called GIF or JPEG and most movies are in a format called MPEG. An XML document would just refer to those files in their native GIF, JPEG or MPEG formats. If you were transcribing an existing print document into XML, you would most likely represent the character-text parts as XML and the graphical parts in these other formats.

1. Sorry about that.

2.2 | Elements: The logical structure

Before we can describe exactly how we are going to represent documents, we must have a model in our heads of how a document is structured. Most documents (for example books and magazines) can be broken down into components (chapters and articles). These can also be broken down into components (titles, paragraphs, figures and so forth). It turns out that just about every document can be viewed this way.

In XML, these components are called *elements*. Each element represents a logical component of a document. Elements can contain other elements and can also contain the words and sentences that you would usually think of as the text of the document. XML calls this text the document's *character data*. This hierarchical view of XML documents is demonstrated in Figure 2-1.

Markup professionals call this the *tree structure* of the document. The element that contains all of the others (e.g. `book`, `report` or `memo` is known as the *root element*. This name captures the fact that it is the only element that does not "hang" off of some other element.

The elements that are contained in the root are called its *subelements*. They may contain subelements themselves. If they do, we will call them *branches*. If they do not, we will call them *leaves*.

Thus, the `chapter` and `article` elements are branches (because they have subelements), but the `paragraph` and `title` elements are leaves (because they only contain character data).[1]The root element is also referred to as the *document element* because it holds the entire logical document within it. The terms *root element* and *document element* are interchangeable.

Elements can also have extra information attached to them called *attributes*. Attributes describe properties of elements. For instance a `CIA-record` element might have a security attribute that gives the security rating for that element. A CIA database might only release certain records to certain people depending on their security rating. It will not always be clear which aspects of a document should be represented with elements and which should be represented with attributes, but we will give some guidelines in Chapter 54, "Creating a document type definition", on page 748.

---

1. This arboreal metaphor is firmly rooted in computer science. However, markup experts have recently extended it with the term "grove". This term recognizes that a single document may best be viewed as multiple trees.

©2000 THE XML HANDBOOK™

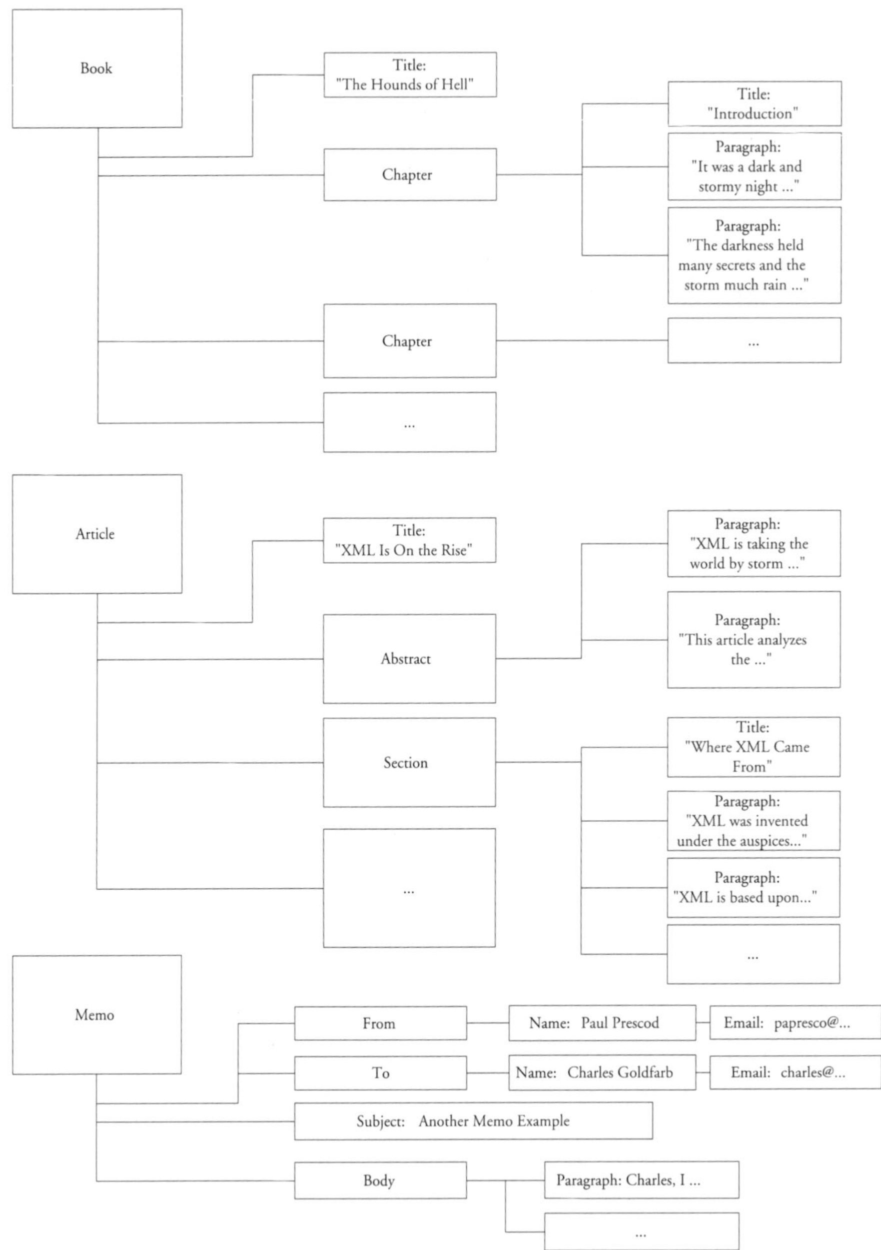

Figure 2-1 Hierarchical views of documents

Real-world documents do not always fit this *tree* model perfectly. They often have non-hierarchical features such as cross-references or hypertext links from one section of the tree to another. XML can represent these structures too. In fact, XML goes beyond the powerful links provided by HTML. More on this in 2.8, "Hyperlinking and addressing", on page 36.

2.3 | Unicode: The character set

Texts are made up of characters. If we are going to represent texts, then we must represent the characters that comprise them. So we must decide how we are going to represent characters at the bits and bytes level. This is called the *character encoding*. We must also decide what characters we are going to allow in our documents. This is the *character set*. A particularly restrictive character set might allow only upper-case characters. A very large character set might allow Eastern ideographs and Arabic characters.

If you are a native English speaker you may only need the fifty-two upper- and lower-case characters, some punctuation and a few accented characters. The pervasive *7 bit ASCII character set* caters to this market. It has just enough characters (128) for all of the letters, symbols, some accented characters and some other oddments. ASCII is both a character set *and* a character encoding. It defines what set of characters are available and how they are to be encoded in terms of bits and bytes.

XML's character set is *Unicode*, a sort of ASCII on steroids. Unicode includes thousands of useful characters from languages around the world.[1] However the first 128 characters of Unicode are compatible with ASCII and there is a character encoding of Unicode, *UTF-8* that is compatible with 7 bit ASCII. This means that at the bits and bytes level, the first 128 characters of UTF-8 Unicode and 7 bit ASCII are the same. This feature of *Unicode* allows authors to use standard plain-text editors to create XML immediately.

---

1. It also includes some not-so-useful characters – there is an entire section dedicated to "dingbats" and there is a proposal to include "Klingon", the artificial language from Star Trek™.

2.4 | Entities: The physical structure

An XML document is defined as a series of characters. An XML processor starts at the beginning and works to the end. XML provides a mechanism for allowing text to be organized non-linearly and potentially in multiple pieces. The parser reorganizes it into the linear structure.

The "piece-of-text" construct is called an *entity*. An entity could be as small as a single character or as large as all the characters of a book.

Entities have *names*. Somewhere in your document, you insert an *entity reference* to make use of an entity. The processor replaces the entity reference with the entity itself, which is called the *replacement text*. It works somewhat like a word processor macro.

For instance an entity named "sigma", might contain the name of a Greek character. You would use a reference to the entity whenever you wanted to insert the sigma character. An entity could also be called "introduction-chapter" and be a chapter in a book. You would refer to the entity at the point where you wanted the chapter to appear.

One of the ideas that excited Ted Nelson, the man who coined the word *hypertext*, was the idea that text could be reused in many different contexts automatically. An update in one place would propagate across all uses of the text. The feature of XML that allows text reuse is called the *external entity*. External entities are often referred to merely as entities, but the meaning is usually clear from context. An XML document can be broken up into many files on a hard disk or objects in a database and each of them is called an entity in XML terminology. Entities could even be spread across the Internet. Whereas XML elements describe the document's logical structure, entities keep track of the location of the chunks of bytes that make up an XML document. We call this the *physical structure* of the document.

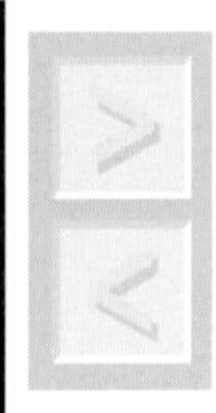

Note *The unit of XML text that we will typically talk about is the entity. You may be accustomed to thinking about files, but entities do not have to be stored as files.*

For instance, entities could be stored in databases or generated on the fly by a computer program. Some file formats (e.g. a *zip* file) even allow multiple entities to reside in the same file at once. The term that covers all of these possibilities is entity, *not* file. Still, on most Web sites each entity will reside in a single file so in those cases external entities and files will functionally be the same. This setup is simple and efficient, but will not be sufficient for very large sites.

Entities' bread and butter occupation is less sexy than reusing bits of text across the Internet. But it is just as important: entities help to break up large files to make them editable, searchable, downloadable and otherwise usable on the ordinary computer systems that real people use. Entities allow authors to break their documents into workable chunks that can fit into memory for editing, can be downloaded across a slow modem and so forth.

Without entities, authors would have to break their documents unnaturally into smaller documents with only weak links between them (as is commonly done with HTML). This complicates document management and maintenance. If you have ever tried to print out one of these HTML documents broken into a hundred HTML files then you know the problem. Entities allow documents to be broken up into chunks without forgetting that they actually represent a single coherent document that can be printed, edited and searched as a unit when that makes sense.

Non-XML objects are referenced in much the same way and are called *unparsed entities.* We think of them as "data entities" because there is no XML markup in them that will be noticed by the XML processor. Data entities include graphics, movies, audio, raw text, PDF and anything else you can think of that is not XML (including HTML and other forms of SGML).[1] Each data entity has an associated *notation* that is simply a statement declaring whether the entity is a GIF, JPEG, MPEG, PDF and so forth.

Entities are described in all of their glorious (occasionally gory) detail in Chapter 55, "Entities: Breaking up is easy to do", on page 780.

1. Actually, a data entity could even contain XML, but it wouldn't be treated as part of the main XML document.

©2000 THE XML HANDBOOK™

2.5 | Markup

We have discussed XML's conceptual model, the tree of elements, its strategy for encoding characters, Unicode, and its mechanism for managing the size and complexity of documents, entities. We have not yet discussed how to represent the logical structure of the document and link together all of the physical entities.

Although there are XML word processors, one of the design goals of XML was that it should be possible to create XML documents in standard text editors. Some people are not comfortable with word processors and even those who are may depend on text editors to "debug" their document if the word processor makes a mistake, or allows the user to make a mistake. The only way to allow authors convenient access to both the structure and data of the document in standard text editors is to put the two right beside each other, "cheek to cheek".

As we discussed in the introduction, the stuff that represents the logical structure and connects the entities is called markup. An XML document is made up exclusively of markup and character data. Both are in Unicode. Collectively they are termed *XML text.*

This last point is important! Unless the context unambiguously refers to data, as in "textual data", when we say "XML text", we mean the markup and the data.

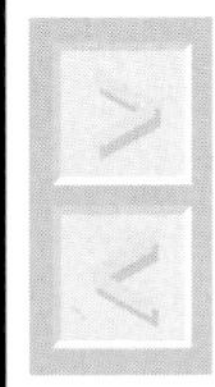

Caution *The term XML text refers to the combination of character data and markup, not character data alone. Character data + markup = text.*

Markup is differentiated from character data by special characters called *delimiters.* Informally, text between a less-than ("<") and a greater-than (">") character or between an ampersand ("&") and a semicolon (";") character is markup. Those four characters are the most common delimiters. This rule will become more concrete in later chapters. In the meantime, Example 2-1 is an example of a small document to give you a taste of XML markup.

Example 2-1. A small XML document

```
<?xml version="1.0"?>
<!DOCTYPE Q-AND-A SYSTEM "http://www.q.and.a.com/faq.dtd">
<Q-AND-A>
<QUESTION>I'm having trouble loading a WurdWriter 2.0 file into
WurdPurformertWriter 7.0. Any suggestions?</QUESTION>

<ANSWER>Why don't you use XML?</ANSWER>

<QUESTION>What's XML?</QUESTION>

<ANSWER>It's a long story, but there is a book I can
recommend...</ANSWER>
</Q-AND-A>
```

The markup between the less-than and greater-than is called a *tag*.

You may be familiar with other languages that use similar syntax. These include HTML and other SGML-based languages.

2.6 | Document types

The concept of a document type is fairly intuitive. You are well aware that letters, novels and telephone books are quite different, and you are probably comfortable recognizing documents that conform to one of these categories. No matter what its title or binding, you would call a book that listed names and phone numbers a phone book. So, a document type is defined by its elements. If two documents have radically different elements or allow elements to be combined in very different ways then they probably do not conform to the same document type.

2.6.1 *Document type definitions*

This notion of a document type can be formalized in XML. A *document type definition* (or *DTD*) is a series of definitions for element types, attributes, entities and notations. It declares which of these are legal within the document and in what places they are legal. A document can claim to conform to a particular DTD in its *document type declaration.*[1]

©2000 The XML Handbook™

DTDs are powerful tools for organizational standardization in much the same way that forms, templates and style-guides are. A very rigid DTD that only allows one element type in a particular place is like a form: "Just fill in the blanks!". A more flexible DTD is like a style-guide in that it can, for instance, require every `list` to have two or more `items`, every `report` to have an `abstract` and could restrict `footnotes` from appearing within `footnotes`.

DTDs are critical for organizational standardization, but they are just as important for allowing robust processing of documents by software. For example, a letter document with a `chapter` in the middle of it would be most unexpected and unlikely to be very useful. Letter printing software would not reliably be able to print such a document because it is not well defined what a chapter in a letter looks like. Even worse is a situation where a document is missing an element expected by the software that processes it. If your mail program used XML as its storage format, you might expect it to be able to search all of the incoming email addresses for a particular person's address. Let us presume that each message stores this address in a `from` element. What do we do about letters without `from` elements when we are searching them? Programmers could write special code to "work around" the problem, but these kinds of workarounds make code difficult to write.

2.6.1 *HTML: A cautionary tale*

HTML serves as a useful cautionary tale. It actually has a fairly rigorous structure, defined in SGML, and available from the World Wide Web Consortium. But everybody tends to treat the rules as if they actually came from the World Wrestling Federation – they ignore them.

The programmers that maintain HTML browsers spend a huge amount of time incorporating support for all of the incorrect ways people combine the HTML elements in their documents. Although HTML has an SGML DTD, very few people use it, and the browser vendors have unofficially sanctioned the practice of ignoring it. Programming workarounds is expensive, time consuming, boring and frustrating, but the worst problem is that there is no good definition of what these illegal constructs mean. Some

1. The document type declaration is usually abbreviated "DOCTYPE", because the obvious abbreviation would be the same as that for document type definition!

incorrect constructs will actually make HTML browsers crash, but others will merely make them display confusing or random results.

In HTML, the `title` element is used to display the document's name at the top of the browser window (on the title bar). But what should a browser do if there are two titles? Use the first? Use the last? Use both? Pick one at random? Since the HTML standard does not allow this construct it certainly does not specify a behavior. Believe it or not, an early version of Netscape's browser showed each title sequentially over time, creating a primitive sort of text animation. That behavior disappeared quickly when Netscape realized that authors were actually creating invalid HTML specifically to get this effect! Since authors cannot depend on nonsensical documents to work across browsers, or even across browser versions, there must be a formal definition of a valid, reasonable document of a particular type. In XML, the DTD provides a formal definition of the element types, attributes and entities allowed in a document of a specified type.

There is also a more subtle, related issue. If you do not stop and think carefully about the structure of your documents, you may accidently slip back into specifying them in terms of their formatting rather than their abstract structure. We are accustomed to thinking of documents in terms of their rendition. That is because, prior to GML, there was no practical way to create a document without creating a rendition. The process of creating a DTD gives us an opportunity to rethink our documents in terms of their structure, as abstractions.

2.6.3 *Declaring a DTD*

Example 2-2 shows examples of some of the declarations that are used to express a DTD:

Example 2-2. Markup declarations

```
<!ELEMENT Q-AND-A (QUESTION,ANSWER)+>
<!-- This allows: question, answer, question, answer ... -->

<!ELEMENT QUESTION (#PCDATA)>
<!-- Questions are just made up of text -->

<!ELEMENT ANSWER (#PCDATA)>
<!-- Answers are just made up of text -->
```

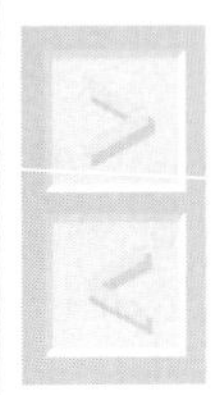

Caution *A DTD is a concept; markup declarations are the means of expressing it. The distinction is important because other means of expressing DTDs are being proposed. However, most people, even ourselves, don't make the distinction in normal parlance. We just talk about the declarations as though they are the DTD that they describe.*

Some XML documents do not have a document type declaration. That does not mean that they do not conform to a document type. It merely means that they do not claim to conform to some formally defined document type definition.

If the document is to be useful as an XML document, it must still have some structure, expressed through elements, attributes and so forth. When you create a stylesheet for a document you will depend on it having certain elements, on the element type names having certain meanings, and on the elements appearing in certain places. However it manifests itself, that set of things that you depend on is the document type.

You can formalize that structure in a DTD. In addition to or instead of a formal computer-readable DTD, you can also write out a prose description. You might consider the many HTML books in existence to be prose definitions of HTML. Finally, you can just keep the document type in your head and maintain conformance through careful discipline. If you can achieve this for large, complex documents, your powers of concentration are astounding! Which is our way of saying: we do not advise it. We will discuss DTDs more in Chapter 54, "Creating a document type definition", on page 748.

2.7 | Well-formedness and validity

Every language has rules about what is or is not valid in the language. In human languages that takes many forms: words have a particular correct pronunciation (or range of pronunciations) and they can be combined in certain ways to make valid sentences (grammar). Similarly XML has two different notions of "correct". The first is merely that the markup is intelligible: the XML equivalent of "getting the pronunciation right". A document with intelligible markup is called a *well-formed* document. One important goal of XML was that these basic rules should be simple so that they could be strictly adhered to.

The experience of the HTML market provided a cautionary tale that guided the development of XML. Much of the HTML on the Web does *not* conform to even the simplest rules in the HTML specifications. This makes automated processing of HTML quite difficult.

Because Web browsers will display ill-formed documents, authors continue to create them. In designing XML, we decided that XML processors should actually be prohibited from trying to recover from a *well-formedness* error in an XML document. This was a controversial decision because there were many who felt that it was inappropriate to restrict XML implementors from deciding the best error recovery policy for their application.

The XML equivalent of "using the right words in the right place" is called *validity* and is related to the notion of document types. A document is *valid* if it declares conformance to a DTD in a document type declaration and actually conforms to the DTD.

Documents that do not have a document type declaration are not really *invalid* – they do not violate their DTD – but they are not valid either, because they cannot be validated against a DTD.

If HTML documents with multiple titles were changed over to use XML syntax, they would be *well-formed* and invalid (presuming the HTML DTD was also converted to XML syntax). If we remove the document type declaration, so that they no longer claim to conform to the HTML DTD, then they would become merely well-formed but neither valid nor invalid.

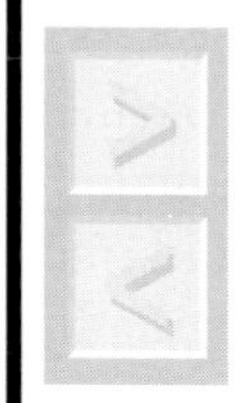

Caution *For most of us, the word "invalid" means something that breaks the rules. It is an easy jump from there to concluding that an XML document that does not conform to a DTD is free to break any rules at all. So for clarity, we may sometimes say "type-valid" and "non-type-valid", rather than "valid" and "invalid".*

You should think carefully before you decide to make a document that is well-formed but not valid. If the document is one-of-a-kind and is small, then making it well-formed is probably sufficient. But if it is to be part of any kind of information system (even a small one) or if it is a large document, then you should write a DTD for it and validate whenever you revise it. When you decide to build or extend your information system, the fact that the document is guaranteed to be consistent will make your programming or stylesheet writing many times easier and your results much more reliable.

2.8 | Hyperlinking and addressing

If you have used the Web, then you probably do not need to be convinced of the importance of hyperlinking. One thing you might not know, however, is that the Web's notions of hyperlink are fairly tame compared to what is available in the best academic and commercial hypertext systems. XML alone does not correct this, but it has an associated standard called *XLink* that goes a long way towards making the Web a more advanced hypertext environment.

The first deficiency of today's Web links is that there are no standardized mechanisms for making links that are external to the documents that they are linking from. Let's imagine, for example that you stumble upon a Web page for your favorite music group. You read it, enjoy it and move on. Imagine next week you stumble upon a Web page with all of the lyrics for all of their songs (with appropriate copyrights, of course!). You think: there should be a link between these two pages. Someone visiting one might want to know about the other and vice versa.

What you want to do is make an *external link*. You want to make a link on your computer that appears on both of the other computers. But of course you do not have the ability to edit those two documents. XLink will allow this external linking. It provides a representation for external links, but it does not provide the technology to automatically publish those links to the world. That would take some kind of *link database* that would track all of the links from people around the world. Needless to say this is a big job and though there are prototypes, there is no standardized system yet.

You may wonder how all of these links will be displayed, how readers will select link sheets and annotations, how browsers will talk to databases and so forth. The simple answer is: "nobody knows yet."[1]

---

1. But we've got some ideas. See Chapter 44, "Extended linking", on page 588.

Before the first Web browser was developed there was no way to know that we would develop a convention of using colored, underlined text to represent links (and even today some browsers use other conventions). There was also no way to know that browsers would typically have "back" buttons and "history lists". These are just conventions that arose and browser features that became popular.

This same process will now occur with external links. Some user interface (perhaps a menu) will be provided to apply external link sheets, and there will probably be some mechanism for searching for link sheets related to a document on the Web. Eventually these will stabilize into standards that will be ubiquitous and transparent (we hope!). In the meantime, things are confused, but that is the price for living on the cutting edge. XLink moves us a notch further ahead by providing a notation for representing the links.

Another interesting feature of XML extended links is that they can point to more than one resource. For instance instead of making a link from a word to its definition, you might choose to link to definitions in several different dictionaries. The browser might represent this as a popup menu, a tiny window with the choices listed, or might even open one window for each. The same disclaimer applies: the XML Link specification does not tell browsers exactly what they must do. Each is free to try to make the most intuitive, powerful user interface for links. XML brings many interesting hypertext ideas from university research labs and high tech companies "to the masses." We still have to work out exactly how that will look and who will use them for what. We live in interesting times!

2.9 | Stylesheets

To a certain extent, the concerns described above are endemic to generalized markup. Because it describes structure, and not formatting, it allows variations in display and processing that can sometimes disturb people.

However, as the Web has evolved, people have become less and less tolerant of having browser vendors control the "look and feel" of their documents. An important part of all communication, but especially modern business communication, is the idea of style. Stylesheets allow us to attach our own visual style to documents without destroying the virtue of generalized markup. Because the style is described in a separate entity, the stylesheet, software that is not interested in style can ignore it.

For instance most search engines would not care if your corporate color is blue or green, so they will just ignore those declarations in the stylesheet. Similarly, software that reads documents aloud to the sight-impaired would ignore font sizes and colors and concentrate on the abstractions – paragraphs, sections, titles and so forth.

The Web has a very simple stylesheet language called *Cascading Style Sheets* (CSS), which arose out of the early battles between formatting and generalized markup in HTML. Like any other specification, CSS is a product of its environment, and so is not powerful enough to describe the formatting of documents types that are radically different in structure from HTML.

Because CSS is not sufficient, the World Wide Web Consortium is working on a complementary alternative called the *Extensible Stylesheet Language* (XSL). XSL will have many features from CSS, but will also borrow some major ideas from ISO's DSSSL stylesheet language. XSL will be extensible, just as XML is, so that it will be appropriate for all document types and not just for HTML. Like the linking specification, XSL is still under development so its exact shape is not known. Nevertheless, there is a general design that we will review later on.

2.10 | Programming interfaces and models

This subject may seem intimidating if you are not a programmer – possibly even if you are! But we are just going to take a high-level view of a few constructs that will be helpful in understanding the chapters that follow. We'll cover the XML geek-speak Top Term List: Parsing, APIs, DOM, and SAX.

2.10.1 *Parsing*

Great as XML is for representing data, eventually that data has to be processed, which requires the use of one or more programs. One of the nice things about writing XML applications is that there is an abundance of reusable component and utility software available to help.

All great programmers try to reduce their work! If every programmer reinvented the wheel when it came to basic processing of XML, no programmer would ever get around to building applications that *use* XML. Instead of implementing basic XML processing over and over again, programmers tend to download or buy packages that implement various types of XML services.

The most basic reusable service is parsing. Parsing is about ripping apart the textual representation of a document and turning it into a set of conceptual objects.

For example, a parser looking at the document in Example 2-1 would recognize the characters `<QUESTION>` to be a start-tag, and would know that they signaled the start of a `QUESTION` element. The tag is part of the representation; the element is the conceptual object.

If the parser were also validating the document according to the DTD in Example 2-2, it would make sure that an `ANSWER` element followed the `QUESTION` element.

As a human being, you do parsing subconsciously. Because you've learned about elements and attributes, when you look at XML text you can think about the document in those conceptual terms.

But without an XML *parser*, a computer program can only see the characters. It's sort of the opposite of not seeing the forest for the trees. Without some form of parsing, an XML application cannot see the tree because of all of the characters!

2.10.2 *APIs*

There are many good XML parsers out there for use with many different programming languages. There are so many that it is hard to choose. A software developer would hate to pick one and be wedded to it forever. The programmer might want to change some day to a faster or cheaper one, or from a non-validating parser to a validating one.

Switching parsers (often also called *processors*) is easy if the two "look" the same to the programmer. You can plug in different brands and types of light bulbs into the same socket because of the standardization of the socket. The equivalent concept in software components is the standardization of *Application Processing Interfaces (APIs)*.

2.10.2.1 The DOM

The World Wide Web Consortium has standardized an API for working with XML. It is called the *Document Object Model* and it is available in Version 5 Web browsers. If you write code for Microsoft's *DOM* implementation, it should be relatively easy to make that code also work on Netscape's DOM.

But the DOM is not only for use in browsers. It can also be used on the server side. You can use the DOM to read, write and transmit XML on your Web server. DOM-based programs can talk to some XML content management systems. The DOM is very popular for general XML processing. It has been implemented, for example, for use with Python and Perl scripts and with the C++ and Java™ programming languages, among others. In fact, Microsoft's DOM implementation is a built-in part of Windows 2000 itself.

2.10.2.2 SAX

The DOM is popular and useful but it is not the be-all and end-all of XML parsing APIs. It is a little bit like putting a plane on automatic pilot. You point your DOM-building processor at an XML document and it returns you an object tree based on the structure of the document.

But if the document is five hundred megabytes of text and resides on the "other side" of the Internet, your program will just wait. And wait. And wait. When you finally get the data it will fill your computer's memory and some of its disk space. If you are having a bad day it might fill up everything and then crash the computer.

In a situation like this, you would rather just get tiny bits of the data as they come in. An *event-based parser* allows this mode of operation. Event-based parsers let your application work on the bit of the data that the parser finds at each "event" in the document.

For example, each XML start-tag corresponds to a "start element" event. Each end-tag corresponds to an "end element" event. Characters and other constructs have their own events. The event-based XML parser tells the application what it sees in the document as if through a peep-hole. It does not try to describe the larger picture to the application.[1]

The most popular event-based API is the *Simple API for XML. SAX* was developed by XML processor users and developers in an open discussion group called *XML-DEV*. Despite the name, SAX is not actually any simpler than the DOM. It is much more efficient and low-level, however. The price for efficiency is convenience. The processor only provides you with a peephole view, so if your application needs more than that, you'll need to write your own code to understand the "big picture" of the parsed document.

These two APIs are pervasive in the XML processing world. There are many other services that we could envision for XML handling: link management, searching and so forth. It is likely that these will be built either on top of or as extensions to these two popular APIs.

2.11 | Conclusion

There are a lot of new ideas here to absorb, but we'll be repeating and reemphasizing them as we move along. At this point, though, we're ready to look at where XML is going and the ways that it is being used in the real world.

1. If you concluded from this description that a DOM processor in effect uses an event-based parser as it constructs the DOM, you are right.

Where is XML going?

Introductory Discussion

- Beyond HTML
- Database publishing
- Electronic commerce and EDI
- Multimedia
- Metadata
- Content syndication
- Science on the Web

Chapter 3

The XML effort is new ground in many senses. The Web has never before had access to the new features that XML offers. It will take a while for the Web culture to understand the strengths (and weaknesses) of the new language and learn how to properly deploy it. Still, XML is already becoming a building block for the next generation of Web applications and specifications.

3.1 | Beyond HTML

XML was originally conceived as a big brother to HTML. As its name implies, XML can be used to extend HTML or even define whole new languages completely unlike HTML.

For instance, a company might want to offer technical manuals on the Web. Many manuals have a formatting for tables (e.g. a table listing a software product's supported languages) and repeat the formatting on several tables in the manual (perhaps once per program in a package). The formatting of these tables can be very intricate.

The rows, for example may be broken into categories with borders between them. The title of each column and row might be in a particular font and color. The width of the columns might be very precisely described. The final row ("the bottom line") might be colored. HTML could provide the formatting markup that the layout would require, but it would require a lot of duplication. In fact, it would be such a hassle that most companies would choose to use a graphic or an *Adobe Portable Document Format* (PDF) file instead.

To demonstrate how XML can help, we will use a sample table from the specification for HTML tables, shown in Figure 3-1. We will simplify the table somewhat, but the XML solution will still be shorter (in characters) and easier to read than the HTML source in Example 3-1.

CODE-PAGE SUPPORT IN MICROSOFT WINDOWS

Code-Page ID	Name	Windows NT 3.1	Windows NT 3.51	Windows 95
1200	Unicode (BMP of ISO 10646)	X	X	
1250	Windows 3.1 Eastern European	X	X	X
1251	Windows 3.1 Cyrillic	X	X	X
1252	Windows 3.1 US (ANSI)	X	X	X
1253	Windows 3.1 Greek	X	X	X
1254	Windows 3.1 Turkish	X	X	X
1255	Hebrew			X
1256	Arabic			X
1257	Baltic			X
1361	Korean (Johab)			X

Figure 3-1 A rendered table (from the HTML 4.0 Recommendation)

If there are many of these tables the cumulative effort of doing this manual work can add up to a large burden, especially since it must be maintained as products change. Even with an HTML authoring tool, you will probably have to do the layout manually, over and over again. As if this internal expense was not disturbing enough, every person who reads the annual report over the Web must download the same formatting information row after row, column after column, table after table, year after year. Right thinking Web page authors will understand that this situation is not good. The repetition leads to longer download times, congested servers, dissatisfied customers and perhaps irate managers.

Example 3-1. HTML markup for the table in Figure 3-1

```
<TABLE border="2" frame="hsides" rules="groups">
<CAPTION>CODE-PAGE SUPPORT IN MICROSOFT WINDOWS</CAPTION>
<COLGROUP align="center">
<COLGROUP align="left">
<COLGROUP align="center" span="2">
<COLGROUP align="center" span="3">
<THEAD valign="top"><TR><TH>Code-Page<br>ID<TH>Name
<TH>Windows<br>NT 3.1<TH>Windows<br>NT 3.51<TH>Windows<br>95
<TBODY>
<TR><TD>1200<TD>Unicode (BMP of ISO/IEC-10646)<TD>X<TD>X<TD>
<TR><TD>1250<TD>Windows 3.1 Eastern European<TD>X<TD>X<TD>X
<TR><TD>1251<TD>Windows 3.1 Cyrillic<TD>X<TD>X<TD>X
<TR><TD>1252<TD>Windows 3.1 US (ANSI)<TD>X<TD>X<TD>X
<TR><TD>1253<TD>Windows 3.1 Greek<TD>X<TD>X<TD>X
<TR><TD>1254<TD>Windows 3.1 Turkish<TD>X<TD>X<TD>X
<TR><TD>1255<TD>Hebrew<TD><TD><TD>X
<TR><TD>1256<TD>Arabic<TD><TD><TD>X
<TR><TD>1257<TD>Baltic<TD><TD><TD>X
<TR><TD>1361<TD>Korean (Johab)<TD><TD><TD>X</TABLE>
```

The XML solution would be to invent a simple extension to HTML that is customized to the needs of the manual. It would have table elements that would only require data that varies from table to table. None of the redundant formatting information would be included. We would then use a sophisticated stylesheet to add that information back in. The beauty of the stylesheet solution is that the formatting information is expressed only in one place. Surfers only have to download that once. Also, if your company decides to change the style of the tables, all of them can be changed at once merely by changing the stylesheet. Example 3-2 shows what that might look like.

The difference between this XML version and the HTML version is not as dramatic as in some examples, but the XML version is clearer, has fewer lines and characters and is easier to maintain. More important, the stylesheet can choose to format this in many different ways as time goes by and tastes change. All the XML version represents is the actual information about Windows code pages, not the tabular format of a particular presentation of it.

One thing to note is that the extra download of a stylesheet does take time. It makes the most sense to move formatting into a stylesheet when that formatting will be used on many pages or in many parts of the same page. The goal is to amortize the cost of the download over a body of text.

©2000 THE XML HANDBOOK™

Example 3-2. XML version of the table in Figure 3-1

```
<CODE-PAGE-TABLE>
<CP NUM="1200" NAME="Unicode (BMP of ISO/IEC-10646)"
   PLATFORMS="NT3.1 NT3.51"/>
<CP NUM="1250" NAME="Windows 3.1 Eastern European"
   PLATFORMS="NT3.1 NT3.51 WIN95"/>
<CP NUM="1251" NAME="Windows 3.1 Cyrillic"
   PLATFORMS="NT3.1 NT3.51 WIN95"/>
<CP NUM="1252" NAME="Windows 3.1 US (ANSI)"
   PLATFORMS="NT3.1 NT3.51 WIN95"/>
<CP NUM="1253" NAME="Windows 3.1 Greek"
   PLATFORMS="NT3.1 NT3.51 WIN95"/>
<CP NUM="1254" NAME="Windows 3.1 Turkish"
   PLATFORMS="NT3.1 NT3.51 WIN95"/>
<CP NUM="1255" NAME="Hebrew"
   PLATFORMS="WIN95"/>
<CP NUM="1256" NAME="Arabic"
   PLATFORMS="WIN95"/>
<CP NUM="1257" NAME="Baltic"
   PLATFORMS="WIN95"/>
<CP NUM="1261" NAME="Korean (Johab)"
   PLATFORMS="NT3.1 NT3.51 WIN95"/>
```

A similar caveat applies to the time it takes to make the stylesheet and design the table elements. Doing so for a single table would probably not be cost effective. Our example above basically shifts the complexity from the document to the stylesheet, on the presumption that there will probably be many documents (or at least many tables) for every stylesheet. In general, XML is about short-term investment in long-term productivity.

What if you are not interested in the extra investment that XML usually requires? You can get some of its benefits "on the cheap" with XHTML. XHTML is a version of HTML that uses XML syntax. The element types are all identical to those in ordinary HTML, so you do not have to learn new ones.

XHTML's major benefit is the availability of XML parsers. HTML's definition has always been very loose. Major browsers do not offer a way to validate documents and often accept non-conforming HTML-like text as if it were really HTML. XHTML disallows this practice. XHTML documents must always be well-formed and valid. At least one browser can already validate XHTML documents and report errors. Because of this "cleanliness", XHTML is much easier to work with than old-fashioned HTML. Future versions of XHTML will be extensible so that you can add a few of your own element types to the standard XHTML mix.

The real savings come when you move to a full-fledged industry- or company-specific XML document type. Once you have made that investment you can sometimes realize more radical productivity gains than you first intended. That's because your documents, like your database, now holds abstract data – not rendered, as in HTML.

Imagine that you use XML tables to publish the financial information in your company's annual report. Your accountants may be able to use their software's report writing feature to directly transfer accounting information into the XML table. This can save one more opportunity for typos between the accountants' printout and the Web author's keyboard. There might also be opportunities for automation at the other end of the spectrum. Other software might transform the XML table directly into a format required for submission to some government agency.

3.2 | Database publishing

The last example hints at the way XML can interact with systems that are not typically associated with documentation. As documents become abstractions, they can become integrated with the other abstract data in an organization. Some of the same techniques can be used to create them (such as report writing software or custom graphical user interfaces) and some of the same software will be able to read them (such as spreadsheets and database software). One already popular application of XML is the publishing of databases to the Web.

Consider for instance a product database, used by the internal ordering system of a toy manufacturer. The manufacturer might want the database to be available on the Web so that potential clients would know what was available and at what price. Rather than having someone in the Web design department mark up the data again, they could build a connection between their Web server and their database using the features typically built into Web servers that allow those sorts of data pipes.

The designers could then make the products list beautiful using a stylesheet. Pictures of the toys could be supplied by the database. In essence, the Web site would be merely a view on the data in the database. As toys get added and removed from the database, they will appear and disappear from the view on the Website. This mechanism also gives the Website maintainer the freedom to update the "look and feel" of the Website without dealing with the database or the plumbing that connects it to the Web server!

XML is already becoming an important tool for interchange of database information. Databases have typically interchanged information using simple file formats like one-record per line with semi-colons between the fields. This is not sufficient for the new object-oriented information being stored and generated by databases. Objects must have internal structure and links between them.

XML can represent objects by using elements and attributes to provide a common representation for transferring database records between databases. You can imagine that one database might produce an XML document representing all of the toys the manufacturer produces. That document could be directly loaded into another database either within the company or at a customer's site. This is a very interesting way of thinking about documents, because in many cases human beings will never see them. They are documents produced by and for computer software.

One is shown in Example 3-3.

Example 3-3. A products database in XML

```
<TOYS>
<ITEM>
<TITLE>GI John</TITLE>
<MANUFACTURER>War Toys Inc.</MANUFACTURER>
<PRICE>50.95</PRICE>
<IN-STOCK>3000</IN-STOCK>
</ITEM>
<ITEM>
<TITLE>Leggo!</TITLE>
<MANUFACTURER>Grips R US</MANUFACTURER>
<PRICE>64.95</PRICE>
<IN-STOCK>2000</IN-STOCK>
</ITEM>
<ITEM>
<TITLE>Hell On Wheels</TITLE>
<MANUFACTURER>Li'l Road Warriors</MANUFACTURER>
<PRICE>150.95</PRICE>
<IN-STOCK>3200</IN-STOCK>
</ITEM>
</TOYS>
```

3.3 | Electronic commerce and EDI

Assume that a retailer decides that it wants to start selling a line of toys from the database. It might contact the manufacturer to organize the sale. The two could agree on an XML-based product-request message format and formalize it in an XML document type. In fact, there might already be an industry standard XML document type appropriate for the task.

Once the document type has been defined, orders for the part can be sent automatically from the purchaser's computer to the supplier's. This sort of electronic commerce has been possible for years, but XML allows it to be easily standardized, highly extensible and wired into the backbone technologies of the Internet. The easy availability of the software and standards will allow much smaller organizations to use electronic commerce.

Example 3-4 illustrates such a possible "toy order" document.

Example 3-4. An order for a toy

```
<Toy-Order>
<Order-No>967634</Order-No>
<Message-Date>19961002</Message-Date>
<Buyer-EAN>5412345000176</Buyer-EAN>
<Toy><Number>523953-432</Number><Quantity>18</Quantity></Toy>
<Toy><Number>438312-716</Number><Quantity>13</Quantity></Toy>
<Toy><Number>232332-136</Number><Quantity>23</Quantity></Toy>
</Toy-Order>
```

There are several initiatives to build an infrastructure for electronic commerce. The first group on the scene was an informally organized group called XML-EDI.[1] These industry experts work together to promote the use of XML for electronic commerce and data interchange.

CommerceNet is a non-profit corporate membership organization that does research and development of XML e-commerce technologies and methodologies.[2]

Microsoft is also very interested in e-commerce. Its strategy is based on a framework called *BizTalk*.[3] Technically, *BizTalk* is a set of specifications for sending e-commerce messages over the Web. The specifications do not

1. http://www.geocities.com/WallStreet/Floor/5815/
2. http://www.commerce.net
3. http://www.biztalk.org

address the contents of the messages; those will vary between industries. They address only the routing information – the electronic envelope.

The *BizTalk* initiative also includes a portal and repository for industry-specific schemas. The *Organization for the Advancement of Structured Information Standards (OASIS)* has established *XML.org*[1] for similar purposes.

3.4 | Multimedia

XML can be a central component in a rich multimedia system. Consider the *Scalable Vector Graphics (SVG)* specification. This World Wide Web Consortium specification allows vector graphics to be represented entirely in XML, as shown in Example 3-5.

Vector graphics are described in terms of lines and shapes instead of individual points. This makes them relatively efficient (compared to bitmaps) and much easier to work with. Once the Web adopts this standard vector graphics notation, it will be easy to move these graphics between software products like *Adobe Illustrator*™ and *CorelDraw*™. SVG support is not yet built into browsers but is available through plug-ins.

Example 3-5. Diagram represented in SVG

```
<?xml version="1.0" standalone="no"?>
<!DOCTYPE svg PUBLIC "-//W3C//DTD SVG August 1999//EN"
"http://www.w3.org/Graphics/SVG/SVG-19990812.dtd">
<svg width="4in" height="3in">
<desc>Two groups, each of two rectangles
</desc>
<g style="fillcolor:red">
 <rect x="100" y="100" width="100" height="100" />
 <rect x="300" y="100" width="100" height="100" />
</g>
<g style="fillcolor:blue">
 <rect x="100" y="300" width="100" height="100" />
 <rect x="300" y="300" width="100" height="100" />
</g>
</svg>
```

1. http://www.xml.org

The *Synchronized Multimedia Integration Language (SMIL)* is an XML document type for describing multimedia presentations. SMIL allows sequencing of audio, video, text and graphic components. SMIL is used in the *RealPlayer G2*™ product.

3.5 | Metadata

There is a special type of data that interests owners and users of large information collections. It is called *metadata*: information about information. Metadata is starting to become crucial to Web searching and navigation.

3.5.1 *Channel Definition Format*

One of Microsoft's early forays into metadata is called the *Channel Definition Format*. CDF describes things about Web channels, such as their schedules and logos, and can carry a description of the channel (Example 3-6). This may seem familiar to you. If you think about it, you will notice that even *TV Guide* is metadata! Some future online version might use either CDF or a new RDF-based vocabulary.

Example 3-6. Channel Description Format

```
<?xml version="1.0"?>
<CHANNEL HREF="http://www.rocktv.com/channels">
<ABSTRACT>
RockTV is your 24-hour rock station! Nothing but geology,
geography and rock collecting. All day! All night!
</ABSTRACT>
</CHANNEL>
```

XML is convenient for these tasks for several reasons. It can be edited in standard text editors and specialized XML word processors. XML's syntax will be familiar to the millions of Web maintainers who must eventually learn to apply metadata. XML expresses the hierarchy and links of these documents nicely. It is also well suited to representing the textual portions of specifications. For instance, every channel will have a textual description hoping to convince you to subscribe. XML can allow these descriptions to use hypermedia features to create very compelling displays.

3.5.2 *Platform for Internet Content Selection*

The first standardized metadata specification for the Web was developed before XML and is called the *Platform for Internet Content Selection (PICS).* PICS allows the filtering of inappropriate material from computer screens based on external descriptions of content.

The "violent content" label on a video tape is a perfect example of metadata. The data provided, "violent content" describes the contents of the tape – it is data about data. PICS is an electronic version of that label.

PICS is not yet an XML application but it is scheduled to become one.

3.5.3 *Resource Description Framework*

PICS has not yet been converted to XML because the World Wide Web Consortium decided to invent an intermediate layer first. The intermediate layer is called the *Resource Description Framework* (RDF).

RDF is not a document type: it is a convention for designing XML documents so that they can more easily be interpreted as metadata.

RDF's central concept is the "property". An RDF document can associate many properties with documents on the Web. Some of those properties will eventually be from the PICS vocabulary but there will be other RDF vocabularies that are unrelated to content filtering, such as those used in Example 3-7.

Example 3-7. Describing the owner of a document in RDF

```
<RDF:assertions href="http://www.bar.com/some.doc">
    <bib:author>
 <RDF:resource>
   <bib:name>John Smith</bib:name>
 <bib:email>john@smith.com</bib:email>
 <bib:phone>+1 (555) 123-4567</bib:phone>
      </RDF:resource>
 </bib:author>
</RDF:assertions>
```

In one sense, this sounds very complicated: PICS is based on RDF which is based on XML. But on the other hand, it will not be so complicated in practice. PICS and CDF will have a set of element types that you must learn to apply according to the XML syntax described in this book. RDF, the middle layer, will only be visible to the wizards who invent new ways of cataloging, describing and organizing information – the librarians of the future.[1]

3.5.4 *Topic maps*

A related development comes from the *International Organization for Standardization (ISO)*. *Topic maps* are a specific type of metadata designed to allow the construction of logical "maps" of information. Topic maps are designed to help us navigate through the massive amounts of information on the Web. You can think of topic maps as a very sophisticated indexing mechanism for online information.

Topic maps' sophistication comes in the idea of *scoping*. With scoping, you can label a particular characteristic (roughly, an index entry) as only being applicable within a certain context.

For example, if you label characteristics as being applicable only in a particular language, a query for information on a topic would only return occurrences in your native tongue. If you labeled characteristics as being either "biological" or "psychological", then a search for the word "evolution" would return only biological topics or only psychological ones, depending on your query.

Topic maps are discussed in Chapter 46, "Topic maps: Knowledge navigation aids", on page 618, which includes a tutorial.

3.6 | Content syndication

Content syndication is about using metadata to move documents, such as news articles, from place to place. It is a problem domain that is tailor-made

---

1. Luckily, the librarians of the present are very much involved in these standardization efforts.

©2000 The XML Handbook™

for XML because when you put XML and the Internet together you have a powerful information distribution infrastructure.

The alphabet soup of competing and cooperating standards is too long to cover in depth, but we can name a few:

- *ICE* is the *Information Content and Exchange* specification from the vendor consortium of the same name.
- *XMLNews* from Wavo and David Megginson has its roots in the newspaper business. It is described in Chapter 22, "XMLNews: A syndication document type", on page 288.
- *RSS*, the *RDF Site Specification* is a lightweight standard from Netscape that has been embraced by the Open Source and Linux communities.

3.7 | Science on the Web

Although the Web was originally invented in a physics laboratory for communication among physicists, it never developed into a great system for communicating mathematical formulae. Markup for mathematics is more complex than it seems at first to non-mathematicians.

The World Wide Web Consortium has created an XML-based language called *MathML*. Although the major browsers do not support MathML directly, you can get MathML support through Java applets, browser plug-ins and specialized browsers.

A rendition of a mathematical formula is shown in Figure 3-2. Its MathML markup is illustrated in Example 3-8.

$$x^2 + 4x + 4 = 0$$

Figure 3-2 Rendition of a mathematical formula

The *Chemical Markup Language* (CML) is an XML-based language for describing the management of molecular information on computer net-

Example 3-8. MathML markup for the formula in Figure 3-2

```
<mrow>
  <mrow>
    <msup>
      <mi>x</mi>
      <mn>2</mn>
    </msup>
    <mo>+</mo>
    <mrow>
      <mn>4</mn>
      <mo>&invisibletimes;</mo>
      <mi>x</mi>
    </mrow>
    <mo>+</mo>
    <mn>4</mn>
  </mrow>
  <mo>=</mo>
  <mn>0</mn>
</mrow>
```

works. Using a Java viewer that is under development, users can view and manipulate molecules in 2 and 3 dimensions. *Bioinformatic Sequence Markup Language* is a standard for representing DNA, RNA and protein sequence information.

As you can see, XML is branching out into a wide variety of problem domains. Whatever your discipline, you should consider if there is some part of your work that could be made more efficient with part of your work that could be made more efficient with standardization based on XML. In subsequent parts of this book, we will explore in detail a wide array of applications of the kinds we have been describing.

XML in the real world

Introductory Discussion

- Real-world concepts
- Documents vs. data
- Message-oriented middleware (MOM)
- Presentation-oriented publishing (POP)

©2000 THE XML HANDBOOK™

Chapter 4

Applications are the reason for using technology, so it makes sense to get a good idea of what XML is used for before digging into the details of the language.

And since XML may be somewhat different from the technologies that you are accustomed to using, it is also helpful to see how people actually work with it; how the tools are used.

We're going to cover those subjects at length in the remainder of the book. In preparation, we need to examine some often elusive – but vital – concepts relating to real-world use of XML.

4.1 | Is XML for documents or for data?

What is a document?

The dictionary says:

> "Something written, inscribed, engraved, etc., which provides evidence or information or serves as a record".

Documents come in all shapes and sizes and media, as you can see in Figure 4-1. Here are some you may have encountered:

- Long documents: books, manuals, product specifications
- Broadsides: catalog sheets, posters, notices
- Forms: registration, application, etc.
- Letters: email, memos
- Records: "Acme Co., Part# 732, reverse widget, $32.50, 5323 in stock"
- Messages: "job complete", "update accepted"

An e-commerce transaction, such as a purchase, might involve several of these. A buyer could start by sending several documents to a vendor:

- Covering note: a letter
- Purchase order: a form
- Attached product specification: a long document

The vendor might respond with several more documents:

- Formal acknowledgment: a message
- Thank you note: a letter
- Invoice: a form

The beauty of XML is that the same software can process all of this diversity. Whatever you can do with one kind of document you can do with all the others. The only time you need additional tools is when you want to do different kinds of things – not when you want to work with different kinds of documents.

And there are lots of things that you can do.

4.2 | A wide spectrum of application opportunities

Sorry about that, we've been reading too many marketing brochures. But it's true, nevertheless.

Figure 4-1 Documents come in all shapes and sizes.

At one end of the spectrum we have the grand old man of generalized markup, *POP* – Presentation-Oriented Publishing. You can see him in Figure 4-2.

At the other end of the spectrum is that darling of the data processors, *MOM* – Message-Oriented Middleware. She smiles radiantly from Figure 4-3.

Let's take a closer look at both of them.

Figure 4-2 POP application.

4.2.1 *Presentation-oriented publishing*

POP was the original killer app for SGML, XML's parent, because it saves so much money for enterprises with Web-sized document collections.

POP documents are chiefly written by humans for other humans to read.

computer
generates
MOM
document
wrapped
in tags to
preserve
data
to be utilized
by another
computer

Figure 4-3 MOM application.

Instead of creating formatted renditions, as in word processors or desktop publishing programs, XML POP users create unformatted abstractions. That means the document file captures what is *in* the document, but not how it is supposed to look.

To get the desired look, the POP user creates a stylesheet, a set of commands that tell a program how to format (and/or otherwise process) the document. The power of XML in this regard is that you don't need to choose just one look – you can have a separate stylesheet for every purpose.[1] At a minimum, you might want one for print, one for CD-ROM, and another for a website.

POP documents tend to be (but needn't be) long-lived, large, and with complex structures. When delivered in electronic media, they may be interactive. How they will be rendered is of great importance, but, because XML is used, the rendition information can be – and is – kept distinct from the abstract data.

4.2.2 *Message-oriented middleware*

MOM is the killer app – actually, a technology that drives lots of killer apps – for XML on the Web.

Middleware, as you might suspect from the name, is software that comes between two other programs. It acts like your interpreter/guide might if you were to visit someplace where you couldn't speak the language and had no idea of the local customs. It talks in the native tongue, using the native customs, and translates the native replies – the messages – into your language.

MOM documents are chiefly generated by programs for other programs to read.

Instead of writing specialized programs (clients) to access particular databases or other data sources (servers), XML MOM users break the old two-tier client/server model. They introduce a third tier, the "middle tier", that acts as a data integrator. The middle-tier server does all the talking to the data sources and sends their messages in XML to the client.

That means the client can read data from anywhere, but only has to understand data that is in XML documents. The XML markup provides the metadata (i.e. information about the data) that was in the original data source schema, like the database table name and field names (also called "cell" or "column" names).

The MOM user typically doesn't care much about rendition. He *does* care, though, about extracting the original data accurately and making some use of the metadata. His client software, instead of having a specialized module for each data source, has a single "XML parser" module. The parser is the program that separates the markup from the data, just as it does in POP applications.

---

1. We know that all office suites offer some degree of stylesheet support today, but XML (well, GML) did it first, and still is the only way to do it cleanly.

And just like POP applications, there can be a stylesheet, a set of commands that tell a program how to process the document. It may not look much like a POP stylesheet – it might look more like a script or program – but it performs the same function. And, as with POP stylesheets, there can be different MOM stylesheets for different document types, or to do different things with message documents of a single document type.

There is an extra benefit to XML three-tier MOM applications in a networked environment. For many applications, the middle-tier server can collect all of the relevant data at once and send it in a single document to the client. Further querying, sorting, and other processing can then take place solely on the client system. That not only cuts down Web traffic and overhead, but it vastly improves the end-user's perceived performance and his satisfaction with the experience.

MOM documents tend to be (but needn't be) short-lived, non-interactive, small, and with simple structures.

4.3 | Opposites are attracted

To XML, that is!

How is it that XML can be optimal for two such apparently extreme opposites as MOM and POP? The answer is, the two are not really different where it counts.

In both cases, we start with abstract information. For POP, it comes from a human author's head. For MOM, it comes from a database. But either way, the abstract data is marked up with tags and becomes a document.

Here is a terminally cute mnemonic for this very important relationship:

Data + Markup = DocuMent

Aren't you sorry you read it? Now you'll never forget it.

But XML "DocuMents" are special. An application can do three kinds of processing with one:

- *Parse it*, in order to extract the original data. This can be done without information loss because XML represents both metadata and data, and it lets you keep the abstractions distinct from rendition information.

- *Render it*, so it can be presented in a physical medium that a human can perceive. It can be rendered in many different ways, for delivery in multiple media such as screen displays, print, Braille, spoken word, and so on.
- *Hack it*, meaning "process it as plain text without parsing". Hacking might involve cutting and pasting into other XML documents, or scanning the markup to get some information from it without doing a real parse.

The real revelation here is that data and documents aren't opposites. Far from it – they are actually two states of the same information.

The real difference between the two is that when data is in a database, the metadata about its structure and meaning (the schema) is stored according to the proprietary architecture of the database. When the data becomes a document, the metadata is stored as markup.

A mixture of markup and data must be governed by the rules of some *notation*. XML and SGML are notations, as are RTF and Word file format. The rules of the notation determine how a parser will interpret the document text to separate the data from the markup.

Notations are not just for complete documents. There are also *data object notations*, such as GIF, TIFF, and EPS, that are used to represent such things as graphics, video (e.g., MPEG), and audio (e.g., AVI). Document notations usually allow their documents to contain data objects, such as pictures, that are in the objects' own data object notations.

Data object notations are usually (not always) in *binary*; that is, they are built-up from low-level ones and zeros. Document notations, however, are frequently *character-based*. XML is character-based, which is why it can be hacked.

In fact, a design objective of XML was to support the "desperate Perl hacker" – someone who needs to write a program in a hurry, using a scripting language like Perl, and who doesn't use a real XML parser. Instead, his program scans the XML document as though it were plain text. The program might search for markup strings, but can also search for data.

A hacker[1] often uses cues that have special meaning to him, like giving special treatment to a tag that occurs at the start of a line, even though those cues have no meaning to a parser. That's why serious hackers do their XML editing with programs that can preserve a document's source and reproduce it character-for-character. They don't let the software decide which characters are important enough to preserve.

Since databases and documents are really the same, and MOM and POP applications both use XML documents, there are lots of opportunities for synergy.

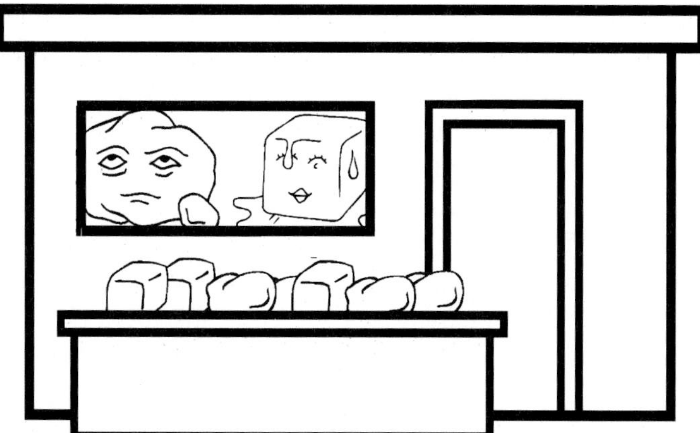

Figure 4-4 Dynamic servers: The MOM and POP store.

4.4 | MOM and POP – They're so great together!

Classically, MOM and POP were radically different kinds of applications, each doing things its own way with different technologies and mental models. But POP applications frequently need to include database data in their

1. As used here, and by most knowledgeable computer people, "hacker" has none of the "cracker" stigma given the term in the popular press. The only security compromised by a desperate Perl hacker is his job security, for leaving things to the last minute!

document content – think of an automotive maintenance manual that has to get the accurate part numbers from a database.

Similarly, MOM applications need to include human-written components. When the dealer asks for price and availability of the automotive parts you need, the display might include a description as well.

With the advent of generalized markup, the barriers to doing MOM-like things in POP applications began to disappear. Some of the POP-like applications you'll read about later in the book appear to have invented the middle tier on their own. And now, with the advent of XML, MOM applications can easily incorporate POP functionality as well.

What is now emerging is a new generation of composite systems, dynamically serving both persistent POP information and dynamic MOM data. They use databases to store information components so they can be controlled, managed, and assembled into end-products in the same way as components of automobiles, aircraft, or other complex devices. Think of them as the MOM and POP store (Figure 4-4).[1]

In fact, we'd go so far as to say there is no longer a difference in kind between the two, only a difference in degree. There really is "an endless spectrum of application opportunities". It is a multi-dimensional spectrum where applications need not be implemented differently just because they process different document types. The real differentiators are other document characteristics, like persistency, size, interactivity, structural complexity, percentage of human-written content, and the importance of eventual presentation to humans.[2]

At the extremes, some applications may call for specialized (or optimized) techniques, but the broad central universe of applications can all be implemented similarly. Much of the knowledge that POP application developers have acquired over the years is now applicable to MOM applications, and vice versa. Keep that in mind as you read the application descriptions and case studies.

That cross-fertilization is true of products and their underlying technologies as well. All of the product descriptions in this book should be of inter-

1. Generations ago the Mom and Pop store (grocery, convenience, etc.) was the achievement of the entrepreneurial couple who'd lifted themselves out of the working class. Today they'd have an Internet start-up and be striving for a successful IPO!

2. The relationship between documents and data is explored further in 35.1, "Documents and data", on page 469.

est, whether you think of your applications as chiefly being MOM or being POP. It is the differences in functionality and design that should cause you to choose one product over another, not their marketing thrust or apparent orientation. We've included detailed usage examples for leading tools in each category so you can look beyond the labels.

4.5 | Conclusion

We've covered the key concepts of XML itself, and of the ways in which it is used in the real world. Now we are ready to examine those real-world uses in depth, with application scenarios, case studies of actual users, and detailed descriptions of the tools of the tag trade. You need just one more vital bit of preparation, our *XML Handbook Jargon Demystifier*™, which is coming up next.

XML Jargon Demystifier™

Introductory Discussion

- Structured vs. unstructured
- Tag vs. element
- Document type, DTD, and markup declarations
- Document, XML document, and document instance
- Schema and schema definitions
- Metadata and metalanguage
- Notations and characters
- Coding, encoding, and markup

©2000 The XML Handbook™

Chapter 5

One of the problems in learning a new technology like XML is getting used to the jargon. A good book will hold you by the hand, introduce terms gradually, and use them precisely and consistently.

Out in the real word, though, people use imprecise terminology that often makes it hard to understand things, let alone compare products. And, unlike authors,[1] they sometimes just plain get things wrong.

For example, you may see statements like "XML documents are either well-formed or valid." As you've learned from this book, that simply isn't true. *All* XML documents are well-formed; some of them are also valid.[2]

In this book, we've taken pains to edit the application and tool chapters to use consistent and accurate terminology. However, for product literature and other documents you read, the mileage may vary. So we've prepared a handy guide to the important XML jargon, both right and wrong. Think of it as a MOM application for XML knowledge.

---

1. We should be so lucky!
2. So does that mean a merely well-formed document is "invalid"? No, for the reasons described in 2.7, "Well-formedness and validity", on page 34. Hey, we didn't promise to justify XML jargon, just to explain it.

5.1 | Structured vs. unstructured

Structured is arguably the most commonly used word to characterize the essence of markup languages. It is also the most ambiguous and most often misused word.

There are three common meanings:

structured = abstract

XML documents are frequently referred to as structured while other text, such as renditions in notations like RTF, is called *unstructured.* Separating "structure from style" is considered the hallmark of a markup language. But in fact, renditions can have a rich structure, composed of elements like pages, columns, and blocks. The real distinction being made is between "abstract" and "rendered".

structured = managed

This is the meaning that folks with a database background usually have in mind. Structured information is managed as a common resource and is accessible to the entire enterprise. Unfortunately, there are also departmental and individual databases and their content isn't "structured" in quite the same sense.

structured = possessing structure

This is the dictionary meaning, and the one used in this book. There is usually the (sometimes unwarranted) implication that the structure is fine-grained (rich, detailed), making components accessible at efficient levels of granularity. A structure can be very simple – a single really big component – but nothing is unstructured. All structure is well-defined and "predictable" (in the sense of consistent), it just may not be very granular.

These distinctions aren't academic. It is very important to know which "structured" a vendor means.

What if your publishing system has bottlenecks because you are maintaining four rendered versions of your documents in different representations? It isn't much of a solution to "structure" them in a database so that modifying one version warns you to modify the others.

You'll want to have a single "structured" – that is, abstract – version from which the others can be generated. And if you find that your document has scores of pages unrelieved by sub-headings, you may want to "structure" it more finely so that both readers and editors can deal with it in smaller chunks.

Keep these different meanings in mind when you read about "structured" and "unstructured". In this book, we try to confine our use of the word to its dictionary meaning, occasionally (when it is clear from the context) with the implication of "fine-grained".

5.2 | Tag vs. element

Tags aren't the same thing as elements. Tags describe elements.

In Figure 5-1 the package, metaphorically speaking, is an element. The contents of the package is the content of an element. The tag describes the element. It contains three names:

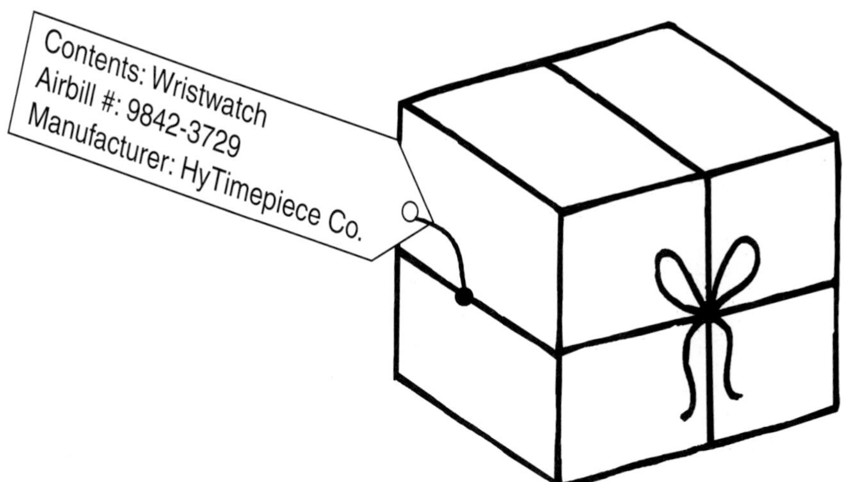

Figure 5-1 What's in a tag?

- The *element-type name* (`Wristwatch`), which says what type of element it is.

©2000 The XML Handbook™

- A *unique identifier*, or ID (`9842-3729`), which says which particular element it is.
- The name of an attribute that describes some other property of the element: `Manufacturer="Hy TimePiece Company"`.

When people talk about a *tag name*:

1. They are referring to the element-type name.
2. They are making an error, because tags aren't named.

5.3 | Document type, DTD, and markup declarations

A *document type* is a class of similar documents, like telephone books, technical manuals, or (when they are marked up as XML) inventory records.

A *document type definition* (*DTD*) is the set of rules for using XML to represent documents of a particular type. These rules might exist only in your mind as you create a document, or they may be written out.

Markup declarations, such as those in Example 5-1, are XML's way of writing out DTDs.

Example 5-1. Markup declarations in the file `greeting.dtd`.

```
<!ELEMENT greeting (salutation, addressee) >
<!ELEMENT salutation (#PCDATA) >
<!ELEMENT addressee  (#PCDATA) >
```

It is easy to mix up these three constructs: a document type, XML's markup rules for documents of that type (the DTD), and the expression of those rules (the markup declarations). It is necessary to keep the constructs separate if you are dealing with two or more of them at the same time, as when discussing alternative ways to express a DTD. But most of the time, even in this book, "DTD" will suffice for referring to any of the three.

5.4 | Document, XML document, and instance

The term *document* has two distinct meanings in XML.

Consider a really short XML document that might be rendered as:

Hello World

In one sense, the *conceptual document* that you see in your mind's eye when you read the rendition is the *real document*. Communicating that conception is the reason for using XML in the first place.

In a formal, syntactic sense, though, the complete text (markup + data, remember) of Example 5-2, is the *XML document*. Perhaps surprisingly, that includes the markup declarations for its DTD in Example 5-1. The XML document, in other words, is a character string that *represents* the real document.

In this example, much of that string consists of the markup declarations, which express the greeting DTD. Only the last four lines describe the real document, which is an instance of a greeting. Those lines are called the *document instance*.

Example 5-2. A greeting document.

```
<?xml version="1.0"?>
<!DOCTYPE greeting SYSTEM "file://greeting.dtd">
<greeting>
<salutation>Hello</salutation>
<addressee>World</addressee>
</greeting>
```

5.5 | Schema and schema definition

The programming and database worlds have introduced some new terminology to XML.

We now speak of a document type as a kind of *schema*, a conception of the common characteristics of some class of things. Similarly, a DTD is a *schema definition*, a representation of a schema.

A notation for schema definitions is called a *schema definition language*. Markup declarations serve that purpose for DTDs, while XML instances do the job for schema definitions. And as with DTDs, the word "schema" can serve for all these purposes when there is no ambiguity.

5.6 | What's the meta?

Nothing. What did you think was the meta?[1]

There are two "meta" words that come up regularly when computer types talk about XML: metadata and metalanguage.

5.6.1 *Metadata*

Metadata is data about data. The date, publisher's name, and author's name of a book are metadata about the book, while the data of the book is its content. The DTD and markup tags of an XML document are also metadata. If you choose to represent the author's name as an element, then it is both data and metadata.

If you get the idea that the line between data and metadata is a fluid one, you are right. And as long as your document representation and system let you access and process metadata as though it were data, it doesn't much matter where you draw that line.

Be careful when talking to database experts, though. In their discipline "metadata" typically refers only to the schema.

5.6.2 *Metalanguage*

You may hear some DTDs referred to as languages, rather than document types. HTML is a prominent example. There's nothing special about them, it is just another way of looking at the way a markup language works.

Remember that an XML document is a character string that represents the conceptual document. The rules for creating a valid string are like the rules of a language: There is a *vocabulary* of element type and attribute names, and a *grammar* that determines where the names can be used.

---

1. Sorry about that!

These language rules come from the DTD, which in turn follows the rules of XML. A language, such as XML, which you can use to define other languages (such as DTDs), is called a *metalanguage*. XML document types are sometimes called *XML-based languages*.

5.7 | Notations and characters

Normally, the characters in a document are interpreted one at a time. They are given the meaning assigned by the document character set, which for XML documents is Unicode. So the character `a` is interpreted as the letter "a" and the character `<` is interpreted as the mathematical symbol "less-than".

A character-based *notation* is a set of rules for interpreting a *sequence* of characters at once, and giving the sequence a meaning that is different from the character-set meaning of the individual characters. The HTML notation, for example, interprets `<a name=b>` as the start-tag of an "a" element.

Computer languages (including markup languages and languages defined by markup languages), document and data formats like RTF and JPEG, and the string representations of datatypes, are all examples of notations.

The distinction between various kinds of notations can be rather esoteric. The important thing is that characters don't have their usual meaning. You need a *parser* to figure out what that meaning is. But XML is simple enough that, after reading Part Eleven of this book, you should be able to parse XML documents yourself.

5.8 | Coding, encoding, and markup

People refer to computer programs as *code*, and to the act of programming as *coding*.

There is also the word *encoding*, which refers to the way that characters are represented as ones and zeros in computer storage. XML has a declaration for specifying an encoding.

You'll often see (in places other than this book) phrases like "XML-encoded data", "coded in HTML", or "XML coding".

But using XML isn't coding. Not in the sense of programming, and not in the sense of character encoding. What those phrases mean are "XML document", "marked-up in HTML", and "XML markup".[1]

5.9 | And in conclusion

The matrix in Figure 5-2 ties together a number of the concepts we've been discussing.

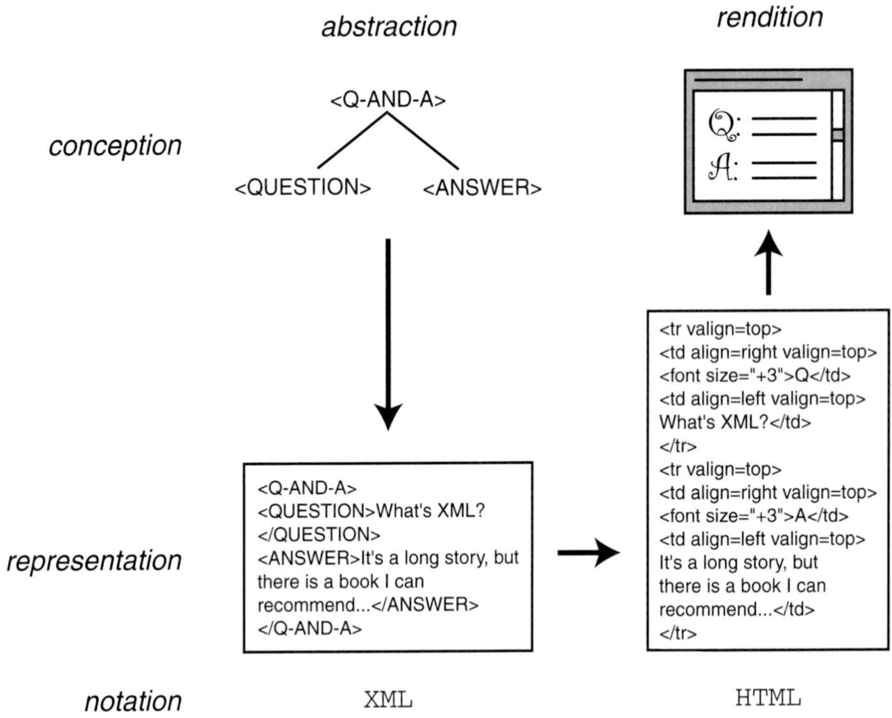

Figure 5-2 A rendition can be generated from an abstraction

1. Although dynamic HTML pages contain so much scripting that the phrase "HTML coding" is sometimes warranted.

is available for use by both middle-tier and client-side processing based on member queries.

Example 6-2. XML document generated from award specials database

```
<special_item
  economy="50000"
  business ="60000"
  first   ="70000"
  partner_name="Sperling Airlines"
  from_city="Vancouver"
  to_city="Paris"
  start   ="02/Apr/1998"
  end   ="Aug 30"/>
<special_item
  economy="52000"
  business ="62000"
  first   ="72000"
  partner_name="Sperling Airlines"
  from_city="Vancouver"
  to_city="Frankfurt"
  start   ="02/Apr/1998"
  end   ="Sep 30"/>
<special_item
  economy="50000"
  business="60000"
  first="70000"
  partner_name="Trillium Airways"
  from_city="Vancouver"
  to_city="London"
  start="01/Apr/1998"
  end="Jul 30"/>
```

The middle-tier server can also request all planned flight point earnings from all remote flight information databases, as shown in Example 6-3. We can easily see the number of points that would be earned from each flight, the partner airline name, the city of origin, the destination, and the date of flight and class of service. This information is available for use by middle-tier and client-side processing.

The information that is sent to the middle tier is compact, personalized, and precise. It differs from HTML because it contains the actual abstract data, not the look of the screen. Middle-tier software acts to assemble and deliver the right information at the right time, minimizing Web traffic and providing a higher degree of user interaction and satisfaction.

©2000 THE XML HANDBOOK™

Example 6-3. XML document with flight point earnings

```
<flight
   points="10000"
   partner_name = "Sperling Airlines"
   from_city = "Vancouver"
   to_city = "New York"
   depart="Jun 01"
   flightclass="business"/>
<flight
   points="15000"
   partner_name = "Trillium Airways"
   from_city = "Vancouver"
   to_city = "New York"
   depart="Jul 21"
   flightclass="business"/>
```

6.6 | Towards the Brave New Web

The World Wide Web continues to evolve rapidly. Today the hottest websites are still those that provide multimedia sizzle. But as the shift continues from simply providing entertainment value to facilitating business transactions, dynamic personalized content is increasingly becoming hot.

Products like those described in this book allow the website developer to add a new middle-tier server to the Web model. It is this middle tier that enables business transactions in a way that was simply not possible before XML.

The *Softland Air* scenario shows how a middle-tier server, using XML as a structured information interchange representation, enables personalized data aggregation and organization from multiple remote databases, and interactive delivery to client browsers based upon end-user requirements.

©2000 THE XML HANDBOOK™

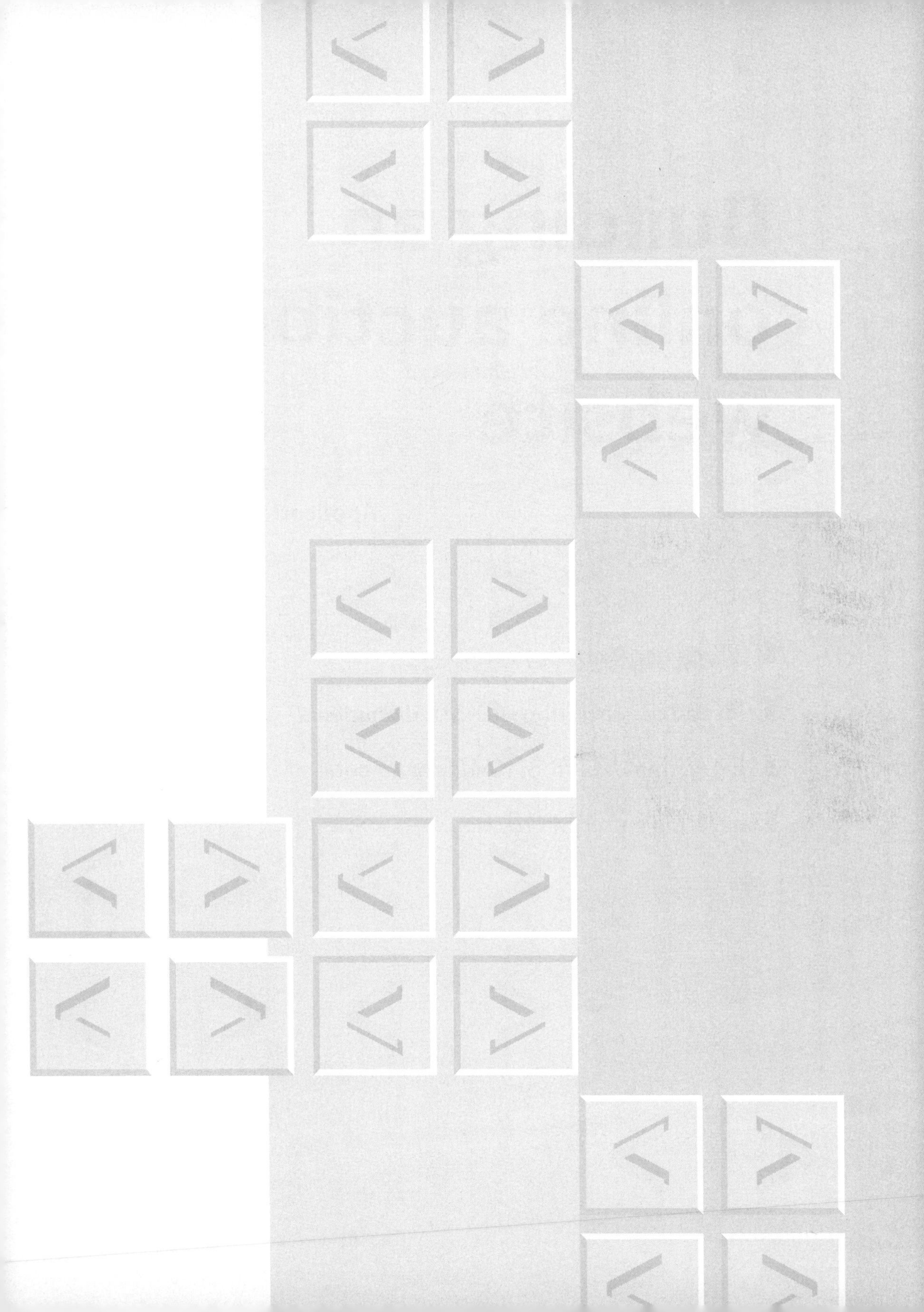

Building an online auction website

Application Discussion

- Three-tier Web application
- Dynamic generation of XML documents
- Extracting data from XML documents
- Creating a user interface

©2000 THE XML HANDBOOK™

Chapter 7

An online auction is the epitome of a complex real-time interactive application, so the Microsoft Web Applications Team built a realistic *Auction Demo* to show how simply one can be implemented as an XML three-tier Web application. This chapter is sponsored by Microsoft Corporation, `http://msdn.microsoft.com/xml`, and was prepared by Charles Heinemann.

The Auction Demo is a three-tier Web application that simulates an online auction using technologies that are available in Internet Explorer 4.0 (IE 4.0). It allows you to view the items available for auction, place bids on those items, and monitor the bids placed by fellow bidders.

Like other three-tier Web applications, the *Auction Demo* has data sources on the back end, a user interface on the client, and a Web server in the middle. We'll see how it was developed, using just three permanent Web pages:

userInterface.htm
This page uses *Dynamic HTML* (DHTML) to allow the Web browser to present the auction information to the user. It contains scripts that collect or update data on the middle tier by requesting *Active Server Pages* (ASP).

auction.asp
This page is an ASP file. When userInterface.htm requests this page, the scripts in it are executed on the server. The scripts

generate auction.xml, an XML document that contains the latest auction data, which is delivered to the client.

makebid.asp
This page is requested by userInterface.htm when the user wants to make a bid. It is executed on the middle tier, causing the data source to be updated with the new bid information.

The user interface (UI) for the *Auction Demo* is shown in Figure 7-1. It is the rendition of the userInterface.htm *Dynamic HTML* page, which is downloaded to the client when the user clicks on a link to the auction.

That page has scripts within it that handle all the client-side activity. That includes requesting data from the middle tier in order to display the most current values of the items and bids. We'll see later how the UI page does its thing, but first let's look at how the middle tier collects and transmits the data. It does so by packaging the data as XML documents.

7.1 | Getting data from the middle tier

The role of the middle tier in a Web application is to gather information from data sources and deliver it in a consistent manner to clients. In the *Auction Demo* we start with a single data source, an ODBC-compliant database. (Later we'll see how multiple data sources of different kinds can be accessed.)

The "Auction" database used for the *Auction Demo* is a relational database with two tables, an "Item" table and a "Bids" table. The "Item" table contains data about each of the items up for auction. It is shown in Figure 7-2.

For the sake of clarity, we'll just cover the "Item" table in this chapter (the "Bids" are handled similarly). You can see the full demo in the Microsoft folder on the CD-ROM. We want to deliver the data in that table in the form of an XML document, so the client's user interface page won't have to know anything about the actual data source.

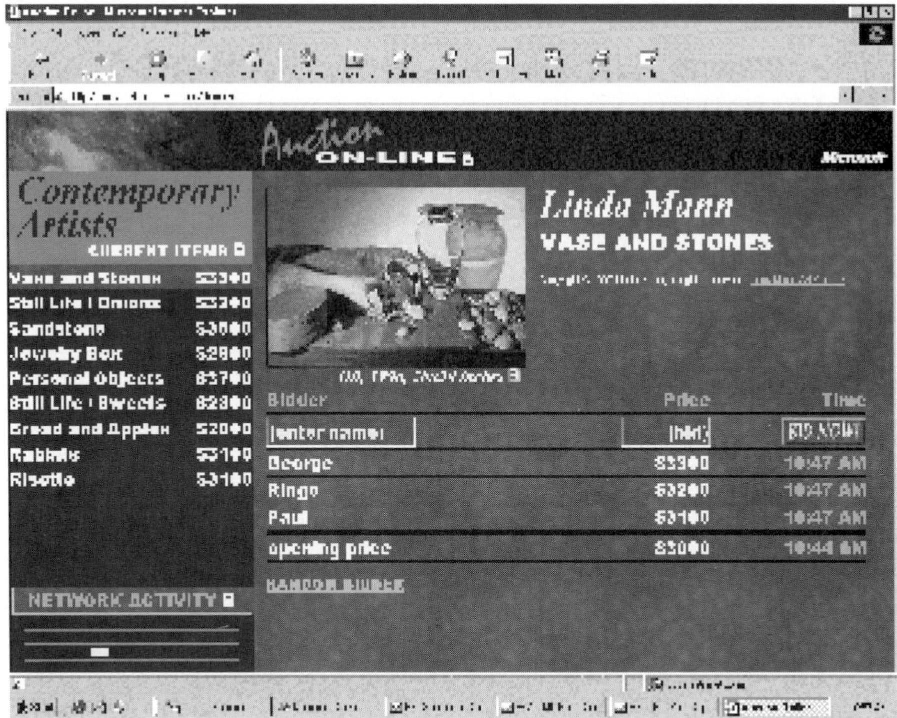

Figure 7-1 The *Auction Demo* user interface.

Title	Artist	Dimensions	Materials	Year
Vase and Stones	Linda Mann	20x30 inches	Oil	1996
Still Life / Onions	Linda Mann	20x30 inches	Oil	1997
Sandstone	Linda Mann	20x30 inches	Oil	1995
Jewelry Box	Linda Mann	20x30 inches	Oil	1994
Personal Objects	Linda Mann	20x30 inches	Oil	1995
Still Life / Sweets	Linda Mann	20x30 inches	Oil	1994
Bread and Apples	Linda Mann	20x30 inches	Oil	1995
Rabbits	Linda Mann	20x30 inches	Oil	1996
Risotto	Linda Mann	20x30 inches	Oil	1995

Figure 7-2 The *Auction Demo* item table.

7.1.1 *Defining the XML document structure*

The key to creating useful XML documents is the proper structuring of the data. For the *Auction Demo*, that means deciding how a record in the "Item" table will be represented as an ITEM element in XML. There is a straightforward mapping, shown in the data-less element in Example 7-1.

Example 7-1. Template for an ITEM element.

```
<ITEM>
  <TITLE></TITLE>
  <ARTIST></ARTIST>
  <DIMENSIONS></DIMENSIONS>
  <MATERIALS></MATERIALS>
  <YEAR></YEAR>
</ITEM>
```

For each field in the "Item" table, there is a corresponding subelement of the ITEM element.

To generate XML documents with these ITEM elements, the *Auction Demo* uses ASP files.

7.1.2 *Using ASP files to generate XML documents*

XML can be generated on the middle tier using *Active Server Pages*. ASP offers an environment in which Web authors can create documents dynamically by intermixing markup languages with in-line scripts. The scripts can be written in a variety of scripting languages, including *JScript* and *VBScript*, and can invoke server-side components to access databases, execute applications, and process information.

When a browser requests an ASP file, it is first processed by the server, which delivers a generated Web page containing standard markup.

Example 7-12. Generating one XML document from a database and another XML document.

```
<%@ LANGUAGE = VBScript %>
<?xml version="1.0"?>
<AUCTIONBLOCK>
<%
Set Conn = Server.CreateObject("ADODB.Connection")
Conn.Open "Gallery1","Gallery1","Gallery1"
Set ItemRS = Conn.Execute("select * from item")
Do While Not ItemRS.EOF
%>
  <ITEM>
    <TITLE><%=ItemRS("Title")%></TITLE>
    <ARTIST><%=ItemRS("Artist")%></ARTIST>
    <DIMENSIONS><%=ItemRS("Dimensions")%></DIMENSIONS>
    <MATERIALS><%=ItemRS("Materials")%></MATERIALS>
    <YEAR><%=ItemRS("Year")%></YEAR>
  </ITEM>
  <%
  ItemRS.MoveNext
  Loop
  %>
<%
'Here the connection to the Gallery3 data is made
Set XML = Server.CreateObject("msxml")
XML.URL = "http://datasource3/Gallery3.xml"
Set Items = XML.root.children
For I = 0 to Items.length - 1
%>
  <ITEM>
    <TITLE><%=Items.item(I).children.item("TITLE").text%>
    </TITLE>
    <ARTIST><%=Items.item(I).children.item("ARTIST").text%>
    </ARTIST>
    <DIMENSIONS><%=Items.item(I).children.item("DIMENSIONS").text%>
    </DIMENSIONS>
    <MATERIALS><%=Items.item(I).children.item("MATERIALS").text%>
    </MATERIALS>
    <YEAR><%=Items.item(I).children.item("DATE").text%>
    </YEAR>
  </ITEM>
<%Next%>
</AUCTIONBLOCK>
```

7.2.1 Using procedural scripts

Internet Explorer 4.0 includes the *MSXML* parser, which exposes the parsed XML document as a *document object model.*[1] Once exposed, scripts can access the data content of the XML elements and dynamically insert the data into the user interface.

The userInterface.htm code in Example 7-13 applies *MSXML* to auction.xml, the XML document generated by auction.asp. That creates an *ActiveX* object representing the parsed document.

Example 7-13. Creating the auction document object.

```
var auction = new ActiveXObject("msxml");
auction.URL = "http://Webserver/auction.asp";
```

In Example 7-14, the script next retrieves the root element. It then navigates the tree until it locates the TITLE element within the first ITEM element of auction.xml. The `innerText` property is used to insert the data content of TITLE into the user interface as the value of the "item_title" attribute, which appears on a DIV element.

Example 7-14. Extracting data from the auction document object.

```
var root = auction.root;
var item0 = root.children.item("ITEM",0);
var title = item0.children.item("TITLE").text;
document.all("item_title").innerText = title;
<DIV ID="item_title"></DIV>
```

One of the benefits of using procedural scripts to display XML documents is that you can manipulate the data content of an XML element before you display it. For example, if you wanted to display the dimensions of each painting using the metric system, rather than feet and inches, your

1. The Auction Demo was developed before the W3C completed development of the common document object model (DOM) for XML and HTML. However, the IE 4.0 Document Object Model attempted to maintain compliance with the W3C draft as it evolved and IE5 supports the W3C DOM. The final spec for the DOM is on the CD-ROM.

script could simply convert the content of the DIMENSIONS element from inches to centimeters.

7.2.2 Using descriptive data binding

The *IE 4.0 XML Data Source Object* (XML DSO) is a declarative alternative to the procedural scripts described in the last section. The XML DSO is an applet (see Example 7-15) that enables the data of XML elements to be bound as the content of HTML elements.

Example 7-15. The *IE 4.0 XML Data Source Object* applet.

```
<APPLET ID=auction CODE=com.ms.xml.dso.XMLDSO.class MAYSCRIPT
      WIDTH=0 HEIGHT=0>
   <PARAM NAME="url" VALUE="auction.asp">
</APPLET>
```

In Example 7-15, the "url" parameter points the XML DSO to auction.asp, which causes auction.xml to be generated on the middle tier. A persistent XML source could also have been used.

In Example 7-16, data binding is used to populate the part of the user interface that shows the painting and the caption beneath it.

Example 7-16. Data binding with the XML DSO.

```
<TD>
  <DIV STYLE=
  "margin-left:16px;margin-top:16px;margin-right:16px">
    <DIV ID=pict></DIV>
    <DIV CLASS="details">
      <SPAN DATASRC=#auction DATAFLD=MATERIALS></SPAN>,
      <SPAN DATASRC=#auction DATAFLD=YEAR></SPAN>,
      <SPAN DATASRC=#auction DATAFLD=DIMENSIONS></SPAN>
    </DIV>
  </DIV>
</TD>
```

With the XML DSO applet embedded in the Web page, no scripting is required to bind the data content of XML elements to HTML elements. Instead, the name of the document object (ID of the APPLET in Example

7-15) is specified as the value of the DATASRC attribute, and the generic identifier of the XML element is specified for the DATAFLD attribute.

One advantage of displaying XML with the XML DSO is that the XML document is processed asynchronously to the rendering of the page. Therefore, if the inventory of paintings were very large, the initial elements of the XML document could be displayed even before the last elements were processed.

7.3 | Updating the data source from the client

We have seen how userInterface.htm on the client obtained data to display to the user by invoking auction.asp on the middle tier. It can also enable the user to make his own bid by invoking another middle tier page, makebid.asp.

In the *Auction Demo*, the user bids by overwriting the price and bidder name in the first row of the bid table. A bid therefore consists of the "title" of the item currently displayed, the "price" of the new bid, and the name of the new "bidder".

These data items must be passed as parameters to makebid.asp, which executes a script to process them and update the database. The script returns to the client a "return message" XML document: a single element containing information about the status of the processing.

The script in userInterface.htm (see Example 7-17) begins by assigning the title of the current item up for auction to the "title" variable, the value of the "price" text box to the "price" variable, and the value of the "bidder" text box to the "bidder" variable.

It then creates the return message document object, which will state whether makebid.asp successfully updated the database. The three variables are passed as parameters to the ASP file when it is invoked.

Example 7-17. Sending a new bid to makebid.asp.

```
var title = current_item.children.item("TITLE").text;
var price = price.value;
var bidder = bidder.value;
var returnMsg = new ActiveXObject("msxml");
returnMsg.URL = "http://auction/makebid.asp?title=" +
  title + "&price=" + price + "&bidder=" + bidder;
```

In Example 7-18, makebid.asp (called by userInterface.htm in Example 7-17) assigns the values of the parameters "title", "price", and "bidder" to variables with the same names.

The "BidRS" record set object is then created and a connection to the "Auction" database is made. Note that the connection is made for both reading and writing. The "Bids" table is then opened and the new information is added to the record set, after which the connection is closed. The process is much the same as it was for auction.asp, except that the database is written to instead of just being read.

Finally, makebid.asp generates the return message document with the status of the update.

7.4 | Conclusion

The entire *Auction Demo* was built using the methods described above. You can get a head start on building a similar Web application by modifying these scripts to suit your particular requirements.

XML enables Web applications by providing dynamic, accessible content that can be navigated and manipulated on the client. In addition, it enables the updating of content without having to refresh the entire user interface. This ability saves time by reducing round trips to the server for information that already exists on the client.

With XML, users can manage data over the Internet just as they presently do on their local machines. As a result, the Web is made a more interactive and interoperable medium. As the information superhighway is

Example 7-18. The makebid.asp file updates the database.

```
<%@ LANGUAGE = VBScript %>
<%
  title = Request.QueryString("title")
  price = Request.QueryString("price")
  bidder = Request.QueryString("bidder")

  Set BidRS = Server.CreateObject("ADODB.RecordSet")
  connect = "data source=Auction;user id=sa;password=;"
  BidRS.CursorType = 2
  BidRS.LockType = 3   ' read/write
  BidRS.Open "Bids", connect

  BidRS.AddNew
  BidRS("item") = title
  BidRS("price") = price
  BidRS("bidder") = bidder
  BidRS.Update
  BidRS.Close
%>
<STATUS>OK</STATUS>
```

transformed into the data superhighway, Web applications similar to the *Auction Demo* will allow for better utilization of the vast resources made available by the Web.

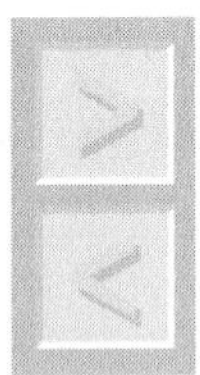

Analysis *The Auction Demo clearly illustrates the architecture of a three-tier application. It uses the middle tier as a transient data aggregator and normalizer. In other chapters you'll see different approaches to the middle tier, including persistent storage of metadata and the use of object paradigms rather than data paradigms.*

8.1.3 *Supply chain integration*

A *supply chain*, as the name implies, is a relationship in which one partner supplies things to another. An aircraft manufacturer, for example, is supplied with electronic equipment and other parts from various vendors and subcontractors, and then in turn supplies the aircraft to an airline. Records must be kept of all of this activity, including documents with legal significance, such as purchase orders and invoices.

Traditional business-to-business technology for this purpose, such as electronic data interchange (EDI), is gradually being supplemented or supplanted by Web-based versions, which are much more flexible. We will discuss these issues at greater length in Part Three, "E-commerce".

An information server should allow you to modify the content, products, customers, etc. of your supply chain applications without requiring any changes to the application code itself. These modifications should be possible dynamically, without disrupting the operation of your application.

8.1.4 *Enterprise application integration (EAI)*

In an ideal world, all of the business applications of an enterprise – purchasing, invoicing, general ledger, inventory, etc. – would be designed to work together and share data. Indeed, many companies have deployed Enterprise Resource Planning (ERP) systems to accomplish this very objective.

But despite the enormous popularity of ERP software, most enterprises are very far from that ideal state. In fact, the separate departmental systems of most companies are no better able to communicate with one another than are the systems of independent participants in a supply chain. And just as supply chain integration has become a killer app for the public Web, enterprise application integration is becoming the killer app for intranets.

An EAI system requires a *data hub*, which provides a single point of access and unified view of all enterprise data that you can query, update, delete, etc. An information server can fulfill this role.

8.1 | Requirements for an information server

From this brief survey of some key e-business application categories, we can identify several requirements for an information server. A common thread is flexibility with respect to data handling, something that use of XML facilitates.

access to all kinds of data

Corporate data can be found in a variety of sources, including relational databases, flat files, the Web, email, and prepackaged applications. Because of the flexibility of XML, any information on a hard drive or any shred of information that is thought up can be turned into well-formed XML. An information server should present and support a single view of all information as being well-formed XML documents, thereby making all data usable as e-business information.

extensibility

E-business applications require the ability to add new attributes to a data model in an ad hoc fashion, akin to scribbling an isolated fact in the margins of an incident report. XML allows you to extend individual elements by adding subelements and attributes independently without breaking existing query and retrieval operations. A server should exploit the extensibility of XML by enabling you to build extended applications without impacting database administration.

development tools

Server software should include a suite of tools to facilitate application development and the adoption of XML. The technology is evolving rapidly, so well-designed tools that can guide you through adopting and successfully employing new technology tend to be a necessity, not a luxury.

persistence and granularity

The server should store and manage XML documents either as well-formed XML document strings (whether or not valid), or in a pre-parsed form from which the original strings can be restored. The document should be accessible at any level of granularity needed by an application.

8.3 | How *eXcelon* works

eXcelon, from Object Design, is an example of an information server that addresses these e-business requirements. It has three components: *eXcelon Data Server*, *Xconnects*, and *eXcelon Toolbox*. The data server is the core run-time component that supports the applications, while *Xconnects* are modules that provide back-end connectivity to data sources. The *Toolbox* is a suite of tools to speed application development.

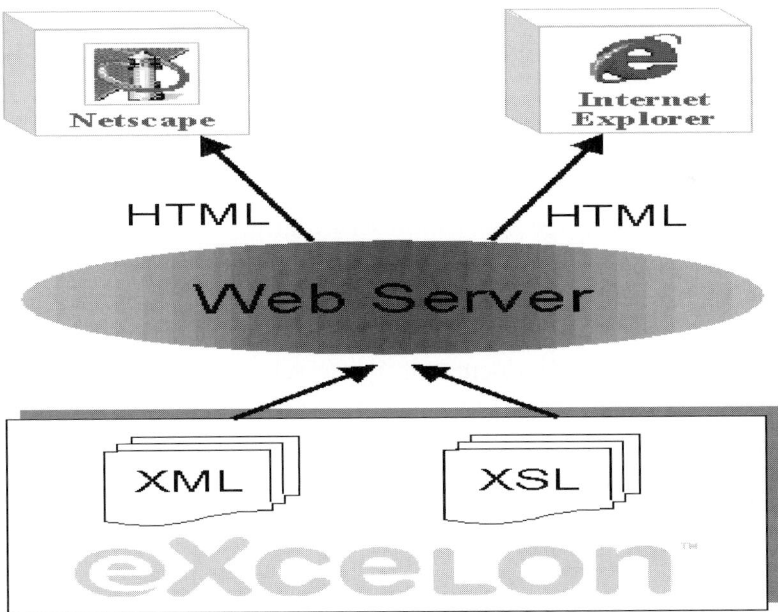

Figure 8-1 *eXcelon Data Server*

8.3.1 *eXcelon Data Server*

At run time, the *eXcelon Data Server* (shown in Figure 8-1) supports the applications. It includes a complete XML database and manages, stores, and delivers information directly to applications either through Web server extensions, or to an application server through component object model (COM) or *Java* interfaces.

It also supports XML-based queries using XQL, XPath, and XSLT, which give highly-granular access to XML data. Query performance can be enhanced with XML indexes, which are content-based and therefore do not compromise concurrency.

The heart of the *Data Server* is the data engine, which stores XML documents as hierarchically-linked objects. It stores files that use other document and data representations, such as images, audio, and HTML files, as binary large objects (BLOBs). The data engine supports basic create, read, update, and delete functionality, which you can enhance with *Java* or COM server extensions.

The *eXcelon Data Server* can be the actual managed repository for non-relational data and/or a front-end that manages access to existing sources of data. It can also work in parallel with relational databases.

The server also creates and maintains caches for each Web server and application server to provide high performance, in-memory database support. It keeps these caches up-to-date and transactionally consistent even when scaling across a large application server farm.

eXcelon supports the extensibility of XML by enabling you to extend an XML data record without disrupting any applications that are connected to the *Data Server*. If you extend the knowledge base, either through *Studio* or by simply editing an XML document, the server will store and manage that new attribute without requiring a schema evolution and without breaking any current requests.

8.3.2 *eXcelon Xconnects*

Xconnects are modules that convert data into XML and load it into *eXcelon*. The modules can be designed to incorporate any method of translation as well as two-way synchronization, and can be built to custom requirements with an array of third-party tools and APIs.

8.3.3 *eXcelon Toolbox*

eXcelon Toolbox is an integrated tool set for building and managing XML e-business applications. It includes three tools, which are described in this section.

8.3.3.1 *eXcelon Studio*

eXcelon Studio, shown in Figure 8-2, allows you to define XML document types for your application graphically. You can describe document and element types with their attributes and connect them with one-to-one or one-to-many relationships.

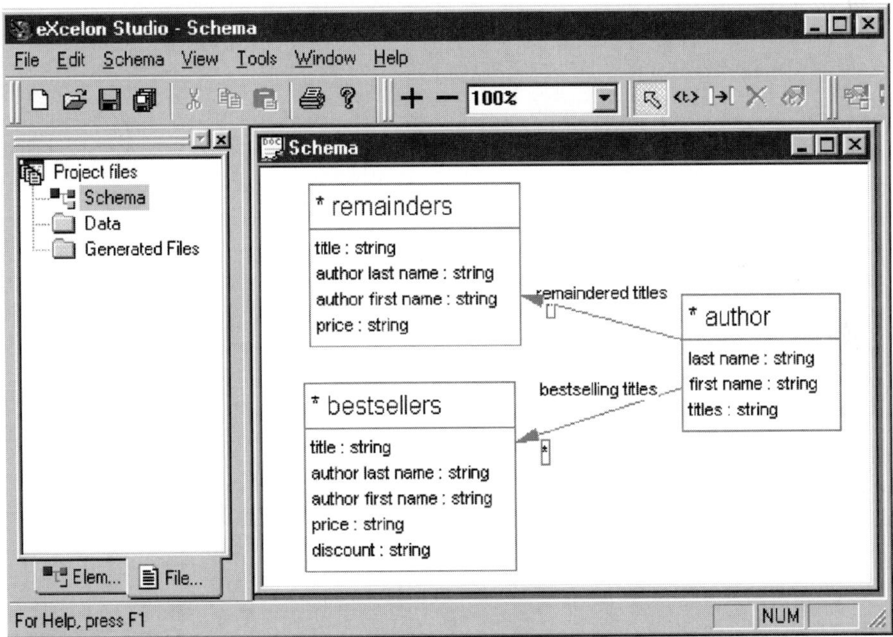

Figure 8-2 A schema being defined in *eXcelon Studio*

The tool automatically generates *eXcelon Server* extensions in both *Java* and COM to manipulate your XML data using the W3C Document Object Model (DOM). It also generates HTML forms for data entry.

Studio is using XML Document Content Description (DCD) as its schema representation until one is approved by the W3C. It can read an existing XML document, reverse engineer the schema, and allow you to extend it. This facility makes it easier to incorporate new information.

8.3.3.2 *eXcelon Explorer*

The *eXcelon Explorer*, shown in Figure 8-3, is a graphical user interface (GUI) for organizing and browsing your XML data. It has a familiar file system metaphor: you can create folders and move both XML and non-XML files with a simple drag and drop.

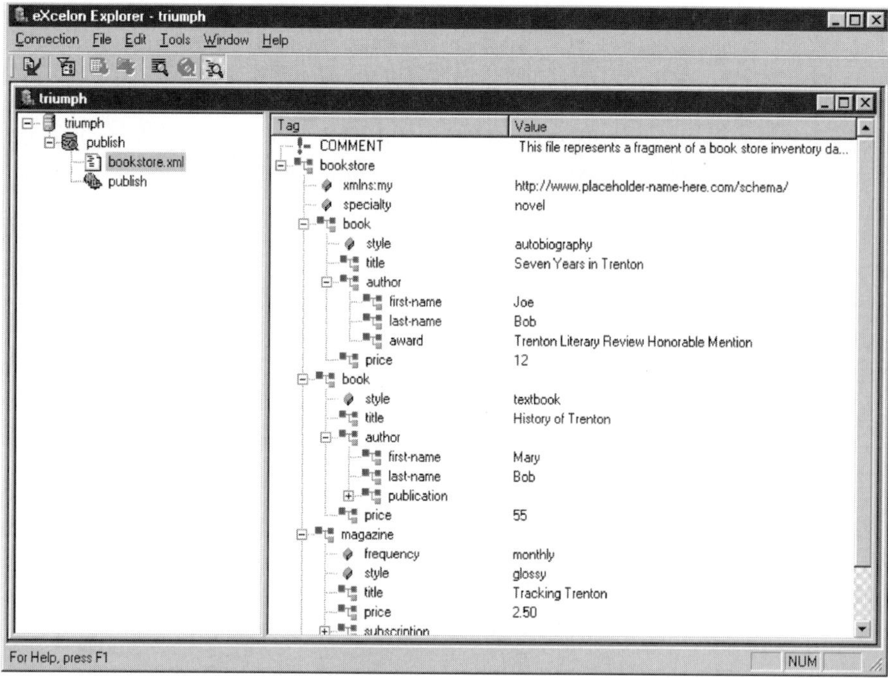

Figure 8-3 A book store inventory in *eXcelon Explorer*

Explorer includes a *Query Wizard*, shown in Figure 8-4, to build queries visually. It supports ad hoc querying by dynamically generating a list of the attributes provided by the applicable schema. If you take advantage of

XML's extensibility and add an attribute to even a single element, *eXcelon* updates the document type schema and the *Query Wizard* dynamically adapts to the change.

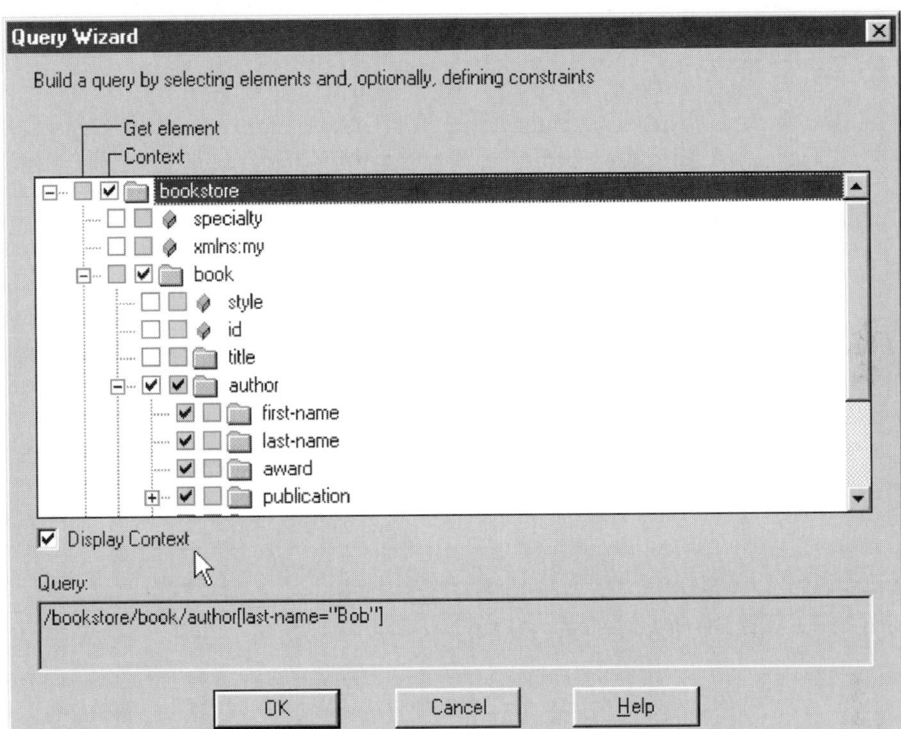

Figure 8-4 Using *Query Wizard* to search for books by Bob

8.3.3.3 *eXcelon Manager*

The *eXcelon Manager*, shown in Figure 8-5, provides a central point for all administration. You can create XML document stores, define users and assign their access rights, distribute and load-balance across multiple servers, and create additional caches for increased concurrency.

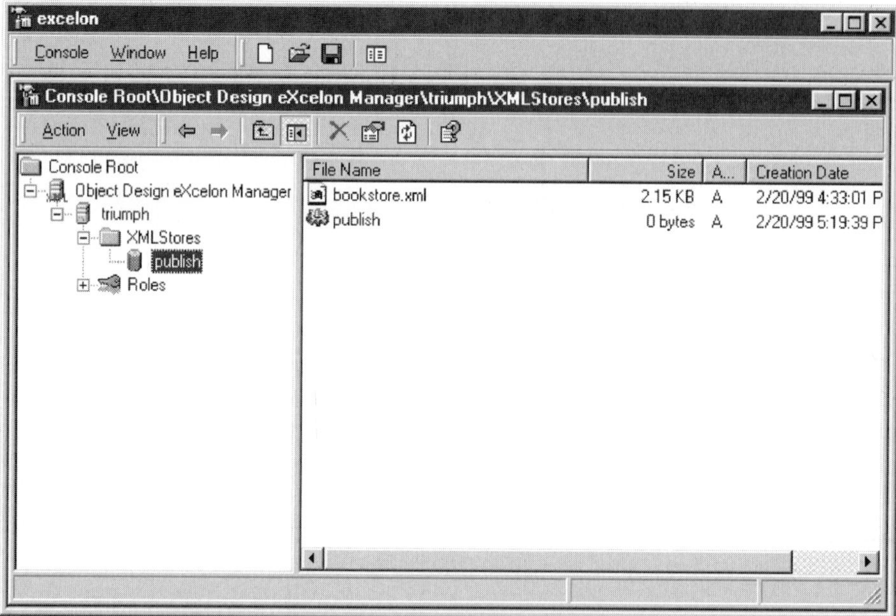

Figure 8-5 *eXcelon Manager* administration tool

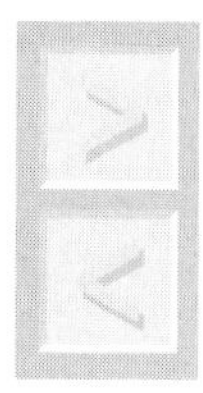

Analysis *eXcelon can be thought of as a persistent information server, one that is optimized for information assets with a long, indefinite, or even permanent life span. In the next chapter, we'll examine a server with a different orientation.*

method, to run when the XML document is received. There are also methods for "acknowledgePurchaseOrder" and "cancelPurchaseOrder".

Example 9-1. XML e-mail from the bike shop

```
<?xml version="1.0"?>
<?sapphire method="submitPurchaseOrder"?>
<Purchase-Order>
  <Buyer>
    <Buyer-id>123-44-5678</Buyer-id>
  </Buyer>
  <PO-Number>YZ789</PO-Number>
  <Item-list>
    <Item>
      <Qty>2</Qty>
      <Part-Number>AB123</Part-Number>
      <Description>Blue Boy's 26 inch 10-speed</Description>
    </Item>
    <Item>
      <Qty>1</Qty>
      <Part-Number>43QX</Part-Number>
      <Description>Red Mountain Bike</Description>
    </Item>
  </Item-list>
</Purchase-Order>
```

In effect, the bike shop and the distributor are conducting an EDI transaction, but without the overhead of a traditional private network EDI system. And they could easily do more.

For example, they could use e-mail certificates to assure security, both encryption of the message and authentication of the participants. Or the bike shop could install a server of its own, which would let it receive purchase order acknowledgments automatically and store them in a database. The shop would then be able to give exact delivery dates to its customers.

9.3 | Architecture of a dynamic data server

Figure 9-2 illustrates the architecture of a system built around an XML dynamic data server. There is a large amount of detail because the particular server depicted, *Bluestone XML-Server*, was designed for general-purpose

©2000 The XML Handbook™

use. However, even a simple application-specific server would have the same kinds of components.

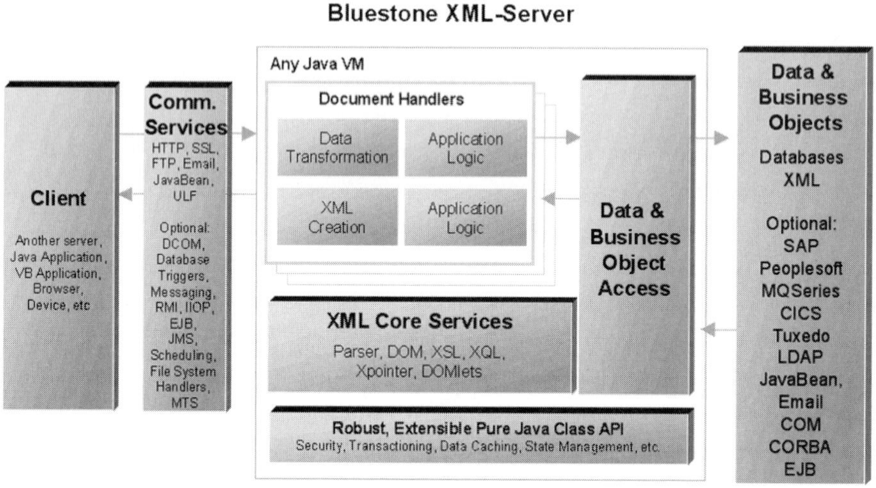

Figure 9-2 Architecture of the *Bluestone XML-Server*

For example, a "Document Handler" might be some lines of a Perl script that would use a parser ("XML Core Services") to extract data from an XML document. The script, based on its built-in "Application Logic", would then issue a database query to a data source ("Data & Business Object Access"). The returned query results would be put into DOM format (another "XML Core Service") from which an XML document is generated (another "Document Handler").

Unlike the Perl script, which is a "hard-wired" (i.e., monolithic) single-purpose application, the server in Figure 9-2 is modular. Its individual components (document handlers, etc.) can be reused and replaced, which should facilitate coping with changes as XML and its related standards evolve over time.

©2000 THE XML HANDBOOK™

9.4 | Server components

Let's take a closer look at the components, starting from the left-hand side of Figure 9-2.

9.4.1 *Client*

A client can take a variety of forms. It can be a browser, an application, or even another XML server. It may also be a device, like a *Palm Pilot* or cell phone. In fact, there is a specific XML document type called Wireless Markup Language (WML) that servers can use for communicating with wireless devices.

9.4.2 *Communication services*

XML documents can be transferred by a variety of protocols. For low cost reliability, as in the bike shop scenario, e-mail may be useful. For distributed interactions, the HTTP and SSL protocols are very good for moving documents across firewall boundaries and leveraging the cost advantages of the Internet. Other applications might need to multicast or broadcast XML documents to a large number of clients. Or guaranteed messaging might be needed.

A server product should provide a framework that allows communications protocols to be plugged in as transport layers without changing the dynamic data server, its code or interface. Such a framework could allow a single application to handle multiple communications protocols without any changes to the application.

In *Bluestone XML-Server*, the framework is called *Communication Services.* It can handle all of the protocols listed in the "Comm. Services" box in Figure 9-2. It also has a *Universal Listener Framework* that allows large e-commerce sites to monitor, or "listen on", multiple communication flows concurrently and to work with other sites to build large work flows and supply chains.

9.4.3 *Document handlers*

The key component of an XML dynamic data server is called a document handler. Figure 9-3 shows the role of one in an application. There is typically a different document handler for each type of document processed.

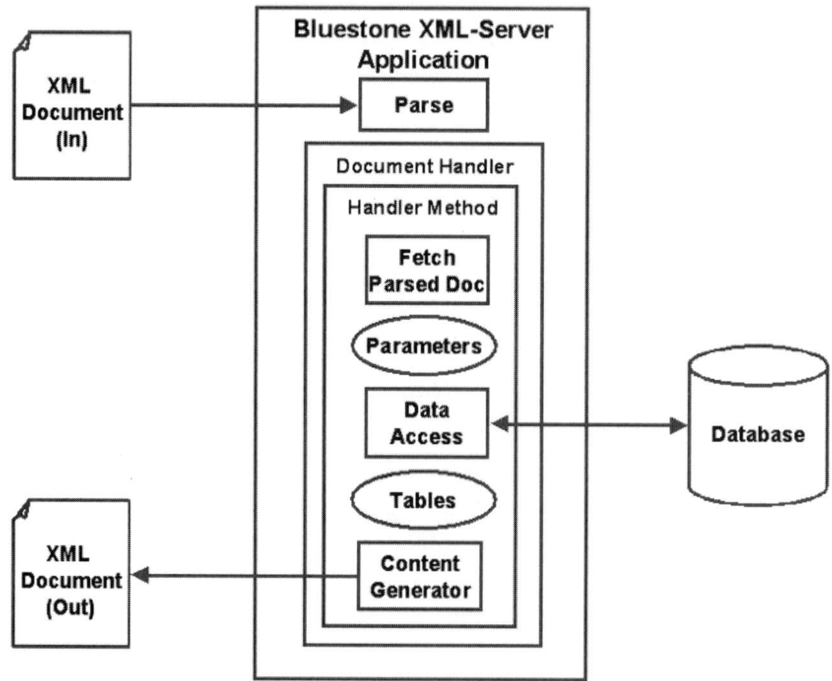

Figure 9-3 Document handler in an application

Each handler supports multiple methods that can operate on its document type. In the bike shop scenario, for example, the purchase order handler provides "submit", "acknowledge" and "cancel" methods. Each method runs specific application logic and can call different back-end objects such as data sources and stored procedures.

When the server receives a document it invokes the handler associated with that document type and tells it to execute the appropriate method. These two pieces of information – document type and method – could be communicated to a server by the application that invokes it. However, a server should be able to determine an XML document type from the start-tag of the root element, and the method by a convention such as the processing instruction used in the document in Example 9-1. For that document, the server would invoke the document handler for `Purchase-Order` to execute the method for `submitPurchaseOrder`.

In *Bluestone XML-Server*, document handlers can also be *chained* and *forwarded*. Chained handlers are invoked to operate on particular element types during the original processing, while forwarded handlers operate on the document after the original handler is done.

For example, the handler for a document with `equation` elements might chain a specialized document handler for them. The equation handler might transform those elements in some way, in which case a request would be forwarded to another handler to process the transformed document.

9.4.4 *XML core services*

In order for computers to solve real-world problems, real-world concepts, like "purchase orders", must be available to them in a form that they can manipulate. That is, there must be *representations* of those concepts in the computer.[1]

So the sequence of characters in Example 9-1 isn't really a purchase order. It is an XML document that *represents* a purchase order.

The conceptual purchase order is a richly-structured hierarchy: The PO contains a buyer, a number, and a list of items; each item contains a quantity, a part number, and a description. But the representation – the XML document – is a perfectly flat character string. In order to find the rich structure described by that string, the XML document must be *parsed* according to the rules of the XML language.

A character string is an easily visualized structure that is very familiar to humans. It is easy for programmers to work with because it is accessible with ubiquitous plain text editors – software that does not have to understand the representation in order to let you manipulate the characters.

That's why the character string is such a good basis for a universal data representation like XML. But while an application is processing the data, it

1. File formats, data formats, and MIMEtypes are examples of representations. We try to avoid the use of "format" in this context, though, because it is more commonly used in the context of stylesheets.

is better to have a representation that tracks the structure of the conceptual object more closely, so that programmers can more easily access relevant parts of it. That way a program could step through the list of item elements in the purchase order, rather than the sequence of characters in the XML document.

Such a representation is called an *object model.*[1] A program that processes an XML document both parses it and constructs an object model in order to operate on the elements.

Depending on its processing needs, the model it constructs might be very simple or very detailed. An application that needs to count the number of bicycles on order might include only quantity elements in its model, while one that analyzes buyer preferences in bicycle models and colors would need a more complex model.

The W3C has standardized an object model for XML, known as the *Document Object Model*, or DOM. A standard model makes it possible for programs to operate with different implementations, such as those in different Web browsers or servers. The trade-off is that the standardized model needs to include everything, which could require more processing time and resources than the simpler specialized model that an application might construct for itself.

Bluestone XML-Server provides the W3C DOM application programming interface (API) in its *Core XML Services*. Through the DOM interface, document handlers can operate concurrently on the same document.

For document handlers that do their own parsing, the *Simple API for XML* (SAX) interface is also provided. SAX gives the programmer control at each "event" in the XML document string, such as the start or end of an element. A program might be able to do all of its processing as each event occurs, in effect creating a piece of the object model, processing it, then discarding it. Alternatively (or in addition), it could preserve the pieces of the model that it builds at each event and be able to process the entire model when the document is parsed.

---

1. At least it is called that by the W3C. Computer scientists may call it a parse tree. Markup experts call it a grove because it has more than one tree: the content tree of elements and their child elements, plus separate attribute trees for those elements that have attributes.

9.4.5 *Data & business object access*

After a document handler extracts data from a received document, through either the DOM or SAX interfaces, it will want to do something with that data. It uses a server's so-called "back-end" access services for this purpose.

For example, the handler may call an SQL statement that inserts a new customer into a database, an ERP API to create a new sales order, or a mainframe application that is doing bill processing. The data might be filtered and/or translated in the process.

Bluestone's server offers access to the data and business objects shown at the far right of Figure 9-2. In addition, it provides production-level features such as connection pooling, secure database login, error handling, and transactioning.

The reverse process takes place when data is retrieved from a back-end data source. The data items must be represented as elements or attributes in a dynamically generated XML document. The rules for binding data to XML can be provided by a mapping or binding service, a template, or an XSLT transform.

For example, a "`pur_num`" database field could be bound to a `PO-Number` element type. If multiple rows of data are returned, then multiple `PO-Number` elements would be generated. As with the complementary receiving process, it may also be appropriate to filter and translate some of the data.

For Web publishing of the data, an XSL stylesheet could be applied to the generated XML document.

9.5 | Bluestone Visual-XML

A server should provide development tools. Bluestone's tool is unusual in that it can be used with or without the server.

As a stand-alone tool it can browse databases and generate XML documents and DTDs from them. It also contains XML, DTD, *Java*, and SQL editors, plus other capabilities.

©2000 The XML Handbook™

In conjunction with *Bluestone XML-Server* it provides a drag-and-drop interface for binding database objects to element types and automatically generating pure *Java* code for document handlers.

Tip *A free copy of Bluestone Visual-XML is on the CD-ROM, along with a database of 40 XML application specs to try it on.*

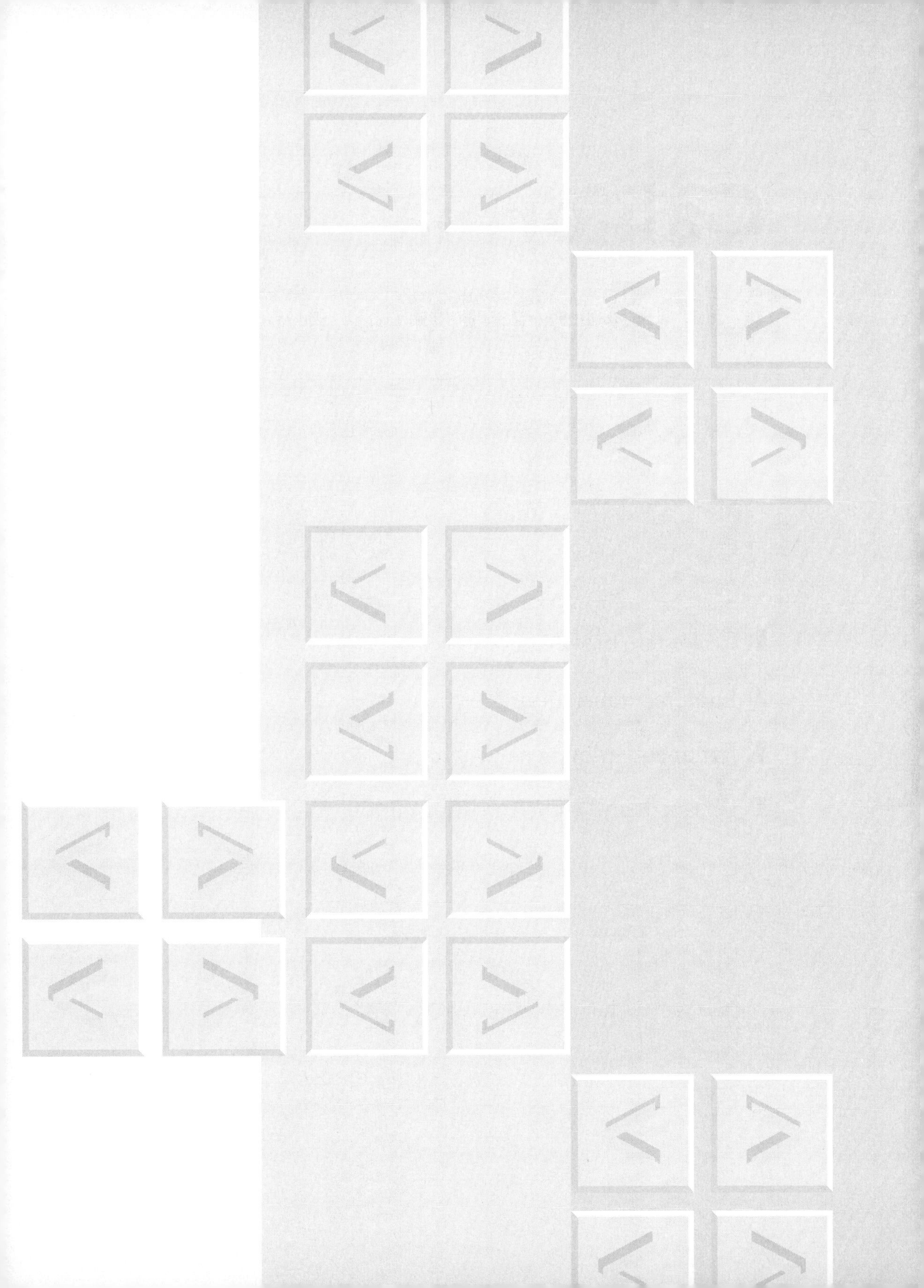

California UnRealty

Case Study

- Real estate brokerage
- Loss-free translation
- Extranet deployment
- Persistent and transient information

©2000 The XML Handbook™

Chapter 10

The ability to move data from one system to another without losing anything in translation is one of XML's strengths. It makes a whole new class of applications possible, such as the sophisticated real estate information system described in this chapter. IBM Corporation, `http://www.ibm.com/xml`, is the sponsor; it was prepared by Toufic Boubez and Doug Tidwell.

Without a generalized markup language, translating data from one representation to another invariably entails information loss. With XML, though, such losses can be avoided, which opens the door to a variety of new applications, such as the one we will now describe. It was built for California UnRealty, a fictitious realty company, and one of its branch offices, San Jose UnRealty.[1]

California UnRealty needs to keep an updated database of listings, sales data, and new home starts. San Jose UnRealty needs to keep its agents up-to-date with the latest listings, keep its local systems in sync with the central office, and display listings on a variety of remote devices.

10.1 | System overview

The California UnRealty central office stores its listings in a *DB2* database and uses IBM's *WebSphere Application Server* to serve that data to branch

1. Although the company is unreal, the application has been implemented and is very real indeed!

offices. The branch offices use Lotus *Domino* databases, which they must keep in sync with the central office database.

The branch offices use a transcoding servlet to deliver the data to real estate agents, clients, banks, insurance companies, and builders. These end users employ a variety of device types (desktop computers, laptops, palmtops, cellular phones, etc.) and connect to the network in various ways (T1 lines, dial-up lines, wireless connections, etc.).

10.1.1 *Data collection*

The central office server gets input from a wide range of sources in a wide range of formats. Some brokers submit new listings using the OpenMLS XML document type; other brokers use their own document types or non-XML formats. The system parses XML documents as they come in and maps the data to fields in the *DB2* database.

10.1.2 *Data synchronization*

The San Jose office database contains all listings, sales data, and new home starts for the San Jose area. These are synchronized daily with the *DB2* database in the central office. Synchronization is done with a *Java* servlet that queries *DB2*, converts that data into XML, and stores it in the local office database.

10.1.3 *Rendering XML documents*

To find specific data, users invoke a *Java* servlet that runs a *Domino* query and serves the results to the client. The servlet transcodes the data to HTML for older browsers, DHTML for more modern ones, and XML for clients that understand it. Precision Graphics Markup Language (PGML) is used for browsers that support that nascent markup standard for professionally-rendered text and graphics.

10.2 | System architecture

Figure 10-1 depicts the system architecture, which has several data flows. Beginning in the upper left, the central office gets data from a variety of sources, including the OpenMLS service and the Mansions 'R' Us brokerage.

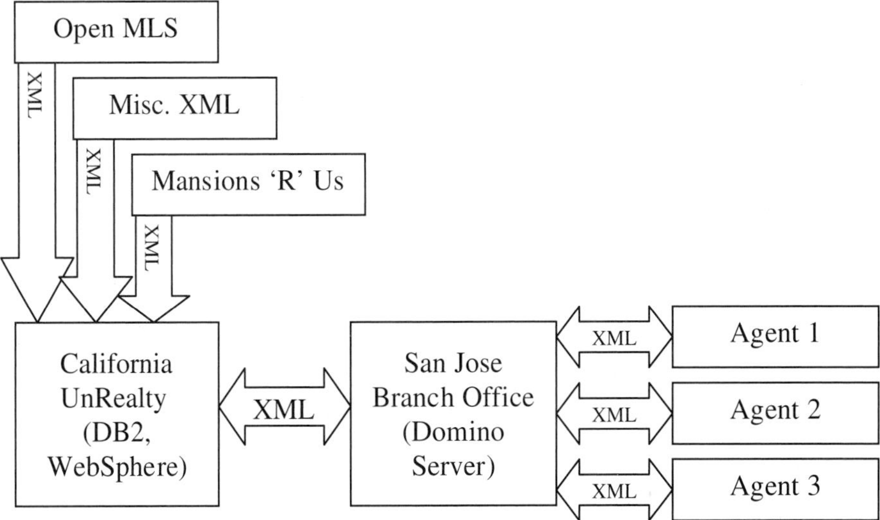

Figure 10-1 System architecture

All sources deliver XML documents to the central office, which uses a document "shredder" to parse the documents and map their data to the appropriate fields in the *DB2* database. This process generates Structured Query Language (SQL) statements for the elements that cause them to be stored as records in the database.

The document shredder (Figure 10-2) enables the central office to gather data from disparate sources in a variety of XML document types. Once the central office has the data, the branch offices can begin the task of replicating that data to their local systems.

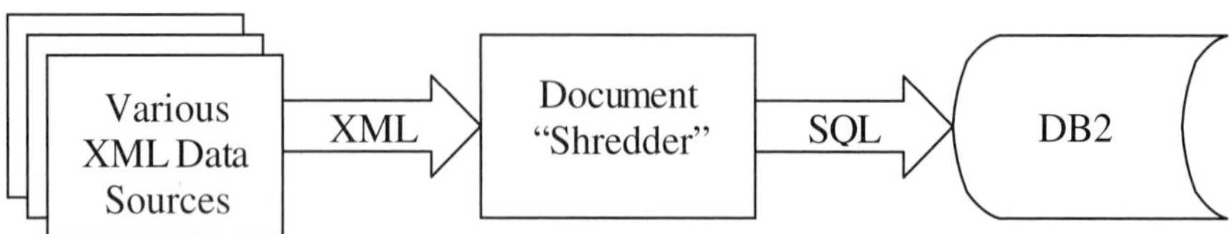

Figure 10-2 The document "shredder" processes XML and stores data in DB2

A *Java* servlet (Figure 10-3), running on IBM's WebSphere Application Server, replicates the central office database to the branch office's *Domino* database. This servlet knows how to query the *DB2* server in the central office and translate the query results into XML to be sent to the branch office.

Figure 10-3 Data flows between the central office and the branch office

The final data flows, shown in Figure 10-4, are between the *Domino* server in the branch office and various client devices. A builder might retrieve house plans and view them through a PGML-enabled browser. A loan officer at a bank might retrieve the details of a house (heated square feet, number of bedrooms, etc.) and view them in a traditional browser. Because all the metadata is preserved as the data moves through the system, other renditions (a voice response system for telephone users, for example) could be generated easily.

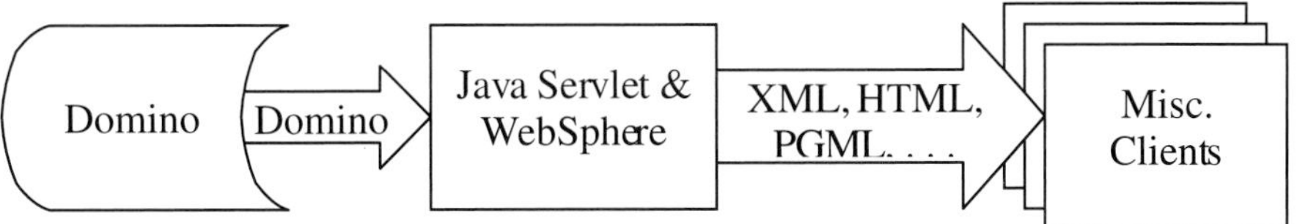

Figure 10-4 Data flows between the branch office and various clients

10.3 | The document shredder

The document shredder transforms real estate listings from XML into the *DB2* database used in the central office. Listings are received from a variety of sources, but most of them use the DTD outlined in Figure 10-5:

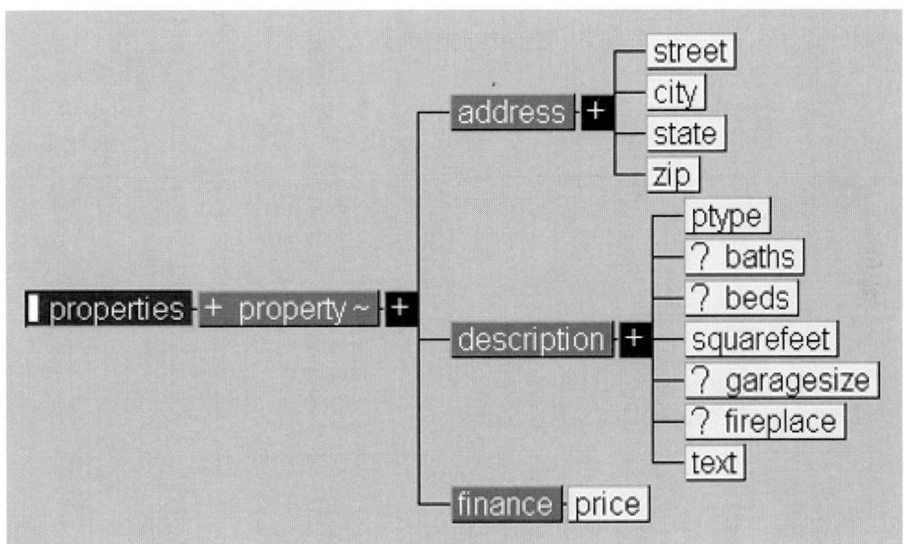

Figure 10-5 Structure of the listings DTD

As listings are received, the shredder analyzes the description of each property and stores the various pieces of information in the central database. As described earlier, the replication scheme ensures that those listings find their way to the servers in the appropriate branch offices. The shredder works similarly for listings that conform to other DTDs.

Because of XML, no repetitive data entry is required. A listing agent somewhere in California originally enters each listing; once a listing is created, it moves from one system to another without losing anything in translation. Just within California UnRealty, the data moves between *DB2* and *Domino* and is rendered on a variety of client platforms, with no manual intervention required. XML is the technology that enables the entire system.

10.4 | Generating renditions

Once the listings documents are shredded and stored in the branch offices, renditions must be generated for the agents in the field. This is a two-step process: First, an XML document is generated containing the results of an agent query; then it is rendered in the appropriate format for the agent's browser.

A *Domino* view template specifies which fields in the database must be returned, along with rules for representing them as XML. The structure of the simplest result DTD is shown in Figure 10-6.

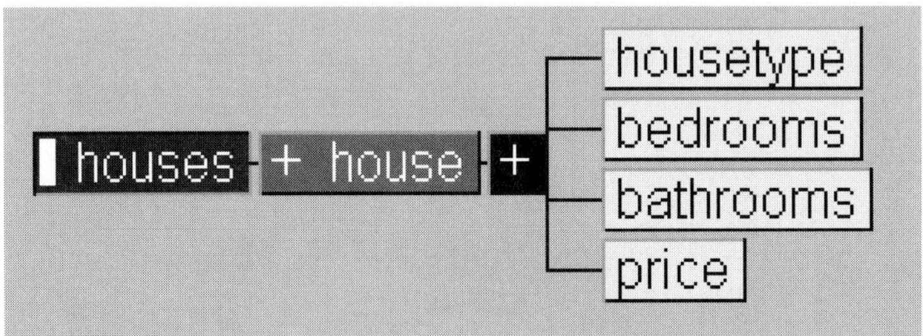

Figure 10-6 Structure of XML output from *Domino*

This DTD defines a simple document type containing only the essential information about each listing for an inquiring agent. Other applications might require more detailed DTDs, which are handled similarly.

For example, a loan officer at a bank would certainly want more information than is defined by the DTD above. Because the database contains all the data and the appropriate metadata, it is easy for us to generate different XML documents using different DTDs.

Another servlet creates a rendition of the XML document in the appropriate format for the browser being used by the requesting agent. Because the data is in XML, the system can render it as HTML, DHTML, PGML, or some other XML document type.

The end result is that requestors gets the correct data in a format optimized for the browser in use at the time they need the data. Best of all, because of XML there is no need for custom views for each combination of real estate listing and browser type. IBM simply wrote code that describes how the data should be manipulated for various clients, then let that code do all the work.

10.5 | Summary

XML enables California UnRealty to import, manipulate, translate, and export complicated data without any manual intervention. This sample application demonstrates how an XML information server system can move data from one data store to another, regardless of the underlying architecture of those data stores.

In addition, the ability to translate XML documents from one document type to another enables the system to deliver custom views to a variety of clients using disparate browsers and devices. Despite the many document types, the common XML syntax meant that a significant portion of the required code (parsing, transforming, etc.) came from off-the-shelf tools that needed little customization. XML made this application much easier to build and maintain, and much more efficient to operate.

©2000 The XML Handbook™

Wells Fargo & Company

Case Study

- Intranet deployment
- XSL stylesheets
- Persistent information server

©2000 THE XML HANDBOOK™

Chapter 11

The Web may be the world's library, but as it grows it becomes increasingly difficult to keep the shelves organized. Instead of stocking them with static HTML pages, why not generate the pages as needed, from your ever-changing content? This chapter is sponsored by Object Design, Inc., `http://www.objectdesign.com/excelon`, to show how one company did it.

Retirement plans are big business!

Wells Fargo & Company's Institutional Trust Group (ITG) is one of the world's largest, with more than $260 billion in assets under administration and more than 650,000 people participating in its IRAs and other retirement plans. The ITG is consistently top-ranked for customer satisfaction among all U.S. institutional retirement organizations.

11.1 | Website requirements

In order to make its services more competitive, Wells Fargo realized that there was an enormous amount of useful information in the company that needed to be used more effectively. But there was no system in place that could deliver this information to employees. If the company could devise such a system, it would go a long way toward ensuring that the ITG would continue to maintain its leading position.

Specifically, the company needed a system that could do the following:

- Access and use any piece of information in the company, whether located in a database, on someone's desktop, or on a Web server...anywhere.
- Enable customization of the information so that specific content is delivered to specific users, right down to the level where different users get different paragraphs within personalized versions of the same document.
- Capture knowledge by allowing users to append information to documents and contribute ad hoc content to the system dynamically.
- Provide highly targeted searching capabilities so people can get the exact information they need, when they need it.
- Enable new audiences and information to be added dynamically, without disrupting the rest of the system.

Wells Fargo met these requirements by implementing an XML-based knowledge management system based on Object Design's *eXcelon* (see Chapter 8, "eXcelon: Serving information", on page 110).

11.2 | The challenge: Leverage all the information

Wells Fargo's new knowledge management system is replacing the company's old intranet, which was based on static HTML pages and was too rigid to accommodate the company's requirements.

There was an enormous amount of valuable information, such as newsletters, memos, requests for proposals, etc., scattered throughout the organization. It was not being leveraged because there was no practical way to deliver this information, which was increasing by dozens of documents every week. It was virtually impossible to publish and manage it using static HTML pages.

XML was chosen as the solution to the problem because it could be used to represent any kind of information – both managed (i.e., information kept in a formal database) and unmanaged (everything else). Furthermore, because information constantly changes, XML's extensibility would enable the bank to constantly update and extend its knowledge base without disrupting the system.

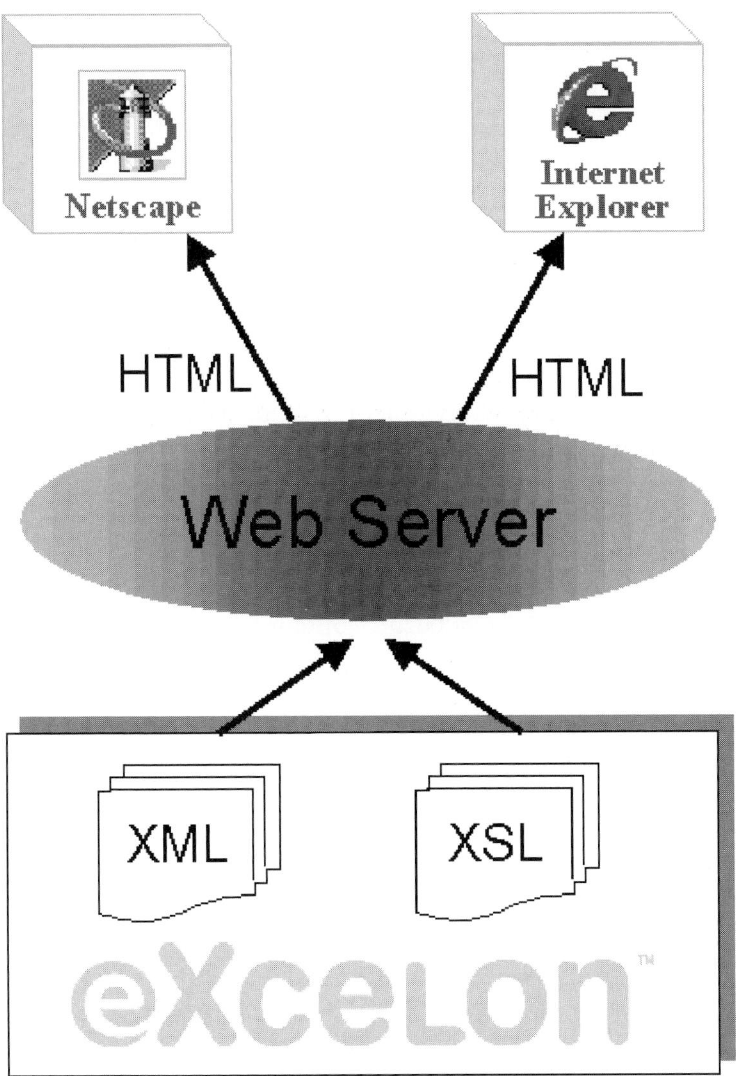

Figure 11-1 Information flow in the Wells Fargo intranet

11.3 | The new intranet system

The new system, which is shown in Figure 11-1, was deployed in just two months using the development tools in the *eXcelon Toolbox*. It currently supports three distinct audiences: general Wells Fargo employees, general employees who are frequent visitors, and ITG employees.

The system meets all of the requirements, and then some. capabilities, including:

Universal information access
: Because *eXcelon* is not restricted to a single data representation, virtually every piece of information in the organization can be used in the knowledge management system. These range from *Word* documents and email messages to finely-structured and managed relational database information.

Highly targeted content delivery
: The bank added "audience type" attributes to its content, which enables the system to deliver specific content to specific users.

Enhanced sales support
: The company is now able to implement a "service selector" feature. It enables salespeople to enter profile information for prospective customers (number of employees, etc.) and to receive a customized package of the product and service marketing materials that are most appropriate.

Continually evolving content
: Wells Fargo can exploit XML's extensibility to continuously evolve and improve the content on the site. For example, the sales force now has access to the multitudes of newsletters and management memos generated each week. And individuals can append information to the content, thereby enabling them to share their knowledge with the rest of the sales force. This will get easier in the future when a new extension is deployed that will enable employees to publish *Microsoft Office* content directly into *eXcelon*, in XML.

Example 11-1. Service description document

```
<?xml version="1.0"?>
<?xml:stylesheet type="text/xsl" href="Service.xsl"?>

<ITGServiceTypes>
<Service>
<Name>Small Business 401K</Name>
<Description>Small Business 401(k) is a cost-effective
retirement plan program that offers small businesses many of
the features normally available only in larger plans.
Features include daily valuation, a toll-free number and
employee communication services.</Description>
<PlanType>401k</PlanType>
<Link>http://cartalk.cars.com/columns/cc/latest.html</Link>
</Service>

<Service>
<Name>OMNI Bundled Regional Services</Name>
<Description>ITG ranks in the top 20 providers of plan
administration, recordkeeping and investment
services.</Description>
<PlanType>OMNI</PlanType>
<Link>http://www.microsoft.com/msdn</Link>
</Service>

<Service>
<Name>OMNI Bundled National Services</Name>
<Description>ITG ranks in the top 20 providers of plan
administration, recordkeeping and investment
services.</Description>
<PlanType>OMNI</PlanType>
<Link>http://www.netscape.com</Link>
</Service>

</ITGServiceTypes>
```

11.4 | How the system works

The system uses XML and XSL so that both the content and the Web layout can be changed independently. This strategy allows new services and information to be added without the assistance of a webmaster.

The data flow is shown in Figure 11-1. The client completes a search form that requests an *Active Server Page* from the Web server, which interprets the page and issues a data request to *eXcelon*. The latter returns an

XML document and an XSL stylesheet to the Web server, which processes them and generates HTML pages that are delivered to the client.

The abbreviated illustration of such an XML document in Example 11-1 shows how Wells Fargo describes its services. Note the element called `PlanType`, which assigns each service to a category.

The XSL stylesheet with which the Web server creates the HTML rendition of the document is shown in Example 11-2. It uses the `PlanType` element to select and display only services that are associated with OMNI plans.

Example 11-2. Stylesheet to display only OMNI plans

```
<?xml version="1.0"?>
<xsl:stylesheet xmlns:xsl="http://www.w3.org/TR/WD-xsl"
                xmlns="http://www.w3.org/TR/REC-html40">
   <xsl:template match="/">
      <xsl:for-each select="//Service[PlanType='401k']">
         <xsl:apply-templates/>
            <a>
               <xsl:attribute name="href">
                  <xsl:value-of select="Link"/>
               </xsl:attribute>
               <xsl:value-of select="Name"/>
            </a>
            <p></p>
            <xsl:value-of select="PlanType"/>
            <blockquote>
               <font size="-1">
                  <xsl:value-of select="Description"/>
               </font>
            </blockquote>
      </xsl:for-each>
   </xsl:template>
</xsl:stylesheet>
```

11.5 | Conclusion

Wells Fargo's *eXcelon*-based knowledge management system is enabling its employees to be better informed and better prepared to do their jobs. They can respond more quickly to customer inquiries and deliver better sales offerings to prospective customers. Furthermore, the company no longer incurs the expense of maintaining and revising static HTML pages.

©2000 THE XML HANDBOOK™

E-commerce

- Electronic Data Interchange (EDI)
- Business-to-business
- Supply chain integration
- Web storefronts
- Online catalogs with ERP integration
- Schemas for Web storefront catalogs

©2000 The XML Handbook™

Part Three

E-commerce is all about the elimination of manual procedures among trading partners. The eventual goal is to have each partner's system exchange information directly with all the others.

Today, the most visible manifestations of e-commerce are *Web storefronts* – websites where an online catalog replaces a paper catalog and mailed-in order forms. These sites enter transactions directly into the vendor's system, but the purchaser must do everything manually. Increasingly, as brick-and-mortar companies go online, these website catalogs will exist in print as well.

Historically, though, business supply chain automation, in the form of Electronic Data Interchange (EDI), has been the major driver of e-commerce. EDI is vital to those companies rich enough to have implemented it, but for smaller trading partners it is unattainable.

In the following chapters, we'll see why traditional EDI has reached its limit and how XML and the Web can help it realize its full potential. We'll also examine the production of catalogs for concurrent use in Web storefronts and in print, including the design of the DTD or schema definition. Finally, we'll see how the *Discovery Channel* discovered a way to shop at a hundred Web storefronts at once.

XML and EDI: The new Web commerce

Application Discussion

- Traditional EDI: Built on outdated principles
- Ubiquitous EDI: A quantum leap forward
- The New EDI: Leveraging XML and the Internet

©2000 THE XML HANDBOOK™

Chapter 12

XML and the Internet will dramatically reshape the Electronic Data Interchange (EDI) landscape. By driving down costs and complexity, EDI will become a truly ubiquitous technology that will reshape business as we know it. This introduction to EDI was prepared by Mike Hogan of POET Software Corporation, `http://www.poet.com`.

Over the past several decades, corporations have invested trillions of dollars in automating their internal processes. While this investment has yielded significant improvements in efficiency, that efficiency has not been extended to external processes.

In effect, companies have created islands of automation that are isolated from their vendors and customers – their trading partners. The interaction among companies and their trading partners remains slow and inefficient because it is still based on manual processes.

12.1 | What is EDI?

Electronic Data Interchange (EDI) has been heralded as the solution to this problem. *EDI* is defined as the exchange of data between heterogeneous systems to support transactions.

EDI is not simply the exportation of data from one system to another, but actual interaction between systems. For example, Company B is a supplier to Company A. Instead of sending purchase orders, bills and checks in hard copy form, the two might connect their systems to exchange this same data electronically.

In the process they could benefit in many other ways, including faster turnaround on orders, better inventory control, reduced financial float, complete real-time information about orders and inventory for improved decision-making, reduced costs for manual data input, and more. Companies that have implemented EDI rave about the various benefits.

In fact, these benefits can be expanded to a chain of suppliers. For example, Company C might be a supplier to Company B above. If companies B and C implement EDI, then Company A gains the additional benefits of superior integration with their entire *supply chain* of suppliers.

12.1.1 *Extranets can't hack it*

There is a significant gap between the business benefits described above and the actual implementation of EDI. This is because the actual implementation of "traditional EDI" is fundamentally flawed. It is difficult and costly to implement and, even worse, it requires a unique solution for each pair of trading partners. This situation is analogous to requiring a unique telephone line to be wired to each person to whom you wish to speak.

Many people falsely proclaimed the Internet as the solution to this problem. By implementing EDI over a single network, our problems would be solved. This "solution" was so exciting it was even given its own name, the extranet. Unfortunately, a network with a common protocol is still only a partial solution.

This is because the systems implemented in each company are based on different platforms, applications, data formats (notations), protocols, schemas, business rules, and more. Simply "connecting" these systems over the Internet does not, by itself, solve the problem. To use the phone system analogy again, this is analogous to wiring each business into the global phone network, only to realize that each company's phone system is unique, and incompatible with every other phone system.

And given the trillions of dollars companies have invested in automation, they are not simply going to replace these systems with new "compatible" solutions, assuming such things existed.

12.1.2 *XML can!*

The eXtensible Markup Language (XML) provides a solution for EDI over the Internet. XML is a universal notation (data format) that allows computers to store and transfer data that can be understood by any other computer system. XML maintains the content and structure, but separates the business rules from the data. As a result, each trading partner can apply its own business rules. This flexibility is critical to creating a complete solution for EDI.

There are additional technologies that are also part of the complete solution. Security, for example, is critical to EDI. Transactional integrity, connection stability, authentication and other services are also critical to implementing a complete solution. These requirements are addressed by technologies that are layered on top of the Internet. We refer to them generically as *Internet-based services.*

The final piece of the EDI solution is data storage. XML introduces a unique set of requirements for hierarchical naming and structure. It also requires rich relationships and complex linking. XML's use in EDI adds further requirements for metadata and versioning. These requirements levy heavy demands on database technology.

12.1.3 *The new EDI*

By combining XML, the Internet, Internet-based services and database connectivity, we have a complete solution for *New EDI*. Together, these technologies will not only change EDI, they will change our entire business landscape. EDI will metamorphose from a handful of unique interconnections, defined by the supply chain, into a "supply web". The supply web is an intelligent common fabric of commerce over the Internet.

According to Metcalfe's Law – formulated by Robert Metcalfe, the inventor of *Ethernet* – the value of a network is roughly proportional to the square of the number of users. Imagine what this means when your EDI "network" expands from a one-to-one proposition, to a true network that encompasses practically every company in the world. Suddenly, the trillions of dollars companies have invested in internal automation increase in value by several factors. By the same token, this information can also be extended to customers, adding significant value to the vendor-customer relationship, thereby enhancing customer loyalty.

This is a pivotal time in the history of technology. With the emergence of XML, all of the pieces are available to create a universal mechanism for EDI. The Internet provides the transport. XML provides the flexible, extensible, structured message format. Various Internet-based services provide solutions for security, transactional integrity, authentication, connection stability, network fail-over and more.

Add to this sophisticated data storage and you have all of the pieces necessary to unite corporate islands of automation into a single coherent fabric of electronic commerce. This will result in dramatic improvements in efficiency, cost-savings, superior access to real-time data for analysis and decision-making, superior inventory management, and more.

We will be examining these propositions in detail, and the technology that makes them possible. The new EDI is already emerging as the driving force behind the use of XML on the Web.

12.2 | The value of EDI

While traditional EDI is very costly and difficult to implement, the potential benefits are very significant. Companies that have implemented EDI rave about benefits like improved efficiency, vendor management, cost savings, superior access to information for decision making, tighter inventory control, customer responsiveness, and it is a competitive advantage that can be marketed to attract new customers.

12.2.1 *The 20/80 rule*

EDI was initially implemented to improve efficiency by enabling companies to eliminate costly and slow manual methodologies, like the processing of purchase orders and bills. It was thought that by allowing the computers of two or more companies to share this information, they could achieve dramatic improvements in efficiency.

However, the largest savings are derived from a complete shift to EDI that allows companies to completely eliminate their hard copy processes. The traditional 80/20 rule applies in reverse to EDI, meaning that it is the last 20% of your trading partners to convert to EDI who account for 80% of the potential savings.

This is because even with 80% of your trading partners using EDI, you must still maintain the same manual processes for the remaining 20% who don't. While most companies have not been able to completely convert from hard copy processes to EDI, the 20% savings companies have realized have still been very significant. With ubiquitous EDI enabling companies to completely eliminate their manual processes, the savings will improve dramatically.

With EDI, companies are also able to manage their supply chains much more efficiently. Through EDI, companies have been able to reduce the average time from issuance of an order to receipt of goods from several weeks, to a matter of days. By improving inventory control, companies are able to minimize their investment in costly inventory, while still being able to address spikes in business. For industries where inventory costs are a significant part of their business, like manufacturing, this represents a significant cost savings.

EDI also reduces the financial float by eliminating the typical order generation, delivery and processing, by 5-7 days. By combining EDI with Electronic Funds Transfer (EFT) companies can also reduce the financial float by 8-10+ days. Based on the amount of money involved, this can represent a significant savings.

EDI also provides companies with superior real-time information upon which to base decisions. Everyone recalls stories of companies who simply didn't have the data to realize how bad things were, until it was too late. With EDI, companies have access to complete data in real-time. The ability to collect, manipulate and measure information about your relationships with vendors and customers can be critical to your company's success.

Customer responsiveness is becoming increasingly important. Many companies have leveraged technology to dramatically improve customer responsiveness. A good example of this is Federal Express, which has created a website where customers can track the status of their packages.

This is only accomplished through FedEx's end-to-end dedication to EDI. By capturing information about the package status at each step in the process, and making this information accessible to customers, they have made themselves leaders in customer support. This is critical to building and growing businesses, especially in the Internet age.

Some companies who have implemented EDI with one supplier, have gone on to market this capability to other potential customers, as a unique selling point. This has enabled them to grow their business. As EDI becomes more ubiquitous, the tide could shift to the point where compa-

©2000 The XML Handbook™

nies will not accept vendors who are not EDI-capable. That is because of the dramatic savings that can be achieved by a complete conversion to EDI.

12.2.2 *Ubiquitous EDI: A quantum leap forward*

Ubiquitous EDI will have a profound impact on business-to-business and business-to-consumer relationships. The many problems with current implementations of EDI have relegated it to large enterprises and selected industries. However, the combination of the Internet, Internet-based technologies, and XML will open up EDI not only to small-to-medium enterprises (*STME*s), but also to individuals (Example 12-1).

Through deployment of these technologies, EDI will experience growth and market penetration that will rival the e-mail market. Electronic commerce will finally blossom on the Web and become an everyday part of our lives. In short, EDI will usher in a new era in computing. The Internet will metamorphose from a transport for Web pages into a ubiquitous and seamless foundation for every imaginable transaction. In the future, EDI will touch every aspect of computing.

The term *data interchange* has many meanings, and many forms of data interchange have been implemented. For example, OLE and DDE are used for sharing data among heterogeneous applications on the same computer, while CORBA, Java RMI, COM, and COM+ support data interchange among computers. But the acronym "EDI" invariably refers to the traditional "Electronic exchange of data to support business transactions".

In focusing on traditional EDI, the seminal questions are: "What is the real value of EDI?" and "Why should I care?"

12.3 | Traditional EDI: Built on outdated principles

The phrase *traditional EDI* refers to the use of rigid transaction sets with business rules embedded in them. This model simply does not work in today's rapidly changing business environment.

Example 12-1. The value of data interchange.

Mike opens his company expense report, and in the microsecond it takes to launch, he reminisces about the old days when he had to fill out these things himself. Now the computer does it for him. Mike recently took a trip to Utah to close a major deal. In the process he purchased a plane ticket, a rental car and various meals. In the old days, he used to enter all of these charges manually into an expense program...not any more.

Mike uses a corporate American Express card for these purchases. When he opens the expense report, it automatically connects to American Express, via EDI, and presents a list of new charges. Mike selects the charges that are appropriate for this expense report.

American Express sends this data to Mike's computer, which automatically formats the data into his expense report. Mike then clicks the send button and the expense report is sent to his manager to approve. Then the company's bank instantly wires the money to Mike's bank account.

Behind the scenes, all these companies are establishing connections, as needed, to share information in a secure and reliable manner using XML and the Internet. But Mike doesn't concern himself with what goes on behind the scenes, he's off to close another big deal in Washington.

This problem is compounded by the fact that companies have chosen to interpret these transaction set standards in ways that suit their unique business requirements. As a result, vendors who engage in EDI with multiple customers typically must create a unique solution to handle the transaction sets from each company. This makes the implementation of EDI far too expensive, especially for STMEs.

These and other problems have hindered the growth of EDI. However, by solving the problems of traditional EDI, we will usher in a new era, where EDI is as common as an Internet account is today.

12.3.1 *The history of EDI*

EDI is a process for exchanging data in electronic format between heterogeneous applications and/or platforms in a manner that can be processed without manual intervention.

EDI dates back to the 1970s, when it was introduced by the Transportation Data Coordinating Committee (TDCC). The TDCC created transaction sets for vendors to follow in order to enable electronic processing of purchase orders and bills.

At the time, the technology landscape was very different from what it is today. Lacking ubiquitous powerful CPUs, a common transport, and a file format that allows for flexibility, they defined strict transaction sets. These transaction sets addressed the needs for data content, structure and the process for handling the data. In other words, the business rules were embedded into the transaction set.

The incorporation of business rules into the definition of the transaction set causes many problems, because:

1. Business rules vary from company to company;
2. Business rules for one size company may be completely inappropriate for companies of another size;
3. Business rules are subject to change over time according to changes in market dynamics.

In short, the use of fixed and rigid transaction sets, while necessary at the time, have limited the value of EDI, and therefore stunted its growth.

12.3.2 *EDI technology basics*

Traditional EDI is based on fixed transaction sets. These transaction sets are defined by standards bodies such as the United Nations Standard Messages Directory for Electronic Data Interchange for Administration, Commerce and Transport (*EDIFACT*), and the American National Standards Institute's (ANSI) Accredited Standards Committee X12 sub-group.

Transaction sets define the fields, the order of these fields, and the length of the fields. Along with these transaction sets are business rules, which in the lexicon of the EDI folks are referred to as "implementation guidelines".

To actually implement EDI, the trading partners would follow these steps:

1. Trading partners enter into an agreement, called a trading arrangement.
2. They select a Value Added Network (VAN).

3. The trading partners typically either contract for, or build themselves, custom software that maps between the two data set formats used by these trading partners.
4. Each time a new trading partner is added, new software would have to be written to translate the sender's data set for the recipient. In other words, you start from scratch with each new trading partner.

Transaction sets are typically transmitted over expensive proprietary network service providers called VANs, which generally base charges on a mixture of fixed fees and message lengths. These fees can become quite substantial, but they are typically overshadowed by the cost to build and maintain the translation software. The VANs provide value-added services such as:

1. Data validation (compliance) and conversion
2. Logging for audit trails
3. Customer support
4. A secure and stable network
5. Accountability
6. Transaction roll-back to support uncommitted transactions

It is important to note that EDI is not simply the exportation of data from one system to another, but a bidirectional mechanism for interaction between systems. Because these disparate systems typically employ different file formats (data notations), schemas, data exchange protocols, etc., the process of exchanging data is very difficult.

12.3.3 *The problems of traditional EDI*

Traditional EDI suffers from many problems that have limited its growth. One of the most significant problems is the fact that it is based on the transfer of fixed transaction sets. This rigidity makes it extremely difficult to deal with the normal evolution necessary for companies to introduce new products and services, or evolve or replace their computer systems.

In addition, these transaction sets include strict processes for handling the data. These processes are not universally acceptable to companies in various industries and of various sizes. This problem is compounded by a standardization process that is too slow to accommodate the accelerating pace of business today.

In addition, the high fixed costs of implementation have been too much to justify for STMEs. In short, there are a host of problems which, despite the benefits of EDI, have prevented its universal adoption.

12.3.3.1 Fixed transaction sets

EDI is currently built on transaction sets that are fixed in nature. For example, a contact field might include the individual's name, title, company, company address and phone number. However, the company does not have the flexibility to add or subtract fields.

Why is this important?

Companies cannot be frozen in time by a fixed transaction set. This prevents them from evolving by adding new services or products, changing their computer systems and improving business processes. This inflexibility inherent in the current custom solutions required to map data between each trading partner pair is untenable, despite the significant benefits of EDI (Example 12-2).

Example 12-2. Problems of traditional EDI: Healthcare

The transaction sets created for the healthcare system were defined for the traditional indemnity model, where the insurance company pays the doctor on a per visit basis. However, the movement toward managed care was not foreseen in this transaction set. Since managed care pays the doctor a set fee per patient, but does not reimburse on a per visit basis, the standard transaction set simply doesn't work.

The typical doctor sees a mixture of patients, some having managed care insurance and others with indemnity insurance. In order to accommodate this scenario, the doctor is forced to create a false "per visit" fee for managed care patients. This false fee, which is required in order to "complete" the transaction set, creates havoc with the doctor's other billing systems, which EDI was supposed to help.

Rigid transaction sets that enforce process as well as content are simply not flexible enough to address the ever-changing business environment.

12.3.3.2 Slow standards evolution

EDI standards are defined by standards bodies that are structurally ill-equipped to keep up with the rapid pace of change in the various business environments they impact, as illustrated by Example 12-2.

These standards accommodate many companies with very different needs. They also encompass not just the ontology, but the associated business processes. As a result, it is very slow and difficult, if not impossible, to develop one-size-fits-all solutions.

The current process for defining standards for transaction sets can take years. This simply will not work in today's business environment, which is characterized by accelerated change and increased competition. However, in an effort to jump-start the creation of industry ontologies in the form of DTDs for XML, the work of the traditional EDI standards bodies could be enormously valuable.

Historically, technology standards that are defined and managed in a top-down fashion, like EDI standards, have been replaced by bottom-up standards that allow for independent and distributed development. In other words, technologies like XML, that support greater flexibility and diversity, while providing compatibility between implementations, typically replace inflexible managed solutions like fixed transaction sets. The XML standardization process is managed by the World Wide Web Consortium (W3C).

12.3.3.3 Non-standard standards

Despite the perception of standardization, there remains some flexibility in the interpretation of these standards. The simple fact of the matter is that companies have unique needs, and these needs must be translated into the information they share with their trading partners.

In practical terms, the customer is at a significant economic advantage in defining these "standards", vis-a-vis the supplier. As a result, suppliers are forced to implement one-off solutions for each trading partner. In many of the industries where EDI is more prevalent, the suppliers also tend to be the smaller of the two partners, which makes the financial proposition even worse (see 12.3.3.4, "High fixed costs", on page 164).

Because of the various informational needs of companies, it is impractical to expect that EDI standards can be a one-size-fits-all proposition. The variables of company size, focus, industry, systems, etc. will continue to cre-

©2000 The XML Handbook™

ate needs that are unique to each company. As evidence, consider the amounts companies spend on custom development and customization of packaged applications.

12.3.3.4 High fixed costs

While large companies tout the financial and operational benefits of EDI, these same benefits have eluded the STMEs. That is because of the high fixed costs of implementation, which must be balanced against savings that are variable.

Depending on the level of automation, implementing EDI for a large enterprise is not substantially more expensive than it is for STMEs. In fact, it can be more expensive for the STMEs. Larger companies can often implement a single EDI standard, while the STMEs must accommodate the various standards of their larger partners. This can be very expensive.

Yet, ironically, the benefits are variable. So, if savings are 2% of processing costs, this might not be a substantial number for the manufacturer of car seat springs, but it can be a huge number for GM, Ford or Chrysler. STMEs simply do not have the scale to compensate for the high fixed costs of traditional EDI.

Because of this some of the STMEs that claim to implement EDI are actually print hard copy of the data feeds and re-typing them in their systems. The reason they implemented this faux-EDI is to meet customer requirements, but they simply do not have the transactional scale to justify the investment. Something must be done to bring down these costs (Example 12-3).

12.3.3.5 Fixed business rules

Business rules are encapsulated in the definition of the transaction sets as implementation guidelines. However, business rules are not something that can be legislated, nor can they be rigid.

Business rules that are applicable for a large enterprise, may be completely inappropriate for an STME. To make matters worse, business rules for a medium-sized enterprise may be wholly inappropriate for a small enterprise.

Example 12-3. Problems of traditional EDI: Retail

One large retailer requires its vendors to implement EDI in order to qualify as a vendor. However, like all traditional EDI implementations, the data set is unique to the retailer.

For small companies, implementing this system can be quite an investment. Retail is a very fast-paced industry, because it is forced to cater to ever-changing customer demands. As a result, some suppliers to this retailer have implemented this costly technology, only to later lose their contract with the retailer. In fact, because of the significant investment in technology these companies were forced to make, they have sued the retailer.

If this technology were universally applicable, the vendor's investment in a single customer would be eliminated, as would the retailer's legal liability.

These business rules will also vary between industries. Even companies of the same size that are in the same industry will implement different business rules. What's more, business rules change over time. The earlier healthcare example demonstrates this point.

Traditional EDI focuses too much on process as an integral part of the transaction set. This is a fatal flaw. New technologies, like XML, support the separation of process, or business rules, from the content and structure of the data. Achieving this separation is critical to widespread adoption of EDI.

The linkage between transaction sets and business rules creates additional problems. The real-life implementation of EDI typically requires custom solutions for each trading partner pair. This creates havoc when trying to implement or modify global business rules.

For example, if your company changed business policy to begin accepting purchase orders, which you had refused to accommodate in the past, you would have to manually change the individual software for each trading partner. You could not make these changes on a global basis using traditional EDI.

This problem also impacts your ability to upgrade or replace your internal systems, since they are uniquely woven into the EDI software in place. In essence, you can become locked into systems that may become obsolete by the time you actually implement the total solution.

©2000 The XML Handbook™

12.3.3.6 Limited penetration

EDI penetration has been very limited, when compared to the penetration rates of other automation technologies. Yet the majority of the value of EDI is derived by complete elimination of the hard-copy processes EDI is meant to replace.

As mentioned above, EDI benefits do not follow the 80/20 rule, because converting the first 80% of your vendors to EDI results in only 20% of the potential cost savings. The remaining 80% of the costs remain, since the company is forced to maintain all of the old manual process in tandem with the electronic processes. The most significant savings come only from completely replacing all manual processes with EDI.

The real value of any network is in its adoption by users. Remember Metcalfe's Law: The value of any network is roughly proportional to the number of users squared.

But EDI, in its current state, is *not* a single interlinked network. On the contrary it is a series of one-to-one chains of data flow. As a result, it is vulnerable to alternative "networked" solutions like those enabled by XML, the Internet, Internet-based services, and database connectivity.

12.4 | The new EDI: Leveraging XML and the Internet

Now that we've established the tremendous benefits of EDI, and the structural problems of traditional EDI, the obvious question is: "How can we fix the problems?"

Fortunately, new technologies are coming together to completely reshape the EDI landscape. Today, EDI is currently implemented in a 1-to-1 manner between trading partners. These partnerships can then be extended through tiers to create a supply chain.

This is all changing!

The new paradigm is the *supply web*. The supply web is based on utilization of XML, the Internet, Internet-based services and database connectivity to create a network, or "web", of trading partners.

Implementation and operational costs will plummet, trading partners will implement one-size-fits-all solutions, and adoption will skyrocket And

Using XML, companies can separate the business rules from the content and structure of the data. By focusing on exchanging data content and structure, the trading partners are free to implement their own business rules, which can be quite distinct from one another. Yet, using templates, companies can work with legacy EDI, non-XML datatypes as well (as we will see in Chapter 13, "XML and EDI: Working together", on page 176).

12.4.2 *The Internet*

Many companies heralded the cost savings and ubiquity of the Internet as the death knell for VANs. However, this future has not come to pass...yet.

The boldest of these claims was based on the notion that the extranet would redefine the new computing paradigm. What these pundits failed to realize was that the Internet alone does not address the needs of the EDI community.

The EDI community is generally limited to the largest enterprises. EDI is mission critical, and requires a dependable network. It also requires a level of security that couldn't be found on the Internet. To put it simply, the savings were not sufficient to justify the switch.

Furthermore, connectivity is only a small part of the problem, the largest issue is the exchange of data in a universal fashion.

All these issues have now been addressed.

- Technology is now available to provide dial-up services to support the Internet in addressing up-time and throughput for mission critical information.
- Security has improved dramatically.
- The use of XML will broaden the EDI customer base to include STMEs and individuals. This new group of customers is much more price-sensitive, so they are inclined to seek an Internet-based solution.
- The ability to exchange data in a more democratic and ad hoc manner will cause an explosion in the average number of EDI connections.

The current average number of EDI trading partners, for those companies who utilize EDI at all, is two. Building EDI solutions based on XML, and operating this over the Internet, which offers a low-cost ubiquitous

©2000 THE XML HANDBOOK™

transport, will dramatically expand the value of EDI, according to Metcalfe's Law.

12.4.3 *Internet technologies*

Internet technologies have improved, and continue to improve dramatically, now providing a critical mass of technologies that is capable of replacing the services of VANs. Consider the following list of VAN services, each followed by the Internet-based alternatives that offer greater functionality and flexibility:

Data validation and conversion
: XML DTDs, XML validation, templates, and structure-based data feed interpretation.

Intermediary-based logging for audit trails
: Ubiquitous XML-savvy repositories employed by all trading partners enables rich logging for audit trails. Combining these with electronic signatures ensures system and company identification.

Consulting, customer service and customer support
: This function could be handled by VANs capable of making the transition to Internet technologies, or by the other legions of consultants.

Security and accountability
: Public key cryptography, certificate authorities, digital signatures can assure secure transactions.

Connection reliability, stability
: New technologies in bandwidth allocation, general improvement in the stability of the Internet and alternative fail-over solutions like dial-up continue to move the Internet toward supporting critical real-time data flow. (Remember, it was originally designed to withstand nuclear attack!)

Trading partner negotiation

Directories (X.500, LDAP, NDS, Active Directory), certificate authorities, digital signatures, e-mail, Internet versions of the Better Business Bureau, etc., can support this function.

Transactional support (roll-back, etc.)

The improvements in remote messaging systems and transaction processing monitors provide a layer of transaction support that is capable of adding transactional integrity even on unstable networks.

Because of the knowledge and experience of the VAN community, and because of the anticipated growth of the entire EDI market, the VAN community is well positioned to transition into consulting or systems integrator roles, helping companies implement these new technologies.

12.4.4 *XML data storage*

In other technological transitions, data storage has been a moot point, since the data could be mapped more-or-less directly into relational tables or file systems. More recently, object-oriented database management systems became available for this purpose.

XML data, however, is composed of self-describing information elements that are richly linked, and that utilize a hierarchical structure and naming mechanism. These qualities enable new data-access capabilities based on the tree structure, such as context-sensitive queries, navigation, and traversal.

"Native" XML-based support for these new capabilities can be provided by a value-added content management layer above the DBMS.

12.4.5 *Data filtering*

The source of the vast majority of EDI-related information is currently in mainframes and relational databases. This data will be marked-up on the fly with XML tags. XML data will also come from data sources such as:

- XML content management systems

- Various Internet resources
- EDI-XML documents, both full documents like purchase orders and short inter-process messages
- Result sets from applications, also in XML

These diverse sources must be communicated with by a middle-tier "data filter" that can speak to each source in a manner that the source will recognize. The data must then be filtered in source-dependent ways, based on one's confidence in the data, application of consistent business logic, resolution of the various element-type name ontologies, response mechanisms, security, caching for performance, etc. Only then can the application address the data in a consistent manner and receive consistent responses from the middle tier, as shown in Figure 12-1.

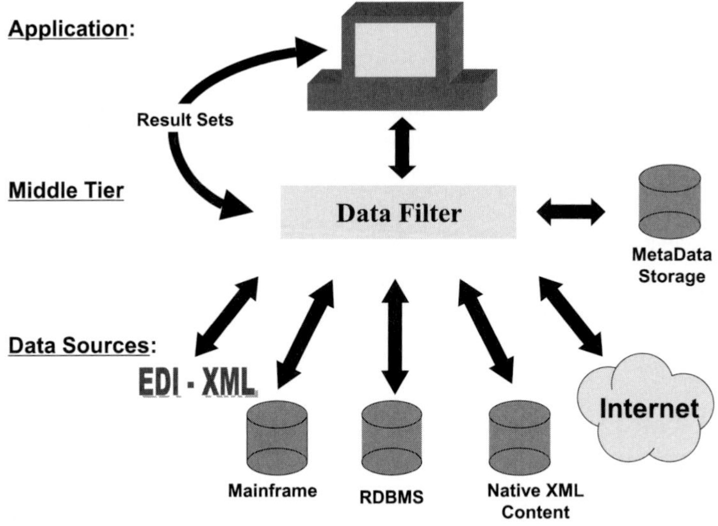

Figure 12-1 Data filter in an XML-based EDI system

The middle tier could maintain valuable meta-information that would add structure and context to the data stream. Such information could include:

- Routing for the query, response, etc.
- Source of the information (to indicate credibility, etc.)
- Time stamps
- Data, DTD, and tag normalization
- Context and navigation aids

Further details on XML content management and the use of object-oriented storage systems in the management of XML data can be found in Part Six, "Content Management".

12.5 | Conclusion

After decades of investment in corporate data centers, we have created islands of automation inside companies. Their isolation from trading partners limits the value companies can recognize from these systems.

EDI offers the ability to change all of this. EDI offers benefits like:

- improved efficiency
- supply chain management
- real-time data and metrics
- better planning
- superior execution
- control systems
- resource management
- cost savings
- superior access to information for decision making
- customer responsiveness
- ... and more.

However, traditional EDI is very difficult and expensive to implement. Because of problems like rigid transaction sets that embed business rules, slow standards development, high fixed costs, and limited market penetration, EDI has not achieved broad adoption. Fortunately, new technology is now available to address these problems and, in the process, reshape the EDI industry.

XML, the Internet, Internet-based services and database connectivity are combining to create a revolution in EDI. Instead of forcing companies to adapt their systems and business processes to the EDI data, this data will dynamically adapt to the companies' existing systems.

EDI will no longer be isolated to certain industries or the largest enterprises, it will become as ubiquitous as e-mail. EDI will evolve from a one-to-one supply chain to a richly interconnected web of trading partners forming the supply web.

This supply web will result in dramatic improvements in efficiency. Companies will slash costs, while improving access to critical information. This information will be pushed all the way to the end-user, providing superior customer support as well.

XML and EDI: Working together

Application Discussion

- Approaches to e-commerce
- Traditional-EDI and XML e-commerce compared
- Leverage existing EDI with XML
- Free software on CD-ROM

©2000 THE XML HANDBOOK™

Example 13-1. Sample EDI purchase order

```
ISA*00*       *00*   *08*61112500TST       *01*DEMO WU000003
*970911*1039*U00302000009561*0*P?
GS*PO*6111250011*WU000003 *970911*1039*9784*X*003020
ST*850*397822
BEG*00*RE*194743**970911
REF*AH*M109
REF*DP*641
REF*IA*000100685
DTM*010*970918
N1*BY*92*1287
N1*ST*92*87447
N1*ZZ*992*1287
PO1*1*1*EA*13.33**CB*80211*IZ*364*UP*718379271641
PO1*1*2*EA*13.33**CB*80211*IZ*382*UP*718379271573
PO1*1*3*EA*13.33**CB*80213*IZ*320*UP*718379271497
PO1*1*4*EA*13.33**CB*80215*IZ*360*UP*718379271848
PO1*1*5*EA*13.33**CB*80215*IZ*364*UP*718379271005
CTT*25
SE*36*397822
GE*1*9784
IEA*1*000009561
```

13.2.2 *The different flavors of XML and EDI*

EDI comes in two distinct flavors, X12 and EDIFACT. X12 is the American standard that evolved over the years from the most basic attempts at exchange in the 1960s to full-blown billion-dollar networks. EDIFACT is the international standard, endorsed by the United Nations and designed from the ground up beginning in 1985. Both flavors have several version releases of their message formats. Compatibility between versions is not always straightforward.

XML e-commerce is currently even more diversified, with proposed standards that use XML only and others that are XML-EDI hybrids. Some of the most important are listed here.

- CommerceNet, a business consortium, is developing ECO.
- RosettaNet, another consortium, is working on XML standards for product catalogs.
- Commerce ONE has created the common business library (CBL), in part funded by a government grant from the US National Institute for Standards and Technology (NIST).

©2000 The XML Handbook™

Example 13-2. Sample XML purchase order

```
<?xml version="1.0" ?>
<?xml:stylesheet?>
<purchase-order>
<header>
   <po-number>1234</po-number>
   <date>1999-02-08</date><time>14:05</time>
   </header>
<billing>
   <company>XMLSolutions</company>
   <address>
      <street>601 Pennsylvania Ave. NW</street>
      <street>Suite 900</street>
      <city>Washington</city>
      <st>DC</st><postcode>20004</postcode>
      </address>
   </billing>
<order items="1" >
   <item>
      <reference>097251</reference>
      <description>Widgets</description>
      <quantity>4</quantity>
      <unit-price>11.99</unit-price>
      <price>47.96</price>
      </item>
   <tax type="sales" >
      <tax-unit>VA</tax-unit>
      <calculation>0.045</calculation>
      <amount>2.16</amount>
      </tax>
   ...
```

- Ariba has rallied several companies around commerce XML (cXML), a proposed standard for catalogs and purchase orders.
- Microsoft has loosely grouped many of these technologies under what it calls *BizTalk*.
- The XML-EDI Group has proposed a naming convention for representing EDI messages in XML. Essentially, they have built-on and preserved the hard-won consensus for the X12 taxonomy by using X12 names in XML tags.
- Still other groups, such as the Open Buying Initiative (OBI), are proposing standards for simply moving EDI X12 messages over HTTP.

13.3 | An XML-EDI trading system

Traditional EDI works. You can rely on it. There is no greater accolade for a technology. Large companies have spent millions on their EDI systems, which are mission-critical and unlikely to be abandoned. The objective now should be to leverage this sound base and extend it to more trading partners.

Sending EDI X12 or EDIFACT messages over HTTP – the Web transport protocol – won't do the job. Although EDI's transport system is primitive, it is not the EDI's governing limitation.

The expense of EDI is rooted in its complexity, and its complexity is based in its compressed, cryptic message formats. XML can overcome this complexity by storing the metadata within the data of the message. And XML also happens to be designed for HTTP.

Traditional EDI users can extend their electronic trading base by installing XML-EDI translators on their Web servers, as shown in Figure 13-5. The translation must go both ways: XML to EDI for messages starting from the small company and EDI to XML for messages starting from the large company traditional EDI user.

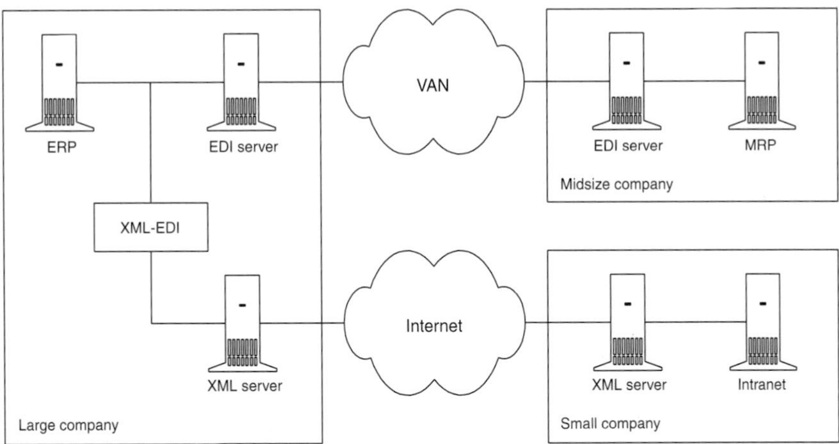

Figure 13-5 An XML-EDI trading system

13.3.1 *XML to EDI*

XML-EDI translators are already available, many relying on proprietary technology and unique scripting languages. Others, including XMLSolutions' *ExeterXML EDI Parser* use XSL to specify the transformation, as shown in Figure 13-6.

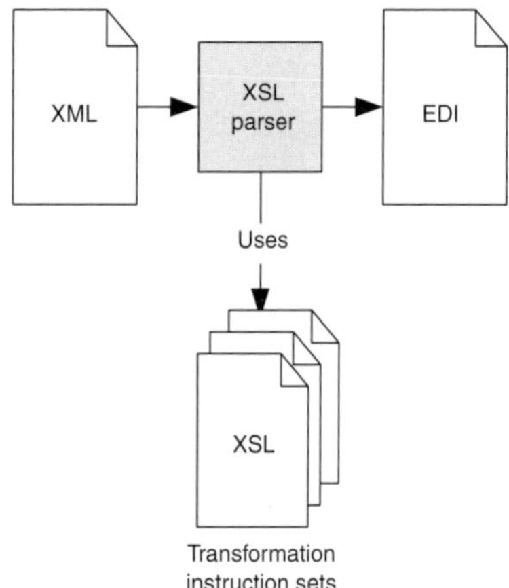

Figure 13-6 XSL is well-suited for transforming XML into EDI

Although XSL is most commonly used to transform XML into HTML for presentation, it is perfectly well-suited to transform XML into any representation, including EDI. And as it is an open standard, it is likely to benefit from the availability of free and open-source implementations and a large body of skilled developers.

13.3.2 *EDI to XML*

XSL cannot be used directly for the inverse conversion, as it can only transform from XML. The problem is well-known from the long experience in SGML and XML systems of having to convert word processing documents to generalized markup. The solution is also well-known: an intermediate trivial translation from the foreign notation to the markup language. A translation, in other words, that changes only the representation of the document, not the meaning. Then XSL can be applied to accomplish more powerful transforms.

This technique is illustrated in Figure 13-7, which shows an EDI parser as the intermediate translator. The EDI parser has an application programming interface (API) very similar to the XSL parser (and the XML parser for that matter). The EDI parser makes an XML message out of the EDI message by replacing EDI codes with their full names and making XML elements out of the EDI segments and elements. This process follows the XML-EDI Group's concept of preserving the X12 taxonomy when translating to XML.

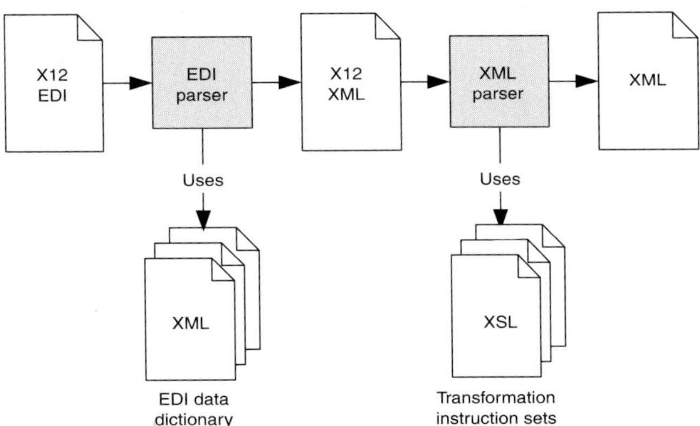

Figure 13-7 Transforming EDI to XML requires an intermediate step

Once the EDI message is a well-formed XML document, XSL can transform it into various XML-EDI message standards, such as cXML, RosettaNet or BizTalk.

Because there are many kinds of XML and many kinds of EDI, an XML-EDI translator is not a one-to-one system but rather a many-to-many system. Such a translator can therefore also serve as an XML to XML translator and an EDI to EDI translator.

13.4 | The future of e-commerce

The objective of e-commerce is to eliminate manual processes by allowing the internal applications of different companies to exchange information directly. Stated more generically, *e-commerce* is systems integration that crosses the boundary of the enterprise.

That definition encompasses more than just the automation of supply chain paperwork. It envisions a future framework that also automates business processes and workflow between trading partners, and that accommodates those few trading partners that might never automate as well.

XML and EDI working together is the first step toward that future.

Supply chain integration

Application Discussion

- Business-to-business communication
- XML messaging
- Web Interface Definition Language (WIDL)
- XML Remote Procedure Call (RPC)

©2000 THE XML HANDBOOK™

Chapter 14

Supply chain management is tricky business for suppliers and manufacturers. Ideally, they should have real-time access to one another's inventory and schedule planning systems, but that is expensive to achieve with traditional EDI. webMethods, `http://www.webmethods.com`, who sponsor this chapter, and Joe Lapp, who prepared it, believe there is a better means of business-to-business communication.

Managing a manufacturing business is in some ways a lot like feeding a family. The home is the factory and grocery stores are the suppliers. Parents manufacture meals for themselves and for their children.

But before they can make a meal they must be sure the refrigerator is stocked with the right foods in the necessary quantities. As they serve dinners, the food levels diminish, so they have to time their shopping to be sure that they always have enough food for the next meal. Sometimes the family must scale up to feed unexpected in-laws, and sometimes the family must scale back when the kids are away at camp.

14.1 | Linking up a supply chain

Manufacturers and suppliers struggle with these issues all the time. Suppliers are caught up in the challenge, as they must feed parts to multiple manufacturers. They must be sure that manufacturers have parts when they're needed, but they have to be careful not to overstock their products when manufacturer demand is not high enough to sell them. The supplier may itself be a manufacturer and have its own suppliers.

A series of businesses that feed parts to one another in sequence is known as a *supply chain.*

Suppose Manufacturer X decides to maximize the efficiency of its link in a supply chain. It wants to integrate its Materials Resource Planning (MRP) system with the planning systems of its suppliers, thereby providing each side with rich inventory information in real-time.

The manufacturer benefits by having access to up-to-date availability information on supplier parts, including parts delivery schedules. That allows it to reduce stock-outs even as it reduces inventory levels.

The supplier benefits by having access to the manufacturer's current parts inventory levels and to the manufacturer's expected rates of inventory depletion. For both parties there is a reduction in costs, as well as an improvement in customer service.

14.2 | Supply chain integration requirements

Manufacturer X does not want to lose an arm or a leg or a bevy of shareholders in the process of implementing the solution. It requires a cost-effective solution that it could put together in a period of weeks, rather than in a period of months or years. One in which all of its trading partners could participate, not just the top few. These requirements rule out traditional methods of electronic business integration, such as Electronic Data Interchange (EDI).

In an earlier time, EDI might have won hearts and ears and pocketbooks, but now the Internet and XML offer better ways to do things. Manufacturer X is aware of what is currently possibly with technology and imposed the following general requirements:

- The system must integrate with Manufacturer X's existing MRP system.
- Manufacturer X must communicate with its suppliers over the Internet. Private network solutions are too costly.
- Access to manufacturer data must be secure. Only registered suppliers may access the data. Suppliers may not access the

data of other suppliers. Data must remain secure in transit over the Internet.
- The effort and expense required of both Manufacturer X and its suppliers must be minimized.

The problem can be solved by employing a tool that allows disparate applications to interoperate over the Web. Let's take a look at one.

14.3 | *webMethods B2B*

webMethods B2B is a suite of components that enable open, Internet-based integration of the information systems of manufacturers and their customers, partners, and suppliers. The principal component is the webMethods *Business-to-Business Integration Server*, which sits between applications to enable them to communicate despite differences between them. The applications need only agree in an abstract sense on the nature of the services they offer, and on the data to be exchanged between these services.

The integration server employs *WIDL* (Web Interface Definition Language) technology for expressing these abstractions. Once the abstractions have been established, any two applications can communicate, regardless of their programming languages, whether they accept and/or receive XML messages, and regardless of the document type definitions (DTDs) to which the XML messages conform.

In other words, *webMethods B2B* makes applications accessible to one another over the Web, and it makes existing Web data accessible to applications. It provides the communications infrastructure needed to do the job, including security, passage through firewalls, and access to proxies. It also translates between message representations, such as URIs, CGI query data, and differing XML message document types.

Let's see how these capabilities can be applied to integrate a supply chain.

14.3.1 *Overview of the system*

A somewhat generalized version of the system architecture is depicted in Figure 14-1.

©2000 THE XML HANDBOOK™

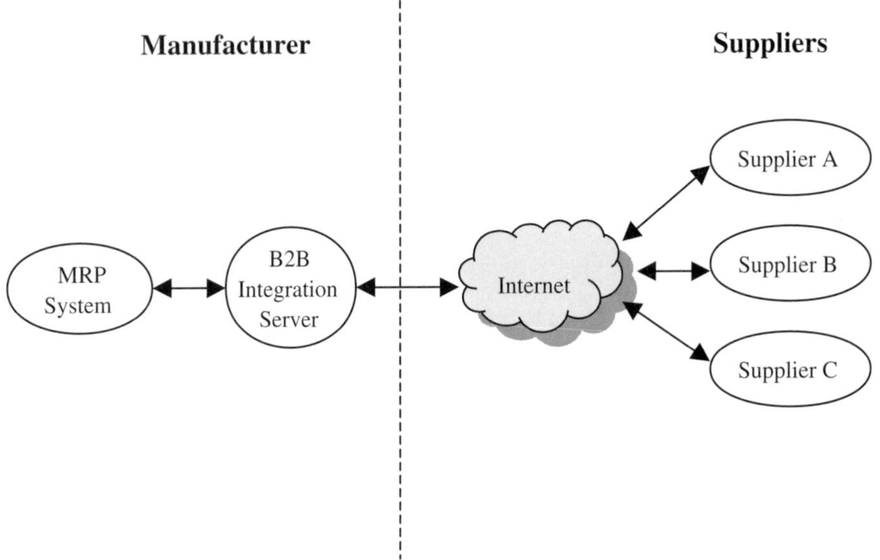

Figure 14-1 Supply chain integration architecture.

The generalization allows us to demonstrate the applicability of the solution to supply chains in general. Here, the integration server sits on the manufacturer's site and mediates all exchanges between suppliers and the manufacturer. It assumes responsibility for hiding network, protocol, and security issues from the supplier and manufacturer systems, and hiding differences in how the systems are interfaced.

Supplier systems access the manufacturer's MRP system to obtain part inventory levels, and communication between the systems is completely automated. The suppliers issue requests to the integration server in the form of XML messages, sending the requests via the standard POST method of HTTP.

The integration server translates these requests into calls to the MRP system. It then translates responses from the MRP system into XML reply messages that it sends back to the supplier. This request/reply mechanism for accessing services is called *Remote Procedure Call* (RPC).

The MRP system must also access supplier data. In order to minimize the impact on the suppliers, B2B uses standard URIs and CGI queries for the requests and allows both HTML and XML to be used in the responses.

(See Chapter 50, "WIDL and XML RPC", on page 672 for more information on these technologies.)

Upon receiving a response, the B2B server uses WIDL to convert the HTML or XML into a data representation that is suitable for the MRP system to consume. It then passes the converted data to the system, completing the request/response circuit.

14.3.2 *The manufacturer services*

The manufacturer services comprise half of the complete integration solution. These services give suppliers access to inventory level information found in the manufacturer's MRP system.

Figure 14-2 shows how the manufacturer provides services to its suppliers. A supplier issues a request to the integration server, which in turn calls upon a piece of software known as an "integration module". The latter acts on the MRP system to perform the request and returns data back to the integration server, which translates the data into the appropriate form for delivery to the supplier.

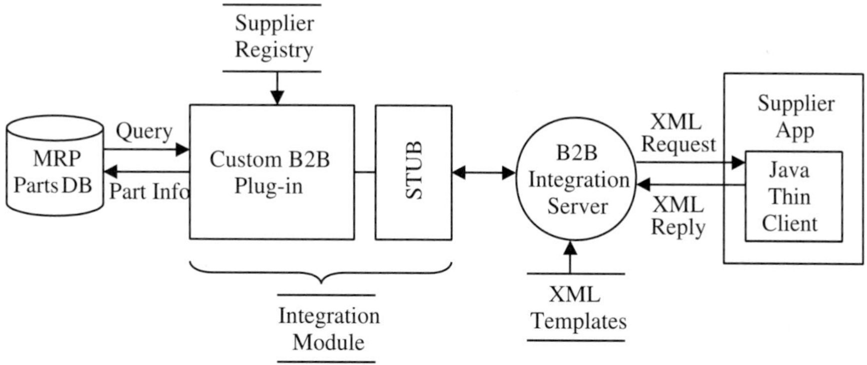

Figure 14-2 Providing manufacturer services to suppliers.

Several pieces shown in Figure 14-2 are key to the solution and merit some discussion.

14.3.2.1 Integration module

An integration module is software that enables MRP packages (e.g. SAP, Baan, etc.) and traditional middleware (MQ Series, MSMQ, etc.) to be extended securely beyond corporate boundaries. It has two components: a plug-in and a server stub.

14.3.2.1.1 Plug-in

The plug-in is code that Manufacturer X wrote to communicate with its MRP system. It is written in Java and exposes an interface to the integration server. The most important "method" (or program function) of this interface is one that retrieves part information from the MRP system when the method is called. The method inputs a part number and outputs information about the part.

The plug-in will only return part information to the suppliers that provide the parts; suppliers cannot acquire information about the parts that other suppliers provide. The plug-in accomplishes this by looking up the supplier's user name in the supplier registry to fetch the associated supplier ID. The retrieved ID must match the supplier ID that the MRP database associates with the part.

14.3.2.1.2 Server stub

A server stub is a portion of code that links into the plug-in and that allows the integration server to invoke an API that the plug-in exposes. Server stubs enable the integration server to communicate with plug-ins written in any programming language. They also benefit the server by hiding the details of the plug-in's method signatures (that is, their names and parameter definitions).

When a supplier requests the integration server to invoke a manufacturer service, the integration server hands the input parameters to the server stub, telling the stub which Java method to invoke on the plug-in. The stub invokes the method and then provides the method's output parameters to the integration server, which creates an XML reply.

14.3.2.2 XML requests and replies

The integration server communicates with the supplier via XML. It receives XML requests from the supplier and it sends XML replies back to the supplier. When it receives a request it translates the XML into a set of input parameters and hands these parameters to the server stub. When the stub returns output parameters, it translates the output parameters into an XML reply.

Manufacturer X chose to represent these XML request and reply messages using a "generic" message DTD. A generic DTD is capable of representing any set of input or output parameters, thereby allowing all message exchanges to use the same DTD. For efficiency, the solution uses an encoder/decoder module to translate XML into input parameters and to translate output parameters into XML.

14.3.2.3 Java thin client

The Java thin client is a piece of software that Manufacturer X developed and distributed to all of its suppliers. It contains the *webMethods B2B Client Classes*, which allows the client to submit and receive XML messages. However, the supplier could choose to use any XML-aware client.

The thin client provides suppliers with default behavior to jump-start their integration efforts with software that understands the generic XML DTD. To use the manufacturer services, the thin client must first establish a secure SSL session and log in to the server with a user name and a password that Manufacturer X provided.

14.3.2.4 Manufacturer interface specification

The solution requires that we define the set of services that the stub offers, and it requires that we state the data inputs and outputs for each service. We accomplish this by using WIDL to define an interface specification.

Example 14-1 shows a portion of the interface specification that does the job. A supplier invokes the "`getInventory`" method to retrieve inventory information as a function of a part number.

webMethods B2B includes a toolkit called the *webMethods B2B Developer*, which can be used to create both the server stub and this interface specification. The toolkit includes GUI-based tools for designing the interface spec-

Example 14-1. WIDL interface specification for the manufacturer services.

```
<WIDL NAME="com.Manufact-X.PartsInventory" VERSION="3.0">
  <RECORD NAME="PartHandle">
    <VALUE NAME="partNumber"/>
  </RECORD>
  <RECORD NAME="PartInventory">
    <VALUE NAME="inventoryLevel" TYPE="i4"/>
    <VALUE NAME="targetLevel" TYPE="i4"/>
    ...
  </RECORD>
  ...
  <METHOD NAME="getInventory" INPUT="PartHandle"
      OUTPUT="PartInventory"/>
  ...
</WIDL>
```

ification and for generating the source code for the stubs, so that the developer does not need to be familiar with either WIDL or XML.

14.3.3 *The supplier services*

The supplier services comprise the second half of the complete integration solution. These services give the manufacturer access to supplier inventory levels and delivery schedules.

Figure 14-3 portrays how the manufacturer utilizes the services of the supplier. Suppliers make their information available from Web servers in the form of HTML or XML pages. The interface to the information on these pages is again provided by an integration module.

14.3.3.1 Integration module

The client stub provides APIs that the plug-in calls to access the information found on the supplier's Web pages. The plug-in runs a background thread that periodically invokes these APIs to retrieve supplier part information. The thread updates the MRP system with the part information that the APIs return.

The integration server uses Web automation to make the supplier Web sites available to the plug-in. *webMethods B2B* can provide Web automation services to any application, not just plug-ins, but Manufacturer X wanted to centralize the entire integration solution within the plug-in.

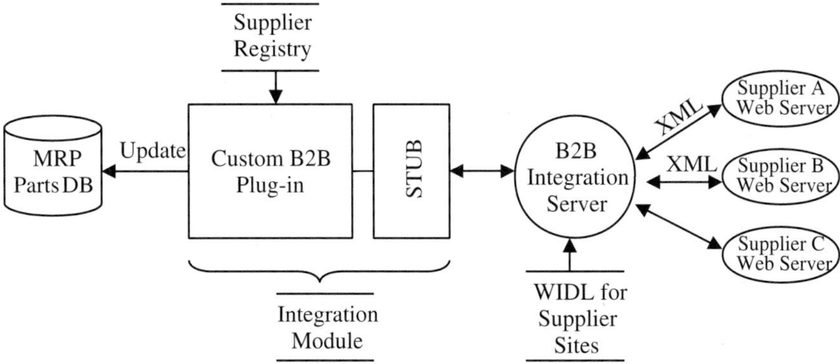

Figure 14-3 Providing supplier services to the manufacturer.

Web automation *wraps a website* so that it looks like a set of APIs (functions). As shown in Figure 14-3, there is no need to put Web automation technology on any of the wrapped websites themselves. The integration server merely sits between the website and the client (in this case, the plug-in) and makes the website accessible to the client through the APIs of a client stub.

14.3.3.2 Supplier interface specification

A developer generates the client stub by first designing a WIDL interface specification for the supplier services. Example 14-2 shows a portion of this specification.

The interface specification defines the APIs that the stub will expose, including the input and output parameters of each API. Since the plug-in is written in Java, the stub implements the APIs as Java methods. The developer links the client stub into the plug-in so that the plug-in can call these methods. The stub methods in turn use the services of the B2B server.

Next the developer uses WIDL to wrap the supplier websites so that each site conforms to the interface specification. The Toolkit does this through direct interaction with a website, and again the developer need not have any knowledge of WIDL. Once the WIDL files have been created, one configures the integration server to wrap the websites by dropping the files into a directory.

Example 14-2. WIDL interface specification for the supplier services.

```
<WIDL NAME="com.Supplier.PartAvailability" VERSION="3.0">
  <RECORD NAME="LoginProfile">
    <VALUE NAME="username"/>
    <VALUE NAME="password"/>
  </RECORD>
  <RECORD NAME="Availability">
    <VALUE NAME="dateRefreshed"/>
    <RECORDREF NAME="parts" DIM="1" RECORD="Part"/>
  </RECORD>
  <RECORD NAME="Part">
    <VALUE NAME="partNumber"/>
    <VALUE NAME="availableInventory" TYPE="i4"/>
    <VALUE NAME="quantityInTransit" TYPE="i4"/>
    ...
  </RECORD>
  ...
  <METHOD NAME="login" INPUT="LoginProfile"/>
  <METHOD NAME="getAvailability" OUTPUT="Availability"/>
  ...
</WIDL>
```

Each supplier site then has the same interface, consisting of the set of methods that the client stub exposes. The input parameters of a method fill out a form on a supplier website. The output parameters of the method contain data extracted from the pages that the site returns upon submitting the form parameters.

This approach allows the suppliers to return the information in many forms: HTML pages using any presentation or XML messages using any DTD. The supplier can even have a *B2B Integration Server* receive the form parameters and reply with XML messages, allowing the supplier to have tight integration with other manufacturers as well. The manufacturer's integration server makes the form of the supplier data transparent to the plug-in.

Once per day, the plug-in iterates over the suppliers listed in the supplier registry. For each supplier it retrieves a supplier ID, a URI, a user name, and a password. The URI specifies the location of the supplier site. The user name and password are items that the supplier provided to the manufacturer; they allow the manufacturer to log in to the supplier site.

For each supplier in the registry, the plug-in invokes methods on the client stub. It first invokes "login" to authenticate with the supplier's site and then invokes "`getAvailability`" to acquire the part availability data.

Finally, the plug-in writes the part availability data to the manufacturer's MRP database, keeping the database accurate to within a day.

14.3.4 *Extending the supply chain*

Suppliers are also often manufacturers and have their own supply chains. For example, computer manufacturers purchase disk drives, and disk drive suppliers are also manufacturers who purchase disk drive components from their suppliers.

Figure 14-4 illustrates such an extended supply chain. In this scenario, when Manufacturer X runs low on inventory, not only would Manufacturer X's suppliers become aware of this, but so would the suppliers of Supplier B.

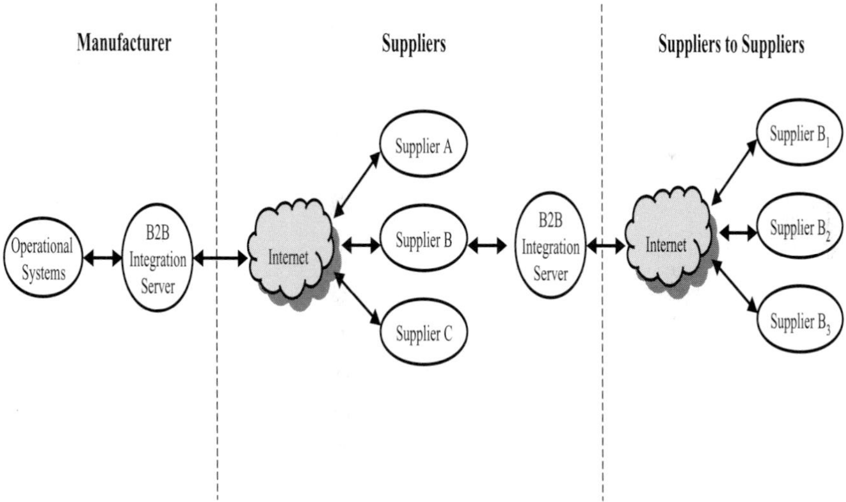

Figure 14-4 Extended supply chain integration.

14.4 | Conclusion

webMethods B2B allows Manufacturer X to integrate tightly with its suppliers. It allows the manufacturer's MRP system to communicate with the supplier planning systems without requiring the MRP system to have any knowledge of the Internet, of XML, or of the supplier system interfaces.

These facilities enabled Manufacturer X to implement the solution in only two weeks. Had Manufacturer X used an integration method like traditional EDI, it would still be negotiating the platform and protocol details with the suppliers. Instead, *webMethods B2B* provided Manufacturer X with a significantly simpler, faster, and less expensive way to get the job done.

Bright Lighting Company

Case Study

- Online and print catalog information system
- Entities for common text and translation
- XPointer application

Chapter 15

As more companies open Web storefronts, product data becomes more important than ever. Now their print catalogs must also be online catalogs and interfaces to their ERP systems. TANNER Dokuments, `http://www.tanner.de`, has implemented many of these catalog systems and sponsors this chapter to show you how to do it.

Even the most traditional of brick-and-mortar enterprises are seeing the Internet light and establishing Web storefronts. Suddenly, local and regional businesses find themselves selling their products all over the world.

15.1 | The challenge

For many companies, this is also the only way to survive in the market. The growing competition leads to smaller and smaller profit margins, which means more products have to be sold in order for companies to be successful.

Product information therefore plays an increasingly crucial role in these businesses. They have an urgent need for a catalog-based information system that not only works on the Web, but that can retain and grow their traditional base of physical world customers as well.

TANNER, located in Lindau, Germany at Lake Constance, develops such catalog systems for its clients. They aren't desktop publishing projects!

In a typical case, TANNER establishes an electronic information and ordering system – much more than an ordinary product catalog – for trading enterprises dealing in a large range of customized products. The first and most important step in this task is to convert product information to a standardized and finely-structured electronic format that can be read and used by different publishing tools for different media, and especially can be published online.

Information on around 100,000 articles must normally be stored, and usually that number continuously increases during the life of the system. Ease of scalability is therefore critical.

15.2 | The scenario

Let's see how TANNER developed a system for an actual German trading enterprise with a worldwide presence. We'll call it the Bright Lighting Company.

Bright sells consumer lighting products and components of all kinds, such as lamps, cables, switches, contacts, etc. Its customers are both resellers of the products and electricians who use them in their work. The two customer sets, of course, have different interests and a different approach to the merchandise. The product catalog is established to comply with the needs and requirements of both these target groups.

15.3 | The information base

The following principles were applied when implementing Bright's system:

- In order to ensure long-term availability of product data, independent of system and application, the ISO standard SGML was used as the data storage representation.
- Data storage was organized strictly by inventory objects (e.g., products), irrespective of the subsequent publication medium.
- The catalog data was the central constituent of an information management system that was designed and implemented in parallel with the initial production of the catalog.

For each single product or product group, an SGML document was prepared containing all applicable information.

15.3.1 *DTD development*

The DTD macrostructure provides information containers for different kinds of product information, as shown in Figure 15-1.

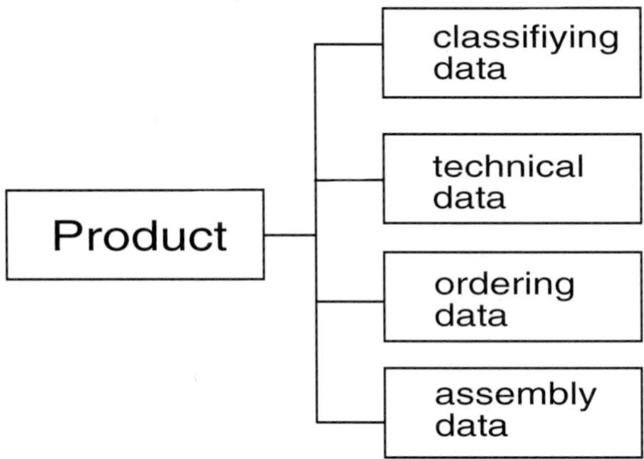

Figure 15-1 DTD macrostructure

The first container in the DTD stores information for the classification of the product. This information includes, for example, whether the product belongs to the category "halogen lamps" and whether it is a "lamp to be built in" a ceiling. Other classifications for identifying the product include the name of the manufacturer, the power consumption of the lamps, and the materials used in its construction.

15.3.2 *Utilization of standard texts*

To ensure utilization of consistent terminology throughout the entire catalog, corresponding to some 5,000 printed pages, a familiar SGML/XML technique was used. A list of product-related internal entities was defined for the terms that occurred most frequently (Example 15-1). Authors enter these terms by selecting them from the entity list.

Example 15-1. Fragment of a German entity list

```
<!ENTITY leistung       CDATA "Leistung">
<!ENTITY helligkeit     CDATA "Helligkeit">
<!ENTITY tiefe          CDATA "Tiefe">
<!ENTITY durchmesser    CDATA "Durchmesser">
```

The utilization of entity lists gives rise to a further advantage: if it is necessary to produce a catalog in another language, the entity lists are translated (Example 15-2). Note that the entity names are the same as in Example 15-2. The terms from the original entity list are replaced in the catalog with the terms of the new language simply by resolving the entity references. By use of this technique, up to 60% of the catalog is translated automatically – and without errors!

Example 15-2. Fragment of an English entity list

```
<!ENTITY leistung       CDATA "power">
<!ENTITY helligkeit     CDATA "brightness">
<!ENTITY tiefe          CDATA "depth">
<!ENTITY durchmesser    CDATA "diameter">
```

15.4 | The print catalog

15.4.1 *Assembly*

The first stage of print catalog production was to assemble the individual product documents into a single catalog document, as shown in Figure 15-2.

The rules for the assembly were written in an XML document and utilized the classification properties described above. For example, it was possible to stipulate that all lamps made by a specified manufacturer should be the first in the catalog, followed by all lamps with a diameter of more than 80mm.

©2000 THE XML HANDBOOK™

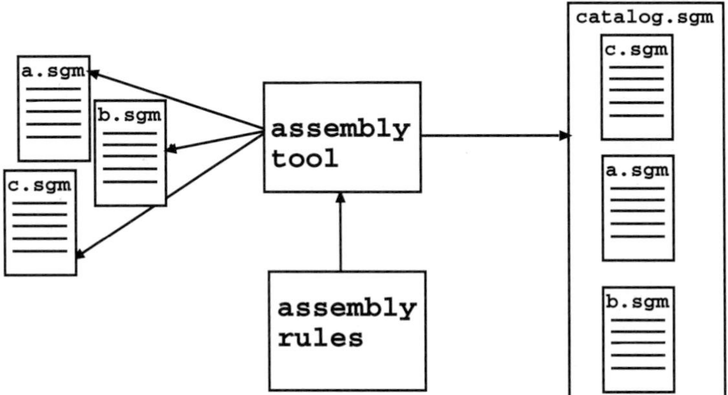

Figure 15-2 Catalog assembly

The assembly was performed by an "assembly tool" utility developed by TANNER that read the "assembly rules" XML document. By substituting other XML assembly rules, product-related or target-customer-related catalogs or catalog extracts could be generated.

15.4.2 *Preparation for rendition*

In the next stage, the catalog document was prepared for rendition by a publishing program. That process was controlled by a *template*, an XML document that specifies which information is extracted from the product descriptions and how and where it is set out on the rendered catalog pages.

The template, in *HyTime* terminology, performs the function of a hub document (see Example 15-3). It consists entirely of links between objects in the catalog and rendition rules. The catalog objects are located by means of XPointers.

A tool written in Perl analyzes these templates and produces a partially-rendered catalog document that contains all information in the desired sequence. All logical processing, such as numbering of list items and generation of text for headers and footers or margin columns, has been performed so that the publishing tool needs to resolve only page numbering.

In order to arrange the information on a page in a different sequence or integrate further information, it is only necessary to write a corresponding

Example 15-3. Template for print catalog

```
<!DOCTYPE PRODUCT
PUBLIC "-//BrightLighting//DTD Publications-DTD Version 1.0//EN" [
<PRODUCT>
<ORDER>
<?xpointer( "descendant(1,ORDER).child(1,ORDERTAB-
NOTICE)" )>
<?startattrset("ORDERTAB", "LAYOUTSP", "1" , "ORDERTAB",
   "ColWidth", "34" ,   "ORDERTAB", "ColWidth2", "@1*")
<?xpointer( "descendant(1,ORDER).(all,ORDERTAB)" )>
<?endattrset>
<?xpointer( "descendant(1,ORDER).(all,ADDINFO)" )>
<?xpointer( "descendant(1,ASSEMBLY).(1,ASSEMBLYINSTR)" )>
<?xpointer( "descendant(1,ORDER).(all,FURTHER-PRODUCTS)" )>
</ORDER>
</PRODUCT>
```

template that provides the desired functionality and then re-start the rendition process.

The partially-rendered catalog is then processed automatically by a publishing tool.

Note that, in the context of catalog production, the term "automatic" refers only to the portion of the job that can successfully be defined by rules. Full automation is possible only when information is uniform, of the same standardized size, and always presented in the same way. In practice, 70% automation is considered an excellent result. In any event, a good publishing tool can record the manual interventions and reproduce them at the next data import.

15.4.3 *Online*

The online version of the product catalog uses the same SGML product descriptions that are the basis for the print catalog.

After starting the online catalog, the user selects a product subdivision from the product range. For example, if he is interested in halogen lamps, a search is made in the product data store in order to determine which types of halogen lamps are available.

After the user selects a halogen lamp, a search mask is generated, as shown in Figure 15-3. The contents of the pull-down menus correspond to the selected product and are extracted from the data store. For performance

©2000 THE XML HANDBOOK™

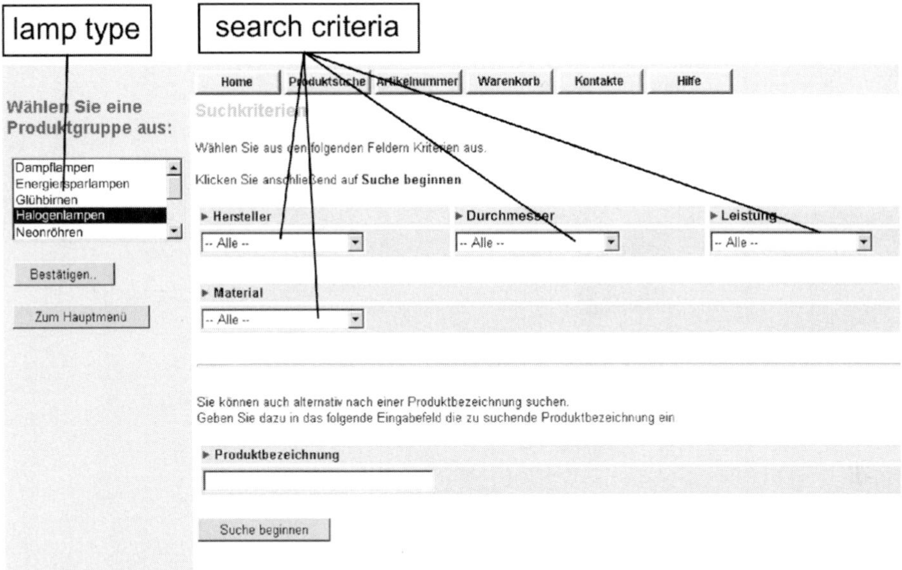

Figure 15-3 Search mask

reasons, the search is not conducted on the product description documents, but rather via a network of indices that contain all search-related information. The indices themselves are XML documents.

As the result of the search, the customer receives a list (Figure 15-4) containing all products that comply with the search terms.

Now the user is only one mouse-click away from the target product. Using the preview picture and additional criteria, he selects his lamp. The product description appears after the preview picture has been clicked on. For this purpose, the corresponding SGML product description is dynamically converted to HTML.

That screen also gives independent access to *product data*, *order data* and *assembly data*, as shown in Figure 15-5.

The *product data* button retrieves technical information, product illustration and dimensional drawings.

The *assembly data* comprises information on ancillaries and technical drawings which interested customers can download from a Web server.

By means of the *order data* button, a user can select products to order and place them in a shopping basket. This shopping basket contains all data relating to the order and a small preview picture that shows the user all of

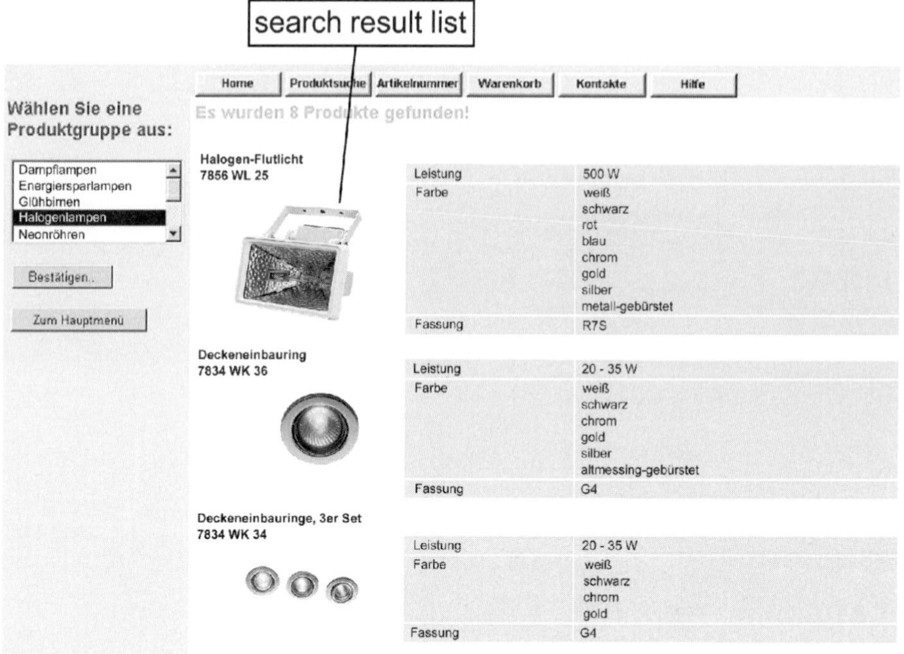

Figure 15-4 Search result list

the products he has placed in the basket. By clicking on the preview picture, he can reach the corresponding product page.

After the user has found his products and finalized his shopping basket, he can send an electronic order. This order is immediately booked in the dealer's ERP system. In reply, the user receives confirmation along with the probable delivery times.

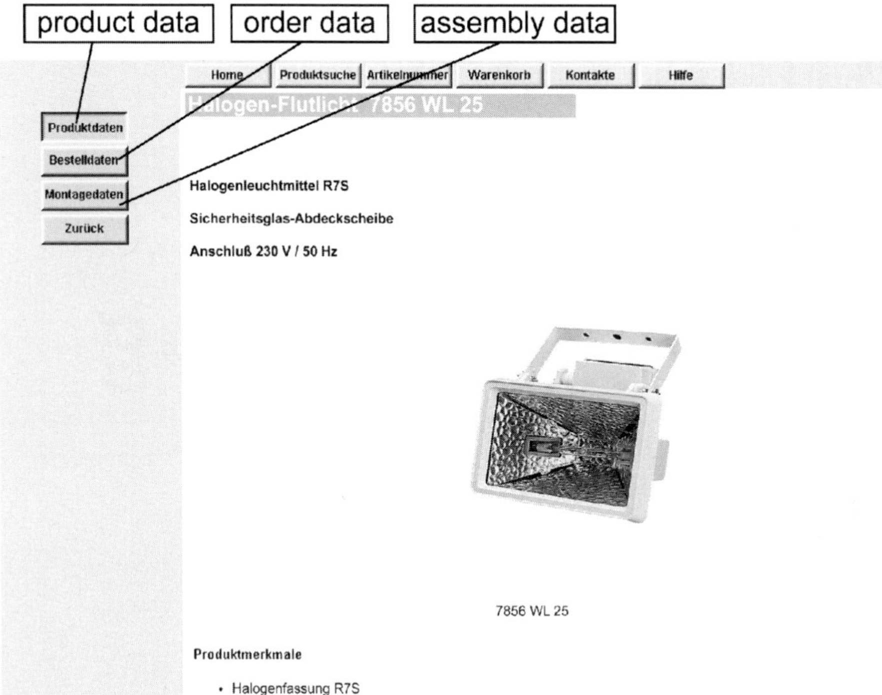

Figure 15-5 Product information

Building a schema for a product catalog

Application Discussion

- Schema design considerations
- DTD declarations and schema notations
- Datatype specification and validation
- Free trial software on CD-ROM

©2000 The XML Handbook™

Chapter 16

The better your schema, the better your data! In the case of product catalogs, you could add: And the better your business! In this chapter we will walk you through the analysis and design of a schema for an online product catalog. It is sponsored by Extensibility, `http://www.extensibility.com`, and was prepared by Lee Buck.

The online catalog is in many respects the heart of electronic commerce. With XML, it can provide a standard and platform independent way of exchanging information between resellers, manufacturers and customers.

Such exchanges can be thought of as information flows between the various organizations. We'll look at one such flow between manufacturers and the folks at a fictitious website called `www.we-sell-everything.com`.

We'll use a schema to define what information may exist in the flow, where it may appear and how it should be used. This schema establishes a vocabulary by which we can exchange information and a contract that ensures that the information conforms to our expectations. It must reflect the requirements of our product catalog application.

16.1 | Online catalog requirements

Online catalogs have no bounds. Electronic catalogs provide resellers and manufacturers the opportunity to personalize the customer's experience. Rather than merely publishing a conventional print based catalog on the

Internet, our catalog example will use XML to build part of the framework for a catalog application. This application will build upon existing information resources to provide enriched content interaction and access.

Because XML objects are simultaneously both documents and data, the catalog can include not only blocks of descriptive text but also database information. The two will allow our site to provide the user with flexible presentation of the information as well as powerful comparison facilities. This content may be in the form of character text, audio and video files.

The components of our online catalog will enable personalized product pricing for prospects and customers. By including promotional codes and rebate information, the reseller and manufacturer gain added pricing flexibility. Additionally, the catalog will link complementary products to create dynamic solution offerings.

By creating an online catalog, results of customer buying habits can be determined quickly. Using the appropriate approach for schema design, changes to the catalog can be deployed quickly, further enhancing results.

16.2 | Design considerations

Whenever we design a schema we confront a number of issues.

Validation

XML 1.0, using DTDs, provides a strong foundation for ensuring that all the necessary pieces of information are present at the right places in a document (i.e. required elements are included, inappropriate ones are not, attributes are supplied when required, etc.). DTDs can also offer some help in constraining the value of a particular attribute or data content of an element. (See 16.3, "Datatypes", on page 218.)

Modularity

Modular schemas are one of the best means to build a flexible and reusable schema repository. A modular approach to schema creation delivers application flexibility and component reuse. Libraries of modular schemas can facilitate e-commerce in heterogeneous environments for e-commerce applications. Taking a modular approach to schema design is an important goal for our little project. In our case it will mean pulling out the notion of an address and placing it into a budding corporate standards schema which will contain such often repeated element types.

Relationship modeling

Schemas provide two facilities to model the relationships between pieces of information. The first is the structure of the document; the context in which an element appears. The second is `ID/IDREF` relationships. These permit all kinds of relationships to be modeled independent of the structure of the document. In our example we'll use both facilities to model the relationships involved.

Collaboration

Collaborative schema design efforts help ensure schemas reflect diverse corporate needs. Schemas will be shared between organizations to help ensure successful e-commerce applications. Resellers and manufacturers will want to collaborate on schemas to establish mutually agreeable rules for data interchange.

Elements vs. attributes

Many pieces of information which we want to model could be represented either as elements or as attributes. While each has its own strengths and limitations, the choice between them is often a matter of style. In our case we'll tend to use attributes for atomic data with a corresponding datatype and use elements for organizing concepts and for representing structures of data items.

Iterative design and schema flexibility

*Schema*s are living documents which must change as the business requirements change. When such change occurs two sets of compatibility issues arise: a) can existing XML documents be validated against the new schema and b) can existing processes handle documents conforming to the new schema? Careful design can maximize the potential for future changes to answer “yes” to both. For our example, we'll design the `promotion` element type to accommodate new kinds of promotions in the future.

©2000 THE XML HANDBOOK™

16.3 | Datatypes

A *datatype* is a category of information, usually the kind that comes in small pieces and is used to build bigger ones. The examples in Table 16-1 will convey the idea better than any formal definition. They are a subset of those defined in the *XML-Data* schema language proposal.

Table 16-1 Common datatypes

`string`	`number`	`dateTime`
`boolean`	`float`	`date`
`uri`	`int`	`time`

It is good for a schema to be able to identify and enforce the use of datatypes because it strengthens the contract between the producer and the consumer of an XML document. In e-commerce applications such as our catalog, we need to assure the integrity of the information to the extent possible at the earliest moment.

16.3.1 *Using datatypes in DTDs*

A datatype name is usually applied to both the conceptual object (the "abstract datatype") and its representation as a character string. That is, in markup language terms, datatypes are notations.

In an XML DTD, you can declare a datatype name by using a notation declaration. You can then use that name as the value of a notation attribute to identify the datatype of an element. However, there are no intrinsic facilities for defining new datatype representations nor for specifying datatypes of attributes, although applications can use conventions provided by the *SGML Extended Facilities* (XFAC) standard.

Furthermore, XML leaves validation of datatypes – as it does all aspects of the data – in the hands of the application. Although, given a common convention for specifying datatypes, a simple datatype validator could be constructed that could be used by all applications.

Tip *Open source software is available on the CD-ROM that lets programmers support this convention with both the DOM and SAX interfaces.*

16.3.2 *Validating datatypes in DTDs*

In our catalog schema, we take the first step to building this capability by specifying the appropriate datatype within the schema. We use the XFAC convention that enables us to associate the name of a datatype with any attribute or element type. Optionally, we can also define a notation of the same name to provide a definitive reference to the datatype's meaning or even to point to the actual utility program that performs the validation.

To do all this we create two new fixed attributes for each element type. The value of the first, `e-dtype`, will be the name of the datatype for the elements. The value of the second, `a-dtype`, will be the names of the datatypes for all the attributes. In order to link each datatype name with its attribute, the `a-dtype` attribute value is a list of pairs, each attribute name being followed by its datatype name.

16.4 | The design

Our catalog is to come from one or more manufacturers. It needs to contain information about each manufacturer, the products available and any special promotions available for the products.

To build the schema we'll use *XML Authority*. A trial version is provided on the CD-ROM. To follow along, install and open the program and click "New Schema".

©2000 The XML Handbook™

16.4.1 *The catalog*

We'll model a catalog as the root element of the document. It contains a repeatable sequence of elements which provide information about each of the concepts: manufacturer, product and promotion. Our model is as shown in Figure 16-1.

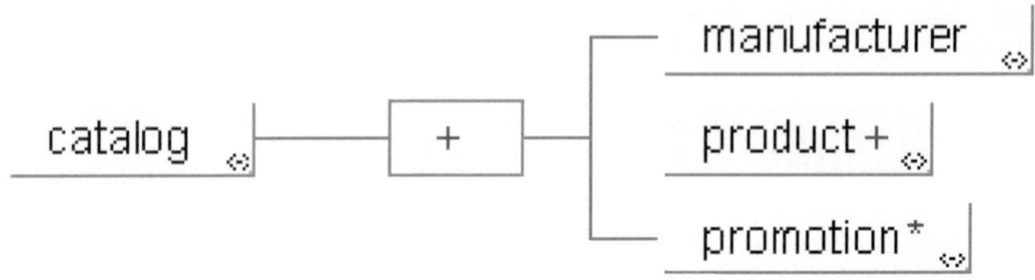

Figure 16-1 Catalog's content model: (manufacturer, product+, promotion*)+

Figure 16-1 is produced by *XML Authority*. It provides a concise visualization of the structure of our schema. A brief explanation of its symbology:

- Square brackets represent a sequence of elements
- Angled brackets represent a choice between elements
- Occurrence symbols alone represent grouping of elements
- The icons at the right of an element represent what an element may contain: other elements, untyped character data, or typed data.

The catalog element type will need various bits of housekeeping information like its effective date and its expiration date. More robust implementations might well contain routing information, authentication and other bells and whistles but we'll keep it simple. We'll model the dates as attributes as shown in Figure 16-2:

Figure 16-2 illustrates an attributes table in *XML Authority*. If you are following along in XA, bring up the window by clicking “Attribute Types” in the toolbar and enter the information as shown above.

Attribute Type	Element	Data Type
date.expires	catalog	date
date.issued	catalog	date

Figure 16-2 Catalog's attributes

16.4.2 *Manufacturer*

The manufacturer element type will contain name and address information, as shown in Figure 16-3. The former we'll model as an ID attribute type since we need it to uniquely identify a particular manufacturer (see Figure 16-4).

The address information provides a simple example of a powerful concept in schema design: modularization. It enables us to build an inventory of reusable chunks that can be referenced from multiple schemas. The address model shown is rather limited and inappropriate to our global audience. By separating it out into its own schema, we'll be able to isolate the necessary enhancements from our design efforts (as long as they are done in a compatible way).

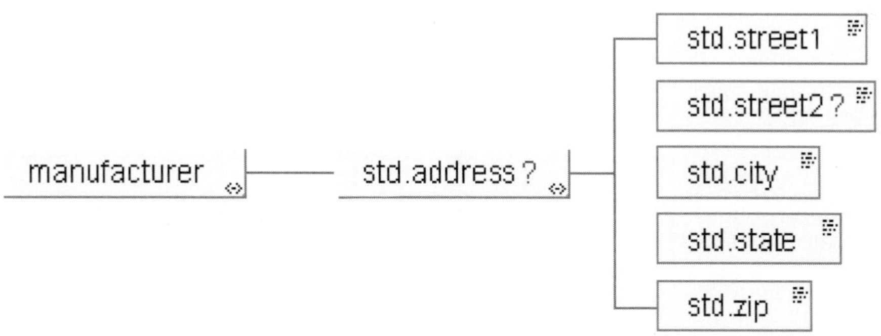

Figure 16-3 Manufacturer's content model: (std.address?) std.address': (std.street1, std.street2?, std.city, std.state, std.zip)

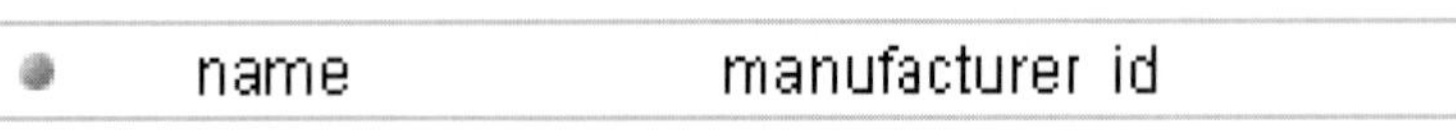

Figure 16-4 Manufacturer's attributes

16.4.3 *Product*

The product element type contains basics like name, SKU (essentially its bar-code), and SRP (standard retail price). These we'll model as attributes. Importantly, we'll model SKU as an ID attribute so we can refer to it later from within a promotion. We can then also use SKUs in a `complements` attribute to refer to other products that are complementary to this product (i.e. taken as a whole they comprise a complete solution). We want to be able to include a picture or other such media about the product so we'll define a media attribute that locates such media.

We'll also include a mixed element type for a product description that permits portions of the description to be marked as a feature or a benefit (see Figure 16-5 and Figure 16-6). This simple refinement of the description enables a much richer set of presentation possibilities on our website. More advanced designs would include a much richer set of potential markup here, providing maximum flexibility to our website designers to present the information in various ways.

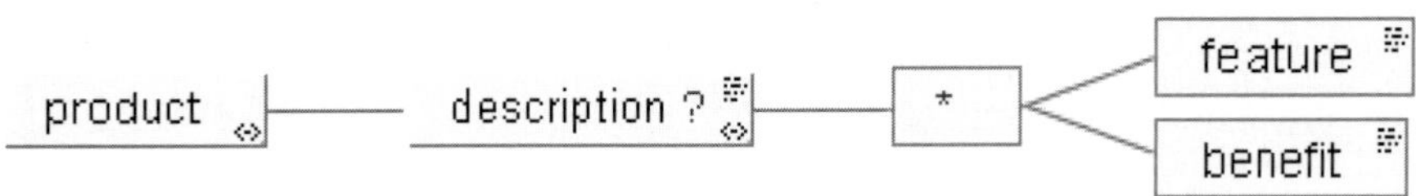

Figure 16-5 Product's content model: (description?) description's: (feature | benefit)*

16.4.4 *Promotion*

Finally we have the promotion element type. It may contain information about two different types of discounts: `bundles`, which provide for a lower price for a particular product when one or more other products are purchased at the same time, and `discounts`, which provide volume-based pric-

•	complements	product	idrefs
•	media	product	entity
•	product.name	product	text (cdata)
•	sku	product	id
•	srp	product	currency

Figure 16-6 Product's attributes

ing (see Figure 16-7 and Figure 16-8). In the future, as shown in Figure 16-7, `rebate` could be added without affecting existing documents.

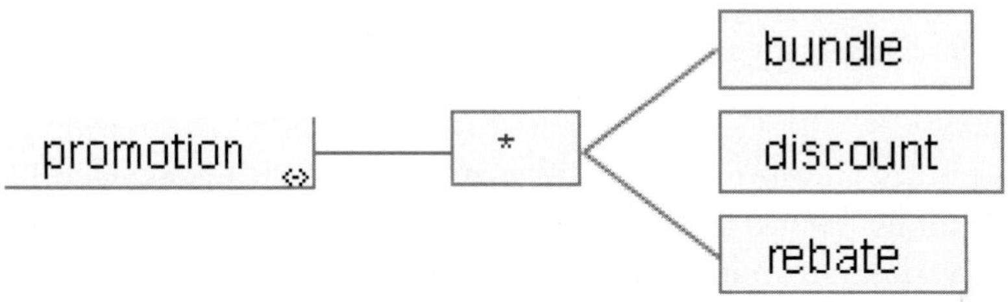

Figure 16-7 Promotion's content model: (bundle | discount | rebate)*

•	other.skus	bundle	idrefs
•	sku	bundle	id
•	price	bundle	currency
•	sku	discount	id
•	min.qty	discount	integer
•	pct.off	discount	float

Figure 16-8 Attributes of promotion's subelements

16.4.5 *The big picture*

We did it. Taken as a whole our schema's structure looks like Figure 16-9:

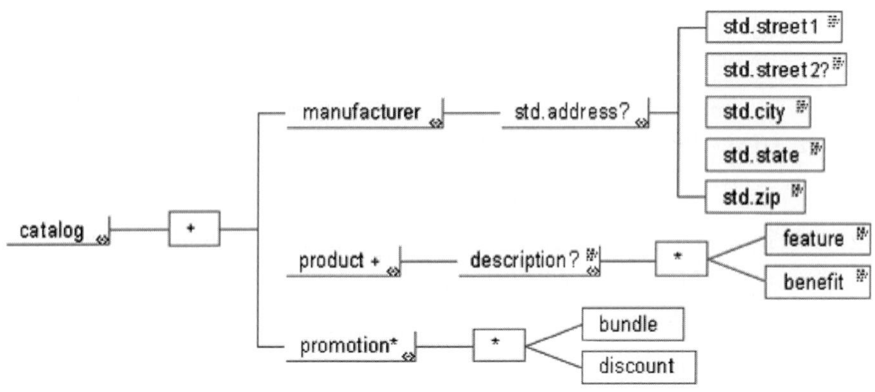

Figure 16-9 Document structure

In Example 16-1 we can take a look at part of the schema expressed as DTD declarations. Notice the use of `a-dtype` fixed attributes to specify the datatype for various attributes. (In *XML Authority* you can view this source at any time by clicking the Source button in the toolbar.)

16.5 | Alternatives to DTD declarations

Alternatives to DTD declarations are beginning to emerge and the W3C is working to standardize one (see Chapter 64, "XML Schemas", on page 928). They provide support for both specifying and validating datatypes, plus other functions that should prove useful in many applications.

Part of our schema, expressed in the *XML-Data* schema notation appears in Example 16-2. The equivalent DTD declarations are in Example 16-3. (With *XML Authority*, you can export your schema in a variety of schema notations by choosing "Export" from the File menu.)

Example 16-1. Schema excerpt expressed as DTD declarations

```
<!ELEMENT catalog  (manufacturer , product+ , promotion* )>
<!ATTLIST catalog  date.issued  CDATA    #IMPLIED
                   date.expires CDATA    #IMPLIED
                   a-dtype      NMTOKENS #FIXED 'date.issued date
                                               date.expires date'>
<!ELEMENT manufacturer  (std.address? )>
<!ATTLIST manufacturer  name    ID       #REQUIRED >
<!ELEMENT product (description? )>
<!ATTLIST product sku           ID       #REQUIRED
                   product.name CDATA    #IMPLIED
                   srp          CDATA    #REQUIRED
                   complements  IDREFS   #IMPLIED
                   media        ENTITY   #IMPLIED
                   a-dtype      NMTOKENS #FIXED 'srp fixed.14.4'>
<!ELEMENT promotion  (bundle | discount | rebate )*>
<!ELEMENT bundle   EMPTY>
<!ATTLIST bundle   price        CDATA    #REQUIRED
                   complements  IDREFS   #REQUIRED
                   sku          ID       #REQUIRED
                   a-dtype      NMTOKENS #FIXED 'price fixed.14.4'>
<!ELEMENT discount EMPTY>
<!ATTLIST discount min.qty      CDATA    '1'
                   pct.off      CDATA    #REQUIRED
                   sku          ID       #REQUIRED
                   a-dtype      NMTOKENS #FIXED 'min.qty int
                                               pct.off float'>
```

Example 16-2. Manufacturer expressed as XML-Data

```
<ElementType name="manufacturer" content="eltOnly" order="seq">
   <element type = "s:std.address" minOccurs="0" maxOccurs="1"/>
   <AttributeType name = "name" dt:type="ID" required = "yes"/>
   <attribute type = "name"/>
</ElementType>
```

Example 16-3. Manufacturer expressed as DTD declarations

```
<!ELEMENT manufacturer  (std.address? )>
<!ATTLIST manufacturer  name ID  #REQUIRED >
```

16.6 | A sample document

A sample document that conforms to the schema looks like Example 16-4. (In *XML Authority*, you can get a head start on such a sample document by choosing `Export->Example XML Document` from the File menu. It will create a template for you to populate.)

Example 16-4. Sample catalog

```
<catalog date.issued = "5-31-2000" date.expires = "6-30-2000">
<manufacturer name = "Stuff-o-rama">
   <std.address>
      <std.street1>127 Walking Way</std.street1>
      <std.city>Chapel Hill</std.city>
      <std.state>NC</std.state>
      <std.zip>27514</std.zip>
   </std.address>
</manufacturer>

<product sku = "12-3783-23" product.name = "foozle" srp = "29.99">
<description>
The foozle is the finest in plastic oven-ware.
Its <feature>patented melt-away containment
</feature>means that <benefit>you'll never have
to wash another dish.</benefit>
</description>
</product>

<product sku = "12-2412-23" product.name = "singey" srp = "19.99">
<description>
The singey aluminum oven mitts are ideal for
accessories for any kitchen. Available in three
sizes with convenient <feature>teflon
coating</feature> to <benefit>ensure a steady
grip.</benefit>
</description>
</product>

<promotion>
   <bundle sku="12-2412-23" price="14.99" other.skus="12-3783-23"/>
   <discount sku = "12-2412-23" min.qty = "10" pct.off = "10" />
   <discount sku = "12-2412-23" min.qty = "20" pct.off = "15" />
   <discount sku = "12-2412-23" min.qty = "50" pct.off = "20" />
</promotion>
</catalog>
```

16.7 | Conclusion

Our catalog schema provides the foundation for building a reseller's website. By formulating and expressing our information flows using XML schemas we are assured that we can connect with our business partners no matter what type of technical infrastructure they may have. We can maximize the business impact of the information and respond quickly to new opportunities as they emerge.

©2000 The XML Handbook™

Agent Discovery

Case Study

- Media industry
- Middle-tier Web application
- Image search and procurement
- Web automation

©2000 THE XML HANDBOOK™

Chapter 17

Here's an application interesting enough to be the subject of one of the Discovery Channel's own programs: How they implemented Web searching for images and automated procurement in just eight days! This chapter is sponsored by webMethods, Inc., `http://www.webmethods.com`, and was prepared by Charles A. Allen.

Electronic commerce on the Web takes many forms. Browser-based purchasing is one form that has proliferated at a healthy pace as businesses large and small have begun deploying electronic storefronts enabling customers to buy direct over the Web.

Aggregating purchasing functions across disparate browser-based purchasing systems is one of the first places where so-called *agent technologies* have begun to establish a foothold.

A next-generation electronic commerce application called *Agent Discovery* illustrates how Web-based procurement can be automated using XML-based technologies. It demonstrates a number of integration principles that will become increasingly important as XML itself proliferates on the Internet.

17.1 | *Agent Discovery*

Agent Discovery automates the procurement of images across the electronic commerce Web sites of numerous photo agencies. The idea for *Agent Discovery* was conceived by Discovery Communications, Inc. (DCI), operators of the Discovery Channel, and AnswerThink Consulting Group (ACG). Web Automation technology from webMethods was employed to deliver a solution that enables *Agent Discovery* to exchange data automatically and simultaneously with different photo agencies' Web sites.

Before *Agent Discovery*, the company's worldwide design group had no alternative but browser-based manually intensive online searches.

Using webMethods' *Web Automation Server* and the Web Interface Definition Language (WIDL), a working system was built in only eight days. It immediately enabled DCI to realize huge savings in the amount of time designers spend searching for and purchasing images over the Web.

Here are the basic steps that were taken to build the image search and procurement functionality of *Agent Discovery*:

1. The target photo agencies' Web sites were identified.
2. The functionality of target Web sites was cataloged.
3. A matrix of functions provided by all photo agencies was created.
4. An aggregate interface of all *Agent Discovery* functions was defined in WIDL.
5. A separate WIDL was developed for each Web site, implementing functions provided by each site and defining conditions for successful invocation.
6. A Java servlet was developed to dynamically invoke the services defined in each WIDL implementing the *Agent Discovery* interface.

Now picture yourself as a designer who might need these functions (Figure 17-1).

17.2 | Picture this

Imagine you're a designer of a Web site, magazine, or corporate branding campaign, tasked with procuring a large number of compelling images to convey messages of "efficiency" and "innovation". Thanks to the Web, you are able to access the image databases of dozens of on-line photo agencies, retrieving images that match your search criteria.

©2000 THE XML HANDBOOK™

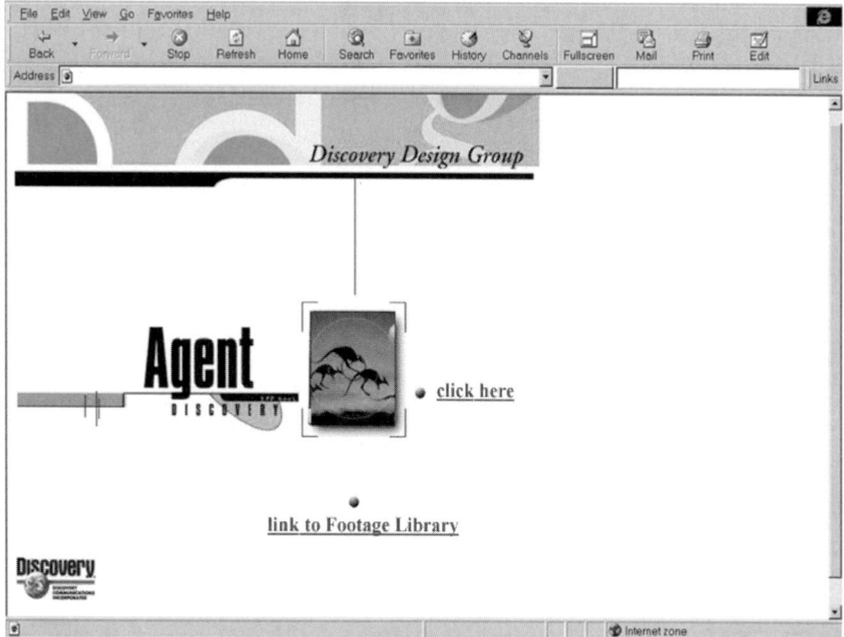

Figure 17-1 The *Agent Discovery* application.

Unfortunately, you have to log into each system separately, submit the search criteria repeatedly, and switch back and forth between multiple browser instances to compare images from each agency.

When you are finally ready to purchase the images you've selected from a number of agencies, there are various mechanisms for payment and delivery. Most commonly, you must right-click and save images to your local disk, losing both the captions that allowed you to find the images in the first place, as well as the rights information associated with each image.

17.2.1 *Access vs. integration*

The Web has provided you with an amazing degree of access, but it has also placed on your shoulders an incredible burden of integration.

You are now responsible for navigating through numerous systems, each with a slightly different usage model. The information, though delivered through a common medium, has no common form. You spend hours of your valuable time performing manually intensive repetitive tasks that have been learned only through hard-won experience in the trenches of the Web. Figure 17-2

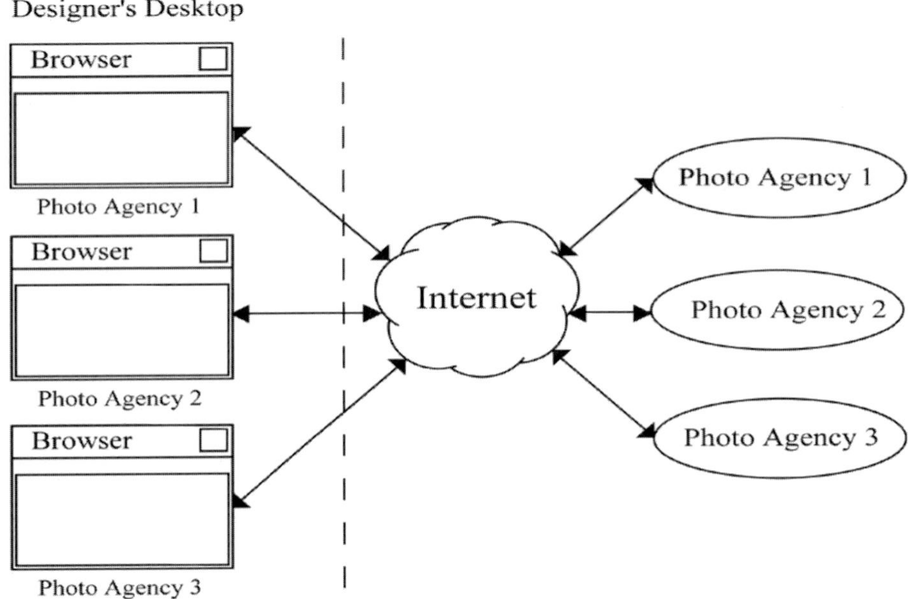

Figure 17-2 Separate browser windows for each photo agency.

This is not the job you signed up for. You're stuck shuffling bits rather than selecting images that fill your needs. There must be a better way. But how do you go about convincing each of the photo agencies to agree on and implement common interfaces and formats? Even if you could convince them that this is, in principle, a good idea, how would you agree on a technology platform?

17.2.2 *The solution: Web automation*

For *Agent Discovery*, photo agencies had already made the investment in Web-based electronic commerce applications; all the necessary functionality was accessible. The shortest path to integration was to leverage the systems that had already been put in place by the various photo agencies, sidestepping the need to achieve consensus among a large number of competing companies.

With this approach, the speed of development was compelling. More impressive still was the immediacy of the return on investment.

Finding the right images quickly and efficiently is a key requirement for any media company, particularly DCI, whose brand is known for compelling images. Designers at DCI were faced with the dilemma outlined in this image procurement scenario. Web automation removed the repetitive tasks from the process of procuring images without impacting the services of the photo agencies. Figure 17-3

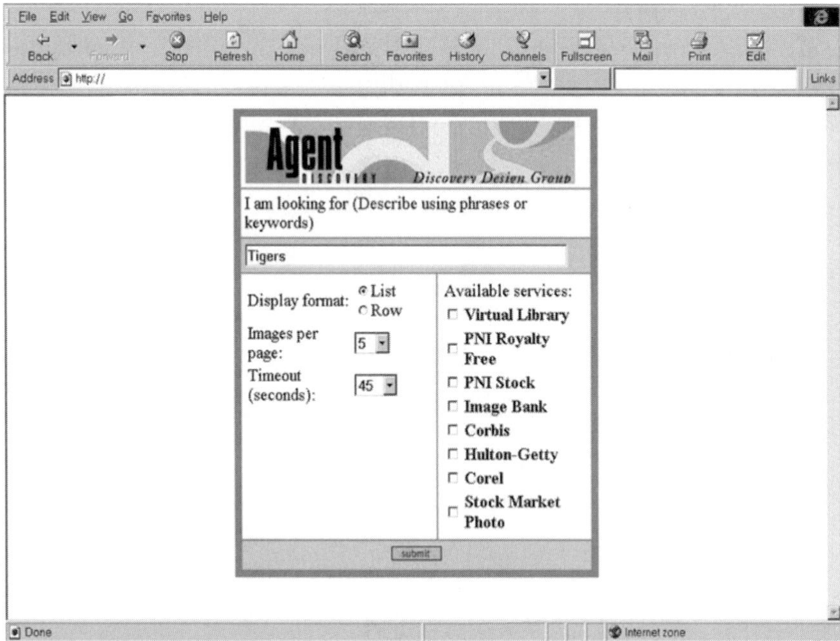

Figure 17-3 Designers can select photo agencies to search.

17.3 | What is Web automation?

Imagine everything a browser can do: sign-on to a secure Web-site; navigate through pages; submit queries; retrieve the results. Now imagine that business applications can do the same thing, automatically, without human intervention and without using a browser. This is the power of *Web automation*.

Interactions normally performed manually in a browser, such as HTTP authentication, entering information into a form, submitting the form, and retrieving HTML or XML documents, are automated. This is done by capturing details such as input parameters, service URLs, and data mapping methods for output parameters. Mechanisms for conditional processing are provided to enable robust error handling.

In essence, the *Web Automation Server* makes the Web look like one large application server. It is a middle-tier component that provides an abstraction layer between business applications and the remote functionality that lives behind Web servers.

The *Web Automation Server* and WIDL transform the Web from an *access medium* into an *integration platform*, providing a practical and cost-effective infrastructure for business-to-business electronic commerce over the Web. Figure 17-4

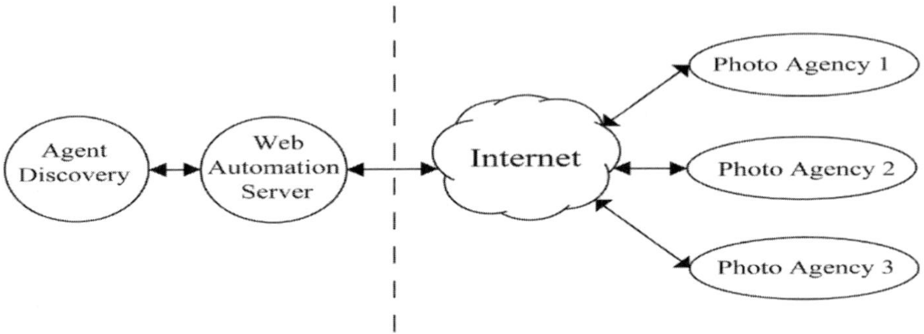

Figure 17-4 The *Web Automation Server* aggregates services.

17.4 | Discovering common ground

In the case of *Agent Discovery*, Web automation enabled the services of various photo agencies to be aggregated into a single logical application interface. Figure 17-5

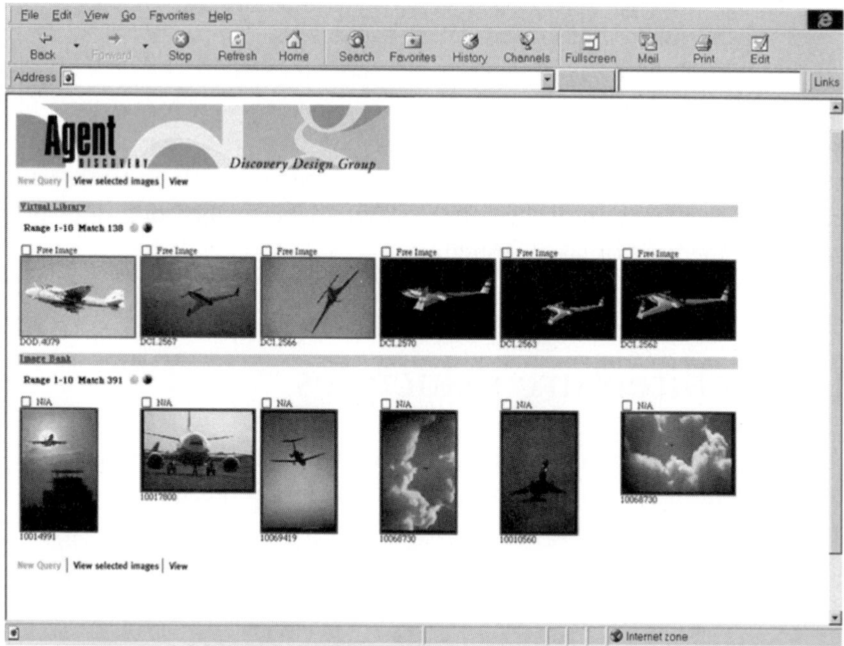

Figure 17-5 *Agent Discovery* enables a "virtual light-box".

Agent Discovery gives DCI's designers a common user interface for searching for and retrieving images across different photo agencies' Web sites; it substantially reduces the time and effort required to procure images, and enables more efficient tracking of DCI's digital assets.

17.5 | What about XML?

The introduction of XML promises to accelerate cross-organizational application and data integration, providing a standard for data representation that addresses many of the concerns raised above. However, XML alone is not a total solution.

The *Web Automation Server* was built using an application of XML called the Web Interface Definition Language (WIDL). Together they lower the barriers to cross-organizational integration by removing the requirement that various organizations agree on data formats up front. (See Chapter 50, "WIDL and XML RPC", on page 672 for the details.)

The only requirement is that data be accessible via HTTP, FTP, or HTTPS. The data representation can be either HTML or XML. Most significantly, product is designed to accommodate dynamic change in data representations, so that applications initially deployed with HTML data sources can be migrated transparently to XML. Client side code does not need to be re-generated or re-compiled.

17.6 | Architecture principles

The ability to manage change dynamically is important because target Web sites are periodically changing. While the mapping mechanism within WIDL can "see thorough" a significant amount of change in document representations, it is sometimes necessary to re-map and re-publish a service definition. Figure 17-6

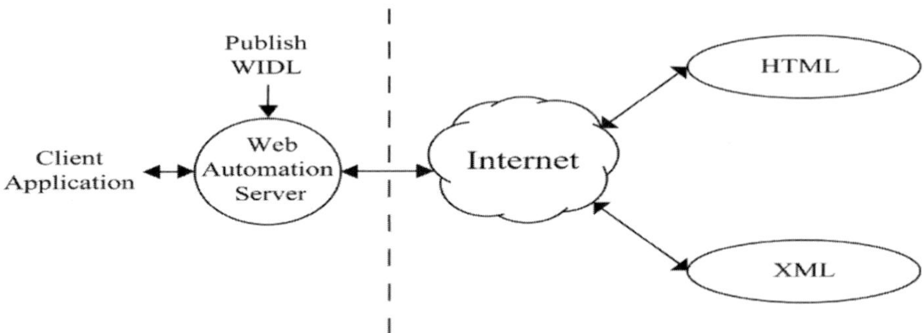

Figure 17-6 WIDL defines a common interface to HTML and XML.

For DCI, the challenge was that each agency presented similar services in different forms. WIDL enabled common interfaces to be defined for different HTML documents. Significantly, WIDL also enables common interfaces to be defined across HTML and XML document structures, and even across different XML DTDs.

Consider the alternative: without the layer of abstraction that WIDL provides, the *Agent Discovery* application could only have been developed by hard-coding routines to handle each different document structure encountered at the various photo agencies' Web sites. If target document structures changed, application code would have to be modified and recompiled. This is roughly equivalent to the situation experienced by developers of two-tier applications when database changes are made.

17.7 | Conclusion

DCI's Designers wanted a process that was automated and centralized. They wanted one program with one user interface that would search, retrieve, and procure images from multiple sources, thereby reducing the time spent navigating several different Web sites. *Agent Discovery* delivered on these goals.

The use of Web automation and WIDL logically separated the act of integration from the act of building the client application. This logical separation enabled *Agent Discovery* to span multiple photo agencies' services, and to be built in record time.

The architecture of the *Agent Discovery* application provides valuable lessons for the development of cross-organizational XML-enabled applications. Waiting for all target systems to support a common format would have significantly slowed the delivery of an application that has had an immediate return on investment.

Just as *Agent Discovery* today must be able to negotiate common interfaces among different HTML document formats, next generation XML-enabled applications may well need to negotiate among different XML DTDs. In addition to removing the barriers to business-to-business appli-

©2000 The XML Handbook™

cation integration, the use of WIDL enforced a three-tier architecture that positions the system for such an eventuality.

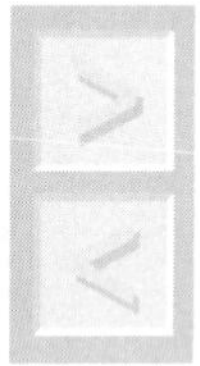

Analysis *For all the promise of XML, there is a lurking danger that some developers will fall into the trap of coding applications so that they cannot easily respond to changes in the DTDs. That would effectively be a return to two-tier client/server architecture, where data access methods are embedded in application code.*

WIDL or similar interfaces may be a cure for such situations. The best prevention is the employment of late-binding stylesheet-like techniques, such as those successfully employed in publishing by XML and SGML users.

Portals

- Doorways to information
- Enterprise Information Portals (EIP)
- Information feed syndication
- XMLNews
- Information and Content Exchange (ICE)

©2000 THE XML HANDBOOK™

Part Four

A portal is a doorway, and in the language of the World Wide Web, a "portal site" is one that users visit first. It acts, literally, as the user's doorway to all of the resources of the Web.

Now organizations are constructing their own portals – not all-encompassing sites for the masses, like traditional Web portals, but *Enterprise Information Portals* (EIP). An EIP is a doorway to a focused set of resources, intended for a specific audience, like the employees, customers, and suppliers of a business. Most importantly, an EIP can serve as a single coherent view of information aggregated from disparate sources by e-commerce systems.

In this part, we'll explore the reasons for EIPs and the systems needed to build them. We'll look at two EIPs in detail: one of the largest and busiest sites on the Web, and an imaginary but possible portal that you'll wish your doctor had. Finally, we'll look at content syndication, the Web equivalent of the newswire, that brings real-time information feeds to portals.

DataChannel: Enterprise portals

Tool Discussion

- Global information economy
- Enterprise information challenges
- Enterprise Information Portal (EIP)
- Framework for EIP development

©2000 THE XML HANDBOOK™

Chapter 18

> The industrial age is dead. Long live the information age! But the information revolution will be as devastating to the unprepared enterprise as the industrial revolution was to cottage industry. DataChannel, `http://www.datachannel.com`, has sponsored this chapter to help you prepare.

We are witnessing an economic transformation that is unparalleled in history. The stabilization and acceptance of the Internet is resulting in its becoming the primary platform for conducting business. Information is at the core of this rapidly emerging transformation as it is presented, shared, and exchanged to transact business everywhere.

Essentially, information is used to support every business decision made within an enterprise. This shift towards a global information economy via the Internet has created a new playing field in the electronic business marketplace. Electronic business is becoming a major defining element of an enterprise's market capitalization.

18.1 | Information is the global economy

Corporations around the globe, large and small, recognize this transformation and the potential power of their information. Over the past five years millions of dollars have been spent to develop ways to better capture and efficiently use existing data. These include:

back office systems
: Enterprise Resource Planning (ERP), financials, human resources, engineering, process automation/workflow, project management, etc.

front office systems
: Sales force automation, customer relationship management, help desk, marketing automation, etc.

personal productivity systems
: Word processor, spreadsheet, presentation, contact manager, Personal Information Manager, etc.

Front office and back office systems capture and create a tremendous amount of managed information. However, with personal productivity tools readily available, company employees, partners, and customers have all created a wealth of unmanaged information as well – some 80% of a typical company's information base! (See Figure 18-1.)

The global information economy discovery is upon us and with it, two distinct realizations:

- The first realization is the fact that this tremendous IT investment in back office, front office, and personal productivity systems has paid off. As a result of investing in the available technology, companies can now create and capture information from every transaction, inquiry, resource, supplier, partner, and customer.
- The second realization as it relates to the first, however, is even more revealing. There are significant barriers to accessing information by the people who need it to make critical business decisions. If not addressed appropriately, these barriers will prevent anyone from intelligently managing the information to its fullest potential, thereby potentially stunting the growth of this economic transformation that has recently emerged.

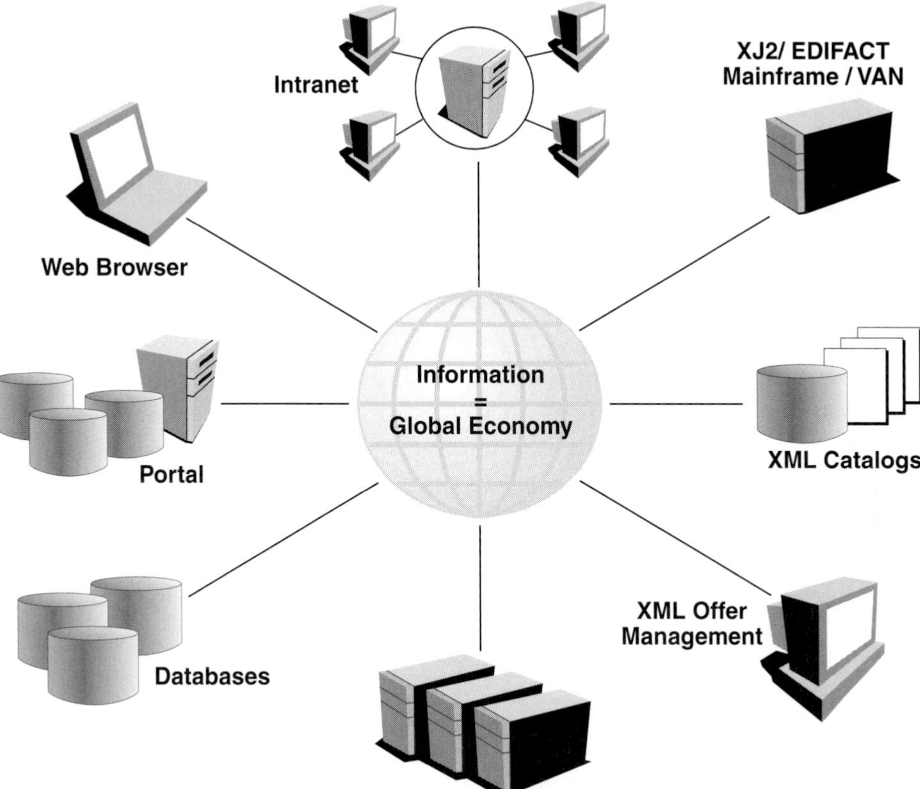

Figure 18-1 Managed and unmanaged data drive the global economy.

Today, this global information economy is one without geographic, industry, or computing boundaries. Intranets, extranets, and the Internet all become arteries of the seamless information highway without specified origins or destinations. The catch is, however, that any enterprise wishing to participate successfully in the new economy must transform itself to enable common access and integration to *all* information from *all* roads.

That it means it must learn how to deal effectively with the many challenges that now exist to the effective utilization of enterprise information.

18.2 | Enterprise Information challenges

There are several challenges and roadblocks preventing information access and the systems interoperability required to unleash critical information. They exist for both managed and unmanaged data.

18.2.1 *Managed data*

Managed data is information that is built and maintained by the enterprise. It consists of controlled repositories of information like business documents, policies and procedures, enterprise applications, and customer and product databases. While managed data has connotations of being more useful than unmanaged data, it presents its own unique challenges to those wishing to access and use it efficiently.

18.2.1.1 Legacy systems

While computing systems tout openness and standards, the fact remains that a significant amount of business information resides in legacy systems, which effectively means proprietary systems. These can be anything from a mainframe or enterprise application, to one of the many customized solutions built by a company's Information Technology (IT) or Management Information Systems (MIS) department.

Even a newly-implemented solution creates a legacy problem if it is not entirely compatible with existing technology. The more such legacy systems are incorporated within the IT infrastructure, the more difficult it becomes to integrate disparate data as needed.

And integrating the data is the primary issue only if the user is lucky enough to find it in the first place! Often, the primary challenge is just being able to *access* the data.

18.2.1.2 Disconnected data sources

Although each managed-data system can demonstrate effectiveness to some degree, they constitute "islands of automation" that are disconnected from each other. Routine reports and access to each individual data source are common and expected. However, creating a report that integrates information from more than one system, and doing it routinely, requires customized development.

It also requires ongoing maintenance, as the various technologies change and upgrade. IT organizations typically spend between 25% and 40% of their budget on application integration and system compatibility.

18.2.1.3 Restricted application development

Even the most heterogeneous system environment requires some degree of integration. It is provided by IT departments, who respond to customization requests and ad-hoc queries from users. IT groups also build proprietary applications to meet the specific needs of their business that cannot be met with generic manufactured software.

To remain competitive, corporations must be able to develop solutions for their exact business model. A company cannot rely on its systems to give it a competitive advantage unless the systems are updated just as quickly as the market changes. Employing incompatible systems in the same environment handicaps IT's ability to respond.

18.2.1.4 Proprietary access

Each of these heterogeneous data sources has its own registry of authorized users and administrators. The administrative burden to manage the limitless permutations of users and systems can be overwhelming.

It is not uncommon to find several machines on the same manager's desktop to help manage users and systems. In a typical back-office scenario, one might find a terminal for accessing account history, a workstation to manage the ERP system, and a PC with Internet access and/or reporting tools.

18.2.2 *Unmanaged data*

While managed data is captured by enterprise applications, it is the day-to-day work that creates the vast majority of information throughout an organization. Most of this work is done using personal productivity tools and is "managed" in an impromptu, even chaotic way.

Moreover, users of these tools frequently take managed data and "unmanage" it by manipulating information from multiple managed sources into a single document or report. These new information resources are stored and shared in numerous ways. File systems, document management systems, e-mail, hard copy, fax, and messaging middleware all contribute to exponential growth of unmanaged data communications and exchange.

18.2.2.1 Ad-hoc productivity tools

Desktop productivity tools have become standard issue in corporations around the world. They free users to manage their own environments and allow them to create documents and files on demand.

However, this freedom comes with a price. Typically, there is no organized way to share, exchange, or validate these outputs. Sometimes a report may be created in a spreadsheet, the next time in a word processor, or even specially programmed and faxed in a hard-copy version.

18.2.2.2 Chaotic access and exchange

Access to personally-created information is haphazard. Such disjointed access mechanisms cause uneven distribution and, as a result, misunderstandings. Groupware solutions have addressed this problem with only limited success. While they create a collaborative platform for creating and exchanging data, managing access for persons outside the group is still a challenge. Furthermore, information must be kept in the application's proprietary representation, limiting those who can access the data.

18.2.2.3 Restricted publication rights

Once information has been compiled and processed, it can be published to a community of users. Today's intranets provide the useful function of allowing end-users to store critical, unmanaged information and make it available to a community of users. However, the administrative burden of maintaining these systems can become cost-prohibitive.

A bottleneck occurs when users who want to publish to the corporate intranet are required to do so through administrators who control the access rights. There are further difficulties when they want to publish to only a subset of the corporate community and there is no way to manage access rights on a per-user basis.

18.3 | Enterprise information portals

Tying together diverse and proprietary systems presents significant challenges. Breaking down the barriers erected by disparate applications, intranets, extranets, and the Internet is the final step in creating an enterprise ready for the global information economy. The result is the Enterprise Information Portal (EIP).

A *portal* – a system to manage access to information – is nothing more than a door to the information of the enterprise. If the information is not readily accessible or organized, the door opens to a wall. An information portal is, therefore, only as good as the information it can access.

Legacy systems, enterprise applications, database systems, and other applications may provide portals to the information they store. The failure comes, however, when those systems must communicate with each other, or the information in them must contribute to a greater application.

For an EIP to succeed, it must be properly designed to access all the information. A single standard of computing is the elusive Holy Grail of IT professionals, yet, it is now within grasp. In the same way that enterprises around the globe have accepted the Internet Protocol (IP) as the standard for *transmitting* data, they now have the opportunity to adopt a global standard for *representing* the data that is transmitted – XML.

18.3.1 *The role of XML*

XML is not only the Web standard for exchanging data, it is also becoming the standard for business transactions in legacy systems environments. When an enterprise wants to move data across dissimilar systems, transforms are required. As we have seen, XML makes it possible to create such transforms quickly.

The power and beauty of generalized markup languages is that they maintain the separation of the rendition seen at the user interface from the structured abstract data, allowing the seamless integration of data from diverse sources. Customer information, purchase orders, research results, bill payments, medical records, catalog data and other information can be converted to XML on the middle tier of a three-tier enterprise architecture, allowing abstract data to be exchanged online as easily as HTML pages display rendered data today.

18.3.2 *The golden rule of content*

A single rule can save countless hours of work and vast expense. This rule, put simply: *Content must be abstract and kept separate from rendition.*

By following this rule, after some preparation, users, developers, and IT professionals will be able to create *dynamic applications*. In these applications, the rendition of the information may differ each time a query is made, or may change depending on the profile of the user.

But because the rendition is independent of the content, the interface need not depend upon the access rules or the structure of the data being presented. Content sources maintain their integrity while dynamically becoming integrated with data from other sources, as illustrated in Figure 18-2. This is possible only because there are no ties to the presentation that might otherwise encumber the processing of the data content.

The rule can also eliminate integration overhead when maintaining data. Typically, when an update routine from a single transaction affects data in more than one system, heavy integration is required.

However, when the golden rule of content is observed, multiple data sources can be updated dynamically without requiring a user to have explicit rights to each of them. That's because user access rights are associated with specific reports and other presentations, which are no longer connected with the abstract content.

18.3.3 *EIP empowers the enterprise*

Abstract data content makes the EIP possible, which empowers the enterprise in new ways:

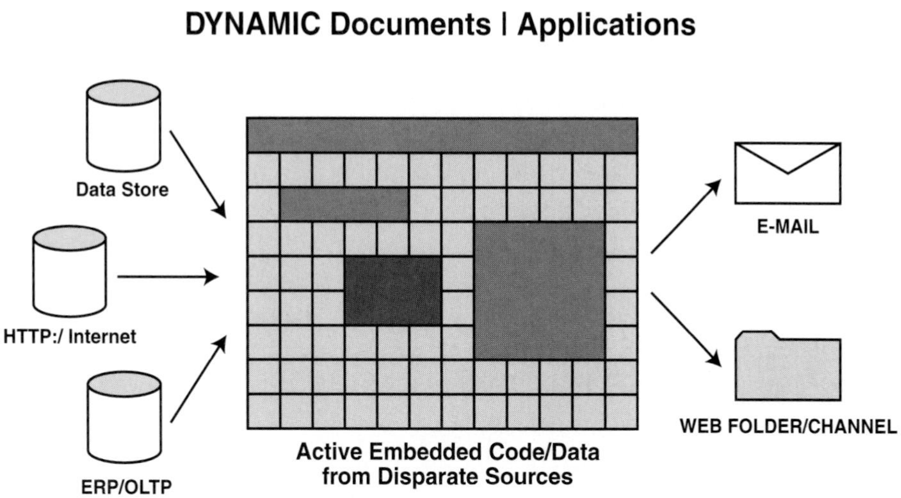

DYNAMIC Documents | Applications

Data Store

HTTP:/ Internet

ERP/OLTP

Active Embedded Code/Data from Disparate Sources

E-MAIL

WEB FOLDER/CHANNEL

Figure 18-2 Integrating reusable elements from disparate sources

- Business managers can now engage their customers using data from formerly isolated distinct systems, and consolidate the information for delivery to the customer's browser.
- The information infrastructure can be extended beyond the boundaries of a corporation and include an extended community of customers, partners, and suppliers.
- New offers can be configured literally in a moment's notice and back office support systems can readily respond to the new requirements.

The latter prospect is especially critical for commodity-type businesses that rely on services and fast response to maintain a competitive edge. Financial institutions and telecommunications companies in particular must adapt their offerings quickly because of the tremendous competitive threat that exists in their markets.

18.4 | A framework for portals

To transform an enterprise's computing environment into an EIP capable of capitalizing on the information economy requires a well-architected

©2000 THE XML HANDBOOK™

strategy and a framework in which the necessary software and services can be applied. DataChannel's approach, which is based on the consulting and training experience of its ISOGEN division, is called *XMLFramework*.™ It is pictured in Figure 18-3.

The critical horizontal layers ("Training" and "Professional Services") are required to support each of the other solution offerings to one degree or another, depending on the customer's unique business and IT infrastructure requirements.

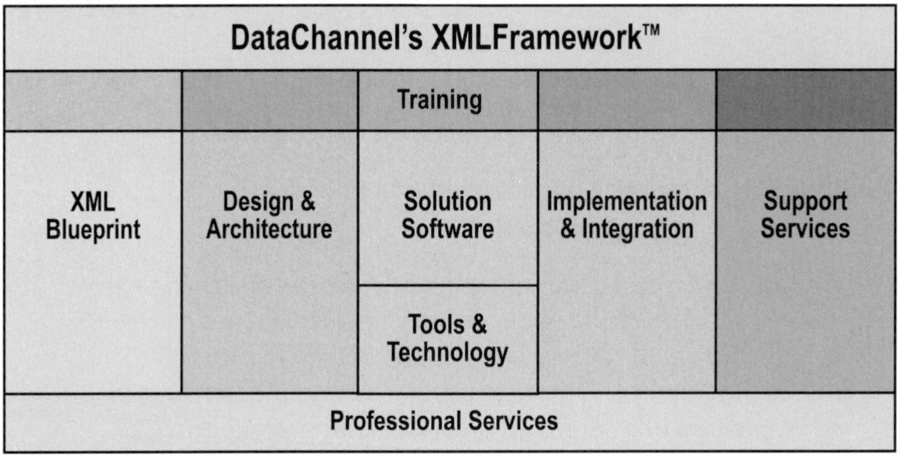

DataChannel's XMLFramework™
Training
XML Blueprint
Design & Architecture
Solution Software
Tools & Technology
Implementation & Integration
Support Services
Professional Services

Figure 18-3 The DataChannel *XMLFramework*

18.4.1 *Strategy*

A cornerstone of the solution is a comprehensive, customized strategy, which DataChannel calls the *XMLBluePrint*.™ Designed by both business management and IT professionals, the blueprint identifies and describes the roadblocks to realizing the enterprise's strategic imperatives, and how XML can be applied to address strategic and technological challenges.

18.4.2 *Design & architecture*

IT design and architecture are then developed that support the *XMLBlue-Print*. XML metadata markup and integration design criteria are defined for the customer's entire cross-platform environment.

18.4.3 *Software*

There is a multitude of software offerings for EIP development, much of it described in this book and/or available on its CD-ROM. They tend to fall into two broad categories:

Focused software
: This is software designed for a specific function, such as editors, parsers, publishing systems, etc.

Platforms
: These are systems of various kinds that provide a platform into which focused software can be plugged and integrated (Figure 18-4). There are lots of platform systems in this book, targeted for specific application domains, such as middle-tier servers, commerce integrators, portal systems, and content management systems.

For example, DataChannel offers *RIO*, shown in Figure 18-5, as an XML-enabled platform for publishing, managing, and retrieving information. Its functions include end-user Web publishing, personalized information delivery with notification, multi-tier administration, and an extensible security architecture.

DataChannel also offers focused software that plugs into *RIO*, such as the following programs:

WEBView Extensions
: This offering allows seamless viewing of over 200 document file formats through a standard Web browser without installing additional applications.

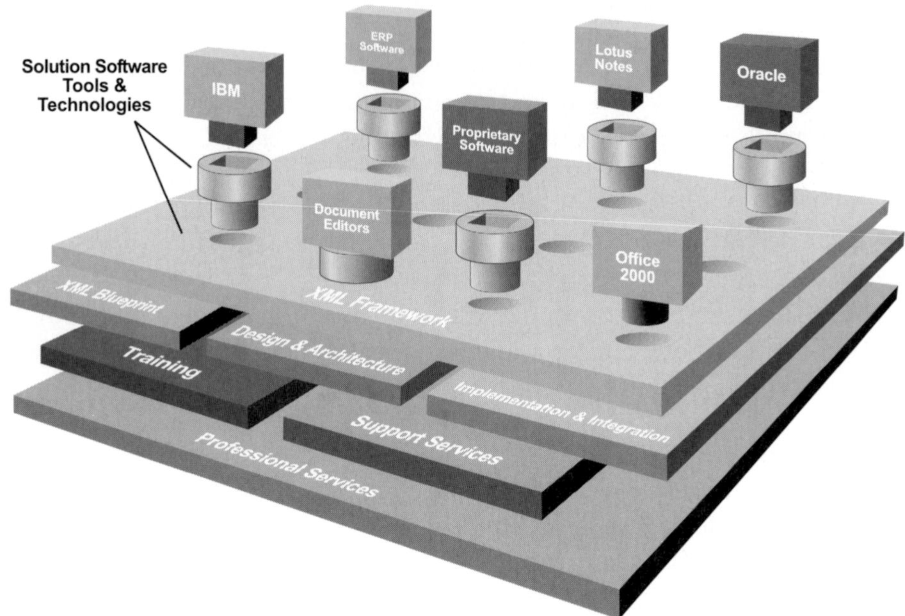

Figure 18-4 Platforms support and integrate other software.

XJParser

This is a validating parser for the *Java* platform that enables server-side and client-side parsing. It is based on Microsoft's XML parser technology. DTD/schema, XML-data subset, and namespaces capabilities allow application developers to integrate XML support into existing or new products through the W3C DOM interface.

XSL Processor

This is a server-based XSL engine that provides XML-to-XML or XML-to-HTML transformations. It includes support for pattern matching as well as Microsoft's proposed query language specification.

XML Generator

This product can automatically transform character data from tab- or comma-delimited files into XML documents. By means of

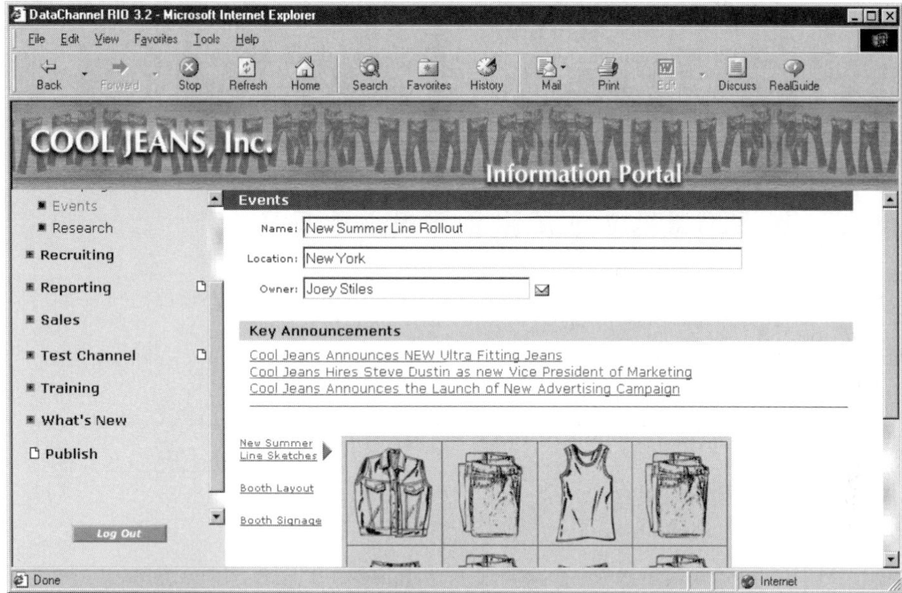

Figure 18-5 *DataChannel RIO* client interface

a template, the *XML Generator* can automatically map your data fields to XML elements.

18.5 | Summary

A company must mobilize its resources to compete effectively in today's global information economy. With IT infrastructure encompassing such a large percentage of those resources, there is a compelling case for an organization to transform its enterprise architecture to adapt to its changing business requirements, overcome computing boundaries, and truly leverage its information, both managed and unmanaged. XML technology and a systematic approach like that embodied in DataChannel's *XMLFramework* can accomplish that goal.

©2000 The XML Handbook™

Sequoia: Portal development system

Tool Discussion

- Enterprise Information Portal (EIP)
- True aggregation
- Portal system architecture

©2000 The XML Handbook™

Chapter 19

The first portals were Web search engines, searching all kinds of information for all kinds of users and returning groups of links. The new portals are more selective in both respects, and they don't just tell you where to link, they aggregate the relevant data for you. This chapter shows what goes into a modern portal system. It is sponsored by Sequoia Software Corporation, `http://www.sequoiasw.com`, and was prepared by Bryan Caporlette

The data environment in enterprises today brings to mind the lament of Coleridge's Ancient Mariner:

Water, water everywhere,
Nor any drop to drink

Organizations deploy a multitude of disparate and proprietary systems. They have us swimming in a sea of data, but thirsting for the information that we need to make better, more informed decisions.

Data is only valuable when it can be transformed into useful information and then into knowledge. So, we are faced with answering this question: How do we sift through all the data of the enterprise to isolate the information that is pertinent to the needs of a specific audience?

The answer lies in the Web-based concept of portals, and a class of products that can serve as portal development systems. More specifically, it lies in the Enterprise Information Portal (EIP), which we will investigate more closely in this chapter.

19.1 | What is an EIP?

A *portal* is a Web-based solution for gathering information from different sources and providing a user-specific view of that information.

First generation portals were created by Internet search engines like *Yahoo*, *Excite*, and *Alta Vista*. These services allow you to search for a keyword and then provide a group of links to information that satisfies your search criteria. Essentially, these search engines act as portals, or doorways, to the World Wide Web.

19.1.1 *Vertical portals*

Web portals can be thought of as horizontal, because of the breadth of both their search domain and the audience they serve. Now a second generation of portal is emerging that is more vertical in nature, called the Enterprise Information Portal (EIP).

EIPs are less general than the portals developed by the Internet Search Engines. They are created for specific audiences as opposed to the general population. Their search domain is narrower as well, as it is limited to the data of a single enterprise or individual, or perhaps to a specific subject area.

But EIPs are significant not just because they are vertical, but because they introduce technology that allows the portal to take on a new role. An EIP does not just provide access to data; it also facilitates the electronic interaction between various departments and organizations.

EIPs are automating the information relationships that are key to business to business e-commerce. That is because EIPs not only *group* information as first generation portals did; they support the true *aggregation* of information.

19.1.2 *Grouping vs. aggregating*

Grouping is merely the bundling together of links that are specific to the needs of a designated audience. The user must traverse each link to find the needed information.

True aggregation, however, means that elements from a variety of documents are pulled together to create a new document, thereby obviating the need to traverse the links.

To build an EIP that can aggregate, an enterprise must be able to acquire data from a variety of different and distributed sources. Once acquired, the data must be managed so that it can support search and retrieval. And it must be possible to present the data in a manner that is specific to the needs of the user.

Let's take a closer look at the software that can help you build an EIP.

19.2 | Portal development system

A *portal development system* is an application platform used for the acquisition, management, and presentation of tailored, audience-specific information.

Sequoia Software Corporation makes such a system, called *Sequoia XML Portal*, that is based on representing all data in XML. It is shown in Figure 19-1. We will use it to illustrate our examination of the components of a portal development system.

19.2.1 *Data acquisition*

By *data acquisition* we mean the act of gathering data from multiple data sources. To successfully acquire data, a system must support a multitude of industry protocols and provide robust data extraction and transformation capabilities.

The data acquisition component in Figure 19-1 is labeled *iAcquire*. It is an object-oriented fifth-generation language tool that allows the creation of interfaces to receive data and transform it to XML. The transformed data is then passed to the management facility, labeled *iManage* in the diagram.

The acquisition component is also responsible for receiving requests for information from outside the system and forwarding those requests to the management facility. The response to such requests is an XML document, which the acquisition component transforms into a message and protocol that the requesting system can understand.

The acquisition component provides both back-end and front-end support, allowing information to be gathered not only from enterprise applica-

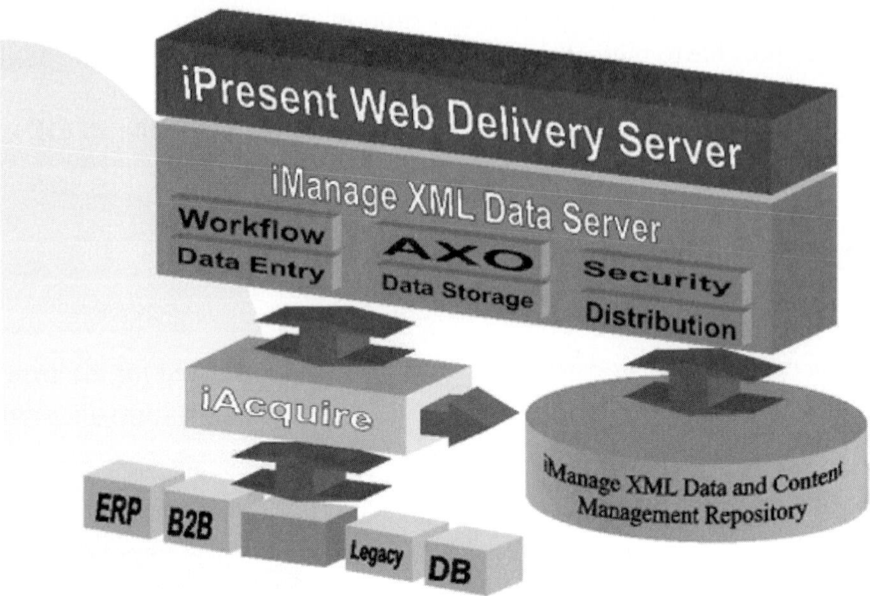

Figure 19-1 *Sequoia XML Portal* system overview

tions like ERP systems and legacy systems, but also end-user applications like office suites and Web page editors.

19.2.2 *Data management*

Data management refers to functions for dealing with various information types once they have been made accessible by the data acquisition component. These include:

- A persistent data repository.
- Index capabilities for data stored in the repository.
- Search facilities for both data stored in the repository and data captured dynamically.
- Functionality for security, workflow, data distribution, data linking, and data aggregation.

The *Sequoia XML Portal* management facility accepts data in the form of an XML document. It extracts the data, indexes it, stores it and/or the document, manages the workflow and access control. This division of labor insulates the enterprise back-end systems from the excessive transactional traffic that can result from the establishment of an EIP.

Applications access the management facility via its transaction processor, labeled *iManage XML Data Server* in Figure 19-1. For example, if a request is made to search information, the transaction processor makes the appropriate requests to the repository for data stored there, in addition to querying external systems via the acquisition component. The multiple search result sets then are collated and returned back to the requesting system or end-user.

19.2.2.1 Embedded XML repository

The system repository is labeled *iManage XML Data and Content Management Repository* in Figure 19-1.

This database utilizes technology currently in place on the World Wide Web, such as indexing spiders, harvest-like caches, etc. It also stores and manages information in document form and can provide access to the unindexed data content that is often required for searching.

The index and search functions provided by the repository include:

- High-recall search and retrieval of document content data.
- Comprehensive, full-text indexing.
- Fuzzy, wildcard, phonetic, and thesaurus searching.
- XML attribute-value pair indexing, allowing searches on every element of an XML document

19.2.2.2 Aggregate XML objects

The heart of an Enterprise Information Portal is its facilities for true aggregation. *Sequoia XML Portal* provides a template mechanism for defining XML documents that are created and revised automatically, as data in other XML documents is received and updated. They are called *aggregate XML objects* (AXO).

Figure 19-2 illustrates how information from the billing system and the sales management system can be combined into a single object for a report.

The template in the lower-left corner determines the elements that will be included in the AXO, which is shown in the lower-right. When data in the two systems changes, the revised data is reflected in the AXO, which is always up-to-date.

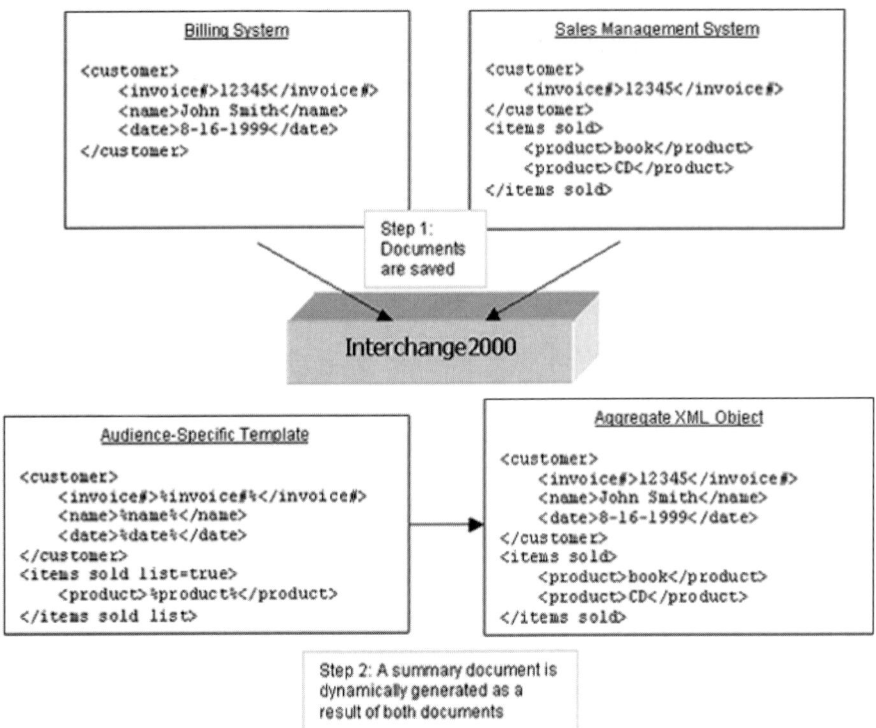

Figure 19-2 An AXO with up-to-date data from two separate sources.

As the AXO contains only the data elements of interest, the user is spared from sifting through documents with irrelevant information. Moreover, the data elements can be reused repeatedly in other AXOs.

19.2.2.3 Workflow and content-based routing

The system's workflow facility is driven by a rules-based repository for routing XML documents. Administrators can define rules that manage the life-cycle of XML documents based on the data they contain. For example, the rules could cause documents generated by one application to be processed automatically by another.

Consider the document shown in Example 19-1, which was generated by a group calendar application. An administrator could define a rule that routes all XML documents that are generated by that application, and where the "`service_rep`" element equals "John Smith", to Mr. Smith's desktop.

Example 19-1. Generated XML document

```
<Client>
    <ID>12345</ID>
</Client>

<Appointment>
   <Time>11:30am</Time>
   <Date>12/13/1997</Date>
</Appointment>

<Meeting>
    <service_rep>John Smith</service_rep>
    <topic>acct balance</topic>
</Meeting>
```

19.2.3 *Data presentation*

Data presentation is the process of delivering data to the end user, rendered in a way that best suits his needs. It is what makes a portal system a portal!

The *Sequoia XML Portal* presentation module, labeled *iPresent Web Delivery Server* in Figure 19-1, provides personalization features to end-users via a Web-based interface. This interface adapts dynamically to customized templates that are set up by administrators.

Views of information are created by stylesheets, which act as filters that affect the presentation of an XML document without modifying the document itself. In addition to controlling rendition (fonts, layout, etc.), stylesheets may do things like suppress selected data, highlight key element types, or create a summary of a document.

Administrators can associate particular stylesheets with a document, depending on which user or application is requesting it. Users can select styles as well, so that an accountant and a sales manager, for example, can have different views of the same document.

Personalization functionality includes the ability for users to subscribe to specific channels. The presentation module uses the popular channel definition format (CDF) to allow users to set up automatic delivery of specific content to their desktop.

ibm.com

Case Study

- Major commercial website
- Combining navigation with data content
- Strategies for rendering and serving XML
- Free software on CD-ROM

©2000 The XML Handbook™

Chapter 20

One of the largest and busiest portal sites on the World Wide Web is gradually converting to XML to solve significant content management problems. In doing so, several different strategies were prototyped for rendering and serving XML efficiently. The details are described in this chapter, which is sponsored by IBM Corporation, `http://www.ibm.com/developerWorks`, and was prepared by Maciej Wisniewski and Doug Tidwell.

The ibm.com site is the entry point to IBM's Internet presence. It is one of the busiest portals on the Web, receiving an average of 8 to 10 million hits a day. Given the importance of the site to IBM, any experiment with XML would have to be fast, reliable, and scalable. As with most production applications, end-user performance is paramount; use of new technologies is of secondary importance.

20.1 | The challenge

20.1.1 *Content management*

Currently IBM manages more than 2 gigabytes of information. Obviously, with such a large site, content management is a constant problem. Although there are many new pages added to the site each month, there are also a number of pages from the dawn of time (the mid-1990s); those pages have very little metadata or useful structure. In addition to the base of existing information, several megabytes of new content are added to the site each month.

20.1.2 *Maintenance and redesign*

In addition to the normal problems involved with managing an enormous Web site, *ibm.com* undergoes a major redesign twice a year. As IBM's presence on the Web, it is vital that the site be visually appealing and up-to-date with the latest in Web technologies and trends. Unfortunately, the site contains many thousands of static pages that aren't easily updated when new style guidelines are announced. IBM's goal is that a major redesign should mean simply rewriting a few stylesheets, with the new stylesheets reflected in every page on the site.

20.2 | Using XML

Any XML aficionado viewing IBM's list of concerns and issues will immediately recognize XML's potential to address these problems. Given the state of the Web, the company had several goals in mind when it began to design an XML strategy:

- Provide a useful, manageable set of metadata about each page on the site.
- Use XML to combine data content and navigation.
- Use XSL stylesheets to minimize the impact of redesigns.
- Use XML to manage content more effectively.

20.2.1 *News documents*

Figure 20-1 shows a sample page containing IBM's XML-based news feed.

The DTD for news (not shown) uses a simple set of element types that describe both the content and information about the content. There is a `Head` section whose elements summarize and categorize the document, and a `Body` section with the text of the article itself. An `Xlink` element uses the emerging XLink standard to refer to related articles.

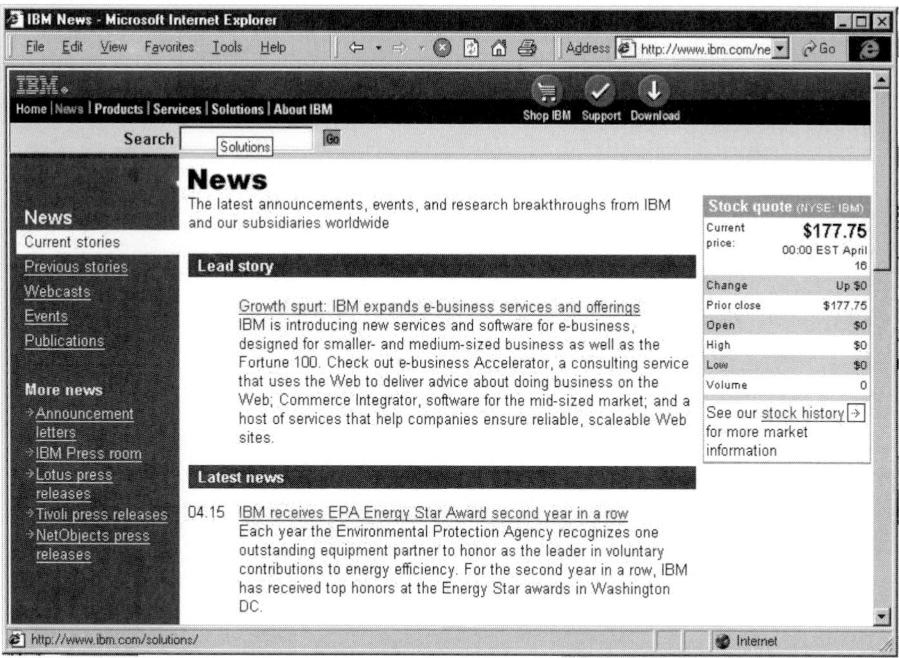

Figure 20-1 Sample news page on *ibm.com*

To keep things simple, the `Body` section element types are very limited. There are no lists (`ol`, `ul`, etc.) or formatting elements (`b`, `i`, `u`, etc.) to complicate rendering. The simple document type also makes it easy to manage the stylesheets that generate HTML.

20.2.2 *Shop documents*

The shop DTD is designed to standardize the description of all products orderable through *ibm.com*. This DTD needs to give a consistent view of all IBM products, whether they are built by the same IBM division or not (or whether they are built by IBM at all). That consistency makes it easy to retrieve information about IBM products, and it makes comparing similar products easier as well.

Example 20-1 is a fragment of a document that describes the *ThinkPad 770*. The `ActionNotebooks` element is interesting because it defines the items that should appear in the navigation area on the left-hand side of the screen.

Example 20-1. Shop document (excerpts)

```
<?xml version="1.0"?>
<!DOCTYPE IBMSHOP SYSTEM "IBMshopV0.4b1.dtd">
<IBMSHOP countrycode="us" language="en">
<NotebooksPDAs>
<CategoryName>ThinkPad</CategoryName>
<NotebookPDAmodel><ModelName>ThinkPad 770</ModelName>
...
<ActionNotebooks>
...
<OrderNotebooks
 buy="http://www.pc.ibm.com/us/thinkpad/howtobuy.html"
 overview="http://www.pc.ibm.com/us/thinkpad/"
 support="http://www.pc.ibm.com/support?page=IBM+ThinkPad"
 news="http://www.pc.ibm.com/us/news/thinkpad/index.html"
 comparison="http://www.direct.ibm.com/cgi-bin/ncommerce/SalesNav?
             family=ThinkPad+770&amp;cntry=840&amp;lang=en_US"
 specs="http://www.pc.ibm.com/us/thinkpad/spec_brochure.html"
 accessories="http://www.pc.ibm.com/us/access/thinkpad/index.htm"
 upgrades="http://www.pc.ibm.com/us/access_upgrades/index.html"
 contact="http://www.ibm.com/contact/"
 href="http://www.pc.ibm.com/us/notebooks/"
 library="http://www.pc.ibm.com/us/thinkpad/tech_library.html"
 resources="http://www.pc.ibm.com/us/thinkpad/mrc/resources.html"
/>
...
</ActionNotebooks>
...
</NotebookPDAmodel>
```

The most important point behind the shop DTD design is that the content and navigation are combined in a single document. All the information needed to build a custom navigation area for this document is included in the document itself. Placing both kinds of information in a single document makes maintenance much easier, and simplifies redesigns as well. If a redesign dictates that the navigation area should be on a different part of the screen, it is simple to generate different HTML markup from the document shown in Example 20-1.

20.2.3 *Search Results*

The search results DTD was written to simplify searches across the *ibm.com* site. As shown in Figure 20-2, the search input field is part of IBM's home page, making it easy to access the search engine.

Figure 20-2 Accessing search from the IBM home page

When a user asks for information, the results of that request are marked up using the search results DTD. This makes it easy for the user to find further information or related information, based on the original search.

IBM wanted to customize search results in two ways: First, intranet users should see different results from Internet users, and second, IBM wanted certain search results to link to parts of the IBM site instead of to a general search results page. As an example, searching on "*ThinkPad*" takes you to a *ThinkPad* home page, from which you can get information about various *ThinkPad* models and features. A more generic search argument, such as "copper chip," simply takes you to a standard page listing the results of your search.

The index for our search engine uses XML as well.

20.2.4 *Product Navigation*

When an IBM product is mentioned somewhere on the site, it is important that users be able to find more information about that product. While a simple URL pointing to the product's home page is helpful, IBM wanted a more complete set of links allowing users to find specifications, support information, press releases, and other information. The product navigation DTD allowed IBM engineers to define a class of documents to do this. A defined XML fragment completely identifies all the relevant links relating to a given product, as shown in Figure 20-3.

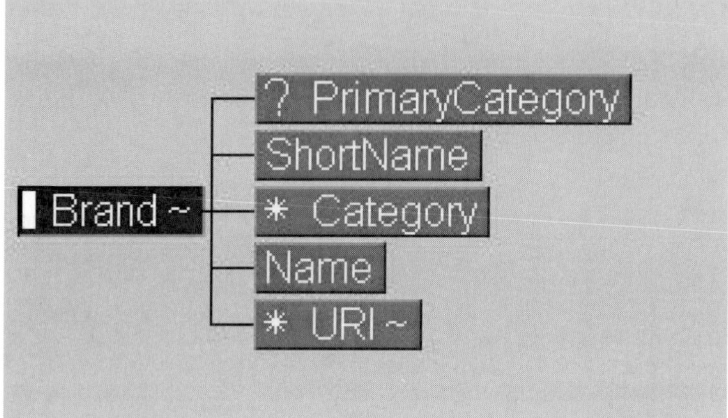

Figure 20-3 Structure of the product navigation DTD

The XML fragments are built on an early specification of the *XML Fragment* standard. Fragments allow for quick independent editing as well as for customized navigational structures.

Example 20-2 shows an example of an XML fragment.

Example 20-2. Sample XML fragment

```
<Name>Web Servers</Name>
<URI name="How to buy"
     href="http://www.software.ibm.com/webservers/howtobuy.html"/>
<URI name="Support"
     href="http://www.software.ibm.com/webservers/support.html"/>
<URI name="Download"
     href="http://www.software.ibm.com/webservers/download.html"/>
```

And Example 20-3 shows the fragment context specification.

20.3 | Implementation strategies

Once the IBM team members developed their DTDs, they built a series of prototypes to deliver XML data to the client. They built prototypes for three strategies, the third of which is used in production today. We'll discuss each strategy, the technologies used, and what was learned from each.

Example 20-3. Context specification for the fragment in Example 20-2

```
<f:fcs xmlns:f="http:w3c.org/TR/WD-xml-fragment"
       extref="http://www.ibm.com/data/xml/ProdNav.dtd">
  <Brand>
    <PrimaryCategory/>
    <ShortName/>
    <f:fragment
     ref="http://www.software.ibm.com/webservers/NavFrag.xml"/>
  </Brand>
</f:fcs>
```

20.3.1 *Client-side rendering*

The first strategy processed the XML markup on the client. Figure 20-4 depicts the flow of code and information across the connection.

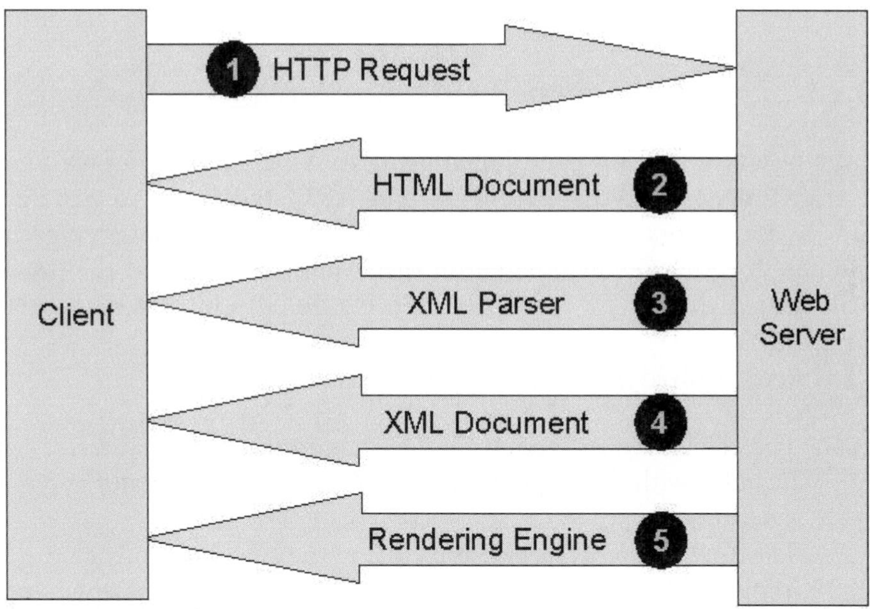

Figure 20-4 First strategy: client-side rendering

The steps involved in this strategy are as follows:

©2000 The XML Handbook™

1. The client sends an HTTP request to the Web server.
2. An HTML document is returned. That document contains an `applet` element that downloads other components to the client.
3. The Web server sends an XML parser to the client.
4. The Web server sends the XML document to the client.
5. The Web server sends a simple rendering engine to the client, which parses and renders the document on the client.

Although this prototype successfully rendered XML documents on the client, there was far too much overhead in downloading all the software components. In addition, the rendering engine was homegrown and supported a limited number of constructs; to fully implement this would have been a major software development effort. This was done only as a proof-of-concept; having shown the power of XML, the IBM engineers proceeded to build another prototype that used XSL to process the XML documents on the server.

20.3.2 *Dynamic server-side rendering*

IBM's next strategy was prototyped using its *XML Enabler*, a Java servlet that processes XML documents and XSL stylesheets to generate HTML documents dynamically. The XML Enabler chooses a given stylesheet for each request, based on the requested URL and the `User-Agent` field in the HTTP request header. Figure 20-5 illustrates the network flow.

The steps involved in this strategy are as follows:

1. The HTTP request goes from the client to the *XML Enabler*. Included with this request is a `User-Agent` field that identifies the browser type.
2. The *XML Enabler* retrieves the URL of the XML document from the HTTP request, then opens that URL to request the document.
3. The requested XML document is returned.
4. Based on the value found in the User-Agent field, the *XML Enabler* selects an XSL stylesheet.

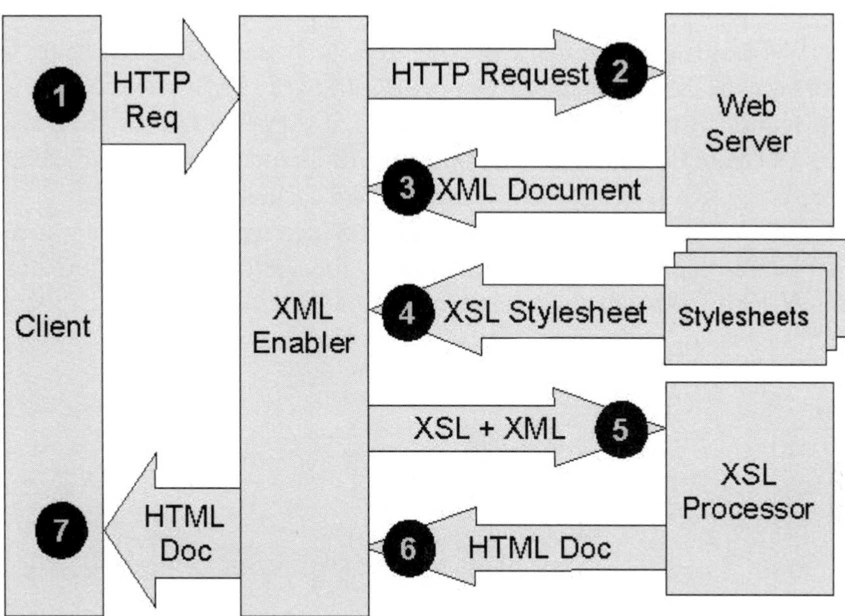

Figure 20-5 Second strategy: dynamic server-side rendering

5. The *XML Enabler* sends both the XML document and the XSL stylesheet to the XSL processor. The processor transforms the XML document according to the rules in the XSL stylesheet.
6. When the transformation is complete, the XSL processor sends the HTML document back to the *XML Enabler*.
7. The *XML Enabler* sends the transformed document back to the requesting client. The client displays the HTML, having no idea that the page began life as an XML document.

The main advantage of this approach is that the client sees only an HTML document. It has no idea that the document it receives began its life as XML. This approach also greatly minimizes the amount of data that flows across the network connection. Unfortunately, the performance of the version of *XML Enabler* that was available at the time wasn't suitable for the high traffic volumes of *ibm.com*.

20.3.3 *Cached server-side rendering*

The IBM team's final strategy, the one ultimately used on the website, was to convert the XML documents into the various HTML pages before any client requests were processed. For example, if they had five different stylesheets to create five different views for five different client types, then they generated all five views of each document and cached them.

When requests come in, the server quickly determines which pre-generated HTML document matches a request, then returns that document to the user. Figure 20-6 depicts the network flow for this strategy.

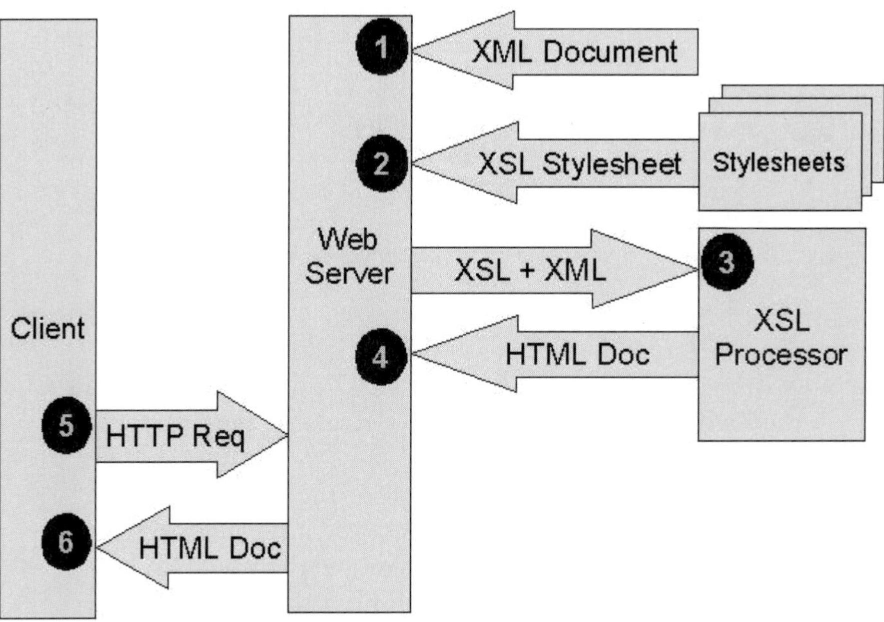

Figure 20-6 Production strategy: cached server-side rendering

The steps involved in this strategy are as follows:

1. Before any HTTP requests are served, an automated process on the Web server retrieves each XML document.
2. As each XML document is retrieved, one or more XSL stylesheets are also retrieved.

3. The XML document and one of the XSL stylesheets are sent to the XSL processor.
4. The XSL processor returns its results. In our case, HTML documents are returned, although documents of any arbitrary XML document type could be generated.

Lather, Rinse, Repeat: Steps 1 through 4 are performed on all of the combinations of documents and stylesheets on the site.

5. An HTTP request comes in from the client. As with the *XML Enabler*-based strategy, the server uses the value found in the `User-Agent` field to determine which previously-generated HTML document to return.
6. The Web server sends the appropriate HTML document to the client.

Because XML- and XSL-enabled browsers are beginning to appear on the market, the IBM team set up the caching mechanism to serve the original XML and XSL documents to those browsers capable of rendering them. This allows the client machine to provide additional function, such as extracting data for processing, that is not possible with the generated HTML file.

This strategy proved scalable to the traffic volumes enjoyed by *ibm.com*.

Tip *XML Enabler is available on the CD-ROM, along with lots of other free XML tools from IBM alphaWorks.*

RxML: Your prescription for healthcare

Application Discussion

- Health portal system
- Dynamic patient summary
- Information aggregation
- Supply chain automation

©2000 The XML Handbook™

Chapter 21

When it comes to electronic information processing, the U.S. medical system is "terminally" ill, so to speak. Systems rarely share data, even in the same medical organization, and there is little chance that your doctor can usefully access all your records for a diagnosis. Sequoia Software Corporation, `http://www.sequoiasw.com`, is sponsoring this chapter to prescribe a cure. It was prepared by Bryan Caporlette

Imagine you're feeling under the weather, so you make an office visit to your primary care physician.

Dr. Caps enters the examination room with a portable device instead of a clipboard. From that device he can access a patient summary record that contains your complete medical history, follow-up visits, current medications, and your favorite pharmacy. This information has been pooled together from various sources in the ABC Medical Center to create a single integrated logical view.

After an initial evaluation, Dr. Caps orders a throat culture to check for streptococcus bacteria. A laboratory order request, in the form of an XML document, is transmitted to the microbiology department. A culture is obtained by the nurse and sent to the lab. The culture results will be sent directly to the doctor's electronic in-basket, where he can evaluate them to determine the appropriate course of action.

Until determination of the culture result, he prescribes Keflex for coverage. He chooses Keflex, rather than amoxicillin, because the patient summary indicates that in a previous "encounter" (office visit, etc.) you reported an adverse reaction to amoxicillin.

The prescription is sent electronically to your local MRC pharmacy, where it will be awaiting your arrival as you head home for some much needed rest. Following your departure, the billing department will automatically generate an XML invoice that is electronically submitted to Blue Triangle, your healthcare provider.

That all-important patient summary is made possible for Dr. Caps through a collection of electronically stored medical information, aggregated and distributed through a *health portal system*, as shown in Figure 21-1. It enables you, as a patient, to receive the best service, and clinicians to make the most informed decisions regarding your care.

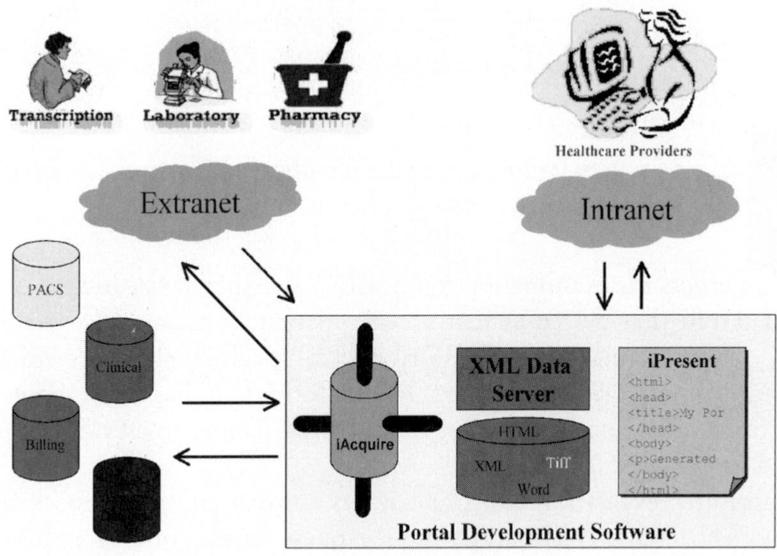

Figure 21-1 Health portal system

21.1 | Doing as well as can be expected – Not!

As you have probably noticed, real-world experiences with the healthcare industry do not resemble the integrated environment portrayed above. Let's say you were born in upstate New York, went to school in Ohio, and now live in Silicon Valley. More likely than not, you have had to receive medical attention at each of these locations.

Most of us have been asked repeatedly to fill out the same forms, with our demographic and medical histories. The onus has been on us to remember our doctors' names, dates of injury and illness, arcane names for medications we are taking, and allergies that have been discovered over a lifetime. This information has been stored multiple times, in multiple systems, in multiple geographic locations.

Unless you have been fortunate enough to have the same doctor your whole life, your physicians probably haven't had all the information necessary to render the best diagnosis. Stories of duplicate laboratory tests, negative reactions to unknown medical allergies, and misdiagnosis due to missing or incorrect information abound within the industry.

There are many reasons the care we receive falls short of our expectations. Organizations have to deal with a copious amount of information. However, providing access to this information to the correct person at the correct time is often impossible.

The typical healthcare organization information system deploys between 30 and 70 applications. These applications are spread across multiple functional departments, hardware platforms, and geographical locations, which impedes effective use of their information. Other barriers include security considerations and the cost of software licenses.

21.2 | The prescription: a health portal system

Fortunately, there is a cure for this condition. Health portal systems like the one used by Dr. Caps in our example can exist. They are just examples of Enterprise Information Portals, which organizations can build using portal development products like *Sequoia XML Portal*.

©2000 The XML Handbook™

A *health portal system* provides a single point of access for all your medical information. Clinicians log into the portal, after which they have sophisticated search and navigation capabilities to access a comprehensive library of information.

These capabilities enable the clinician to locate your patient summary record quickly. The patient summary is an aggregate view of your complete medical history, made up of information components extracted from the numerous systems deployed by the health enterprise. Figure 21-2 depicts what Dr. Caps saw in our example.

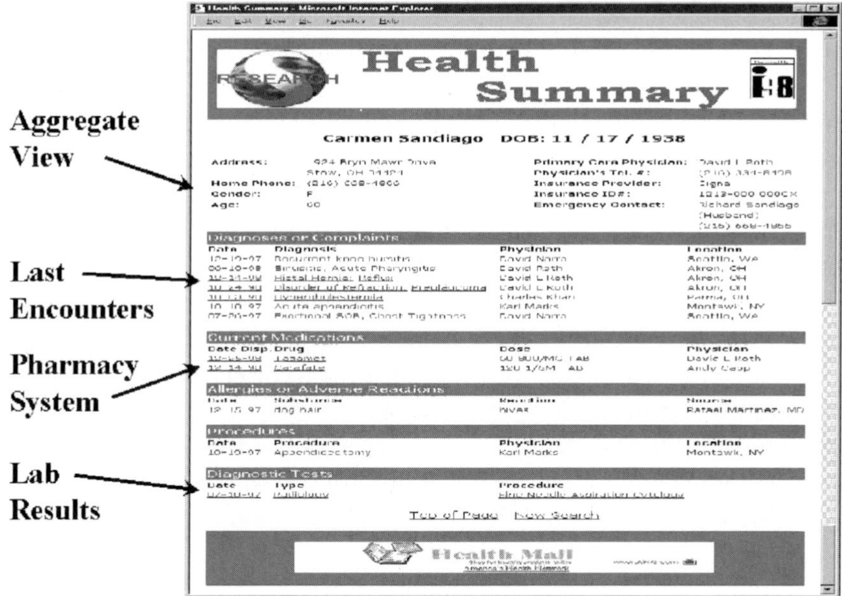

Figure 21-2 Rendition of patient summary

In addition to those internal systems, the portal provides access to medical libraries and external systems, such as laboratory results and pharmaceutical ordering systems. Its all done by the portal system's acquisition component and its connectors.

21.3 | Connectivity counts

The portal software in Figure 21-1 is *Sequoia XML Portal*; its acquisition component is labeled *iAcquire* and it has connectors that tap into various disparate systems. The connectors communicate with software applications, extract data from them, and transform that information into XML. The XML documents are then passed on to the XML data server.

The connectors are a flexible bunch. One might be communicating directly with a radiology system, capturing the images and routing them into the portal. Another connector could be listening through a TCP/IP port for health industry standard (HL7) messages being transmitted from the "admit, discharge, transfer" application.

Yet another connector might poll an FTP directory that has been set up for our transcription service company to submit operative reports and other transcribed documents. As the documents are sent into the directory, the connector grabs them and converts the information into XML.

This functionality doesn't just happen. The portal administrator must train the system to perform the transformations by defining connectors. Systems typically provide a graphical user interface (GUI) that enables easy mapping of source data elements into their target XML document. Some, like *Sequoia XML Portal*, provide other features that make the administrator's life easier, such as DTDs that allow automatic import of standard HL7 messages. Once defined, the connectors are deployed across the enterprise to begin collecting the data needed by Dr. Caps.

But these connectors are not just one-way data pumps. The administrator can also enable connectors to dynamically query data stored in an electronic medical records (EMR) application. When Dr. Caps needs to find out if you have had streptococcus recently, the data server can formulate a search request. This request is serviced in real-time by the connector, communicating to the EMR application through an ODBC interface. Perhaps he will recommend a vitamin C supplement to your diet.

Figure 21-3 illustrates the acquisition component of *Sequoia XML Portal* and its connectors, which are labeled *Accessor* in the diagram.

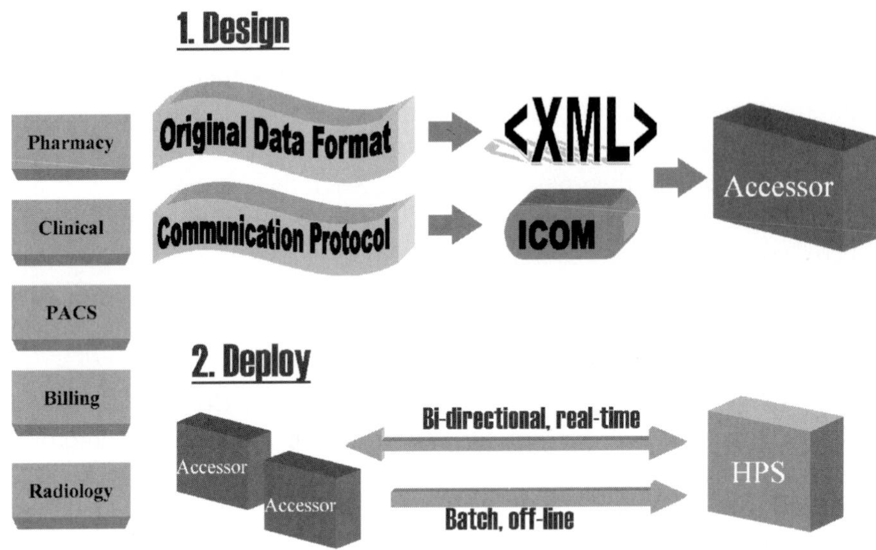

Figure 21-3 *Sequoia XML Portal* and its *Accessor* connectors

21.4 | Aggregation adds value

As information flows into the portal's XML data server, it must be organized in a way that facilitates easy, intuitive access by Dr. Caps.

Information overload could become a problem, if information is not properly presented to the physician. The obvious first step is to provide a categorization facility to help organize the data into folders. XML provides the ability to define element types such as patient name, encounter date, and attending physician that can be used to place documents into a particular folder.

However, the unique capability of a true enterprise information portal is that it can aggregate data from disparate sources to create a comprehensive view of your overall health. This is where XML really plays a significant role.

Imagine trying to assimilate information from a proprietary ASCII format, the results of an SQL query, and an operative report in some word processor format. But, if the connectors are doing their transformation job properly and sending only XML into the portal, a new breed of aggregate XML objects can be built dynamically from these sources.

The aggregate XML object in this case is a patient summary. The template that causes it to be created is shown in Figure 21-4. The template is an XML document with no data. The empty elements act as queries that retrieve the data of the same element types in other documents – the "data sources".

Actual patient summaries are constructed by filling in copies of the template with data extracted dynamically from the data sources as they enter the system. The patient summary becomes the universal access point for all information, with hyperlinks into the original data source documents supplementing the summary where appropriate.

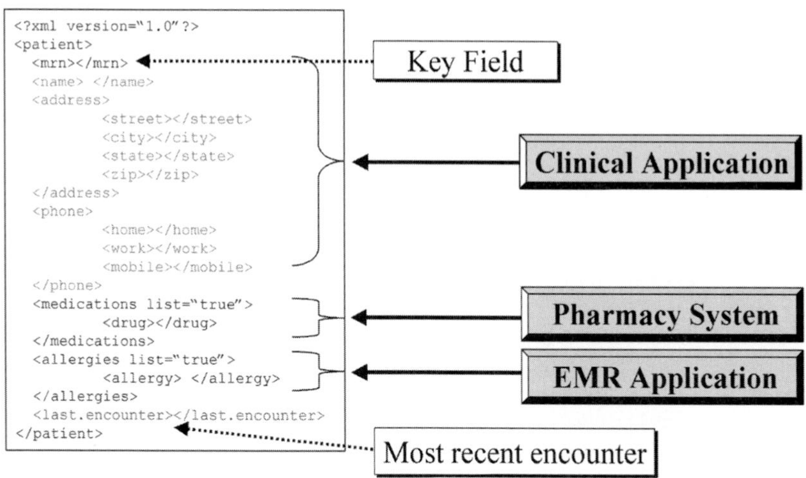

Figure 21-4 Template for patient summary

21.5 | Personalization assures usability

Not everyone needs to see, or should see, all the information flowing into the system. The portal can deliver personalized renditions of the XML information to the clinicians by using XSL stylesheets. These provide very granular personalization, applying transformation rules at the element level.

The portal applies XSL on the server-side, where it can employ a powerful rules engine to associate multiple stylesheets with the same document. Users can define profiles that choose their preferred stylesheet.

Personalization doesn't only apply to the presentation. Access and document routing can be controlled through XML documents so that physicians can automatically be sent a "today's appointments" report listing the day's schedule.

The portal can also limit access to patient records to their own doctors. For example, the access rule in Example 21-1 ensures that only Dr. Caps has access to the lab report in Example 21-2, where he is identified as the attending physician. The `%doctor_name%` variable accesses the user's login identity.

Example 21-1. Access rule for lab reports

```
Access Rule: Grant Read where
   Lab.report\attending.physician$eq$%doctor_name%
```

Example 21-2. Lab report

```
<lab.report>
<patient>
<name>John Smith</name>
<mrn>ID939393</mrn>
</patient>
<attending.physician>Dr. Caps</attending.physician>
<result>
<test>
<name>Throat culture</name>
</test>
</result>
</lab.report>
```

21.6 | Linking up the supply chain

Healthcare enterprises struggle constantly with managing all their external suppliers. The typical organization must deal on a daily basis with laboratories, physicians, transcription services houses, and most importantly, the benefit providers (Blue Triangle in your case).

The portal's ability to automate the relationship with provider organizations is one of the key benefits to the healthcare facility. The billing department will extract XML information from the portal to create an electronic billing invoice, passing it through an XML-enabled transaction server for transmittal over a secure extranet connection to Blue Triangle. Blue Triangle, in processing the invoice, verifies your benefits eligibility with Healtheon prior to transmitting a payment voucher back to ABC Medical Center.

Internet banking services will also impact the payment system. Soon you might be able to authorize electronic payment of your co-pay amount directly from your checking account.

21.7 | Conclusion

XML-powered health portals with dynamic patient summaries transform the healthcare experience. Patients receive better, faster healthcare service while clinicians gain greater access to information that enables them to make the best decisions.

Healthcare organizations also realize significant benefits. Their service reputation improves even while they cut costs because doctors don't order the same tests multiple times. In addition, automated billing lowers costs further while improving cash flow.

Hint *You can learn more about building enterprise information portals with Sequoia XML Portal in Chapter 19,* *"Sequoia: Portal development system", on page 256.*

XMLNews: A syndication document type

Application Discussion

- News syndication initiative
- *XMLNews-Story* document type
- Instances with varying degrees of markup

©2000 THE XML HANDBOOK™

Chapter 22

Portals feed on *feeds* – continuous information streams like the newswire, which has carried syndicated articles from services like Reuters and the Associated Press since the dawn of the telegraph. Now the news feed is being updated for the Internet, thanks to XML. This chapter is sponsored by Corel, `http://www.corel.com`, and was prepared by Bonnie Robinson and David Megginson.

The XMLNews initiative promotes the use of XML in the news syndication industry, building on existing specifications and providing new ones where needed. To date, two specifications have been published: XMLNews-Meta and XMLNews-Story.

XMLNews-Meta

This XML application defines metadata records for news objects. It conforms to the Resource Description Framework (RDF), developed by the World Wide Web Consortium for the exchange of metadata.

XMLNews-Meta is not limited to traditional, character-based wire stories. Because it holds the metadata in a separate document, you can use it for any kind of news information, including textual news stories, photos, audio or video clips, or even virtual 3-D worlds and interactive scripts.

XMLNews-Meta is described in Chapter 23, "Wavo Corporation", on page 300.

XMLNews-Story

This specification defines the representation of news stories in XML. It is a streamlined but fully-compatible subset of the larger News Industry Text Format (NITF) standard, developed by the International Press Telecommunications Council (IPTC; `http://www.iptc.org/iptc/`) and the Newspaper Association of America (NAA; `http://www.naa.org/`).

NITF itself is designed to replace ANPA 1312, a modem format currently used by most major wire services.

This chapter illustrates *XMLNews-Story* (and NITF) by showing how to create and then enhance a simple news story.

22.1 | Structure of a news story

Although there is a lot of variety in presentation, most news stories share a basic logical structure. Figure 22-1 shows the parts of a basic news story.

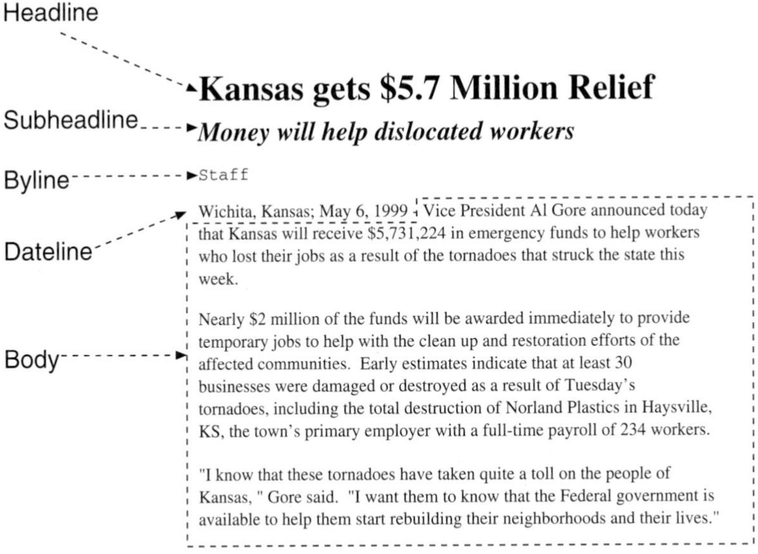

Figure 22-1 Structure of a news story

headline

The headline "Kansas gets $5.7 Million Relief" is the main title of the story. The purpose of a headline is both to grab a reader's attention and to provide some information about what will appear in the story. As a result, the headline is usually presented in such a way that it stands out from the rest of the story.

subheadline
In addition to the headline, this story contains a subheadline "Money will help dislocated workers," which provides additional information about the contents of the story. The subheadline is usually rendered so that it is less prominent than the headline, but more prominent than the rest of the news story. In certain rare cases, a story might have more than one subheadline.

byline
The byline credits the author of the story. It is called the "byline" because, in English, it often begins with the word "by". Many news stories do not have bylines, and for those that do, the byline might contain a person's name, several people's names, an organization's name, or just a generic word like "staff", as is the case with this story.

dateline
Some news stories contain a dateline, like "Wichita, Kansas, May 6, 1999." If the dateline is present, it contains the location (or locations) from which the story was filed, and sometimes, the date as well.

body
The body (or "copy") contains the actual news story itself. A simple news story consists only of character text divided into a series of paragraphs. More complicated news stories contain other types of information, such as photographs, figures, and tables.

22.2 | Structure of an XMLNews-Story document

The XML element types used in an *XMLNews-Story* document (and in a full NITF document) reflect this basic story structure. Figure 22-2 shows

©2000 The XML Handbook™

the top-level element structure, which borrows heavily from HTML. The root element type, `nitf`, contains two subelements, `head` and `body`.

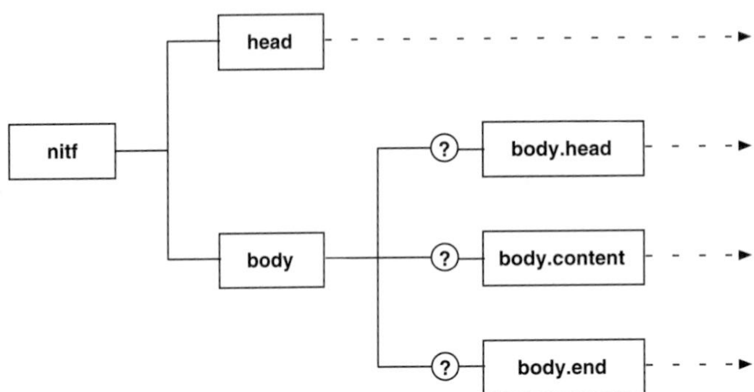

Figure 22-2 *XMLNews-Story* top-level structure

As in HTML, the `head` element contains non-printing information about the document, such as the title for cataloging purposes (which may or may not be the same as the headline).

Unlike HTML, though, the *XMLNews-Story* `body` element is further subdivided into three parts:

`body.head`
: This element contains the headline, subheadlines, byline, and dateline, together with other (optional) information.

`body.content`
: This element contains the actual story body.

`body.end`
: This element contains the (aptly-named for XML) `tagline`, a small copyright or distribution notice that often appears at the end of a printed story.

To actually create a story, you need to insert the root `nitf` element; it is also a good idea to include the XML declaration, stating the version of

XML used (currently, "1.0") and, optionally, the character encoding, as seen in Example 22-1:

Example 22-1. XML declaration and `nitf` root element

```
<?xml version="1.0" encoding="UTF-8"?>
<nitf>
</nitf>
```

If you wish to create a valid XML document, you must also include a document type declaration with the system identifier for the *XMLNews-Story*, as shown in Example 22-2.

Example 22-2. Adding the document type declaration

```
<?xml version="1.0"?>
<!DOCTYPE nitf SYSTEM
  "http://www.xmlnews.org/dtds/xmlnews-story.dtd">
<nitf>
</nitf>
```

An XML-aware editing tool, such as *WordPerfect®9*, can insert all of this for you automatically (see Figure 22-3). (See Chapter 36, "WordPerfect: The information supply chain", on page 482 for more information on this tool, which includes a template for *XMLNews*.)

You must include a `head` element followed by a `body` element. The `head` element contains a `title` element with the title of the news story, as shown in Example 22-3. This is the title for cataloging purposes; it may be the same as the headline, but does not have to be.

Example 22-3. `head`, `title`, and `body` elements

```
<head>
<title>Gore announces Emergency Relief</title>
</head>
<body>
</body>
```

©2000 The XML Handbook™

The body of the story is divided into three parts. The body.head element contains the headline, subheadline, byline, and dateline, together with the name of the distributor, as shown in Example 22-4.

Example 22-4. The body.head element

```
<body.head>
  <hedline>
    <hl1>Kansas gets $5.7 Million Relief</hl1>
    <hl2>Money will help dislocated workers</hl2>
  </hedline>
  <byline>
    <bytag>Staff</bytag>
  </byline>
    <distributor>ACME Newswire</distributor>
  <dateline>
    <location>Wichita, Kansas</location>
    <story.date>May 6, 1999</story.date>
  </dateline>
</body.head>
```

The body.content element contains the main body of the story, divided into paragraphs, as shown in Example 22-5.

Example 22-5. The body.content element

```
<body.content>
<p>Vice President Al Gore announced today that Kansas will
receive $5,731,224 in emergency funds to help workers who
lost their jobs as a result of the tornadoes that struck the
state this week.</p>
<p>Nearly $2 million of the funds will be awarded
immediately to provide temporary jobs to help with the clean
up and restoration efforts of the affected communities.
Early estimates indicate that at least that at least 30
businesses were damaged or destroyed as a result of
Tuesday's tornadoes, including the total destruction of
Norland Plastics in Haysville, KS, the town's primary
employer with a full-time payroll of 234 workers.</p>
<p><q>I know that these tornadoes have taken quite a toll on
the people of Kansas,</q> Gore said. <q>I want them to know
that the Federal government is available to help them start
rebuilding their neighborhoods and their lives.</q></p>
</body.content>
```

The body.end element contains a tagline with a copyright notice for the fictional provider ACME Newswire, as shown in Example 22-6.

Example 22-6. The body.end element

```
<body.end>
<tagline><copyrite>Copyright (c) 1999 by ACME Newswire. All rights
reserved.</copyrite>
</tagline>
</body.end>
```

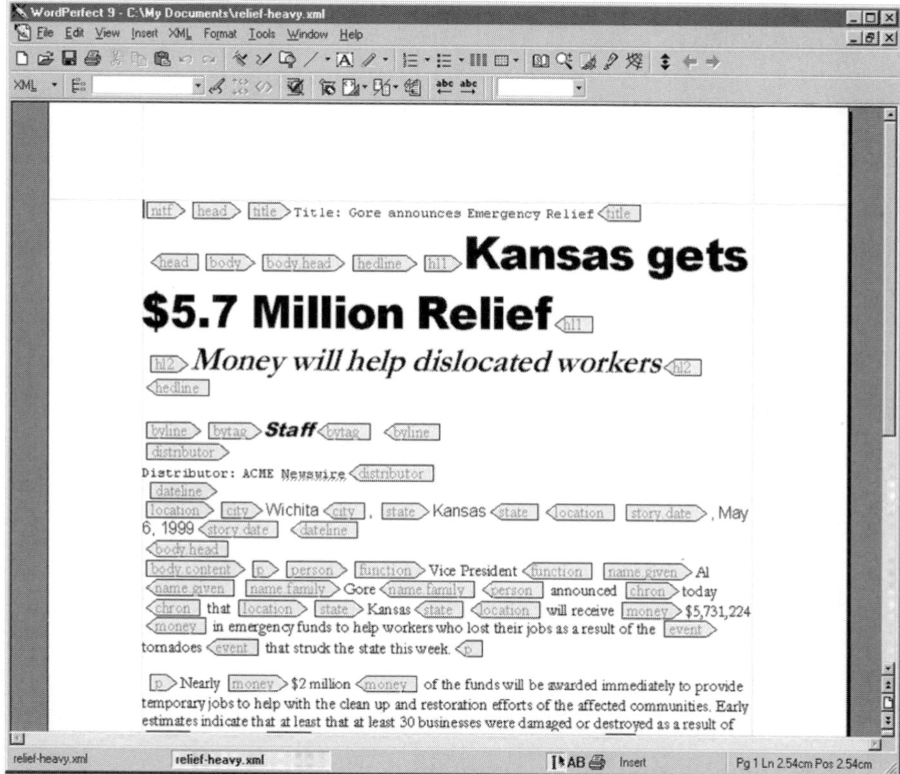

Figure 22-3 Creating an *XMLNews-Story* document in *WordPerfect*.

22.3 | Rich inline markup

In addition to basic, high-level structural markup, the *XMLNews-Story* document type also supports rich inline markup, which can improve the quality of news feeds.

The existing ANPA 1312 standard allows newswire stories to contain some presentational inline codes, to mark font shifts within a paragraph for example. NITF and *XMLNews-Story* replace these codes with XML elements specifying not how a word or phrase should look, but what it actually means.

There are seventeen inline elements allowed (but not required) in the body of a news story:

chron
: A phrase that refers to a specific date and time (such as "today", or "last February"). It optionally includes a normalized date and time in ISO 8601 format.

copyrite
: A copyright statement.

event
: A word or phrase referring to an event, such as a holiday, a natural disaster, an election, or an awards ceremony.

function
: A word or phrase referring to a person's function, such as "President," "well-known reporter," "astronaut," or "right-wing lobbyist."

location
: A word or phrase referring to a geographical location, such as a country, city, town, region, neighborhood, or building.

money
: A word or phrase referring to a monetary item. It optionally includes the currency in ISO 4217 format.

num

A word or phrase referring to a quantity, including fractions.

object.title

A word or phrase referring to the title of an object such as a book, movie, television show, or song.

org

A word or phrase referring to an organization such as a government, a non-profit organization, a university, or a publicly-traded company.

person

A word or phrase referring to a person.

virtloc

A word or phrase referring to a virtual location such as a URL or an e-mail address.

a

A word or phrase that is the source of a hyperlink (from HTML).

br

A line break (from HTML).

em

An emphasized word or phrase (from HTML).

lang

A word or phrase in a different language or dialect from the main story. It may optionally include the ISO 629 language code, with or without an ISO 3166 country code as a qualifier.

pronounce

A word or phrase that may be difficult to pronounce. It includes a phonetic spelling or other guide to pronunciation.

q

A direct quotation. (It is not necessary to add quotation marks when you use this element).

None of the additional markup is required. However, including it can make the news story much more valuable, because consumers can perform more intelligent indexing, filtering, cataloging, and searching. For example, an online news service could generate an index of every person mentioned in the day's news, and a user could search for "Buffalo" the city without finding matches for "buffalo" the animal.

Example 22-7 is the first paragraph of the body of the original story:

Example 22-7. The first paragraph of the body of the original story

```
<p>Vice President Al Gore announced today that Kansas will
receive $5,731,224 in emergency funds to help workers who
lost their jobs as a result of the tornadoes that struck the
state this week.</p>
```

For many uses, simply delimiting the paragraph is sufficient; however, a news distributor could add value to a news story by introducing some basic inline markup, as shown in Example 22-8:

Example 22-8. Introducing some basic inline markup

```
<p><person>Vice President Al Gore</person> announced today
that <location>Kansas</location> will receive
<money>$5,731,224</money> in emergency funds to help workers
who lost their jobs as a result of the
<event>tornadoes</event> that struck the state this week.</p>
```

Now, a news filtering system can tell that this story discusses the `event` "tornadoes" rather than, say, the airplane, and the `person` "Gore" rather than a street or town with the same name.

An archivist might choose to add even more markup to the same paragraph to allow highly-sophisticated searching and analysis, as shown in Example 22-9:

With this rich inline markup, it would be possible for a British publication to perform automatic currency conversion from U.S. dollars to pounds sterling; for a search engine to distinguish the word "Kansas" as a state name from the word "Kansas" as part of a city name; or for an filtering program to find stories about people with "Gore" as a last name but not a first name.

Example 22-9. An archivist's additional markup

```
<p><person><function>Vice President</function>
<name.given>Al</name.given>
<name.family>Gore</name.family></person> announced <chron
norm="19990506">today</chron> that
<location><state>Kansas</state></location> will receive
<money unit="USD">$5,731,224</money> in emergency funds to
help workers who lost their jobs as a result of the
<event>tornadoes</event> that struck the state this
week.</p>
```

Initially, at least, most news providers and distributors will likely not adopt markup as rich and complex as that in the last example, but the markup is available when needed.

22.4 | Media objects

Even traditional printed news stories often contain non-textual items such as photographs or illustrations, and a news story from a new media provider might also contain live content like audio or video clips. NITF and *XML-News-Story* provide support for photographs, images, and audio and video clips.

Tip *You can find the full details on XMLNews on the CD. Point your browser to* `d:/WAVO/INTRO.html`, *where "d:" is your CD-ROM drive.*

Wavo Corporation

Case Study

- *NewsPak* Internet syndication service
- From delivery service to value-added aggregator
- Automatic markup
- XMLNews-Meta document type
- Information and Content Exchange (ICE)

©2000 The XML Handbook™

Chapter 23

The "wire" in newswire used to refer to telegraph wires. Nowadays it's virtually virtual, as news increasingly moves by other means, including the Internet. Learn how one company went from being a wire substitute to a value-added data aggregator with the help of XML. This chapter is sponsored by Wavo Corporation, `http://www.wavo.com/`, and was prepared by Deren Hansen.

For more than 15 years, Wavo Corporation has been in the business of moving media, particularly news. Every day it distributes thousands of stories from major newswire providers like the Associated Press, Dow Jones, and Reuters.

In the fall of 1998, the company launched a strategic initiative to integrate the technologies from its various divisions into an industry-standard system for aggregating, normalizing, and delivering commercial news services via the Internet. From the beginning, it was clear that XML would be the glue that bound these technologies together into a system whose whole was greater than the sum of its parts.

23.1 | The challenge

Wavo's business initially revolved around delivering a provider's data to customers in the provider's own format. To that end, the company developed a system to broadcast streaming, real-time data via satellite or FM transmitter. As shown at "A" in Figure 23-1, broadcasts are made to a proprietary receiver (IDR) that, in turn, feeds client computer systems.

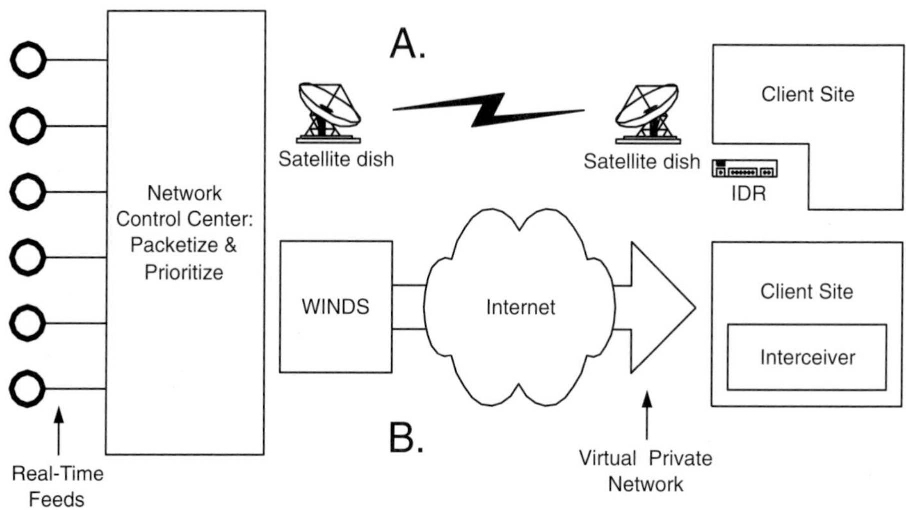

Figure 23-1 Wavo's streaming, real-time data delivery systems.

With the advent of the Internet, the company expanded its palette of delivery mechanisms by creating the Wavo Internet News Delivery Service (WINDS). The WINDS system creates a virtual private network to deliver real-time, streaming information across the Internet. It is shown at "B" in Figure 23-1

Once the distribution infrastructure was in place, the company discovered there was a market for news aggregation services. Commercial news consumers, such as major corporations, wanted one source from which they could receive news feeds from a number of providers.

Those providers deliver their data using proprietary (sometimes idiosyncratic) formats. And where they do use one of the several pre-XML standards for news, Wavo found, they follow the standard rigorously – except when they don't!

Shielding downstream data consumers from the idiosyncrasies of the various raw feeds turned out to be a real opportunity. Syntactic normalization, or having a single representation for all delivered data, was the obvious first step. It is shown in Figure 23-2.

Some information providers send metadata to classify their stories by categories, such as industry, location, and subject. As one might expect, each provider that generates metadata has its own taxonomy and data representation. Wavo realized that semantic normalization, or classifying stories

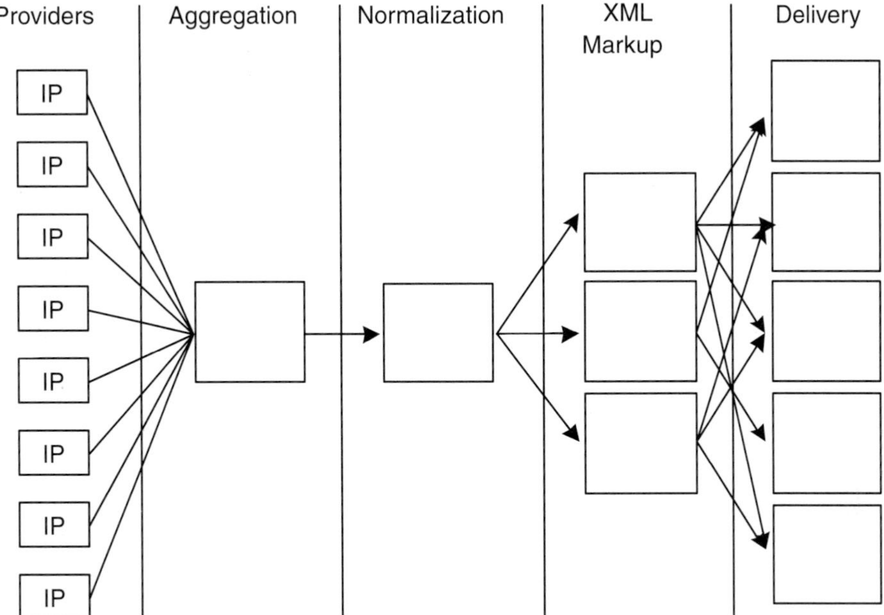

Figure 23-2 Data flow through Wavo's Newscast Global Information Server.

according to a common metadata scheme regardless of the source of the story, would add tremendous value to what up till then had been simply a delivery business.

In reviewing this mix of problems and capabilities, Wavo formulated this list of required characteristics of its new system:

consolidated
: News from multiple providers is available from a single supplier.

blended
: Data is delivered on a single channel; packets are commingled to allow news delivery from multiple sources in a timely fashion.

standardized
: A single industry-standard data representation is used for all news sources.

structured
The structure of the abstract content is preserved in the data representation.

faithful
The provider's original representation is either preserved or can be reconstructed.

consistent
The terminology used in the markup means the same thing for all sources.

richly-marked
The context of proper nouns, such as company names, locations, product names, etc. is identified by markup in the running text.

classified
Stories are classified for easier retrieval.

23.2 | Wavo's *NewsPak* service

Wavo's strategic initiative was named *NewsPak* and was put into production in the summer of 1999. It resulted in the three-layer system shown in Figure 23-3.

Layer 1
High-volume transport services for real-time data.

Layer 2
Content acquisition and normalization at the network head-end and an application framework for the client site.

Layer 3
Business and administration layer.

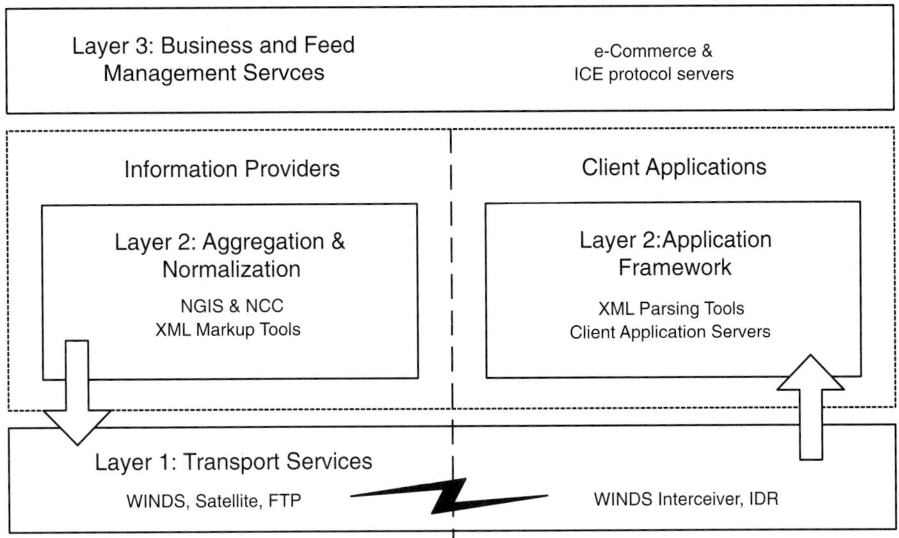

Figure 23-3 The *NewsPak* system

23.2.1 *Transport layer*

Transport services are available in a variety of configurations, ranging from premium services like satellite broadcast and WINDS to ancillary mechanisms such as FTP and HTTP. The feed distribution system enforces usage, re-distribution, and syndication policies.

The system can provide real-time data delivery without sacrificing the benefits of rich markup. Real-time data is processed at the network head-end and immediately broadcast via WINDS or the satellite network. Receivers running at the customer site automatically produce a minimally marked XML version of the story.

At the same time, that same data stream is also processed at the head-end to create richly marked versions of the real-time stories, complete with metadata and inline tagging. The new versions of the real-time stories are then sent to replace the minimally marked versions of the story delivered earlier.

23.2.2 *Content layer*

The information feeds are translated from their original format into richly marked-up XML documents. There are two kinds of automatic markup applied: normalized associated metadata, and contextual inline markup of significant elements.

On the client side, in addition to transport layer components like WINDS receivers, the service includes a set of applications, demonstration systems, and sample code.

23.2.2.1 Metadata normalization

Some information providers supply metadata with their stories. Such metadata sets typically include fields for geographic region, industry, company name, company code (usually its ticker symbol), and so on. Each information provider has its own set of metadata symbols and usage policies. For example, one provider may only report the geographic region with which a story is concerned, while another might indicate all the countries mentioned in the story.

All provider metadata is preserved, but *NewsPak* also provides normalized metadata as follows:

- Company names are extracted from the stories and associated with their standard ticker and other symbols.
- Geographic regions are extracted and associated with standard aggregate geographic codes.
- All other proper names are extracted and associated as metadata.
- Detailed industry and event categories are assigned after content analysis.

23.2.2.2 Contextual inline markup

NewsPak marks up proper nouns (i.e., persons, places, and things) in the body of a story so that one can distinguish between persons and organizations. For example, a sentence such as:

Example 23-1. One word in several contexts.

```
Professor Rice, of Rice University, is an authority on rice.
```

after automatic markup would become:

Example 23-2. Tags identify contexts of words.

```
<person>Professor Rice</person>, of <org>Rice University</org>, is
an authority on rice.
```

23.2.2.3 Markup languages

NewsPak uses *XMLNews-Meta* and *XMLNews-Story* as its XML document types.

XMLNews-Story, which is described in Chapter 22, "XMLNews: A syndication document type", on page 288, is a subset of the News Industry Text Format (NITF), an XML document type under development by the International Press Telecommunications Council (IPTC) and the Newspaper Association of America (NAA). It is used for news stories themselves.

However, the value-added metadata and other elements needed by the system to transmit and process a story are included in a second XML document. You can think of it as a work order and envelope for the story itself. This companion metadata document conforms to the *XMLNews-Meta* document type, which is an application of RDF. An example is shown in Example 23-3.

The relationship between *XMLNews-Meta* and *XMLNews-Story* is shown in Figure 23-4. Decoupling the two provides a great deal of flexibility.

For example, *XMLNews-Story* is limited to associating a single story with its media elements, such as images, audio, and video. *XMLNews-Meta*, however, can associate multiple stories with one another, such as a main article and several sidebars. It can also deliver other document types, such as database records of stock quotes.

©2000 THE XML HANDBOOK™

Example 23-3. XMLNews-Meta document

```
<?xml version="1.0"?>
<rdf:RDF xmlns:rdf="http://www.w3.org/1999/02/22-rdf-syntax-ns#"
 xmlns:xn="http://www.xmlnews.org/namespaces/meta#">
   <rdf:Resource
    about="199903300001K00002DK000031000009.xml">
      <xn:resourceID>199903300001K00002DK000031000009
        </xn:resourceID>
      <xn:format>text/xml</xn:format>
      <xn:providerName>Dow Jones &amp; Company, Inc.
        </xn:providerName>
      <xn:providerCode>73</xn:providerCode>
      <xn:serviceName>Today's Business Sections via DowVision
        </xn:serviceName>
      <xn:serviceCode>97</xn:serviceCode>
      <xn:receivedTime>1999-03-30T00:01-05:00
        </xn:receivedTime>
      <xn:publicationTime>1999-03-30T00:01-05:00
        </xn:publicationTime>
      <xn:title>When the stock market plunged in October 1987
        </xn:title>
      <xn:subjectCode>DOW:N/LCL</xn:subjectCode>
      <xn:locationCode>DOW:R/US</xn:locationCode>
      <xn:copyright>Copyright 1999</xn:copyright>
   </rdf:Resource>
</rdf:RDF>
```

XMLNews-Meta is also extensible. By employing XML namespaces, users can add their own metadata and document associations.

23.2.3 *Business layer*

NewsPak has an e-commerce system that allows customers to acquire software, pay for continuing service, and purchase content from participating publishers without human intervention.

The Information and Content Exchange (ICE) protocol is employed to handle information subscriptions, user counts, usage logs, delivery schedules, updates, event logs, trouble reports, redistribution, re-syndication, and so on. The ICE protocol supports automatic negotiation of delivery schedules and requests to resend content.

©2000 THE XML HANDBOOK™

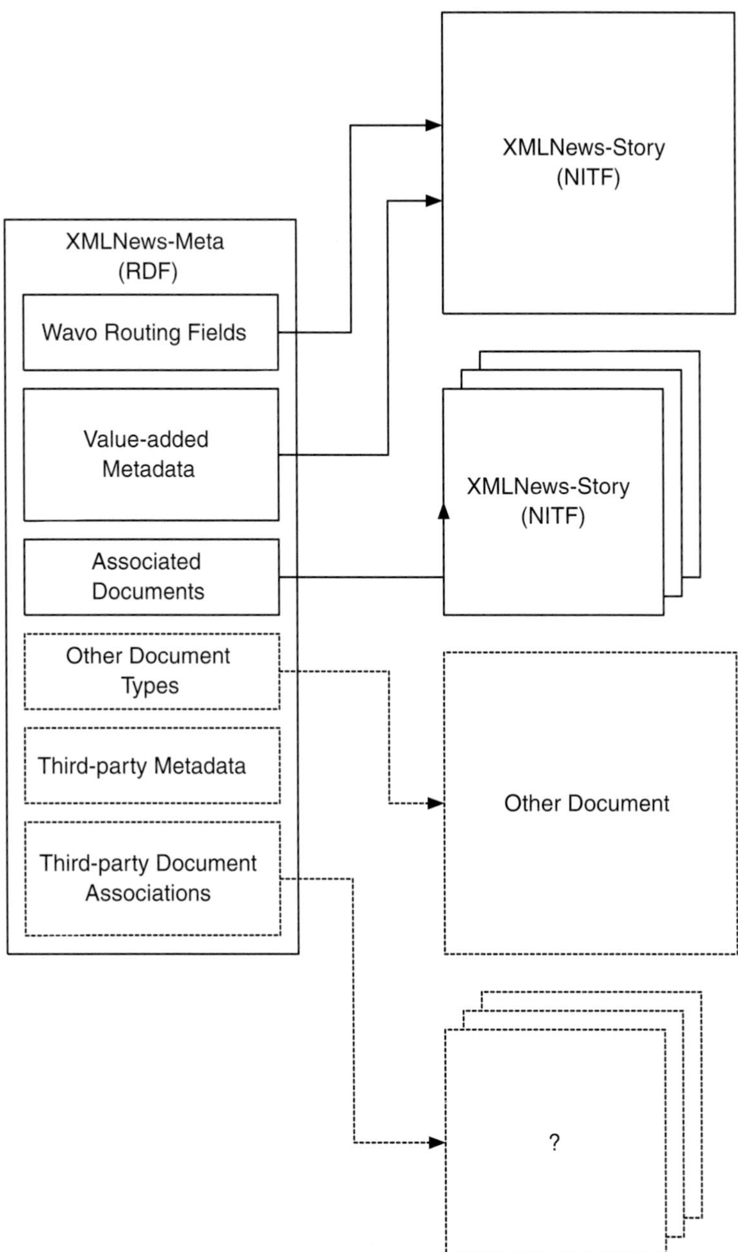

Figure 23-4 Relationship between *XMLNews-Meta* and *XMLNews-Story*

23.3 | Summary

Wavo's *NewsPak* service is an ambitious undertaking whose success depends on XML. XML is the organizing principle that brings a number of formerly separate technologies together into a cohesive system. All data, regardless of its provider, enjoys the benefit of standardized XML markup, consistent metadata associations, and rich contextual inline markup.

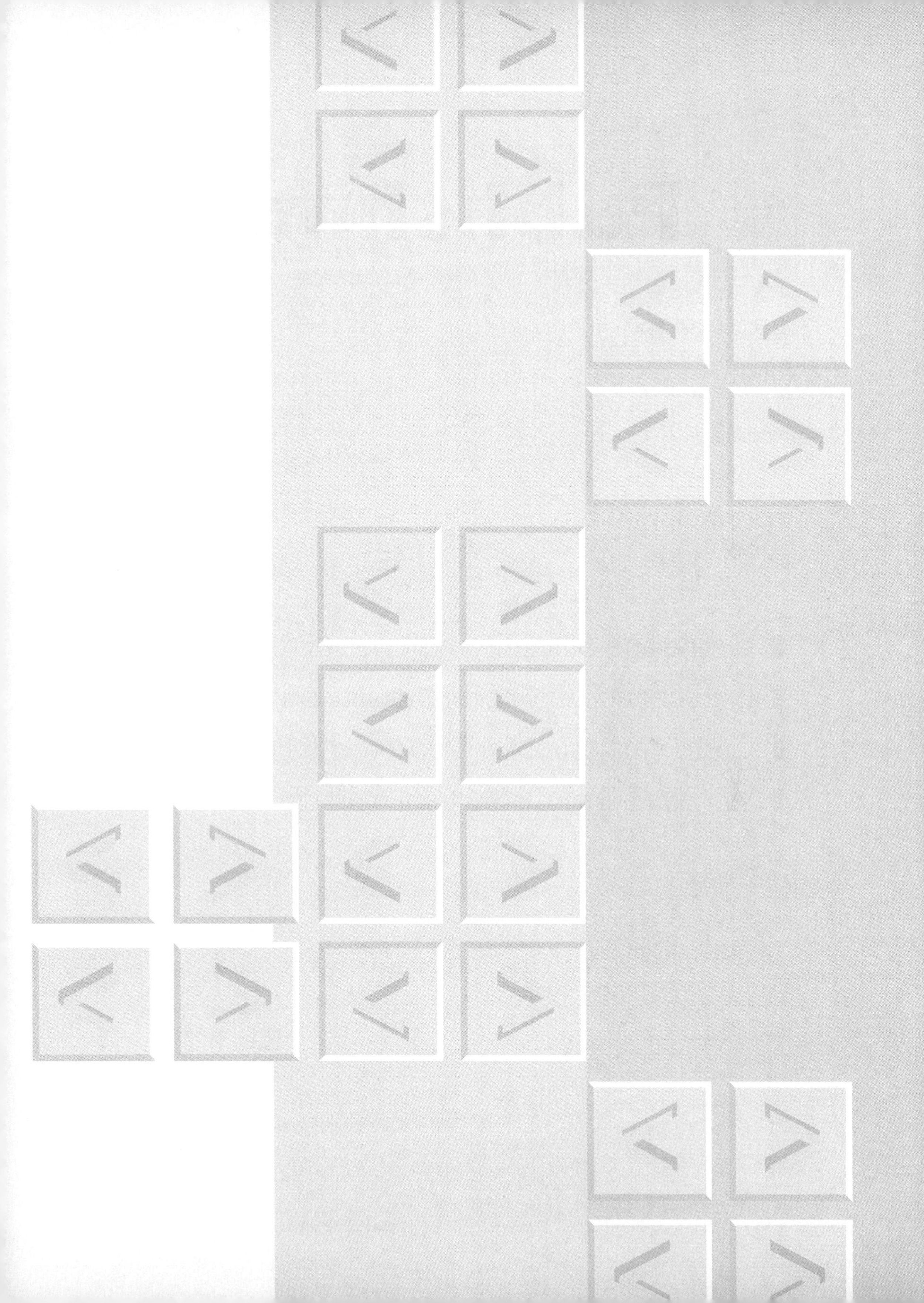

Publishing

- Online and offline from single source
- Extranet delivery of high-quality printing
- Customizing supplier's documentation
- WYSIWYG plus structural markup

©2000 THE XML HANDBOOK™

Part Five

Publish or perish!

For decades that has been the mandate for academics seeking an assured career path. Today it is the mandate for enterprises of all kinds that are hostage to documentation requirements. If the manuals, reports, and marketing materials aren't ready, it is the products and business opportunities that will perish – not the career of some assistant professor.

And publishing today doesn't necessarily mean just a uniform static message on the corpses of dead trees: It means websites, CD-ROMs, multimedia, personalized delivery, and – yes – paper as well.

In this part we'll see how several companies have used XML to meet the demands of this new publishing environment, on and off the Web, in industries as diverse as semiconductors, financial management, travel promotion, and computer magazine publishing. We'll also look at a problem of the information supply chain: How can you customize your supplier's documents safely and seamlessly? Finally, we'll examine an editing and composition tool that combines WYSIWYG with structural markup.

Hitachi Semiconductor

Case Study

- Semiconductor industry
- Product data sheets
- Automating transformations
- Web-based searching

©2000 THE XML HANDBOOK™

Chapter 24

Distributing the right document to the right customer at the right time presents a formidable challenge for a semiconductor manufacturer. This chapter is sponsored by Adobe Systems Incorporated, `http://www.adobe.com`, and was prepared by Lani Hajagos.

Hitachi Semiconductor (America), Inc. maintains nearly 1,000 data sheets comprising a total of 70,000 pages, and each must be made available to prospective customers, primarily design engineers, on the Web, CD-ROM, and on paper. The publishing function is mission-critical because the data sheets provide the chips' performance characteristics and interface specifications. Without them, Hitachi Semiconductor's customers cannot use the chip in their designs. Therefore, the chip cannot be released to market without the data sheet.

24.1 | Introduction

The company urgently needed a way to simplify version control and publish on all media from a single, manageable source file. "In the fast-paced semiconductor industry, we revise our documents an average of four times a year, so version control is challenging enough with 970 publications," says Bob Tabone, program manager for marketing communications. "With 970 times three versions-Web, CD-ROM, and paper-it would be nightmarish."

HM511664C Series

2. $\overline{CAS}$ = V_{IH} to disable Dout.

AC Characteristics (Ta = 0 to +70°C, V_{CC} = 5 V ±10%, V_{SS} = 0 V)*1, *14, *15, *17, *18

Test Conditions

- Input rise and fall time : 5 ns
- Input levels: V_{IL} = 0 V, V_{IH} = 3.0 V
- Input timing reference levels : 0.8 V, 2.4 V
- Output load : 1 TTL gate + C_L (50 pF) (Including scope and jig)

Read, Write, Read-Modify-Write and Refresh Cycles (Common parameters)

		HM511664C							
		-6		-7		-8			
Parameter	Symbol	Min	Max	Min	Max	Min	Max	Unit	Notes
Random read or write cycle time	t_{RC}	105	—	125	—	145	—	ns	
$\overline{RAS}$ precharge time	t_{RP}	40	—	50	—	60	—	ns	
$\overline{RAS}$ pulse width	t_{RAS}	60	10000	70	10000	80	10000	ns	23
$\overline{CAS}$ pulse width	t_{CAS}	15	10000	20	10000	20	10000	ns	22, 24
Row address setup time	t_{ASR}	0	—	0	—	0	—	ns	
Row address hold time	t_{RAH}	10	—	10	—	10	—	ns	
Column address setup time	t_{ASC}	0	—	0	—	0	—	ns	
Column address hold time	t_{CAH}	15	—	15	—	15	—	ns	
$\overline{RAS}$ to $\overline{CAS}$ delay time	t_{RCD}	20	45	20	50	20	60	ns	8
$\overline{RAS}$ to column address delay time	t_{RAD}	15	30	15	35	15	40	ns	9
$\overline{RAS}$ hold time	t_{RSH}	15	—	20	—	20	—	ns	
$\overline{CAS}$ hold time	t_{CSH}	60	—	70	—	80	—	ns	25
$\overline{CAS}$ to $\overline{RAS}$ precharge time	t_{CRP}	10	—	10	—	10	—	ns	
$\overline{OE}$ to Din delay time	t_{ODD}	15	—	15	—	15	—	ns	

Figure 24-1 Original process: Printed data sheet.

Hitachi Semiconductor solved its challenge using Adobe's *FrameMaker+SGML* software, an integrated SGML editing and publishing tool that shields the end user from the technicalities of SGML (see Chapter 29, "FrameMaker+ SGML: Editing+ composition", on page 382). In phase one of the solution, the company adopted the product to create a single source file for multiple output formats, including SGML, HTML, PDF, and RTF. In phase two, the company added XML.

24.2 | The business case

The company's product data sheets are created in Japan by 200 design engineers who use a word processing application that creates RTF files. The documents, ranging from 3 to 1,000 pages, are complex: typically 40 percent tables, 40 percent graphics, and 20 percent free text (see Figure 24-1). Structure is crucial for semiconductor documentation, so detailed stylesheets help the authors comply. The files reference external graphics in EPS format, created by *Adobe Illustrator*.

Publishing occurs at Hitachi Semiconductor's headquarters in Brisbane, California. The RTF and EPS files are checked into a document management system, which stores all the text and graphics files related to a publication as a single compound document.

The publishers convert the RTF files to SGML and the EPS files into GIF files. After this conversion, the company publishes its documents in hard copy and three electronic formats for the Web and CD-ROM: HTML for browsing, PDF for printing, and SGML for downloading – for example, for inclusion in the customer's design automation tool.

24.3 | Phase 1: Creating a single source file

The main drawback of the original process was that Hitachi Semiconductor could not render PDF files from the SGML source, and had to render them from the RTF file instead. "Without a single source file, we could not have a high confidence level that we were producing PDF files from the same version as the SGML file," says Tabone. "That was unacceptable from a quality standpoint."

In addition, the company had to manually add bookmarks and links to the PDF files that were created from RTF, a process that required an average of five hours per document. At 40 documents per month, this meant the company spent 200 person-hours recreating information that already

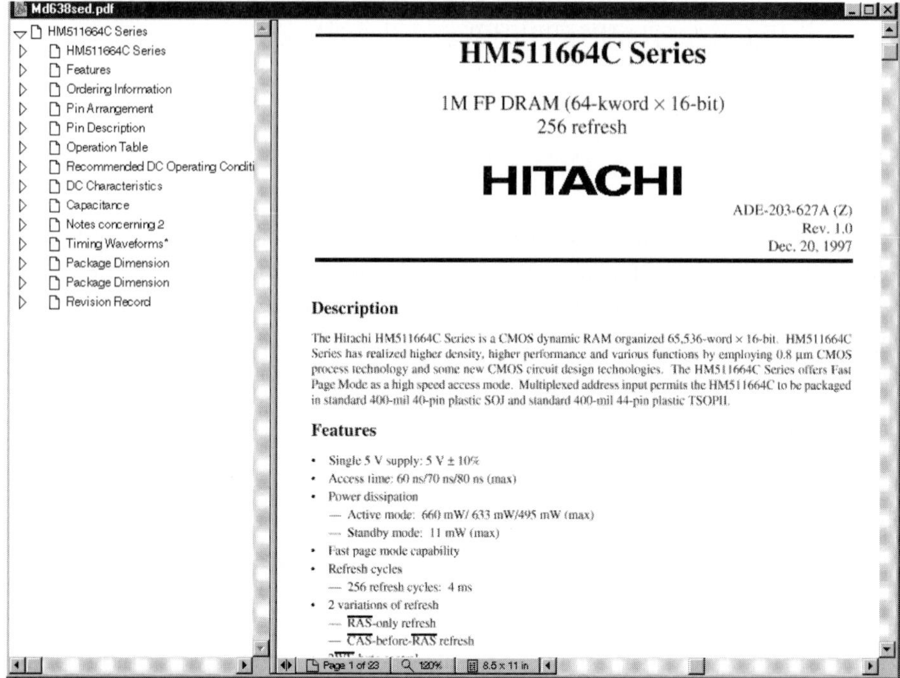

Figure 24-2 Revised process: PDF rendition of a data sheet displayed in *Adobe Acrobat.*

existed in another format. Long publishing lead times left the company with out-of-date documents: approximately 30 percent of published pieces became obsolete while on the company's shelves.

When Hitachi Semiconductor adopted the use of Adobe *FrameMaker+SGML* software in late 1996, the company became able to maintain a single source file and to shorten lead times. The product has since become one of the most important tools in Hitachi Semiconductor's publishing suite.

Hitachi Semiconductor can now produce PDF files from the SGML source, simply by choosing the "Save As PDF" command (see Figure 24-2). By saving the hyperlinks from the SGML file and automatically creating bookmarks, *FrameMaker+SGML* eliminates a labor-intensive process. Hitachi Semiconductor is able to provide print vendors with production-ready files because *FrameMaker+SGML* handles composition and pagination of the data sheets and automatically generates indexes and tables of contents.

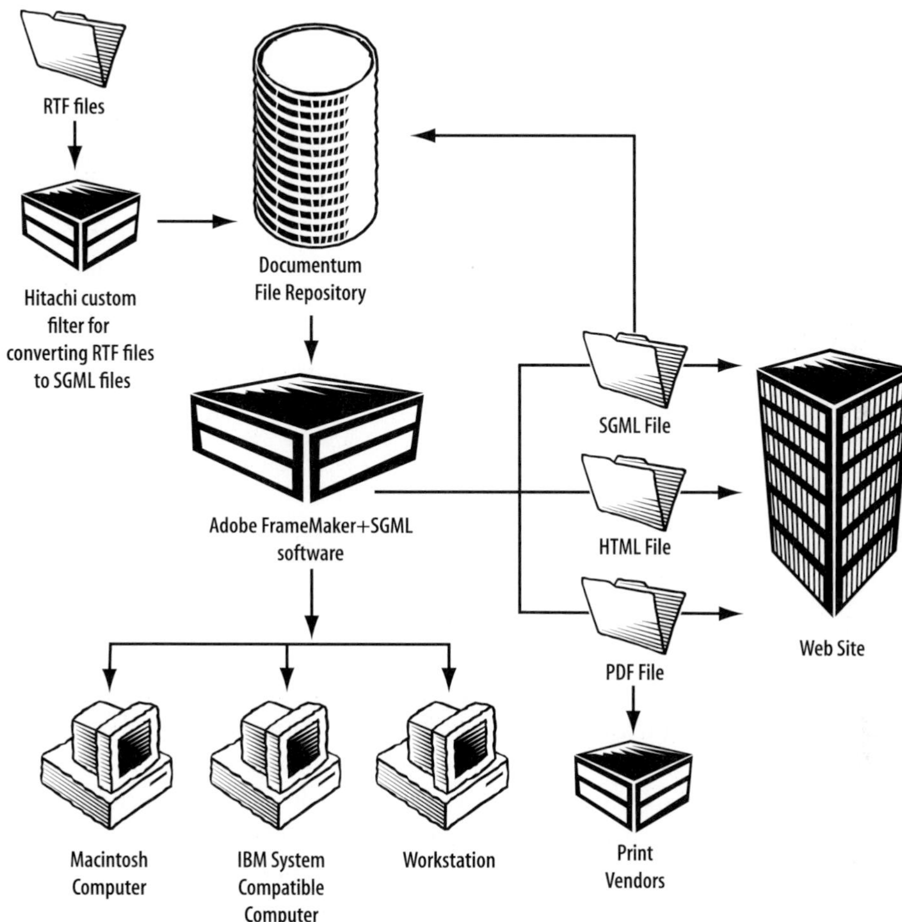

Figure 24-3 RTF/SGML workflow employed by Hitachi Semiconductor.

Hitachi Semiconductor wrote a Perl script to automate the check-in process into the document management system. The script validates the SGML files, notifying their creators if any errors are present, and converts EPS files to GIF files. This automated process gives the company confidence it is using the correct source file and also dramatically reduces the time required for editing, proofing, and publishing (see Figure 24-3).

24.4 | Phase 2: Automating transformations with XML

While *FrameMaker+SGML* solved the initial challenge – creating a single source file for multiple delivery mechanisms – SGML still imposed certain limitations for Hitachi. Its wide range of options and specialized features were overkill for the Web environment.

"In addition", says Tabone, "no Web tools are available to allow customers to take advantage of an SGML document's rich data format. For example, there is nothing today that will enable our customers to search our document set for all chips with performance in a certain range." The answer to these problems came in the form of XML.

"XML provides the structure of SGML without its complexity," says Tabone. An added benefit for the company, whose authors are in Japan, is that XML accepts only integrated double-byte character support.

24.5 | "Publishing on steroids"

When the eXtensible Style Language (XSL) specification (see Chapter 60, "Extensible Stylesheet Language (XSL)", on page 872) is complete, Hitachi Semiconductor will use it to automate data transformations – for example, specifying the location and appearance of an element of type "author."

"XSL will enable us to specify the production process as well as the content – in the same markup language," says Tabone. "We'll acquire a sure, solid methodology for automating the processes throughout the production environment, from input to delivery. No longer will we need special filters and dedicated people to run the transformations. It's publishing on steroids". (See Figure 24-4.)

Adobe recently added the capability to save *FrameMaker+SGML* files as XML. Prior to this availability, Hitachi set up a process, using commercially-available parsers, to adapt its SGML documents for use with XML. Around 80 percent of the parsing happened without any manual intervention, so Hitachi completed the adaptation process in about four months.

File Production Exchange System With XML

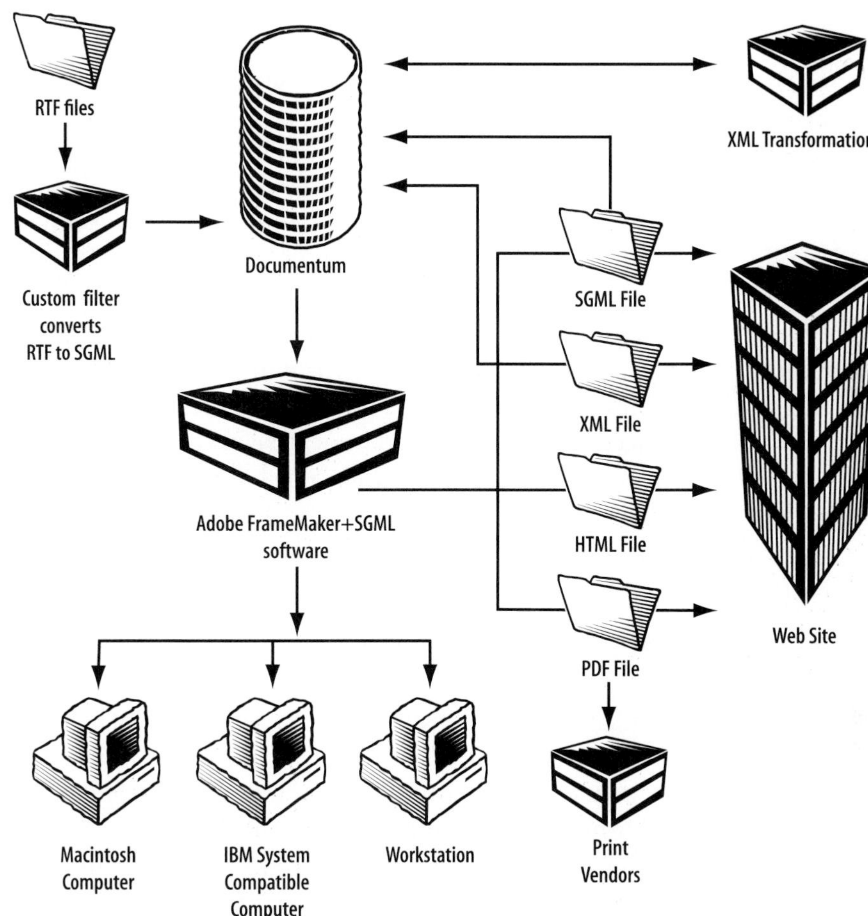

Figure 24-4 Workflow incorporating XML.

24.6 | Facilitation of Web-based searching

XML not only improves the production process, it also benefits Web site visitors by enabling them to search for products by type and significant characteristics. Hitachi Semiconductor tags the searchable characteristics during the RTF-to-SGML conversion process. The tags are retained when the file is exported as XML. As soon as developers introduce the appropriate tools, Hitachi Semiconductor plans to add the tags automatically to an index data file, and customers will be able to perform queries and searches against the index file.

By publishing XML documents on the Web, Hitachi Semiconductor will combine the accessibility of HTML with much of the richness of SGML. Customers who previously downloaded SGML will be able to download the XML instead. Those who need styles will be able to separately download the XSL stylesheet. Customers who do not have XML-enabled browsers will be able to view HTML, which a Web-based application will create from XML on the fly.

24.7 | Quantifiable savings

When Hitachi Semiconductor began using *FrameMaker+SGML* and gained the ability to create PDF files directly from the SGML source documents, the company reduced print costs 40 percent. It also reduced its print cycle 66 percent – from three months to one month. "With shrinking product design cycles, faster time-to-market is not just a nice benefit for our customers, it's a business imperative," says Tabone. Customers download an average of 19,000 product data sheets as PDF files each month, saving the company $19,000 in postage costs.

Tabone found that XML augmented those gains. He calculates that XML reduced printing costs another 15 percent, and shaved another two weeks from lead time for a 50 percent gain.

Hitachi Semiconductor also benefits from the ability to create all its deliverables – paper, PDF, and XML – from a single source. That is, the company can manage a larger volume of information more reliably and accurately. The publication process is more automated, freeing employees with high-level publishing skills to apply their talents to other projects.

24.8 | Conclusion: A new dimension of automation

Tabone views XML as an important publishing technology for the next decade. "Three things will matter in the 21st century: information, information, and information. If you can't deliver information on time, correctly, reliably, and in the format the customer wants, you're out of business. By providing structure and rich information about the document, XML lets companies better serve their consumers' information requirements."

The use of XML also positions Hitachi Semiconductor to meet anticipated recommendations from the Electronic Component Information Exchange (ECIX) Project, an association of eight leading semiconductor manufacturers, including Hitachi Semiconductor, seeking to standardize the way semiconductor product information is presented to consumers.

©2000 The XML Handbook™

Frank Russell Company

Case Study

- Extranet XML financial publishing
- Business and technical requirements identification
- Structure-driven style

©2000 THE XML HANDBOOK™

Chapter 25

This chapter is the chronicle of an extraordinary project: demanding requirements, ambitious goals, leading-edge technology, business school management techniques, and – did we mention "mission-critical"? – a trillion dollars riding on the outcome. And XML figures in it as well. The chapter is sponsored by Frank Russell Company Advanced Technology Labs, `http://www.russell.com`, and was prepared by Bryan Bell and Randy Kelley.

As a leading investment management and asset consulting firm, Frank Russell Company improves the financial security of people throughout the world. Russell provides investment solutions for institutions and individuals, guiding the investment of more than $1 trillion for clients in more than 25 countries.

25.1 | Background

During the eighties, Russell pioneered the use of color presentations and "high touch" relationship management with its group of clients. Recently, Russell has experienced explosive growth in the investment management division, marketing private mutual fund products to the institutional marketplace, and retail funds through a group of selected distribution partners.

Immediately you can visualize the tension between high quality/high touch and explosive growth. There needed to be a strategy to address the increasing production volume demands without sacrificing quality or profit margins. This led to a requirement for automation.

Russell traditionally viewed its printed client books as products. This project was the first to begin to stress that the importance of the book is really Russell's content, and that the book itself is merely a rendition.

Russell had been using the "print, then distribute" metaphor for decades. But as the newer digital technologies and communication processes were taking hold, and the World Wide Web's popularity became undeniable, the Russell Advanced Technology Lab began an effort to evangelize, design, produce and deliver a new metaphor: "distribute, then print".

Along with this shift in metaphors come real quality control issues, especially revolving around color printing. Not only were the traditional problems of re-purposing content for different media (i.e. for paper, CD-ROM, electronic, FAX, and email) an issue, but also an entirely new set of workflow and editing issues was recognized with respect to the re-use of component objects from within the created documents.

Also, the trend to customizing the content product – moving from generic content to a specialized product for an individual information consumer, a "market of one" – was extremely interesting to Russell.

This chapter chronicles both the team's journey and the Russell solution that is currently in production.

25.2 | Project strategy considerations

Russell has steadily been increasing its own awareness that it truly is a large publishing concern, producing millions of pages of color and black and white output for its clients every year. And as a major financial intellectual property publisher, it is also realizing that printing and electronic delivery systems play a very strategic role in its continued growth and success.

There were five principle strategic considerations for the conduct of the project:

- Proceeding from a theoretical abstraction to practical applications.
- Phasing deliverables with measurable return on investment.
- Continuing research in parallel with focused development projects.
- Alignment with overall corporate strategies.
- Executive sponsorship.

25.2.1 *Proceeding from a theoretical abstraction to practical applications*

The project team, though capable of grasping both the short- and long-term objectives for the enterprise, required a methodology to manage scope creep. It chose to divide the tasks into two clear groups:

- the theoretical research and related effort towards general solutions; and
- day-to-day development.

The team was always able to have discussions from the abstract down to the practical by mapping them onto the architecture and life cycle models. When new technologies or vendor products came onto the radar, it was able to discuss them in the context of both the theory and practical project impact using a systematic method.

25.2.2 *Phasing deliverables with measurable return on investment*

This concept may sound similar to the concept of milestones, but is really quite different. This method assumes that there is *no* other project beyond the goals of this one.

It also assumes that this project must justify its own return on investment and bear management review based on its own merits.

Another key element is the openness of each phase's architecture, so that later phases can be bolted on seamlessly with very little trauma to users or developers.

25.2.3 *Continuing research in parallel with focused development projects*

Scope creep is an ever-present danger in technology. Change is a constant. Managing new inputs from press, rumors, research, and outside influence is a constant pressure on fixed milestones and deliverables.

©2000 THE XML HANDBOOK™

The project team chose discretion as the better part of valor by separating the tasks of research and development into two distinct activities. The development tasks have clearly documented milestones, schedules, and budgets, with methodology in place to monitor their success weekly.

The research tasks are managed more loosely, with overall topics of interest. They use annual funding, rather than project-based funding, and measure deliverables by the published output from the team.

The team believes that this separation keeps developers on the hook for cleaner deliverables and return on investment, while still allowing a response to the crucial happenings that are a day-to-day part of the technology world.

25.2.4 *Alignment with overall corporate strategies*

Any technology project can be fraught with risk. Any technology project can solve a specific technical application and add value if properly executed. Russell's experience was that the real grand slam winner projects are the ones that support the overall mission, culture, vision, and business objectives of an enterprise.

In theory every part of an enterprise is supposed to be working on things that contribute to the goals of the entire enterprise. Straying too far from this principle increases risk and confuses observers, whereas following this principle makes a project's justification much easier to defend and publicize.

25.2.5 *Executive sponsorship.*

For several reasons, this is the most powerful thing you can do to enhance a project's chance for success:

- Executives are generally seasoned professionals who have earned a place of authority by knowing how to exploit strengths and manage around weaknesses.
- Executives are generally the best funded portion of an enterprise.

- Executives generally have a clear understanding of the long-term objectives of the enterprise.
- Executives generally have a feeling for the short-term pressures on operations.

These executive qualities enhance a group's ability to make sure their work is done with the support and point-of-view of the senior management and shareholders.

25.3 | Identifying the needs

Russell began to realize the extremely high importance of publishing to the company when it found out the cost. A study determined that almost 1/3 of every expense dollar worldwide was attributable to documents and their production, printing and distribution.

25.3.1 *Business requirements*

The question then became: "How to distribute financial services publications better to a geographically diverse audience, while maintaining premium typographical quality, data integrity, security and compliance?"

Compliance
Russell operates in a heavily regulated environment. There is a legal requirement to reproduce documents related to a customer from many years in the past.

Premium typographic quality
Russell customers typically evaluate large amounts of financial information in a limited time. Russell adds tremendous value for their customers by simplifying and clarifying these numbers through the use of text, graphics, charts, and color.

Data integrity
It is extremely important that the document received by a customer is identical to the one that was sent to it.

©2000 The XML Handbook™

Security
Because of the confidential nature of financial information, it is imperative that only the appropriate people can view these files.

25.3.2 *Technical requirements*

There were significant technical requirements to be met in addition to the business requirements.

Scalability
At Russell, a *Quarterly Investment Review* (QIR) runs from 20-125 pages, averaging around 50 pages. There are hundreds of clients who each get a customized QIR each quarter. Multiple writing, editing, assembly, and compliance steps are required throughout the process.

Low licensing impact for reader software
The problem with end-user licensing of software is that it penalizes a business for the success of a document.

Ease of use
To us, the lab team, ease of use is the single most important factor in the true success of a product.

Cross-platform
Russell cannot control the platforms that its customers use. It has to provide its information in an easily accessible form on virtually every platform available.

Multilingual capability
Russell has offices in London, New York, Winston-Salem, Paris, Hong Kong, Toronto, Tokyo, Sydney, and Auckland. Russell has clients in 25 countries.

25.4 | Create an abstract architecture

Russell's Advanced Technology Lab team set off to learn about the state of the art in publishing systems, SGML, PDF, and document delivery systems.

Russell had been a pioneer of Postscript assembly and color graphics in the financial services industry. Now the Lab team desired to modernize Russell's publication capabilities to support lower than page granularity and the "distribute then print" metaphor. The team felt that this type of system could meet Russell's business objectives.

The team, working with consultants, created a "Request For Information and Statement of Direction" for a system to purchase (Figure 25-1).

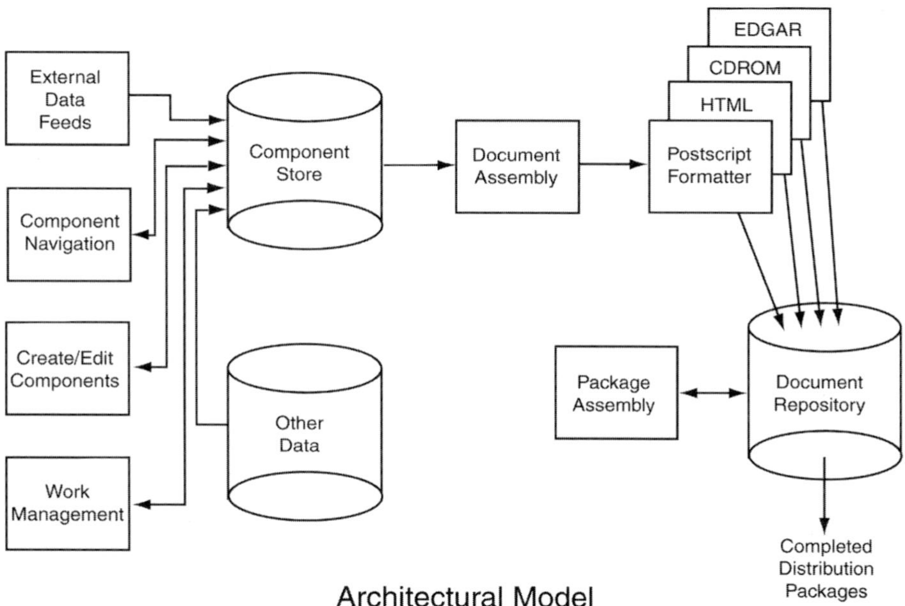

Figure 25-1 Architectural model of desired system.

The team also performed research on document life cycles and included the life cycle requirements shown in Figure 25-2.

Russell searched the SGML community for a publishing solution to meet its requirements and found no single commercial product in the marketplace. It then asked the big question: "Why isn't there one already"? The

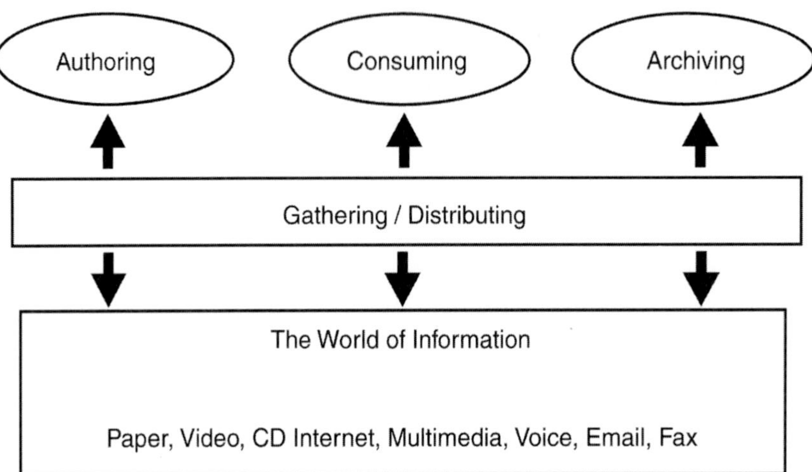

Figure 25-2 Document life cycle requirements.

team felt that there were many companies and institutions with document problems similar to, if not more complex than, Russell's.

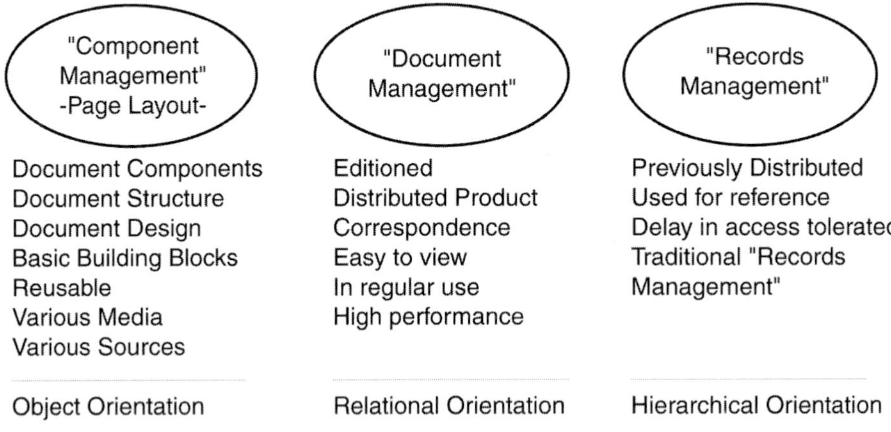

Figure 25-3 Document system orientations.

So the team spent several more months analyzing vendor capabilities and mapping them onto the life cycle graphic until it finally found what it felt was a possible reason. Namely, that the creating, consuming, and archiving stages of a document's life require different system capabilities and orientations: component management, document management, and records management, respectively (Figure 25-3).

Armed with this insight, the team developed the knowledge management model shown in Figure 25-4.

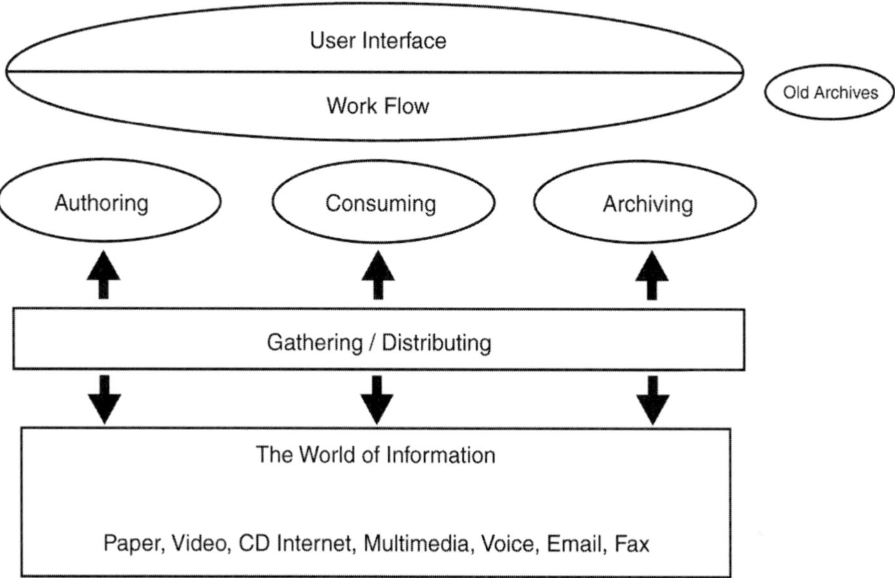

Figure 25-4 Knowledge Management Model

Russell's management and the Lab team then decided to build and integrate a solution out of *commercially available off-the-shelf* (*COTS*) products. The team decided to break the deliverables into different phases that would be integrated upon completion.

25.5 | Implement applications

The team's initial choice for an application was the *Quarterly Investment Review*. The QIR is representative of many of Russell's publications because it consists of a combination of generic, proprietary, customer-specific, and reusable components.

©2000 The XML Handbook™

25.5.1 *Real-world design issues*

In order to apply the theoretical architecture to specific application designs for the QIR publications, the team had to come to grips with real-world issues of internetworking and document representation (file format) standards, to name a few.

25.5.1.1 Internetworking

The WWW family of technologies was chosen for its popularity. Its open-standard nature met the team's basic technical requirements for global electronic delivery, easy access, cheap per-seat licensing costs, cross-platform availability, and security.

The extranet model best served Russell's clients in this application. That is, WWW technologies connected, via public and/or private networks, to a restricted website.

25.5.1.2 Document representation

The Russell team is very firmly attached to the notion that document representation is the key to an organization's success with knowledge management. In the *SGML Buyers Guide* (1998), the authors clearly express this point: *"Don't let the software you buy determine the representation. Let the representation you need determine the software you buy".*

In Russell's case, they needed to choose document representations for all three stages of the document life cycle.

During the creation stage, documents are most useful in an abstract unrendered representation, in which the data can easily be reused and reprocessed. During the consumption and archiving stages, however, the document must be in a rendered form so that it can be presented and displayed quickly and consistently.

25.5.1.2.1 Abstract document representation

At the time the work began, SGML was the only document representation that preserved the abstract data and had the "industrial strength" for Russell's requirements. So Russell used it.

XML, as a streamlined subset of SGML, is by definition, not as feature-rich. However, like its parent it preserves the abstraction, and it seems to be more than adequate for Russell's purposes. XML's capabilities, along with its new-found popularity, promise to bring great momentum to the entire document industry.

25.5.1.2.2 Rendered document representation

Portable Document Format (PDF) was chosen for the rendered document representation. The archiving requirement, that it must be readable for a minimum of ten years time, was the dominant deciding criterion.

Large document collections have been faced with this need for some time; for example, those of the Library of Congress and Department of Defense in the U.S. At Russell and many other enterprises, the final formatted image of a document must be retrievable to meet business needs for compliance and reference. Russell's strong desire to use electronic documents to meet its goals was dependent upon a satisfactory decision in this single topic.

Russell first considered using SGML to meet its archiving requirements. It has successfully been used for simple partial renditions (e.g., HTML), but fully rendered final-form and graphics are outside its design objectives. Although it is undeniably the best representation for long-term preservation of text, that is not what Russell meant by archiving. To be compliant, from Russell's archive it must be possible to retrieve exactly what the client printed originally.

Russell made the choice to use PDF because it met the rendered image requirement for both text and graphics, was widely used across many platforms, had a publicly specified format, and supported a large set of the world's languages. It was also attracted to PDF's usability for email distribution and on-screen display.

PDF supports full text search, linking, and page by page loading. It has a development kit available, a compressed file size, interactive forms, cheap seats, and also prints extremely well.

©2000 The XML Handbook™

25.5.2 *Phased implementation plan*

The work involved some parallel processing, with secondary teams doing research and advanced studies on upcoming phases. The implementation teams, however, focused on the deliverables.

One team was assigned to create archiving requirements for the corporation. Another team worked on object databases and SGML abstractions.

A third team worked on graphical design. Its goal was to constrain the number of presentation layouts in order to optimize for batch processing. Finally, a fourth team had the task of tracking and understanding key standards like SGML, XML, Hytime, and various related W3C activities.

25.5.2.1 Phase I: Records management business study

The technical work on this phase was deferred. The main candidate for an archiving product was in the middle of an acquisition, which created an unacceptable business risk.

However, Russell did conduct a two-year study on document archiving requirements for its Investment Management Business. Once the business case for records management was made, Russell hired a full-time professional archivist to champion the deployment of the technology.

25.5.2.2 Phase II: Document management of PDF files

Russell's corporate Information Technology department had previously deployed a document management system. The project team used it in the interests of corporate harmony, and worked with its vendor's R&D department on the beta version of an application to make documents available over the Web.

This product allows you to build a query on a Web-based form (Figure 25-5), which can be tailored to meet application requirements.

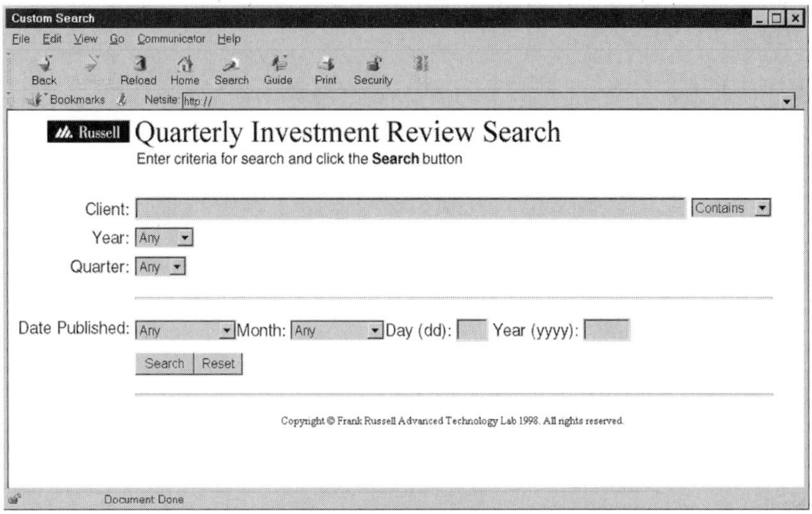

Figure 25-5 Document management search screen.

The query results are delivered as an HTML frame (Figure 25-6), the form of which can also be customized. Russell's users found that it made the interface to the product's library services, particularly document check-out, much more appealing than it had been.

25.5.2.3 Phase III: Document assembly and formatting

The objective of this phase was to create structured documents in SGML that could be auto-assembled, and to implement auto-check-in to the document management system.

As the assembly and formatting phase of the project began, the team focused on the issues of: How much structure is needed?, What are the quality levels required for the publication in its final form? What should the user interface experience be like for editing sections, book assembly and releasing books to the document management system?

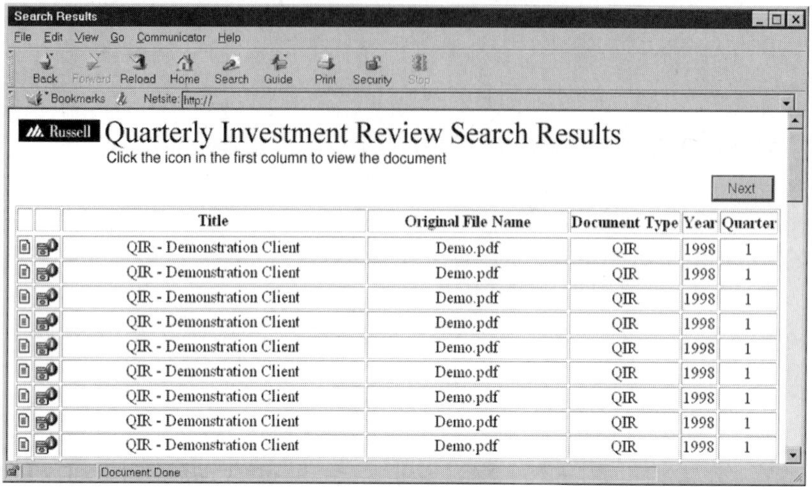

Figure 25-6 Document management search results.

Russell decided to purchase a product that supported integrated structured editing, layout, and typographic control.

The users for this phase are a small group of document editors who compile and author the QIR documents for clients at Russell. Their typical quarterly work cycle involves revising the previous quarter's document files, graphics, and tables, and launching a new composite book for each client. New document pages are created approximately 10% of the time.

The users are trained in popular word processors, spreadsheet, and graphics packages, but have no experience in SGML. They are accustomed to setting the indents, font style, size of a page, and common typography settings. They are often under the spotlight to make a production deadline in hours and therefore must be able to make edits quickly with minimal amount of new steps. They are only interested in software that makes their life easier.

The team quickly found that the system must make the SGML transparent to the user, that the layout must be WYSIWYG, and that the application should assist in the creation of a consistent layout throughout the book.

25.5.2.3.3 How structure was used

The approach taken was to replace the use of paragraph style codes with meaningful SGML element-type names. The document was then formatted in real time, based on the element types, thereby giving the users their customary WYSIWYG effect.

A welcome side-effect was that the list of element-type choices was much smaller than the full list of paragraph styles typically presented by a WYSIWYG editor, because of the context enforced by the DTD. In addition, the product has a guided creation feature, which automatically inserts required elements. It allowed us to lay out a typical page easily, and still allowed deviations by making choices permitted by the DTD.

One area of improvement to the overall professionalism of the book was in the consistency of format and layout. In the old system, each page was laid out individually and it often deviated slightly as editing continued over several quarters of revisions.

The new system, however, used a series of matched templates created by a professional typographer, and it used structure to drive the formatting of the text. The resultant books were consistent, and compliant with corporate guidelines. This achievement was a significant win since "document police" (people trying to enforce style quality control issues from a corporate perspective) are not often welcome.

25.5.2.3.4 Document editing

With all of these facilities available, the team found that it needed to simplify the application menus. Doing so would limit access to designer pallets and provide users with a simpler interface to this complex and powerful tool.

Simplifying was done by using the application's custom user interface feature. It required no programming, although some developer expertise is required.

Training the users on the new system consisted of five sessions of one day in length, including hands on lab sessions. The editing tool took 50% of the training time, with the remaining time being spread on a general introduction, graphics, book building, and lab sessions. The users quickly grasped the system's capabilities and found it to be a huge improvement over the previous system.

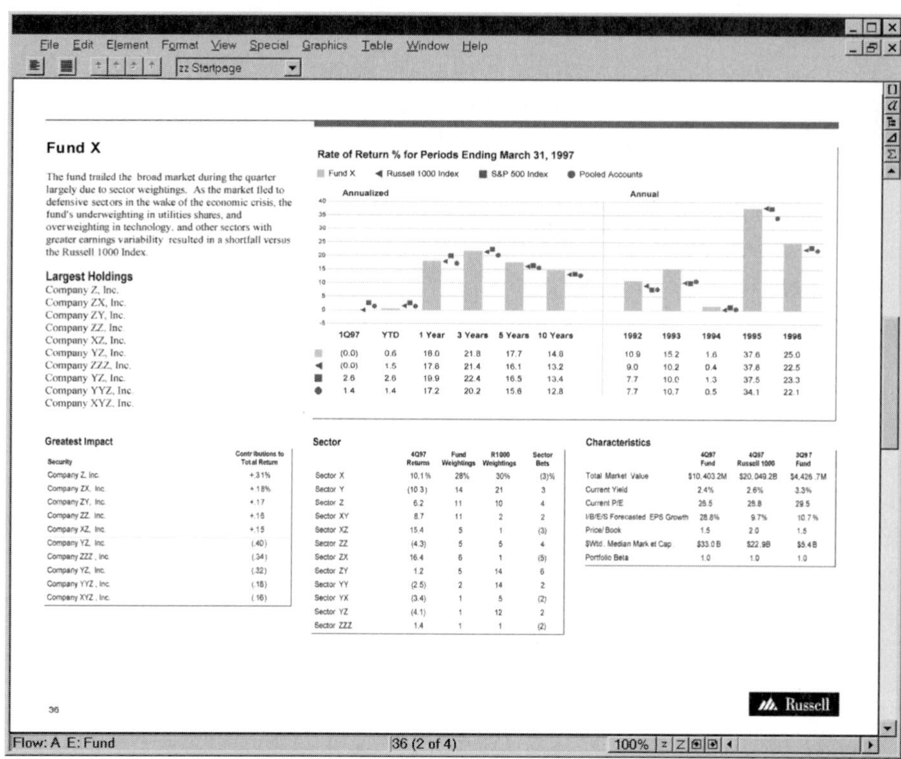

Fund X

The fund trailed the broad market during the quarter largely due to sector weightings. As the market fled to defensive sectors in the wake of the economic crisis, the fund's underweighting in utilities shares, and overweighting in technology, and other sectors with greater earnings variability resulted in a shortfall versus the Russell 1000 Index.

Largest Holdings

Company Z, Inc.
Company ZX, Inc.
Company ZY, Inc.
Company ZZ, Inc
Company XZ, Inc.
Company YZ, Inc.
Company ZZZ, Inc.
Company YZ, Inc.
Company YYZ, Inc.
Company XYZ, Inc.

Rate of Return % for Periods Ending March 31, 1997

Fund X · Russell 1000 Index · S&P 500 Index · Pooled Accounts

	Annualized						Annual				
	1Q97	YTD	1 Year	3 Years	5 Years	10 Years	1992	1993	1994	1995	1996
Fund X	(0.0)	0.6	18.0	21.8	17.7	14.8	10.9	15.2	1.6	37.6	25.0
Russell 1000 Index	(0.0)	1.5	17.8	21.4	16.1	13.2	9.0	10.2	0.4	37.8	22.5
S&P 500 Index	2.6	2.6	19.9	22.4	16.5	13.4	7.7	10.0	1.3	37.5	23.3
Pooled Accounts	1.4	1.4	17.2	20.2	15.6	12.8	7.7	10.7	0.5	34.1	22.1

Greatest Impact

Security	Contributions to Total Return
Company Z, Inc.	+.31%
Company ZX, Inc	+.18%
Company ZY, Inc	+.17
Company ZZ, Inc	+.16
Company XZ, Inc	+.15
Company YZ, Inc	(.40)
Company ZZZ, Inc	(.34)
Company YZ, Inc	(.32)
Company YYZ, Inc	(.18)
Company XYZ, Inc	(.16)

Sector

	4Q97 Returns	Fund Weightings	R1000 Weightings	Sector Bets
Sector X	10.1%	28%	30%	(3)%
Sector Y	(10.3)	14	21	3
Sector Z	6.2	11	10	4
Sector XY	8.7	11	2	2
Sector XZ	15.4	5	1	(3)
Sector ZZ	(4.3)	5	5	4
Sector ZX	16.4	6	1	(5)
Sector ZY	1.2	5	14	6
Sector YY	(2.5)	2	14	2
Sector YX	(3.4)	1	5	(2)
Sector YZ	(4.1)	1	12	2
Sector ZZZ	1.4	1	1	(2)

Characteristics

	4Q97 Fund	4Q97 Russell 1000	3Q97 Fund
Total Market Value	$10,403.2M	$20,049.2B	$4,426.7M
Current Yield	2.4%	2.6%	3.3%
Current P/E	26.5	28.8	29.5
I/B/E/S Forecasted EPS Growth	28.8%	9.7%	10.7%
Price/Book	1.5	2.0	1.5
$Wtd. Median Market Cap	$33.0B	$22.9B	$5.4B
Portfolio Beta	1.0	1.0	1.0

36

Russell

Figure 25-7 Fund page example in editing system.

25.5.2.3.5 How much structure is needed?

Once Russell made the decision to use a structured representation of its publications, the challenge became to decide how much structure was appropriate and for what reasons. The team approached this from two viewpoints: long-term and short-term.

The long-term objectives of using structure were to add value to the intellectual property and aid with repurposing, navigation, automation and archiving.

The short-term goals were to enforce consistency in the typography, assure better quality control, and facilitate the aggregation of disparate content sources into single publications with a high degree of automation. Other short-term goals were to facilitate document assembly with automation, and to improve the user's experience.

25.5.2.3.6 Final-form quality requirements

Russell's output quality requirements are extremely high (Figure 25-7). When it looked at the commercially available database-driven publishing systems and dynamic Web page assemblers, none were capable of presenting publications as well as Russell's legacy systems. Also, although the Web publishing systems were great for producing pages from the current state of the database, they were not capable of satisfying Russell's compliance requirements.

25.5.2.3.7 Book assembly

The team wanted to make the user experience during book building as straightforward as possible by presenting only immediately relevant information. It built a simple windowing scheme, based on a customer database, that presented the bookbuilding experience on two screens (Figure 25-8 and Figure 25-9).

Along with the customer name and the component bill of materials list selections, the book building interface also gathers the metadata required for check-in to the document management system and stores it for later use. This may seem trivial, but it completely removes the user pain from the document management check-in process.

25.5.2.3.8 Releasing books to the document management system

Final preparation of a book for review and release is invoked by a single custom menu item, `Publish`, on the *File* menu. The `Publish` command creates a PostScript file of the book, which is then distilled into a PDF file (Figure 25-10). During this process, the PDF file is updated with the document management system check-in metadata that was gathered during the book building.

The `Publish` command eliminates a large number of print and configuration item choices for the user and controls the way PDF files are created. This plug-in also automatically generates bookmark hyperlinks for the PDF table of contents from the SGML structural element hierarchy.

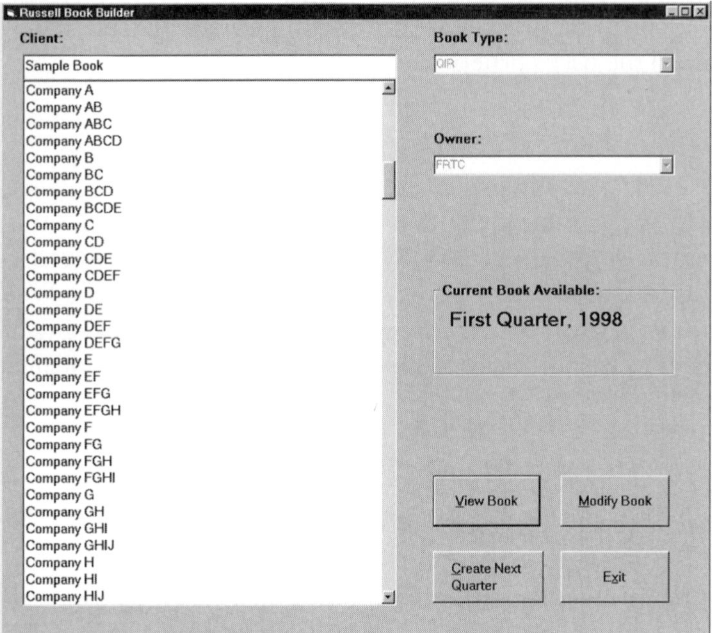

Figure 25-8 Russell BookBuilder (1 of 2)

25.5.2.4 Phase IV: XML and the future

In 1995 Russell began a pure research project into the notion of "Knowledge Management Systems". These are automated systems that would be the next logical extension for publishing, collaborative creation, and electronic delivery.

Russell believes that XML systems are the beginning of an entirely new age of documents. In the same way that ASCII allowed people to interchange bits in the past, adoption of XML as the data representation will allow people to exchange "bits with meaning" in the future.

That was the original promise of SGML, but Russell feels the SGML community, for whatever reasons, fell short on realizing that promise to its fullest commercial degree. Russell's view is that XML is SGML done right for the masses, which still leaves SGML there for those for whom XML falls short.

Russell believes the marriage of XML, databases, WWW, EDI, and publishing technologies is going to be the cornerstone of extremely significant

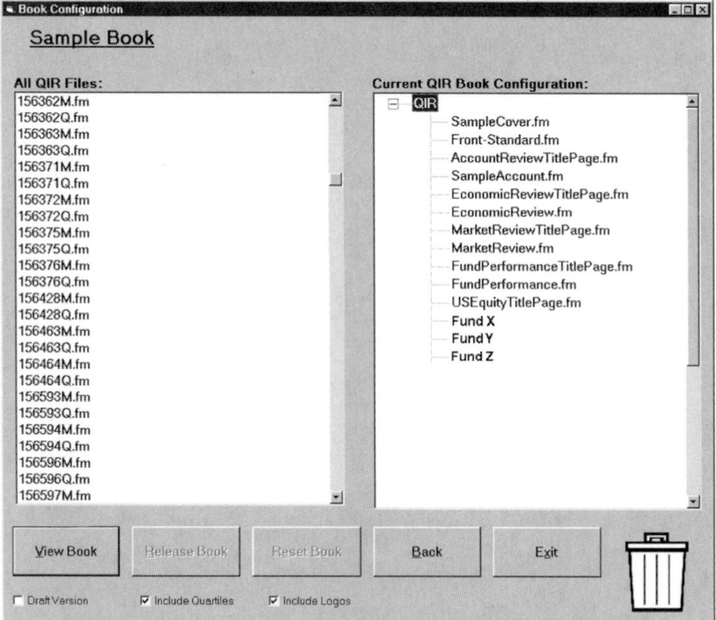

Figure 25-9 Russell BookBuilder (2 of 2)

developments over the next decade. Areas most likely to be affected will include content aggregation, simplified database connectivity, document distribution, and electronic commerce.

Russell also feels there is great danger in "almost open" or "almost standard" representations and technologies. The power and future of information technologies is determined by the degree of vendor and platform independence that they offer for the long term.

For the long term – not one version or two versions, but years and decades later. At Russell, they never lose sight of that goal. It is the company's information, stored in an open representation, that Russell expects to bring it true value in the future.

©2000 The XML Handbook™

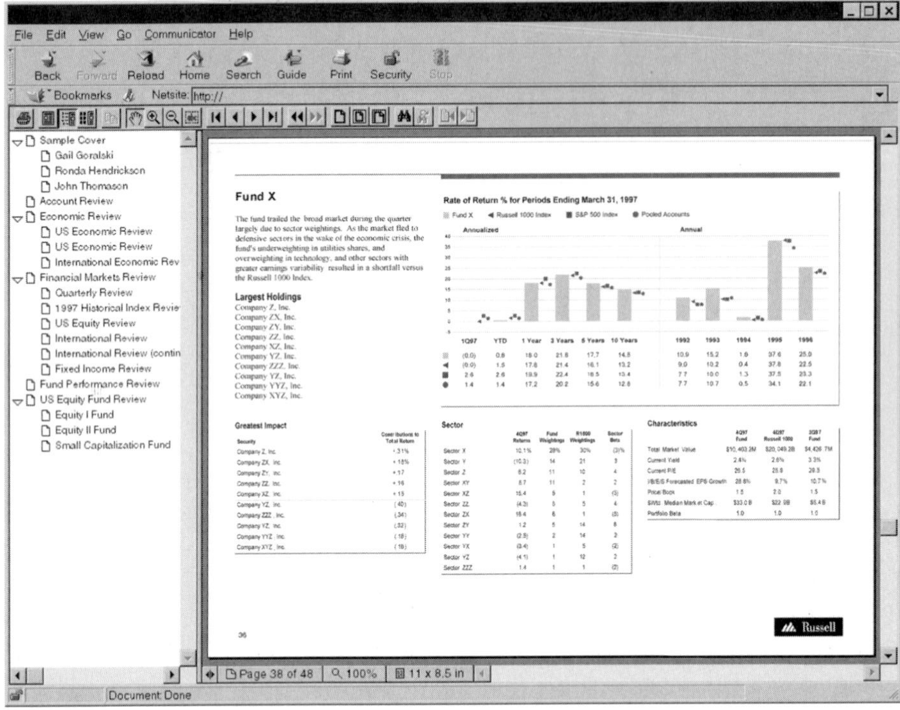

Figure 25-10 Fund page example in PDF book.

25.6 | Conclusion

In the past internetworking of systems was complex. Now, with the World Wide Web and TCP/IP, internetworking is routine and affordable. The next frontier is content interoperability.

Interoperability has always been a challenge. The people at Russell Advanced Technology Labs believe that XML is the interchange/interface language of the future, and that it will do for content interoperability what the WWW and TCP/IP did for internetworking.

Russell says: "We built an SGML application three years ago because it was the right thing to do. We have now converted it to XML because it is the right thing to do. The SGML to XML conversion took one developer three days."

While others discuss the potential values of XML, Russell is already enjoying the benefits of a production extranet XML publishing system.

©2000 The XML Handbook™

City Of Providence

Case Study

- Travel industry
- Repurposing content
- Republishing in multiple electronic media
- Linking static and dynamic Web sites

©2000 The XML Handbook™

Chapter 26

This chapter has more information than you ever wanted to know about the nightlife in Providence, Rhode Island. But it has lots that you need to know about publishing that kind of dynamic information in multiple electronic media. The chapter is sponsored by Inso Corporation, `http://www.inso.com`.

Cities throughout the world have turned the Web into a gigantic rack of travel brochures. But unlike their paper alternatives, Web brochures are expected to be up-to-date, dynamic, and customizable. And cities that want to be competitive have to maintain the Web sites along with the traditional media, which creates new pressures for already overworked staffs and budgets.

26.1 | The *Providence Guide* prototype

City chambers of commerce work to attract local residents, tourists and business travelers to the city to spend their travel and entertainment dollars. Today, they market themselves through multiple media. Paper brochures can be supplemented with Web sites and CD-ROMs mailed to convention planners, travel agents, and others with the potential to bring in hosts of visitors.

Different aspects of a city are of interest to different visitors. Some are interested in historic sites, others in attractions, and the business traveler might only have time to sample a couple of restaurants and night spots during a busy convention. Of particular interest is the question, "what special events are going on during my visit?"

How can a chamber of commerce with a limited marketing budget and staff provide dynamic, up-to-date information for a multitude of visitors with different interests, and on multiple media? Inso Corporation has prototyped a solution for the city of Providence, Rhode Island, where its Electronic Publishing Solutions division is located. This solution repurposes the same XML content about Providence that can be republished three ways:

- A *Providence Guide* on CD-ROM, viewed with the *DynaText* Browser.
- The same guide served on the Web with *DynaWeb*, which links to...
- A dynamic Web site with current club listings and on-line restaurant reservations, using *DynaBase*.

In addition, XML support in these products enables contextual searching, hypertext navigation aids, and multiple views that allow different readers to reuse the publications to meet their own specific needs.

Finally, XML-enabled links between related content in the different publications helps draw the user into a call to action: to visit and spend money at Providence's restaurants, clubs, and other attractions.

To make changes to the *Providence Guide* content in all three forms, the author need only update a single source document with a word processor. These documents are then converted and the content "rescued" (adding XML structure and intelligence) using *DynaTag*.

Extremely volatile data, such as this week's events, are stored and updated in a database and inserted dynamically into the Web pages using *DynaBase*'s built-in scripting language. The city could even allow club promoters to enter their own events directly into the database via a Web-based form, thus reducing work for city employees even further. The club promoters might even be willing to pay an advertising fee for the privilege of listing their events on the city's Web site.

26.2 | Information architecture

The first step in creating the prototype application was to architect the information. Style templates were developed for the word processors with descriptively-named paragraph styles that could easily be converted to XML element-type names.

For example, a club listing consists of three styles: EntertainmentName, EntertainmentAddress, and EntertainmentDescription. These are mapped to similarly named XML element types, inside a containing element type, `ENTERTAINMENT`.

Mapping is not limited to one-to-one mapping of styles to element types. For more information, see Chapter 38, "DynaTag: Visual conversion environment", on page 502.

26.3 | Conversion to XML

After the *Providence Guide* is written and formatted, it is converted with *DynaTag*.

The initial conversion established the mapping rules for converting word processor styles (and any unstyled formatting) to XML elements. It also generated a DTD for the *Guide*.

This information was saved as a "project", which can be re-used for subsequent conversions as the information in the *Guide* is updated. The same project handles conversion of documents created in any of the supported word processing formats, as long as they are similar document types.

26.4 | Generating the electronic book

After converting the *Guide* to XML, *DynaText* was used to generate an "electronic book"; that is, a product-specific compiled form of XML with a fulltext index, optimized for online viewing and navigation.

©2000 THE XML HANDBOOK™

26.4.1 *Using multiple stylesheets*

A stylesheet editor is then used to create stylesheets for viewing the content in various ways. One stylesheet formats the Standard Contents view in the *DynaText* Browser, formatting the text for online display (larger fonts, increased line spacing). This stylesheet also provides hypertext cross-reference links and other features unique to online texts, such as icons that pop up graphics and tables in separate windows.

Another stylesheet generates a hypertext table of contents (TOC) for navigating the electronic book. The table of contents is simply a filtered view of the XML content that shows only title elements, and links them to their related chapters and sections.

Figure 26-1 shows the *Providence Guide* as an electronic book, with its TOC and Standard Contents views.

A third stylesheet formats the text for on-demand printing, including typical print features such as running headers and footers.

Additional stylesheets were also created for specialized views of the information, such as the "Entertainment only" views for readers who aren't interested in (or don't have time to explore) the city's history or other attractions.

26.4.1.1 Contextual searching and personalization

In addition to providing various views of the content, the *DynaText* Browser also allows the user to search for information, taking full advantage of the XML structure.

Imagine that a visitor to Providence heard that there was a new club opening, but all he knew was that the name was "(something) fish". A simple word search for "fish" would find a slew of seafood restaurants and possibly a listing for the nearby Boston Aquarium.

However, using a *DynaText* search form that restricts the search to club names, the user could quickly find "Blue Fish Red Fish", the new club.

The user can also annotate the site to record his favorite dishes at Al Forno. Or he can create a link between the Trinity Rep theater and L'Elizabeth, his preferred spot for after-theater coffee and dessert.

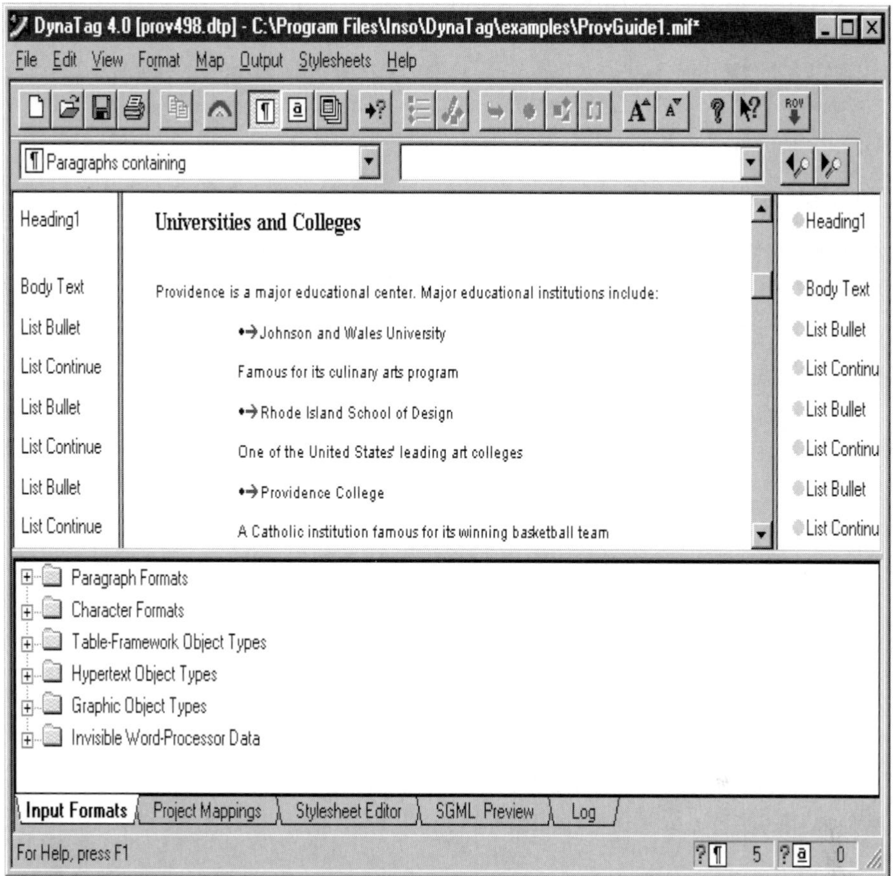

Figure 26-1 The *Providence Guide* electronic book.

26.5 | Web delivery

The same *Providence Guide* is served to Web browsers using *DynaWeb*. For this purpose, a different kind of stylesheet down-translates the XML markup to HTML on the fly. Because this translation is handled in the stylesheet, it is very easy to modify the HTML representation of the data when browsers add support for new tags.

It is not necessary to have a copy of the source tagged as HTML and chunked into small files for serving. The product breaks large documents into chunks based on XML containers such as chapters and sections.

©2000 The XML Handbook™

Also provided on the Web is electronic book functionality: fulltext and contextual searching, and an automatically generated table of contents.

Links in the Web version of the *Providence Guide* take the user to related content on the dynamic *This Week in Providence* Web site, described in the following section. Figure 26-2 shows the *Providence Guide* on the Web.

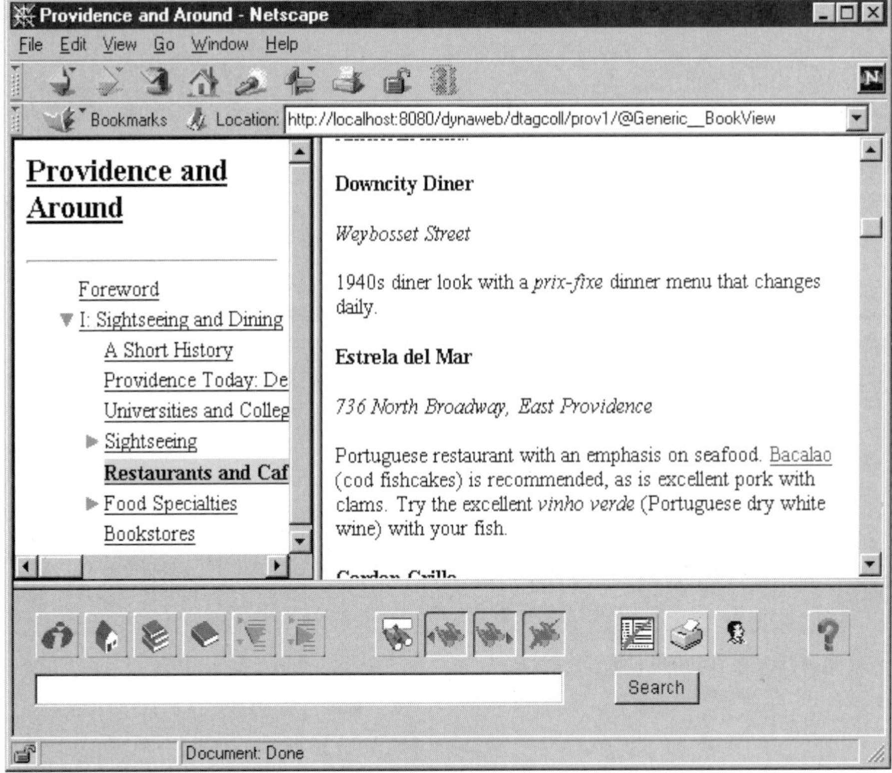

Figure 26-2 The *Providence Guide* on the Web.

26.6 | Dynamic Web delivery

The third deliverable in the three-in-one publishing prototype is the *This Week in Providence* Web site. It contains restaurant listings, online reservations, club listings, and information about this week's performers at each club.

Less volatile information, such as restaurant and club names, locations, and descriptions, are written in word processors and converted to XML as described above. The online restaurant reservations are handled with an HTML form that mails the request to the appropriate restaurant.

The most interesting and unique aspect of the site is the dynamic generation of this week's club listings from the database. The data is integrated with the XML-based club descriptions for presentation. This result is accomplished by a script written in the *DynaBase* scripting language, which is similar to Visual Basic in its syntax.

Here's how it works. Before serving the XML club listings, a fragment of whose source is shown in Example 26-1, *DynaBase* processes the file through a script called `buildnite.wbs`. This script looks up each club (tagged as <ENTERTAINMENTNAME>) in the database, and if there are bands scheduled to appear this week, the script puts out the names of the bands and the dates they are scheduled to appear at the bottom of the club listing.

Example 26-1. XML fragment for club listings

```
<?xml version="1.0" ?>
<CHAPTER><CHAPTERTITLE>II: Entertainment, Night Life, and Dining
</CHAPTERTITLE>
...
<ENTERTAINMENT><ENTERTAINMENTNAME>Aiden's Pub and Grub
</ENTERTAINMENTNAME>
<ENTERTAINMENTADDRESS>5 John Street, Bristol, RI
</ENTERTAINMENTADDRESS>
<ENTERTAINMENTDESCRIPTION>
A small Irish Pub that features local Irish Bands.
Atmosphere is cozy and quaint. Located 20 minutes from Providence.
A large selection of fine Irish Beer and other European brews.
</ENTERTAINMENTDESCRIPTION>
</ENTERTAINMENT>
...
</CHAPTER>
```

The script also transforms the relational data and XML document to HTML so that a wide range of Web browsers can display the information. Furthermore, the script inserts HTML "anchor" tags that enable the links from the *Providence Guide* book on *DynaWeb*.

Any time a new band is added to the database, it will appear immediately on the Web page the next time the page is reloaded. Figure 26-3 shows the

©2000 The XML Handbook™

Entertainment page from the Web site, with the club listings and this week's scheduled bands.

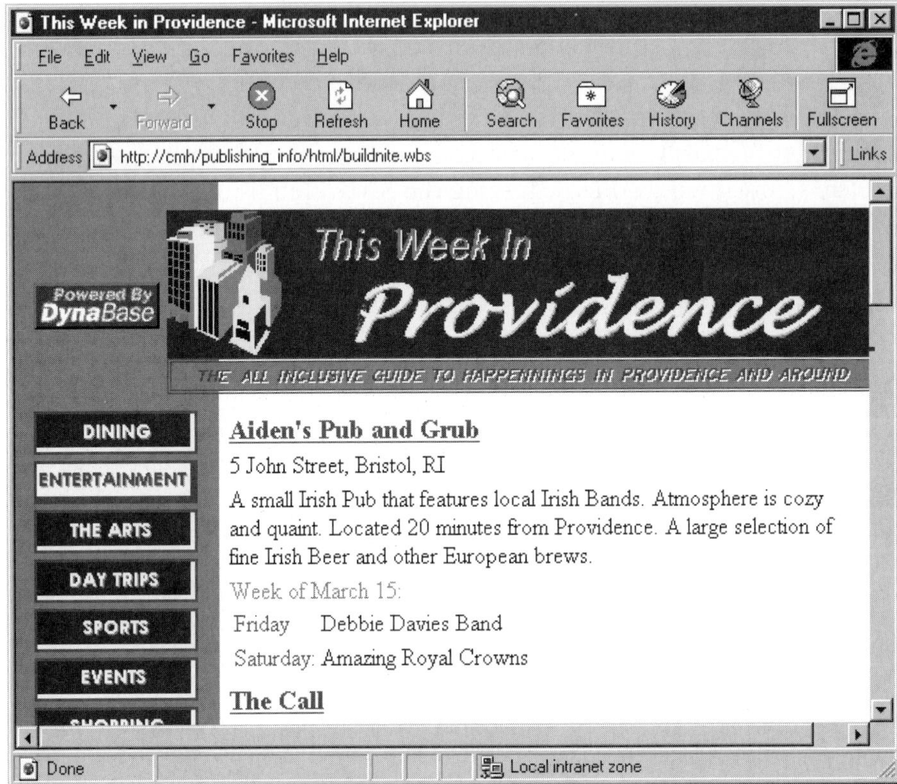

Figure 26-3 The entertainment page is dynamically updated with this week's bands

26.7 | Updating the XML data

The data stored in XML is less volatile than the relational data on this week's bands, but it still needs to be updated whenever a new restaurant or club opens. Let's examine how updates are managed.

The word processing source files for the *Providence Guide* and their XML counterparts (created by *DynaTag*) are stored in the *DynaBase* repository.

When an update is required, an author checks out both files. This checkout process ensures that only one author is updating a file at a time. The interface is shown in Figure 26-4.

The author then opens the word processing file and makes the change. For example, let's say a new club called Blue Fish Red Fish is opening. To ensure consistent use of word processor styles, the author copies an existing club listing and edits the name, location, and description to create a brand new listing.

Next, the author runs the project batch script to convert the updated word processing file to XML. Then, the author checks the XML document and the word processing file back into the repository.

DynaBase updates the revision information for the files and prompts the author for a comment. The author types "added Blue Fish Red Fish" and the checkin process is complete.

The author needs no special training in XML and doesn't need to know all the ways the information will be used. She only needs to know to use the correct word processor styles and to follow the checkout/revise/convert/checkin process.

At this point, the new content may be reviewed by an editor, and additional changes can be made using the same checkout/revise/convert/checkin process. Once all changes are approved, the Web site can be published.

Unlike some file-based Web sites, there aren't separate development and production servers, and no movement of updated files from one server to another. Instead, you simply publish a new "edition" of your Web site, and all the approved content (which may be the latest updates, or previous versions if the latest updates aren't ready for publishing yet) is served as the production site on the Web.

26.8 | Revising the Electronic Book

Now we need to get the latest revisions into the *Providence Guide* electronic book for Web delivery and publication on CD-ROM. Of course, CD-ROM updates would be published less frequently, but for those without Web access, the CD may be the only way to learn about Providence's attractions.

Also, the *DynaText* Browser provides features (such as an annotation capability) that are not available in Web browsers. Because the CD and

©2000 The XML Handbook™

Figure 26-4 The *DynaBase* interface for content management.

Web versions of the information do not include the dynamically generated club schedules, the information does not become outdated as quickly.

To publish the electronic book, the publisher exports all the XML entities that comprise the book from *DynaBase*. Then, a script is run that builds the electronic book. The various stylesheets for creating different views of the information are also incorporated at this point.

26.9 | Summary

The *Providence Guide* that we've examined in this chapter illustrates how XML and suitable products (like the *Inso Electronic Publishing Solutions* suite) can be integrated together to form an XML-based, end-to-end publishing solution that allows for:

- Republishing across media, such as the CD-ROM and Web versions of the *Providence Guide*.
- Repurposing of document components to create multiple publications, such as the club and restaurant descriptions that appear in both the *Providence Guide* and on the *This Week in Providence* Web site.
- Reuse of publications for different user needs, such as the entertainment-only view in the electronic book, and contextual searches that restrict the information to only what is sought.
- Links and navigation aids that lead the reader through your content; for example, the links from club descriptions in the *Providence Guide* to this week's scheduled bands.

PC World Online

Case Study

- Major commercial website
- Dynamic content delivery
- Print and online

©2000 The XML Handbook™

Chapter 27

It is hard enough to keep a website on any subject current and interesting. But when you are the world's largest computer monthly, keeping up with your subject matter is an immense challenge. Learn how *PC World Online* does it from this chapter, which is sponsored by Arbortext, Inc., `http://www.arbortext.com`, and was prepared by Susan Örge.

The website PC World Online is the electronic version of PC World magazine, one of the world's foremost sources of computer information and the largest monthly computer publication. It maintains over 8,000 pages and draws nine million page views per month (Figure 27-1). In addition to deriving diverse and often complex content from its print counterpart, the PC World Online group originates online news and features, a shareware library, and more. PC World Online also repackages content for several third party licensees.

The site serves its readership well by offering timely, useful information that encourages repeat visits. As more competition enters the arena every day, sites such as *PC World Online* must continually strive to sustain their competitive edge.

27.1 | The challenge

Because of a changing landscape of increasingly sophisticated audience expectations, Matt Turner, Director of Applications Development, and Rebecca Freed, Managing Editor, faced a challenging task in 1998. How

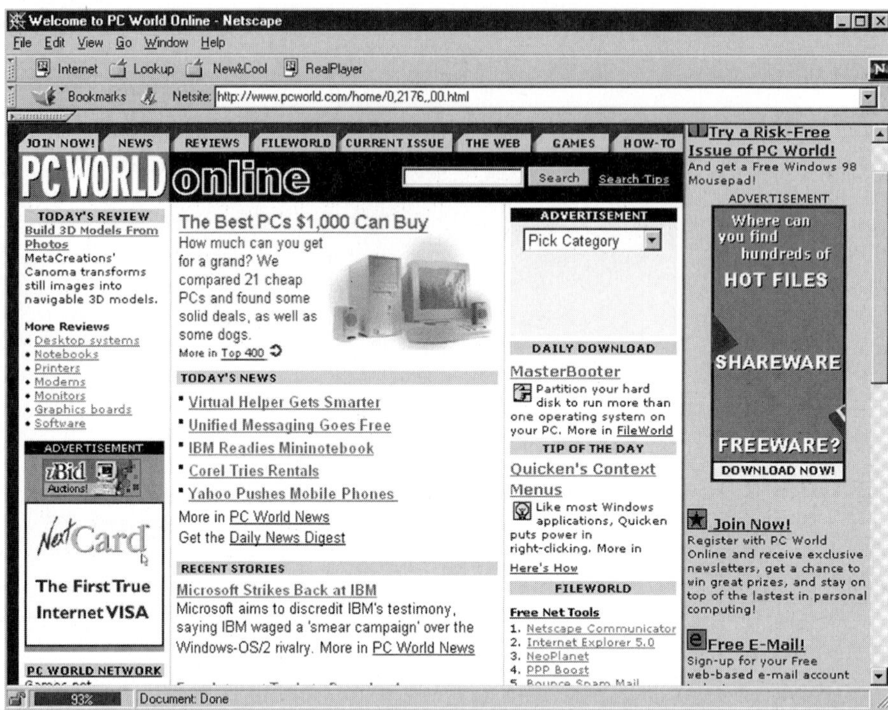

Figure 27-1 *PC World Online* home page

could *PC World Online* pull information from multiple sources, in many different formats, and serve it dynamically on the web, while keeping up with the breakneck speed of the publishing business?

On top of all of this, how could the online publication transform the thousands of pages of then static information into a more useful, dynamic site? After investigating a number of different solutions including standard template/database HTML Web publishing tools, Turner felt that XML was the only technology that rose to this challenge. Today, XML is the basis for all of *PC World Online*'s diverse content delivery needs.

27.1.1 *Complex conversion requirements*

PC World Online's editorial management process is painstakingly complex. The edit team is a central point where a variety of content types come from many different unstructured sources and formats, which the team must then deliver in other formats.

Before it implemented an XML-based publishing system, *PC World Online* had been using a home-grown production process that required four to five people to manually convert each month's *PC World* print articles into HTML (Figure 27-2). Among other problems, this process caused an unacceptable drain on resources while not allowing the group to create, store or access metadata about the content. As a result, the team was kept from building personalized content views or reusing content in different areas of the site.

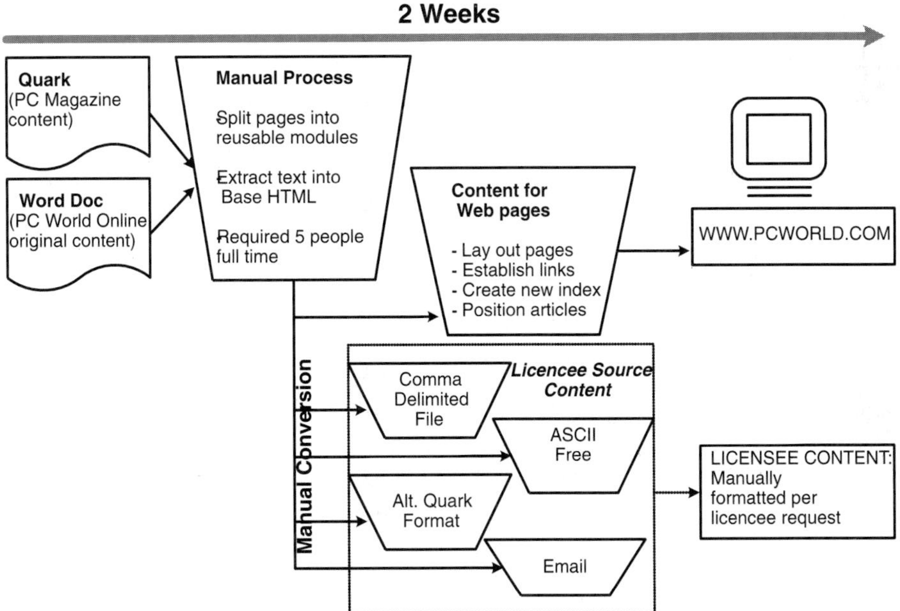

Figure 27-2 Converting articles before XML

Here are some examples of articles in the different source formats:

- **From the magazine**: A feature article from the magazine that is nine pages long, has sidebars, five charts, four screen shots and four art images. The print magazine delivers all of its content to *PC World Online* as a *Quark* document. The edit team must then convert that content to HTML and several other licensee-specific formats while maintaining consistency in style and content between the print version and the Web version.

- **From the online editors**: An online feature article of the same length and complexity, but on a different topic. This article may also have unique structures and layout for the online medium.
- **From the online editors**: A four-paragraph online news story.

These articles must be delivered dynamically in the following formats:

- **To the Web**: *PC World Online* produces HTML formats for at least five different Web site sections, as well as special formats such as an HTML "Print from Browser" version.
- **Via email**: These are text versions sent to readers who subscribe to information on specific topics of interest.
- **To licensees**: Licensee content in several formats including delimited ASCII and *Quark*.
- **To future formats**: *PC World Online* intends to deliver content using technologies, such as DHTML and XML, that are supported by newer browsers.

27.1.2 *Time-consuming HTML markup*

Even for articles originally written for online use, the editors' copy flow and review process was painstaking, as shown in Figure 27-3.

27.1.3 *Richly-structured information sources*

The *PC World Online* group wanted a system that could store these documents with their complexity intact so they could easily publish high-quality information electronically. For example, the print version uses spot art, color and placement cues, which conveys a strong sense of structure to the reader. Matt Turner was convinced that he could preserve this structure so

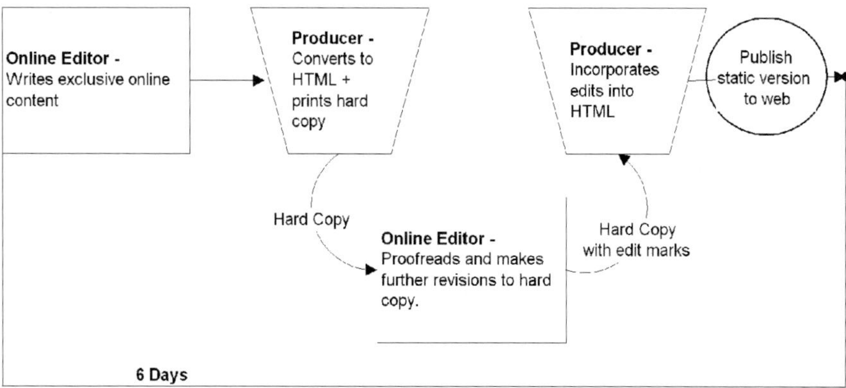

Figure 27-3 Workflow for original online content before XML

that the Web versions could display the same information-rich layouts as the print counterpart.

27.2 | Templates and databases were not enough

PC World Online was already producing some of its simpler information using a template and database Web publishing system, a traditional method of Web site production. Turner suspected that he could implement a more sophisticated version of this system for all of *PC World Online*'s content.

A typical template and database system for Web publishing combines a database that stores information content along with templates that specify where the content will go when it is rendered. When a site is published, the system automatically flows the information from a database through the template to generate a series of HTML pages. This type of tool has allowed many sites to automate the delivery of Web content.

Turner, however, found that his more complex information required transformation of the content, something that a template and database system could not accomplish. For example Turner found it impossible to use this kind of software to generate from the HTML markup the special marks that his licensees required.

Additionally, since a template and database system typically stores an entire body of an article in one "field," the editors lacked the fine granularity they needed to control the formatting of the more elaborately-structured article elements. Instead, the editors had a propensity to insert "rogue" tags arbitrarily to achieve specific formatting results. It was therefore impossible for Turner to base any automated procedure on the article content markup, and therefore impossible to control the format automatically at the time of publication. This situation also hindered *PC World Online* from producing the many diverse delivery formats that were required.

27.3 | XML provides a solution

In reviewing document management approaches, Turner learned about XML and chose it as the means of managing *PC World Online*'s complex content. Instead of forcing content into the rigid tabular structure of a relational database, XML can describe any document in terms of its natural structure as a hierarchy, or "tree", with links among the leaves and branches. This model allowed *PC World Online* to preserve the full richness of an article's structure.

27.3.1 *Content creation and storage*

Within three days, the team, working with a consultant, created a DTD for the Web site's content. The DTD defines element types, such as headlines and paragraph, that are common to most articles, It also defines more specialized element types, such as tips and product reviews, that are particular to a specific kind of article. These relationships are illustrated in Figure 27-4.

Within days, and with almost no training, editors were using this DTD in conjunction with Arbortext products to create their first issue in XML. Figure 27-5 shows an article and its XML markup as it appears when edited using Arbortext software.

Figure 27-6 shows the same article when rendered on the *PC World Online* site.

Soon after, the group began transforming all of its content to XML. The new system significantly reduced the time spent preparing the documents

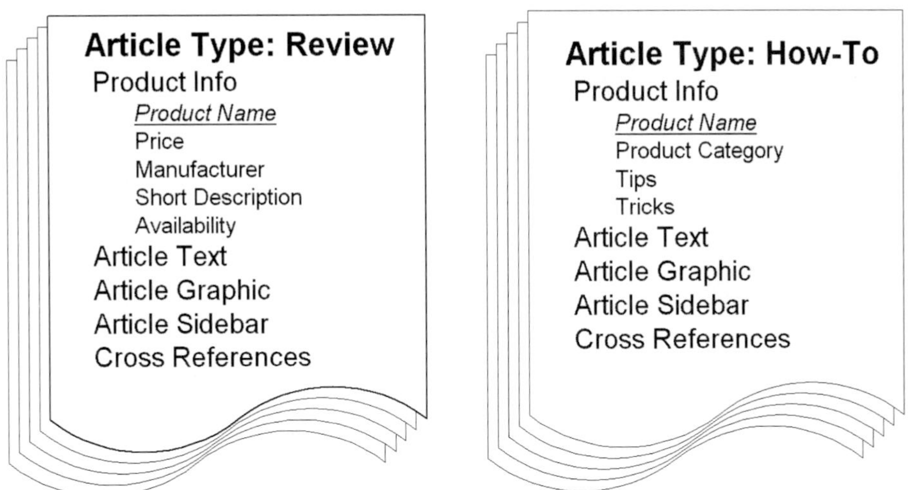

Figure 27-4 Articles can contain reusable elements.

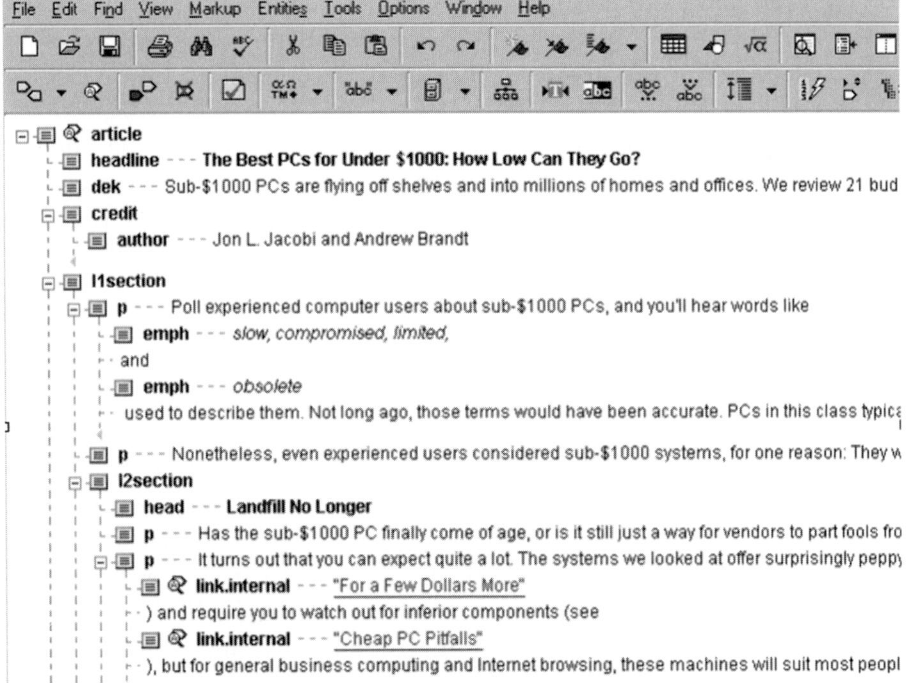

Figure 27-5 An article being edited with Arbortext software

Figure 27-6 The article in Figure 27-5 on the *PC World Online* site

for the Web and licensee formats. *Quark* desktop publishing documents were first converted to an equivalent XML document type, then processed with Arbortext software to refine the XML to conform to the *PC World Online* DTD.

This conversion process not only preserves the richness of the original article, but often allows the team to enrich it even further. For example many stories now include links to the URLs of companies whose products are reviewed, plus charts and product images that are tailored for the Web.

27.3.2 *Data delivery*

Once the articles are in XML, content delivery becomes a much easier, more effective task. That is because an XML-aware database system stores the actual XML document intact. This differs from the template and database system, which can only store lightly-tagged HTML data in simple "fields." One advantage of true XML storage is that data retrieval is much more powerful. Because of the hierarchical structure of XML data, it is just as easy to retrieve complete articles as it is to retrieve a single headline.

But there are additional rewards beyond powerful retrieval. While data is extracted, it is transformed to HTML or other representations by processing it according to an XSL stylesheet. Since *PC World Online* must transform the XML documents into a myriad of output formats, this ability to do it automatically makes for a tremendous time-savings over the previous method of conversion and cleanup of articles. Additionally, it gives the added power of transforming the actual data content depending on the output.

27.3.3 *Improved workflow*

The new XML system has changed the way *PC World Online* produces its Web site. Today, every page is generated from the data store of XML documents. The group now uses the workflow illustrated in Figure 27-7, a significant change from the original workflow in Figure 27-2.

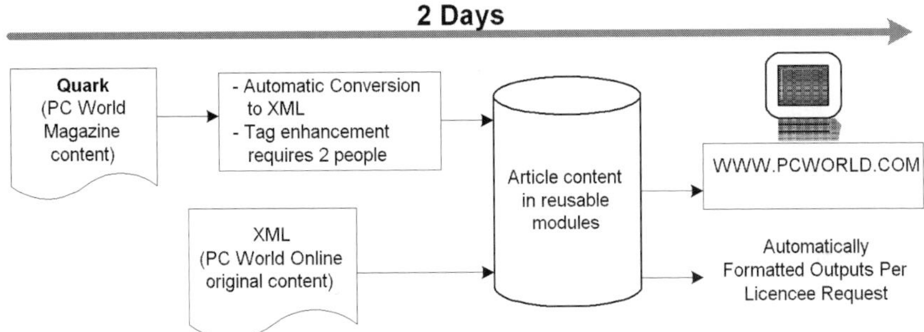

Figure 27-7 XML-based workflow

Once *PC World Online* editors sign off on the valid XML documents they have created, these documents are checked into a relational database and article-level attributes are decomposed into index fields. Although the database is similar to that in a traditional template and database system, there are significant differences. Whereas the traditional systems store lightly-tagged HTML, here a valid, richly-tagged XML document is stored.

When a request is made to view an article, the appropriate XSL stylesheet is invoked and the record containing the article is retrieved from the database. The XSL stylesheet then governs the processing and translation of the XML data to the selected format, such as HTML, and combines the returned fields for presentation. This workflow is the same for all uses of the content, including the Web pages and the licensee format.

The new workflow has been particularly effective for original online content. Contrast the flow in Figure 27-8 with that in Figure 27-3.

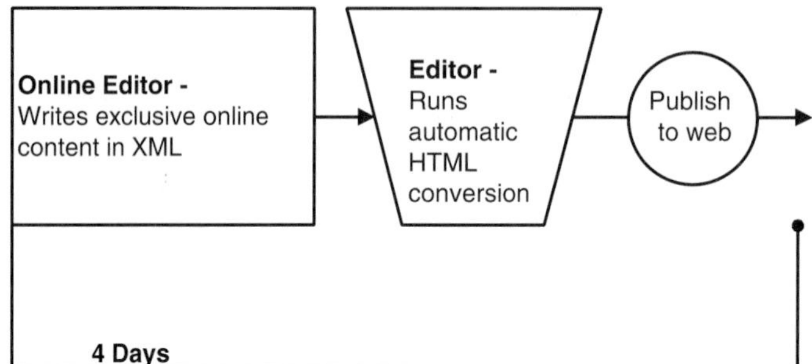

Figure 27-8 Workflow for original online content with XML

27.4 | Results and benefits

PC World Online's new XML system has satisfied the original requirements and yielded a number of significant benefits.

27.4.1 *Publish to and from multiple formats*

XML has enabled automatic conversion of documents from other formats, greatly reducing the time spent doing manual conversions. Converting content into the forms required by licensees had been as time-consuming as producing the articles in the first place. Now the same system that produces the articles can automatically produce the licensee content in whatever format is needed.

As a bonus, *PC World Online* is able to offer a variety of renditions just for the Web. These include a simplified printable Web page format and modified renditions for affiliated Web sites. All of these are simply alternative results from the automatic processing of XML.

PC World Online is always seeking ways to raise the visibility of its brand. That often means disseminating excerpts from its trove of content through affiliate sites that can reach audiences that its primary Web site would not reach. XML has made this a much easier process.

27.4.2 *Reuse*

Reuse from a central data store avoids the integrity problems of duplicated data. If information is derived from an original article, there is only one source version to create and maintain and therefore no need to manage and synchronize multiple versions of the same information. One example of reuse is the website's "product finder" (shown in Figure 27-9), with which site visitors can choose a product category and view a list of products and their review ratings. The product finder is automatically compiled from existing product review articles, so there is no need to create and maintain multiple versions of the information.

27.4.3 *Tailored information for site visitors*

Because *PC World Online* articles are marked up with information-rich tags, tailored subsets of the content can be presented to users. This is a radical departure from the usual method of search and retrieval, where a list of documents is returned when a keyword is searched.

As shown in Figure 27-10, with XML, an individual reader can request and receive only specific elements of the articles of interest. For example, a site visitor may ask for modems, their ratings, and their prices, and get only the parts of articles that contain this information.

Readers can also choose from different assemblies of the same content; for example, it is now easy for *PC World Online* to add a "product tips and tricks" section to its site, showing only the `tips` and `tricks` elements of `How-To` articles. This is a new presentation of the content that is separate from the articles themselves.

And at last, with the help of XSL stylesheets, the group can automatically transform complicated articles (some have a dozen or more highly specialized sections) so they can be displayed differently in different sections of the website.

©2000 THE XML HANDBOOK™

Product Finder
Select one of the following Budget Notebooks manufacturers:
AMS
AMS Tech
ARM
Acer
CTX
Submit
Or, get a list of all of the Budget Notebooks capsule reviews
List All
Changed your mind? To start a new search, select another hardware category:
(Select a Category)
15 Inch Monitors
17 Inch Monitors
19-21 Inch Monitors
Desktops
New Search

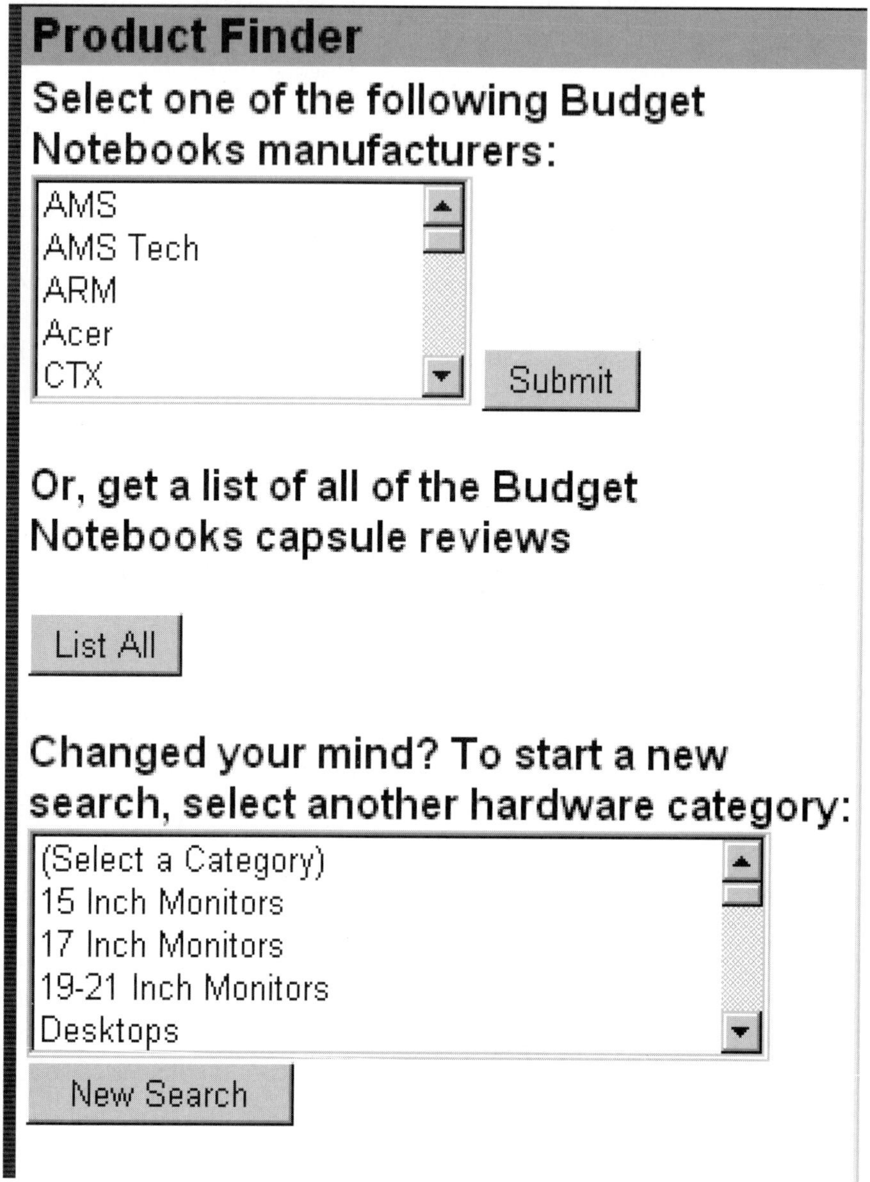

Figure 27-9 Product finder

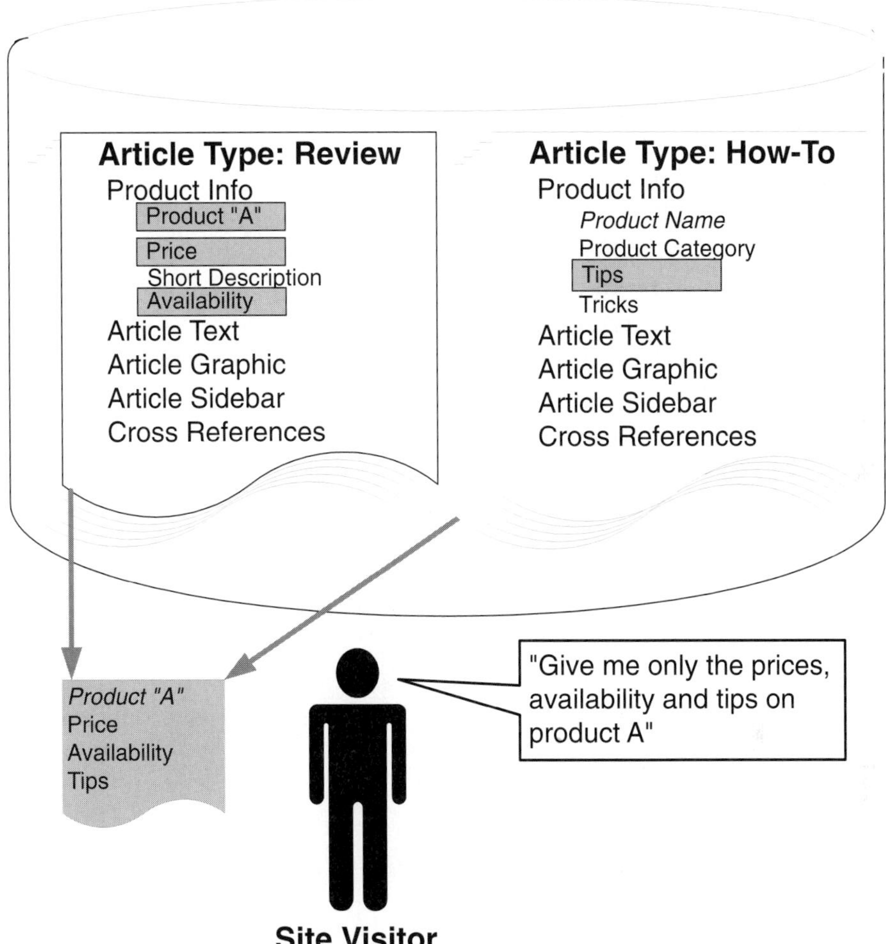

Figure 27-10 Querying for specific data elements

27.4.4 *Reduced cost and time to market*

By simplifying the process of creating, locating, and delivering information, the *PC World Online* team has increased productivity while reducing costs. Rebecca Freed, Managing Editor, reported that their XML system has cut the time to go from print to Web from two days to two hours. They have reinvested this time in creating higher-quality articles.

Additionally, editors now enter copy directly into the XML system, while server-side programs write out the actual HTML pages. Once the article is created, it is ready to go to the Web with little or no manual tagging or reformatting required on the part of the site producers. This is a huge savings in time that used to be spent updating index pages and pouring text into templates by hand.

Editors also handle the entire correction process, saving time and minimizing additional rounds of corrections. Granting this direct access to editors has streamlined production 100 percent.

Using Arbortext's structured editing environment, editors can access the articles and change the markup, while maintaining conformity to the document structure outlined in the DTD.

27.4.5 *Improved quality*

The editors and production staff are constantly seeking ways to enrich the ways in which their content can be accessed, navigated, presented and used. XML has been the key to fulfilling this goal.

Moreover, the easy-to-use, XML-based, automated system allows editors – who understand the content – to do their own markup, resulting in better quality control.

27.4.6 *Future-proofing with a standard*

The new XML system has allowed quick adaptability to new delivery formats as they evolve. For example, with some simple stylesheet adjustments, the system could produce content in forms that future browsers will accept. These might include XML versions for client-side XSL processing, or renditions for users of hand-held PDA devices such as the *Palm Pilot*.

27.4.7 *Job satisfaction*

Formerly, site producers spent time formatting and reworking what the editors had already written. Now they can use that time to add new capabilities to the site, while editors can exercise a greater degree of control over the final presentation of the articles.

27.5 | Summary

PC World Online must create original Web content as well as flow content from its print-based publication into electronic formats. With XML and Arbortext products, the company was able to overhaul production, allowing editors to edit and produce their own content to improve production efficiency.

Additionally, the new system laid the groundwork for a complete XML data store, which will enhance the repurposability of data and become the backbone of *PC World Online* for years to come. Results to date include faster content delivery, editor efficiency, design consistency, flexibility, improved reuse of information, customized content, and elimination of Web production bottlenecks.

Turner and Freed predict that the advantages that *PC World Online* has reaped from XML will cause it to be adopted by *PC World Magazine* as well.

©2000 The XML Handbook™

MTU-DaimlerChrysler Aerospace

Case Study

- Aerospace industry "green pages"
- Customizing supplier documentation
- Information supply chain

©2000 THE XML HANDBOOK™

Chapter 28

How do you introduce your own changes to someone else's documents and see a seamless result? The fine-grained structuring of XML made it possible for DaimlerChrysler, as you'll see in this chapter. It is sponsored by Enigma, Inc., `http://www.enigma.com`.

The relationship between equipment manufacturers and the independent and customer organizations that service their equipment is highly dependent on the transfer of knowledge for maintenance operations. In most cases, unique knowledge is maintained by both the manufacturer and the servicer. To fully utilize this knowledge, manufacturers must be able to deliver intelligent publications, and servicers must be able to customize these publications.

28.1 | The challenge

The MTU-Maintenance division of DaimlerChrysler Aerospace is a maintenance and repair organization for aircraft engines. It performs maintenance on engines produced by the leading engine manufacturers and receives maintenance manuals and parts catalogs from each of them.

As with all airlines and maintenance facilities, DaimlerChrysler has tasks, procedures and parts information that are specific to its operations. These modifications are commonly referred to as "Customer Originated Changes", or COCs.

Historically, COCs have been maintained as paper documents, that are 'slip-sheeted' into the manufacturer's larger paper publications. These added pages were printed on green paper so they would stand out from the original publication, and are still known in the industry today as "green pages".

As the manufacturers began to deliver "intelligent" SGML- and XML-based publications, the green page paper COCs still needed to be referenced. Thus, the full benefit of digital data could not be realized.

An intelligent electronic publication is characterized by tables of contents, hyperlinking, topic specific searching and navigation. DaimlerChrysler sought a way to integrate its own modifications, while maintaining all the intelligence and usability features available in the manufacturer publications.

28.2 | The solution

Using Enigma's *Xtend* software, DaimlerChrysler implemented a complete digital maintenance publication process. Its workflow is shown in Figure 28-1.

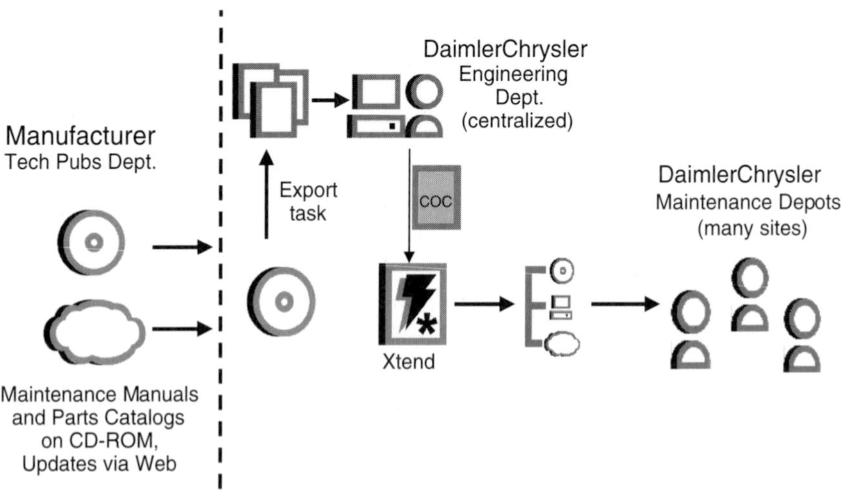

Figure 28-1 Xtend workflow

The system allows authorized DaimlerChrysler employees to update the publications that are used by all the staff mechanics. The process for adding COCs to these publications is as follows:

1. First, the authorized employee selects a task to be customized, using the original publication.
2. Next, the original content is modified with an editor, with templates used to automate the capture of XML metadata.
3. The modified content is dynamically integrated into the original publication and made available to all employees.

Let's look at each step more closely.

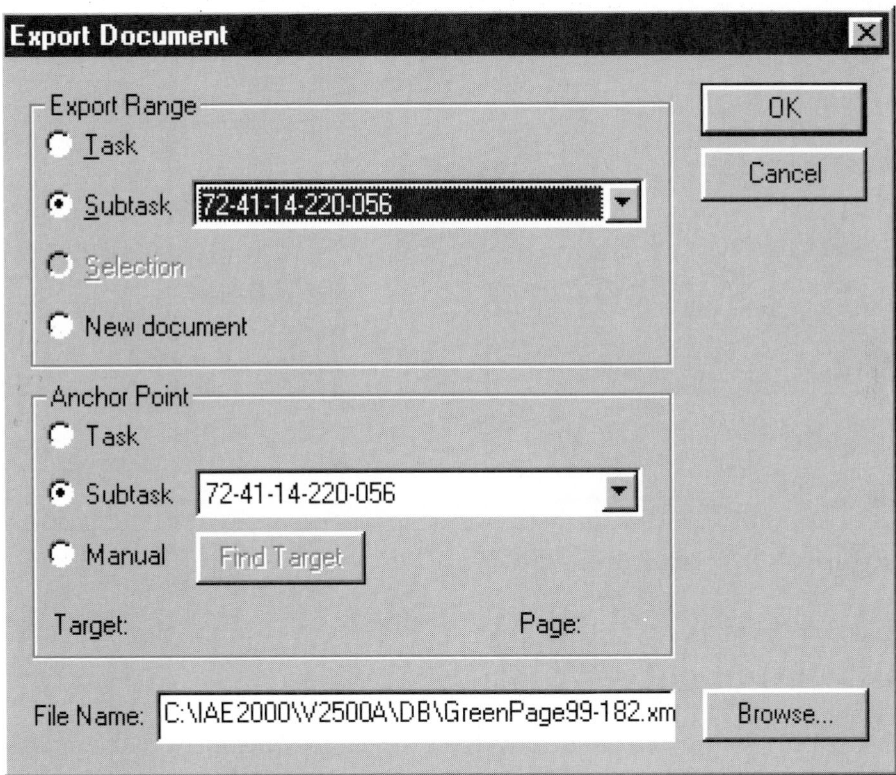

Figure 28-2 Subtask selection for customization

28.2.1 *Selecting content to be customized*

The authorized user can select any task or subtask to export for customization, as shown in Figure 28-2. The customized COC will be anchored to the original for referencing purposes.

Once the desired subtask is selected, the dialog box shown in Figure 28-3 is presented, enabling the capture of XML metadata. This information is maintained for document management purposes and is also automatically placed within the document content.

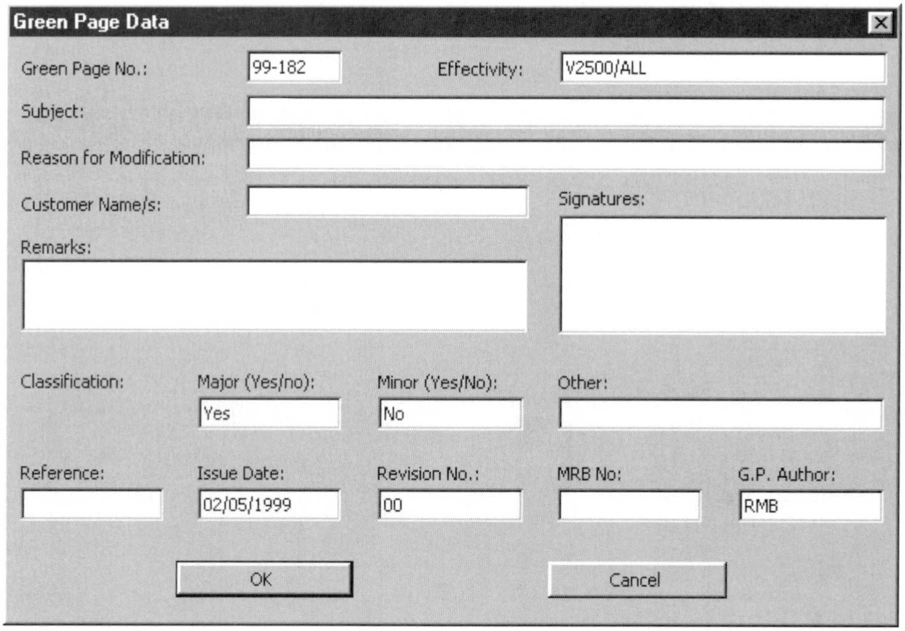

Figure 28-3 Metadata capture

28.2.2 *Content editing*

In Example 28-1 we see an excerpt from the source document that contains the text of the exported subtask.

The author can modify or add any content to this text. However, some elements, such as the `grphcref` graphic reference, are significant in order to reintegrate the COCs into the original publication. To assure that such

Example 28-1. Source document structure

```
<task chapnbr="72-41-14" func="200">
  <title>Examine the HP Compressor Rotating Air Seal</title>
  <subtask chapnbr="72-41-14" func="220" seq="056">
    <title>Maintenance Equipment Specification</title>
    <list1>
      <l1item>
        <para>Identify proper engine bay utilization as follows:
        </para></l1item>
      <l1item>
        <para>Remove access cover as shown in
          <grphcref refid="GR94030">Figure 901</grphcref>
        </para></l1item>
    </list1>
  </subtask>
```

information is not accidentally modified in the editing phase, it is marked as non-editable.

In addition to adding and modifying textual data, the author can add new hyperlinks and graphics.

28.2.3 *Integration and republishing*

After creating the COCs, the content is updated for distribution via the network to all maintenance users. Since the original publication typically is very large (100's of megabytes), it is critical that the update process be able to work with just the new and modified content.

28.3 | The result

As a result of the customization process, technicians at DaimlerChrysler have access to the entire knowledge-base of maintenance information - both from the original manufacturer as well as accumulated knowledge from within their organization.

©2000 THE XML HANDBOOK™

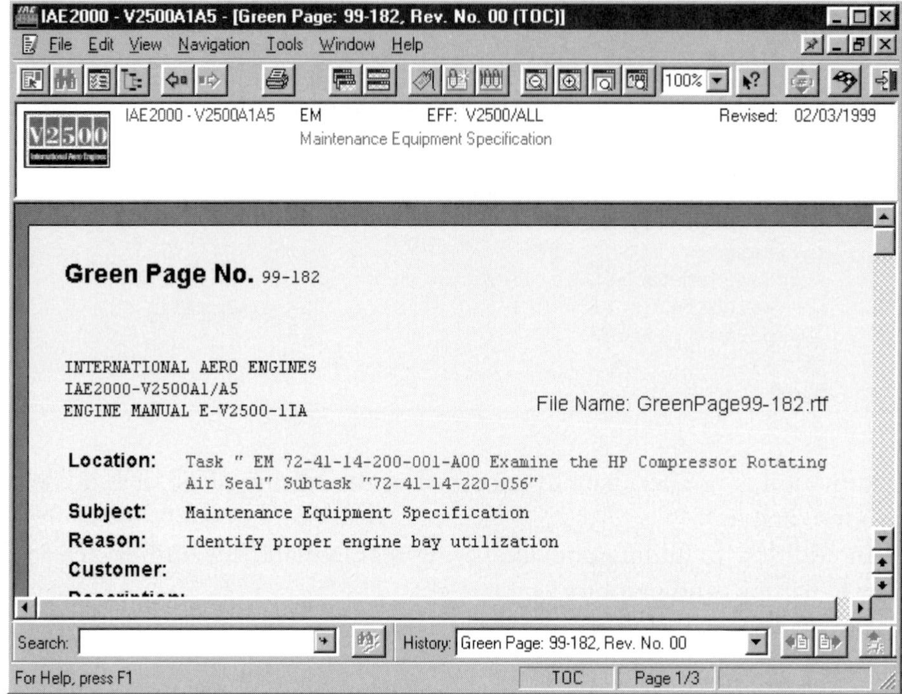

Figure 28-4 Customized information for the maintenance technician

Because all the content is available within a single publication (as shown in Figure 28-4), the technician no longer needs to correlate manually between multiple information sources.

Tip *Other aspects of the Enigma publishing solution are described in Chapter 41, "INSIGHT: The role of stylesheets", on page 550.*

FrameMaker+ SGML: Editing+ composition

Tool Discussion

- XML editing
- Automated WYSIWYG formatting and composition
- Multi-platform publishing
- Free trial version on CD-ROM

©2000 THE XML HANDBOOK™

Chapter 29

One approach to XML editing is modeled on the convenience of word processing. The editing and formatting are integrated, but XML structural facilities are provided. This chapter is sponsored by Adobe Systems Incorporated, `http://www.adobe.com`, and was prepared by Lani Hajagos.

Whether delivering data on the Web or large documents on paper, every corporation today is a publisher. Yet corporations face a daunting publishing challenge: the demand to publish information is quickly surpassing the ability to create, manage, and distribute it.

29.1 | Leveraging information

Delivering content quickly to global markets puts intense pressure on corporate publishing systems. Vast numbers of documents, some thousands of pages long, must be revised, translated, and formatted before business-critical information can reach customers around the globe. Some of these documents must be maintained for many years – far beyond the life-span of any software application or hardware platform.

XML and its parent standard, SGML, have demonstrated the ability to meet this challenge by enabling information reuse. There are many examples of this:

- Multiple outputs can easily be created from a single source. A manufacturer might produce a public parts catalog and a private-label catalog from a common XML source. In addition to the printed versions, electronic versions in HTML and PDF may also be generated, for publishing on CD-ROM and the World Wide Web.
- Information may be shared among numerous documents. A diagnostic and repair procedure for a certain assembly may appear in the trouble-shooting manuals of several devices that incorporate that assembly. The information about the assembly is created and maintained once, and changes are automatically reflected in each manual that references it.
- XML allows users to define markup that identifies components of information within a document. This enables intelligent searching of the information. For example, a user might search for a particular temperature within an "operational tolerances" element. The results from this type of search are far more accurate than simply searching for the string "24°C".
- XML is software and hardware platform-independent, protecting the investment in long-lived information and facilitating the sharing of information in a heterogeneous environment.

When choosing XML tools, you should take into consideration the extent to which the tool can help you obtain those benefits of XML that are important to you. That should be in addition to considerations of how well the tool provides the functionality that you need.

29.2 | XML editing functions

In this chapter, the discussion of tool capabilities is illustrated by Adobe *FrameMaker+SGML*, an integrated XML editing and composition product. It is designed to shield the user from the technicalities of XML and to support a workgroup environment. The tool includes a robust composition capability that can handle complex page layouts with a high degree of automation, even such professional graphic arts requirements as spot and process color separations.

29.2.1 *Guided editing*

Guided editing features help authors create documents that conform to the rules for a document type. In Figure 29-1, the element-type catalog shows which element types are valid for the current location in the document. The interactive structure view lets the author manipulate the structure of the document. It graphically advises whether a proposed move will invalidate the structure. These devices make it possible to create and manipulate the structure of the document without ever working directly with, or even looking at, a markup tag.

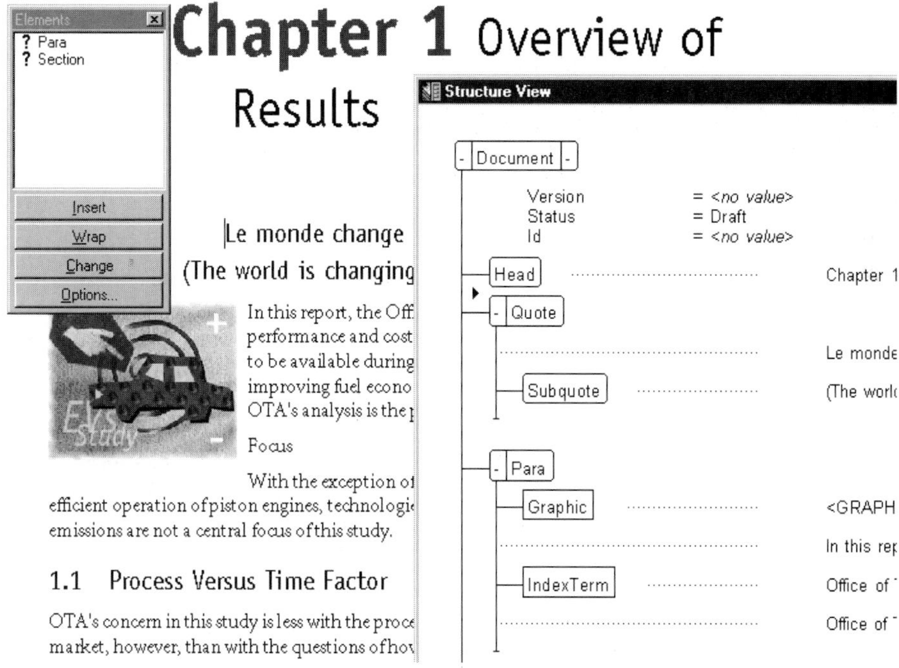

Figure 29-1 Structure view and element-type catalog.

29.2.2 *Editing flexibility*

When creating type-valid XML documents, an editing tool might require that the document be valid at all times, even if that means putting in empty elements when information is not yet available. Maintaining validity in this way means that the author has to start at the beginning of the document, and write everything in order, not skipping any required elements.

However, this isn't what happens in the real world. All too often, the information a writer needs simply isn't available. So the writer may skip some parts of the document and write others out of order. As more and more of the information becomes available, the gaps are filled in and eventually the document is complete. This is easy to do in a word processor, but difficult if your editing tool insists that validity must be maintained.

Some editors address this requirement by allowing information to be entered in any order and allowing required information to be skipped. The document can be saved as a work in progress even if it is not valid. The software keeps track of what is missing and what is in the wrong place, and helps the writer fix things. So the end result is a valid, complete document, without the hassle of having to fight with an inflexible editing tool.

With *FrameMaker+SGML*, when working in the guided editing mode, the element-type catalog shows only those element types valid at the current location in the document. However, as shown in Figure 29-2, the element-type catalog can also be set to display all element types, or any element type that may be valid within a parent element, even further down in the hierarchy. The valid element types are indicated by a checkmark.

29.2.3 *Problem correction*

By definition, a product that allows editing flexibility allows errors, because the user can write a portion of the document out of context when necessary. For example, while working on an introduction, a writer who wants to enter a new term into the glossary can simply insert a glossary element in the middle of the introduction.

As shown in Figure 29-3, from that point the element-type catalog would show the valid element types for a glossary. However, the structure view would indicate, by a dashed vertical line, that the glossary is out of context.

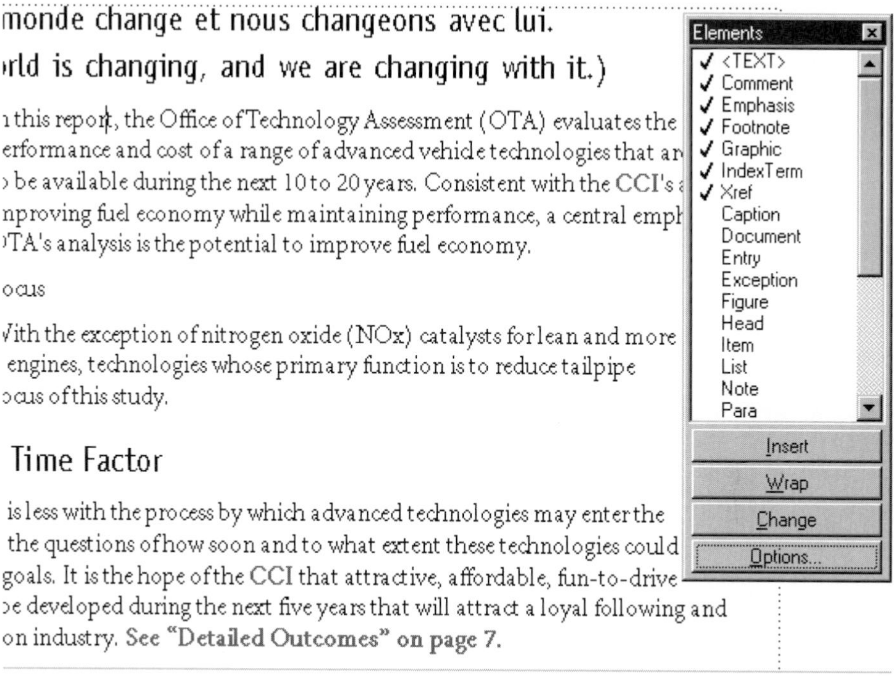

Figure 29-2 Element-type catalog displaying all element types; valid ones are checked.

Editing flexibility also means that a writer can omit required elements. Figure 29-4 indicates that information is missing by an open box in the structure view.

A product that allows the writer to bend document rules when creating and manipulating structured information, should also help to fix problems so that the document can become valid with as little effort as possible. In our example, the user should be allowed to move the glossary to its correct location at any time, thereby correcting the structure.

On the other hand, the writer ought not to be obligated to fix problems immediately. It should be possible to save an invalid document and resume work on it later.

As we have seen in Figure 29-3 and Figure 29-4, a product's structure view can indicate problems with visual clues. However, with long documents, it's not very efficient to scroll through the structure view looking for problems.

©2000 THE XML HANDBOOK™

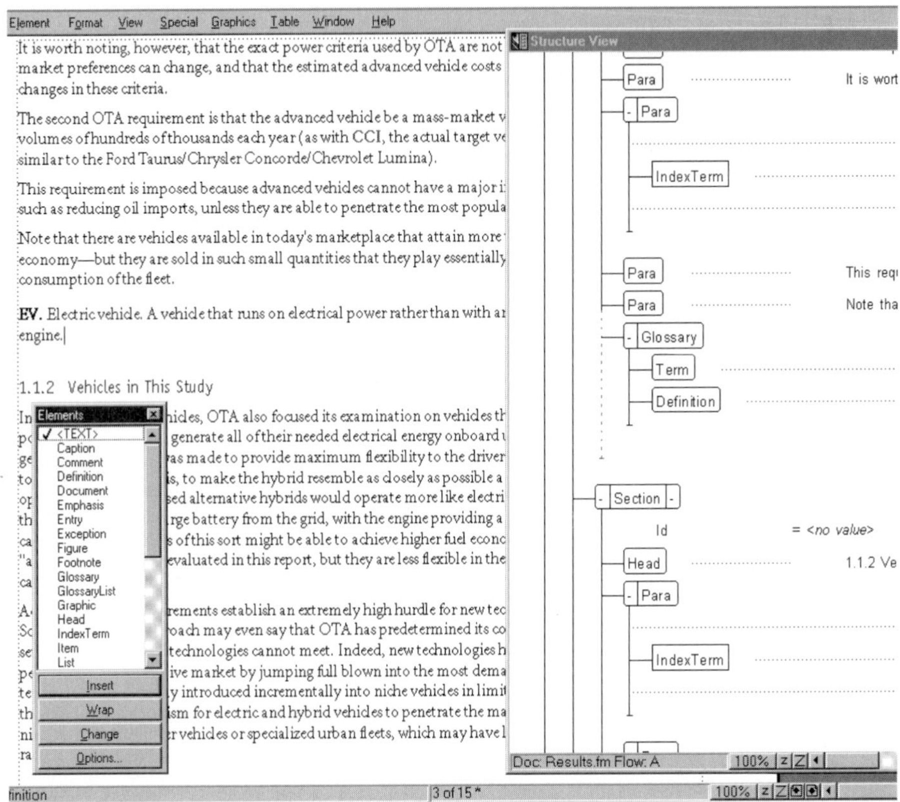

Figure 29-3 Dashed vertical line indicates out-of-context glossary element.

For this reason, a product might provide a batch validator in addition to interactive validation. A validator scans the document looking for problems, such as elements out of context, missing elements, and illegal or missing attribute values.

In Figure 29-5 we see that when the *FrameMaker+SGML* validator locates a problem, it displays a message and sets the insertion point at the problem area. The element-type catalog displays valid element types for that location, so that the author has help in fixing the problem.

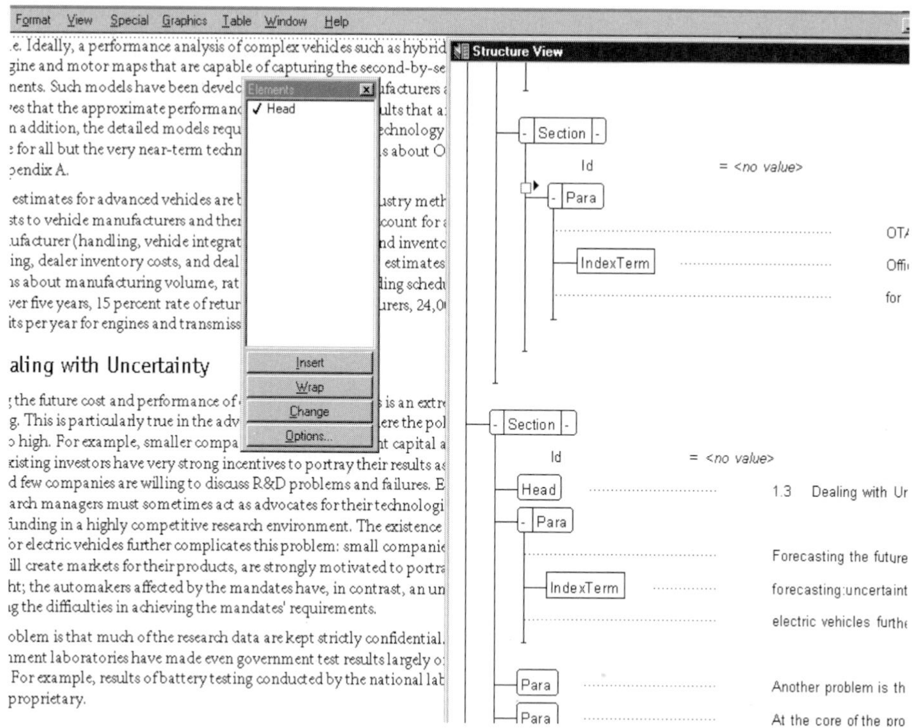

Figure 29-4 Open box indicates missing elements.

29.2.4 *Editing utilities*

Today's XML editing tools offer a variety of useful aids for such tasks as spelling checking, indexing, and cross-referencing. A close look at what our illustrative product offers in this area may help you determine your own needs.

For example, *FrameMaker+SGML* users can access an online thesaurus, and also check spelling in 17 languages. The document template can be set to automatically delete redundant spaces, and to turn "straight quotes" into open and close quotes.

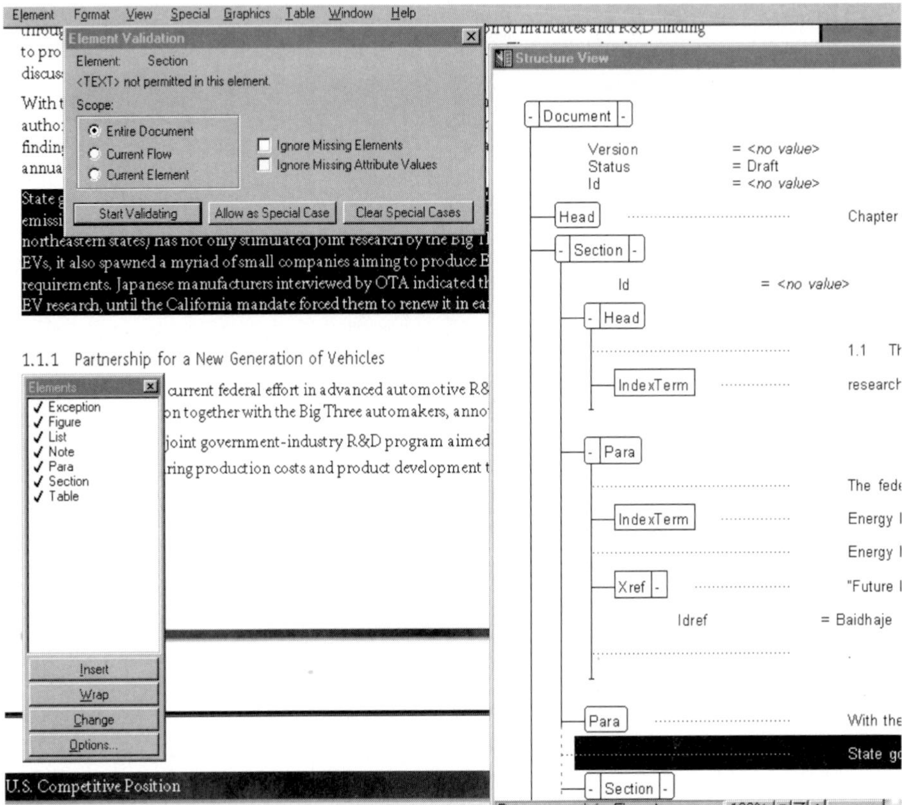

Figure 29-5 Validator identifies problems and provides corrective advice.

29.2.4.1 Cross-references

The cross-reference tool makes it easy to link pieces of information, either within a document or across documents, using standard XML methodology. The user inserts a cross-reference element, and selects a target element type from a list. The tool (Figure 29-6) shows all the instances of that element type in the document.

The user selects the appropriate element and the format of the generated text (e.g., "see table 5 on page 23"), and the generated string is placed in the document. For the XML markup, a unique ID value is automatically generated and placed in the ID attribute of the target element, as well as in the IDREF attribute of the referencing element.

©2000 THE XML HANDBOOK™

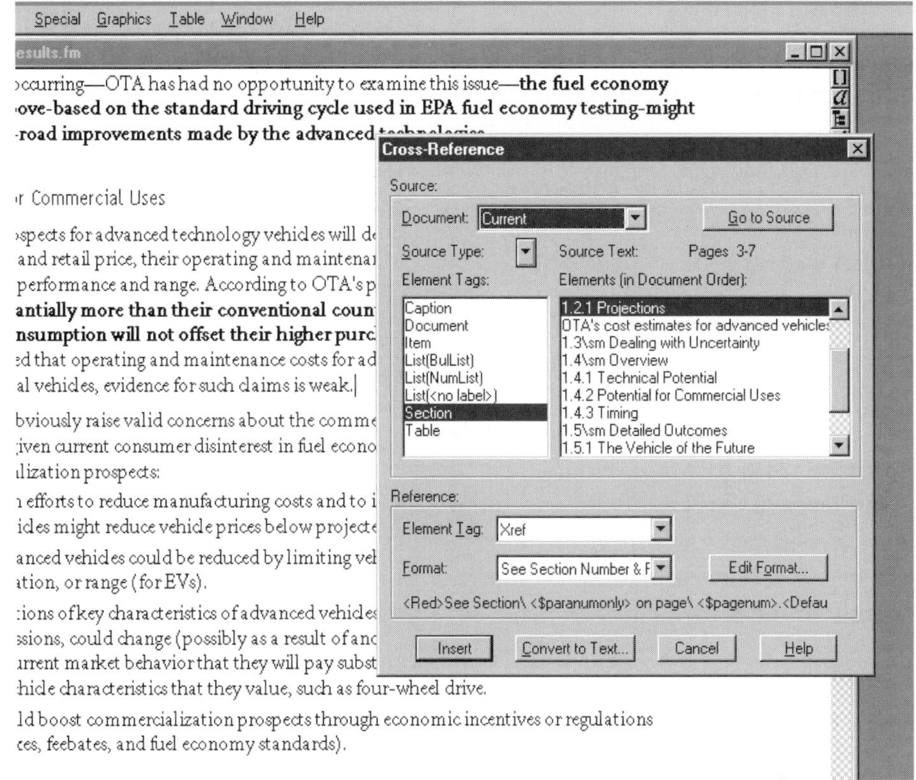

Figure 29-6 Cross-reference interface.

Users can easily modify the generated text, simply by editing the cross-reference format. Table, paragraph, and page numbers are automatically updated as content is inserted into or removed from the document.

29.2.4.2 Indexing

FrameMaker+SGML also provides a powerful index generation utility. This utility can handle complex, multi-level indexes like the following example:

Example 29-1. Multi-level index entry

```
Continental drift
  Fossil evidence, 57
  Rock structures, 62, 80
```

Writers enter index entries at the appropriate locations in the document. These entries are used to compile indexes automatically, either for a single document or a group of documents.

Writers can easily generate trial indexes to check whether use of terms has been consistent. Each item in the generated index is automatically hyperlinked to its source entry. So, if the writer finds a problem, it is easy to jump directly to the source entry to make modifications.

29.2.4.3 Hypertext

FrameMaker+SGML provides a number of tools for creating hypertext documents. Many of the links are created automatically. Hyperlinks are automatically created for all cross-references, while generated files such as indexes and tables of contents are also automatically hyperlinked. In addition, users can insert arbitrary hypertext links. A number of link commands are provided to control the behavior of the link, and they can be tested within the product.

29.2.5 *Managing external content*

A good XML editing tool makes it easy to incorporate external text and graphics into a document. *FrameMaker+SGML* supports a substantial number of text and graphic file formats, allowing input from many different sources. And you can actually see the contents of the external text or graphics in your document, rather than just a reference.

A link is maintained from the reference back to the source document. Any changes made in the source document can automatically be reflected in the referencing document.

To bring in external content, you simply select the appropriate file from a scrolling list. The product automatically creates an entity declaration, if one doesn't already exist, and inserts the entity reference in the XML instance.

29.2.6 *Well-formedness support*

An XML editing tool normally supports creation and manipulation of type-valid documents, using structured editing capabilities such as we've described. You might also need the option of working in a DTD-less mode, creating only well-formed documents.

In *FrameMaker+SGML*, this is accomplished by using an "unstructured template". Elements of information are identified by applying the product's own style codes in a consistent manner. These codes allow a well-formed XML document to be generated.

29.3 | Automated formatting and composition

The purpose of style is to communicate the content of a document. A rendition must therefore convey the document's structure as well as its words. Because XML documents are well-structured, they allow you to take advantage of rule-based formatting, in which the composition is driven automatically by the document's structure and other attributes. Rule-based formatting not only produces a consistent and communicative result, but it does so with far less effort.

29.3.1 *Rule-based formatting*

Rule-based formatters allow the appearance of the document to be modified easily by importing a new formatting *template*. Writers might initially develop the contents using a simple template with a one-column format. When the contents are complete, they may apply a different template that

©2000 The XML Handbook™

utilizes more elaborate formatting such as two-column, and then output the document to PostScript for hard copy production.

If additional layouts are desired, other templates can be applied; for instance, one designed specifically for online presentation. The document can then be output to PDF or HTML to create the electronic version.

29.3.2 *Interactive formatting*

On the other hand, interactive formatting allows minute degrees of adjustment, possibly to communicate in ways too fine-grained to be expressible in rules. More usually, though, interactive styling is used for copyfitting and similar compensations for the medium used, rather than as an expressive device.

An XML formatter should be rule-based. Web browsers are, for example. Interactivity is a plus, but the way in which it relates to the rule-based processing must be considered when evaluating a product.

In *FrameMaker+SGML*, the appearance of the document is fundamentally rule-based. It is controlled through formatting rules stored in the document template. Whenever an element is inserted into the document, the formatting defined for its context is automatically applied. If the element is moved to a new location, its appearance is automatically adjusted to fit its new context.

The product also has an interactive WYSIWYG environment. The user can see what the document will look like and can change the formatting specifications when needed. For example, the user can force a table or graphic to be on the same page with some text by simply selecting several paragraphs and reducing the interline spacing. This can be done without in any way affecting the structure of the document, or by using processing instructions. Therefore, the XML document remains clean.

29.4 | Document fragments

Many enterprises that use XML do so because of a requirement for collaborative editing and workgroup production. XML's structure provides a disciplined basis for writers to work on various pieces of content and then assemble them into a document. The document type designer specifies which elements in the document can be treated as fragments.

An XML editor can support fragments in many ways, for the benefit of both people and content management systems. *FrameMaker+SGML*, for example, not only allows elements to be treated as fragments, but also entities, XML's unit of storage. The product maintains a link to the fragment, and if the fragment is modified, the document incorporating that entity is automatically updated. This is demonstrated in Figure 29-7.

Business as Usual

Assuming that gasoline prices rise very gradually in real dollars, to $1.50 a gallon in 2015, OTA believes that new mid-size autos will gradually become more fuel efficient-reaching about 30 mpg by 2005 and 33 mpg in 2015-despite becoming safer, roomier, more powerful, and cleaner in this time period.

Because both the cost effectiveness of fuel economy technologies and customer preference for efficient vehicles will vary with gasoline prices, other gasoline price assumptions will generate different future fleet fuel economies. If gasoline prices were to reach $3 a gallon by 2015, OTA projects that new car fleet fuel economy would increase by 42 percent over 1995, to 39 mpg. In contrast, were gasoline prices to stagnate or decline in real dollars-as they have during the past decade or so-fuel economy improvements would be far less.

Furthermore, fleet fuel economy will depend on a host of additional factors (some of which are influenced by fuel prices) such as government safety and emissions regulations, consumer preferences for high performance, relative sales of autos versus light trucks (when considering the light-duty fleet as a whole), and so forth. OTA's estimate presumes no additional changes in regulations beyond what is already scheduled, gradually weakening demand for higher performance levels, and no major shifts in other factors. Obviously, another set of assumptions would shift the fuel economy estimates.

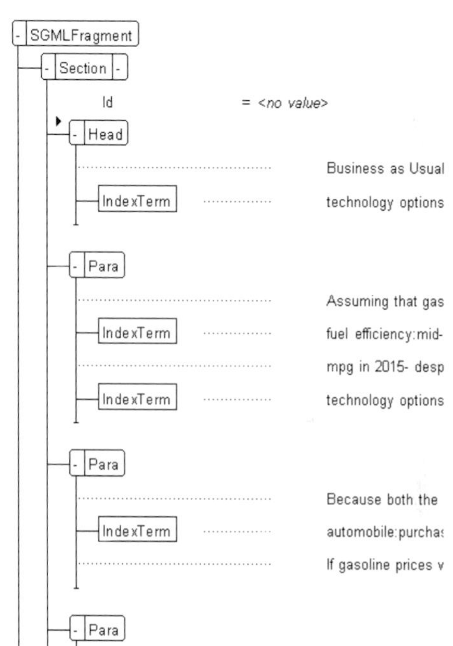

Figure 29-7 Editing a document fragment.

FrameMaker+SGML also has a book utility that allows users to divide a long volume into several individual components. The components are arranged in the desired order in a structured book file.

The book generation utility processes all of the components to assign page, section, and figure numbers, and to resolve cross-references among the components. The utility can also compile a table of contents, lists of figures and tables, and indexes for the book. All of the generated lists are automatically hyperlinked to sources in the book, providing an excellent navigation facility for online documents.

29.5 | Publishing the document

As XML documents can be independent of any style or presentation medium, it is easy to publish them in a variety of forms, enabling users to distribute information on many different media using an assortment of tools. Both paper and electronic distribution can be significant considerations when choosing XML products.

29.5.1 *Paper publishing*

While online distribution is becoming increasingly common, most enterprises still publish a substantial amount of information on paper. An XML product's ability to support paper printing may therefore be important to you.

FrameMaker+SGML, for example, has a composition engine that is quite robust, handling complex formats for both gray-scale and color paper output, as well as simpler online formats. In addition, the product allows you to define colors using Pantone and other standard color libraries. As Figure 29-8 illustrates, spot or process color separations can be created as well, and registration marks can be generated automatically in either Western or Japanese style.

29.5.2 *Online publishing*

In addition to XML itself, a composition package should support distribution in other online formats. *FrameMaker+SGML*, for example, supports publishing to CD-ROM or online in *Portable Document Format* (PDF) and HTML.

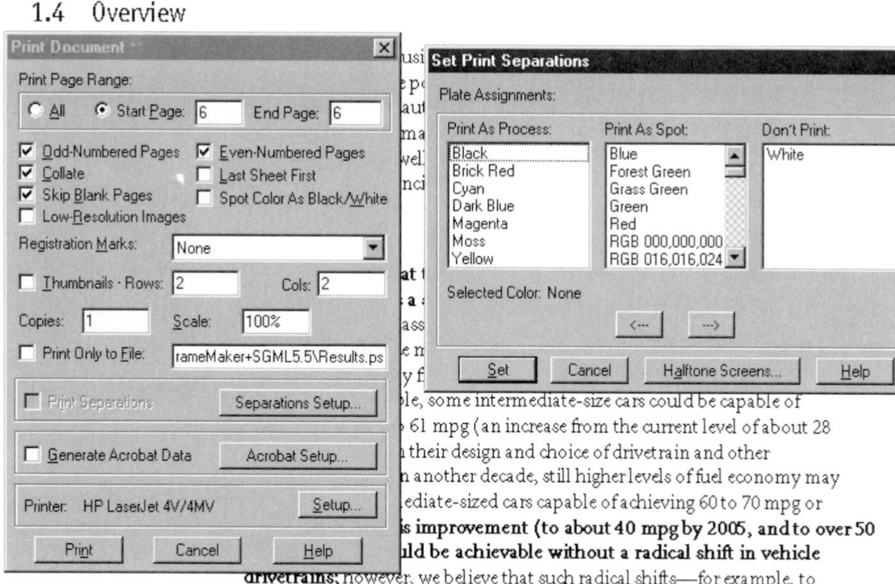

Figure 29-8 The print menu provides numerous options.

29.5.2.1 XML

Well-formed XML instances can be generated so that the original structure of the document is preserved. Visual fidelity can be maintained as well, by means of a Cascading Style Sheet that matches the rule-based format specifications of your *FrameMaker+SGML* document. Generation of both the stylesheet and the XML itself is also rule-based and can be customized.

29.5.2.2 PDF

Hyperlinks and cross-references in the document are automatically converted to PDF links, and hypertext alerts are converted to PDF sticky notes. PDF bookmarks can be generated automatically based on a list of element types. PDF document information, including keywords, can also be generated automatically, resulting in a fully hyperlinked PDF file without post-processing.

29.5.2.3 HTML

FrameMaker+SGML proposes an initial mapping of element types in a document to corresponding HTML elements. The user can review the mapping and make changes as required. In addition, long documents can automatically be divided into smaller files on specified element type boundaries. The files are hyperlinked, and a table of contents is created to aid navigation.

Hyperlinks and cross-references in the document are automatically converted to HREF attributes, and graphics are converted to GIF, JPEG, or PNG. In addition, the product generates a Cascading Style Sheet.

29.6 | Customization and preparation

XML offers much richer possibilities for processing than do unstructured document representations such as word processing files. Couple that fact with the generally rich function set of XML editing and composition products, and you get a sometimes overwhelming set of options as a result. Accordingly, the ability of a product to allow customization and setup can be a major criterion in deciding whether it is right for your environment.

29.6.1 *DTD customization*

Many DTDs are standardized by particular industries for interchange of information among industry members. These DTDs may contain element types that are not used by a particular organization, or within a particular group of documents.

An interchange DTD might also use short, cryptic names, or a terminology that differs from that used at a particular site. (Perhaps because the DTD uses English while the site is in France, or Germany, or Sweden.)

FrameMaker+SGML addresses these situations with a utility that allows the DTD to be customized within the editing environment without affecting the original. The customizer can create a simple *read/write rule* that will cause specified element types to be dropped as the DTD is brought into the editing environment. The software also removes references to that element type in all content models.

Similarly, read/write rules can be used to rename element types or attributes. For example, the rule to rename the element type "Foo" to "Bar" is:

Example 29-2. Read/write rule to rename an element

```
element "Foo" is fm element "Bar";
```

All of these changes are made without actually revising the DTD. When the edit is complete, the same read/write rules can be applied in reverse to save the document with its original element type and attribute names.

29.6.2 *Defining formatting rules*

When rule-based formatting is desired, as it almost always is when XML is used, the means by which a product allows formatting rules to be expressed becomes very important. As an example of the techniques employed for this purpose, let's look at those offered by *FrameMaker+SGML.*

- Page size and layout, column layout, table styles, cross-reference styles, and styles for indexes and tables of contents can be associated with element types and attributes in an *Element Definition Document* (EDD). As the EDD is a structured document, the application developer can take advantage of guided editing to ensure that the format rules are entered properly.
- As an alternative to putting formatting specifications in the EDD, paragraph and character styles can be created in a formatting template (stylesheet) and referenced by the format rules of the EDD.
- Attributes can be mapped to object properties. This is especially useful for setting up display of graphics.
- Style association can be context-sensitive. For example, a paragraph element in a table can be associated with different formatting from a paragraph element in a list item.
- Formatting specifications can be inherited. For example, all the items in a list will inherit the formatting specified for the

list itself, modified by any specific formatting for the first, last, and/or middle list items.

29.6.3 *Extensibility*

Your applications or business environment may require customization beyond what a product makes available out of the box. XML editing and composition products may offer scripting or programming languages for this purpose. A proprietary language usually offers the advantage of product-specific functions, while a standard language can be utilized more easily by a large body of developers who are already familiar with it.

For example, further customizing or extending the functions of *FrameMaker+SGML* can be accomplished by developing a "plug-in" using a C-based application programming interface (API). The API is accessed through a developers kit that provides an application development environment incorporating a library of function calls and makefiles. The kit supports a machine-independent layer that allows plug-ins to be coded once and then recompiled for multiple platforms.

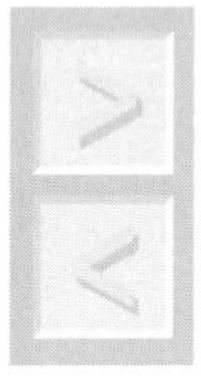

Analysis *Here's an interesting contradiction. One of the most important aspects of XML is that it can preserve data in the abstract; that is, it won't accidentally intermingle your data with rendition information. On the other hand, the style of a rendition is important, because that is what makes communication of the data effective.*

This chapter illustrated an approach to XML editing that seeks to resolve that contradiction. The product is structure-driven, but provides a WYSIWYG rendered view and sophisticated graphic arts functionality. Other XML editors make different trade-offs. Understanding them all will help you determine your own requirements more accurately.

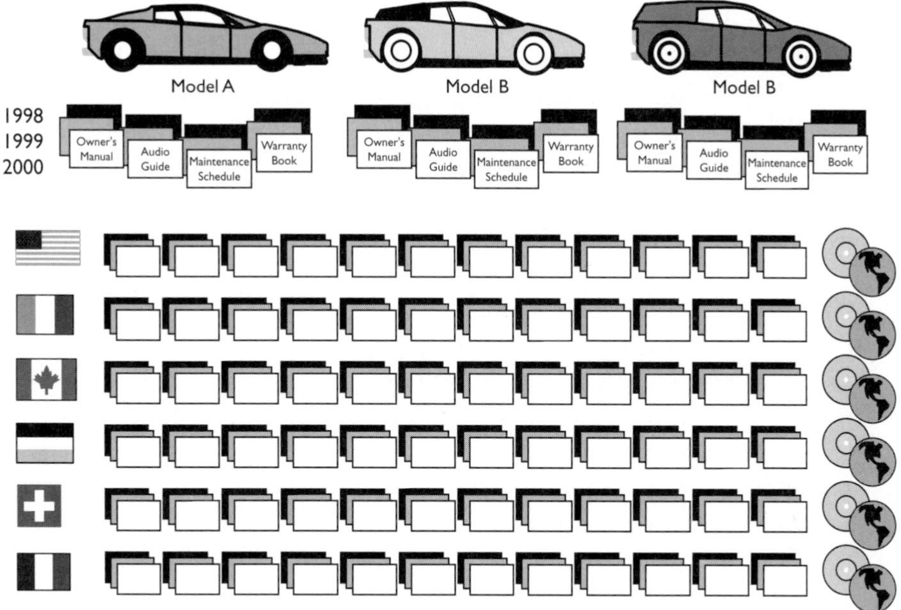

Figure 30-1 Managing information for multiple models and model years in many languages and three delivery formats is a complex task.

30.2 | Global markets, global information

As Tweddle's business grew, so did the requirements for internationalizing the information it managed for its customers. It soon became acquainted with the difficulties of the translation process:

- Passing information to translation houses, communicating about "what was really meant", and answering questions about context
- Tracking the status and progress of the translations underway – and what had been returned
- Retranslating what had already been translated – and hadn't changed – when only a small portion of a document was modified

Managing the process manually was time consuming and prone to error. It also required a large editorial staff.

In 1997 Tweddle undertook to find and apply a technology that would strategically position it to solve the large-scale problems of its customers. Tweddle knew it had to be prepared to support a vehicle release in 30 languages in 60 countries simultaneously. It needed to support 40 vehicle lines with a total of 6000 books. The information management team defined a number of objectives:

- Designing a friendlier more appealing visual style for the owner's manuals
- Creating a global, culturally neutral style
- Meeting local regulations (engineering, regulatory/safety, environmental)
- Reducing time to produce the information
- Reducing overall cost
- Increasing usability of the information
- Anticipating future uses of the information
- Managing artwork

Not everything on their list could be addressed by software, but the issues of time, cost, and reuse of the information could. They concluded that proper management of their information assets required generalized markup and a component-based information management system that could handle it.

30.3 | Needed: An XML component management system

By delimiting and labeling each of the individual elements of a document, XML enables both people and software to manipulate information as units useful for the purpose at hand. No longer is it necessary to deal with a whole document or even a complete chapter when only a small piece – perhaps only one or two paragraphs, a table, or step or two in a procedure – changes.

These units of information are called *components*. Figure 30-2 shows how XML identifies them.

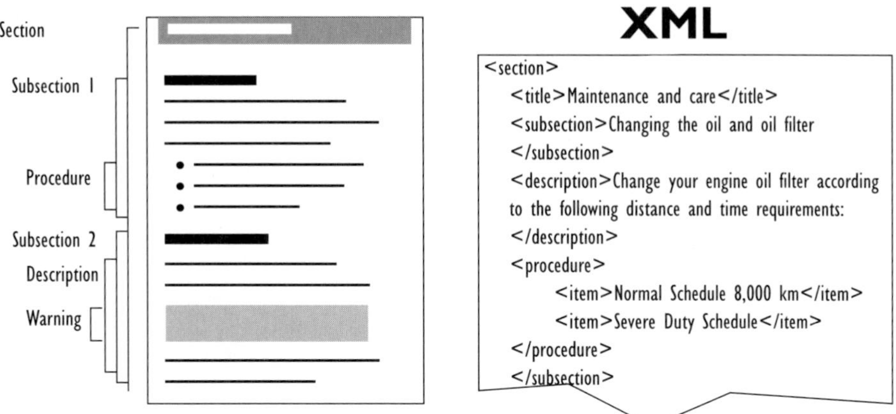

Figure 30-2 XML supports the use of document components

By managing these units separately and combining them into larger chunks of information – sections or chapters or books – only when needed, Tweddle could give only those units that changed to the translators. That level of precision enormously reduces redundant work.

In addition to providing the focus they needed for translation, a component management approach also let them reuse information in multiple documents. They could write a piece once, use it in several different places, and when changes occurred, update the component only once and have the changes replicated in each place it was used.

Even more, a component-based management system allowed them to build different views of the data. For example, a technical writer may be focusing on air conditioning or braking systems for a given auto model. The writer can look into the database and find all the procedures for that kind of system. Another writer, creating a view for a different model, might find that it included many of the same procedures because the systems were similar in both autos.

Tweddle developed its solution using *Parlance Document Manager*. The architecture for component storage is shown in Figure 30-3.

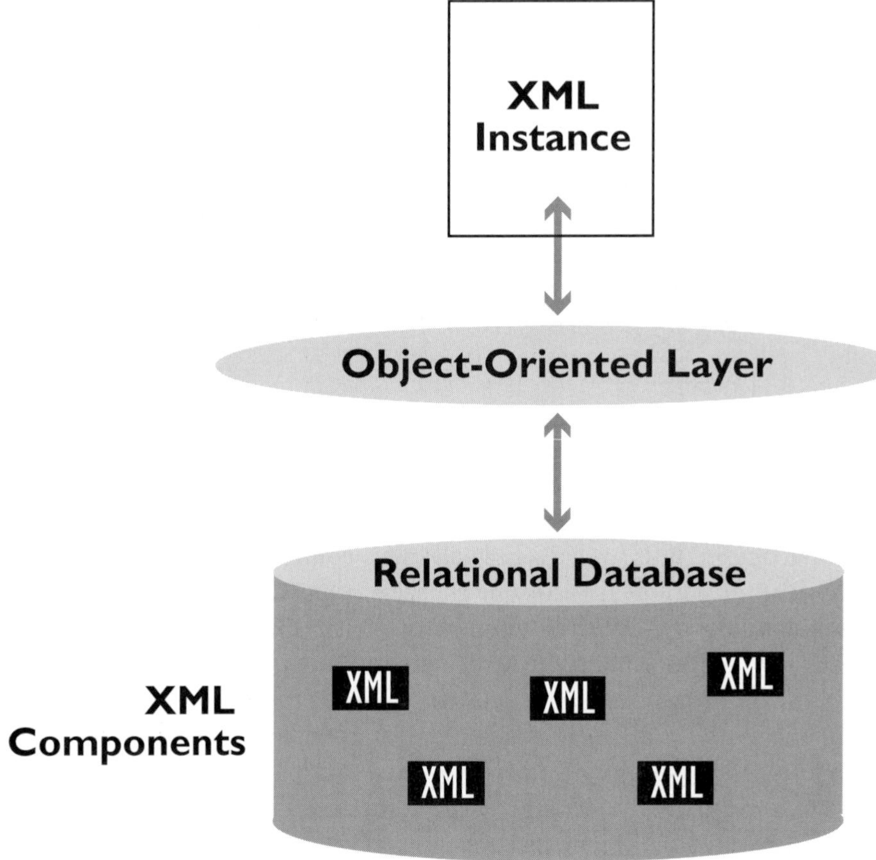

Figure 30-3 Content storage with *Parlance Document Manager*

30.4 | Improving the translation process

Component management allowed translation to be focused on revised components only, a concept illustrated in Figure 30-4.

The translation workflow at Tweddle is based upon the use of in-country translators; that is, native speakers of a language living in the country for which the information is destined. In this workflow, there is a significant exchange of information at "arm's length" between Tweddle and the translators. A key aim in managing the translation process is to preserve context so that the translator has sufficient information to make sound decisions about which word to choose in rendering one language into another.

When changes are made to a previously translated document, *Parlance* creates a translation package for the translator that includes a proof version that shows how the component looked in the last printed book, the previous XML source file for the component, the revised XML source file, and a list of differences. The package provides the context the translator needs.

The system creates the translation package automatically, triggered by the changes made when the revised component is returned to the repository. It is checked out for translation and the translation package is delivered electronically to the translator. Once the translation is complete, the revised translation component is checked back into the database and its status is automatically noted by the workflow manager.

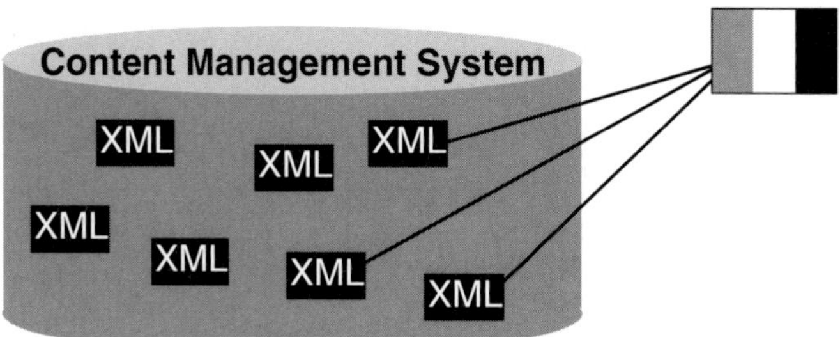

Figure 30-4 Only revised components are sent to the translator.

A further advantage of component management is the ability to coordinate parallel work on the same document. "One of our European car manufacturers does some of its own writing using the system," said Tom Dupont, Vice President of Sales at Tweddle Litho. "It writes some parts in German while we continue to write other parts in English. We have the ability to do original source writing in two different languages and still maintain the common use of data."

30.5 | One Source, multiple delivery formats

A key advantage of using XML is that markup reflects the structure of an element, totally apart from how it is to be rendered. This separation of abstract content from rendered format allows delivery of the information in multiple formats from a single source.

30.5.1 *Printed delivery*

When all revisions and translations are complete, *Parlance* assembles a complete version of the book from its components. This XML instance is then sent to XPP, which automatically composes and paginates the XML instance into finished documents.

"In the past, it took up to six months to deliver a translated book," said Dupont. "We are now getting the same results in 3 weeks and we are even able to support the release of a foreign language document prior to release of the domestic English version."

Tweddle has been setting up remote printing facilities around the world in response to a growing need for on-demand printing. "One of our European customers routinely has us prepare its service literature in 22 languages and then prepare deliverables in both print and CD-ROM formats," said Dupont. "Instead of shipping a large quantity of bulky books, we send the files electronically to be printed in Belgium for European distribution, in Singapore for Asian distribution, and so on."

30.5.2 *Online delivery*

Owner's literature will probably stay a paper-based product for quite some time because inside a car, at present, there are few practical alternatives for viewing it electronically. However, a few of the auto manufacturers have already eliminated paper deliverables completely for documents other than the owner's manuals.

"Another big trend is the move away from paper toward electronic files for customer assistance representatives," said Dupont. "Rather than sorting through one hundred manuals, each 1,400 to 2,000 pages long, the cus-

©2000 THE XML HANDBOOK™

tomer service representative today expects to access a searchable database to quickly find the appropriate procedure for a specific problem."

30.6 | Conclusion

XML enables solutions to complex information management problems such as Tweddle's because:

- XML can enforce the strict separation of abstract content from rendered format.
- XML enables the management and manipulation of small units of data that can be reused and assembled into multiple documents.
- XML can represent the structure of the abstract content, which is the same regardless of the natural language of the text.

Together with a component management system that supports and uses these advantages, XML solves immediate business problems while preserving a flexible and open foundation for whatever changes technology may bring.

©2000 The XML Handbook™

Epic: Efficient content management

Tool Discussion

- Efficient production and efficient consumption
- File conversion
- Component management
- Personalized delivery

©2000 THE XML HANDBOOK™

Chapter 31

Moving at Web speed requires efficiency for information publisher and information consumer alike. XML-based content management systems can help you achieve that goal. This chapter, sponsored by Arbortext, Inc., `http://www.arbortext.com`, will show you how. It was prepared by PG Bartlett.

Organizations that publish large amounts of vital business information face several challenges in keeping that content fresh, accurate and relevant. Whether that information includes internal documents such as engineering specifications, manufacturing instructions or human resource policies, or external documents such as diagnostic manuals or product catalogs, the information is vital to the smooth functioning of an organization.

The Web has dramatically and forever altered the expectations of those who receive information - the information consumers. They have learned that the Web has the power to deliver information that suits their individual needs for accessibility, content and form. They have learned that the Web can deliver all the information they need - and only the information they need - at the moment of need. And they want that information delivered in the form that's most useful to them: print or electronic, online or offline.

In a word, both the producers and consumers of information today seek *efficiency*. The producers need efficient creation, management and utilization of the information. The consumers want the delivery of the information to be efficient for them: personalized and targeted to their needs.

Tools, systems and processes designed for the relatively slow pace and inflexibility of a print-oriented world are not efficient in either respect. Unfortunately for most enterprises, that is all they have.

31.1 | How today's process works

Today's corporate publishing systems are typically based on print-oriented tools that were developed before the Web.

31.1.1 *Original creation workflow*

To meet the need for Web delivery of information, organizations usually try to bolt on additional tools and processes. The result? A workflow that resembles Figure 31-1 for the creation of their vital business information.

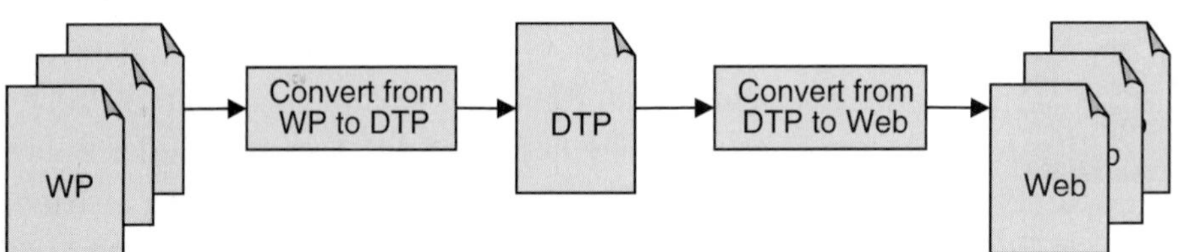

Figure 31-1 Original creation workflow

There are three steps:

1. Contributors, such as subject matter experts, capture their knowledge in word processor (WP) files.
2. Technical writers import the word processor files into their desktop publishing (DTP) systems, aggregate the content from various contributors and illustrators, refine and enhance the content to meet the needs of the ultimate consumer, adjust copy and formatting to create attractive page layouts, produce master copies for printing, and send their electronic files to the Web publishing group.

allows profiles to be defined that represent a combination of such criteria as audience personal characteristics, delivery media, and operating system. A component with an applied profile can be viewed only if the criteria are satisfied. Profiles can be applied to components at three stages (Figure 31-7):

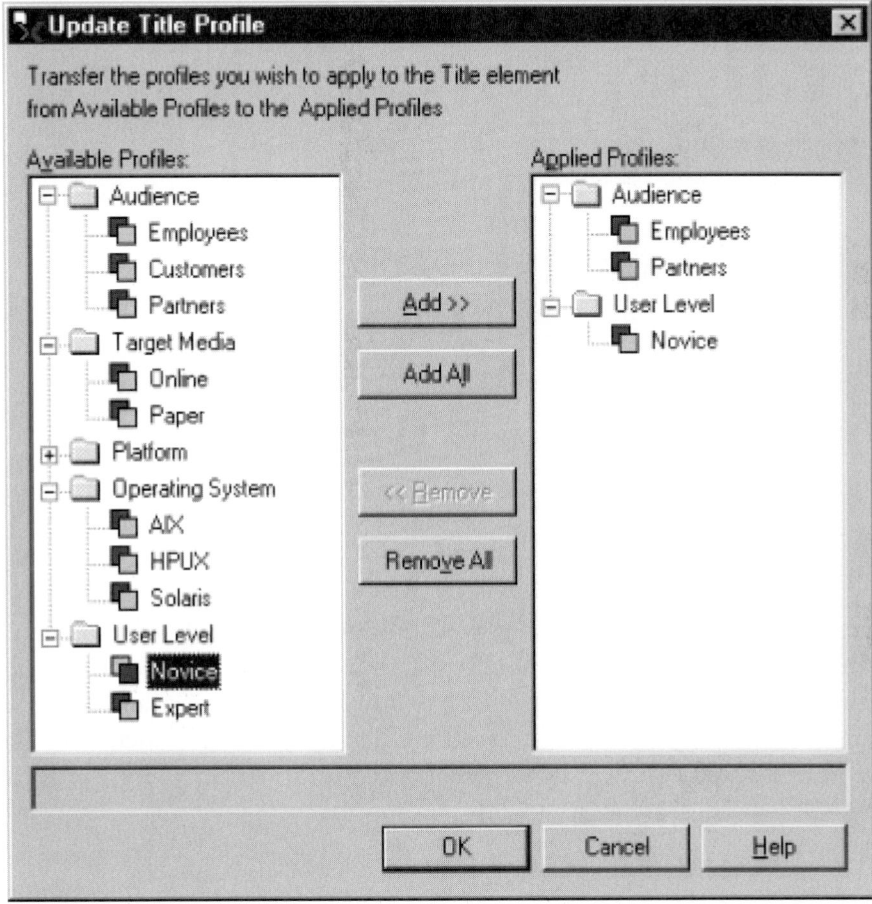

Figure 31-7 Authors can apply profiles to components with *Epic*

Create

Components can be written with a specific profile in mind. For example, some sections may be for internal distribution while others may apply only to a single product model.

Publish
: The author can specify any combination of profiles and the system will omit any components that do not match them.

Access
: The information consumer can be allowed to choose profiles when accessing the document on the Web or a CD-ROM (Figure 31-8).

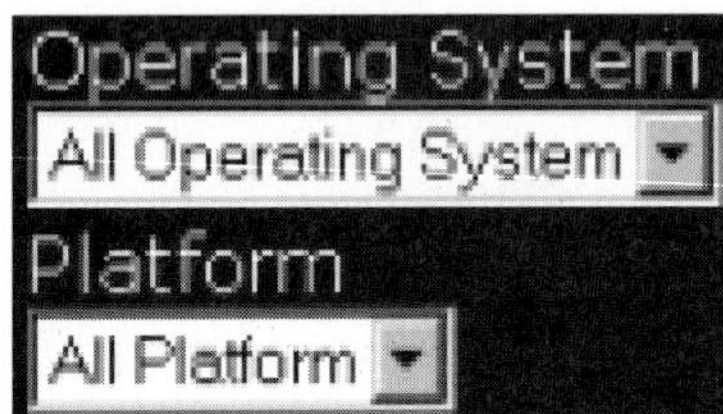

Figure 31-8 Consumers can select profiles when viewing on the Web or CD-ROM.

31.3 | Conclusion

Efficient content management can be attained with XML-based content management systems like *Epic*. Such systems enable organizations to create, manage and present their vital business information in a variety of media formats. The efficiencies these systems offer are dramatic, including the ultimate efficiency of delivering personalized information to the constituents who rely on that vital business information.

©2000 THE XML HANDBOOK™

BladeRunner: The content life cycle

Tool Discussion

- End-to-end content management
- Document management and component management
- Word processor to XML conversion
- Component repository

©2000 THE XML HANDBOOK™

Chapter 32

There was a time when publishing a document was a well-defined project, with a specific corpus of information and a starting and ending date. Today, information is an enterprise asset that grows and changes on a life cycle of its own, with publications generated as needed from the current state of the information. Barry Briggs prepared this chapter, which is sponsored by the e-content company, `http://www.xmlecontent.com`.

Increasingly, large enterprises are faced with a daunting array of tools and skyrocketing requirements for managing vast arrays of online content. As new documents, along with updates, corrections and revisions stream in, the content must be reformatted and restructured to suit an ever-increasing range of publications. And the need to distribute data via the World Wide Web in virtually real time adds yet another demanding dimension to this problem.

A "piece-s" approach is unlikely to meet this challenge. Instead, XML-based content management (CM) systems like the e-content company's *BladeRunner*™, have been constructed to provide a complete solution. Such support all aspects of the content life cycle. With a CM system, customers can manage data at a granular level, and by exploiting XML and XSL technologies, can repurpose content for multiple target media.

32.1 | Document management and content management

A CM system achieves its goals by managing content, as opposed to documents.

32.1.1 *Document management*

In traditional document management systems, the usefulness of the data kept in the repository is limited, as different representations of the finished document must be kept for each possible output medium. That is to say, for each desired output rendition, there must be one full, finished copy of the document.

Updating the content requires that the document be revised and regenerated in each representation, a process that is both expensive and inefficient.

32.1.2 *Content management*

In contrast, content management is a much more powerful technology. It enables enterprises to maintain a single copy of the content as an XML abstraction and to reuse it as necessary to generate any needed representation, be it HTML, PostScript, RTF, XML itself, or even plain text. It is XML's ability to enforce the separation of the abstract data content from style that suits it for this use.

Moreover, XML-based CM systems manage information at a level more granular than a document. For example, a CM system might parse (decompose) an invoice into:

- A customer name and address element,
- A bill of materials element,
- An issue date, and
- A due-by date.

New invoices can then reuse the customer name and address element, thereby saving space in the database. And doing so also improves database integrity, as a change to the name or address will automatically be reflected in all documents that include it. It is XML's ability to identify data elements with semantically-significant metadata tags that recommend it as a representation for highly-granular reusable content.

These capabilities for content reuse and highly-granular access enable content management systems to dramatically enhance the value of corporate information assets.

32.2 | Content life cycle

In most organizations, the production of documents – be they parts lists, sales brochures, catalogs, or what have you – is an elaborate process involving the creation or capture of content, assembly, styling, online management and publishing. Often, many different professionals participate in each of these tasks.

A CM system like *BladeRunner* is designed with this notion of an "end to end" content life cycle in mind, as shown in Figure 32-1. Each major component is targeted at a specific stage in the content life cycle:

- Content capture
- Editing and styling
- Management
- Publishing

Note that this breakdown can vary from one CM system to another. Systems differ both in where the bounds of the stages lie, and also in the terminology used to describe each stage. For example, a system architecture might combine editing with content capture and styling with publishing, or keep all of them separate, rather than utilizing the combinations used here.

We'll now look at each of the stages in detail.

32.2.1 *Content capture*

This stage is where content enters the system. This can happen in many ways. For example, the document might be written within the system, imported as a document from outside the system, converted from legacy

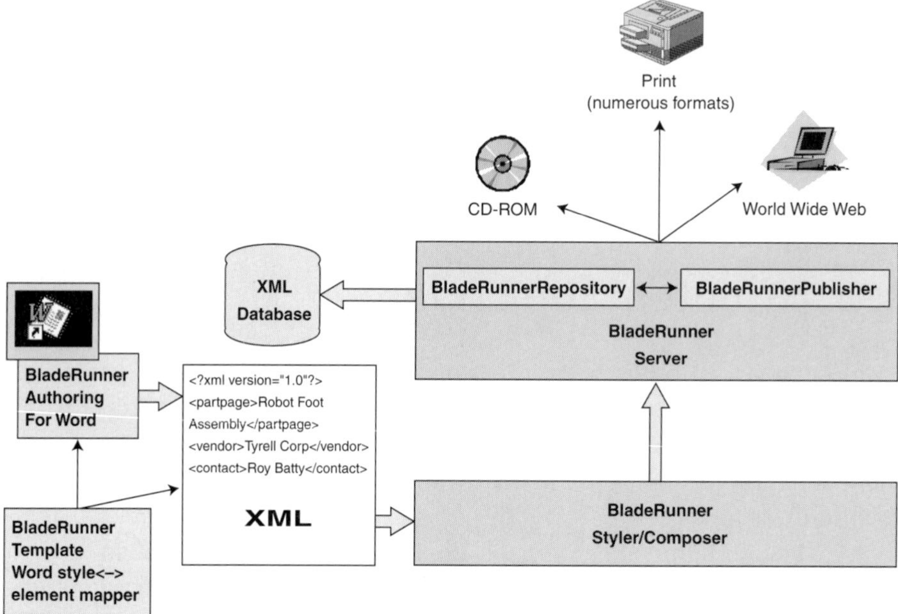

Figure 32-1 Content life cycle

documents or generated from data in a database. These techniques are covered in detail in Part Seven, "Content Acquisition". Here we focus on the first step in document creation, which, of course, is writing.

32.2.1.1 Creating XML documents with Word

While it would be ideal for writers to create XML directly, few of them use tools that do so. The tool they use the most for content creation is *Microsoft Word*™. Unfortunately for our purposes, *Word* is a word processor and is optimized for creating renditions, not for preserving abstract information content the way that databases or XML editors do.

Nevertheless, by disciplined use of *Word* stylesheets, a writer can create a finely-structured, semantically-identified abstraction. With a suitable tool, that abstraction can be converted to XML without information loss. Many CM systems incorporate or can accommodate such tools.

Let's examine the one supplied with *BladeRunner*, which functions as an add-in to *Word*. It is called *BladeRunner Authoring for Word* and it enables both import and export of valid XML. It works by mapping *Word* style codes to XML element-type names in a manner that will be described shortly.

In Figure 32-2, the style codes are exhibited in the style bar on the left side (a standard *Word* feature). Each style code applies to the content on its right.

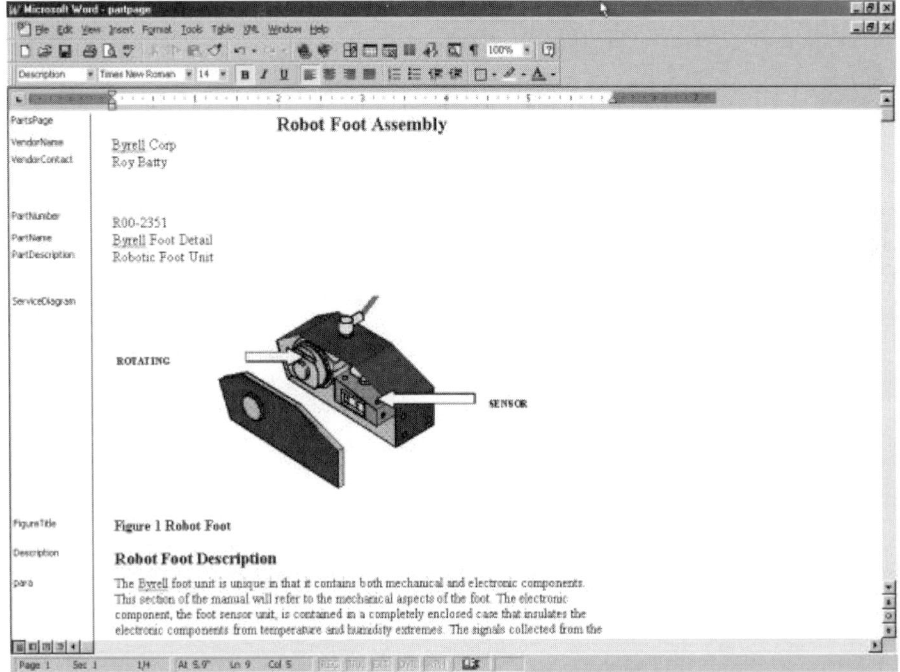

Figure 32-2 *Microsoft Word with BladeRunner Authoring*

Also note `XML` in the menu bar at the top. It appears when a user creates or edits a document using a *BladeRunner*-enabled stylesheet. It has two menu items: `Validate` and `Save As XML`.

When the user selects one of these, macros behind the scenes invoke code that converts the document to XML, validates it, and optionally saves it. Should a validation error occur, the cursor is positioned at the location of the error and an explanatory message is displayed.

32.2.1.2 Mapping Word styles to XML element types

The mapping between the style codes and XML element types is created using a tool called *BladeRunner Template*. Consider Example 32-1:

Example 32-1. *BladeRunner Template*

A heading in *Microsoft Word* such as:

1.3.3.1 This is not important.

can map to markup such as:

```
<heading4>This is not important</heading4>.
```

If the heading were emboldened, as in:

1.3.3.2 This is important.

the tool could recognize the emphasis change and add an appropriate XML attribute, as in:

```
<heading4 priority=important>This is important</heading4>.
```

Mappings are bidirectional so that documents can round-trip between *Word* and *BladeRunner*.

32.2.2 *Editing and styling*

In an XML-based CM system, content is stored as abstractions. In order to publish the content, it must be rendered and presented. Rendition requires the application of *style*, typically by means of an XSL stylesheet. XSL lets you specify the styling and other processing rules that should apply to the elements of an XML document.

Table 5 Mother Board Custom Technology

Device	Description	Vendor
XL33	Array Logic device containing the programs that determine signals relayed to the robot motion mechanisms. These programs can be customized.	ArrayTech
MP99	Microprocessor managing entire Control Center operations. The rated speed is 300 MHz. Special ceramic packaging is used to sheild other circuitry from electromagnetic effects.	Miptronics
XL21	Array Logic device containing the data pattern for signal generation. The data patterns may be customized to redirect the robot.	ArrayTech

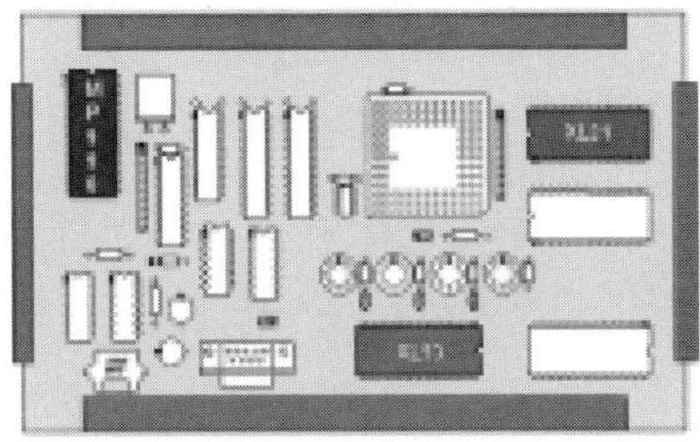

4.3 General Procedures

CAUTION: Always where a static guard wrist protector when working with the electronic components of the Robot Control Center. Any electrical surges could severely damage processor chips or ROMs. Many of these are custom designed components and are expensive to replace.

CAUTION: Always disconnect the negative battery cable when working on the electrical system. The battery system can contain up to 40,000 volts. Although the amperage is very low, this voltage could stun you or set off other reactions within the body.

It is important to follow all procedures in this manual very carefully. Trying to rush through a repair job by cutting corners will only cause harm to both you and your robot.

Always follow the procedures outlined below to ensure a safe, clean and productive environment:

Before opening any of the robot units, clean the entire outside of the unit, preferably with a high pressure washer such as a motor wash spray unit. Dirt entering the internal units will negate any time and effort spent on repair.

During inspection and re-assembly all parts should be thoroughly cleaned with solvent and then dried with compressed air. Wiping cloths and rags should not be used to dry parts. These rags typically contain contaminants which will damage robot parts.

Do not use wheel bearing grease to lubricate parts. Use ordinary un-medicated petroleum jelly to hold the thrust washers in place. Petroleum jelly will not leave a harmful residue as grease often will.

Before installing screws or bolts always dip the threads into clean oil.

Always use properly maintained tools. Excessively worn screwdrivers, spread opened wrenches, cracked sockets , or frayed electrical cords can cause accidents.

Figure 32-4 Motherboard description rendered for printing

Now consider the rendition of the same document that is shown in Figure 32-5. Here the layout is optimized for a Web browser, where the actual width of the display is unknown to the publisher and can be modified dynamically by the reader. In this environment, a two-column layout would not achieve the same results as it does on the printed page. Moreover, the reader would likely consider it a nuisance because of the need to scroll back up from the bottom of column one in order to continue reading at the top of column two.

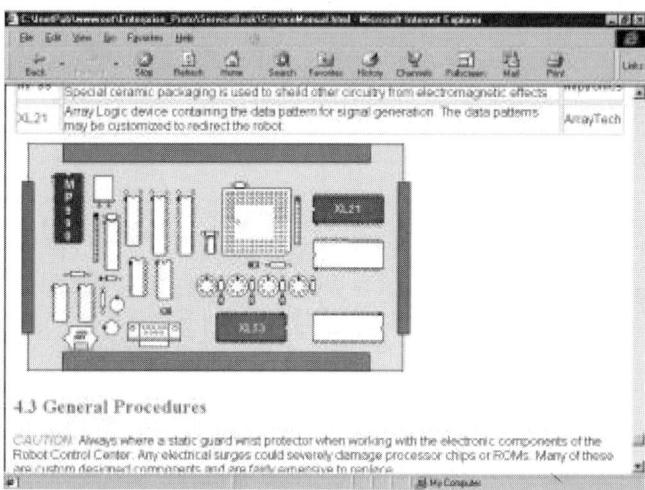

Figure 32-5 Motherboard description rendered for Web browsing

With *BladeRunner*, users can publish documents directly from the repository. They can also publish content they are currently editing. In the latter case, the system keeps track of which components of the published document are currently checked out and residing on the user's client machine and accesses the repository only for the remainder of the document.

Once the content has been fully assembled it is transformed and styled using the selected XSL stylesheet. The result of this operation is either HTML, or an intermediate rendition-oriented processing language that is then directed to the publishing engine.

The publishing engine of *BladeRunner* supports a range of output representations, including Rich Text Format (RTF), PostScript (distillable into PDF), HTML, XML and many others. It can be configured in various ways to best meet the needs of the application and the enterprise.

For example, based on site configuration parameters, any number of publishing engine instances can be configured. That way a very large print job will not block others from running.

Access to the publishing engines is controlled via persistent queues, which log their information to disk. In the event of a system failure, the publishing request can be restarted and no data will be lost.

32.3 | Conclusion

An XML-based CM system, such as the e-content company's *BladeRunner*, can utilize and exploit XML and XSL in ways that dramatically enhance the value of information resources. They turn the content of publications and websites into a true managed corporate asset.

©2000 The XML Handbook™

SigmaLink: Links and workflow

Tool Discussion

- Link management
- Workflow integration
- Open architecture and APIs
- Specialty functional modules

©2000 THE XML HANDBOOK™

Chapter 33

The purpose of a content management system is to manage content efficiently throughout its life cycle. In the new age of online information, that means managing hyperlinks and complex processes as well. Petra Leuser and Hans Holger Rath explain these and other aspects of content management in this chapter, which is sponsored by STEP Electronic Publishing Solutions, `http://www.step.de`.

The arguments for representing information in XML have been presented in various forms throughout this book. Structure and standards are necessary preconditions for the efficient management of information, and efficient information management is vital in today's knowledge-based economy.

The rationale for using content management systems is that, for enterprises that manage large amounts of information, it is not enough merely to create order in the information itself. It is necessary to bring order to the creation, maintenance, and publishing processes as well.

In this chapter we will focus principally on aspects of content management (CM) systems that we have not so far addressed.[1] These include link management, workflow integration, architecture and APIs, and specialized vertical-market functions.

Our illustrative system, STEP's *SigmaLink*, is a client/server system that has CM capabilities in addition to those we will describe here. All the facil-

1. For this reason it is well to reiterate a general principal of this book: a chapter is not a full description of a product. Instead, aspects of products are used to illustrate the concepts in the chapters; in this case, additional capabilities of CM systems.

ities on the client side are accessed through the user interface called the *SigmaLink Workbench*, shown in Figure 33-1. It provides the mechanisms for browsing and viewing, editing, and annotating, as well as for linking to and from information objects. Its basic components consist of an SGML/XML editor, an SGML/XML viewer, and a workflow task list.

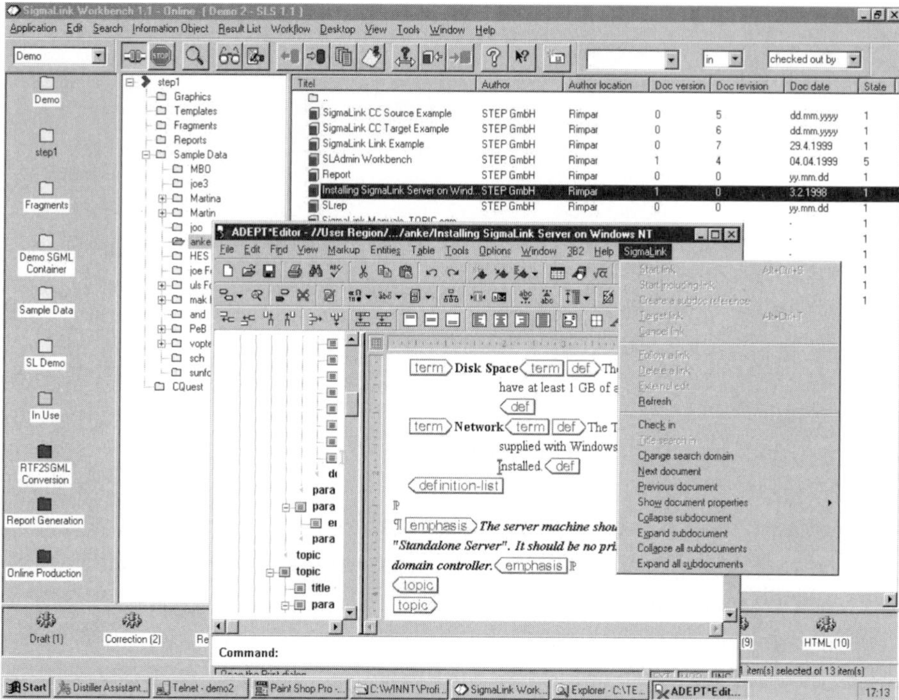

Figure 33-1 Client GUI *SigmaLink Workbench*

33.1 | Link management

Electronic publications on media like CD-ROM or the Web make heavy usage of hyperlinks. It therefore follows that link creation and link management should be important kernel functions of a CM system.

SigmaLink, for example, makes it possible to create, track and control a range of link types. These go beyond the simple linking of HTML in that they indicate why the objects are being linked.

The link types in the following list are supported only for SGML/XML objects, except for the "object link", which does not require understanding of the object's data format (representation).

Object link
A link between complete information objects, such as a document originally written in *MS-Word* with its converted XML equivalent.

Including link
A link to an image to be located at a certain text position.

Subdocument reference
A kind of including link, but to an SGML/XML document which becomes a subdocument of the current document (its master document). The linking might be recursive, such that a subdocument can also be a master document of another subdocument, and so on. The subdocument reference is the key feature for real information reuse on an SGML/XML document level. It is the base for flexible assembly of new publications.

Link into objects
A link to a target element in another object.

Link out of objects
Links from random positions in one object to or into another object.

Links to database contents
These links are bidirectional. In one direction, the contents of an SGML/XML element or value of an attribute are obtained from a database query (e.g. the number of purchases by a customer) when the SGML/XML document is checked-out/exported. In the other direction, both data content and attribute values can be stored in the database when the SGML/XML document is checked-in/imported.

All link information is recorded in the database. That enables the system to ensure link integrity and give warnings or deny access when deletion of a link anchor is attempted.

©2000 The XML Handbook™

Links can be assigned to user-defined categories to aid in their management and processing, as shown in Figure 33-2. The assignment of link categories can be automated; e.g. by defining a rule that every link between an *MS-Word* document and an XML document will be assigned the link category "original document".

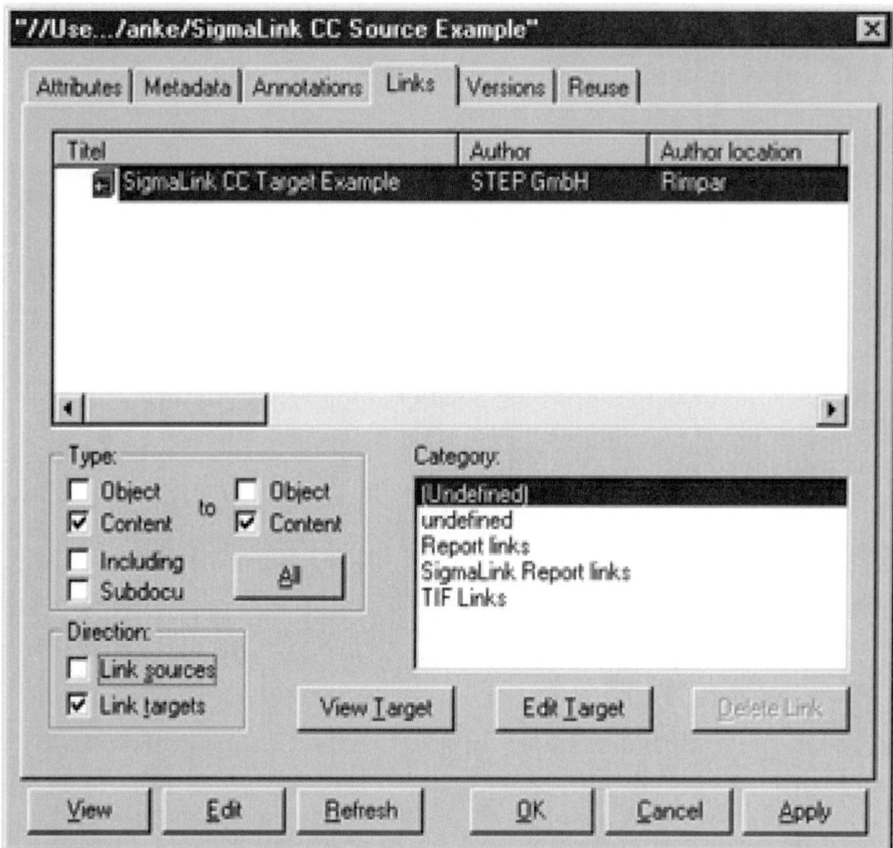

Figure 33-2 Link management in *SigmaLink*

33.2 | Workflow integration

The portion of a CM system that schedules and manages the processing of the data is called *workflow*. Example 33-1 shows a simple workflow for a "pre-publication review" process.

Example 33-1. Workflow for pre-publication review

1. The project manager selects XML files for review and correction and assigns each to a reviewer.
2. Each XML file is booked in its reviewer's task list with the delivery information: "due within the next five days". The task list is shown in the reviewer's *SigmaLink Workbench*. The reviewer can directly edit the information object to work on the corrections.
3. The deadline approaches. The project manager receives an automatically generated message reminding him which information objects are due back from review on the following day. The reviewers receive a message reminding them which objects they must finish by the next day.
4. The deadline arrives. The project manager receives an automatically generated message warning him which information objects have not been received. The offending reviewers receive a message that they are late with delivery.
5. All reviewed information objects have been sent back. The corrected XML files are checked back into the database and their status information is recorded as "ready".
6. A procedure is started to send the selected information objects to the managers who must sign off on the correctness of the information.
7. The workflow waits until each information object has been signed off by its respective manager.
8. The status of all the signed-off information objects is changed to "approved for publication".

Workflows can be substantially more complex. For example, the workflow in Example 33-1 can be augmented with workflows for reviewing the pictures, videos, and audio clips referenced by the XML files. The added

©2000 THE XML HANDBOOK™

workflows can be quite different from those for the XML files, and from one another.

Figure 33-3 shows *SigmaLink* with a workflow engine. Alternatively, a workflow system running in the database could be used.

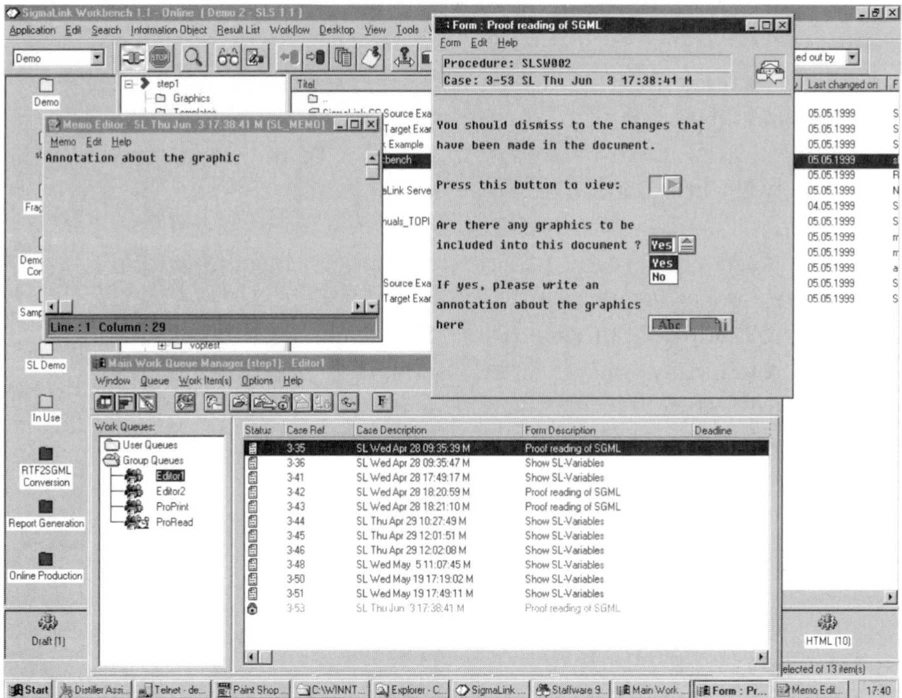

Figure 33-3 Workflow engine in *SigmaLink*

33.3 | Open architecture and APIs

An open architecture allows third-party products to be integrated into the CM system. It therefore allows a system to be tailored initially to the specific needs of a purchaser, and later upgraded to new technology regardless of its source.

For example, with an open architecture, the CM system is not committed to a specific database model: object-oriented, relational or object-relational. The buyer can use the database product that best meets his needs.

In this section we'll examine some of the characteristics of *SigmaLink*'s open architecture.

33.3.1 *Client server communication via HTTP*

The system server normally consists of a database, a full-text search engine, an SGML/XML transformation engine, a workflow management system, and an HTTP server (Web server). All these are standard third-party products that are integrated by the *SigmaLink* server software which is 100% *Java*.

Communication between the server and its clients is implemented with the HTTP protocol. The server provides about 80 different requests that perform all the server's work. All communication data, except the contents of the information objects, is exchanged as well-formed XML instances.

The client is designed for minimal dependence on the server. Only central functions, such as search and navigation via the database, require an active link to the server. Time-consuming processes such as editing take place locally.

33.3.2 *Server extensions*

The set of server requests can be enhanced by adding or replacing complete requests with customized requests, or by "hooking" functions on existing requests. All extensions are created with *Java* code.

customized requests

The customized requests function like regular server requests but implement specialized server behavior needed by the user. For example, a customized request might be added to communicate with a separate image database. When the user wants a thumbnail of a graphic to be inserted into an XML document as an "including link", he indicates this by selecting an image in the GUI of the image database. That causes the image database to send the customized request to the *SigmaLink* server with the thumbnail, metadata values, and user name as parameters. The server responds to the request by importing the graphic, inserting the thumbnail in the document, and setting the metadata values appropriately.

hooked functions

Each server request has two "hooks" on which functions can be hung: a pre-process hook and a post-process hook. The functions hung on the hooks are called when the server performs the request, either before or after its processing. The hooked functions have access to the request parameters and, if needed, the pre-process hooked function can even change them.

33.3.3 *Client APIs*

There are two client-side APIs, supporting communication with the server and with other client-side software, respectively.

client-to-server

The client-to-server API "understands" the client server protocol and both interprets and generates requests. It is capable of supporting the development of a completely customized client, should that be necessary. It includes the Open Document Management API (ODMA), which allows applications like *Microsoft Office* and *FrameMaker+SGML* to access the server through their normal file menu "New", "Open", and "Save" commands.

client-to-client

The client-to-client API is an interface for communication with other client applications. Almost every server request can be started through this interface.

33.4 | Specialty modules

Content management system vendors may offer specialized extensions to meet specific market requirements. Sometimes these were developed in conjunction with users of their products, who acted as subject matter experts.

This section describes some specialty modules that are available for STEP's *SigmaLink*.

33.4.1 *Reference works module*

A consortium of leading European reference works publishers designed this module, which includes:

semantic validation
: Checking metadata values, element content, and attribute values against predefined values.

fact base
: Extracting facts from database tables into SGML/XML instances as single value, list, or table.

virtual documents
: Temporary collection of several instances within a larger instance.

alphabetization
: Sorting of large numbers of articles.

33.4.2 *Journal publishing module*

Kluwer Academic Publishers publishes some 600 scientific journals from offices throughout the world. It is the pilot customer for this module for the highly distributed and complex process of journal production.

33.4.3 *Legal publishing module*

Wolters Kluwer, one of the largest legal publishers, helped design this module which offers the following legal publishing functions:

- Time Engine: manages the different time-versions of a legal document (valid from yy/mm/dd to yy/mm/dd).

©2000 The XML Handbook™

- Support for releases covering all the data belonging to a publication.
- Difference calculation between two versions of a legal document, showing the added, deleted, and changed text portions.
- Independent links for adding commentary to legal documents.

33.4.4 *Loose-leaf module*

Loose-leaf publishing is widely used in technical documentation, management literature, legal publishing, and other areas. It requires maintenance of the published rendition of a document, so that pages can be revised and added individually. Packages of revised and new pages are published as supplements on a regular basis.

A loose-leaf system must maintain a mapping between the XML/SGML abstraction and the structure of the published rendition. This module, for which Kluwer Law International is pilot customer, offers an interface to SGML/XML-aware typesetting systems calculating the loose-leaf information, and a Web browser-based planning interface supporting the selection of changed pages for the supplements.

33.4.5 *Topic map module*

This module supports the new topic map International Standard (ISO/IEC 13250). Topic maps add context to searches. They can describe the knowledge structures inherent in information in such a way as to enable much more intelligent navigation of large information pools. See Chapter 46, "Topic maps: Knowledge navigation aids", on page 618 for an introduction to topic maps.

33.5 | Conclusion

Today most information is still produced in word processing and desktop publishing systems. They are typically renditions, rather than abstract data, and are represented in proprietary file formats. A CM system must therefore be designed to support not only SGML/XML, but any document or data representation that may be used in an enterprise.

A system like *SigmaLink* can do this, and therefore provide the basis for enterprise-wide information management. It can support extensive linking of the information resources, can trigger external processes like publication production through its integrated workflow, and can receive and send information to other applications using its open APIs.

The potential purchaser of a CM system has to weigh the tradeoffs between adjusting to a fully-integrated complete system he can buy off the shelf, or developing one that is perfectly tailored to his needs. It is a balance between, on the one hand, predictability coupled with restrictiveness and on the other, project risks coupled with flexibility. A CM system with an open architecture and suitable APIs could offer a way to get nearly the best of both worlds.

©2000 The XML Handbook™

Oracle8i: Enterprise data management

Tool Discussion

- Enterprise data management requirements
- Mapping XML to databases
- Internet file system
- Complete data integration

©2000 THE XML HANDBOOK™

Chapter 34

Scratch the surface of a content management system and underneath you'll find a database. The same is true for middle-tier servers, portals, commerce integrators, and publishing systems. In this chapter we get below the surface for a close look at how databases deal with XML. It is sponsored by Oracle Corporation, `http://www.oracle.com/xml`.

Application developers face a significant challenge. Their business applications accumulate data at an incredible rate – a rate that is only increasing thanks to the growth in Internet-deployed applications.

And this data is not homogeneous: It comes in different datatypes, representations, and protocols. Application developers must find efficient ways to integrate all this data, store it, and use it within their applications.

XML helps by providing a universal representation of data for inter-application information exchange. However, it does not address the issues of how to store and administer the data, nor how to leverage existing data. And it does not eliminate the need for other views of data, such as object, relational, or the traditional file system view.

Let's look at the data management needs of enterprise applications and the requirements they impose on database support for XML. Then we'll see how those requirements are addressed by the *Oracle8i*™ database.

34.1 | Enterprise applications and XML

Enterprise applications are those that automate a series of business processes, including finance, sales force automation, order processing, warehouse management, etc. Most enterprises use several such applications, often from different vendors.

Enterprise application developers are using XML for two main reasons:

- Data sharing and communication between different applications
- Customized presentation of data

34.1.1 *Data sharing and communication*

As we have seen, in order to achieve the promise of e-commerce, an organization needs to bridge its "islands of automation". For example, its order processing application must be able to pass information to the inventory management system. And both of them must be able to access the existing customer accounts database.

Businesses do not have to convert their existing databases and applications to XML databases to satisfy this need. Instead, they can "XML-enable" the data and systems they already have. In other words, XML can provide an open application communication framework for message transport between applications, while each application continues to operate on its own private data store and data model.

These XML messages can be highly structured, ranging from simple single element structures to complex, multi-level structures as in EDI. Efficient facilities must therefore be provided to convert enterprise data into XML form and parse XML messages into a data model on which enterprise applications can easily operate.

34.1.2 *Customized presentation of data*

The technologies available for end-users to view information are evolving rapidly. Information presentation must now be optimized for different browsers or for other devices, such as Personal Digital Assistants (PDAs) and cell phones.

An XSL processor, either on the client or server, can transform an XML document into an appropriate form for any given client. It can thereby insulate the business application from the means of data delivery and consumption. Transforming information and generating it in multiple forms is key to the effective management of data.

34.2 | Requirements for enterprise data management

We will discuss four categories of requirements:

- Data storage and management
- Data views and interchange
- Query facilities
- Integration with existing systems

34.2.1 *Data storage and management*

The requirements for data storage and management are discussed in this section.

34.2.1.1 Management of structured data

Databases must be able to "read" and "write" XML without losing the structure of the data. Data stored in relational form is structured as a table, and can be mapped to tree-structured XML documents. Likewise, simple XML documents can be mapped to a relational schema, although more complex XML structures may require the use of object-relational technology to fully represent all the data relationships.

34.2.1.2 Performance, reliability, availability and scalability

A datastore that is to be used by enterprise Internet applications must meet very high standards of performance, reliability, availability, and scalability. It should be developed to run 24x7 under heavy loads and come with a broad set of management tools. These should include, for example, transparent application failover with no loss of performance even in the event of hardware failure.

34.2.1.3 Rich datatypes

XML document types are, in fact, custom datatypes. As they can be made up of atomic typed data, character text, multimedia, etc., the storage system must be able to support all these datatypes and optimally provide a single location for their storage and management.

Oracle8i, for example, handles character text, images, audio and video natively. It also provides an extensibility framework that includes interfaces to the type manager, storage manager, indexing and optimizer facilities. These interfaces allow users to:

- Define arbitrarily complex datatypes,
- Plug them into the database,
- Define their own indexing, sort and search algorithms for the data, and
- Leverage the data management and transaction facilities of the database.

34.2.1.4 Security and data integrity

Enterprise applications, as they are accessed by large numbers of people, require the type of access security, transaction management, locking and concurrency control that is typical of modern databases.

34.2.2 *Data views and interchange*

A datastore should be able to satisfy these requirements for supporting renditions and interchange.

34.2.2.1 Multiple clients

A datastore for enterprise data should be able to easily exchange XML documents with a variety of clients, including browsers, e-mail clients, enterprise messaging systems, FTP clients, and server-to-server communication (via HTTP).

34.2.2.2 Rendition and conversion

An XML datastore should provide facilities to *render* business data for presentation to an end-user. It should also be able to *convert* business data into the appropriate XML messages for interchange with applications. Both requirements can be met by running an XML parser and an XSL processor on the server and/or the client.

34.2.2.3 Persistent messaging

As XML becomes widely used for inter-enterprise communication, users will want to store, track, and audit XML message information. Therefore, the enterprise datastore must provide integrated persistence facilities for XML messages that are being exchanged between applications. Since the raw data for the XML messages is being held in the database, it is simple to provide an audit trail for inter-application and inter-enterprise messages.

34.2.3 *Query facilities*

For querying, an enterprise datastore must meet two important requirements:

©2000 THE XML HANDBOOK™

34.2.3.1 Universal query domain

An enterprise datastore must be able to perform complex queries over data from multiple sources. For example, providing book recommendations based on subject classification or keyword, availability, price, or previous purchases requires the integration of information from multiple systems into one delivery system. As all data may be integrated into a single datastore, queries may be run against all datatypes and sources.

34.2.3.2 Query performance and scalability under load

Enterprise applications typically need to execute queries quickly across large datasets. Moreover, performance must remain high even when large numbers of concurrent users access the system, which requires an efficient and fine-grained locking model.

34.2.4 *Integration with existing systems*

In deploying XML for enterprise data management, a difficult tradeoff must be made between deploying completely new systems and XML-specific datastores, or extending existing systems and databases with XML capabilities. For the latter option to be viable, the existing database must have suitable tools for working with XML.

34.3 | Reading and writing XML

In the preceding sections, we have discussed the requirements for enterprise data management and where XML can be of benefit. As most of these requirements rely on the ability to efficiently "read" and "write" XML to and from a database, let's look at the tools and techniques used by *Oracle8i* to accomplish these tasks.

First, some definitions:

- *Read XML from a database*: Export database objects or schemas and represent them as XML documents.

- *Write XML into a database*: Parse an XML document and store its components in a database without losing the metadata that describes the properties of the components and the relationship among them.

34.3.1 *Reading XML from a database*

The ability to represent a database object in XML requires infrastructure components that can use SQL to request the object and transform it into an XML document.

Figure 34-1 depicts a claim form stored as an object in a database using the relational tables shown.

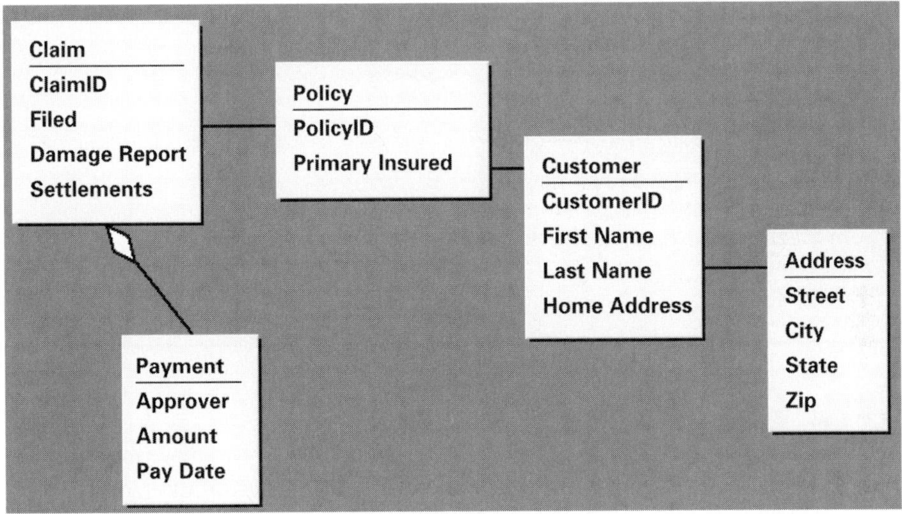

Figure 34-1 A claim form in a relational database

This object can be represented as the XML document shown in Example 34-1, which preserves the data relationships set up by the database schema. The document was produced using the *Oracle XSQL Servlet for Java.*™

Example 34-1. XML representation of a claim form

```
<?xml version="1.0"?>
<CLAIM>
  <CLAIMID>123456</CLAIMID>
  <FILED>1999-01-01 12:00:00.0</FILED>
  <CLAIMPOLICY>
    <POLICYID>8895</POLICYID>
    <PRIMARYINSURED>
      <CUSTOMERID>1044</CUSTOMERID>
      <FIRSTNAME>John</FIRSTNAME>
      <LASTNAME>Doe</LASTNAME>
      <HOMEADDRESS>
        <STREET>123 Cherry Lane</STREET>
        <CITY>San Francisco</CITY>
        <STATE>CA</STATE>
        <ZIP>94100</ZIP>
      </HOMEADDRESS>
    </PRIMARYINSURED>
  </CLAIMPOLICY>
  <DAMAGEREPORT>
    The driver lost control of the vehicle.
    This was due to <CAUSE>faulty brakes</CAUSE>.
  </DAMAGEREPORT>
  <SETTLEMENTS>
    <PAYMENT id="0">
      <PAYDATE>1999-03-01 09:00:00.0</PAYDATE>
      <AMOUNT>7600</AMOUNT>
      <APPROVER>JCOX</APPROVER>
    </PAYMENT>
  </SETTLEMENTS>
</CLAIM>
```

34.3.1.1 Oracle XSQL Servlet for Java

The *XSQL Servlet* is a program that generates XML documents from one or more SQL database queries. It can be loaded into a database that supports *Java*, such as *Oracle8i* (as shown in Figure 34-2), or into a middle-tier server or other Web server that supports servlets.

The query is included in a document of type XSQL, an instance of which is shown in Example 34-2. That document contains a query that searches for insurance claims submitted by Mr. Doe. Note that the query may be written as regular SQL or, as in this case, using object dot notation.

The servlet uses the XML Parser to parse this file and passes any XSL processing statements to the XSLT Processor. It also passes the attributes and data content of the `query` element to the *XML SQL Utilities*.

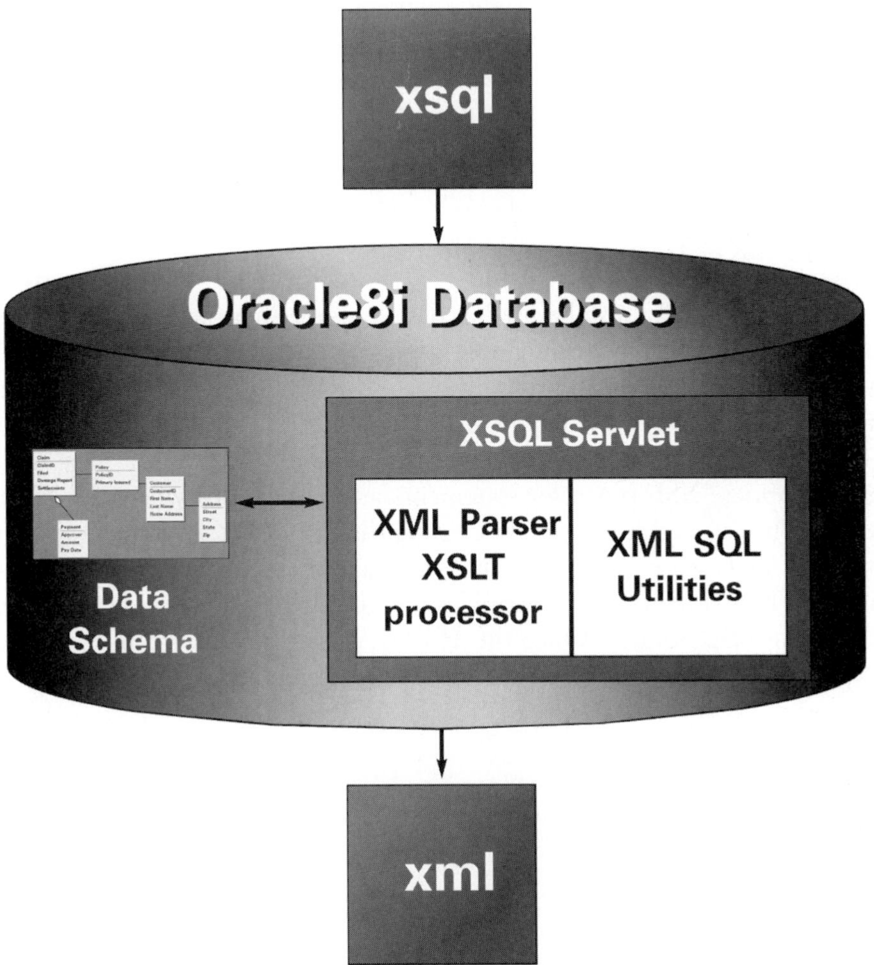

Figure 34-2 Structure of the *XSQL Servlet*

Example 34-2. An XSQL document that searches for insurance claims

```
<?xml version="1.0"?>
<?xml-stylesheet type="text/xsl" href="claim.xsl"?>
<query connection="xmldemo">
  select value(c) as Claim from insurance_claim_view c
  where c.claimpolicy.primaryinsured.lastname = 'Doe'
</query>
```

The query results are received either as an XML document or a JDBC `ResultSet` object. If necessary, the query results may be parsed with the parser and/or transformed using the XSLT processor.

The parser can also be loaded independently into the *Java* virtual machine in *Oracle8i*, run from a middle-tier server, or run on the client as a *JavaBean*.

34.3.1.2 XSLT transformations

XML documents can also be used as data messages between heterogeneous databases, with XSLT providing the translation from one message format to the other. While this capability is particularly useful for e-commerce, XSLT can also be used to render documents in HTML.

This is done by creating a template that is simply an HTML page with the appropriate XSL processor statements at the locations where the XML data is to be displayed. For example, using the insurance claim document in Example 34-1, we can create an HTML page to render selected data elements. While developing the template, we initially use dummy data as page formatting placeholders. Once the HTML is satisfactorily formatted, the dummy data is replaced with XSL processor statements, as follows:

JCOX

```
<xsl:value-of
select="claim/settlements/payment/approver"/>
```

7600

```
<xsl:value-of
select="claim/settlements/payment/@amount"/>
```

123456

```
<xsl:value-of select="claim/@claimid"/>
```

34.3.2 *Writing XML into a database*

Utilizing application generation utilities such as *Oracle XML Class Generator for Java*™, Web-based applications can create XML documents to be stored in databases.

There are two ways to store an XML document: as a single object with its markup intact; or distributed across a set of tables. Distributing across tables maps XML data into the relational schema.

Oracle8i can accept an XML document as a single object, and through its *interMedia* text option, can search for data based upon the XML tags. Using the insurance claim in Example 34-1 as the search domain, the SQL statement in Example 34-3 searches for all settlements approved by JCOX. It uses the CONTAINS SQL function to find those where "faulty brakes" were the cause.

Example 34-3. SQL statement

```
SELECT SUM(Amount)
  FROM Claim_Header ch, Claim_Settlements cs,
       Claim_Settlement_Payments csp
WHERE csp.Approver = 'JCOX'
AND CONTAINS(DamageReport,'faulty brakes WITHIN cause')>0;
```

This technique is quite useful when there are elements whose content includes both data and other elements, such as the DAMAGEREPORT element in our CLAIM document. However, when there is no such mixed content, the document can be parsed and stored in tables, where it can easily be accessed and revised. An XSL stylesheet determines the appropriate SQL insert and update statements for storing the parsed data.

For the claim document in Example 34-1, for example, the stylesheet fragment shown in Example 34-4 could create the entry for the Payment table.

Example 34-4. Stylesheet fragment

```
insert into PAYMENT values
   ('<xsl:value-of
select="claim/settlements/payment/approver"/>',
     <xsl:value-of
select=""claim/settlements/payment/@amount">,
     <xsl:value-of
select="claim/settlements/payment/@paydate"/>);
```

Alternatively, the OracleXMLSave class within the *XML SQL Utilities* can return an XML document into any database table or view. It maps the tag names to the column names and handles structured types, collections and references appropriately.

34.4 | Internet file system

We point out in Chapter 4, "XML in the real world", on page 56 that XML documents are an alternative representation for abstract data, one that is independent of the application or database that created it. The ubiquitous practice on the World Wide Web, of serving HTML documents that are constructed dynamically in response to queries, shows that documents can be representations of rendered data as well.

Such documents have no persistent existence as files in a file system. In fact, they suggest that for an enterprise with a sufficiently capable database, such as *Oracle8i*, it may make sense to avoid the traditional file system even for persistent files. Oracle's *Internet File System*™ utilizes the XML infrastructure in a more general way, for the storing and generating of documents in any representation, not just XML.

The system parses incoming documents with an appropriate parser and inserts the data into a database schema. Documents are then generated from database tables on demand, looking like normal file system files. The file view from *Windows Explorer* is shown in Figure 34-3.

This facility makes data available to both relational and file-oriented applications as required. Although documents can be viewed and retrieved as if they were files in the file system, they may also be updated directly in the database. And, because their content is stored in the database, they can also participate in searches over a unified domain of data and documents.

34.5 | Conclusion

Over the past 15 years, businesses have overwhelmingly chosen relational databases as the infrastructure to support their enterprise applications. This is because of the flexibility and broad applicability of the technology. XML is now becoming popular for largely the same reasons.

Databases such as *Oracle8i*, by providing XML interchange, styling, and support facilities, can allow enterprises to adopt XML without changing

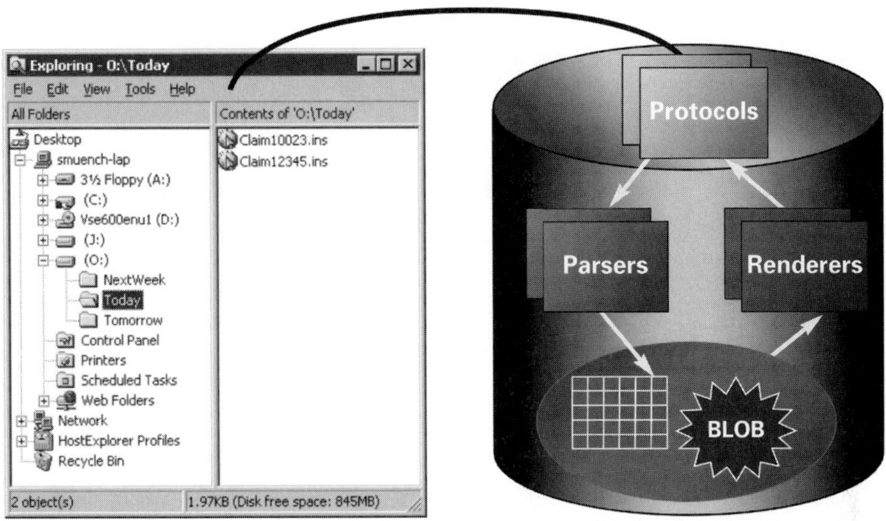

Figure 34-3 File view from *Windows Explorer*

their existing systems or databases. They are able to include XML – along with object, relational, and file system – in the list of supported alternative views of the same managed data.

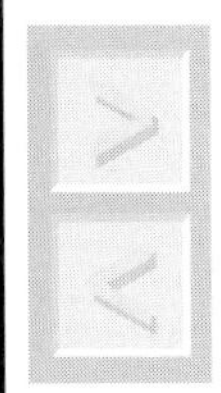

Tip *You can obtain the XML infrastructure components described in this chapter, including the Oracle XML Parser, XML Class Generator, XSQL Servlet, and XML SQL Utilities, from Oracle's website at* `http://technet.oracle.com/tech/xml`.

Congressional Quarterly

Case Study

- News organization and publisher
- Documents and data: the real difference
- Document feed processing
- Dynamic product delivery

©2000 THE XML HANDBOOK™

Chapter 35

One the most powerful aspects of markup languages is their ability to abandon the artificial distinction between data and documents that earlier technologies required. This chapter describes how to exploit that power when designing an information system. The chapter is sponsored by Reed Technology, `http://www.reedtech.com`, and was prepared by Lisa Bos.

Congressional Quarterly Inc. (CQ) is a national news organization and book publisher that reports on American government, politics, and national affairs. In the fall of 1998, it teamed with Reed Technology to build a system that manages its information and produces CQ's many print and electronic products. In developing CQ's content management system the team ignored the distinctions traditionally made between documents and data.

35.1 | Documents and data

It's worth reviewing the document/data relationship at the outset because it is so crucial to this story. The complete easy illustrated explanation is in Chapter 4, "XML in the real world", on page 56, but we'll summarize the high points here.

35.1.1 *It's all data!*

In an XML document, the text that isn't markup is data. You can edit it directly with an XML editor or plain text editor. With a stylesheet and a rendering system you can cause it to be displayed in various ways.

In a database, you can't touch the data directly. You can enter and revise it only through forms controlled by the database program. However, rendition is similar to XML documents, except that the stylesheet is usually called something like "report template".

The important thing is that, in both cases, the data can be kept in the abstract, untainted by the style information for rendering it. This is very different from word processing documents, of course, which normally keep their data in rendered form.

35.1.2 *Comparing documents to data*

Since documents contain data, what are people doing when they compare or contrast documents and data?

They are being human. Which is to say, they are using a simplified expression for the complex and subtle relationship shown in Table 35-1. They are comparing the typical kind of data that is found in XML and word processing (WP) documents with business process (BP) data, which usually resides in databases.

Table 35-1 (typical data in) **Documents and** (business process) **Data**

	XML data	**BP data**	**WP data**
Presentability	Abstraction	Abstraction	Rendition
Source	Written	Captured	Written
Structure	Hierarchy+ links	Fields	Paragraphs
Purpose	Presentation	Processing	Presentation
Representation	Document	Database	Document

Note that the characteristics in the table are typical, not fixed. For example, as we've shown many times in this book, XML data can be a rendition and WP data can be an abstraction. In addition, XML data could:

- Be captured from a data entry form or a program (rather than written);
- Consist of simple fields like those in a relational table (rather than a deeply nested hierarchy with links among the nodes); and
- Be intended for processing (rather than presentation).

In casual use, the term "document" connotes the data characteristics shown in Table 35-1 for "XML data" or "WP data", whichever is being referred to.

When "data" is contrasted with "document", it means the "BP data" column of the table. However, in other contexts, it could refer to "XML data" or all data.

We are more specific whenever a different meaning is intended in this chapter (and elsewhere in the book).

35.1.3 *A word of caution*

The true relationship between documents and data isn't as widely understood as it ought to be, even among experts. That is in part because the two domains existed independently for so long. This fact can complicate communication.

However, the team at CQ and Reed Technology understood the relationship and took advantage of it to satisfy CQ's requirements.

35.2 | Requirements

CQ needs a content management system that is flexible enough to allow news reporters to write, index, and publish breaking news within a matter of hours, or sometimes even minutes. That same system also must allow production of elaborately formatted and complex print publications with a much longer production cycle.

35.2.1 *Multiple products from multiple sources*

The system requirements for the information itself get even more complicated. CQ does produce and manage documents, ranging from short, simple news stories to large books containing statistical information. However, much of CQ's information is what is more typically called "data": what Table 35-1 calls "BP data".

Ever since CQ's first online service, *Washington Alert*, was created in 1984, CQ has been managing its data at a very granular level in multiple databases. The existence of these databases has made it possible for CQ to produce new electronic products that kept pace with the technology used to view those products. A short list includes:

- The Internet-based "*CQ Gopher*" (1994)
- CQ *NewsAlert* website, `http://newsalert.CQ.com` (1996)
- CQ.com *On Congress* website, `http://oncongress.CQ.com` (1998)

The company also had positive experience with the use of SGML as an intermediate representation between their databases and the static HTML in their websites.

As these experiences and requirements were considered, it became clear that CQ's information sources should be combined into a unified data repository (UDR) from which all delivery products could be produced.

35.2.2 *Unified data repository (UDR)*

The team broke CQ's information into five data collections or "data sets", as shown in Figure 35-1, and attempted to understand their relationship to CQ's document collection.

Here are some examples of what the team encountered.

- Users told the team that what was currently stored as a document (file) should actually be stored as multiple fields (data) in the new database because the relationships among the fields were complex and not expressed by the document

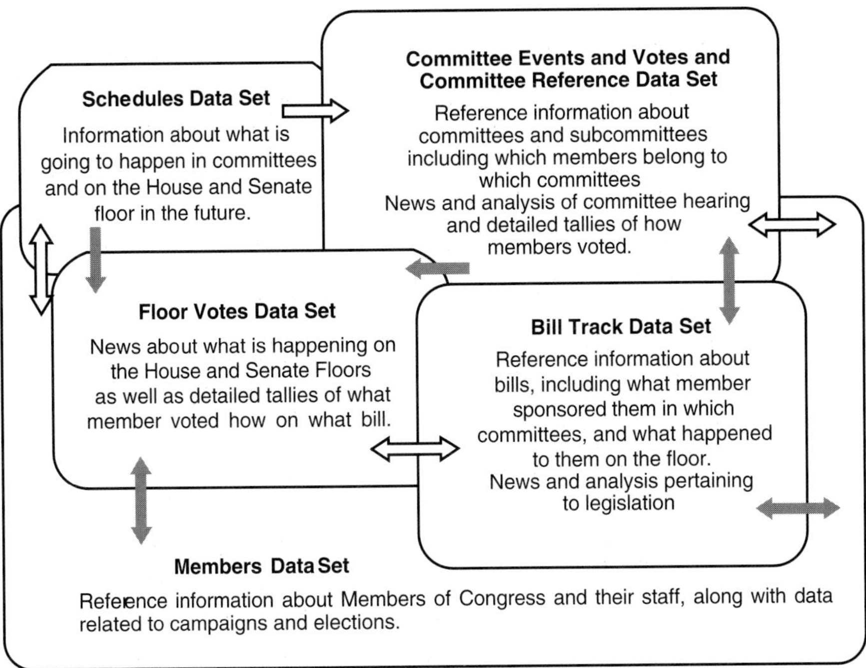

Figure 35-1 CQ data sets and their relationships

structure, and because the users wanted functionality that they associated with data in forms and not with documents.

- Users typically thought of a certain block of text as a field, but on the occasions when the text grew too large to be manageable in a text box in a form, they wanted to treat it as a document.
- Some fields were used in products independently of the rest of a document that otherwise should have contained them. To support these product requirements, the fields were currently being stored in databases, separated from their logical parent documents.
- CQ wanted to develop new products that would combine document and data content in novel ways that would have been very difficult in the original system.
- Website design was limited by a lack of intelligence in existing documents. In some cases, CQ had been forced to trade snazzy Web layouts for reliable processes that converted database

content to HTML. In other cases, documents were sourced from external systems and run through conversion processes that failed to capture the structure of the abstract data at the desired level of granularity.

35.2.3 *Product extraction and delivery*

The following requirements emerged as the driving factors in designing UDR product extraction and delivery component.

1. Editorial staff must be able to build new products and maintain the system.
2. Product delivery must be extremely reliable.
3. It must be possible to initiate product delivery by manual launching, triggering by an event in the database, or scheduling it to occur on a routine basis.

35.3 | System design

Two areas of the system design exhibited the benefits of understanding the document/data relationship: document feed loading and product delivery.

35.3.1 *Document feed loading*

CQ receives more than ten document feeds every day, throughout the day. The team designed a single solution framework, shown in Example 35-1, that supports the conversion and loading of these documents into the UDR.

Over time, it became apparent that some of the feeds contained more BP data than just the metadata that describes the documents. For example, a large number of the fields in the *BillTrack* data set could be automatically populated by data in the *Congressional Record*, a government publication that CQ receives every day. Having the system load this data, would avoid costly (and boring!) daily data entry. Fortunately, the *Congressional Record*

Example 35-1. Procedure for handling document feeds

1. A document and its images arrive at a UNIX server as one or more files. A daemon hands them off to a control process.
2. The control process reads a configuration file (in XML) containing process information specific to that feed, such as which conversion scripts should be used.
3. The control process launches the conversion scripts, which produce XML files. They also extract feed metadata from the body of the document and capture it in the XML output using a common UDR DTD.
4. The control process launches the load process, which is common to all feeds. This load process populates the database with the XML file and its metadata.
5. The control process notifies the user that loading is done.

feed, though it is a rendition, is structured in such a way that much of the desired data could be parsed out of it.

The system was easily extended to support cases such as this. First, the metadata DTD was extended to become a data DTD, and was constructed to ensure that a computer program could map it to the database model. Second, specifications for the load process were changed to support the modified DTD. The outcome was a process by which XML could be used as a means to move data from documents to the database.

35.3.2 *Product extraction and delivery*

An overview of the product delivery design is pictured in Figure 35-2.

To summarize, a product component "extractor" extracts product information from the database into an intermediate XML representation. The XML files are then converted to product-specific forms by product component generators.

These generators are the part of the system that is expected to change over time. When a new product is developed, developing a new generator is the biggest task. Both maintenance and new development of generators will be within the capability of technical members of the CQ editorial department, which was a major design objective.

The complete process is described in Example 35-2.

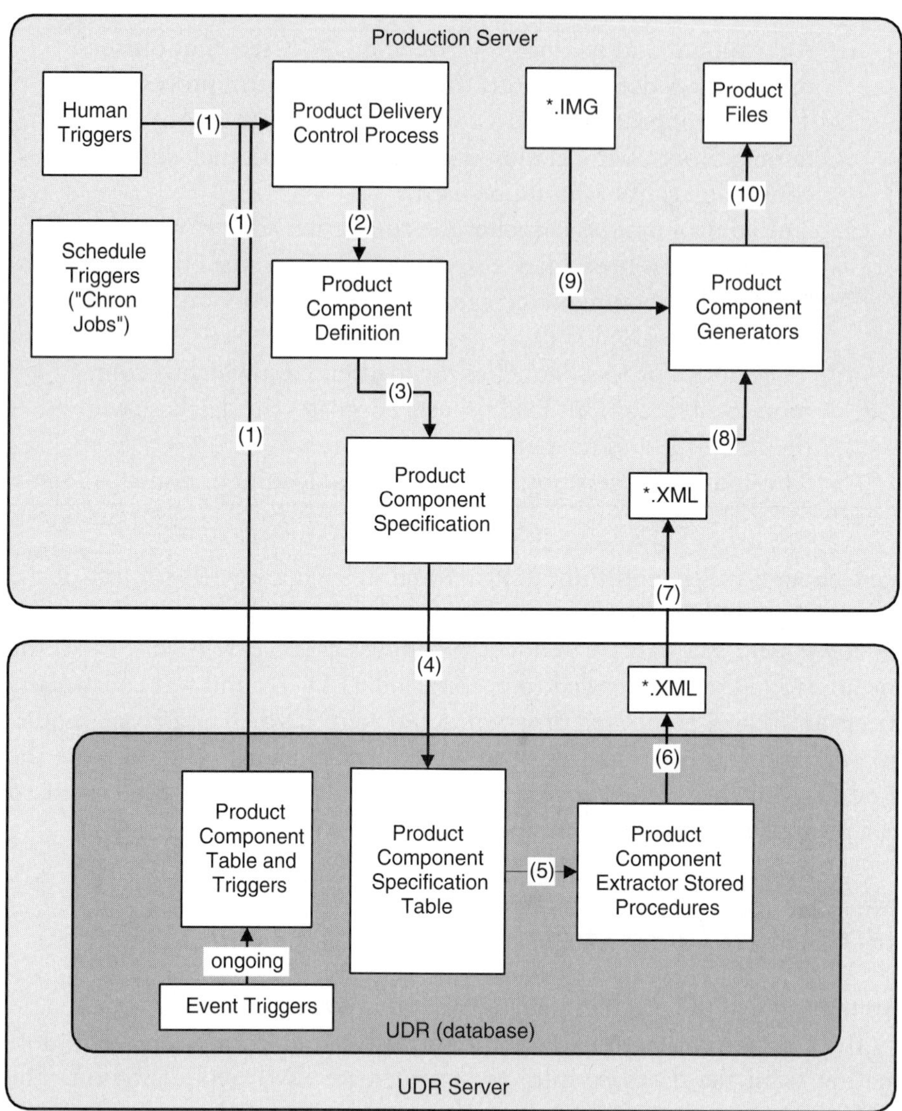

Figure 35-2 Product extraction and delivery system

Example 35-2. Explanation of Figure 35-2

Step numbers correspond to those in the figure.

Step (1): The product delivery control process script is triggered in one of the three ways indicated.

Step (2): The control process reads the appropriate product component definition file (XML).

Step (3): The control process reads the product component specification (XML), which identifies the data that should be extracted. (See Example 35-3 and Example 35-4.)

Steps (4), (5) and (6): The product component specification is duplicated in a database table. The product component extractor reads the table, extracts the data, and writes it to an XML file on the UDR server.

Step (7): The control process copies the XML to the production server.

Steps (8) and (9): The control process launches the product component generator, which produces product files and retrieves any necessary images.

Step (10): The generator copies the product files and images to the directory specified in the product component definition file. Product daemons move the files to the appropriate location so they can be loaded into the publishing system for print publication, processed for inclusion on a website, or FTPed to a site license client.

35.4 | Conclusion

The distinction between data and documents may be complex and subtle, but it is not an academic exercise. As Table 35-1 shows, document and database are really two ways to *represent* information, not two *kinds* of information.

That insight had positive impacts on the range of solutions available to the project design team. For CQ, it was neither possible nor helpful to choose a representation based on content characteristics. Indeed, Table 35-1 makes it clear that many variations of content characteristics are possible for either representation. There is no one-to-one mapping.

Trying to formulate content-based rules for what to represent as a document versus what to store in a database merely limits a designer's options. Consider CQ's experience with extracting information from the *Congressional Record* about nominations made in the U.S. Senate.

©2000 The XML Handbook™

Example 35-3. UDR product component specification DTD

```
<!ELEMENT product-spec     (table+)   >
<!ATTLIST product-spec
          name              CDATA     #REQUIRED >

<!ELEMENT table            (table*)   >
<!ATTLIST table
          name              NMTOKEN   #REQUIRED
          where             CDATA     #IMPLIED
          order-by          CDATA     #IMPLIED
          group-by          CDATA     #IMPLIED
          select            CDATA     #IMPLIED
          keys              NMTOKENS #IMPLIED
          key-values        NMTOKENS #IMPLIED
          if-null-suppress NMTOKEN   #IMPLIED   >
<!--
TABLE ATTRIBUTES
================
name             Current table name.
where            SQL restriction clause.
order-by         Sorting column(s).
group-by         Grouping column(s).
select           Arbitrary SQL statement.
keys             Key(s) linking current table to its parent.
key-values       Key value(s) linking current table to
                  its parent; these are parent-table keys
                  if names are different from those in
                  the key attribute (if same omit).
if-null-suppress If current table has no key-valued rows,
                  suppress this ancestor and all
                  intervening tables.
-->
```

Originally, this information was captured in great detail and stored as BP data. Later, it became clear that simply copying the information and representing it as a document could satisfy CQ's needs. Doing so eliminated much of the effort and made it unnecessary to build a special user interface for the data entry: a stylesheet and XML editor were sufficient.

The leap from data to document was easy to make because the team did not think of the terms as being inherently connected to the information itself. Instead they thought of them as two options for the way the information could be accessed and edited.

One of the lessons of this project is that XML and databases are both ways of harnessing information so that it can be used by people and systems. What people call that information at any place in a system flow is

Example 35-4. UDR product component specification

```
<!DOCTYPE product-spec SYSTEM "file://product-spec.dtd">
<product-spec name="SCHEDULES">
 <table name="EVENT">
  <table name="EVENT-SPONSOR" keys="EVENT_ID">
   <table name="COMMITTEE" keys="COMMITTEE_ID"/>
   <table name="ORGANIZATION" keys="ORG_ID"/>
   <table name="PERSON" keys="PERSON_ID"/>
  </table>
  <table name="AGENDA" if-null-suppress="EVENT" keys="EVENT_ID">
   <table name="AGENDA_BILL" keys="EVENT_ID AGENDA_ID">
    <table name="BILL" keys="BILL_SYS_ID"/>
   </table>
   <table name="AGENDA_PANEL" keys="EVENT_ID AGENDA_ID">
    <table name="PARTICIPANT" keys="EVENT_ID AGENDA_ID PANEL_ID">
     <table name="PERSON" keys="PERSON_ID"/>
    </table>
   </table>
  </table>
 </table>
</product-spec>
```

much less relevant than the fact that the data is intelligently represented, and that tools exist to transform, render, and search that data.

The information itself does not change, only the way we interface with it: Databases are better for some tasks than XML tools, and vice versa. But this might well become less true over time. The distinction between databases and documents may even cease to have meaning when tools exist that allow a user to decide on the fly whether to interface with information through a form or an editor.

Eventually, modeling techniques for databases, objects, and XML will converge, and we will have to settle on new ways of talking about information. While the practical application of such change might be years away, the structure and relationships of CQ's information will remain meaningful, regardless of whether it is represented in a database, in XML, or in both. Whatever the change, CQ's intelligently represented information will ensure that new technology can be deployed whenever it does come.

Content Acquisition

- Creating abstract XML documents directly
- Converting legacy documents
- Accessing dynamic data

©2000 THE XML HANDBOOK™

Part Seven

Content is king!

Yes, we said that before, but now we can tell the whole truth.

Actually, content is a royal family. There is *persistent information*, which you find in documents, and *dynamic data*, which is a by-product of business processes. Ideally, we want the documents to be unrendered abstractions, represented in XML, just as we want the data to be in sharable enterprise databases.

But much of the time, the documents are *legacy documents* – either rendered or not XML (or both!) – and the data is *legacy data*, usable only by the application that created it.

In this part, we look closely at the different ways of acquiring usable abstract content for XML systems: creating it directly in XML, converting legacy documents, and accessing dynamic data.

First, we look at the information supply chain and what you can do to help your suppliers create the XML documents you need. We also examine XML editing functions, with particular attention to structure. We then consider both technical and managerial aspects of converting legacy documents. Finally, we see how XML can make legacy data an integral part of the enterprise's information resources.

WordPerfect: The information supply chain

Tool Discussion

- Direct creation of XML by partners
- XML editing facilities
- Customized XML editing environments

©2000 THE XML HANDBOOK™

Chapter 36

It isn't just purchase orders that create a supply chain. In the increasingly interconnected world of e-business, the documents you publish are likely to have as many components and suppliers as the products you sell. Helping your information suppliers to give you what you need is the subject of this chapter, which is sponsored by Corel Corporation, `http://www.corel.com`, and was prepared by Kelly Fraser.

The best XML documents for your organization are the ones you create from the outset in XML, using your own DTDs.

For many enterprises, however, that truism is virtually an unattainable dream. Information gets created in many forms and you often have to take what you can get. That is why the systems we have been discussing – servers, portals, e-commerce, publishing, and content management – all put considerable emphasis on importing data into XML.

For dynamic data, which is produced as a by-product of business transactions, translation to XML is unavoidable. But for information that is created expressly for your system, there ought to be a better way. And in fact, there are many companies where information is created directly in XML or SGML in controlled environments, frequently in conjunction with a content management system.

Unfortunately, such systems can't often be used when the people creating the information are your trading partners rather than your employees. Or even when they are employees of your company but not full time creators of content for your system.

In most of these cases, the solution is for you to accept word processing files and convert them. This task is easier if your information supply chain partners are encouraged to use stylesheets in a disciplined way, and when conversion aids are employed, as we have discussed earlier (and will review in more detail in a later chapter).

But there is still another approach: Give your suppliers a word processing tool that is customized to create XML directly, using your own DTD. The author gets a familiar interface and you get exactly the valid XML document you need – without conversion!

Let's examine the requirements for such a tool, both for customizing editing environments for the information supply chain, and more general requirements for XML-based word processing. To illustrate, we'll use *WordPerfect®9*, the current version of a word processor that has supported SGML since 1992.

36.1 | Customizing editing environments

The editing environment customization objects for a word processor are aggregated into an object that is typically called a *template*. For this discussion, we will focus on three significant components:

- The template itself;
- Document type definitions; and
- Stylesheets.

36.1.1 *Templates*

The purpose of the template is to provide the expertise and assistance of the using organization to its information supplying partners. A well-designed template can reduce the cost of training and support and limit the likelihood of invalid documents being submitted. If, in addition, the environment created is comfortable to the non-XML savvy end-user, it will increase the likelihood that the partner will cooperate.

XML editors often ship with templates for popular document types. For example, *WordPerfect* includes, among others, a template for the document type discussed in Chapter 22, "XMLNews: A syndication document type", on page 288.

36.1.1.1 Template objects

For an XML environment, a template must at a minimum include a DTD. In *WordPerfect*, templates may also include custom toolbars, menus, embedded macros, prompts, and the default view setting of the document instance. Multiple stylesheets can also be included.

36.1.1.2 Associating templates with document types

An association must be maintained between the template and the document type to which it applies. *WordPerfect* does so with catalog files in the form defined by the Organization for the Advancement of Structured Information Standards (OASIS).[1]

36.1.2 *Document type definitions*

Merely well-formed documents are considered to be "simpler" than valid ones. But paradoxically, writers untrained in XML are most effective when creating valid documents – those that explicitly conform to a DTD.

That is because an XML-aware editor can use a DTD to guide an author, by showing which element types and attributes are permitted at each point in the document. *WordPerfect*, for example, provides a DTD compiler (Figure 36-1) that enables document type information to be embedded in the template for that purpose.

The DTD compiler can handle any DTD and can verify whether it conforms only to SGML, or to XML as well. It provides a log of errors and warnings to the DTD creator. Double-clicking on any error or warning brings up an explanation to help correct the situation.

36.1.3 *Stylesheets*

Applications, for the most part, need to deal with abstract data. When a program is comparing dates or calculating inventory levels, information

1. OASIS is an industry consortium, formerly known as SGML Open. Its catalog spec is on the CD-ROM.

©2000 The XML Handbook™

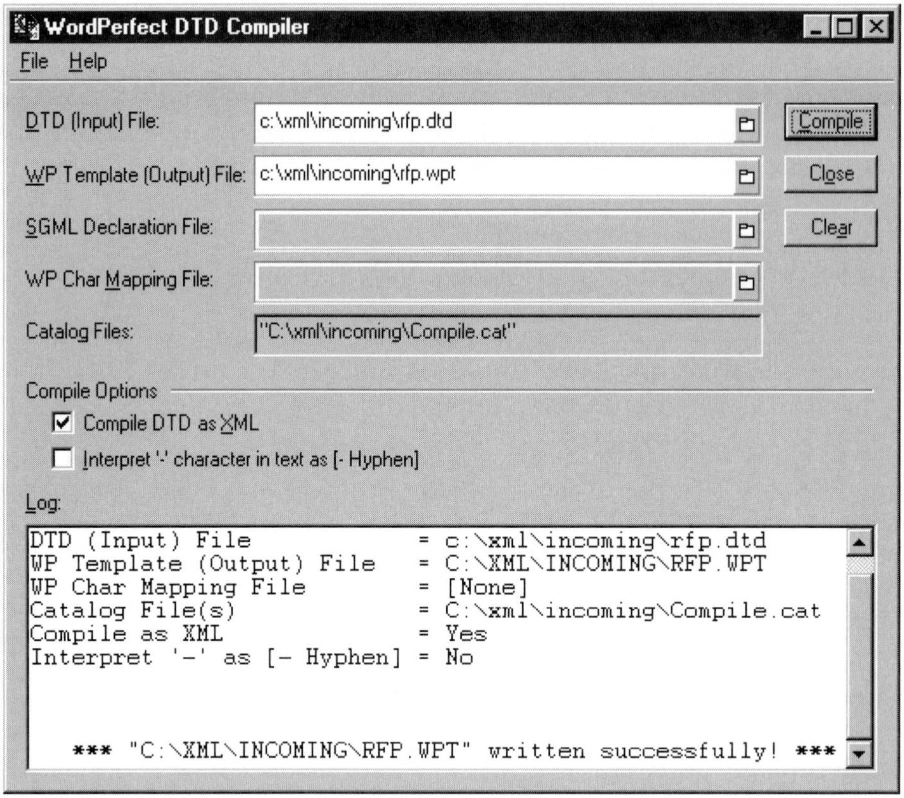

WordPerfect DTD Compiler

File Help

DTD (Input) File: c:\xml\incoming\rfp.dtd

WP Template (Output) File: c:\xml\incoming\rfp.wpt

SGML Declaration File:

WP Char Mapping File:

Catalog Files: "C:\xml\incoming\Compile.cat"

Compile Close Clear

Compile Options

☑ Compile DTD as XML

☐ Interpret '-' character in text as [- Hyphen]

Log:

```
DTD (Input) File              = c:\xml\incoming\rfp.dtd
WP Template (Output) File     = C:\XML\INCOMING\RFP.WPT
WP Char Mapping File          = [None]
Catalog File(s)               = C:\xml\incoming\Compile.cat
Compile as XML                = Yes
Interpret '-' as [- Hyphen]   = No

   *** "C:\XML\INCOMING\RFP.WPT" written successfully! ***
```

Figure 36-1 *WordPerfect* DTD compiler

about fonts, colors, or layout styles would only get in the way. XML documents, like databases, are excellent representations of abstract data.

Humans, however, understand data best when it is rendered in a style that brings out its structure and other characteristics. That's why the inventors of the first markup language had to invent computer stylesheets at the same time – they needed a way to render and present the abstract information in the GML documents.

36.1.3.1 Style requirements

The principal requirement for stylesheets in XML word processors is that they should be maintained separately from the XML document and not affect its representation. The word processor should also provide the usual formatting capabilities for font, color, page layouts, margins, and so on, but these needn't be as capable as what one would expect from a high-end publishing system.

What is more important for our purposes is the capabilities for *associating* those style facilities with the document. It is a minimimal requirement, for example, to make the data of elements of a given type red and bold everywhere that such elements appear.

But it is more useful to be able to specify that the format of the data will vary depending on where the element appears in the hierarchy; for example, make this type of element bold when it is contained in a paragraph element but underlined when it appears in a heading element. It is also helpful to be able to condition an element's style on the value of its attributes; for example, to use bold type if `priority=urgent`.

36.1.3.2 Specifying behavior

As we have seen, with XML there is no reason to limit stylesheets to specifying style. They are actually "specification sheets" that can associate any kind of processing with components of a document. In object-oriented programming parlance, this capability is called *specifying behavior.*

For example, when you format a document for use as a Web page and you cause a cross-reference element to act as a hyperlink, you are specifying the behavior of that element. Behavior specification can be especially useful in creating editing environments for information suppliers, as we'll see momentarily.

One of the benefits of separating style from abstract data is that a template can contain multiple stylesheets. These are normally used for tailoring the rendition of the document to accommodate a user's experience level, national language, or the presentation medium in which he perceives the document (paper, online, etc.).

But one of the more powerful benefits is having specialized stylesheets for use during the creation and editing of the document itself. Databases also have this facility; they call a rendition for data creation a "form" and a rendition for presentation a "report".

It is in the creation-time renditions that specifying behavior can be particularly useful. For example, the behavior for an element type could be to display a dialog box that will assist the author in specifying attribute values or entering subelements.

36.1.3.3 The XML Project Designer

To see how these requirements are addressed in a real word processor, we'll take a quick tour of the *WordPerfect XML Project Designer*, shown in Figure 36-2. This tool is for designing style rules[1] and associating them with the document components to which they will be applied. The rules are stored in stylesheets (which the product calls "layout specification instance files") which in turn are embedded in templates.

36.1.3.3.1 Element rule list

This is a list of the element types that have style rules assigned to them. Several different rules can be defined for the same element type, depending on where a specific instance of the element occurs in the hierarchy, or the attribute values exhibited by that instance.

The rule list can be sorted in three ways:

- By element type name;
- By the hierarchical context in which the rule applies; or
- By descriptive names that can be assigned to a style rule.

36.1.3.3.2 Descriptive name

Since style rules do not have a one-to-one relationship with element type names, it is useful to be able to give a rule a name of its own.

36.1.3.3.3 Content model

The content model of the element type is displayed as a convenience, since it can influence the style designer's decisions.

---

1. In the emerging XSL standard, the rules for specifying styles (and other processing) and associating them with document content are called "template rules". We call them that elsewhere in the book, but we'll use "style rules" in this chapter because of the special meaning of "template" here.

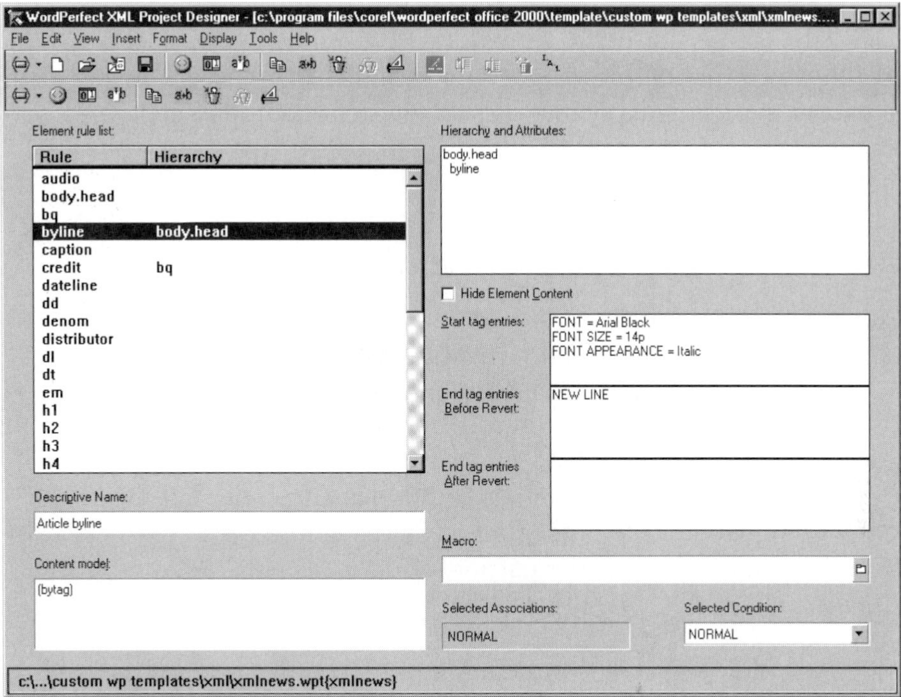

Figure 36-2 *WordPerfect* XML Project Designer

36.1.3.3.4 Hierarchy and attributes

This area displays the hierarchical context and attribute assignments that must exist for an element in order for the defined style rule to be applied to it. If this area is empty, the style applies to all elements of the type selected in the element rule list.

36.1.3.3.5 Hide element content

There are several reasons why it may be desirable to keep the content of an element out of the rendition. One reason is when the rendition is intended to be an overview of a detailed document and the hidden content is part of the detail.

Another reason is that the template creator may want to include alternative data in the rendition instead of the hidden content.

36.1.3.3.6 Start-tag and end-tag entries

These three areas are where formatting commands can be specified. The area in which the command appears determines where it will execute with respect to the associated element. From top to bottom, they are:

Start-tag entries
These commands execute before the content of the element is processed.

End-tag entries before revert
These commands execute after the content of the element is processed, but before the element ends.

End-tag entries after revert
These commands execute after the element ends, but before continuing with the processing of the parent element. They can change the format of the portion of the parent that follows this element.

This capability is superior to rendition-oriented word processors, which offer the designer only a flat structure of sequential paragraphs to work with. *WordPerfect* not only recognizes the hierarchical nesting of elements when associating style rules, but when positioning individual commands within those rules as well.

36.1.3.3.7 Macro

A style designer can specify behavior by invoking a macro when an element is created or rendered.

36.1.3.3.8 Selected associations

Most word processors and publishing programs have an implicit model of rendered output that includes components like footnotes, page headers and footers, tables, etc. This area allows your style rule to generate or modify such components.

36.2 | XML editing

The requirements for XML-specific aspects of editing affect two classes of user:

- The writer creating or editing an XML document.
- The template designer customizing an environment for an information supplier.

36.2.1 *Automatic environment initialization*

When the user edits an XML document of a given type, the product should be able to initialize itself automatically for that type of document. In *WordPerfect*, for example, a template is associated by means of the document type declaration, if one is present, or else the root element type name. The template contains the compiled DTD for the document type, as well as the preferred configuration and stylesheets that were defined by the template creator.

36.2.2 *Structured editing*

In addition to a rendered WYSIWYG view, which provides a familiar word processing interface, an XML editor should provide the ability to switch to one or more structured views. These can include a tree view, such as that shown in the left pane of Figure 36-3, and an enhanced rendered view in which tags are displayed, shown in the right pane. It should be possible to turn the tag display on and off, in order to restore true WYSIWYG.

The tree view serves many purposes. It allows navigation of the document, it displays the element hierarchy to provide context, and it displays attributes and their values. In case of markup errors, it also provides users with context-sensitive help to identify why the document is not valid in its current state.

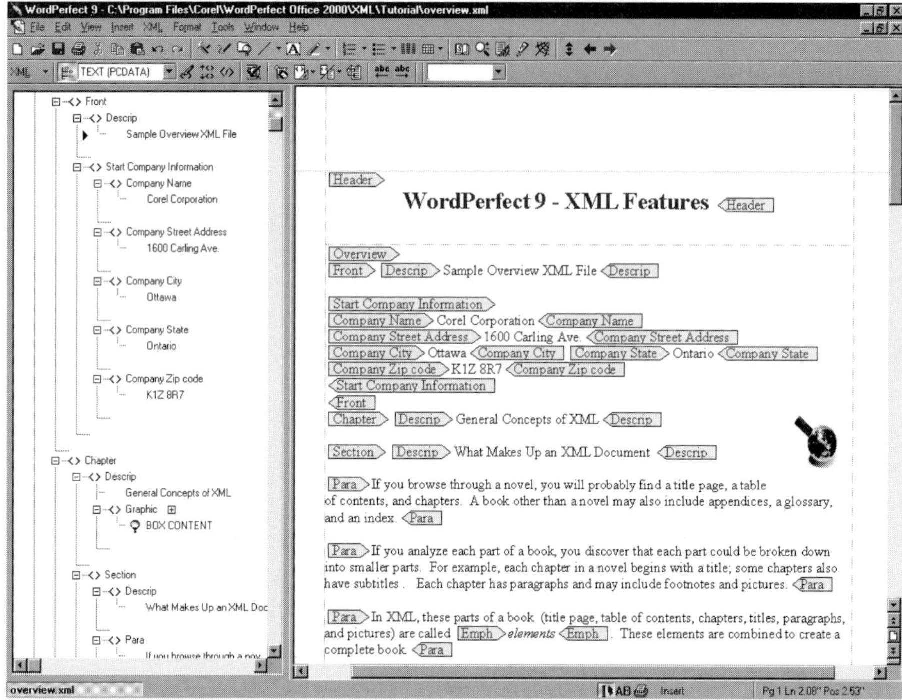

Figure 36-3 Structured editing

36.2.3 *Changing the rendition*

The benefits of XML include the ability to have multiple stylesheets for different renditions. The editing environment should be similarly customizable so that users can test the various presentation-time renditions, or use edit-time renditions that make it easier to work on the documents.

36.2.4 *Tables*

An XML editor should be able to support tables without requiring you to design your own mechanism, or locking you into the specific functionality of the editor. *WordPerfect*, for example, supports the industry-standard CALS and HTML table models. Although the product provides a visual interface for working with tables, the file representation conforms to the standard models and is independent of the product.

36.2.5 *Special characters*

XML supports the Unicode character set, which is far greater in size than any keyboard. It is helpful if the editor can support the insertion of characters not normally found on the keyboard without requiring the user to determine the character numbers. In *WordPerfect* this is done through the "Insert Character or Symbol" dialog boxes.

36.2.6 *Element and attribute insertion*

It can be helpful for the editing tool to be able to insert required elements automatically, and to indicate which elements are valid at any given point in the document. It should also be able to prompt for attribute values and display default values when they exist.

36.2.7 *Validation*

It must be possible to validate a document when saving it, and at other times during editing.

36.3 | Empowering the information supply chain

XML allows validated documents to be exchanged, which allows dynamic data to be integrated automatically with existing data repositories and workflow processes. However, acquiring purpose-written valid XML documents from information suppliers has been difficult because of the specialized editing tools and training typically required.

Now these barriers can be overcome with the availability of low-cost validating XML editing tools, with familiar user interfaces. By providing tem-

©2000 The XML Handbook™

plates for such tools that guide the user through the writing process, organizations can now empower more of their information supply chain.

This seamless and automatic integration of information is rapidly becoming a requirement for all businesses, as information becomes the most valuable commodity and response time becomes the most important service.

Documentor: Hyperlinked XML editing

Tool Discussion

- Personal Portals
- Structural aspects of editing
- Web-based editing
- WebDAV
- Free trial on CD-ROM

©2000 The XML Handbook™

Chapter 37

There's more to documents than just data – structure matters as well. And since the purpose of structure is to facilitate access and navigation, an editor that exploits structure well should offer innovative ways of getting around in and among documents. This chapter is sponsored by Excosoft, `http://www.excosoft.com`, and was prepared by Håkan Lothigius.

Selecting an editing tool to cope with ever-increasing information management demands is not an easy task. In other chapters we examine XML editing features in detail; here we consider some other aspects of these tools:

- Presentation of structural relationships.
- Access to documents and files that are related to the one you are editing.
- Development and use of Personal Portals.
- Web-based editing.

37.1 | Presentation of structural relationships

Traditional word processors are paper rendition oriented while markup editors mainly focus on tagging individual documents and, in some cases, embedded fragments. But information consists of both data and structure, so the means by which an editor provides access to structure can be significant.

For example, the successive disclosure of structure levels shown in Figure 37-1 has long been a feature of SGML browsers. These products allow you to navigate from a high-level overview down to the content details with just a few mouse-clicks, while still keeping the overview intact and visible. XML editors like Excosoft's *Documentor* can allow editing as well as browsing editing on every level of the structure, and they can present those levels in a way that reflects the hierarchy, as shown in Figure 37-2.

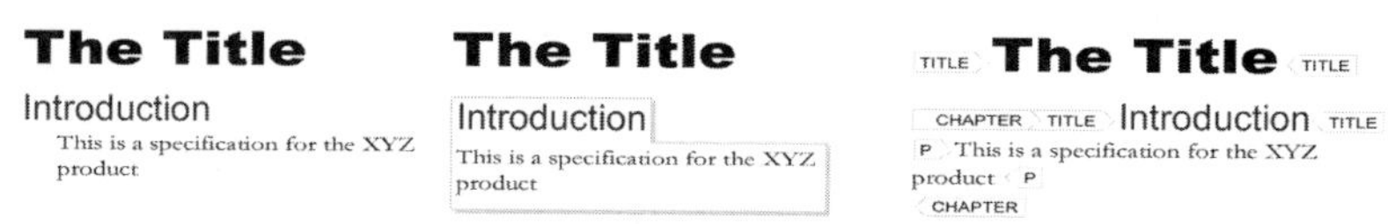

Figure 37-1 Successive disclosure of structure

37.2 | Access to related files

Information professionals may spend as much as 25-30% of their time searching for information. We are all conscious of time spent working at the computer, browsing directories and network drives in a quest for files with cryptic names.

Even with a document management system, too much time can be spent in searching for needed documents.

With a Web-based XML editor, however, you can access documents via hyperlinks. You can build your own personal form of Enterprise Information Portal, a *Personal Portal* with which you can access documents that you use on a daily basis with just one or two hyperlink steps.

37.3 | Personal Portals

A Personal Portal is something between a static home page and a dynamic search. Home pages are great for navigation and building basic structures,

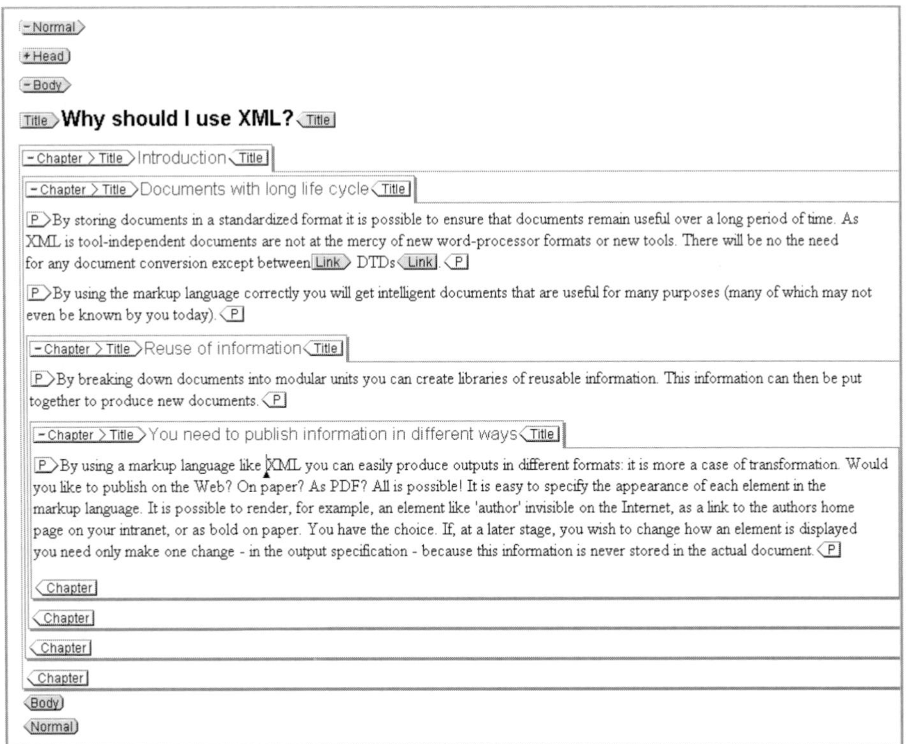

Figure 37-2 *Documentor* shows expansions on several levels.

but are not easy to keep up-to-date. A search engine's results are current, but possibly unpredictable and irrelevant unless you can frame your query precisely.

The Personal Portal is dynamic in the sense that you can fine tune it to suit your needs, include links to your favorite documents and project portals, and structure it to create your personal view of your company's knowledge resources. With products like *Documentor* it is possible to use several different link mechanisms (URL, XLink, file references, etc.) to construct the portal, and you can edit it in XML with or without a DTD.

37.4 | Web-based editing

In the hyperlinked information world, an editor must be able to support workgroups interacting with common information resources, even if the workgroups are spread all over the world. A distributed editing standard, such as Web Distribution, Authoring and Versioning (WebDAV), can help to accomplish this goal. *Documentor*, for example, can be integrated with any WebDAV server to access information over the Internet as easily as on a local area network.

This capability means that whether you are working on a local network or over the Internet, you can access the exact same documents that your colleagues do, virtually eliminating the risk of having several similar copies of the same document in existence.

Sharing the original document ensures consistent information and eliminates the need to update copies of the same document in several places. Sharing the same document archive with other projects can also boost reuse, which can improve the return on your information investment.

37.5 | Conclusion

In this short chapter we've touched on a few editing concepts related to document structure and the Web: presentation of structure, hyperlinked access, Personal Portals, and remote editing.

An XML editing tool with strong support for these concepts can reach a wider audience in your enterprise than just the specialists who understand the value of XML. Moreover, it can open the door to a variety of interesting application possibilities, which we explore further in Chapter 47, "The universal collaborative Web", on page 636.

Tip *You can experiment with Documentor using the free trial version on the CD-ROM.*

©2000 THE XML HANDBOOK™

DynaTag: Visual conversion environment

Tool Discussion

- XML conversion tool
- Document conversion concepts

©2000 THE XML HANDBOOK™

Chapter 38

A lot of the world's documents are in XML, but a lot more aren't and need to be. This chapter is sponsored by Inso Corporation, `http://www.inso.com`, who have a tool for getting them there.

Word processor file formats faithfully record how data should look, but they are useless as reliable sources for processing that data. That's why so many of them need to be converted to XML.

Middle-tier data aggregators need to do it dynamically, and publishers need to do it as part of the editing process. Both groups can benefit from understanding the concepts involved.

38.1 | Concepts of document conversion

An XML document consists of data intermixed with markup. The purpose of the markup is to describe the data: its meaning, structure, and other attributes.

When data originates in a database, as in middle-tier applications, it is straightforward to incorporate it in an XML document. That is because a database keeps data in an *abstract* state; it isn't mixed up with reports, entry forms, or other rendition information. Moreover, the database schema knows how to associate meaning with the data – meaning that is easily represented as element types and attributes when creating the XML document.

Creating an XML document is also straightforward with an XML structured editing system. Such systems, like databases, keep the data in an abstract state internally even if they present a rendered WYSIWYG view to the author.

But the real garden variety word processors, beloved of authors and typists the world over, have no concept of data. They exist solely to create renditions and will happily mingle formatting commands with data, given the slightest opportunity.

But despite that fact, many XML-savvy organizations use word processors regularly to create XML documents. They prefer not to invest in the retraining and process changes that switching editing environments requires.

Which is why XML conversion tools were invented. Many of them are essentially programming languages with varying degrees of XML-awareness. (There are some on the CD-ROM accompanying this book.) They often require a programmer's skills to create rules for parsing word processing formats, and they don't provide visual feedback.

We'll see a different approach later in this chapter, but first we need to look at two key concepts: *data rescue* and *style serves meaning*.

38.1.1 *Data rescue*

Converting a word processing document to XML typically involves more than just changing from one representation ("file format") to another. Instead of simply translating the document's formatting characteristics and content, it is necessary to isolate the real information content – the abstract data and its structure – from the style information. In other words, the data must be rescued from the rendered form, and stored in a notation – XML – that is capable of preserving structured data as an abstraction.

Data rescue restores rendered content so that it can serve as dynamic information for many uses in a variety of delivery environments. (For an example, see Chapter 26, "City Of Providence", on page 346.)

38.1.2 *Style serves meaning*

The basic principle behind data rescue is that the purpose of the style in word processing documents is to help convey the meaning of the data. In other words, as an example, the reason for using a particular set of formatting instructions (such as bold, centered, 18 point type) is to show that the data in that style is a "title".

By taking advantage of this principle, it is possible to transform word processing styles to XML markup. That task is made easier when the word processing documents use style templates consistently, but even in their absence, combinations of formatting instructions can be used, as we have seen.

38.2 | Converting documents with DynaTag

DynaTag is a graphical environment for converting word processing (WP) documents to XML. (It also contains other components, described later, that prepare the converted documents for electronic publishing on CD-ROM and the Web.) It converts WP documents in Western European languages and Japanese.

The product is designed to simplify the often complex task of mapping word processing style conventions to XML. Once a conversion is defined with *DynaTag*, it can be reused for other documents of the same type.

Figure 38-1 illustrates one view of the product interface. The upper half of the window shows the input word processing file with its original formatting. Names of input formats appear on the left, and output objects (usually element types) appear on the right. The bottom portion of the screen changes depending on the current stage of the process. Here, the input formats tab is displayed.

38.2.1 *Getting started*

In *DynaTag*, the set of rules for transforming a class of WP documents is called a "project". Using the *New Project Wizard* shown in Figure 38-2, the user specifies the project and its initial WP source files. The WP document

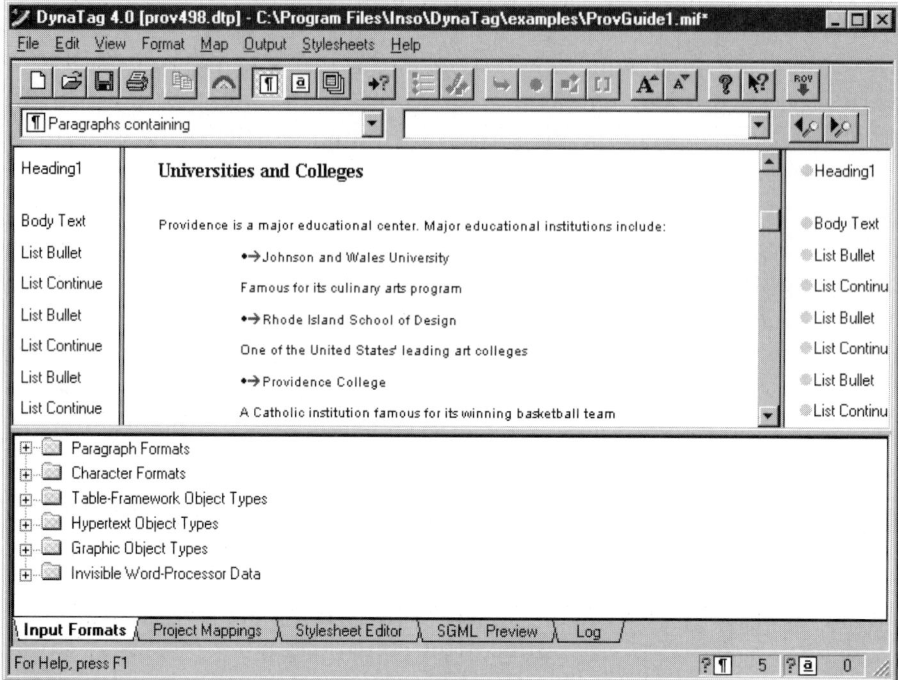

Figure 38-1 *DynaTag* interface to mapping rules

is analyzed and converted into an intermediate tagged form that retains all the content and formatting information. The product then displays a document preview, formatted with the original WP styles. The document is now ready for mapping.

38.2.2 *Mapping*

Document conversion is driven by mapping rules. A *mapping* rule specifies how to convert an input format (a WP style) to the correct output object, which may be an XML element type. Multiple rules may yield the same output object.

Several views are provided for sorting, organizing, and managing these mapping rules. Mapping rules from other projects can be used as a starting point for a new project.

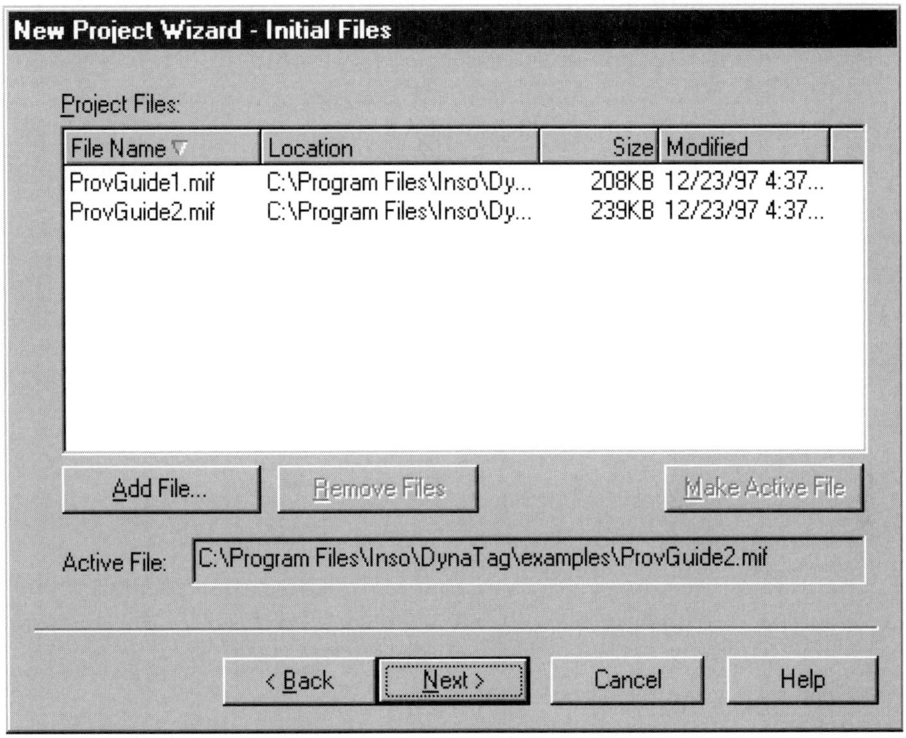

Figure 38-2 New project wizard.

DynaTag's mapping tools provide a number of features for handling different input formats and creating the desired output.

38.2.2.1 automatic mapping

The product automatically maps WP styles to XML element-types with the same names. This is a fast, easy way to get to well-formed XML when a specific DTD is not a requirement. Those with specific DTD requirements can choose their own element-type names and selectively map each input format to the desired type.

©2000 The XML Handbook™

38.2.2.2 Variant detection

DynaTag detects not only WP styles, but also overrides of these styles, or *variants*. Variants can be mapped to unique element types or treated as equivalent to other instances of the WP style.

For example, an author may have used a standard body text style, but applied extra indentation to indicate a block quotation. The product can detect this override and allow the user to map this instance to a `BLOCKQUOTE` element, while other body text maps to `PARA` elements.

In other instances, the variant formatting may be meaningless. The author may have decreased the space before a paragraph to fit text on the printed page, or inserted a page break to force it to the next page. *DynaTag* can be instructed to ignore such variants.

38.2.2.3 New-mapping helper

A wizard helps users map WP styles to XML element types by guiding the creation of each mapping rule.

38.2.2.4 Conditional mapping

Conditional mappings create different mapping rules for different "conditions" in the text. For example, an initial text pattern, such as the word "Warning" followed by a tab, can be used to map certain instances of the body text style to a `WARNING` element. Context (e.g., the preceding or following element type) and formatting properties can also be used for conditional mappings.

38.2.2.5 List wizard

This wizard, shown in Figure 38-3, helps users map list formatting conventions to element types. It can recognize different kinds of lists (ordered, unordered, term/definition), multiple list levels, and parts of lists (e.g., markers, paragraphs, continuation paragraphs). Different styles and levels of lists in the WP document may be identified and mapped using regular expression matching on the list markers (e.g., different types of bullets, sequence numbers and letters).

©2000 THE XML HANDBOOK™

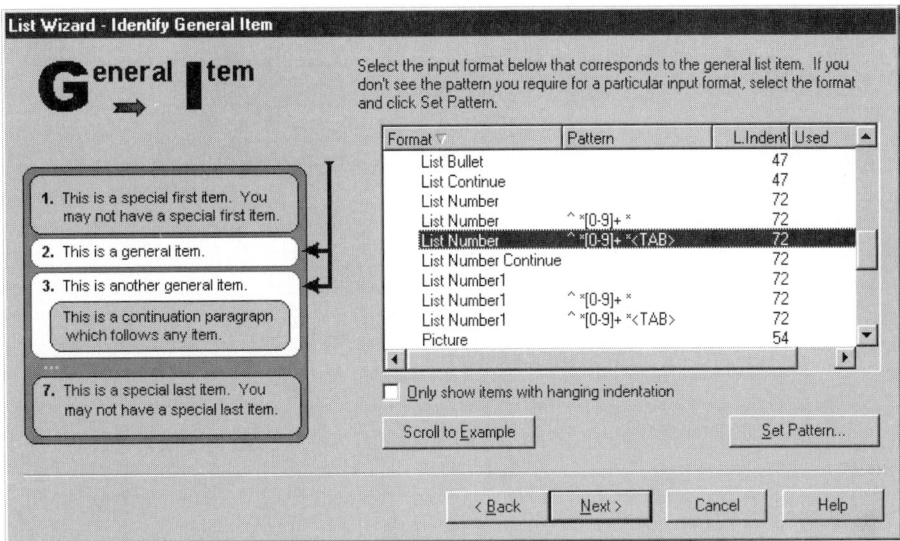

Figure 38-3 List wizard.

38.2.2.6 Tables

Tables are mapped automatically. However, if needed, tables may be divided into classes for special handling. For example, the table's width can be specified with attributes. Later, when the document is rendered in a browser, narrow tables can be formatted to display inline while wide tables are iconized for display in popup windows.

38.2.2.7 Character mapping

Styles that make format changes at the character level (e.g., emphasized text, book titles) can easily be mapped to proper, descriptive XML elements. In cases where authors simply used formatting overrides to create bold, italic, or underlined text, bulk character mapping can be used to create consistent XML markup for each different format.

For example, in Figure 38-4, bold text is mapped to an output object called EMPH.BOLD, which in turn generates an XML element with the start-tag <EMPH TYPE="BOLD">.

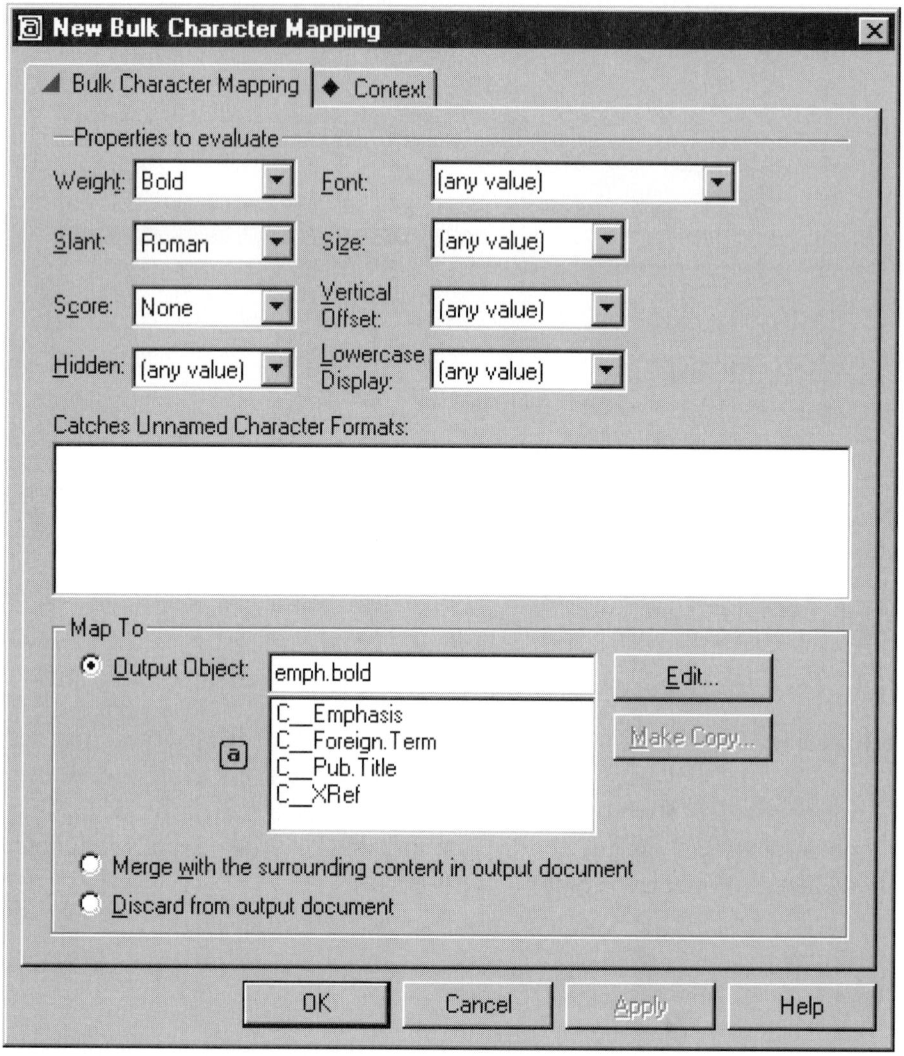

Figure 38-4 Bulk character mapping.

38.2.2.8 Cross-references

Each word processor has a recommended way to create automatic cross references, typically printed as a reference to a page or a section title. If authors follow the recommendations of their word processor, *DynaTag* automatically converts the cross-references to hypertext links. In the resulting XML, tags and attributes identify the source and destination of the link.

38.2.2.9 Searching

DynaTag provides fulltext searching for finding specific content that needs to be mapped.

38.2.2.10 Comments

All mappings can be annotated with comments for managing mapping tasks and for project documentation.

38.2.2.11 XML markup features

Users can view XML markup inside the user interface. They can also specify attributes, create entities, and use other markup options to enrich the XML output.

38.2.2.12 Capturing structure

XML elements that contain other elements are sometimes called (surprise!) *container elements*. The complete structure of containers and containees can nest to many levels. Computer scientists refer to such a structure as a *hierarchy*, or *tree structure*.

The element structure of an XML document is the basis for much powerful processing. The content of containers can be hidden, or displayed in popup windows in a browser. Containers for chapters and sections are the basis for automatically generating a hypertext table of contents and for selective, on-demand printing.

Most importantly, the concept of containment enables *structured searches*: highly efficient queries that narrow down searching to given elements for maximum precision in finding information.

For example, a boolean search for “chocolate and milk” inside any one `RECIPE` element provides much more precision than searching for the same words across an entire cookbook.

DynaTag's *Container Wizard*, shown in Figure 38-5, makes it easy to assign result element types to their proper level in the document structure. This panel of the Wizard shows that chapter, section, and subsection element types have been created, and illustrates their hierarchical relationship.

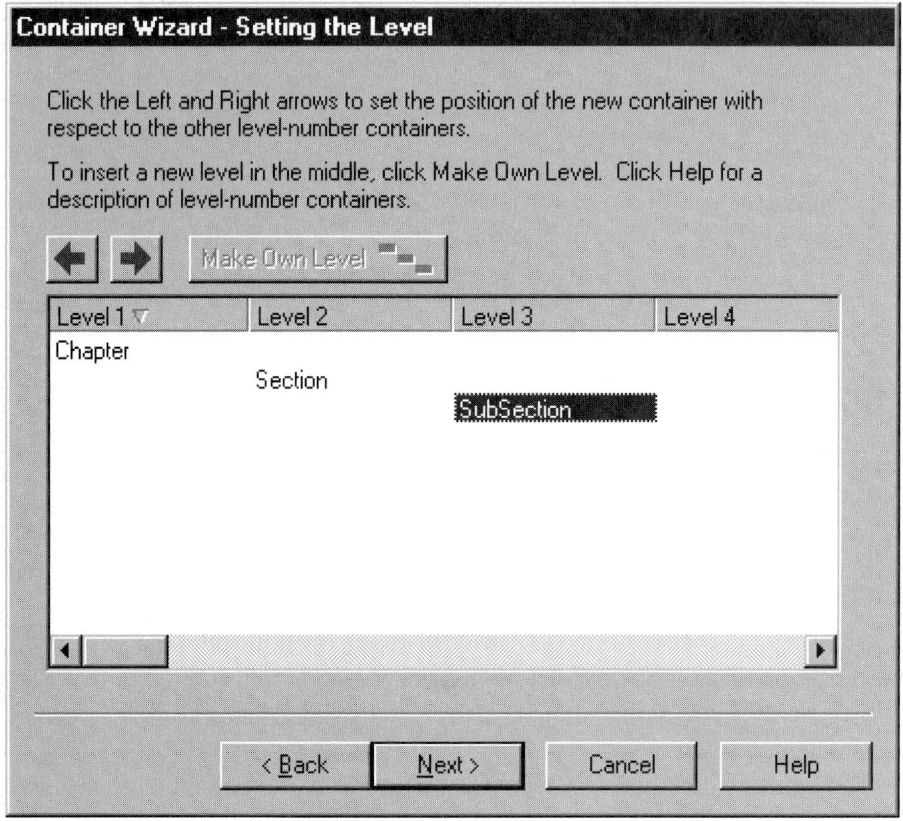

Figure 38-5 Container wizard.

38.2.2.13 Reuse

Once a project is finished, its mapping rules can be re-used for similar documents. *DynaTag*'s batch converter processes groups of WP documents that share the same rules. The only human intervention required is starting the batch script and checking the log file upon completion.

38.3 | Preparing for electronic publishing

DynaTag also includes facilities to prepare a converted document for electronic distribution on CD-ROM and the World Wide Web, using Inso's suite of electronic publishing tools. Those facilities include a stylesheet editor with preview capability, graphics data format conversion to JPEG and TIFF, and a helper for developing contextual search forms. You can see the full suite in action in Chapter 26, "City Of Providence", on page 346.

©2000 THE XML HANDBOOK™

Planning for document conversion

Application Discussion

- Methodology for large-scale conversion projects
- Concept and planning
- Proof-of-concept
- Analysis, design and engineering
- Production

©2000 THE XML HANDBOOK™

Chapter 39

Legacy document conversion is a jungle, and the next best thing to a personal guide through it is an accurate map made by someone who's been over the ground many times. This chapter provides such a map for you. It is sponsored by Data Conversion Laboratory, `http://www.dclab.com`, and was prepared by Mark Gross and John Lynch.

Whether you're building an e-commerce site with an online catalog containing 1,000,000 products, publishing journals online or on CD-ROM, or maintaining a huge legal citation database, it is highly likely that the existing documents you wish to use are renditions. That means the real data in your files is mixed in with style information and can't be processed reliably.

The solution, of course, is to make this legacy content useful by converting it to XML.

But simply converting those files to XML syntax will not gain the benefits you are seeking. To be useful, your converted XML documents must preserve the integrity of the abstract information that the renditions are trying to convey; that is, the real data and its structure.

As we have seen, there are techniques available to assist with extracting data from renditions. However, the effectiveness of those techniques tends to vary with the consistency of the rendition files. Effectively, the more control over their creation and the more discipline used, the greater the chance that simple rule-based conversions will do the job.

Legacy documents, however, are often amassed over a period of many years and written by multiple authors. There can be huge volumes of materials, produced in a multitude of electronic formats. Worse still, they may include mountains of pre-computer paper documents as well.

In this kind of an environment, on this kind of scale, mastering the technical aspects of the conversion is only part of the job. For the project to be successful requires a disciplined methodology, which is what this chapter is about.

The methodology we will describe was developed by Data Conversion Laboratory, based on its experience with more than 25,000 projects, converting some 50 million pages. With it you can hope to avoid pitfalls like that shown in Figure 39-1.

Figure 39-1 It is easy to underestimate a large-scale conversion project.

39.1 | The Data Conversion Laboratory methodology

While you might build a tool shed without a blueprint, it is not likely that you would construct a 20-story building without one. Large conversion efforts are quite similar to large construction projects and many of the techniques to ensure that the final product meets the end-user's needs are common to both.

No matter how well you think it's going to go, a conversion project has many unknowns. By following the phased approach shown in Figure 39-2, there will be specific checkpoints at which you can reconsider the project in terms of such new information and redirect the project appropriately.

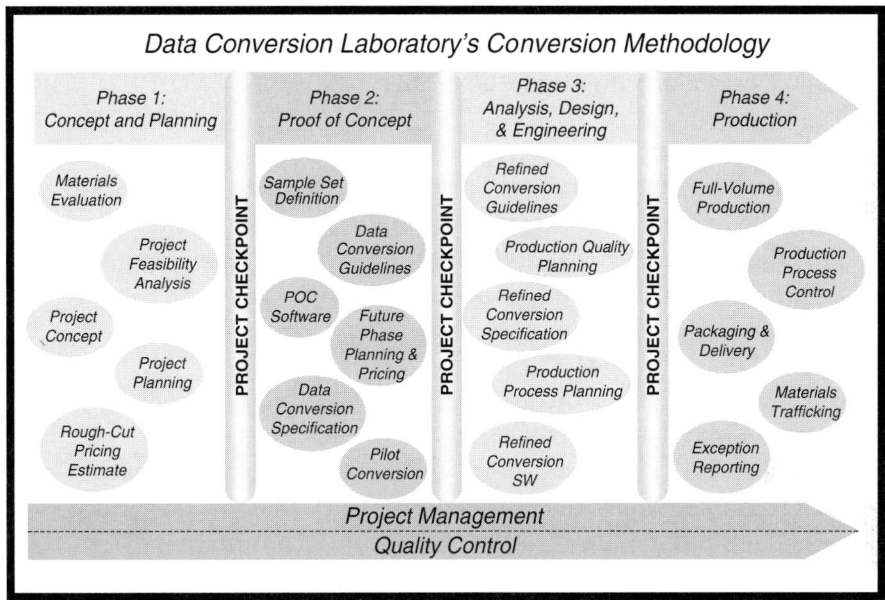

Figure 39-2 A phased approach to document conversion

Phase 1: Concept and planning

The purpose of this phase is to get everyone to agree to a common definition of what the project is. You'll want to lay out the project objectives and expectations, define the success criteria, lay out a preliminary approach, identify the risk areas, estimate approximate cost ranges and define a preliminary budget.

Phase 2: Proof-of-concept

The purpose of this vital step is to test your approach on a limited scale, paying particular attention to the areas identified as potential risk areas. The results of this phase will help you arrive at a more detailed plan, while further fleshing out functional requirements. Based on the results of the test, preliminary software is prepared, and cost projections are fine-tuned.

Phase 3: Analysis, design, and engineering
This is the critical step where all the details get worked out and the project is prepared for volume production. Specifically, keying and conversion specifications are finalized, cleanup and review guidelines are defined, and final production costs are confirmed. More generally, the entire conversion process is finalized and tested, and production ramp-up begins.

Phase 4: Production
This is the objective that was planned for in the other phases – data flowing smoothly at 500 or 50,000 pages a week. If the preceding phases were done well, this phase can focus on monitoring quality and productivity with an eye towards improvement.

In addition to the four phases, there are two other important aspects to this methodology. These are the disciplines shown as two stripes at the bottom of Figure 39-2. As in any large project, management and quality control are critical and apply to every phase. Ideally, a single dedicated person will oversee both disciplines in order to guarantee continuity.

39.2 | Phase 1: Concept and planning

Although it is an important step, this can be a pretty short one if you've carefully thought through exactly what you want to happen. It may just be a day or two, though it's more likely to be several weeks. The major elements of this phase are described below.

39.2.1 *Project concept*

Everybody needs to be on the same page.

The first step is to define the project clearly, and to get an agreement that people's various expectations are the same. You simply cannot meet a goal that you don't know about in advance. At this point, the project concept is discussed at a high level, without getting bogged down in detail. The following are the critical questions that need to be answered honestly.

- What do you need to do, and how quickly do you need to do it?
- Do you have a technical approach in mind?
- What are the goals and what are the success criteria?
- What's critical and what's nice to have?
- What's the expected budget? And what are the estimated costs?
- Where are the tradeoffs in time, budget, and functionality?

The end result of this analysis is a project concept document.

39.2.2 *Materials evaluation*

While a detailed inventory of materials does not usually get done until the proof-of-concept phase, it is critical to get an early understanding of the project's scope. Design and implementation decisions on where best to focus resources will be based on this information. This is illustrated by the chart in Figure 39-3. While the specific questions will vary from project to project, typical questions are:

- How big is the project? You need to quantify in terms you're used to thinking in – pages, books, journal issues, products, etc.
- How much source variation is there? Materials may have been produced in a multitude of electronic formats, on different computer operating systems, or by different typesetters. Some of it may even live as paper, under dust, in huge warehouses.
- How much format variation is there? How often has the rendition style changed over the years? Invariably, different authors choose different styles. While it would be nice to have a strictly enforced template, if you're dealing with legacy

documents, you're bound to find a lot of formatting inconsistency.

- What are the special issues? Tables, formulas, cross-referencing and graphics are all areas that need special attention in the planning process.

All of these critical issues will differ slightly from project to project; it's a good idea to lay them out explicitly in a format like Figure 39-3.

Materials Evaluation Worksheet			
Document Set	**% of Total**	**Average Frequency of Elements Per Page**	**Other Special Issues**
FrameMaker	25%	Characters = 3,023 Tables = .92 Equations = None X-Refs = 5 Images = .28	Text Boxes, Complex Tables, Cross Refs
WordPerfect	12%	Characters = 4,009 Tables = 1.2 Equations = 2.2 X-Refs = 7 Images = .5	Equations, Complex Tables
Ventura	30%	Characters = 3,540 Tables = 1.1 Equations = None X-Refs = 5 Images = 1.4	Multiple Authors, No Stylesheet Used, Poorly Formatted
Quark	13%	Characters = 5,806 Tables = .05 Equations = None X-Refs = 2 Images = 1.27	Mac Files, Text Boxes,TIFF Images
Paper	20%	Characters = 3,877 Tables = .3 Equations = .51 X-Refs = 8 Images = .2	Old - Not Suitable For OCR, Equations, Tables

Figure 39-3 Materials evaluation sheet

39.2.3 *Rough-cut pricing estimate*

Usually, there is not enough information available this early in the process to allow an accurate prediction of the project's overall production costs. There are simply too many variables that will not be finalized until well into Phase 2. However, it is possible (and useful) to start assembling rough-cut costing parameters.

You can use a chart like the one shown in Figure 39-4 to lay out what the major tasks in the production process are. Alongside each task, indicate its historic cost range.

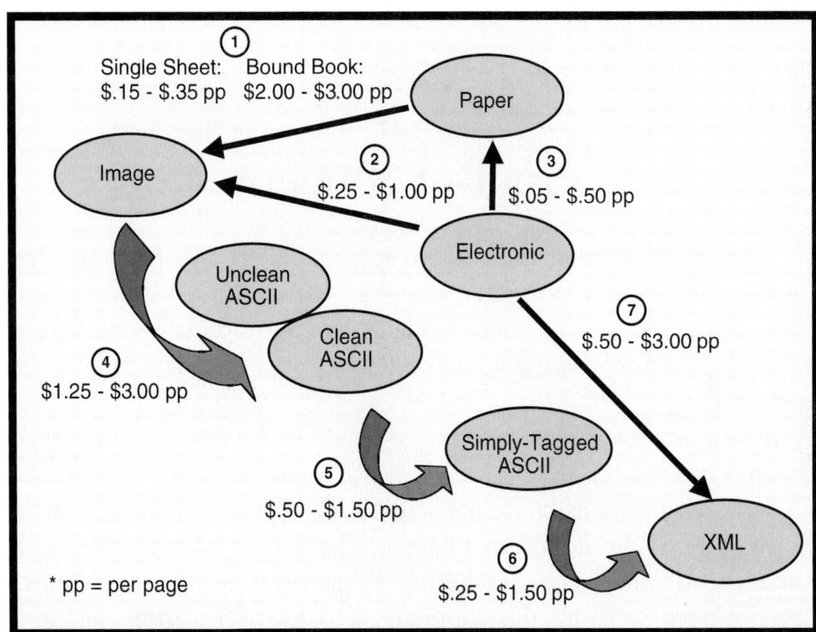

Figure 39-4 Rough-cut cost ranges for major tasks

You now have a guide for both feasibility analysis ("I didn't know we were talking about a $2,000,000 project!") and sensitivity analysis ("If we didn't have to do that step we could save $2.00 per page"). If budgeting has not yet been done for your project, these ranges will also prove to be useful guides for setting budgets.

39.2.4 *Project feasibility analysis*

While the information collected so far is fairly sketchy, this is an early opportunity to assess, based on those broad parameters, whether the project is still feasible. You'll typically need to answer questions like the following:

- If this is a $1-$2 million project, does it still make good business sense to proceed?
- If it's way over budget can you redefine the project's scope? Is there another way to do this?
- Can you do without certain elements in order to bring down the cost? If so, does the project make sense at a reduced level?
- And most importantly, does it make sense to go on with Phase 2?

39.3 | Phase 2: Proof-of-concept

So Phase 1 has told you that the project may actually be worth pursuing. You've got the rough-cut estimate, and even your CFO admits that it sounds like a pretty sound business model. Most importantly, everyone is agreed on what the broad strokes of the project are. The next step is the proof-of-concept.

The purpose of the proof-of-concept phase is to test your planned approach on a limited scale. This will be your opportunity to test out the areas that were identified as being particularly risky, and to test on a small scale, the hypothesis developed in Phase I. The results of this phase will provide a more detailed plan, including fleshed-out functional requirements, preliminary software development, a converted sample set, and more finely-tuned cost projections.

Returning to the building analogy again, this is the step where the preliminary design is laid out, and a model built so that everyone can get an idea of what the building will look like. Additionally, a test boring is done to ensure that the soil will be able to support the building.

Figure 39-5 shows a typical project timeline for this phase. For a significantly larger project, this phase might take up to ten weeks. Let's look at the key stages and deliverables.

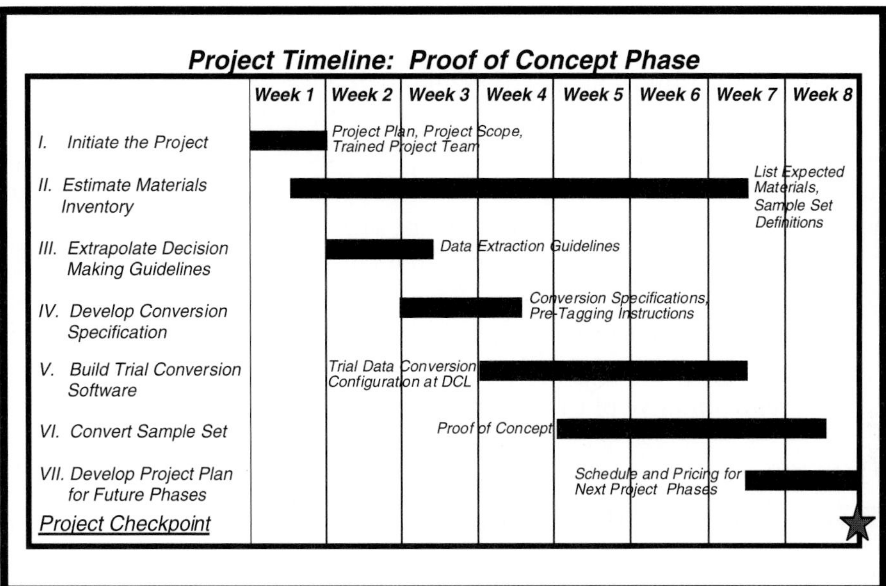

Figure 39-5 Project timeline for proof-of-concept phase

39.3.1 *Project initiation*

You always need a project kickoff meeting. One of the main purposes of this meeting is to make sure that everyone on the expanded team has the same understanding of the project concept. The team should include a project manager, a domain expert, a data analyst, a programmer and a senior editor.

The project initiation is also where the detailed task plan is created and reviewed. The task plan will help ensure that everyone understands his role and responsibilities as a member of the team.

39.3.2 *Sample set definition*

Important questions need to be answered in order to define the proof-of-concept. Be patient here; you probably won't be ready after the kickoff meeting.

Ask yourself the following questions: What's intended to be proven? How big should the sample be? Which project elements are known technology and therefore don't need to be part of this exercise? Which elements are particularly risky or unknown and need special focus?

Beware the common mistakes. While there may be a tendency to try to do everything at once, or to do the easy parts first, remember that the real purpose is to focus on a small data set, and on the risky and unknown areas. Fail to identify where your project's critical challenges are now, and the hypothesis of your whole project might be off.

With this in mind, it may be better to focus on 10 pages of difficult bibliographic references or complex tables, rather than 100s of pages of straightforward or repetitive text. And if there are 20 major variations of material, don't try to analyze them all. Instead, pick the two or three that are most representative of the issues.

39.3.3 *Inventory materials*

This task invariably provokes groans, but someone has to do it. You need to have a good idea of how big the pile of documents is, and a clear understanding of the variation contained within the pile. The exact methodology you use to collect this information will vary depending on the project.

While it would be ideal to get a detailed list of everything that needs to be done, that's not usually the case. What you are trying to do at this stage is get an understanding of how much of each type of material there might be. That's because each type of material will probably require its own programming and conversion process. And while building conversion software to help automate much of the conversion makes sense, you don't want to invest lots of programming time automating for a particularly difficult type of material when you only have 10 pages of it.

39.3.4 *Data conversion guidelines*

This is usually the heart of the proof-of-concept phase. The extent to which you can develop rules and guidelines for transforming your source materials into "properly tagged data" will be the most important determinant of the final cost of this project. In other words, the development must be done with care.

The domain expert and the data analyst should work closely together here, to try to generalize the rules and condense them into as small a set as possible. What you are trying to do at this stage is build a functional set of rules. Don't make the mistake of turning this into a programming exercise; that will just bog you down.

Equally importantly, don't give up too early. While the usual tendency is to think there are no rules – "it's just common sense and you either know it or you don't" – that's rarely the case.

39.3.5 *Data conversion specification*

It is useful at this stage to formalize the guidelines derived to this point into a single document. The conversion specification document will become the primary repository of project information; it will be continually consulted and reviewed by the end user, the domain expert, the analyst, and the programmer.

This document expands the previously established guidelines into a set of rules that can be programmed for. It also identifies areas that are ambiguous or difficult to define; these areas will then need to be reviewed by the domain expert.

The conversion specification document typically circulates among the various parties involved, and becomes the central discussion document until issues are resolved. It is also the document that defines the programming efforts.

39.3.6 *Software and pilot conversion*

O.K., the conversion specification document is written. Hopefully it addresses all the major issues of the conversion. Now it's time to see if you can really use those guidelines and specifications to convert anything.

As in the project initiation phase, you need to be cautious here. While most successful conversion projects combine automation with manual effort, programming should be done sparingly at this point. There simply isn't time during the proof-of-concept phase to program for everything you'd like to. In addition, there will be a tendency to program for the easy things first.

©2000 The XML Handbook™

The best approach is to select a few complex areas which people doubt can be converted in an automated manner. For these areas, invest time testing out programmatic approaches to the unique problems. This learning process will be invaluable and will help tremendously when you move on to Phase 3.

For the rest of the sample set, however, it probably makes sense for people to follow the conversion specification manually, rather than investing heavily in writing and testing programs.

The end result of this phase should give you a good feel for what can and should be automated, and what will need to be done manually. It will also yield some valuable timings for the likely labor elements of the project.

39.3.7 *Pricing*

If all has gone well thus far, you'll now be able to estimate the project's costs more closely and lay out a realistic timeframe in which it can be done. As more materials are tested and converted in the next phase, these estimates will be further refined.

Keep in mind that programming costs will rise in the next phase as you start to expand your efforts toward automation. However, if the materials you initially selected for the sample are truly representative, and you've taken into account people's learning curves as they started working with your sample data, what you have now is pretty accurate.

39.3.8 *Go/no-go decision*

This phase is also the checkpoint at which to determine whether the project still makes sense. You'll be able to address these issues:

Time to market
: You'll have a realistic estimate of how long this project will take, as well as your options for speeding it up.

Quality
: You'll be able to demonstrate expected results while there's still time to make modifications.

Cost

You'll have an understanding of the project costs and what the tradeoffs are.

Scalability

You'll understand the extent to which the size of the project can scale.

39.3.9 *Planning for future phases*

By now, you will have a clear understanding of what you want to achieve from this conversion. The proof-of-concept has yielded valuable clues as to where and how to refine the conversion guidelines. Mistakes have been identified and concepts proven.

More than anything else, the proof-of-concept should land the entire conversion team on the same page and become the foundation upon which the remainder of the project will be built. You now have:

- Improved conversion guidelines.
- Refined conversion specification.
- Refined conversion software.
- More finely-tuned cost projections.

39.4 | Phase 3: Analysis, design and engineering

Phase 3 is primarily a matter of refining the various deliverables produced from the conversion sample, for the fuller set of materials. Additionally, you now program for all the things you did not have time for (or did not need to prove) during the proof-of-concept phase. Planning for gradual ramp-up and full volume production processing will also be done in this phase.

A typical project timeline for this phase is shown in Figure 39-6. For the typical larger project, this phase will likely take 6-10 weeks. Let's take a look at the key tasks.

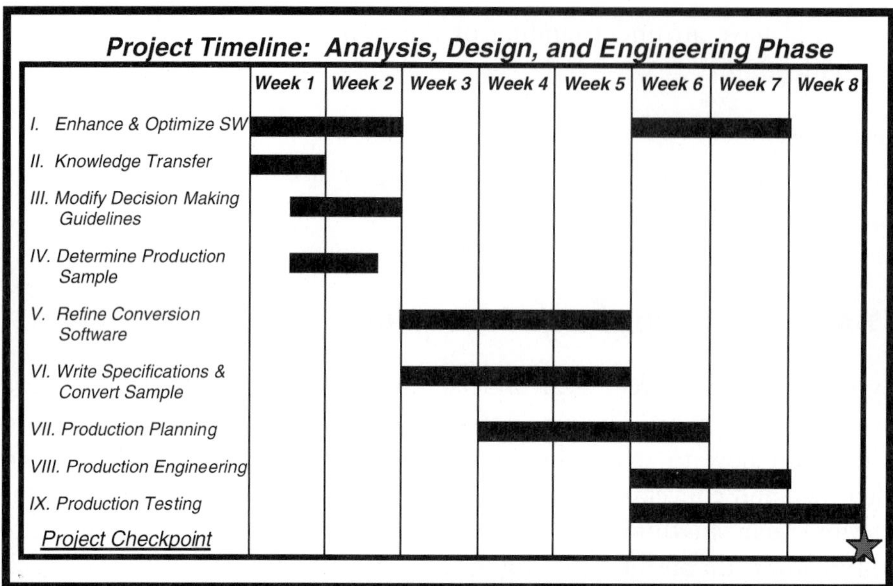

Figure 39-6 Timeline for the analysis, design and engineering phase

39.4.1 *Production process planning*

Integrating the various elements of the conversion process is too often an afterthought. That can be an expensive mistake. The most mundane things, such as agreeing upon filename conventions and basic data trafficking procedures, are too often not properly planned in advance.

Typically, a large conversion effort consists of some 30 to 50 independent steps, requiring multiple skills and often multiple vendors. There are also time dependencies that need to be integrated in order to ensure a smooth production flow.

In planning the production process, there are also a number of important logistical considerations:

- How many pages a week can each step in the process handle?
- What's the weak link in the chain?
- Can you keep up with reviewing and inspecting converted materials as they're delivered?

- Technical questions will arise; will there be a dedicated point of contact for them?
- How will materials be transported back and forth?

Another important question to ask is: How much time will it take? If you already have, or can contract, an ongoing production facility that handles thousands of pages a day, you still need to allow 4-6 weeks for the integration to take place. You'll therefore need to start early in Phase 3. And if you're going to be building a process from scratch, you should allow at least 6 months.

39.4.2 *Production quality planning*

While many of the standard quality control processes apply to conversion projects, there is a significant difference. Your favorite cookie baker may make the best cookies, but he'll attribute it to using the choicest chocolate chips and the finest flour. Unlike a cookie factory, you can't really control the quality of ingredients coming into your machine.

No matter how well you select your samples and trial materials, you are unlikely to find every significant variation. Therefore, it is expecting too much to hope to account for all the possibilities in advance. The documents will typically have been written by many individuals, at several different locations, in many different editing packages, over a long period of time, and on a variety of systems. So, like the people who made them, the documents will have personalities. And, like people, their behavior may not always be exemplary.

Ensuring quality control in this environment means building feedback loops at each step of the process. These checkpoints are designed to report when things are not meeting expectations, and provide guidelines, rather than rules, to the people inspecting the results. Information needs to flow back and forth easily in order to allow refinement of this process. You'll also need to collect statistics in order to tell how much sampling will be needed as the process improves.

39.4.3 *Production ramp-up*

Just as we advised in Phase 1, caution is critical at this stage. The best approach is usually to plan for a few weeks of low-volume production through the initial production process. This will help to identify any weaknesses in the process.

The entire production team needs to be aware that the purpose of the first weeks of production is to provide feedback in order to help engineer a smoother process. This is not yet the time to put dozens of people to work, but rather a time to assign a select few individuals who are capable of figuring out where improvements can be made.

39.5 | Phase 4: Production

You're there at last, but you do need to monitor results continually and make sure that quality and productivity stay where you expect them to be.

Full-volume production
Even after the production ramp-up stage, it is not necessarily prudent to plan for full production volumes immediately. Increase volumes gradually, thereby allowing ample time for people to be trained and to come fully up to speed.

Production process control
You need a method to track production through the various phases. For smaller projects, spreadsheets may be sufficient. But for larger projects, you probably need something more sophisticated. At a minimum you need to know where in the process each batch of materials is, how long it is taking a batch to go through, and how much material is awaiting each phase of processing.

Materials trafficking
It is very rare that you have everything that needs conversion ready in a pile at the beginning of a project. More likely, materials will be readied gradually as the project progresses. In order to avoid slowdowns later in the process, someone needs to be in charge of

trafficking the materials, making sure that materials are ready and complete, and forwarding them appropriately.

Process improvement feedback

The process certainly won't be perfect when you first go into production. You will need a method to formally collect information on exceptions and on what's not working properly. This method will need to be quite flexible as different parts of the process will report exceptions at different times.

Exception reporting

You'll also have to allow for exception reporting. Exception reports are delivered to the end-user along with the converted documents. Because of the wide variance and inconsistencies of the materials being converted, there will inevitably be materials that need special handling by the recipient. And it would seem wise to have a mechanism more sophisticated than yellow stickers to deal with this.

Packaging and delivery

This doesn't seem like a big deal, but you need to get the finished materials to the right person. The right materials! Otherwise frustration can set in. This is also a convenient point at which to do some final quality checking, and to document any specific procedures the person you're delivering to needs to follow.

39.6 | Conclusion

Data Conversion Laboratory's methodology for large-scale conversion is highly detailed, as would be expected from an organization that's been through so many conversions. But there are some major principles that stand out and can be kept in mind:

- Don't just do it. Figure out exactly what you want to accomplish before you start planning, then plan it before you do it. (Don't be the company in Figure 39-7).

Figure 39-7 Maybe everyone involved should read this chapter.

- Project management and quality assurance are key. To ensure that the project proceeds properly and on time, you'll need a dedicated team. Don't think of this as a part-time job; your critical team members need to be dedicated to the project.
- Communications are vital. The domain expert, the technical expert and management all need to be on the same page.
- Select your sample set carefully. It is better to pick 200 truly representative pages than 5000 random ones.
- Plan the production process. Work through the details before you ramp up to volume processing.
- Be sure that it's working. Build feedback loops into every step to monitor, control and continually improve the production process.

Integrating legacy data

Application Discussion

- Legacy data defined
- Profiting from the Y2K problem
- Legacy data flow
- Free software on CD-ROM

©2000 THE XML HANDBOOK™

Chapter 40

The infamous Y2K problem has a secret good side. Because of the efforts made to solve it, enterprises have better knowledge of their legacy data than ever before. XMLSolutions Corporation, `http://www.xmls.com`, sponsors this chapter to show how that knowledge can produce valuable XML data and metadata. It was prepared by Sowmitri Swamy.

The overwhelming fact of legacy data is that there is a lot of it, and it is critical to the operations of the enterprises that own it. It has been a dominant theme in this book, as we have examined the task of dynamic data acquisition in the context of middle-tier servers, e-commerce, portal systems, and publishing.

40.1 | What is legacy data?

Simply put, *legacy data* is data that is generated and used by specific business processes and that is not directly available to other processes. The shared data in enterprise databases is *not* legacy data, although it is business process data.

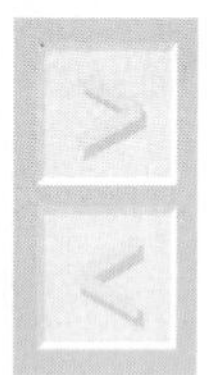

Caution *Legacy data is not the same thing as legacy documents, which are documents that are either renditions, or are not represented in XML, or both. However, legacy documents usually contain legacy data, which is why there is such interest in converting them to XML abstractions.*

40.1.1 *Unlocking legacy data*

Legacy data is a critical revenue-generating asset in many corporations, but for reasons that are largely historical and technological, it is not easily accessed by any application but the one that created it.

Web-enabling of legacy applications and data is a goal of many companies, who look forward to leveraging their legacy data assets by migrating to a Web-based communication paradigm. However, although Web-enabling provides access, it does not necessarily provide knowledge of what the data means. Knowing what the data means leads to methods to transform and use it effectively.

The correct enterprise goal should be to *unlock* legacy data – not only provide access, but also an idiomatic understanding of the data for both human and computer use. Synergy is achieved when legacy data can be accessed, understood and utilized throughout the enterprise in a timely manner.

40.1.2 *The benefit of Y2K*

Such sharing of legacy data as exists in an enterprise is often in a specific context, such as a report, memo, or other document. Documents, however, are usually summaries or extracts from larger data sources and they tend to be formatted to suit the reporting context. Extracting complete data from a rendered document is often difficult or impossible. When it is possible, the data may not be current because of the lead time to produce and distribute the document.

So the only completely reliable means of utilizing legacy data is to go directly to the data itself, which in effect means analyzing the legacy applications that understand its structure and semantics. Fortunately, as a result of the otherwise completely unfortunate Year 2000 (Y2K) bug, enterprises have recently expended vast resources to do just that.

This valuable knowledge is being applied a second time – to making legacy data a sharable enterprise resource through the use of XML. Consultants with extensive Y2K backgrounds, such as XMLSolutions Corporation, are leveraging their Y2K experience to offer a systematic approach to legacy data integration. Their model, called *legacy data flow*, provides conceptual underpinnings and heightened potential for dynamic data acquisition and EDI (see Chapter 13, "XML and EDI: Working together", on page 176).

40.2 | E-commerce with legacy data

Unlocking legacy data for use in e-commerce is valuable for business growth because it provides timely information on products, pricing, policy, and availability. Let's examine some e-commerce applications with an eye towards developing a model of automated legacy data flow.

Figure 40-1 provides a capsule view of the enabling architecture. Two legacy applications are interfaced to an XML-based e-commerce network implementation through special modules, identified in the figure as *metadata engines*.

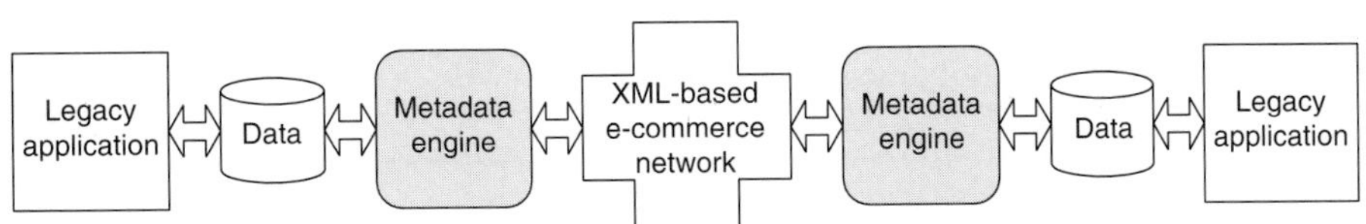

Figure 40-1 XML-based e-commerce integrates legacy data

The e-commerce network uses XML to convey data and metadata between two XML servers anchoring the e-commerce implementation at either end (represented by the two stubs protruding from the e-commerce box).

The roles played by the metadata engines are critical in the proper functioning of the scheme because their role is to convert between XML metadata and legacy data so that the legacy applications can perform their normal processing.

We will use three simple examples to illustrate the functionality of the metadata engine: Year 2000 compliant dates, euro currency conversion, and inventory part numbers. In all three examples, legacy data is changed in an anonymous manner. That means the legacy applications process data in the formats that they are familiar with; they are unaware of the intermediate transformations into and out of XML.

40.2.1 *Y2K-compliant date exchange*

The solution for bringing legacy systems into Year 2000 compliance involves two major techniques: date expansion and windowing. The "expansion" part of the solution involves prefixing the two-digit year with a two-digit century whenever a date is accessed; the "windowing" part determines which century. A common window is "1930-2029", meaning that two-digit years lower than 30 are treated as occurring in the 21st century.

Note that the "compliance" occurs dynamically in the application software. The storage representation of the date is still two digits.

Consider the case of two compliant insurance applications with different internal date representations that need to communicate with one another. One application uses a flat file to store a policy record with the date in MMDDYY format, as shown in Example 40-1.

Example 40-1. Date stored in legacy flat file

```
...052998...
```

This application is written in Cobol. The code declares the date in the `POLICY-ISSUED` field of the `POLICY-RECORD` structure that is partly shown in Example 40-2.

Example 40-2. Legacy Cobol structure for date

```
01 POLICY-RECORD
   ....
   05 POLICY-ISSUED
      10 MM PIC 9(2)
      10 DD PIC 9(2)
      10 YY PIC 9(2)
   ....
```

The two applications interchange dates using the XML representation shown in Example 40-3.

Example 40-3. XML representation of Y2K-compliant date

```
<POLICY>
  ....
  <ISSUE_DATE FORMAT="ISO-8601">19980529</ISSUE_DATE>
  ....
</POLICY>
```

Example 40-4 shows the transformation rules by which the Cobol application's metadata engine produces the date in Example 40-3 from the Cobol record, prior to its transmittal over the XML-based e-commerce network. Note that `CC` refers to the calculated century prefix.

Example 40-4. Semantic transformation rules

```
<POLICY-ISSUED> => <ISSUE_DATE>
<FORMAT ISO-8601> <= CC&&YY&&MM&&DD
```

The metadata engine for the other application uses similar rules (not illustrated) to convert the XML data into a representation that its legacy application can process.

40.2.2 *International invoicing*

With the advent of the euro, a fourth reserve currency has been added to the current three widely-used reserve currencies: the dollar, the pound sterling and the yen. The XML-based techniques we have been examining can be used to enable legacy applications to handle e-commerce in euros.

Consider a U.S. vendor that must invoice a French customer. In addition to the normal conversion between legacy data and XML, the French metadata engine must convert to euros and add French value-added tax (VAT). The scenario would proceed as follows.

The metadata engine for the U.S. invoicing application converts the legacy invoice to the XML document partly shown in Example 40-5, prior to sending it over the e-commerce network.

Example 40-5. U.S. invoice in XML

```
<INVOICE>
....
<INVOICE_DATE format="ISO-8601">19990621</INVOICE_DATE>
<AMOUNT currency="USD">12000</AMOUNT>
<AMOUNT_DUE currency="USD">12000</AMOUNT_DUE>
....
</INVOICE>
```

The metadata engine for the French accounts payable application first transforms the U.S. XML invoice into the French XML invoice shown in Example 40-6 by applying the following semantic transformations:

- Convert U.S. dollars to euros.
- Compute French VAT tax payable.
- Calculate the total amount due in euros.

Example 40-6. Invoice created by French metadata engine

```
<INVOICE>
....
<INVOICE_DATE format="ISO-8601">19990621</INVOICE_DATE>
<AMOUNT currency="EURO">12600</AMOUNT>
<VAT country="FR" currency="EURO">2520</VAT>
<AMOUNT_DUE currency="EURO">15120</AMOUNT_DUE>
....
</INVOICE>
```

The French metadata engine then converts the French invoice data in Example 40-6 into legacy form (not shown) by applying other transformations, similar to those in Example 40-4.

40.2.3 *Automated bid response*

In this e-commerce scenario, a customer puts forth a list of parts on which it invites suppliers to bid. A vendor chooses from the list only those items that it can supply and submits bids on them.

Example 40-7 shows excerpts from the customer's consolidated list of bid requests. It requests bids on three different sizes of the part numbered "12T20-2".

Example 40-7. Customer's bid request

```
<BID_REQUEST>
<UNIT>MD-STLOUIS</UNIT>
<DEPARTMENT>EN</DEPARTMENT>
<CONTACT>J.DOE</CONTACT>
<TEL>8001111111</TEL>
<EMAIL>JDOE@MD-STLOUIS.COM</EMAIL>
<BID_OOB format="ISO-8601" >19990821</BID_OOB>
....
<ITEMNO>24</ITEMNO>
  <PARTNUM dimension="124">12T20-2</PARTNUM>
  <QUANTITY>2000</QUANTITY>
....
<ITEMNO>52</ITEMNO>
  <PARTNUM dimension="28">12T20-2</PARTNUM>
  <QUANTITY>3000</QUANTITY>
<ITEMNO>53</ITEMNO>
  <PARTNUM dimension="52">12T20-2</PARTNUM>
  <QUANTITY>3000</QUANTITY>
</BID_REQUEST>
```

The vendor's metadata engine extracts the `PARTNUM` content and `dimension` attribute value of each item to determine the part numbers and sizes requested. It queries the legacy application to determine which ones the vendor can supply. The application's response is used to prepare the XML bid document shown in Example 40-8.

The vendor uses the same `BID` document type for all its bids to all its customers, which allows it to use the bid data effectively. As a result, some ele-

Example 40-8. Vendor's bid document

```
<BID>
<CUST>MD-STLOUIS</CUST>
<DEPARTMENT>EN</DEPARTMENT>
<ATTN>J.DOE</ATTN>
<TEL>8001111111</TEL>
<EMAIL>JDOE@MD-STLOUIS.COM</EMAIL>
<DUE_DATE format="ISO-8601" >19990821</DUE_DATE>
<ITEMNO>52</ITEMNO>
  <PARTNUM dimension="28">12T20-2</PARTNUM>
  <QUANTITY>3000</QUANTITY>
<ITEMNO>53</ITEMNO>
  <PARTNUM dimension="52">12T20-2</PARTNUM>
  <QUANTITY>3000</QUANTITY>
</BID>
```

ments that appear in both the bid request and the bid have a different element-type name in each. For this reason, before sending the bid to the customer, the vendor's metadata engine will translate the element-type names `CUST`, `ATTN`, and `DUE_DATE` to `UNIT`, `CONTACT`, and `BID_OOB`, respectively.

40.3 | Legacy data flow

Legacy data flow is a concept that underlies much of the promise of XML, and therefore much of what you have been reading about in this book. It is the notion of making legacy data speedily available wherever it is needed in the enterprise, and in a form that is suitable for use at that point.

Specifically:

- Data flows from *data generation points* to *data use points* through the enterprise network.
- Data use points determine the usage of the data. The term "usage" includes aggregation, transformation, rendition, and presentation. Therefore, the same data may be used in different ways at different use points.
- *Data semantics* – the meaning assigned to data – determines its usage. Therefore, a data use point may ascribe its own semantics to the data it receives.

- Data flow is autonomous.

There are many advantages implicit in this concept.

- First and most importantly, it provides a conceptual framework in which enterprise data is truly integrated and thereby becomes a competitive advantage.
- Second, it refutes the notion that an enterprise monoculture in terminology, acronyms, etc., is essential to its success. Data is made available to all groups, and each group interprets it in ways that is useful to its process or task. There is a kind of data ubiquitousness that may prove to be the key ingredient of success.
- Third, data use points may use data in multiple ways: to generate documents as input to their applications, for external use such as e-commerce databases, or for statistical purposes such as data mining.
- Fourth, the concept embraces a full range of data atomicity, structure, and type. For example, data atomicity may range from a single product id to a departmental organizational chart; data structures may range from lists, tables, and tree structures to entire documents; and datatypes may range from conventional numeric data to complex non-numeric data such as company logos.

40.3.1 *Usage scenarios*

In the legacy data flow model, the traditional role of documents as collators and interpreters of data is not diminished; rather it is enhanced. Legacy data flow will simply make documents and enterprise communication more precise, and enterprise processes run faster and less prone to errors or delays. The usage scenarios described below illustrate these points.

Catalog generation

The enterprise product catalog generation process speeds up due to quicker data updates and less need for manual editing and error checking. The "busy-wait" periods in data exchange between enterprise departments are eliminated.

E-commerce server

The enterprise e-commerce server database can better reflect product availability and pricing changes. This is especially true when complex product configurations or multiple pricing models are involved. Human data entry errors, catalog maintenance delays, and other factors that bedevil product databases are reduced.

Corporate merger

A corporate merger can be consummated more efficiently if both corporations' legacy data are organized on legacy data flow principles. Disruption in either partner's operations during the initial days of the merger can be reduced by initially providing bridges between the two data flows. Later, the best practices of each enterprise can be incorporated in the merged organization by retaining the corresponding data flows.

Data event reporting

A tripwire reporting facility based on the occurrence or non-occurrence of data events may be implemented. Examples include triggers based on critical parts availability, financial flows, personnel issues, etc. More sophisticated versions may provide a data filtering mechanism based on the semantic content of data such as e-mail.

40.3.2 *XML-based legacy data flow*

XML provides the ideal technology framework for implementing the legacy data flow concept. XML, through its tagged data and metadata structure, provides the means to "describe" the data to each use point. Two items of essential metadata are needed for legacy data to work. XML can be used to describe both. They are:

- Context metadata
- Semantic property metadata

Context is key because the same data may be interpreted differently in different contexts. A use point may therefore use or ignore data depending on context. Context includes such information as the means by which the data was generated (legacy application name, for example), the data generation point, generation date, time, etc. It would also contain the name of a larger data structure of which it is a part.

Semantic property information on the other hand is metadata that is intrinsic to the data itself; and may therefore remain unchanged in different contexts. Put in the context of legacy data flow, it is the interpretation of the data according to the data generating point.

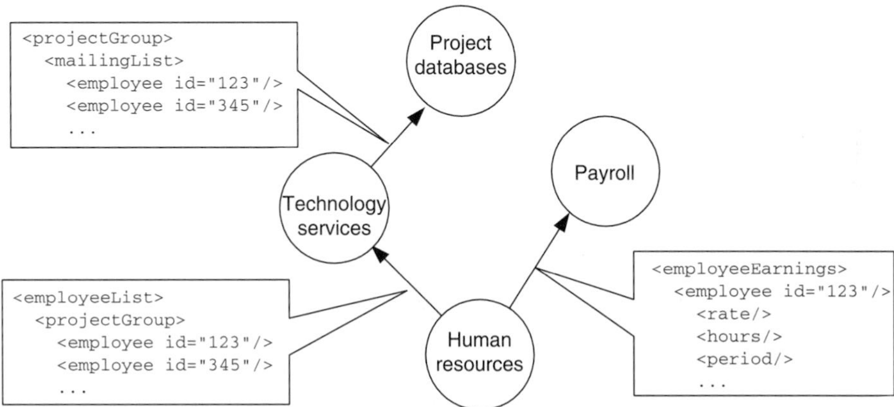

Figure 40-2 XML-based legacy data flow for employee data

Figure 40-2 depicts a simplified partial data flow of employee information between four departments in a corporation: the Human Resources (HR) department, the Technology Services department, the Payroll department, and the Project Group. Each arc represents data flow between its end points. On each arc, the context and semantic property metadata are shown as callouts; the actual data is not illustrated.

The information channel can be implemented as a centralized Information channel. The actual flows that occur may occur at different times: possibly bi-weekly between HR and Payroll, and at unscheduled times between Technical Services and Project Group. Generally, we can expect today's processes to implement efficient data flow when it is regularly scheduled, as between HR and Payroll. However, unscheduled data flows are rarely as successful.

40.3.3 *XML communication server*

One way to implement the concept of legacy data flow is to start with a preliminary list of data elements around which individual flows are then constructed. These flows will be multi-point data flows, unlike the e-commerce examples that we discussed earlier.

Moreover, each data element will have its own individual data flow tree or graph. In addition, we need to decide the mode of initiation of each flow: time-triggered or event-triggered.

To manage these flows simultaneously, we define an *XML communication server*. The XML communication server processes XML metadata just like the metadata engine, so it should not be surprising that many of the functions of the two overlap. Among these are homonymic and synonymic transformations of metadata, data formatting, aggregation, and extraction.

However, managing the individual data flows still remains the most important task handled by the XML communications server. In doing so, it must construct one or more contexts for a given data element at the generation point. Similarly, at each use point, the XML communication server must first evaluate the context, decide the course of action (accept or ignore), extract data and other related information, and then perform the metalanguage transformations necessary to insert the data in the use center's database.

40.3.4 *Data repositories*

The legacy application data repository is a source of information regarding data relationships. Many such repositories were constructed during the analysis phase of Y2K compliance projects. In particular, the data dictionaries are the starting points for building legacy data flows.

Each legacy application has its own data dictionaries, which are relatively isolated from other data dictionaries. In the legacy data flow implementation, care must be taken to ensure that these repositories are not modified in a manner that leaves them incompatible with the legacy applications they serve.

The bridge between these legacy data repositories is the XML communications server metadata repository. This repository consists of one or more metadata dictionaries spanning multiple legacy applications. Data element descriptions, semantic property descriptions, context specifications, and metadata transformation grammars are some of the objects in the metadata repository.

40.4 | Legacy data challenges

Despite the name, legacy applications are not frozen in time, but are continuously evolving. The challenge is therefore in being able to maintain compatibility between legacy data changes and the metadata descriptions of legacy data. Sometimes these changes are very subtle.

For example, the windowing technique described earlier for Y2K fixes involves no change in the structure of the application data, but only in its interpretation. A metadata repository must be able to interpret this change, perhaps at the level of individual date elements.

Another example is where apparently irrelevant data (e.g. Cobol record FILLERS) is interpreted as meaningful data by the legacy application, due to new application enhancements.

High-throughput online transaction-oriented legacy systems may pose another challenge. It may be difficult to design XML modules that will provide metadata transformation synchronized to the transaction rate.

Such examples are not rare scare stories, but rather common occurrences in the world of legacy applications. They are the outcome of a requirement to maintain compatibility with "old" legacy data and the systems that rely on it.

Tip *XMLSolutions Corporation, sponsor of this chapter, has provided a free copy of its Apache-based ExeterXML Server on the CD-ROM.*

Stylesheets

- Styles
- Behaviors
- Active documents
- Website design considerations

©2000 THE XML HANDBOOK™

Part Eight

Style is the dress of thought.

Lord Chesterfield said that over a century ago, but he might have had XML in mind. He knew that the way you present your ideas is important – too important to mix up with the ideas themselves. Different audiences require different presentation styles, so you had better keep your data as an undressed abstraction until you know exactly where you want it to go today.

When you do, it is the stylesheet that spells out how to dress each part of the content – the colors, fonts, flow rules, etc. – and, increasingly, how that part should act as well (what programmers call "behaviors").

In this part we'll first look at the role of stylesheets and how they work, with an emphasis on traditional style specifications. Then we'll see how to use stylesheets in interactive applications, including the specification of behaviors and the use of active documents. Finally, we'll examine the tradeoffs that affect stylesheet design in real-world Web applications.

INSIGHT: The role of stylesheets

Tool Discussion

- Intelligent publications
- Template rules
- Free trial on CD-ROM

©2000 THE XML HANDBOOK™

Chapter 41

Abstract XML documents make it easier to build robust intelligent electronic publications without programming. Instead, designers can specify presentation with declarative stylesheets, often aided by stylesheet design tools. This chapter shows how. It is sponsored by Enigma, Inc., `http://www.enigma.com`.

XML publishing systems are distinguished by their ability to deliver intelligent publications; that is, electronic publications with live tables of contents, hyperlinking, topic searching, and other navigation aids.

Stylesheets play a critical role in delivering these capabilities, from two standpoints:

- Stylesheets aren't just limited to specifying style for renditions (fonts, layout, color, etc.). They are really generalized "specification sheets" that can also control behaviors, such as interactivity, navigation, data processing, and so on. So the word "style" in their name shouldn't be taken too literally.
- Styles are applied to components of an XML document in accordance with *template rules*. The language for creating such rules can be quite powerful and allow for highly-granular application of the styles.

41.1 | The need for intelligent publications

The business need for delivering intelligent publications – such as maintenance and parts information or commercial reference publications – has always existed. The publications too have always existed, even in paper format, with elaborate multiple indexes, various types of lists of illustrations, detailed running headers and footers, and extensive cross-referencing.

However, both the need and the opportunities for more effective implementation, have significantly increased with the advent of corporate intranets. This infrastructure enables content providers to make their intelligent publications more useful, and more widely available. And with the ability to interconnect these publications with ERP and e-commerce systems, content providers and end-users alike are improving productivity and increasing after-market revenues, as we have seen in other parts of this book.

Among the XML systems that have been developed to support this need is Enigma's *INSIGHT* electronic publishing software. It produced the intelligent document shown in Figure 41-1. Note the two panes. The left contains navigation aids and the right shows the material that is accessed by selecting a navigation aid. The bottom part of the left pane is a "live" table of contents that can be collapsed and expanded. The upper part is a list of search items.

In this case, the search item called "Visual Access" has been selected in the left pane, and an exploded graphic is shown on the right. Navigation can also be initiated within the right pane by hyperlinking. Here, any of the call-outs can be clicked in order to access more information about the parts they identify.

41.2 | Creating a stylesheet

We will use *INSIGHT* in this chapter to illustrate the concept of stylesheets and a selection of their capabilities. In order to make use of abstract XML content, a stylesheet must be created that specifies how the content should be presented.

In the terms used in the emerging XSL stylesheet standard, a stylesheet for XML is a set of template rules. A template rule has two parts:

©2000 THE XML HANDBOOK™

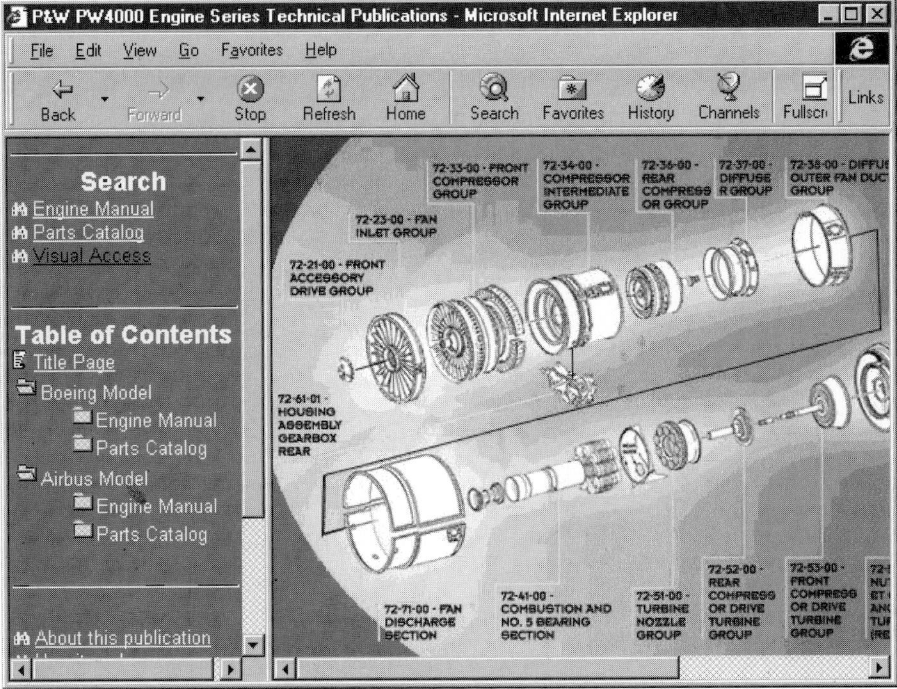

Figure 41-1 Intelligent publication with live navigation aids

- A *pattern*, which selects the content portions to which a rule applies.
- A *template*, which specifies the rendition style, behavior, and/ or other processing to be applied to the selected content.

INSIGHT provides a stylesheet editor to assist in defining these rules. It is illustrated in Figure 41-2.

In the left pane, the document type structure is presented in an expandable tree view. Alternatively, a list of element types could be shown by selecting the appropriate tab.

In the upper-right pane, there is a set of tabbed dialogs for the available style and behavior specifications. The illustrated dialog allows the selected content to be numbered and boilerplate text to precede or follow it. The lower-right pane shows a preview of the applied specification.

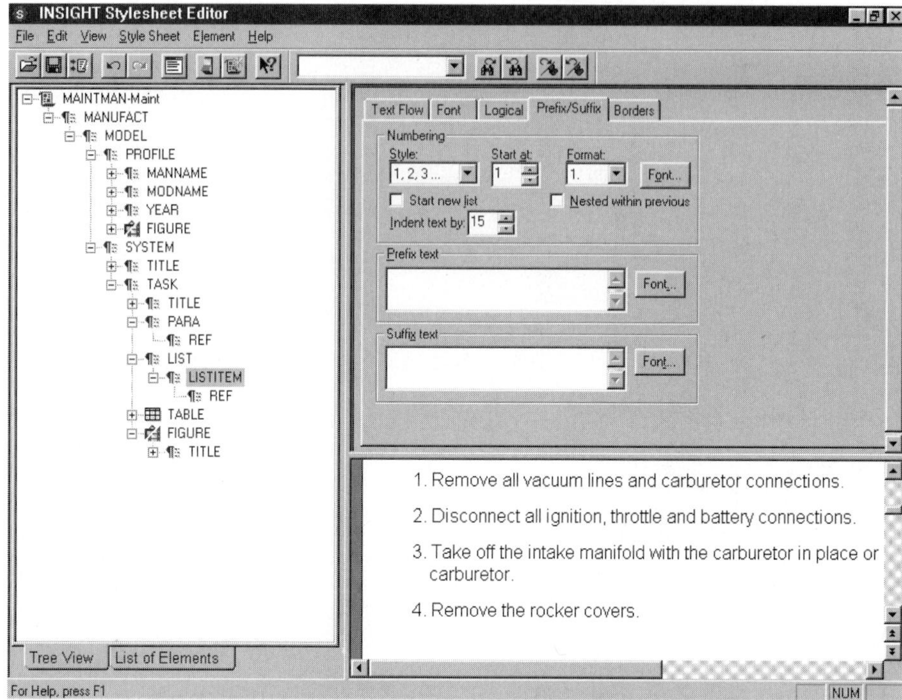

Figure 41-2 Stylesheet editor

41.2.1 *Associating processing with document components*

Let's look at *INSIGHT*'s facilities for applying template rules.

41.2.1.1 Pattern specification

There are several ways to specify a pattern (called a "match-pattern" in the *INSIGHT* product):

element type occurring anywhere
: An example would be: any `PARA` element, no matter where it occurs.

element type in hierarchical context
An example would be: any `TITLE` element that is the child of a `TASK` element.

qualified by attribute value
Patterns of the above types can be further qualified by attribute values. For example: Any `PARA` element that has a `PERIL` attribute whose value is `DANGER`.

41.2.1.2 Rule inheritance

It is not necessary to specify individual template rules for every element type in the document. If no rule applies specifically to an element, it inherits the rule that applies to its parent.

This principle is applied independently to each of the dialogs in Figure 41-2. For example, if you specify only font properties in the rule for an element, it will inherit all prefix, text flow and border properties from its parent.

41.2.2 *Specifying processing*

INSIGHT's facilities for the "template" portion of a template rule include both styling and behaviors.

41.2.2.1 Rendition style

A range of style properties can be specified in a template rule, including:

- Font information (e.g. font, size, bold/italic)
- Text flow (e.g. space before/after, justification)
- Borders and shading
- Prefix/suffix and list numbering
- Table type (CALS, HTML table, user-defined)
- Image/multimedia display (scaling, inline/iconized)

Attribute values can be included in the style specifications (e.g. as a prefix or suffix). Such uses are independent of whether the attribute was used to qualify the rule's pattern specification.

41.2.2.2 Behaviors

In addition to style properties, the following behaviors can be specified for the selected content:

- Search item in the navigation pane
- Table of Contents entry and hierarchy level
- Hyperlink rules (based on ID/IDREF, XPointer, attribute values, or data content)

41.3 | Delivering the results

After the stylesheet is defined, the entire publication is packaged for delivery to the end-user. The publication can be installed on a public Web server, delivered to the owner to be installed on a local intranet, or sent as a stand-alone or networked CD-ROM publication. *INSIGHT* provides a wizard to attend to the details (Figure 41-3).

Note that the source documents that are included in the publication are not restricted to XML or SGML. Rendered documents from common word processors and desktop publishing systems can also be included in the delivered publication, with their content hyperlinked and searchable.

Normally, the document and the stylesheet are served to the end-user and the stylesheet is applied dynamically on the client side. However, for

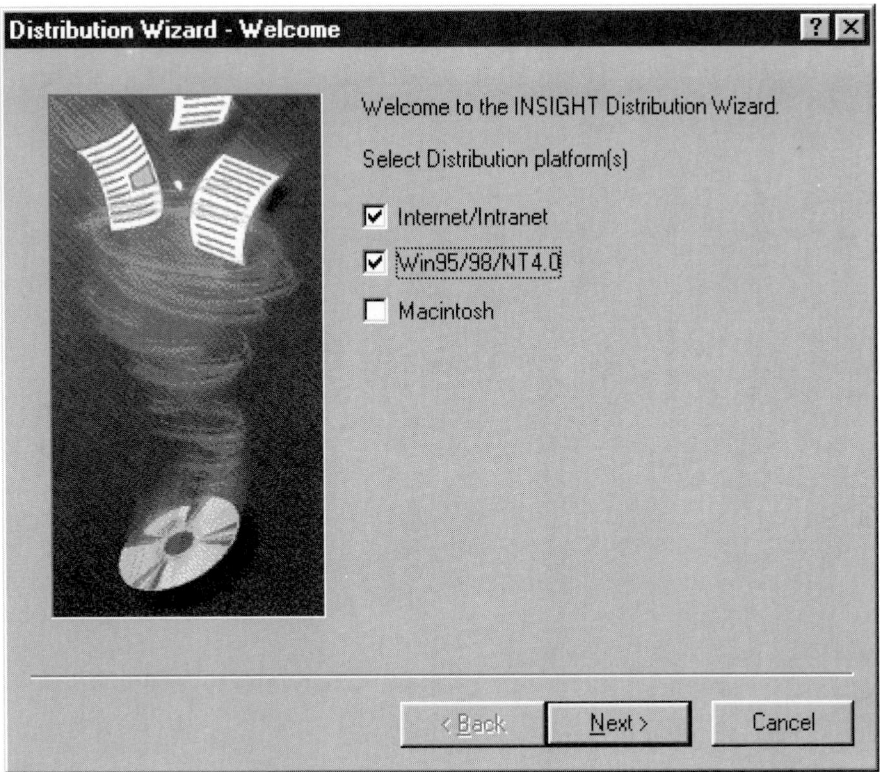

Figure 41-3 *INSIGHT* distribution wizard

browsers that do not support XML, HTML can be generated on the server and delivered to the browser.

Tip *A free trial version of INSIGHT is available on the CD-ROM that accompanies this book.*

Stylesheets for interactive applications

Application Discussion

- HTML and XML compared
- Methodology for interactive XML
- Active documents

©2000 THE XML HANDBOOK™

Chapter 42

When is a document not a document? When it's an entire interactive application – and even then, it's still a document. This chapter will show you what stylesheets can do for interactive applications, and how a document can be data, user interface, and program, all at the same time. It is sponsored by: RivCom, www.rivcom.com, and was prepared by Tony Stewart.

As the Web continues to become the standard medium for business-to-business communication, the Web browser is fast becoming the standard interface for interactive business applications. Therefore, any improvements in the cost, effectiveness or maintainability of browser-based applications will benefit enterprises of every size and type.

Using XML for those interactive applications offers significant advantages over traditional HTML-based methods. Because XML abstractions contain much more information than HTML renditions, the application can do more of its work in the browser without having to go back to the server for additional information. And because client-side XML applications are so efficient, application designers can include functionality that is prohibitively difficult to achieve when HTML is delivered to the browser.

This chapter discusses these issues and describes some illustrative applications.

42.1 | Using HTML

In most interactive Web applications, HTML is generated dynamically on the server and sent to the browser for display. When the user then clicks on a hyperlink or `Submit` button, the browser sends a message back to the server indicating what the user has just done and requesting another page of data. Software on the server reacts to the request, and a new page is generated and sent to the browser.

The pattern of back-and-forth messages and server-side processing continues throughout the user's session, as shown in Figure 42-1.

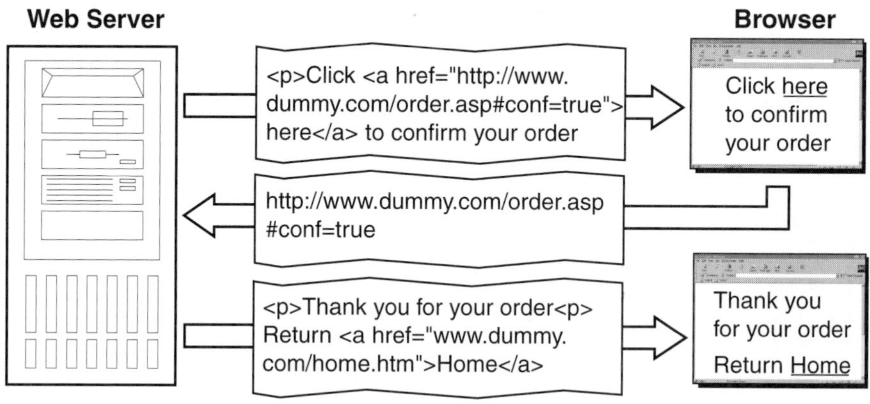

Figure 42-1 HTML messages

42.1.1 *Interactive HTML applications*

The HTML model works fine for relatively simple processes, such as reading static pages, or for transactions where most of the work really should be done on the server. But increasingly there are types of applications in which it makes sense to move more of the processing to the browser.

Let's look at two common scenarios. These are not complete applications. Rather, they represent the kinds of mid-level functionality that occur again and again in a typical Web application. If we want to develop applications that are cost-effective and pleasing, we need to implement this functionality without writing a lot of complicated code, and without making the user wait each time for responses from the server.

42.1.1.1 Validating a form

When you enter data in a Web form, there are usually rules that must be enforced before the form can be processed. For example, as in Figure 42-2, certain fields cannot be left empty, or a password must have a minimum length. In cases like these it is frustrating to press the `Submit` button, wait ten or fifteen seconds, and then receive an error message saying that you have made a mistake. It would be better to have appropriate feedback while you are entering the data in the first place.

*Name:
Address:
City:
State:
Postal Code:
*Email:
*Password:
(at least 5 characters)
* = Required Fields
Submit

Figure 42-2 A form with data-entry rules

42.1.1.2 Multiple-window interactions

Suppose that you are reading an interactive technical manual that uses two windows, as illustrated in Figure 42-3. The navigation window on the left displays an expandable outline of the procedures and tasks in the manual. The content window on the right contains the text of the current task, along with hyperlinks for jumping to other tasks. Obviously, when you click on an item in the navigation window, the text of that item should appear in the content window. But, equally important, when you jump from one task to another in the content window, the navigation window outline should refresh itself (by collapsing and expanding) in order to show the context of the task to which you have just jumped. In a complex manual, this kind of real-time context display can make it much easier to master the material.

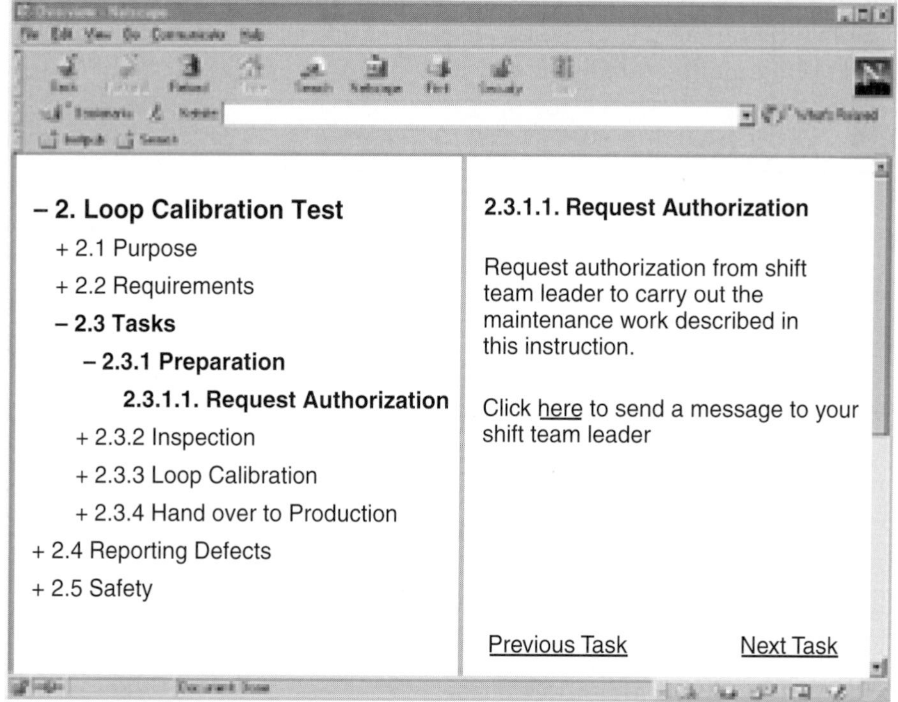

Figure 42-3 A two-window technical manual

42.1.2 *Three strategies for interactivity*

HTML-based Web technologies offer three strategies for interactivity. Let's see how they work with our scenarios.

42.1.2.1 Serve plain HTML

In this strategy, all processing is performed on the server, which sends plain-vanilla HTML to the browser.

This is first-generation Web technology. It can certainly implement the data-entry form, but the server-side processing would lead to delays. It would *not* work for the multi-window technical manual, because there is no way in standard HTML to refresh two windows simultaneously.

42.1.2.2 Serve HTML with *JavaScript*

This is second-generation Web technology, commonly called Dynamic HTML (DHTML). It can handle data-entry forms quite nicely, and it runs in the browser so there are no delays. However, it would be very difficult to refresh the navigation window using only *JavaScript* and HTML, because the HTML would not contain enough information to support the required processing.

42.1.2.3 Serve HTML with a custom applet

This is the "hit it with a big hammer" approach. It will definitely work for both scenarios if the necessary data is sent to the browser as an abstraction, rather than an HTML rendition. But the cost of writing and maintaining custom code for these relatively modest problems is disproportionate to the results.

42.1.3 *HTML limitations*

The vast majority of interactive Web applications use one of the latter two strategies. This means that they rely on expert programmers to write the code, they require significant server-side resources to generate the pages, and the most advanced of them also require the downloading and installation of a specialized *Java* applet or `ActiveX` control in order to use the application.

In many cases this level of activity is appropriate to the problem. However, as our two scenarios demonstrate, there are also many cases when it would be useful to:

- Reduce the number of programmers required to develop interactive documents.

- Allocate appropriate parts of the processing to the user's machine (the client) rather than the server.
- Do without a separate *ActiveX* or *Java* application for each type of interactive application.

42.2 | Using XML

XML opens the door to all of these improvements over the HTML way of doing things.

42.2.1 *Five precepts*

Like other technologies, XML can deliver value when used properly but there are plenty of opportunities to do things the wrong way as well. A proven methodology is to follow these five precepts:

1. Separate abstraction from rendition
2. Use stylesheets for rendition
3. Process on the client side
4. Use stylesheets for behavior
5. Use a generic runtime style engine

42.2.1.1 Separate abstraction from rendition

This is the core concept that motivated the invention of markup languages 30 years ago and it is just as powerful today. Many people think that using SGML/XML is synonymous with creating abstract documents, but HTML is proof that it isn't.

By carefully using element types that describe the *meaning* of the information rather than its *formatting*, you can automatically generate any desired rendition on demand.

This approach, as shown in Figure 42-4, delivers multiple benefits that have been demonstrated repeatedly in this book and in real life:

- Media-independent publishing (i.e. different renditions for Web, CD and print)

XML Abstraction

```
<book>
<title>Winnie The Pooh</title>
<author mailto="aam@am.com">A. A. Milne</author>
<copyright crdate="1926" crby="author"/>
<chapter ID="c1>
<title>We are Introduced to Winnie-the-Pooh and Some Bees</title>
<para ID="c1p1">Here is Edward Bear, coming downstairs now...</para>
...</chapter> ... </book>
```

HTML Rendition

```
<H1 ALIGN="CENTER">Winnie The Pooh</H1>
<P ALIGN="CENTER"><I>A. A. Milne</I></P>
<P ALIGN="RIGHT"><FONT SIZE="-1">&copy; 1926 by
<A HREF=mailto:aam@am.com>A. A. Milne</A></FONT></P>
<H2> We are Introduced to Winnie-the-Pooh and Some Bees</H2>
<P> Here is Edward Bear, coming downstairs now...</P>
```

Figure 42-4 Abstract and rendered versions of a children's classic

- The application of multiple styles to the same information (e.g. "manager's view" vs. "technical view", or "tabular format" vs. "narrative format")
- Easier maintenance of the underlying information over time (edit the information as needed, then re-publish automatically by re-generating a rendition in the desired style)

42.2.1.2 Use stylesheets for rendition

As your XML is an abstraction, you will have to generate the desired formatting programmatically. There are many ways to do this, and the approach taken for any given project will depend on the nature of the project and the types of people available to do the work.

Stylesheets are an extremely efficient way to convert XML information into properly formatted output (see Figure 42-5). As we have seen, a stylesheet is a collection of template rules. Each rule consists of an association between a pattern of information in the document, and some processing that should be applied to it.

For example, a template rule can say that whenever a `title` element is encountered, its contents should be centered and boldfaced on the page or screen. A more complex rule could apply differing treatments to chapter titles and book titles, could filter or rearrange the information being generated, or could generate different results at runtime according to the access rights or the job function of the person reading the output.

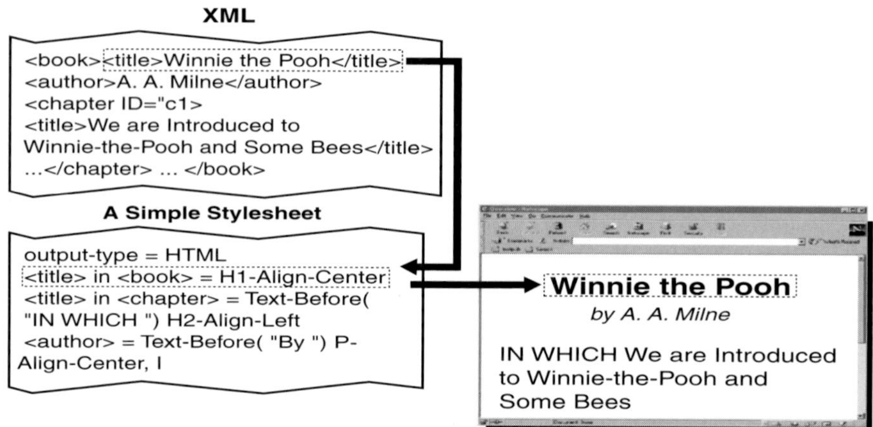

Figure 42-5 Applying a template rule to generate HTML

Template rules are processed by running both the XML and the stylesheet through a "stylesheet processor". This is a generic software component that reads XML text and a stylesheet, applies the template rules, and generates the resulting output(s). It is "generic" in the sense that it can handle any XML document type, and any stylesheet in the stylesheet notation that it supports.

Historically, stylesheet notations have been proprietary and stylesheet processors were built into programs that do formatting. Now formatting programs, following the lead of Web browsers, are starting to support standardized stylesheet notations like XSL. There are also stand-alone stylesheet processors that can be downloaded and plugged into any software architecture.

42.2.1.3 Process on the client side

It is perfectly possible to use XML and stylesheets on the server and then send HTML to the browser for display. Most XML processing is currently being done on the server, and server-side stylesheets are often an improvement on other mechanisms for generating HTML.

But, as noted in our examples above, there are many types of functionality that are made easier if the abstract information, rather than just a formatted view of it, is available in the browser. That means sending the XML and the stylesheets (rather than HTML) to the client machine. The client can then process the stylesheets either in the browser itself (if it supports this functionality) or in a separate stylesheet processor (see Figure 42-6).

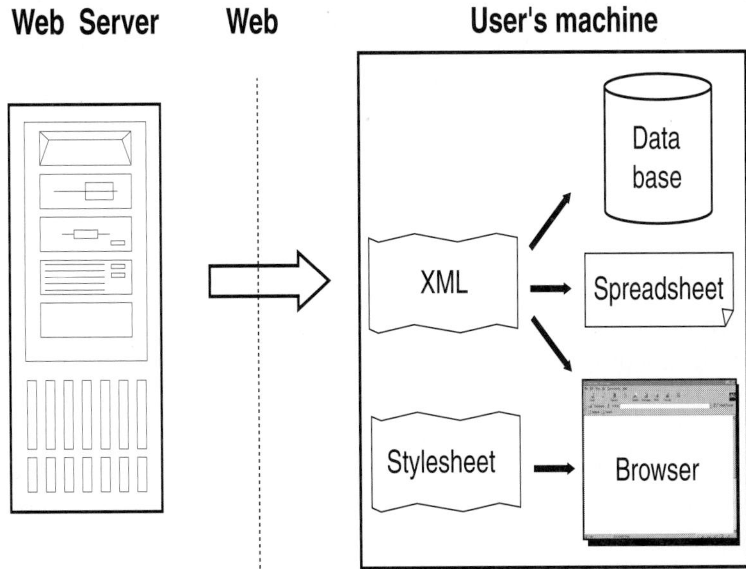

Figure 42-6 Once an XML abstraction is in the client you can do more than just display it

In all cases, moving the stylesheet processing to the browser means that the abstract data in the XML document is available on the client machine and can be used by programs running either inside or outside the browser. That data availability can facilitate EIPs, e-commerce, and other application integration that we have discussed. It also enables other benefits, as we shall see.

42.2.1.4 Use stylesheets for behavior

One of the reasons stylesheets are so efficient is that they are based on rules that bind a particular effect (for example, some style of formatting) to a particular pattern of data (for example, `titles` within `chapters`, or `net-profit` elements that contain negative numbers). Once such a rule has been created, it is automatically applied to all the information that conforms to the pattern specified in the rule.

This same mechanism is an extremely efficient way to bind behavior to XML information. As seen in Figure 42-7, stylesheets can specify not only that a particular type of element should be formatted as a hyperlink or button, but also, what should happen at runtime when the user clicks on that link or button. A *JavaScript* function or a compiled *Java* applet may implement the actual behavior, but it is the stylesheet that performs the critical function of linking these software programs to the information in the document.

The stylesheet approach can be a more efficient way to attach behavior to XML elements than traditional scripting because of its powerful rule-based binding mechanism. It can be less costly because, once a library of generic routines has been developed, non-programmers can attach these routines to the information in documents. Doing so also has the interesting side effect of putting both the visual and behavioral design in the hands of a single designer.

Separating the association rules from the behavior implementation has proven beneficial even in the absence of standardized ways to specify the runtime behavior itself.[1]

42.2.1.5 Use a generic runtime style engine

Traditional rendition-only stylesheets are processed just once, when the page is first displayed. Behavioral stylesheets, however, need to remain

1. The emerging International Standard for Multimedia Interactive Documents (ISMID) addresses this need. It is being developed by the same ISO committee that developed SGML, DSSSL, HyTime, and Topic Maps.

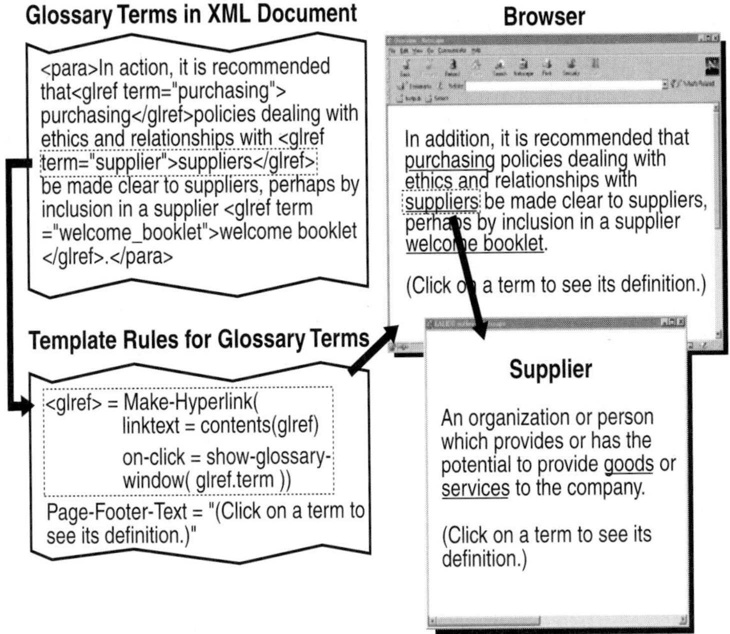

Glossary Terms in XML Document
<para>In action, it is recommended that<glref term="purchasing"> purchasing</glref>policies dealing with ethics and relationships with <glref term="supplier">suppliers</glref> be made clear to suppliers, perhaps by inclusion in a supplier <glref term ="welcome_booklet">welcome booklet </glref>.</para>
Browser
In addition, it is recommended that purchasing policies dealing with ethics and relationships with suppliers be made clear to suppliers, perhaps by inclusion in a supplier welcome booklet.
(Click on a term to see its definition.)
Template Rules for Glossary Terms
<glref> = Make-Hyperlink(linktext = contents(glref) on-click = show-glossary-window(glref.term))
Page-Footer-Text = "(Click on a term to see its definition.)"
Supplier
An organization or person which provides or has the potential to provide goods or services to the company.
(Click on a term to see its definition.)

Figure 42-7 A template rule can specify both formatting and runtime behavior

accessible while the user is interacting with the page. In order to implement robust runtime behavior based on behavioral template rules, there must be a runtime engine (like RivCom's *RivComet*™) that sits outside the Web page and manages the entire process.

With such an engine, when the user activates a hyperlink or presses the `Submit` button, the browser sends a message to the style engine containing instructions that were attached to the link or button when the page was first rendered. Acting on these instructions, the style engine can perform calculations, update the XML information, re-render the page, request new data from the server, or call up any other application to perform necessary tasks.

Despite this power, a runtime style engine does not have to be heavy or complex. Most of its functionality is provided by components, such as an XML parser and a stylesheet processor, that are already present in any XML environment.

Most importantly, unlike custom plug-ins or *ActiveX* controls, the runtime style engine is a generic application whose behavior is driven entirely by the stylesheets. Once the user has installed it – or once the major browsers include such an engine as standard equipment – entire applications can be delivered in the form of XML documents and behavioral stylesheets, with no further software code required.

42.2.2 *XML advantages*

Interactive applications that follow these precepts typically gain advantages like these:

- Easier to build than traditional Web applications.
- Provide additional functionality.
- Lighten the load on the server.
- Enable offline applications that can be run with only a browser.

This last point is particularly significant for dispersed enterprises and supply chain applications. It is often useful to be able to provide mini applications, such as automated bidding forms or engineering worksheets, to vendors or suppliers who do not have access to the enterprise's online databases.

The package of XML information and a controlling stylesheet can be sent by email. The recipient then interacts with it in his browser just as if it were a traditional software application. When finished, the application automatically creates an email containing the modified XML data and sends it back to the enterprise, where it can be integrated into the workflow process that spawned it.

In effect, this methodology uses XML to implement an application generator.

42.3 | Interactive XML applications

In order to demonstrate these advantages, we will describe three real-world projects that RivCom implemented for clients and the architecture they share in common.

42.3.1 *The RivCom projects*

The three applications run the gamut from relatively simple to quite complex.[1]

42.3.1.1 Process plant engineering activity model

This is a high-level description of the activities involved in building an oil refinery or nuclear power plant. The user can select various views of the data, and all navigational links are generated on the fly by the stylesheet.

42.3.1.2 Competence gap analysis tool

This is a human resources application that merges read-only information from the server with values entered at runtime by the user and displays a graphical analysis of the combined data. This is an example of an XML document with active content. It looks and behaves like a traditional software application that just happens to have a browser interface.

42.3.1.3 Storefront website demo

This application was built for an e-commerce start-up company to help raise their second round of financing. The demo shows two windows.

In the first window, the user configures an entire Web storefront, both selecting the inventory and specifying how to display it. In the second window, a mock-up of the resulting site is displayed simultaneously and is modified dynamically as the configuration changes.

The stylesheet performs pricing calculations, cascades updates through multiple open windows, and applies different visual styles based on the user's choices. Meanwhile, the runtime style engine maintains seven parsed XML documents in memory, tracks the user's changes to each of them, and writes the updates to disk only when the user presses the `Save Changes` button.[2]

---

1. A sample version of the applications is available on the CD so that you can install and run them for yourself.

©2000 The XML Handbook™

42.3.2 *The enabling architecture*

All three of these applications rely on the same underlying technology to generate both presentation and behavior. The architecture is shown in Figure 42-8.

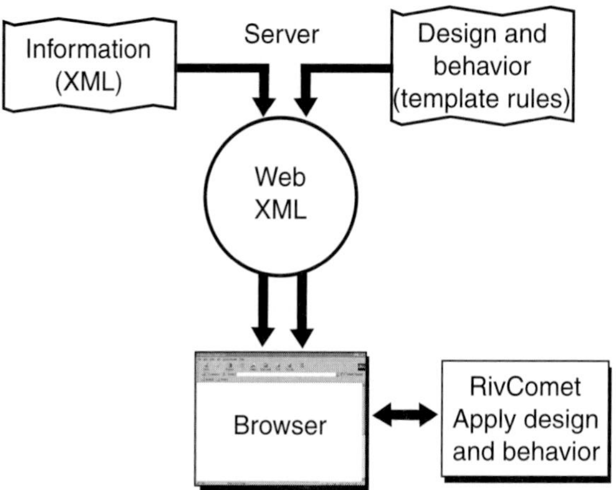

Figure 42-8 The RivComet™ model

The following procedure is executed:

1. The browser issues a request for information to the server.
2. The server aggregates the appropriate information (if necessary) and sends it to the browser as one or more XML documents accompanied by the relevant stylesheets.
3. The stylesheet processor within the browser parses the XML and the stylesheet and loads them into memory as a parsed object model. It then applies the style and behavior template rules to the associated portions of the parsed document and generates the appropriate HTML, DHTML and/or *JavaScript*, which the browser interprets and displays.

---

2. In the original version of this application the changes were sent over the Web to an XML database at a remote location. The application on the CD has been modified so that changes are not saved.

4. Template rules indicate not only what should happen when the page is initially displayed, but also what should happen when the user acts on it, such as by clicking on a button or typing into a field.
5. The stylesheet can call a scripting language to perform calculations, query or manipulate the object model, invoke new template rules, trigger additional calls to the server, etc.
6. Based on the user's behavior and the governing template rules, the browser re-renders the page, displays a new page, transmits information to the server, or takes whatever other action is required.

With this architecture, the user can click on information in the browser and immediately see more details in a user-friendly way, without waiting for a request to be sent the server and fulfilled. The architecture allows applications to be used even in circumstances where the server is half-way around the world or where the application is only available on CD.

Designing website stylesheets

Application Discussion

- IE5 XML Sports demo
- Server delivery strategy
- Navigation in large mixed document sets
- Using XSL for data processing
- Presentation in non-traditional media

©2000 THE XML HANDBOOK™

Chapter 43

XSL offers immense creative possibilities to website developers, far beyond the simple generation of HTML renditions. But real-world conditions relating to a given application and its data can affect your stylesheet design. These issues are explored in this chapter, which is sponsored by Microsoft Corporation, http://msdn.microsoft.com/xml, and was prepared by Charles Heinemann.

Website stylesheets can't be designed in a vacuum. Although modular design and reuse of stylesheet components is a desirable goal, the more specifically a stylesheet focuses on particular documents and their implications for the client/server relationship, the more efficient the stylesheet will be.

The *XML Sports Demo*, which was released with Microsoft *Internet Explorer 5*, demonstrates different techniques for building websites that exploit the XML technology of the browser.

The demo site is data-driven. It hosts a large interconnected set of news stories and statistical information for teams and players in several major American sports. The demo is elaborated in sufficient detail to raise – and resolve – a number of the issues that affect practical stylesheet design.

We will discuss several of those issues in this chapter.[1] They are:

- Server delivery strategy
- Navigation in large mixed document sets
- Using XSL for data processing
- Presentation in non-traditional media

1. The full demo is available on the CD-ROM for further examination.

The discussion assumes knowledge of *Active Server Pages* (ASP), which were explained in Chapter 7, "Building an online auction website", on page 92.

43.1 | Server delivery strategy

The *XML Sports Demo* is an example of a data-driven website. This means that the site offers large amounts of data to the client. The goals of the demo in that respect were to:

1. Provide access to all the data needed by the user.
2. Serve up that data in the most efficient manner.

43.1.1 *Accessing all the data*

Achieving the first goal requires the website to have access to a large amount of data. In the case of the *XML Sports Demo*, this does not create a significant performance problem because all of the necessary files are located on the same server.

The results would be different, however, if the data were stored on other servers somewhere else on the Web. It could take some time to download a large XML document containing, for instance, the statistical information concerning yesterday's Major League Baseball box scores

It is difficult to get around the fact that the user simply must wait for data to be downloaded. However, a Web developer can help the situation by making that wait more palatable. Web surfers have come to accept the initial time hit when a Web page is first loading. However, they soon grow impatient if the website takes a long time to respond to their subsequent actions.

The *XML Sports Demo* solves this problem by loading and parsing most of the XML necessary to drive the website before it sends the user interface HTML page to the client. This means that the user has to wait a little longer for the user interface to appear, but by the time it does, the site that sent it will have all of the data ready in parsed form.

The user's experience begins with the display of the user interface HTML page. The page is generated dynamically by an ASP file. That file

©2000 THE XML HANDBOOK™

also loads and parses the large XML documents that contain all of the data for the demo. To simplify our discussion (but without loss of generality), we will speak as though there were two such documents: one containing all the basketball stories, and another containing statistics on all the basketball teams that are mentioned in any of the stories.

The `XMLDOMDocument` objects that result from parsing the XML documents are assigned to `Application` variables that are instantiated and initialized in `Global.asa`, a file that executes when an ASP file is called in the same directory.

The ASP script that does these things is shown in Example 43-1.

Example 43-1. ASP script to load, parse, and save an XML document

```
var oSource = Server.CreateObject("Microsoft.FreeThreadedXMLDOM");
oSource.async = false;
oSource.load("http://localhost/xmlsports/stry_xml.asp");
Application("xmlsportsXML")=oSource;
```

Once an `Application` variable is set, the server can access it throughout the session. There is no need to reload and reparse the document every time a user needs it.

43.1.2 *Serving the data efficiently*

Although each complete XML document is parsed and ready on the server, it would not be efficient to send them in their entirety to the client. By performing some processing on the server, it is possible to deliver to the client only the information that the user needs.

For example, when the ASP file constructs the user interface, it can create a menu with the headlines in it, as shown in Example 43-2. That by itself doesn't cause any part of the document to be downloaded, other than the headlines in the menu.

A story is delivered only when the user clicks on one of the headlines, which causes the client-side function in Example 43-3 to be executed. The function changes the color of the headline as an acknowledgment of the user's request.

Example 43-2. Script to create a menu from the story headlines

```
oHeadlines = oSource.selectNodes(
              "stories/story[sport='" + sSport + "']/headline"
             );
for (i=0; i < oHeadlines.length; i++)
{
  if (i>0)
    sHeadlines += '<hr color = "ffffff">';
  sHeadlines += '<SPAN CLASS="link" ID="oHead"
                + onClick="fnFillStory(this.innerHTML);">'
             + oHeadlines.item(i).text + '</span>';
}
oTDHeadlines.innerHTML = sHeadlines;
```

Example 43-3. Requesting the specific story

```
function fnFillStory(headline)
{
  var oStory = new ActiveXObject("Microsoft.XMLDOM");
  oStory.async = false;
  // Grab the story with the selected headline
  oStory.load("getStory.asp?headline=" + headline);
  divStory.innerHTML =
    oStory.documentElement.transformNode(oStyle.documentElement);
  // Color this story's headline
}
```

When `oStory.load` in Example 43-3 executes, the server invokes the ASP file `getStory.asp` and passes it the value of the `headline` variable. The ASP file executes the script shown in Example 43-4.

Example 43-4. Selecting the requested story element from a document containing all of them

```
headline = Request.QueryString("headline");
oSource = Application("xmlsportsXML");
oStory = oSource.selectSingleNode("stories/story[headline='" +
            headline + "']");
Response.write(oStory.xml);
```

The script returns an XML document that consists of just the requested story. By extracting only a portion of the comprehensive XML document, the server spares the user from waiting for uninteresting data.

43.2 | Designing document types for navigation

In the *XML Sports Demo*, when the user's mouse pointer hovers over a team name in a story, the statistics for that team are displayed in a pop-up window. Figure 43-1 demonstrates what this looks like to the user.

NBA coaches not enjoying lockout
IT'S A WORKING stiff's fantasy - even rich working stiffs - and yet, most NBA coaches are finding that no work and all pay makes for a dull lifestyle. When you're a basketball junkie and you're used to getting an adrenaline high 82 times a season and you suddenly find yourself separated from the source of your competition, well, it's hard to kick the habit.
"The coaching staff has been working hard twiddling our thumbs," Miami Heat coach Pat Riley s
recently. It must be weird for Riley to have no players tc
at right now. "I actually miss them," Riley said, apparen
surprised at the thought.
Michael Caulfield / AP
Miami Heat
Eastern Conference
55-27
SPORTS
NFL
NBA
MLB
FANTAS
FOOTBA
Join Fantas
Football.con
<XML>

Figure 43-1 A window pops up with team statistics.

This bit of magic is accomplished by designing cross-references into the documents.

43.2.1 *Cross-referencing*

Each of the stories made available on the site contains references to elements in other documents that contain team statistics. For example, let's look at the `story` element in Example 43-5, which was downloaded in response to a headline click.

Note the `team` element in the second `paragraph`. It references an element with the ID `team78`. In this case, the statistics element with that ID is also a

Example 43-5. Story document

```
<story>
  <sport>NBA</sport>
  <headline>NBA coaches not enjoying lockout</headline>
  <image>281073.jpg</image>
  <city>null</city>
  <storybody>
<paragraph>IT'S A WORKING stiff's fantasy - even rich
working stiffs and yet, most NBA coaches are finding that no
work and all pay makes for a dull lifestyle. When you're a
basketball junkie and you're used to getting an adrenaline
high 82 times a season and you suddenly find yourself
separated from the source of your competition, well, it's
hard to kick the habit.</paragraph>
<paragraph>"The coaching staff has been working hard
twiddling our thumbs," <team ref="team78">Miami Heat</team>
coach Pat Riley said recently. It must be weird for Riley to
have no players to yell at right now. "I actually miss
them," Riley said, apparently surprised at the
thought.</paragraph>
  </storybody>
</story>
```

team element, but as it exists in a different XML document there is no conflict between the element type names.

The XML document containing the referenced team statistics element is shown in Example 43-6.

Example 43-6. Team statistics document

```
<team id="team78">
  <city>Miami</city>
  <name>Heat</name>
  <Conference>Eastern</Conference>
  <Division>Atlantic</Division>
  <record>55-27</record>
</team>
```

Because of the cross-referencing between the XML document that contains the story and the XML document that contains the team statistics, we can easily navigate from the story to the statistics. This frees us from having to incorporate all of the statistics repeatedly in every story, and having to download statistics that the user might not ever access.

©2000 THE XML HANDBOOK™

43.2.2 *Traversing to referenced nodes*

Traversal from a team reference to the team statistics that it references is done using the services of the XML Document Object Model (DOM).

A story is processed under the control of an XSL stylesheet that causes the `team` reference elements to be rendered in the form of HTML elements, like that shown in Example 43-7.

Example 43-7. HTML rendition of a `team` reference element in a story

```
<SPAN style="color:#333399;cursor:hand" onmouseout="fnChuckInfo()"
  onmouseover="fnGetInfo('team78')">Miami Heat</SPAN>
```

The `fnGetInfo` function calls the `nodeFromID` method on the team statistics XML document. The string `team78` is passed as a parameter and the function returns the `team` statistics element with that `id` value. The statistics element is rendered as a pop-up window, as we saw in Figure 43-1.

43.2.3 *Defining an ID attribute*

In XML, as we have seen, cross-references can be represented by ID and IDREF attributes. An element with an ID reference attribute is one anchor of a link; an element with an ID attribute is the other.

The attribute of the `team` statistics element in Example 43-7 that is named `id` has to be defined to be of type "id". The name alone has no significance to the XML processor. The attribute definition is included in the definition of the document type schema.

When the demo site processes an XML document, any element exhibiting an `id` attribute is indexed by the attribute value, which allows the element to be located quickly.

43.2.3.1 Using DTD declarations

If the document type were defined using DTD declarations, the relevant fragment would be that shown in Example 43-8.

Unfortunately, this approach is not available to the *XML Sports Demo* in its present form. That's because in a valid XML document, the value of an

Example 43-8. Markup declaration for `id` attribute of `team`

```
<!ATTLIST team id ID #REQUIRED>
```

ID reference (i.e., an attribute of type "IDREF") must be an ID of an element in the same document. In the demo, the team statistics elements are in a separate document from the story elements.

The easy solution would be to change the element type name of `team` in the story document to something like `teamref` and combine the two documents into one. Validity of the combined large document would be checked by the parser during the site initialization in Example 43-1.

43.2.3.2 Using a schema definition language

The *XML Sports Demo* actually addresses the problem by using a schema definition in the XML-Data schema definition language, the relevant fragment of which is shown in Example 43-9.

Example 43-9. XML-Data definition for `id` attribute of `team`

```
<AttributeType
 name="id"
 xmlns:dt="urn:schemas-microsoft-com:datatypes"
 dt:type="id"
/>
<ElementType name="team">
  <attribute type="id"/>
</ElementType>
```

Note that with a schema definition language, unlike DTD declarations, the document is not valid and therefore an ID reference need not be to an ID of an element in the same document.[1]

1. As schema definition languages are still in development, there are still many unanswered questions. One of them concerns the scope of extra-document references. The XML Sports Demo defines that scope to be the demo website, but this is a processing decision that is not reflected in the documents themselves. It works, but it is not a general solution for portable self-describing XML documents.

43.3 | Filtering with XSL

In Example 43-1 we saw that a comprehensive XML document containing all of the statistics for all of the teams is parsed and loaded onto the server when the client requests the initial Web page. The user, however, from that initial user interface page, can select the sports that are of interest. That selection enables the server to filter the comprehensive document so that extraneous data is not served.

The filtering is accomplished under control of an XSL stylesheet that is generated from an ASP file. This custom stylesheet applies templates only to those nodes of the parsed comprehensive document that have data concerning the user's selected sports.

The line of code in Example 43-10 comes from the ASP file that generates the XSL stylesheet. Recall that an XSL stylesheet is itself an XML document, and that XSL components are therefore elements.

Example 43-10. ASP script to generate XSL filtering element

```
<xsl:for-each select="root/sport<%=sMySports%>">
```

When the ASP file executes it substitutes the user's selected value into the XSL pattern. For example, `[@name='NBA']` might be inserted in place of `<%=sMySports%>`. The script would then generate the XSL filtering element shown in Example 43-11.

Example 43-11. XSL filtering element generated by the ASP script in Example 43-10

```
<xsl:for-each select="root/sport[@name='NBA']">
```

The generated XSL stylesheet element selects only those elements in the statistics document that match the pattern `root/sport[@name='NBA']`. Therefore, MLB and NFL statistics and others that don't concern basketball will be ignored. Only the statistics that fit the criteria selected by the user will be displayed.

It is important to note that when an ASP file generates an XSL stylesheet or other XML document, only the generated XML is seen by the parser. All of the ASP code completes execution before the XML or XSL is parsed.

43.4 | Rendering XML documents as speech

An interesting application of XSL in the *XML Sports Demo* produces a sort of *social interface* by using the IE5 agent feature. The demo allows a user not only to view the statistics of interest, but to have them read aloud by the agent of his choice.

The same XML that is rendered as HTML for viewing is transformed under control of an XSL stylesheet into simple lines of text. As in Example 43-10, the XSL stylesheet itself is generated from an ASP file. The generated stylesheet is shown in Example 43-12.

Example 43-12. XSL stylesheet to render simple text for speech synthesis

```
<xsl:stylesheet xmlns:xsl="uri:xsl">
  <xsl:template match="/">
    <xsl:for-each select="root/sport[@name='NBA' $or$ 'MLB']">
    <!-- Write a different bit for each sport -->
      <xsl:if match="root/sport[@name='NBA']">
        In hoops:
   </xsl:if>
   <xsl:if match="root/sport[@name='MLB']">
     Baseball action this week saw:
   </xsl:if>
   <xsl:if match="root/sport[@name='NFL']">
     On the gridiron:
   </xsl:if>
   <xsl:for-each select=
     "game[hometeam/name='Rangers' $or$ awayteam/name='Rangers']"
   >
     The <xsl:value-of select="hometeam/name" /> played the
        <xsl:value-of select="awayteam/name" />.
     The score was <xsl:value-of select="hometeam/name" />
        <xsl:value-of select="hometeam/score" />,
     the <xsl:value-of select="awayteam/name" />
        <xsl:value-of select="awayteam/score" />.
   </xsl:for-each>
    </xsl:for-each>
  </xsl:template>
</xsl:stylesheet>
```

The stylesheet in Example 43-12 could generate the text in Example 43-13, which would then be passed to a text-to-speech engine to generate an audible presentation.

Example 43-13. Text to be passed to the agent's text-to-speech engine

```
 Baseball action this week saw: The Rangers played the
Tigers. The score was Rangers 5 the Tigers 1.
```

Although the transformation of XML to plain text is a relatively simple one, it serves to illustrate an important way to think about utilizing XSL. XSL is not simply a language for rendering XML as HTML. XSL is a means of processing XML documents, not just for traditional rendition, but for data processing and alternative renditions as well.

43.5 | Conclusion

The *XML Sports Demo* demonstrates techniques of website construction using the XML support in *Microsoft Internet Explorer 5*. In particular, it illustrates uses of XSL that go beyond merely generating HTML renditions. The demo reveals real-world issues related to managing very large data collections, navigation among multiple documents, data processing, and audio rendition. These considerations affect the design of optimal stylesheets, and ultimately affect user satisfaction with your website.

Navigation

- Extended linking
- XML Query Language (XQL)
- Topic maps
- The universal collaborative Web

Part Nine

There are only two ways to get there from here: go directly, or go someplace else and then go there.

Or to put it in terms of Web navigation, you can either type in a URL, or keep clicking on links until you reach your destination.

The second kind of navigation is called *link traversal*; the first is a form of query ("Find the Web page whose URL is ..."). Either can operate in physical space, topical (information) space, or a mix.

As practiced on the Web today, both kinds are primitive. The direct access query uses physical addresses (URLs), as do hyperlink anchors. Although the links themselves represent topical associations, there is no hint of the *reason* why things might be linked. Of course there are search engines that operate in topical space, but they are totally undisciplined and routinely return thousands of irrelevant pages.

This part shows how XML can be used today to cure these problems. Extended linking supports meaningful relationships. XML querying operates on logical properties. And topic maps can organize the Web's information space so you can use topical addressing and never get lost. Add the ability to write to the Web, not just read it, and we start to achieve the original vision of the collaborative Web.

Extended linking

Application Discussion

- Extended linking defined
- XLink applications
- XPointers
- Strong link typing
- Topic maps

©2000 The XML Handbook™

Chapter 44

Extended linking and strong link typing will let the Web traverse to locations where it has never been. Those concepts are explained simply and clearly in this chapter, which is sponsored by ISOGEN International, a DataChannel company, http://www.datachannel.com. It was prepared by Steven R. Newcomb of TechnoTeacher, Inc., http://www.techno.com, co-editor of the HyTime International Standard (ISO/IEC 10744).

Future generations of Web browsers and editors will reduce the effort required to keep our personal affairs organized and our corporate memories up to the minute. The productivity of many kinds of work will be enhanced, and in many ways. It's all going to happen basically because of two simple enhancements to the Web paradigm.

The W3C's draft XLink "extended link" facility proposes to give all of us the ability to annotate documents, and to share those annotations with others, even when we cannot alter the documents we are annotating. In other words, we won't have to change a document in order to supply it with our own annotations – annotations that a browser can make appear as though they were written right into the annotated document.

44.1 | The shop notes application

As an example, consider a technician's set of online maintenance manuals. These are electronic books that the technician is not (and should not be) authorized to change. With the Web's existing HTML hyperlinks, the technician cannot write a note in a manual that can take future readers of that manual, including himself, to his annotations. Nor can the technician's annotations be displayed in their proper context – the parts of the manual that they are about.

44.1.1 *What is extended linking?*

By using *extended linking*, when the technician makes an annotation, he does so purely by editing his own document; no change is made to the read-only manual document that he is annotating.

The big difference between "extended" linking and present-day HTML linking is this. With an HTML (or "simple") link, traversal can only begin at the place where the link is; traversal cannot begin at the other end. With an "extended" link, however, you can click on any of the link's anchors, and traverse to any other anchor, regardless of where the link happens to be.

Tip *Extended linking allows the starting anchor of a link to be different from the link itself. Instead of HTML's "A" tagged element that is linked to one other element, you can have (say) an "L" tag that links two or more other elements to one another.*

A simple link (top of Figure 44-1) is always embedded ("inline") in (for example) the InstallLog text from which it provides traversal; the link cannot be traversed by starting at the target anchor (for example, the Installation procedure document).

An extended link (bottom of Figure 44-1) can appear in a separate document, and provide traversal between the corresponding parts of two other documents: for example, the technician's shop notes document ("TechLog") and the read-only installation manual. Because the location of this particular link is not the same as any of its anchors, it is said to be "out-of-line" (not embedded).

In our example, an annotation takes the form of just such an extended link element.

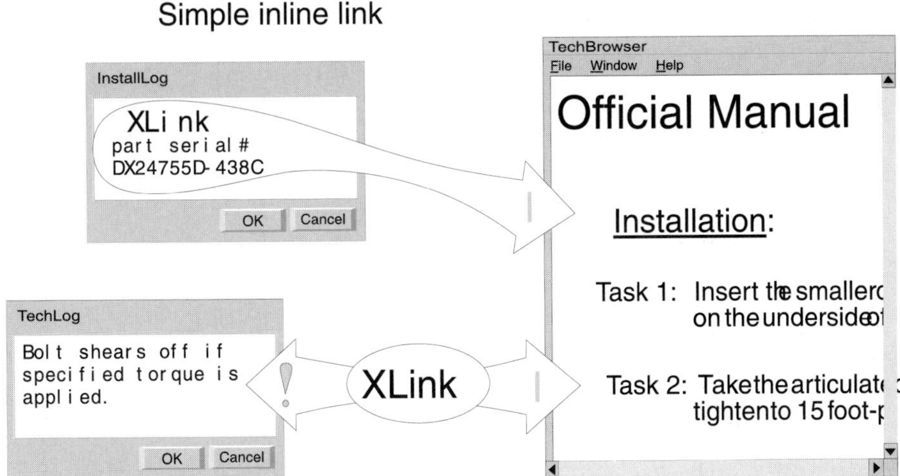

Figure 44-1 Simple vs. extended linking.

44.1.2 *Displaying extended links*

One way to realize the benefits of extended links is to display an icon at each anchor that indicates something about the other anchor. (The mechanism that supports this is discussed in greater detail under "Strong link typing", below.)

For example, as shown in Figure 44-2, a reader of the installation manual on the right will know that, if he clicks on the exclamation point displayed near Task 2, he will see a shop note about that task. If he clicks on the pound sign, he will be shown the serial number of a part that was installed according to the procedure, recorded in an "InstallLog" document.

Similarly, a reader of the annotation in the shop notes document ("TechLog") will know that clicking on the "I" icon will bring him to the installation instruction that the annotation discusses.

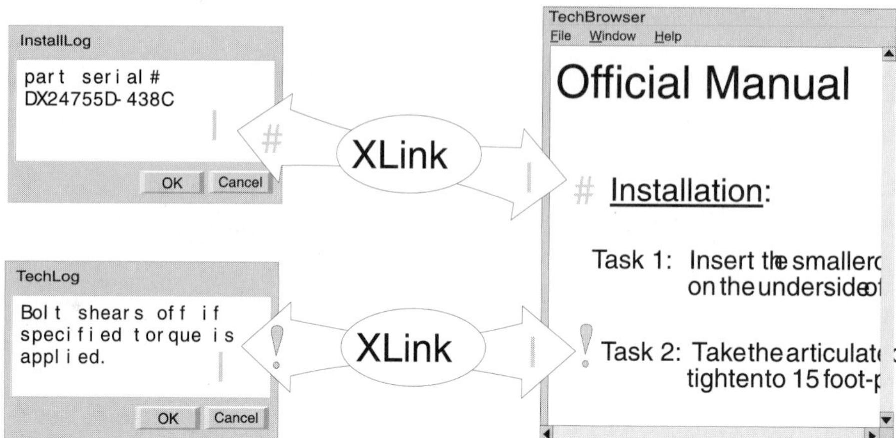

Figure 44-2 The exclamation point icon near Task 2 indicates that a shop note is available.

44.1.3 *Notes survive to new versions of manuals*

The technician's annotations – his "shop notes" – accumulate over time, and they represent a valuable asset that must be maintained. If the technician were to write shop notes inside each manual, when a new version of a manual is received it would be a chore to copy annotations from the old manual to the new manual.

With extended linking, however, the annotations are not in the old version; they are in a separate document. Therefore, the shop notes don't disappear when an annotated manual is replaced by a newer version.

That is because each link is equipped with "pointers" – pieces of information that can tell a browser where (for example) clickable icons should be rendered that indicate the availability of an annotation. Each such "XPointer" (as it is called) can point at anything in any XML document.

In our technician's shop, when a manual is replaced by a new version, the XPointers keep on working, even with the new manual, so the new manual is instantly and automatically equipped with the old manual's annotations.

In most cases, the XPointers don't have to be changed, because they continue to point at the right things, even in the new manual. If, because of differences between the old and new versions of the manual, some XPointers in the shop notes don't still point at the right things (or perhaps have nothing to point at any more), certain techniques can be used to detect each such situation. By dealing with these problem spots, the maintainers of the shop notes can minimize their efforts.

Moreover, XPointers and extended links enhance the potential for achieving high levels of quality and consistency, even when there are voluminous shop notes that annotate many manuals.

44.1.4 *Vendors can use the notes*

Some shop notes may also have value to the vendors of the manuals they annotate; they may beneficially influence subsequent versions of the manual. An editor of the manual can load (i.e., make his browser aware of) all the shop notes of many repair shops; this has the effect of populating the manual with icons representing the annotations of all the shops. The most common trouble spots in the manual will be made obvious by the crowds of annotation icons that they appear to have accumulated (Figure 44-3).

The fact that the shop notes take the form of interchangeable XML documents that use standardized extended links makes the task of sharing internal shop notes with manual vendors as easy as sending them any other kind of file. There is no need to extract them from some other resource, or to format them in such a way that they can be understood by their recipients. They are ready to work just as they are, in the tradition of SGML, HyTime, HTML, and now XML.

44.2 | Other applications of extended linking

The above "shop notes" example is just a sample of the kinds of enhancements that extended linking will bring to our interactions with information resources. Some of the broader implications are a bit more startling.

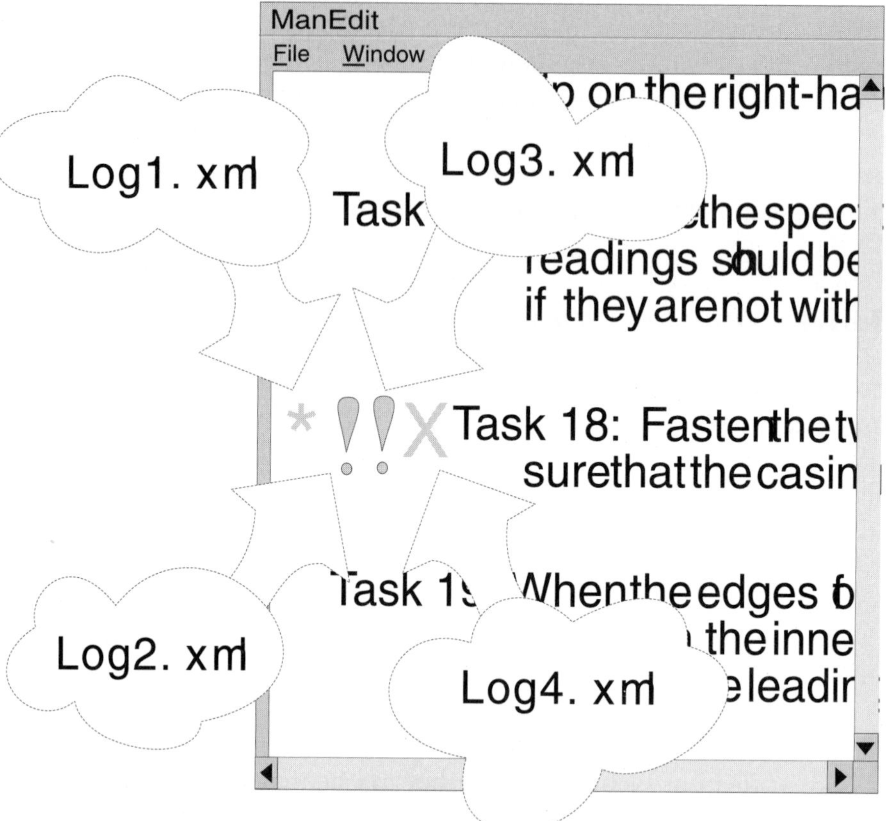

Figure 44-3 Task 18 evidently prompted three kinds of annotations in four different shop logs.

44.2.1 *Public resource communities of interest*

For example, many web sites today contain HTML links to public resources. One is the U.S. Government's online service for translating any U.S. postal code into its corresponding Congressional district and the name of its current incumbent Representative (`http://www.house.gov/zip/ZIP2Rep.html`).

However, if those HTML links were to become XLink extended links, an XLink-enabled browser could render this U.S. government Web page in such a way as to add to it a catalog of the activists and lobbying organizations who refer readers of their websites to this particular U.S. government resource. The "marketplace of ideas" represented by the aggregate of such organizations is thus revealed in a new and interesting way.

44.2.2 *Guidance documents*

Another startling possibility is the association of browser-controlling metadata with any and all Web resources.

In this scenario, a document of annotations (or a set of such documents) can be a user's companion during excursions on the Web. These annotations might make suggestions to users as to where to find more recent material, or they might even take control of the browser's link traversal ability in order to protect children from disturbing material.

While the latter XLink-enabled possibility may sound inimical to the freedom of speech, in fact it enhances liberty. It provides a new public medium for free speech: documents that censor the Web and/or otherwise provide guidance to Web travelers in the form of annotations that appear only in their designated contexts.

Of course, no adult is required to use any such guidance document, just as no one is required to read any particular book, but it's easy to predict that many will pay for the privilege of using many kinds of such "guidance documents".

More importantly, everyone will have the tools to write such guidance documents, so the technical ability to provide guidance (and, yes, even to provide censorship services) will be widely distributed, rather than being dangerously concentrated in a few generalized rating services. The creation and maintenance of guidance documents may well become a thriving cottage industry. Anyone can be a critic.

In the case of electronic commerce, it's easy to imagine that vendors will attempt to provide guidance documents designed to annotate the online sales catalogs of their competitors. In response, some providers of online sales catalogs will take steps to render the pointers in these kinds of guidance documents invalid and unmaintainable.

Regardless of all this, the overall impact on electronic commerce will certainly be positive; increasing the meaningful interconnectedness of the Web will help more people find exactly what they're looking for.

©2000 The XML Handbook™

And it may turn out to be a mistake, in many cases, for catalog owners to attempt to render the pointers used to annotate their catalogs invalid, because similar pointers could be used, for example, by impartial consumer testing organizations to attach "best buy" recommendations to certain products. The guidance documents of consumer testing organizations will probably be quite popular, and well worth the cost of using them.

44.2.3 *Computer-augmented memory*

Extended linking has the potential to make radical improvements in our ability to keep track of what we are doing. Someday, we can expect to automatically annotate each piece of information we work with in such a way that, in effect, it refers future readers to the work we did with respect to it.

In other words, practically everything we do can be usefully seen as an annotation of one or more other pieces of work. If everything we do is, in some sense, an annotation of one or more other things, everything we do can all be found far more easily, starting from any piece of work anywhere in the "chain" (or, more likely, "tree" or "graph") of relevant information.

This is because extended linking allows all links to be bidirectional. (Or, rather, "n-directional", to account for extended links with more than two ends.) All of the connections among our affairs can then be tracked more or less automatically, so that each of us can enjoy a radical reduction in filing, cross-indexing, and other organizational chores, and with vastly increased ability to find what we're looking for quickly and easily.

Obviously, this same idea is even more significant in the realm of corporate memory. Even with today's behemoth enterprise integration technologies, it's still too hard to figure out what has happened, who is doing what, how various plans and projects are going to integrate, and where the relevant paperwork can be found.

Going a step further, there is an nternational Standard (ISO/IEC 13250) that seeks to exploit extended linking in such a way as to create living, easily explored and maintained "topic maps" of sets of information resources (see Chapter 46, "Topic maps: Knowledge navigation aids", on page 618). This goal sounds almost insanely ambitious, but extended linking, in combination with strong link typing (see below), should make it practical and achievable.

The topic maps paradigm elegantly solves consistency and usability problems faced by people who must collaborate in developing indexes and glossaries, or who must merge multiple indexes into master indexes. When applied to the Web, topic maps are analogous to the Global Positioning System provided by earth-orbiting satellites, allowing Web users to determine their current locations in a multidimensional "topic space".

44.2.4 *Intellectual property management*

The advent of extended linking also offers interesting new possibilities for the management and exploitation of intellectual property.

For example, metadata regarding the licensing policies of owners of Web resources could be associated with those resources by means of extended links. Such metadata could be changed when the resources are sold or licensed, without requiring any changes to the assets themselves.

This method greatly reduces the likelihood of inadvertent damage to the assets, and greatly increases the ease with which ownership and/or management policies can change. There is already an official, internationally-ratified ISO standard for using extended linking for exactly this purpose (see `http://www.ornl.gov/sgml/wg8/document/n1920/html/clause-6.7.html#clause-6.7.3`).

Such activity policies, and the means by which they are associated with online assets, could well become a source of private law that will strongly influence the development of intelligent agents (see `http://www.hytime.org/papers/higgins1.html`).

44.3 | Strong link typing

With the XLink extended link facility, there is no limit to the number of links that can be traversed from a single point in a single document. Many different documents can contain links to the very same anchor, with the result that, theoretically, at least, an unlimited number of traversals are possible, starting from a single point. In addition, there are no limits on the kinds of annotations that can be made, nor on the purposes to which such annotations may be put.

Therefore, it makes sense to provide some easy way to sort the annotations (i.e., the links) into categories. For example, some kinds of annotations will be made in order to provide "metadata" about the document, and these will often take effect in some way other than by rendering an icon on the display screen. Some kinds of annotations are interesting only for specialized purposes.

44.3.1 *Hiding the installation log*

Going back to our earlier example, the technician can create an annotation that indicates the serial number of a new part that he installed in accordance with a particular maintenance procedure. The fact that such an annotation is available would be of interest only to someone who was auditing the installation of parts; it probably wouldn't appear even to the technician, despite the fact that it was he who created the annotation.

The technician's installation log annotation can be hidden from most people because it is "strongly typed": it has been clearly and unambiguously labeled as to its intended meaning and purpose, so all browsers can see what kind of link it is. In effect, the link says, "I am a Part-Installation-Log-Entry". People who aren't interested in part installation records can arrange for their browsers to hide them.

44.3.2 *Why do we need strong link typing?*

People may still choose to be made aware of other kinds of annotations made by our technician. For example, other technicians may wish to read our technician's accounts of any special situations that he has experienced when attempting to follow a particular instruction, or about successful and unsuccessful experiments with substitute parts.

The notion of "strong link typing" is virtually absent from HTML links. Basically, in HTML, the browser software knows where the user can go, but not why the author of the document being browsed thought the user might like to go there. The human reader can usually divine something from the context about the material that will be shown if the "anchor" hyperlink is traversed, but the browser itself is basically unable to help the user decide whether to click or not to click, so it can't hide any available traversals.

To be able to hide the availability of unwanted kinds of links can save a lot of time and effort. So the draft W3C XLink recommendation also provides for the addition of strong typing features, not only to extended links, but also to the "simple" links that closely resemble the familiar HTML

©2000 THE XML HANDBOOK™

"anchor" (<a>) element. Thus, browsers can start supporting strong link typing promptly, even before they can handle extended linking.

44.3.3 *Anchor role identification*

The notion of strong link typing includes the notion of "anchor role" designation.

For example, the simple link at the top of Figure 44-1 characterizes its target anchor as an installation instruction; in the diagram, this is indicated by the "I" icon in the arrowhead. Similarly, the extended link at the bottom of Figure 44-1 characterizes one of its anchors as a shop note (the exclamation point) and the other anchor as an installation instruction (another "I" arrowhead).

Thus, a link can do more than just identify itself by saying, for example, "I am a Part Installation Log Entry". It can also specify which of its anchors fulfill which roles in the relationship it expresses.

For example, our Part Installation Log Entry link can say, in effect, "I signify that part [pointer to entry in parts catalog or inventory record] was installed in [pointer to information that identifies the unit being maintained] in accordance with maintenance directive [XPointer to instruction in manual]".

In other words, the log entry link is a three-ended link whose anchor roles might be named "replacement-part" (indicated with a "#" icon), "maintained-unit" ("@" icon), and "maintenance-directive" ("I" icon) (Figure 44-4).

The fact that an anchor plays some specific role in a relationship often determines whether the relationship is interesting or even relevant in a given application context.

44.4 | Conclusion

It is easy to see that the impact of extended linking will be significant, and that technical workers and electronic commerce will be early beneficiaries. Extended linking will enhance the helpfulness and usefulness of the Web environment. The burden of many kinds of paperwork will be very substantially mitigated.

©2000 The XML Handbook™

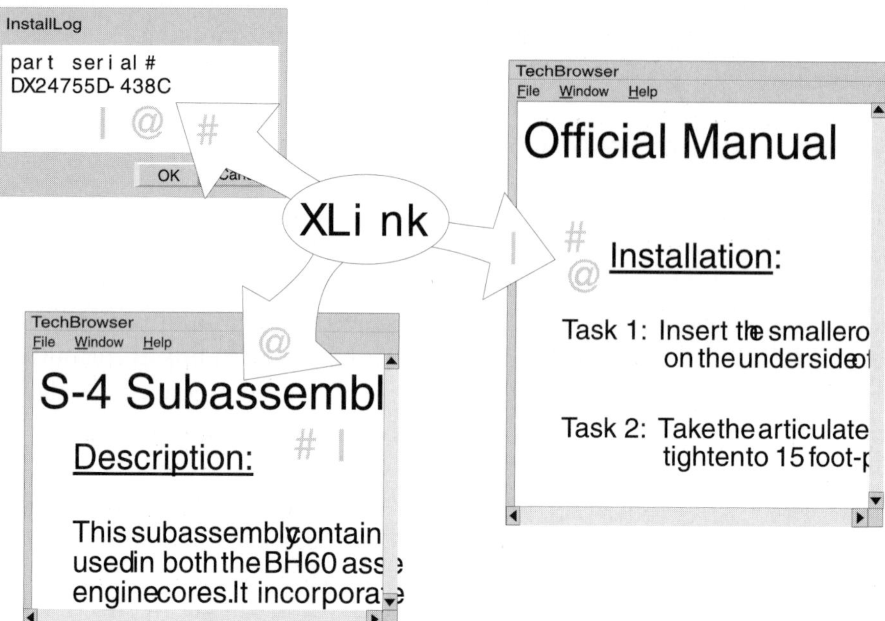

Figure 44-4 Link with two traversal possibilities at each anchor, distinguishable because of anchor role identification.

On the horizon, there appears to be serious potential for significant improvements in the availability of all kinds of knowledge, due to the possibility of creating and interchanging topic maps. Intellectual property management, and the Web-based utilization of intellectual property, will become easier and more orderly.

All of these benefits, and probably many more, emanate from two very simple enhancements of the Web paradigm in the draft XLink and XPointers recommendations of the World Wide Web Consortium:

- Allowing the starting anchor of a link to be different from the link itself; and

- Strong link typing, in which links plainly exhibit the kind of relationship they represent, and the roles their anchors play in that relationship.

Tip *For more on XLink, see Chapter 62, "XML Linking Language (XLink)", on page 902. The text of the XLink and XPointer drafts are on the CD-ROM.*

B2B QueryView: XQL search tool

Tool Discussion

- XML Query Language (XQL)
- Path expressions
- Free software on CD-ROM

©2000 THE XML HANDBOOK™

Chapter 45

An abstract XML document can contain rich information about the structure and other properties of its content data. A query language can let you exploit that information to mine the content in valuable and interesting ways. webMethods, `http://www.webmethods.com/`, sponsors this chapter to explain how. It was prepared by Bob DuCharme.

The database world has used query languages for years to allow fast, simple extraction of useful subsets of databases. The XML Query Language (XQL) proposal from Microsoft, Texcel, and webMethods describes one way to bring this power to XML documents. With the free copy of webMethods B2B QueryView on the CD-ROM, you can use XQL with your own documents to get a feel for XML querying.

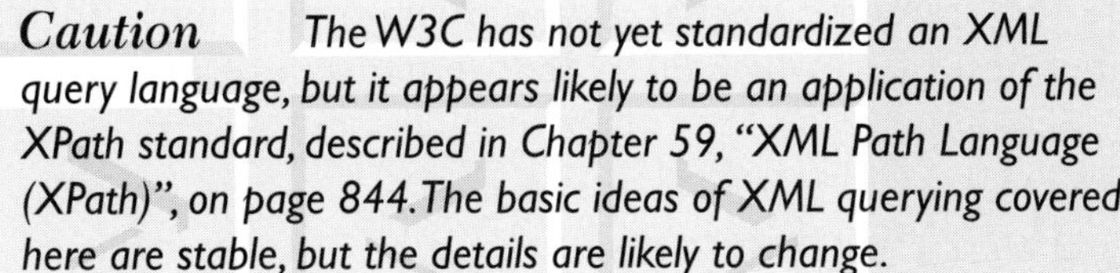

Caution *The W3C has not yet standardized an XML query language, but it appears likely to be an application of the XPath standard, described in Chapter 59, "XML Path Language (XPath)", on page 844. The basic ideas of XML querying covered here are stable, but the details are likely to change.*

45.1 | XQL queries

XQL is a notation for locating information within a document. That information could be:

- An "executive summary" of a longer document.
- A glossary of terms whose definitions are scattered throughout a manual.
- The specific sequence of steps, buried in a large reference work, needed to solve a particular problem.
- The customized subset of information that a particular customer subscribes to.
- All the sections and subsections of a book that were written by a particular author or revised since a specific date.
- For documents holding information from relational databases, all the typical queries made of relational databases: a particular patient's medical records, the address of the customer with the most orders, the inventory items with low stock levels, and so on.
- For documents that are containers for document collections, all the typical queries made in a library catalog or on a website: articles about Abyssinian cats, essays on the proper study of mankind, prospectuses of Internet IPOs with positive earnings, etc.

A programmer working with an XML-aware programming or scripting language could write code to search the document and retrieve the information that meets the specified criteria. The purpose of a query language is to automate this searching so that a non-programming user can retrieve the information just by writing a query that contains the criteria.

45.1.1 *Path expressions*

In order to retrieve something, you need to know where to find it – in other words, its *address*. Addresses in XML documents – whether used in a query, an XSL template rule, or an XPointer – all can be represented in a similar format, called a *path expression*. A path expression can address a single thing, or several things at the same time.

If you use UNIX or Windows, you may already be familiar with path expressions because they are used to address files by specifying the path from the file system's root to a specific subdirectory. For example, the path `/home/bob/xml/samples` identifies a particular one of the four `samples` subdirectories shown in Figure 45-1.

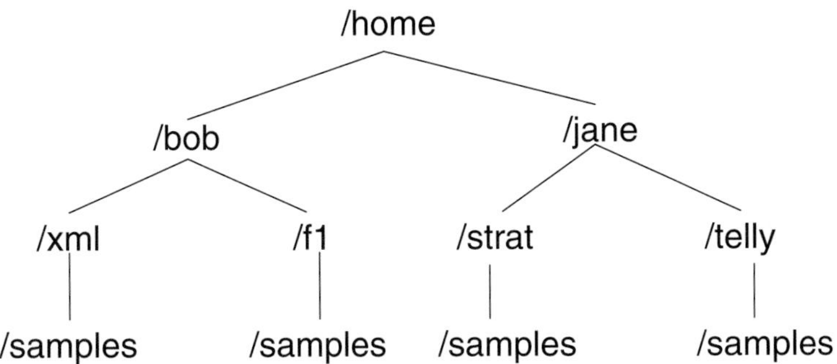

Figure 45-1 File system directory structure

45.1.2 *Patterns*

Because a query is normally intended to retrieve several things, a path expression in a query is usually a *pattern* that several things might match.

For example, the pattern in Example 45-1 matches all `caption` elements within `figure` elements that are within `chapter` elements within `book` elements.

Example 45-1. XML pattern

```
book/chapter/figure/caption
```

In the book whose structure is shown in Figure 45-2, the pattern in Example 45-1 would address the first two `caption` elements, because they are children of `figure` elements. It would not address the third, which is the child of an `example` element.

When a pattern is used in a query, the query engine returns the portions of the document that match the pattern. In this case, the pattern `book/`

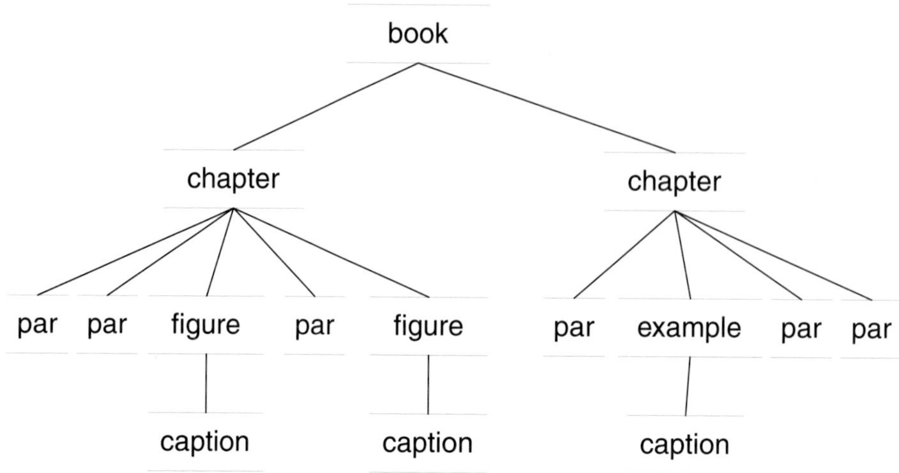

Figure 45-2 Document structure

`chapter/figure/caption` would cause the two figure captions to be returned.

Before continuing with more XQL queries, let's take a brief look at how to use *QueryView* so that you can try the example queries as you read along.

45.2 | Using *QueryView*

When you first start *QueryView*, it will look essentially like Figure 45-3. However, the style of the buttons, slider bars, and other GUI components can be changed by choosing `Look and Feel` from the `Edit` menu and selecting `Standard`, `Windows`, or `Motif`.[1]

45.2.1 *Loading a document*

Load a document using either `Open File` or `Open URL` from the `File` menu. The bottom pane displays either a tree-based rendition of the document or a plain text view, depending on whether the `Tree` or `Source` tab is

1. Illustrations in this chapter use the `Standard` look.

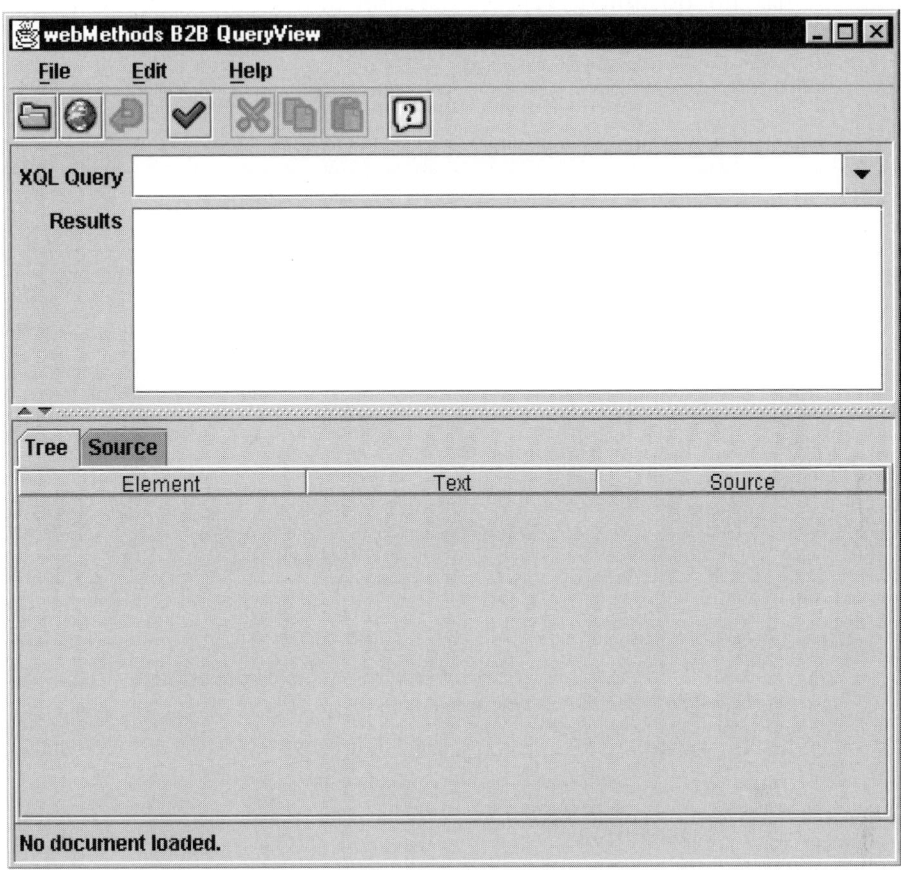

Figure 45-3 *QueryView* main window

selected. The `XQL Query` area near the top is where you enter a query, and the `Results` area below that is where the results are displayed.

Figure 45-4 shows *QueryView* with a short document loaded and a query entered in the `XQL Query` area. Note that the document, though well-formed, has no document type declaration and is therefore not valid. *QueryView* does not require a document it searches to be valid.

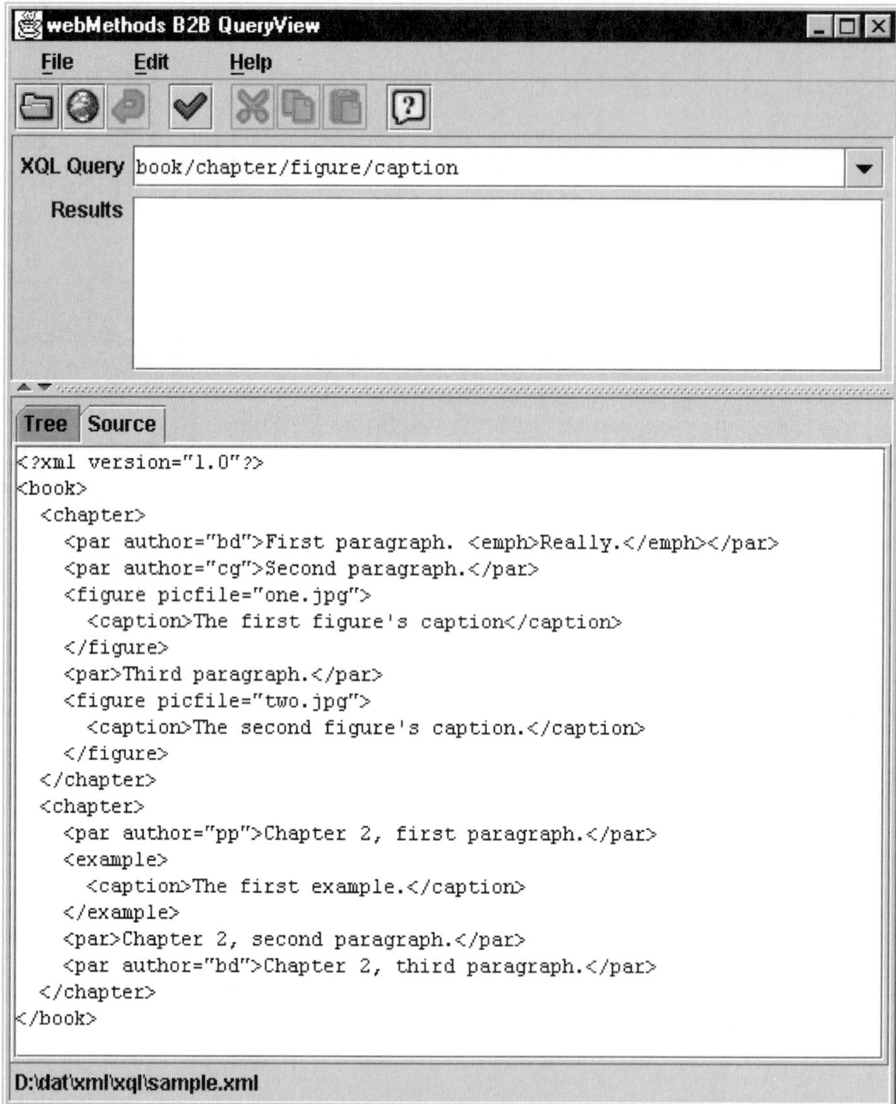

Figure 45-4 A document loaded and a query ready to run

Figure 45-5 shows the document pane when presenting the tree view of the same document.

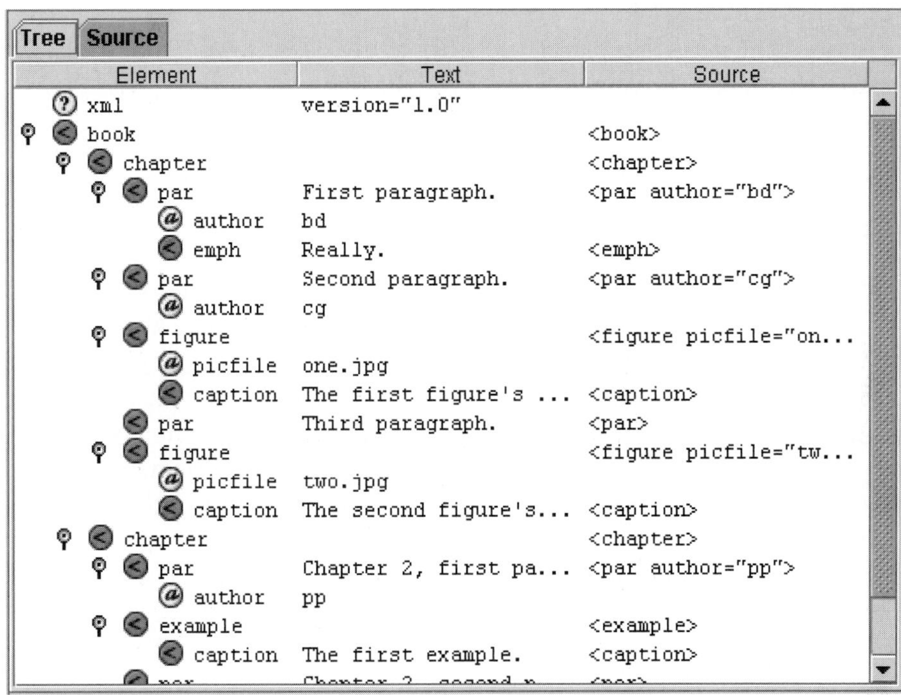

Figure 45-5 Tree view of document in Figure 45-4

45.2.2 *Editing a document*

The `Edit` menu gives you ways to interact with the loaded document. It includes the following choices:

- `Undo` and `Redo` affect edits that you make in the bottom pane's `Source` view.
- `Cut`, `Copy`, `Paste`, `Delete`, and `Select All` perform the same actions that they do in most graphical user interface (GUI) document editors, making it possible to move and copy text. `Select All` and `Copy` in combination are particularly useful as a quick way to copy query results onto the clipboard so they

can be pasted into a text editor and saved as a new XML document.

- `Show Namespaces` displays a listing of the namespaces used in the document.

Although *QueryView* parses each file as it loads it, you may want to reparse the loaded document if you've edited it. To do this, select `Parse Again` from the `File` menu.

45.2.2.1 Running a search

Select `Submit Query` on the `Edit` menu to search the loaded document for things that match the pattern in the `XQL Query` area. (You can also press the **Enter** key or click on the green checkmark icon.)

The query asked for any `caption` element that was in a `figure` element inside a `chapter` element that had a `book` element as its parent. As you can see in Figure 45-6, *QueryView* found two such `caption` elements. It put them in the `Results` area ready for copying and pasting to other applications.

Had there been nothing that satisfied the query, *QueryView* would have returned an empty document, indicated by the string `** Empty **` in the `Results` area.

45.3 | Children and descendants

The `book/chapter/figure/caption` query returned two elements with no children other than data. Submitting a query of `book/chapter/figure`

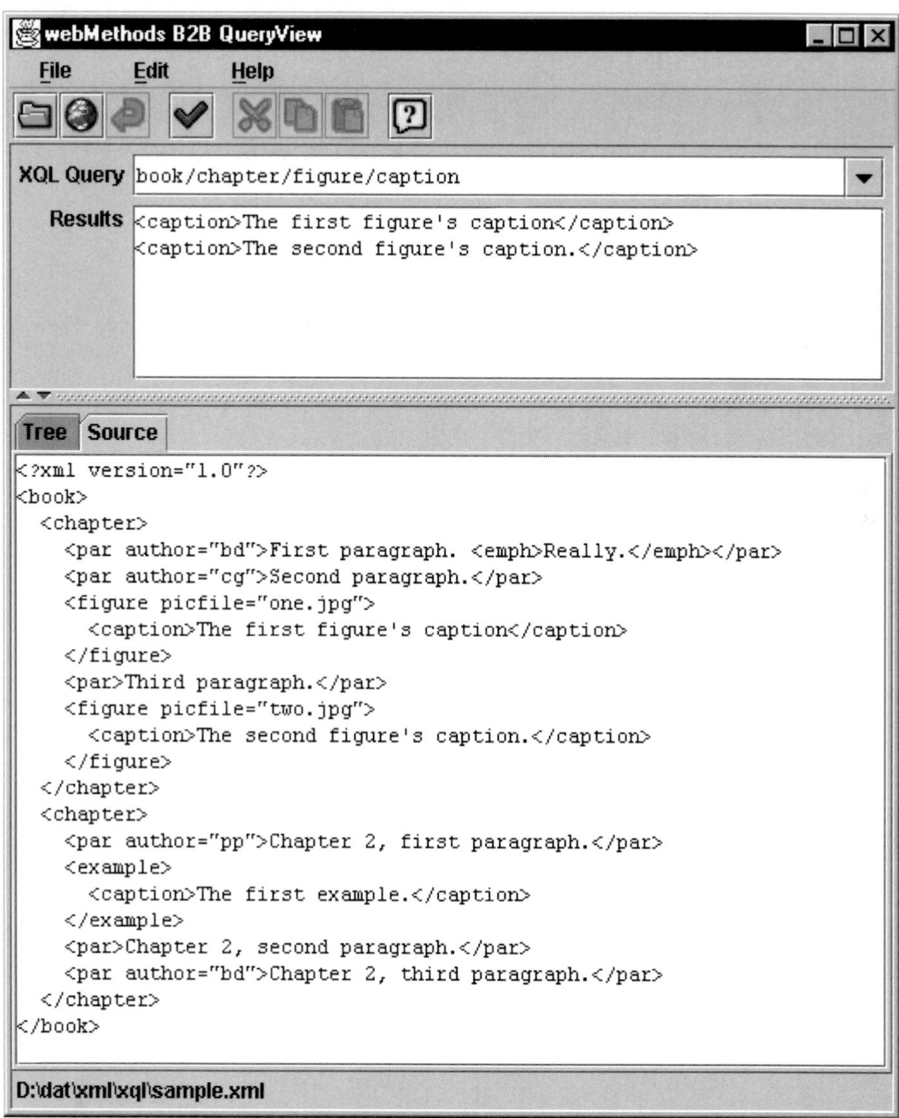

Figure 45-6 Query results are shown.

returns the `figure` elements with their `caption` children, as shown in Example 45-2.

Example 45-2. Figure elements with their caption children

```
<figure picfile="one.jpg">
      <caption>The first figure's caption</caption>
    </figure>
<figure picfile="two.jpg">
      <caption>The second figure's caption.</caption>
    </figure>
```

If you submit an XQL query of `book` the entire source document will be returned as your result document.

In a path expression, the slash character (`/`) means "child of." A double slash (`//`) means "descendant of," which is more flexible. For example, `book//caption` asks for any caption element descended from the `book` element. In the book shown in Figure 45-2 it would return the `example` element's `caption` from the book's second chapter along with the figure elements' two `caption` elements:

Example 45-3. Caption elements descended from the book element

```
<caption>The first figure's caption</caption>
<caption>The second figure's caption.</caption>
<caption>The first example.</caption>
```

45.4 | Attributes

An address in XML document navigation is not a storage address like a file system path, despite the similarity in syntax. An XML address locates objects by their position in a document's structure and other properties, such as the values of their attributes.

A tree rendition of a document often presents an attribute's information as a child of the element exhibiting the attribute. This isn't technically correct, because attributes are not siblings of subelements. For this reason, XQL uses `/@` to show the element/attribute relationship.

For example, the query in Example 45-4 requests all the values of the `par` elements' `author` attributes.

Example 45-4. Query with an attribute

```
book//par/@author
```

Example 45-5. Result of query in Example 45-4

```
bd
cg
pp
bd
```

The equals sign (=) lets you retrieve elements with specific content data. For example, the query in Example 45-6 retrieves all the `par` elements that have "Second paragraph." as their content data.

Example 45-6. Query with specific content data

```
book//par = "Second paragraph."
```

Example 45-7. Result of query in Example 45-7

```
<par author="cg">Second paragraph.</par>
```

The `!=` operator means "not equal to," so that the query in Example 45-8 retrieves all the `par` elements that do not have "Second paragraph." as their content data.

Example 45-8. Query excluding specific content data

```
book//par != "Second paragraph."
```

Example 45-9. Result of query in Example 45-8

```
<par author="bd">First paragraph. <emph>Really.</emph></par>
<par>Third paragraph.</par>
<par author="pp">Chapter 2, first paragraph.</par>
<par>Chapter 2, second paragraph.</par>
<par author="bd">Chapter 2, third paragraph.</par>
```

These patterns can be applied to attribute values as well, but remember: a query like that in Example 45-10 returns the attribute values themselves, which you already know. The real purpose of the query is to let you count the number of elements exhibiting the specified value for the attribute.

Example 45-10. Query that returns the attribute values themselves

```
book//par/@author = "bd"
```

Example 45-11. Result of query in Example 45-10

```
bd
bd
```

To ask for all the `par` elements whose `author` attribute exhibits a particular value, we need a *filter subquery.*

45.5 | Filtering with subqueries

A *data filter subquery* imposes further selection criteria on the elements identified by the path preceding the subquery. The subquery is recognized by the square brackets that delimit it. For example, the XQL query in Example 45-12 retrieves any chapters that have a `figure` element in them.

Example 45-12. XQL query for chapters with a `figure` element

```
book/chapter[figure]
```

The query in Example 45-13 requests all the book's `par` elements whose `author` attribute exhibits a value of `bd`.

Example 45-13. Query for `par` elements exhibiting `bd` as the value of their `author` attribute

```
book//par[@author="bd"]
```

Example 45-14. Result of query in Example 45-13

```
<par author="bd">First paragraph. <emph>Really.</emph></par>
<par author="bd">Chapter 2, third paragraph.</par>
```

These criteria can be applied to any component of a path expression, not just the final one. For example, the query in Example 45-15 asks for the caption of any `figure` element whose `picfile` attribute exhibits "two.jpg" as its value.

Example 45-15. Query for the caption of a specific `figure` element

```
book//figure[@picfile="two.jpg"]/caption
```

Example 45-16. Result of query in Example 45-15

```
<caption>The second figure's caption.</caption>
```

45.6 | Methods

Methods are like built-in functions that let you create more expressive queries. For example, the `text()` method returns the character data of an element, even if that element has subelements; that is, it returns the concatenated data of the element and all its descendants.

For example, we couldn't use a query like that in Example 45-17 to retrieve the first `par` element, because part of the data is in its `emph` child element.

Example 45-17. Thwarted query

```
book//par = "First paragraph. Really."
```

However, the `text()` method's ability to look across subelement boundaries means that a query like that in Example 45-18 would find that first `par` element, returning it with its subelement.

Example 45-18. Query for data of first `par` element and its subelement

```
book//par[text() = "First paragraph. Really."]
```

©2000 The XML Handbook™

Example 45-19. Result of query in Example 45-18

```
<par author="bd">First paragraph. <emph>Really.</emph></par>
```

Some methods identify elements based on their position. The query in Example 45-20 returns the last `par` element within each element that has any `par` elements – in this case, within the two `chapter` elements that have `par` elements.

Example 45-20. Query for last `par` element of every element with `par` elements

```
book//par[end()]
```

Example 45-21. Result of query in Example 45-20

```
<par>Third paragraph.</par>
<par author="bd">Chapter 2, third paragraph.</par>
```

The `index()` method returns the order of an element among its sibling elements. The numbering begins with zero, so the first will be 0, the second, 1, and so forth. The query in Example 45-22 requests the second `par` element of the first `chapter` element.

Example 45-22. Query for second `par` element of the first `chapter` element

```
book/chapter[index() = 0]/par[index() = 1]
```

Example 45-23. Result of query in Example 45-22

```
<par author="cg">Second paragraph.</par>
```

45.7 | Additional XQL features

This chapter has shown you just a small sample of XQL's features. Others include additional methods, query operators, and ways to combine them. The XQL proposal on the CD-ROM can provide further information.

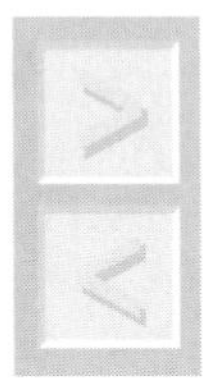

Note *XQL was proposed before the W3C began development of XPath, which is now the addressing language for XSLT and XPTR. However, XQL and XPath are similar enough in their basic syntax and data model that this chapter serves as a useful starting point for learning XPath (which we cover in Chapter 59, "XML Path Language (XPath)", on page 844).*

Topic maps: Knowledge navigation aids

Application Discussion

- Topic maps in a nutshell
- Indexes, glossaries, and thesauri
- Topic map applications
- Tools for topic maps

©2000 THE XML HANDBOOK™

Chapter 46

True story: Charles was searching an online shopping site for a CD by the doo-wop greats, the Flamingos. He was offered a pink neon sculpture. That site needs topic maps! In this chapter, Hans Holger Rath and Steve Pepper, of the ISO topic map standards group, explain why yours does too. It is sponsored by STEP Electronic Publishing Solutions GmbH, `http://www.step.de`.

Ever want to fire your Web search engine for bringing you thousands of useless pages? Or to navigate from one Web page to another on the same subject when there is no link between them? Then you want topic maps.

When you ask your Web browser to search for "Mozart", that composer is the "topic" of your search and you hope to find Web pages that are in some way devoted to it. The browser might actually find such pages, but they will probably be lost among the thousands of pages in which "Mozart" is simply a word that occurs in passing and in no way the main topic of the page.

Similarly, when you look up "Mozart" in the index of a book, you hope to find the pages whose topic is Mozart.

So topics are a familiar concept, one that we work with all the time. What then are topic maps and why do we need them?

Well, suppose you want to find out about operas composed by German composers that were influenced by Mozart. There is no way to formulate such a query in a Web search engine. You can try to use a set of relevant keywords such as "opera + Germany + composer + Mozart", but you are guaranteed to get an enormous number of useless hits. You are also guaranteed to miss some of the most interesting pages. More importantly, even if the search were extremely accurate, you would still have to wade through all the resulting documents simply to find the names of the works you are interested in.

How much easier if you could simply query your index for all *operas* "written by" *composers* associated with *Germany* ("born in" or "lived in") and with *Mozart* ("influenced by")!

The key difference between the two approaches is that the former simply uses a full text index built from the raw content of a set of information resources. The latter, however, utilizes an index that encapsulates the structure of the underlying knowledge.

The latter solution is actually an example of a *topic map*; that is, a structured network of hyperlinks above an information pool. Each node in the network represents a named topic (e.g. Germany, Mozart, Wagner). The links connecting the nodes express the associations between the nodes (e.g. written by, lived in, influenced by).

From this it should be clear that indexes are actually very simple forms of topic maps. So, too, are glossaries and thesauri. This chapter will explain the basic concepts of topic maps, how they relate to the kinds of navigational aids we are already familiar with, what additional benefits they provide, and how to create and use them. We'll also look at some applications and consider requirements for topic map tools.

46.1 | Topic maps in a nutshell

A topic map is an XML or SGML document whose element types represent topics, occurrences of topics, and associations between topics. The document conforms to the International Standard ISO/IEC 13250, which also standardizes the conceptual model for topic maps.

The key concepts are:

- topic and topic type
- topic occurrence and occurrence role
- topic association and association type

Other concepts, which extend the expressive power of the topic map model, are:

- scope
- public subject
- facets

46.1.1 *Topic and topic type*

In the context of an encyclopedia, a *topic* might represent subjects such as "Germany", "Bavaria", "Munich", the king "Ludwig II", or the opera "Lohengrin" by the composer "Richard Wagner": anything that might have an entry (or indeed a mention) in the encyclopedia.

The subject represented by a topic can be any "thing" whatsoever – a person, an entity, a concept, really *anything*, regardless of whether it exists or has any other specific characteristics, about which anything whatsoever may be asserted by any means whatsoever. Exactly what one chooses to regard as topics in any particular application will vary according to the needs of the application, the nature of the information, and the uses to which the topic map will be put.

A topic can have a number of characteristics. First of all, it can have a *name* – or more than one. The standard provides an element form for *topic name* which consists of at least one *base name*, and optional *display* and *sort* names.

A topic also has a *topic type* – or perhaps multiple topic types. Thus, Germany would be a topic of type "country", Bavaria a topic of type "state", Munich and Würzburg topics of type "city", Ludwig II a topic of type "king", etc. In other words, topic types express typical *class-instance* relationships or the *is a* relation (see Figure 46-1).

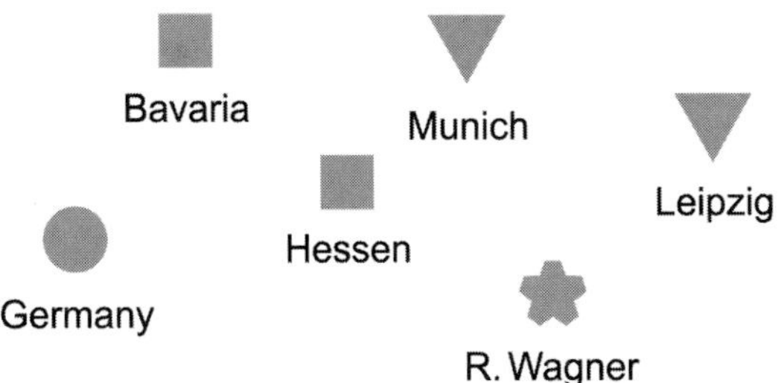

Figure 46-1 Topic names and types (represented by different symbols)

Topic types are themselves defined as topics. In order to use them for typing, you have to explicitly declare "country", "state", "city", etc. as topics in your topic map, and this then allows you to say more about them using the topic map model itself.

46.1.2 *Topic occurrence and occurrence role*

A topic can have one or more *occurrences*. An occurrence of a topic is a link to an information resource (or more than one) that is deemed to be somehow relevant to the subject that the topic represents. It could be an article about the topic in an encyclopedia, a picture or video depicting the topic, a simple mention of the topic in the context of something else, a commentary on the topic, or any of a host of other forms in which an information resource might have some relevance to a given subject.

Such resources are generally outside the topic map document itself, and they are "pointed at" using whatever addressing mechanisms the system supports, typically XPointer or HyTime.

Occurrences may be of any number of different types (we gave the examples of "article", "illustration", "mention" and "commentary" above). Such distinctions are supported in the standard by the concept of the *occurrence role* (see Figure 46-2). As with topic types, occurrence roles are themselves formally considered to be topics, although the actual occurrences are not.

46.1.3 *Indexes and glossaries*

As described so far, topics and occurrences provide a model for explicitly stating which subjects a pool of information pertains to and how. That is basically what an index also does.

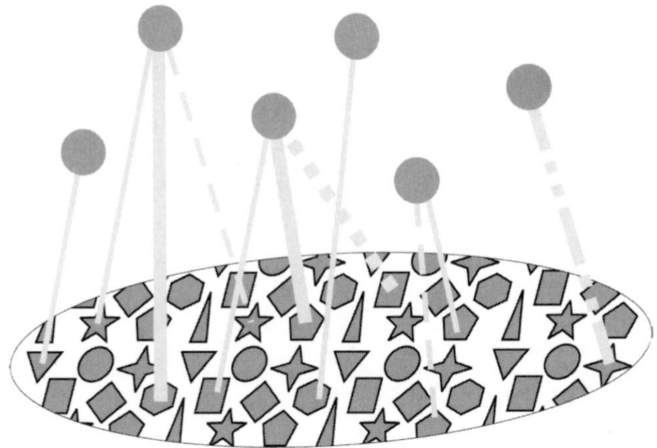

Figure 46-2 Occurrences of topics in an information pool and their various occurrence roles (represented by different line types).

In Example 46-1, the index terms are topics and the page numbers are their occurrences.

Example 46-1. An index is a simple form of topic map.

Germany 17, 77
Mozart 72
Wagner 49
Würzburg 22

But topic maps offer more. Through the concept of *occurrence roles*, they generalize and extend the conventions used to distinguish different kinds of references from one another.

In Example 46-2 the use of different typefaces indicates different *roles* played by the occurrences on pages 17 and 77 (perhaps a *main description* and a *mention*).

Example 46-2. An index with occurrence roles

Germany **17**, 77

Some books contain more than one index (index of names, index of places, etc.). *Topic types* provide the same facility, but extend it in several directions to enable the creation of multiple, dynamic, user-controlled indexes organized as taxonomic hierarchies.

Glossaries, too, can be implemented using just the bare bones of the topic map standard that has been described so far. Like an index, a glossary is also a set of topics and their occurrences, ordered by topic name. Here, though, the occurrence role is "definition".

Example 46-3. A glossary is a topic map.

Federal Republic of Germany: see *Germany.*

...

Germany: Federal republic in the northern part of central Europe, population (1998) approx. 82 million.

...

Würzburg: City in Bavaria, Germany on the river Main, 90 km south-east of Frankfurt. 128.000 inhabitants (1998).

Note that "Federal Republic of Germany" does not have a definition. It is just another topic name for the topic that also has the name "Germany", and in this map there can be only one definition per topic.

The definitions in Example 46-3 are instances of just one kind of occurrence – those that play the role of "definition". With a topic map it is easy to create and maintain much more complex glossaries than this; for example, ones that use multiple kinds of definitions (perhaps suited to different kinds of users).

46.1.4 *Topic association and association type*

Topic maps don't stop here, however. They go far beyond just providing a mechanism for creating more robust and powerful indexes and glossaries. The key to their true potential lies in their ability to model *relationships* between topics, and for this the topic map standard provides a construct called the *topic association.*

A topic association is (formally) a link element that asserts a relationship between two or more topics. Examples might be as follows:

- Munich *is in* Bavaria.
- Bavaria *is in* Germany.
- Wagner was *born in* Leipzig.
- Lohengrin was *composed by* Wagner.
- Wagner was *influenced by* Mozart.

46.1.4.1 Association role

Just as topics can be grouped according to type (country, state, city, etc.) and occurrences according to role (definition, article, illustration, commentary, etc.), so too can associations between topics be grouped according to their type. The *association types* of the five relationships in the list above are "is in", "born in", "composed by" and "influenced by" (see Figure 46-3). As with most other constructs, association types are themselves regarded as topics.

Each topic that participates in an association has a corresponding *association role* which states the role played by that topic in the association. In the case of the relationship "Wagner was born in Leipzig" those roles might be "person" and "birthplace"; for "Lohengrin was written by Wagner" they might be "opera" and "composer".

Like topic types, association roles must be declared as topics in order to be used.

46.1.4.2 Association topology

In the topic map model, associations do not have a direction; that is, they are not one-way (or "unilateral"). The "born in" relationship between Wagner and Leipzig implies what might be called a "fostered" relationship between the city and the composer ("Leipzig fostered Wagner"), and the "composed by" relationship between Lohengrin and Wagner is also a "composed" relationship between the composer and his opera ("Wagner composed Lohengrin").

Sometimes associations are *symmetrical*, in the sense that the nature of the relationship is the same whichever way you look at it. For example, the corollary of "Wagner was a friend of Ludwig II" would be that "Ludwig II was a friend of Wagner". Sometimes the association roles in such symmetrical relationships are the same (as in this case: "friend" and "friend"), sometimes they are different (as in the case of the "husband" and "wife" roles in a "married to" relationship).

Other association types, such as those that express superclass/subclass and some part/whole relationships, are *transitive*: If we say that Munich is in Bavaria, and that Bavaria is in Germany, we have implicitly asserted that Munich is in Germany and any topic map search engine should be able to draw the necessary conclusions without the need for making the assertion explicitly. Much of the real power of topic maps results from using transitive relations between topics, types, and roles for querying the map.

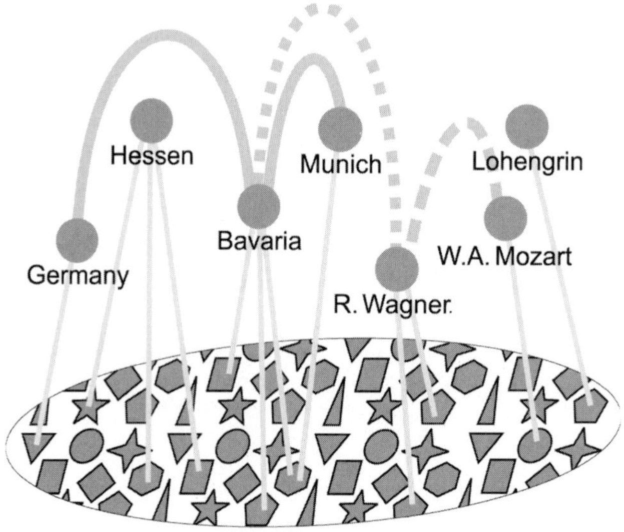

Figure 46-3 Associations of various types between topics (represented by different line types)

46.1.5 *Thesauri and semantic networks*

Typed topic associations extend the power of topic maps to the modeling of thesauri and other networks of information and knowledge.

A *thesaurus* is a network of interrelated terms (along with their definitions, examples, or whatever) within a particular domain. There exist various standards for thesauri that predefine relationship types, such as "broader term", "narrower term", "used for", and "related term", all of which correspond directly to association types in a topic map. Other thesaurus constructs, such as "source", "definition", and "scope note" would be modeled as occurrence roles in a topic map.

One advantage of applying the topic map model to thesauri is that it becomes possible to create hierarchies of association types that extend the thesaurus schema without deviating from accepted standards (for example, by subclassing "used for" as "synonymous for", "abbreviation for", and "acronym for"). Further advantages would be gained from using the facilities for scoping, filtering and merging described in the next three sections.

"Semantic networks", "associative networks" and "knowledge" (or "conceptual") "maps" are terms used within the fields of semantics and artificial intelligence to describe various models for representing knowledge structures within a computer. Many of these already correspond closely to the topic/association model. Adding the topic/occurrence axis provides a means for "bridging the gap" between these fields and the field of information management, thereby establishing a basis for true knowledge management.

46.1.6 *Scope*

When I refer to "Paris", you know immediately that I am talking about the capital city of France. Or do you? How do you know that I'm not talking about the town of the same name in Texas or the hero of Troy? Presumably because you are assuming a *scope* set by some form of context, whether it be a particular subject area under discussion or a generally accepted default.

The concept of scope is important for avoiding ambiguities like this and for increasing the precision with which assertions can be made. In topic maps, any assignment of a characteristic to a topic, be it a name, an occurrence or a role in an association, is considered to be valid within certain limits, which may or may not be specified explicitly. The limit of validity of such an assignment is called its *scope*; scope is defined in terms of *themes*, and themes are modeled as topics.

So, in topic maps where the scope is defined by the themes "France", "USA", and "Greek mythology", the name "Paris" could be used unambiguously. Similarly the association expressing the assertion that "Leipzig *is in* East Germany" could be qualified by giving it the scope "1949-90".

46.1.7 *Public subject*

Sometimes the same subject is represented by more than one topic. This can be the case when two topic maps are merged. In such a situation it is necessary to have some way of establishing the identity between seemingly disparate topics.

This can be done in either of two ways:

- Explicitly, by specifying *identity attributes* of the topic elements that address the same *public subject;* or
- Implicitly, through the *topic naming constraint*, which states that any topics that have the same name in the same scope refer to the same subject.

46.1.8 *Facets*

The final feature of the topic map standard to be considered in this introduction is the concept of the *facet.* Facets basically provide a mechanism for assigning property-value pairs to information resources. A facet is simply a property (such as "language" or "security level"); its values are called *facet values.* Facets are typically used for applying metadata which can then be used for filtering the information resources.

46.2 | Applications of topic maps

We will consider two applications. They both involve publishing, but topic maps have broad applicability in other areas as well.

46.2.1 *Reference work publishing*

In the age of digital information all commercial publishers face major new challenges, but perhaps none more so than publishers of reference works, especially encyclopedias and dictionaries. Not only has the advent of the World Wide Web finally forced all such publishers to think seriously about moving into electronic publishing; it has also turned out to be perhaps their biggest and most threatening competitor.

The reason for this, of course, is that the raw material from which reference works are fashioned consists for the most part of "hard facts" that cannot be owned. The knowledge that Wagner was born in Leipzig or that the population of Germany is about 82 million cannot be copyrighted. Almost every piece of information to be found in any modern, commercial encyclopedia can be found somewhere on the Internet for free. So how is a reference work publisher to compete?

46.2.1.1 Adding value

Paradoxically, the answer lies in the fact that most users today do not need more information – if anything, they need less, because they are already drowning in enormous quantities of it. At the very least, they need the ability to be able to find their way to relevant information as quickly as possible and to be able to filter out the "noise" created by all the information for which they have no use. They also need to be able to trust the information they receive, to know that it is reliable and up-to-date. Thus, two of the most important "value-adds" that commercial publishers can provide are

- tools and methods for finding the required information in a timely manner; and
- the confidence that the information so found can be trusted.

Topic maps can greatly assist the discovery of relevant information. In addition, the topic paradigm turns out to provide an *organizing principle* for many kinds of information that helps ensure its timeliness and accuracy.

46.2.1.2 A typical topic map

Encyclopedia articles are – at a very abstract level – about persons, geographical objects, history, culture, and science. These are the main *topic types*. Existing classification systems list further subclasses of these topic types, such as:

- historic person (monarch [emperor, king, queen], politician, [president, chancellor], explorer), artists (writer [novelist,

poet], painter, sculptor, composer, musician), scientists (mathematician, physicist, chemist, biologist, physician);
- country, state, landscape, city/town, river, mountain, island.

The *occurrence roles* point to the resources of an encyclopedia publisher. Typical data assets are articles, definitions, mentions of the topic in an article, pictures/images, audio, and video clips.

Even more interesting (because of the value added to the publication) are the *association types* that are used to structure the mass of cross-references normally found in such works. Obvious examples are: ruled over, conquered, painted, composed, wrote, played, discovered, invented, parent of, child of, located in, larger than, took place, before, after, discovered by, conquered by, founded by, invented by, etc.

Some of these are simply different names for the same association type viewed from different perspectives (e.g. conquered/conquered by, parent of/child of). Others exhibit the important property of transitivity (e.g. located in, larger than).

It is a good idea to identify transitive relationships like these because the topic map engine can use this information to generate more intelligent answers to the queries of the user.

46.2.2 Technical documentation

Technical documentation for a complex product could consist of thousands of pages, or megabytes of textual data. Corporate publishers have to manage and publish the documentation for different product versions and product variants. More ambitious corporate publishers add reader-related information to the publications ("skill level" is the typical example) or publish different views of the same material ("Overview", "Reference Manual", "Questions and Answers", etc.).

Versions, variants, and views require a more complex organization of the text than the sequential ordering of printed book. XML alone does not meet these requirements; publishers must also change the information management paradigm.

46.2.2.1 Text modules

Modularization of the text is the first step towards an appropriate solution. The existing chapter-section-subject structure of book-oriented technical documentation is split up into hundreds or thousands of separate text modules (information objects). The modules consist of "self-contained" text about a given subject (e.g. "Installation"). Hyperlinks connect the modules.

Hierarchical subject codes – assigned as metadata – allow quick access when querying the database containing the modules.

These two characteristics (self-contained text, hierarchical subject codes) indicate a class of technical documentation that is an ideal candidate for a topic map application.

46.2.2.2 A typical topic map

The identification of *topic types* can be based on the subject code classification. If this is not available, the technical design of the product or semantic markup in the documentation will give the necessary hints. In software documentation for example, the topic types might consist of "program block", "command group", "command", "macro", "parameter", "error", etc.

The *occurrence roles* would relate to existing modularized material. Data modules, functional diagrams, tables, screen shots, error messages, and syntax examples are among the possibilities.

Finally, *association types* can be derived from knowledge of the relationships between the topic types already identified: "command group A *consists of* commands X, Y, and Z", "command X *has parameters* P and Q", etc.

46.3 | Tool support for topic maps

Possibilities for tool support exist at each phase of the topic map life cycle.

46.3.1 *Topic map design*

The design of topic maps is an incremental process. The definition of the various types and roles and sub-/super-classes of them should be done under the control of a topic map design tool. Doing so will help ensure the consistency of the map.

Outside the scope of the topic map standard, but nevertheless very useful, are constraining conditions that can drive consistency checks. They make it possible to check whether transitive associations are used correctly, whether the types of topics in an association correspond to the respective association roles, etc.

Another part of the topic map design is the generation of all the topics, associations, and occurrences. In a large application these can be numbered in the thousands or even millions. The design tool has to offer an easy access to all these objects of the map.

As in a content management system, user access rights play an important role in a topic map design tool. Permission for creating, changing, and deleting parts of the map could be assigned to different user groups with different responsibilities, and the system has to take care that these rules are enforced.

46.3.2 *Creation and maintenance*

The boundary between the design and the creation of a topic map is fluid. Only the initial design will distinguish the declaration of types and roles on the one hand, and the topics, associations, and occurrences on the other. During the maintenance of the map these will be done concurrently – maybe by different user groups.

The editors (designer, author) of the topic map need a visualization tool besides the consistency checker. The visualization tool produces a rendition of the map that is similar to the one the end-users will see. The querying possibilities should also be similar.

The initial creation of the map out of an existing information pool can probably be supported by an automatic rule-based process. This process can be compared to the conversion of word processor files to XML abstractions. Both add structure to "flat" data.

A conversion for topic maps takes as its input information objects in which the topics and associations exist only implicitly, and produces a linked and structured knowledge base as output.

46.3.3 *Exchange of topic maps*

The publication of topic maps will be done electronically, since paper-based presentations of any but the simplest of topic maps are to all intents and purposes impossible. The topic map document architecture defined in the standard is the interface between topic map design and creation tools, and the topic map browser – the rendition and navigation tool of the end-user.

Note that this interchange standard does not address application-specific semantics such as the "association topology" properties described earlier. Eventual de facto acceptance of such semantics may cause them to be supported by topic map tools.

46.3.4 *Navigating a map*

There are two ways to navigate a topic map: by traversing the links or by directly addressing the nodes through queries.

Traversal of a large link network – possibly consisting of millions of nodes and links – requires an easy-to-use and easy-to-understand user interface. Very sophisticated colorful graphical user interfaces with nodes and edges that move in accordance with physical laws (like magnetism or gravity) might be eye-catchers. However, the familiar and easily implemented tree-based metaphor can also be an appropriate interface. Different icons for the nodes will help to distinguish the different types and roles in a map. For example, Figure 46-4 shows the topic management tool that is part of STEP's *SigmaLink* system (described in Chapter 33, "SigmaLink: Links and workflow", on page 442).

Querying a topic map requires a query language covering the concepts of the topic map standard and desirable application-specific semantics (associations, transitivity). The user needs additional support when defining a query – the information available in the map can be offered to the user by the query interface, e.g. in a menu-like style.

There should also be the possibility to "build-in" the knowledge that, say, the (virtual) topic type "clarinetist" is in fact a synthesis of all topics of type "person" that are connected via a "player of" association with the topic "clarinet". This will allow the user to work in a very intuitive manner and ensure very precise query results.

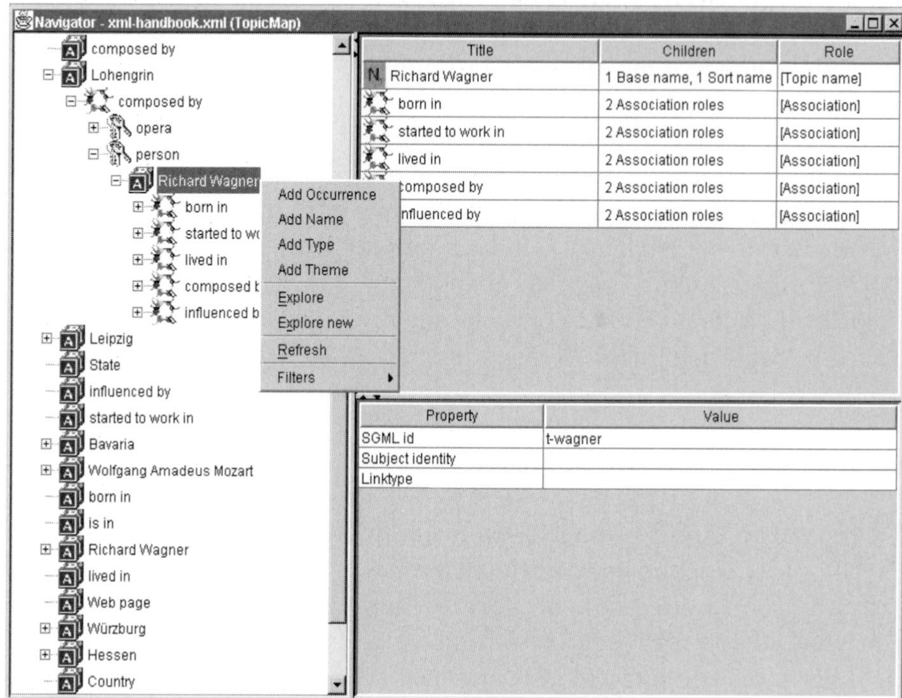

Figure 46-4 STEP's *SigmaLink* topic map interface

46.3.5 *As we think ...*

The human brain always remembers previously recognized things in context. Association is the main way we think. A topic map browser can support our way of thinking by offering related topics when the user looks at a given topic. The related topics can be dynamically calculated just by following the various "links" of the map. The relevancy of a related topic depends on its "distance" to the current one – where the distance could be the number of links to follow from one topic to the other. The "associative navigation" makes topic maps very powerful.

46.4 | Conclusion

The topic map standard provides a limited but complete and implementable set of concepts for organizing and navigating large and continuously growing information pools. The combination of the concepts opens up a wide variety of applications.

Topic maps are information assets in their own right, irrespective of whether they are actually connected to any information resources or not. Also, because of the separation between the information resources and the topic map, the same topic map can be overlaid on different pools of information, just as different topic maps can be overlaid on the same pool of information to provide different views to different users.

Furthermore, this separation provides the potential to be able to interchange topic maps among publishers and to merge one or more topic maps. Because of this, topic maps can stimulate a new business: An "Information Broker" can design topic maps, sell them separately to the information owner (e.g. publisher), or link the topics to resources from contracted information providers and sell both map and resource access to the end-users.

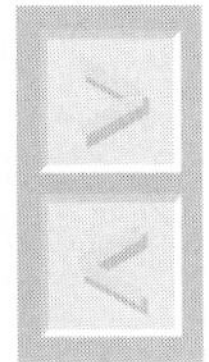

Analysis *The ability to apply multiple topic maps to arbitrary information pools has enormous potential for the World Wide Web. Website owners and independent third parties can develop and apply topic maps to collections of websites, thereby providing an overall information context for them. Instead of relying solely on physical addresses, which have no information context, a surfer could check his location in an applicable topic map to see where he is in an information space. In other words, topic maps can act as the Global Positioning System (GPS) for the World Wide Web.*

©2000 The XML Handbook™

The universal collaborative Web

Application Discussion

- Scenarios for collaboration
- WebDAV: Web-enabled Distributed Authoring and Versioning
- Writable Web archives
- Personal Portals
- Free trial software on CD-ROM

©2000 THE XML HANDBOOK™

Chapter 47

Extended linking, XML queries, and topic maps offer enormous potential for precise and powerful Web navigation, but when you get where you're going, you still can't change anything. New developments like writable Web archives and Personal Portals are starting to change all that, turning the Web into a true collaborative system. This chapter is sponsored by Excosoft, `http://www.excosoft.com`, and was prepared by Håkan Lothigius.

The major contribution of the World Wide Web has been to make information globally accessible. Vast resources of information lie within a mouse-click or two, ready for you to read, view, or listen to – but not to modify.

And that's the problem: The Web is the world's greatest peephole. You can look, but you can't touch.

Now this restriction is starting to disappear and the Web may yet achieve Tim Berners-Lee's original vision of a universal collaborative environment.

47.1 | Some collaborative Web scenarios

Let's look at some scenarios to see what Web collaboration could do for people working in different professions: a project leader, a doctor, a newly-hired programmer, and a car dealer.

47.1.1 *The project leader*

Kim is leading a project developing a new generation of micro-monitors for personal digital assistants (PDAs). The workgroup is spread over France, the U.S., Sweden and China.

Formal management is done by email when reviewing specifications, confirming milestones, giving comments on a prototype, etc. This method makes it easy to follow the project and refer to previous messages.

For quick and direct interaction, members working in overlapping time zones use the *Virtual Corridor*, an advanced video-conferencing system that is always online.

The project-related documentation itself is never dispatched between members. It is stored in distributed archives managed by the configuration manager of the team. The actual location depends on traffic fees, available bandwidth and storage costs, but is never the concern of the development team.

On arriving at her Stockholm office in the morning, Kim receives a message from Paul in Dallas. Paul has finished the interface specification as planned and in the message there is a link to the document. When Kim clicks the link, the updated parts of the document are transferred from the archive currently located in Barcelona. Most of the document was already cached on Kim's PC, as she had looked at it just a few days earlier.

Kim wants to read the specification on her way home, so she drags the link to the document onto the PDA icon of her Personal Portal – her personalized dynamic interface to her company's information resources. The entire document is then copied to her PDA. Because the document is an XML abstraction, its presentation will be generated dynamically and adapted to the smaller screen of the PDA.

Later that evening, Kim makes some comments and alterations to the document and stores a modified version in the archive. Because Paul subscribes to new versions of the document, he is automatically notified that the document is available (Figure 47-1). He can make his final modifications and store the final version of the document without copying a single syllable onto his hard disk.

Figure 47-1 Sharing documents over the Web

47.1.2 *The physician*

Anesthesiologist Caren is working at Rigshospitalet in Copenhagen. She needs to consult the records of Nigel, a patient traveling in Denmark but domiciled in Cambridge, U.K.

Thanks to the distributed Web-based archive of Addenbrook Hospital in Cambridge, Caren needs only to get the password from Nigel's doctor to access Nigel's health portal. From there she can access all relevant information about Nigel's medical condition and details of recent examinations.

Nigel needs special surgery, so prior to the operation Caren and her colleagues access video recordings of a similar operation that was performed on him at the Cambridge hospital. They also access comments and recordings from specialists all over the world.

After the successful operation, Caren again accesses Nigel's health portal and notes her experiences from the operation. Because the health portal is

XML-based, Caren can use the same navigation and editing tools that she uses internally at Rigshospitalet.

This easy access to information allows Caren and her colleagues to be better prepared for any unusual situations, and to be able to share the experiences of colleagues around the world.

47.1.3 *The programmer*

Olof is a new member of a team developing telecom billing applications. He is involved with the communication interface.

The team is using literate programming and maintains both source code and documentation in XML. This means that the documentation is stored and edited together with the code and is therefore always up-to-date.

For reviewing purposes the documentation can be extracted and published as a separate document. When generating the system for the daily build, the source code is extracted and fed to the compiler.

Using an XML representation also makes it easier to add metadata to the code. Some parts of the code are tagged with unique identifiers for tracing purposes. XLinks are used wherever one part of the code calls another, which makes it very easy to follow the logic of the program.

Olof quickly finds that the integrated documentation makes the source code very easy to understand. If he reads a description of a subclass on one structure level, he knows that he can get more details by expanding the next level in the structure.

The team stores all project plans, specifications, code, etc. in a Web-based archive. All members of the project team can access both current and previous versions of all files, and even one another's working files.

This method of information management is completely new to Olof, who is used to disk drive and file-based access. But it does not take him long to see the advantages of full version control, global access, and daily builds of the XML-based system. These capabilities contribute to making him productive from day one.

47.1.4 *The car dealer*

David represents a German car manufacturer in Fairbanks, Alaska. Instead of a large showroom and several salesmen, he demonstrates the cars in a "virtual showroom". He can even display customized configurations of cars that have not yet been manufactured.

Pictures and data for all configurable components are stored in a central archive that is accessible over the Web. The customer can select options and accessories, choose colors and interiors, and visualize the final result in three dimensions in David's virtual showroom.

When the customer makes a final selection, the price and delivery schedule are calculated for the car, based on the cost and known lead-times of the chosen components. A comprehensive owner's handbook is printed on demand, customized for the car's unique configuration. David generates the order and it is instantly entered into the production system in Germany.

Creating the virtual showroom for David wasn't difficult. The car manufacturer was already using the configuration system internally, so setting it up on a secure server was a straightforward job. And the documentation was already maintained in an XML-based content management system that supported customized demand printing.

For David, the virtual showroom means a shorter sales cycle and a much leaner operation. Above all, it means satisfied customers.

47.2 | The missing links

Clearly, the above scenarios don't depict the way the Web is used today. They rely on the combination of two requirements that appear to be far from full realization:

- Geographically unbound secure access to all enterprise information for immediate browsing and editing.
- *Logical* navigation based on the topic of the information, rather than *physical* navigation based on its location.

Fortunately, and perhaps surprisingly, the reality is more positive than the appearance. The technology already exists to make these scenarios real; it is just a question of maturation and wide deployment. Let's examine the components of that technology: writable Web archives and Personal Portals.

47.2.1 *Writable Web archives*

The technology that the Web relies on for distribution – the *Hypertext Transfer Protocol* (HTTP) – is being extended. It will support not only read-access, as at present, but also write-access with document management functions (Figure 47-2).

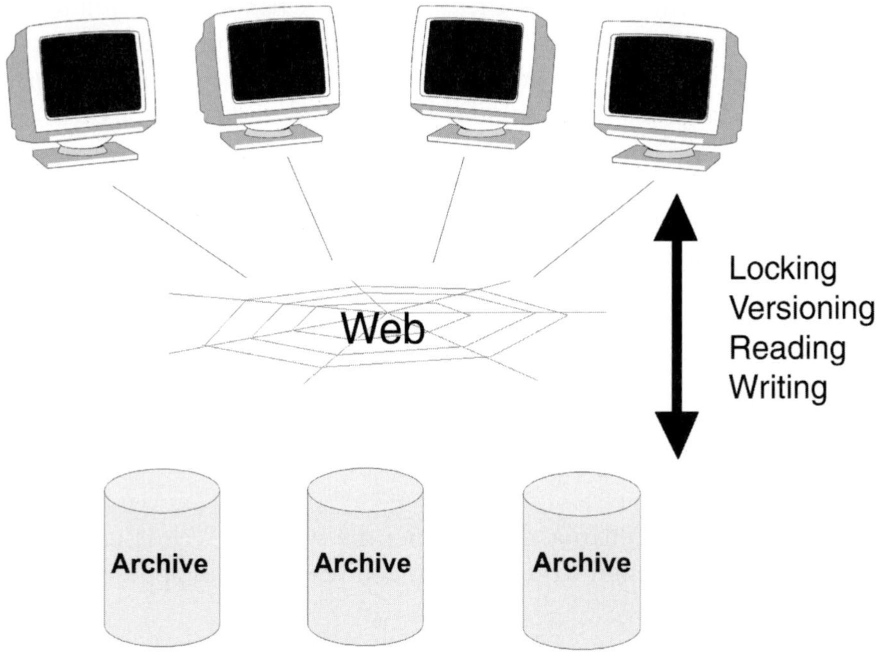

Figure 47-2 WebDAV connects users to writable archives

The new standard is called *WebDAV*, which stands for *Web-based Distributed Authoring and Versioning*. It is a set of extensions to the HTTP protocol that allows users to edit and manage files collaboratively on remote Web servers, thereby enabling the writable archives needed by our scenarios.[1] WebDAV's document management functions are:

1. Actually, WebDAV comprises several different standards, developed by the Internet Engineering Task Force. You can read them at `http://www.webdav.org/` and on the CD-ROM that accompanies this book.

- *Overwrite prevention* by locking documents remotely.
- *Properties handling* for consistent metadata management.
- *Namespace management* to ensure unambiguous and consistent naming of Web resources.
- *Version management* including parallel version branches.
- *Advanced collections* for persistent ordered groups of documents.
- *Access control* to limit access rights for a given resource.

With WebDAV writable archives, information storage can be dispersed either within the company's own network or outsourced, or whatever combination is the most cost-efficient and secure. The users, however, need not care about the physical location of the information. They can access it wherever it is stored from wherever they may be. They can read, update and restore the one and only copy – version controlled of course – which will then become instantly available to any other authorized user.

47.2.2 *Personal Portals*

In Part Four, "Portals", of this book we discussed Enterprise Information Portals (EIP), customized doorways into restricted information sets, such as the health portal in the physician's scenario above. EIPs are not just home pages full of links to other resources; they also contain information that has been integrated from sources within the enterprise, including data gleaned from legacy applications.

An EIP that is customized for an employee's access to the enterprise's intranet is termed a *Personal Portal.* Today it is predominantly for consuming information, with relatively cumbersome facilities for contributing back to the information base.

With WebDAV and writable archives, however, the Personal Portal takes on a whole new meaning. It becomes the user's desktop. As shown in Figure 47-3, all company and personal information is accessible from a single interface, where both information consumption and information production can take place. The keys to that accessibility are logical navigation and hyperlink organization.

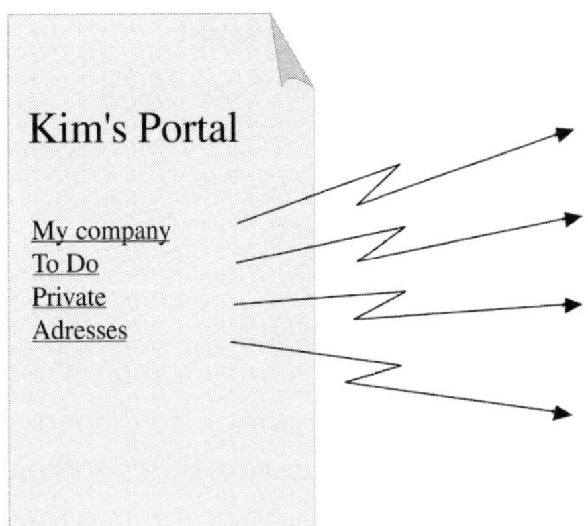

Figure 47-3 A Personal Portal

47.2.2.1 Logical navigation

Since the dawn of the disk drive, the hierarchical file system has been the predominant information storage model. In that model, we search through a structure of networks, drives, folders, and files in search of our information. It is the storage organization of the information and the names given to the storage objects that provide the context for our access to it.

Today, thanks to the World Wide Web, we are in an era of overwhelming information abundance. The very word "Web" connotes the new model it introduced to manage that abundance, a model in which information is interconnected by means of logical associations called *hyperlinks* (Figure 47-4).

47.2.2.2 Hyperlink organization

Hyperlinks permit different types of information to be associated and presented logically. This means that the information no longer is organized depending on its type or its location, but on its logical context. Learning to think this way about information resources can be a difficult paradigm shift.

For hyperlinked access to be effective, the information must be organized so that it is readily accessible within the correct context. For example, if you are browsing through recent correspondence and agreements with a cus-

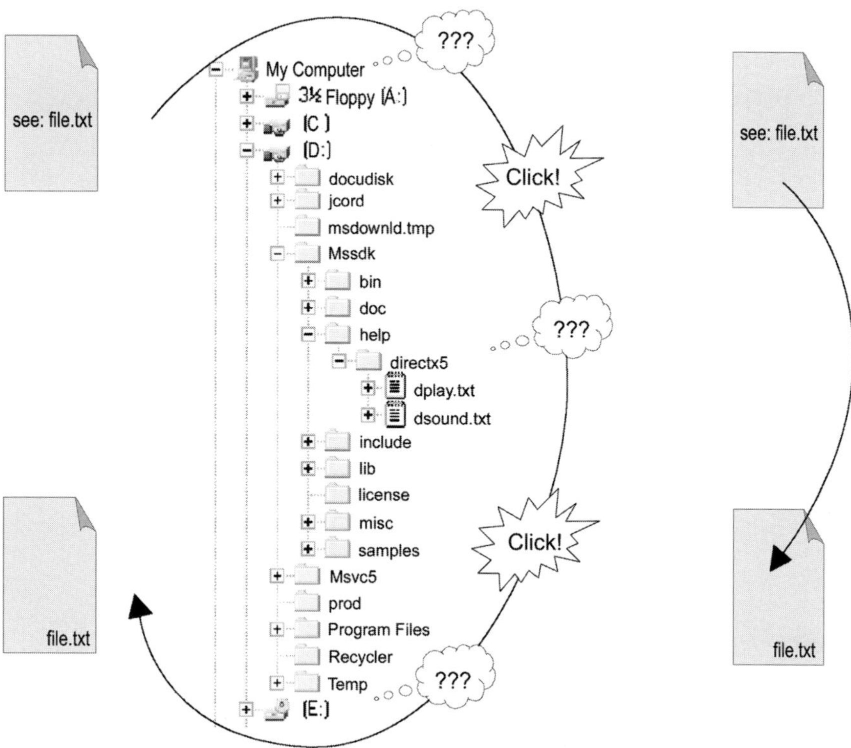

Figure 47-4 File system versus hyperlink

tomer, the financial transactions stored in your ERP system should also be just a mouse-click away (Figure 47-5).

47.3 | Tool requirements

From a purely mechanical standpoint, a collaborative Web could be built with browsers and editors much like today's, simply by adding webDAV support to those products. However, tools that are designed for the new Web paradigm could do a much better job of helping users. Such tools should address three requirements:

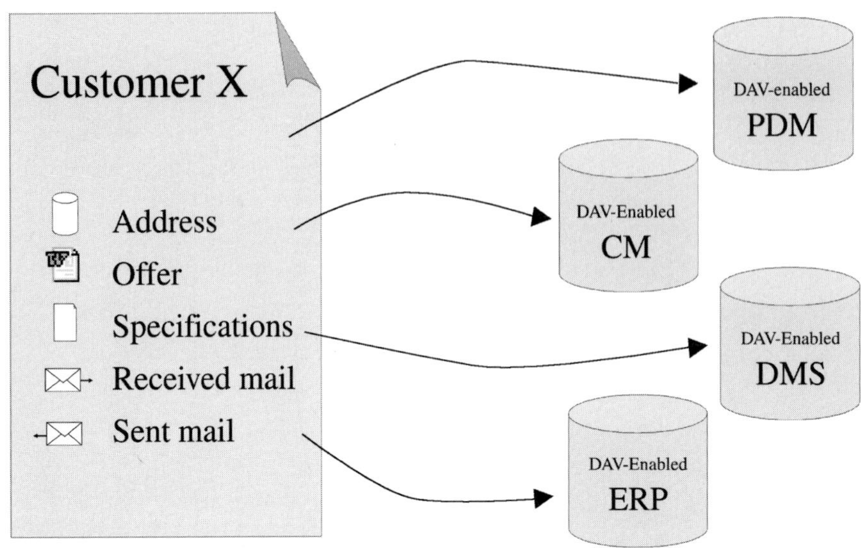

Figure 47-5 Connecting information

Reveal the abstract information
The tool should embrace the concept of working with abstract information structures and presenting them as such, rather than as WYSIWYG renditions of documents.

Use logical navigation
The tool should implement the logical navigation paradigm, rather than the physical filing cabinet.

Support browsing and editing seamlessly
The tool must be an information interaction tool, where both browsing and editing are equally well supported.

The reason for this last requirement is as much philosophical and motivational as it is technical. A tool with which the acts of learning and adding knowledge are as close to one another as they are in real life motivates users to contribute to the enterprise knowledge assets. In other words, it makes information as easy to update as it is to access.

A tool that meets all of these requirements, then, can actually encourage the creation of the collaborative Web by making it easy to add links and organize information in easily navigable structures for everyday use.

Figure 47-6 illustrates the Personal Portal of Figure 47-3 as it might appear in one such tool, Excosoft's *Documentor.* Note that the `To Do` item is expanded. Although two separate files are shown in Figure 47-6, the tool presents them as a single logical information structure.

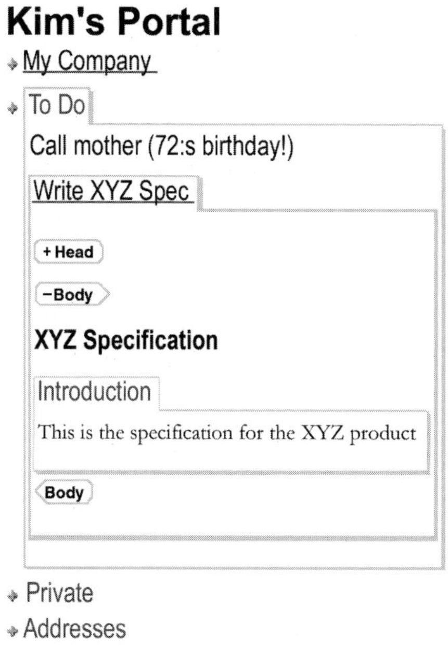

Kim's Portal
My Company
To Do
Call mother (72:s birthday!)
Write XYZ Spec
+ Head
–Body
XYZ Specification
Introduction
This is the specification for the XYZ product
Body
Private
Addresses

Figure 47-6 A transclusion ("XYZ Specification") in the Personal Portal of Figure 47-3

Documentor employs *transclusion*, which means that a hyperlink's target anchor is presented as a replacement for its reference anchor.[1] In the figure, the "XYZ Specification" is the target of a link. It appears within the referencing document, right where the click occurred.

1. The term "transclusion" was coined by Ted Nelson, who also coined the term "hypertext". It is a combination of the word "inclusion" with the prefix "trans", used in the sense of "across" or "beyond".

Documentor also supports the capability – normally found only in navigation panes of two-window views – of expanding and collapsing the document according to its abstract structure. That facility, in combination with hyperlink transclusion, makes it possible to hide subordinate details until you need them. The result is a convenient overview of large amounts of information, combined with easy access to the details.

47.4 | Conclusion

The technologies described in this chapter exist in full or partial form today, and products have begun to support them.

All of which implies that a new generation of powerful and user-friendly information management systems is on the way. It is only the paradigm shift that may prove slow to accomplish: replacing electronic filing cabinets with a web of logically interconnected information.

With these new concepts and tools that support them, users can build the Personal Portals that will revolutionize their way of working and create the universal collaborative Web.

©2000 THE XML HANDBOOK™

XML and Programming

- Programming technology
- Distributed programming
- Interface definition
- Active content
- Comprehensive case study

©2000 THE XML HANDBOOK™

Part Ten

So far our emphasis has been on the *uses* of markup technology, rather than how it works. But now we give in to the nerd that lurks in all of us and look at technology for its own sake: specifically, the relationship of XML and programming.

For a data representation technology, it's a very unusual relationship indeed. We've seen throughout the book how products support XML for content management and data integration, and in this part we'll see how programming technology supports many of those products.

But we'll also look at the counterpart of data integration: *distributed programming*. If you can aggregate data from multiple independent programs, it means (to look at it another way) that you are coordinating the execution of those programs to accomplish a common result.

That coordination is achieved through well-defined interfaces to the programs, and messages sent between them. We'll see how XML is used for both the interfaces and the messages, both in complex system architectures and in a single document with *active content*.

Finally, we'll look at a detailed case study that uses all the virtuoso techniques, including the generation of program code and user interfaces from marked-up documents.

Java technology for XML development

Tool Discussion

- Tools for tool-building
- SAX and DOM APIs
- Middleware development services

©2000 THE XML HANDBOOK™

Chapter 48

This chapter is sponsored by Sun Microsystems, http://java.sun.com/xml.

Several of the products that we've used to illustrate the chapters of this book have something in common: They are written in the Java™ programming language. If they support EDI or other forms of application integration, they may also use the Java 2 Platform, Enterprise Edition (J2EE).

But we don't say much about these common characteristics in those chapters. For one thing, we'd be repeating ourselves a lot if we did.[1] But more importantly, we'd be getting off-topic.

The chapters in which those products appear occur in application-oriented parts of the book. For that reason, we focus on *what* the products do with XML, rather than *how* they accomplish it. In contrast, the purpose of this chapter is to provide – in a single place – a look at some of the *Java* technology that influences their ability to process XML.

Some might argue that the main influence is metaphysical: there is a profound *rightness* about using the two technologies together in that both were designed for the Web, both are internationalized (because they support Unicode), and both are designed for portability.

1. We repeat ourselves a lot as it is, but we generally restrict the repetition to emphasizing important XML concepts.

More than portability! They are designed to *let information be free*, to liberate it from the bonds of operating systems, to let it travel unhindered throughout the network that is the computer ...

Right.

Metaphysics notwithstanding, in this chapter we'll focus strictly on technical capabilities. We'll look at implementations of the SAX and DOM interfaces, and services for developing XML middleware.

Note *In 2.10, "Programming interfaces and models", on page 38, we covered some basic concepts that are necessary for this chapter: parsing, APIs, DOM, and SAX.*

48.1 | SAX and DOM implementations

An XML parser must ensure that the XML document is *well-formed*, which means (in a nutshell) that the tags are properly constructed, every start-tag has an associated end-tag, and the elements they identify are always nested properly, one within the other.

Proper nesting means that the `title` element, for example, is always fully inside or fully outside the `chapter` element, not overlapping. The `title` element can't start outside the `chapter`, and then finish inside it.

When validating, a parser goes even further and verifies that the XML document lives up to the restrictions and specifications declared in the document's DTD (or schema definition). If there is no document type declaration, the document is not valid.

All XML parsers must be able to check for well-formedness. Those that can also validate are known as (surprise!) *validating parsers*. Either kind can be used with the SAX and DOM APIs.

48.1.1 *The SAX API*

You can think of this interface as "serial access" for XML.

Recall from 2.10, "Programming interfaces and models", on page 38 that SAX is "event-driven". The parser reads through an XML document once, from start to finish. At each parsing event, such as recognizing the start or end of an element, it notifies the application. It also provides the information associated with the event, such as the element-type name, attributes and their values, or content data characters.

The SAX API is fast and it uses little memory, which recommends it for server applications and simple programs that only read data or make only small changes to it.

The basic outline of the SAX parser is shown in Figure 48-1. First the `ParserFactory` generates an instance of the parser. The XML text is shown coming into the parser from the left. As the parser runs, it invokes the appropriate operations (called "methods"), which are organized into the four groups (called "interfaces") shown on the right.

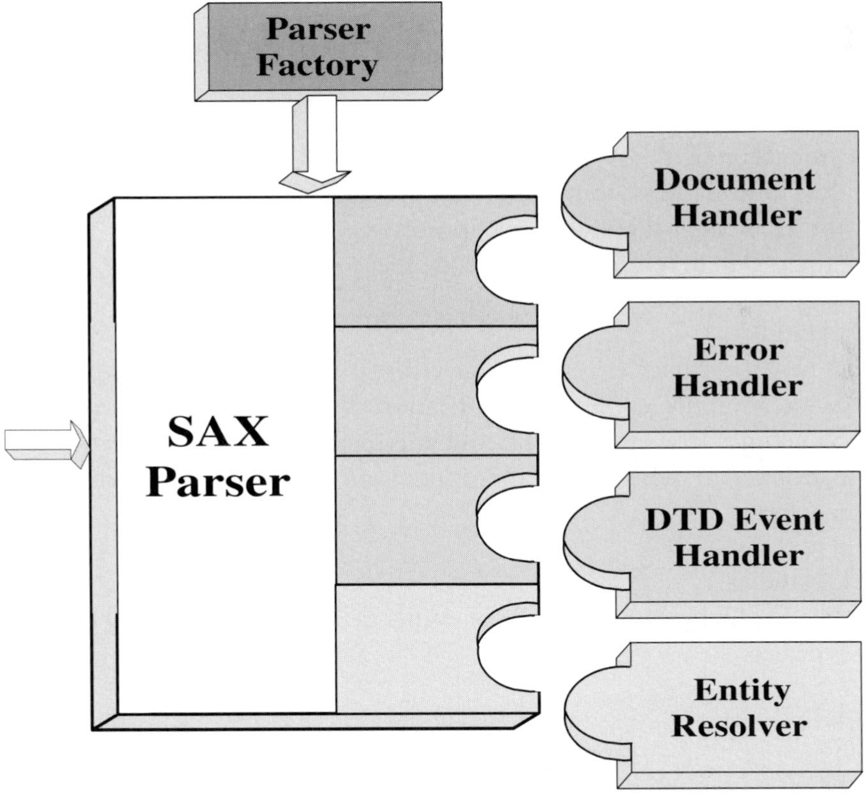

Figure 48-1 SAX API

What those methods actually do is determined by the application programmer, who might not even implement all of them. A typical application provides at least the `DocumentHandler` methods. A robust one will implement the `ErrorHandler` interface as well.

Here is a summary of the major SAX functions, grouped by the interfaces in which they are defined:

ParserFactory
: The ParserFactory class defines the `makeParser()` method, which lets the user determine which parser to use at runtime. For example, the user might choose to use a parser from a different vendor, or choose a validating parser rather than a nonvalidating parser.

Parser
: The parser reads the XML text and recognizes parsing events, as described above.

DocumentHandler
: The information about the events the parser recognizes is sent to the DocumentHandler for processing. This is where the application developer puts the code that processes the data.

ErrorHandler
: When the parser encounters an error, it tells the ErrorHandler. Sometimes the application can ignore the error and continue. Sometimes the error makes it impossible for the parser to continue, in which case the application would issue an error message.

DTDHandler
: The DTDHandler takes care of events that occur when the DTD is parsed.

EntityResolver
: The `resolveEntity` method is invoked when the parser must access text that is outside the document entity.

48.1.2 *The DOM API*

You can think of this interface as "random access" for XML, because you can access any part of the data at any time.

The Document Object Model is a collection of objects in your program. You can manipulate the object model in any way that makes sense. You can modify data, remove it, or insert new data. When your application is through making changes, it can then write the structure out as an XML document. Interactive applications can use the DOM API to maintain the parsed document while displaying a rendition for users to read and edit.

While the SAX API is fast, it is only good for reading data. You can't use it to write XML, or to modify an XML document that has been parsed. The DOM API fills those needs.

On the other hand, the DOM can't be used to read XML. For that it uses SAX, so SAX and DOM work together hand-in-hand.

Figure 48-2 shows how Sun's *Java* XML libraries implement the Document Object Model.

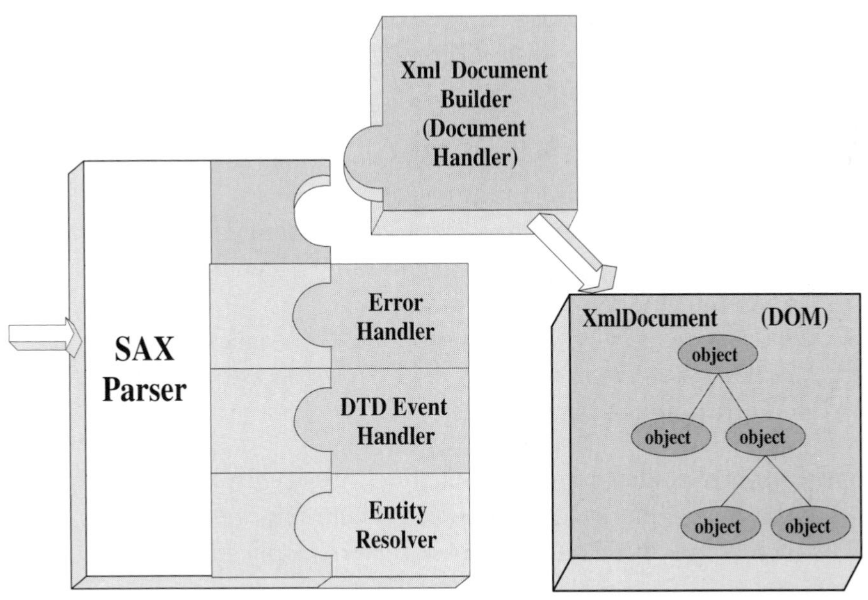

Figure 48-2 DOM API

The `XmlDocumentBuilder` class is just an elaborate SAX `DocumentHandler`. As event information arrives from the parser, the XML-DocumentBuilder uses it to construct a DOM representation of the parsed document.

The DOM API hides the intricacies of the SAX API, and provides a relatively familiar tree structure of objects. It also provides a framework to help generate an XML document from the object tree.

On the other hand, constructing the DOM requires reading the entire XML document and holding the object tree in memory, so it is much more CPU and memory intensive. For that reason, the SAX API may be preferable for server-side applications and data filters that do not require an in-memory representation of the entire document at once.

Implementations of both APIs, together with sample application code, can be found on the CD-ROM.

48.2 | XML middleware services

The *Java 2 Platform, Enterprise Edition* is a set of middleware services for developing enterprise applications. XML is supported in J2EE as a standardized data representation for information interchange.

J2EE includes such technologies as:

- *Enterprise JavaBeans*™ (EJB) technology, for server-centric component-based programming
- *Java Servlets*, for extending web server functionality
- *JavaServer Pages*™ (JSP), for dynamically generating Web content, including XML documents
- *Java Message Service*, for asynchronous XML data messaging.
- *Java Database Connectivity* (JDBC™), for accessing databases and other tabular data sources

Figure 48-3 illustrates how J2EE facilities are used to construct a business-to-business e-commerce application. There are two businesses, each with its own secure intranet of database servers, application servers, client systems, etc.

In both businesses, applications on the intranet communicate across an internal firewall to the company's Web server, using JSP and/or Servlets.

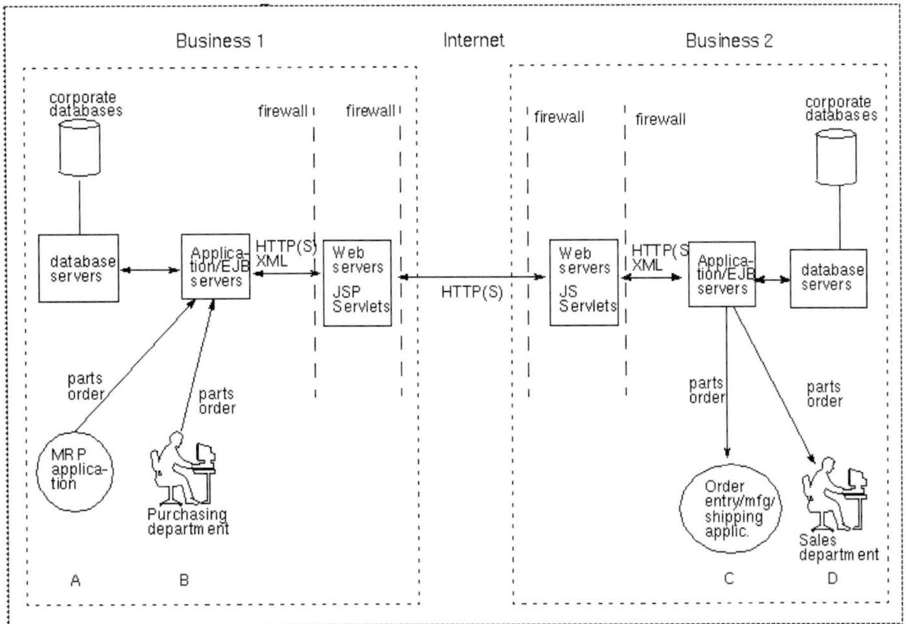

Figure 48-3 Business-to-business e-commerce application

The communication protocol is HTTP(S) and the data is represented in XML.

An external firewall protects the Web server from the Internet. Other businesses can communicate with the Web server only by using HTTP(S) to cross the external firewall.

48.2.1 *Business 1*

Business 1 is an end-product manufacturer. It runs a Materials Resource Planning (MRP) application on its intranet that calculates when to order parts, and in what quantities. It also has a purchasing department that places special orders interactively.

48.2.1.1 Automated parts ordering

Area A of Figure 48-3 illustrates the automated ordering process.

The MRP application generates order data, which is converted to a "parts order" document represented in XML using techniques like those described in Part Three, "E-commerce" of this book. The parts order is transmitted to an EJB server, then to the Web server, and eventually across the Internet to a parts supplier, such as Business 2.

48.2.1.2 Interactive parts ordering

The interactive purchasing process is shown in area B of Figure 48-3.

Purchasing personnel interact with a browser-based application, similar to those described in Part [no number], "Middle-tier Servers" of this book. JSP pages are used to collect the purchasing data and generate "parts order" XML documents that are sent to the parts supplier over the Internet.

48.2.2 *Business 2*

Business 2 is an OEM parts manufacturer. It runs an order-entry, manufacturing, and shipping application on its intranet that automatically books and processes e-commerce orders. However, its application server is programmed to route non-routine orders, such as very large orders and rush orders, to the sales department for interactive processing.

48.2.2.1 Automated sales processing

Area C of Figure 48-3 depicts the automated sales processing. It is essentially the inverse of Business 1's automated order processing and uses similar techniques.

The parts order document is parsed and its data is incorporated in a sales order in the form accepted by the order entry application. That application enters the order into the manufacturing system. It also generates and sends a confirmation of the order to Business 1, including pricing and shipping dates.

48.2.2.2 Interactive sales processing

Interactive sales processing is shown in area D of Figure 48-3.

The parts order XML document is rendered on the client under the control of an XSL stylesheet, using techniques like those discussed in Part [no number], "Stylesheets". Sales personnel review and approve the order and enter it into the system.

©2000 THE XML HANDBOOK™

Distributed programming through XML

Application Discussion

- XML as a component model
- Benefits of XML
- Sample distributed application

©2000 The XML Handbook™

Chapter 49

All that distinguishes an XML workflow system from an XML component framework is the size of the messages and the waiting time for the responses. That intriguing insight is the basis for this chapter, which considers XML in the light of what it does to programs, rather than what programs do to it. The chapter is sponsored by Bluestone Software, `http://www.bluestone.com/`, and was prepared by Jason A. Kinner

In the MOM application discussions in this book – EDI, portals, etc. – XML is presented as a data integration enabler: It allows data from disparate sources, such as databases, ERP systems, and legacy business applications, to be combined into a single XML document for processing and/or rendition.

But there is another way to look at the very same behavior. Because XML is enabling disparate programs to work in combination, it is really (also) a *distributed programming* enabler. In programming terms, it is a *component model* and its implementation is a *component framework*.

In this chapter, we'll discuss some implications of an XML component model and framework and look at a sample application.

49.1 | XML as a component model

Components, of course, are programs – but programs that are designed to do specific tasks, and which are intended to be combined with other components to build complete applications.

Such applications are termed *loosely-coupled*, meaning that their components know nothing about one another's internals or data formats, only about their formally-defined interfaces. In contrast, traditional applications (including components themselves) are termed *tightly-coupled* because their internal objects do have intimate knowledge of one another.

So the key to a component model is the interfaces – the object classes and the messages. In the XML component model, object classes are document types and messages are documents. But these are not the large documents and long message-response intervals of POP workflow applications; in a component model we deal with minute messages that are passed instantaneously among choreographed objects to control the system itself.

Using a character-based notation like XML for this purpose is novel. Historically, the idea of transporting data as text has been dismissed as inefficient, given that a simple message such as `<price>10.00</price>` can represent 300% overhead. On the other hand, in the context of the overall system, including design and maintenance, the textual nature of XML actually improves efficiency by making it easier to design, debug, and create objects, for programs as well as people.

Let's look at some other considerations relating to the use of XML as a component model.

49.1.1 *Version support*

XML intrinsically supports version changes. As long as a message is valid with respect to the current DTD, if either party sends elements not recognized by the other, they can simply be ignored. As long as interfaces only expand and never contract, clients and servers can operate in relative isolation without breaking either old client code or new server code.

This benefit is a direct corollary of the XML performance drawback that every message must be parsed. In a traditional component model, the client and server are tightly-coupled. Both understand the internal structure of individual messages being passed between them, which allows them to find parameters quickly by means of pointer arithmetic.

But there is no free lunch here. Since the message format must be agreed upon beforehand, the client code must be updated if the server revises its interface. Fail to do can lead to unexpected failures of both the client and the server, and such failures are notoriously difficult to debug.

On the other hand, an XML component model is very adaptable to changes in the message structure. Crashes will not occur when the server is expecting more information than a client provides. The parser knows that elements are missing and the server can pass that error message to the client.

49.1.2 *Transactions*

A *transaction* is a logical grouping of actions that must occur on an "all or nothing" basis. Component frameworks support this concept with components that are capable of committing and rolling back transactions.

In a traditional distributed component model, a network request is initiated for each action to be performed. In order to use a component with five properties and two methods, a client in a system using that model would make seven round-trip requests to the server, even if all the actions combined constituted a single logical transaction.

In the XML model, however, the actions could be combined into a single request simply by nesting them in a transaction element. They would receive a single reply, even if an output of the first method were required as input to the next. By abstracting return values on the client side, an asynchronous operation can be created wherein the actual return value is not required until the completion of the entire transaction.

We'll illustrate this capability in an example later on.

49.1.3 *Application server facilities*

Application servers provide services similar to object request brokers, including persistent objects and remote invocation semantics. By front-ending a legacy non-distributed component model with an XML component framework, the features of the application server become available to the previously isolated components. These include real-time monitoring and adaptation (load-balancing, network latency reduction, etc.), legacy component transactions, and security management.

49.1.3.1 Transactions with legacy components

The front-ending technique allows legacy component frameworks to participate in transactional processing. Simply nesting several method calls within a transaction element would indicate to the run-time environment that a transaction is requested by the client application.

For example, suppose a company has a CORBA interface to a billing system and a COM interface to a catalog system. It may be necessary to group updates of the item price in both systems into a single transaction.

By applying the XML component framework, transactional support can be added without changing the original components. As a side benefit, there would be a stronger integration between the COM and CORBA systems through the implied bridging technology inherent in the XML component framework.

49.1.3.2 Security and personalization

An enterprise-level application server will provide some sort of security management mechanism. Typically, a scheme involving users, groups, and roles is used to provide maximum flexibility in assigning permissions. These permissions can be incorporated into the XML component framework.

For example, there may be a single interface to a pricing model component that supports queries, inserts, and updates. In an e-commerce environment it is necessary to protect the database from unauthorized inserts and updates. The implementation of methods on that component could be designed to be filtered by the standard application server security mechanism.

Similarly, the common administrative tools of the application server could be used to define the component permissions at the property and method level.

49.2 | An XML component model sample

In this sample application, we open a new account at a bank. Doing so requires the successful completion of two actions:

©2000 THE XML HANDBOOK™

1. Create a new account.
2. Deposit money into it.

First we will define the object classes, then we will illustrate two ways to open the account: as a sequence of two separate method invocations, and as a single transaction that combines both invocations.

49.2.1 *Object classes*

The application requires object classes for `Bank`, `Account`, `Bank-Reply`, and `Account-Reply`. Their definitions are represented by the DTD fragment in Example 49-1.

Example 49-1. Object class definitions

```
<!ELEMENT Bank ((createAccount|closeAccount)+)>
<!ELEMENT  createAccount  (primary-ssn,secondary-ssn*)>
<!ATTLIST  createAccount  objID  CDATA #IMPLIED>
<!ELEMENT   primary-ssn   (#PCDATA)>
<!ELEMENT   secondary-ssn (#PCDATA)>
<!ELEMENT  closeAccount   (Account)>
<!ATTLIST  closeAccount   objREF CDATA #IMPLIED>

<!ELEMENT Bank-Reply      ((createAccount|closeAccount)+)>
<!ELEMENT  createAccount  (Account)>
<!ELEMENT   Account       EMPTY>
<!ATTLIST   Account       objID  CDATA #IMPLIED>
<!ELEMENT  closeAccount   EMPTY>

<!ELEMENT Account         ((deposit|withdraw|transfer)+)>
<!ATTLIST Account         objID  CDATA #IMPLIED
                          objREF CDATA #IMPLIED>
<!ELEMENT  deposit        (amount)>
<!ELEMENT   amount        (#PCDATA)>
<!ATTLIST   amount        currency CDATA #IMPLIED>
<!ELEMENT  withdraw       (amount)>
<!ELEMENT  transfer       (Account, amount)>

<!ELEMENT Account-Reply   ((deposit|withdraw|transfer)+)>
<!ELEMENT  deposit        EMPTY>
<!ATTLIST  deposit        objID  CDATA #IMPLIED>
<!ELEMENT  withdraw       EMPTY>
<!ATTLIST  withdraw       objID  CDATA #IMPLIED>
<!ELEMENT  transfer       EMPTY>
<!ATTLIST  transfer       objID  CDATA #IMPLIED>
```

©2000 THE XML HANDBOOK™

The children of each object class are methods provided by the class. The children of the methods are their parameters and/or return values, which can themselves be object classes.

Two attributes are used for identifying and referencing persistent objects, objID (object ID) and objREF (object reference). If the user specifies a value for objID, the system receiving the document registers the value.

There is only one instance of a Bank object, which is why the identifying and referencing attributes are not defined for that class.

49.2.2 *Separate method invocations*

The account can be opened by the following sequence of actions.

49.2.2.1 Create an account

Example 49-2 opens an account with the primary SSN "999-99-9999".

Example 49-2. Invocation of createAccount method on Bank object

```
<Bank>
   <createAccount>
      <primary-ssn>999-99-9999</primary-ssn>
   </createAccount>
</Bank>
```

On successful completion, a new Account object named "Acct:999-99-9999" is returned. This name can be used to reference the account at a later time by using the objREF attribute.

Example 49-3. Account object returned by Example 49-2

```
<Bank-Reply>
   <createAccount>
      <Account objID="Acct:999-99-9999"/>
   </createAccount>
</Bank-Reply>
```

49.2.2.2 Make a deposit

Make a deposit in the newly-created account from Example 49-3.

Example 49-4. Invocation of `deposit` method on `Account` object in Example 49-3

```
<Account objREF="Acct:999-99-9999">
    <deposit>
      <amount currency="USD">10.00</amount>
    </deposit>
</Account>
```

Successful completion is confirmed by returning with no data.

Example 49-5. Successful return from Example 49-4

```
<Account-Reply>
   <deposit/>
</Account-Reply>
```

49.2.3 *Single transaction*

The account can also be opened more efficiently by combining the previous actions into a single transaction. To do so, we will need a way for the `deposit` method to reference the not-yet-created `Account` object, which of course doesn't yet have an object ID.

Example 49-6 defines two new attributes for the `Account` element type, `tempID` (temporary-ID) and `tempREF` (temporary-ID reference). If the user specifies a value for `tempID`, the system receiving the document retains the object for at least the remainder of the transaction, so that it can be referenced by a `tempREF` with that value within the transaction.

If, as is the case with `Account`, the object is persistent, it will survive the transaction. However, the `tempID` is not persistent; future references to that object must use its object ID.

Example 49-6. Additional attribute definitions for `Account` object class DTD

```
<!ATTLIST Account tempID  CDATA #IMPLIED
                  tempREF CDATA #IMPLIED>
```

With the new attributes defined, the `open account` transaction can be invoked as shown in Example 49-7. It specifies exactly the same set of operations as the two separate method invocations in Example 49-2 and Example 49-4.

Example 49-7. Transaction for method invocations in Example 49-2 and Example 49-4

```
<?xml version="1.0"?>
<open-account>
  <Bank>
    <createAccount tempID="account-1">
      <primary-ssn>999-99-9999</primary-ssn>
    </createAccount>
  </Bank>
  <!-- The tempREF attribute refers
       to the account just created -->
  <Account tempREF="account-1">
    <deposit>
      <amount currency="USD">10.00</amount>
    </deposit>
  </Account>
</open-account>
```

If all goes well, the reply document should appear as shown in Example 49-8, basically a concatenation of the replies in Example 49-3 and Example 49-5. Note that the `objID` is still accessible and may be retained by the client for future operations on the `Account`; the `tempID` is not.

Example 49-8. Reply returned by transaction in Example 49-7

```
<?xml version="1.0"?>
<open-account-reply>
   <Bank-Reply>
      <createAccount>
         <Account objID="Acct:999-99-9999"/>
      </createAccount>
   </Bank-Reply>
   <Account-Reply>
      <deposit/>
   </Account-Reply>
</open-account-reply>
```

WIDL and XML RPC

Application Discussion

- Application interoperability
- Web Interface Definition Language (WIDL)
- XML Remote Procedure Call (RPC)

©2000 THE XML HANDBOOK™

Chapter 50

XML goes a long way toward allowing applications to interoperate, but some think it needs to go a WIDL further. Among them are webMethods, Inc., `http://www.webmethods.com`, who sponsor this chapter, and Joe Lapp, who prepared it.

Engineers numbered 12-345-68 through 23-457-89 at Oops E-Commerce Corporation say "XML is the solution to interoperability". These engineers gang up on the managers until the corporate gears succumb and reverse direction. Soon the sales reps are saying the words "universal data format" more often than the words "object-oriented." Oops XML-enables its popular Loops product, renames the product to Xoops, and then ships Xoops out the door.

Over the following weeks we eavesdrop on the support engineers: "Well, if you have Company Q's product you can use our XML feature with it... Well, to get it to talk to your purchasing system, you'll have to XML-enable the purchasing system... Well, their program uses a different DTD from ours, so Xoops won't interoperate with it."

Whoops, Oops goofed with Xoops: XML alone is not quite enough.

50.1 | XML alone is not quite enough

A client that hands a server data must tell the server what to do with the data. The client does this by naming a service. A client must also understand the data that the service returns. Two applications may communicate only if they agree on the names of the services and on the types of the input and the output data.

Furthermore, applications must agree on how to represent this data in the messages that transfer between them. XML provides a way to represent the data, but it does not associate input data and output data with service names, and it does not provide a way to map between message types. Something is missing.

50.1.1 *The missing piece*

The obvious solution to the problem is to associate input DTDs with output DTDs and to give these associations service names. This does provide enough information for two applications to communicate, but it requires both applications to be XML-enabled and it requires the applications to conform to the same DTDs. While the number of XML-enabled applications is increasing rapidly, it is unlikely that all will agree on the same DTDs.

A better solution to the interoperability problem is to define application interfaces in an abstract way. Such abstractions are known as interface specifications.

Interface specifications allow developers to create different – but compatible – implementations of interfaces, thereby allowing applications written in different programming languages to communicate. Because the XML language, unlike programming languages, does not have built-in semantics, we need to go a step further. We must also bridge between applications whose XML messages conform to different DTDs.

The missing piece is an IDL – an *Interface Definition Language*. An IDL is a language in which interface specifications are written.

webMethods, Inc. has specified an IDL for this purpose, an IDL called WIDL. WIDL interface specifications enable middleware to map transparently between application interfaces and XML message DTDs. By delegating XML intelligence and accessibility issues to IDL-aware middleware, we also simplify the application. An IDL such as WIDL allows us to maximize an application's accessibility.

50.1.2 *The role of WIDL*

WIDL is an acronym for *Web Interface Definition Language*. It is an IDL that is expressed in XML. OMG IDL and Microsoft IDL are other examples of IDLs, but WIDL differs from them in several respects.

The WIDL design is the result of a principled attempt to provide 80% of the capability of a conventional IDL with only 20% of the complexity. The objective was to make WIDL easy to learn, easy to read, and relatively easy to implement.

This fact provides WIDL with a potentially large user base, but still leaves room for more sophisticated IDLs, including new ones based on XML. WIDL also differs from conventional IDLs by requiring all data items to have names, which simplifies the process of translating documents into interfaces.

webMethods originally developed WIDL to wrap Web sites within APIs, thereby giving applications programmatic access to the Web. Consequently, the WIDL 1.x and 2.x specifications defined a single language that both specified interfaces and defined how interface specifications map onto a website.

WIDL 3.0 places the interface specification and the document-mapping implementation in separate XML documents. WIDL 3.0 therefore defines two components: an IDL component and a document-mapping component. Together these components allow applications to communicate over a network regardless of the programming languages in which the applications are written, regardless of whether the applications speak XML, and regardless of the DTDs to which XML-speaking applications conform.

50.2 | WIDL the IDL

Let's take a look at the IDL component of WIDL 3.0. Example 50-1 shows a short but complete example of a WIDL 3.0 interface specification.

A WIDL document specifies a single interface. Example 50-2 is a DTD that defines WIDL documents sufficiently for our purposes.

Interfaces should have names that are unique within their scope of use. Naming an interface relative to the reverse order of a domain name provides one way to accomplish this. A client may then identify interfaces by name.

Example 50-1. A WIDL 3.0 interface specification.

```
<WIDL NAME="com.Fortunes-R-Us.Purchasing" VERSION="3.0">
  <RECORD NAME="FortuneOrder">
    <VALUE NAME="accountID" TYPE="i4"/>
    <VALUE NAME="zodiacSign"/>
  </RECORD>
  <RECORD NAME="FortuneReceipt">
    <VALUE NAME="orderNumber" TYPE="i4"/>
    <VALUE NAME="fortune"/>
    <VALUE NAME="accountBalance" TYPE="r4"/>
  </RECORD>
  <METHOD NAME="orderFortune" INPUT="FortuneOrder"
      OUTPUT="FortuneReceipt" RETURN="orderNumber"/>
</WIDL>
```

A WIDL element contains one or more RECORD or METHOD elements.

50.2.1 *Methods*

The METHOD element identifies a service that the client may invoke.

Method names must be unique within the document. Methods may optionally have input and output parameters, as indicated by the optional INPUT and OUTPUT attributes.

The INPUT attribute provides a link to a RECORD element that enumerates the method's input parameters. The OUTPUT attribute provides a link to a RECORD element that enumerates the method's output parameters. The tag may optionally indicate that one of the output parameters is the return value of the method when the interface is implemented in a programming language. Methods may also identify the exceptions that they raise in order to report method invocation failures.

50.2.2 *Records*

A RECORD element represents a record and conforms to the DTD shown in Example 50-2. Record names must be unique within a document. A record consists of a collection of zero or more parameter elements, each of which must have a unique name within the scope of the record. If the record provides a BASE attribute, the record inherits all of the named

Example 50-2. WIDL interface DTD.

```
<!ELEMENT WIDL      (RECORD | METHOD)+ >
<!ATTLIST WIDL
          NAME      CDATA #REQUIRED
          VERSION   CDATA #FIXED "3.0"
>
<!ELEMENT METHOD    EMPTY>
<!ATTLIST METHOD
          NAME      CDATA #REQUIRED
          INPUT     CDATA #IMPLIED
          OUTPUT    CDATA #IMPLIED
          RETURN    CDATA #IMPLIED
>
<!ELEMENT RECORD    (VALUE | LIST | RECORDREF)* >
<!ATTLIST RECORD
          NAME      CDATA #REQUIRED
          BASE      CDATA #IMPLIED
>
     <!-- Parameters -->
<!ELEMENT VALUE     EMPTY >
<!ATTLIST VALUE
          NAME      CDATA #REQUIRED
          TYPE      CDATA "string"
          DIM       NMTOKEN "0"
>
<!ELEMENT LIST      EMPTY >
<!ATTLIST LIST
          NAME      CDATA #REQUIRED
          DIM       NMTOKEN "0"
>
<!ELEMENT RECORDREF EMPTY >
<!ATTLIST RECORDREF
          NAME      CDATA #REQUIRED
          RECORD    CDATA #IMPLIED
          DIM       NMTOKEN "0"
>
```

parameter elements found within the RECORD element to which the attribute points.

The parameter element types are VALUE, LIST, and RECORDREF.

VALUE

An element that represents lexical data and has an optional TYPE attribute that identifies the datatype. Datatypes include strings ("string"), integers ("i4"), and floats ("r4").

LIST
: A LIST element represents a vector of arbitrary size consisting of an arbitrary set of types.

RECORDREF
: The RECORDREF element identifies a RECORD element that nests within the RECORDREF's parent record.

Parameters have an optional DIM attribute. When DIM has a value of "1" or "2" the parameter represents a single- or two-dimensional array. When the attribute is absent, the value defaults to "0" to indicate that the parameter is a single data item and not an array.

WIDL provides only a small number of simple data types. These data types are sufficient to represent most of the types available to programming languages. WIDL is compatible with other data definition languages such as XML-Data and Resource Description Framework (RDF), so WIDL may accommodate the sophisticated schema languages that are emerging. This allows WIDL to support complex data types without itself becoming complex.

50.3 | Remote procedure calls

WIDL provides the information that applications need to communicate, but it does not perform the actual communication. An application that requests a service of another application must issue a Remote Procedure Call, or RPC, to the other application. An application issues an RPC by packaging a message, sending the message to the other application, and then waiting for the reply message.

The RPC mechanism requires the applications to agree on the form of the messages and on the transfer protocol by which the messages travel. HTTP provides a POST method that allows a client to submit a document to a server and to receive a document in response, so HTTP is a candidate protocol. Since HTTP is nearly ubiquitous and since it tunnels through firewalls, it's obvious that we should use HTTP. The question is, should XML be the message form?

IIOP and DCE are both industry standards for RPC messages. Either of these would work, as it is possible to send them over HTTP. We might notice that these message representations are inflexible: senders and receivers must agree on how a message decomposes data into arguments, including the positions of the individual arguments and the structures of these arguments.

Yet if the message representation were XML, the applications would still have to agree on the DTDs to which the messages conformed. Just as applications that use different IIOP or DCE message types cannot communicate, applications that use different DTDs cannot communicate. Without looking more closely, we might be inclined to conclude that XML is all hype after all.

However, we *are* going to look more closely. These problems do afflict XML, IIOP, and DCE alike. No reneging here. When we take that closer look we find that, unlike IIOP and DCE, XML provides a way to solve the problem.

That is, XML provides a way to ensure that so long as two applications agree to conform to the same abstract interface specification, then those two applications may communicate – even if the applications are hard-coded to use different DTDs.

50.3.1 *Representing RPC messages in XML*

XML is an ideal notation for RPC messages because it allows us to label the individual data constituents of a message semantically. These labels are XML's tags.

The only semantic labels available in IIOP and DCE are the numeric positions of the constituents. IIOP and DCE do not allow data to move to new positions and they do not allow data to grow or shrink in unforeseen ways. They also do not allow applications to discover the absence of data from a message or to introduce new data items into a message independently.

But the greatest benefit that XML brings to RPC is that XML moves a significant amount of information about a message into the message itself. It is a benefit because it moves an equal amount of information out of the programs that process the messages. This simplifies the programs that integrate applications.

In all probability, industries will never completely agree on standard interfaces or standard DTDs, so it will always be necessary to translate between interfaces. XML provides interoperability by enabling a new class of middleware to serve as generic application integrators.

50.3.2 *Generic and custom message DTDs*

There are two ways to represent RPC messages in XML. A generic document type is capable of representing any message. The interface specification determines the form that a message takes in a generic document type.

More specifically, the definition of a method uniquely determines the DTDs of the request and reply messages that correspond to the method.

On the other hand, a custom document type is designed only to contain the inputs or the outputs of a particular kind of service. There are many possible custom document type definitions for a given interface method.

Let's look at a few examples that are based on the Fortunes-R-Us purchasing interface shown in Example 50-1. Example 50-3 contains three RPC messages.

The first portrays what an instance of a generic document type might look like for a message that invokes the "orderFortune" method. The same document type scheme might be used for the reply message, which is the second message of Example 50-3. The third message shown is an instance of a custom-DTD reply.

Example 50-3. Generic- and custom-DTD RPC messages.

```
<RPC TYPE="REQUEST">
  <VALUE NAME="accountID" TYPE="i4">2001</VALUE>
  <VALUE NAME="zodiacSign">Aquarius</VALUE>
</RPC>

<RPC TYPE="REPLY">
  <VALUE NAME="orderNumber" TYPE="i4">438553</VALUE>
  <VALUE NAME="fortune">You will use XML for RPC</VALUE>
  <VALUE NAME="accountBalance" TYPE="r4">65.00</VALUE>
</RPC>

<FORTUNE-RECEIPT>
  <orderNumber>438553</orderNumber>
  <fortune>You will use XML for RPC</fortune>
  <accountBalance>65.00</accountBalance>
</FORTUNE-RECEIPT>
```

There are many possible generic XML document types, and we can expect to see industries creating them and using them. There are also many possible custom document types for any given method. We can also expect to see applications using custom document types to message other applications.

The trick is to ensure that we can integrate applications that use different document types to represent the same information. Without this we do not have interoperability. XML makes it feasible to provide large-scale interoperability, but only if we design our messages so that integration middleware may robustly identify data constituents by label.

50.4 | Integrating applications

WIDL and XML RPC together enable middleware to integrate applications. We'll use the term *integration server* to refer to middleware that assumes this kind of responsibility.

A WIDL interface specification supplies an integration server with the information the server needs to map between XML RPC messages and native application interfaces. Interface specifications do not themselves define the mappings, but they provide a common language in which to express them.

Figure 50-1 shows how integration servers connect applications.

Integration servers need to integrate a wide variety of application interfaces. One application may implement an interface as a set of Java or C++ methods. Another may implement an interface as a set of functions in C.

Another application may input and output XML documents conforming to custom DTDs. Still another may input and output XML documents in the form of generic RPC messages. Integrating applications requires bridging between programming languages and document representations.

50.4.1 *Stubs*

Conventional RPC bridges programming languages through code snippets known as *stubs*. A stub translates between the details of an interface and a common data representation. One side of a stub speaks the language that is

©2000 THE XML HANDBOOK™

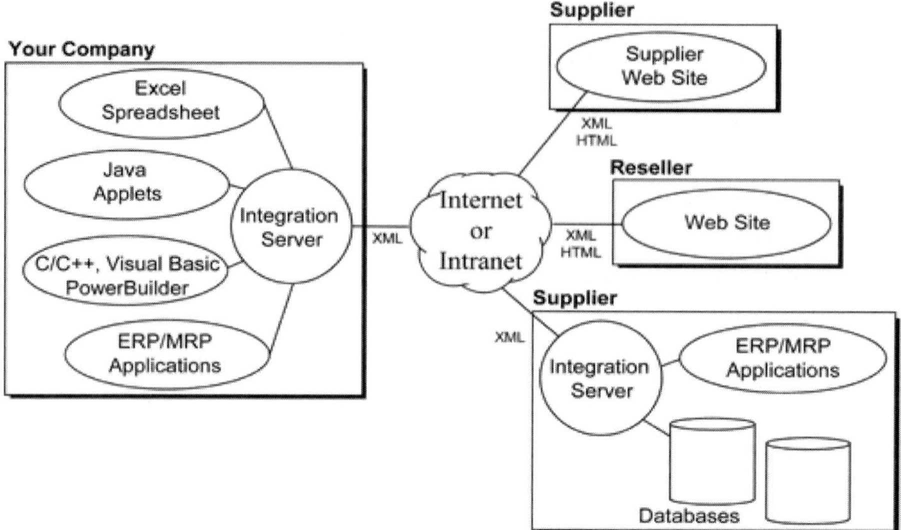

Figure 50-1 Connecting applications with XML RPC and integration servers.

native to an application and the other side speaks a common data representation.

By connecting the data representation ends of two stubs, one may bridge between any two programming languages. In a client stub, the language-specific side consists of a set of APIs (functions) that the client may call. In a server stub, the language-specific side calls APIs that the server itself exposes.

Figure 50-2 illustrates this property of stubs by portraying four stub pairings. Here, XML is the common data representation, but in the usual case intervening middleware will hide knowledge of XML from the stubs.

In diagram (a) an application written in Java is communicating with another application written in Java. Diagrams (b) and (c) show that the same application may also communicate with applications written in C++ or C. Diagram (d) depicts the Java application communicating with an application that speaks XML. In this last scenario the XML-speaking application has no stub, since the XML messages pass directly to the application.

Figure 50-3 portrays how a developer uses stubs to integrate applications. A developer generates an interface specification in WIDL and then runs the specification through a WIDL compiler.

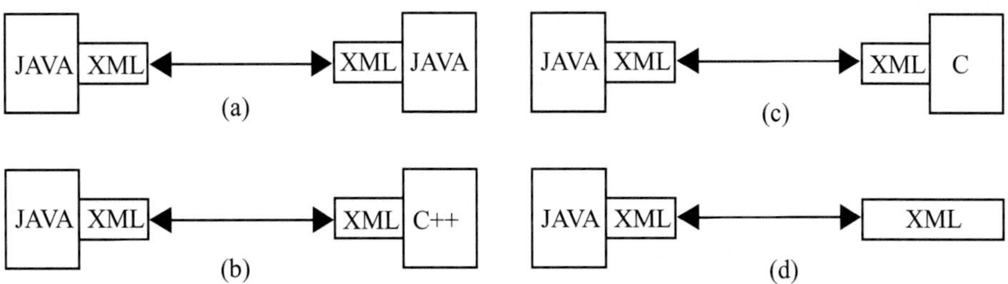

Figure 50-2 Using stubs to make applications interoperable.

The WIDL compiler generates two source files in a programming language of the developer's choice. Both files are stubs, but one file is a client stub and the other is a server stub. The developer then links the appropriate stub into the client or server application. The stubs free the application from knowledge of XML and allow middleware to map transparently between interfaces and different XML document types.

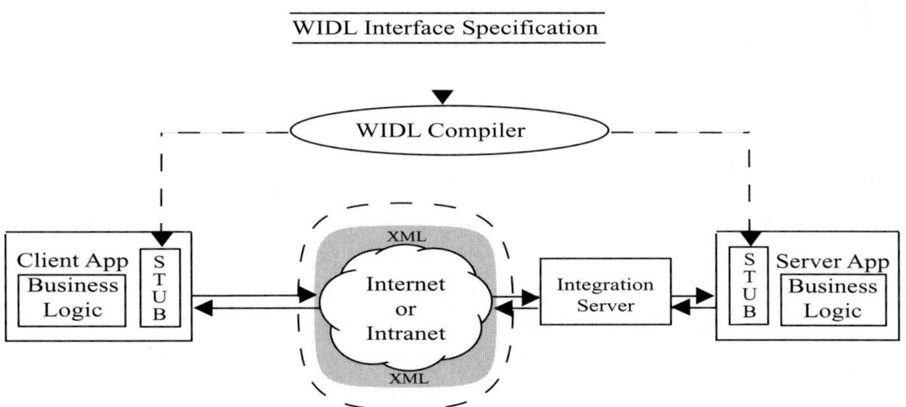

Figure 50-3 Using WIDL for RPC over the Web.

50.4.2 *Document mapping*

The document-mapping component of WIDL defines mappings between interfaces and XML or HTML documents. This is the portion that provides the bridge between XML RPC messages and application APIs; that is, the portion that makes the different XML document types indistinguishable to the application. webMethods originally developed this facility to encapsulate HTML-based websites within APIs, but because XML does a better job of labeling data than HTML does, the technology reaps more benefits from XML.

WIDL document-mapping does its job through *bindings*. A binding specifies how to map raw data into an RPC message or vice versa, where "raw data" means "data represented in a way that is natural to a programming language". The best way to make sense of this is to look at an example, so consider Example 50-4.

Example 50-4. A WIDL binding.

```
<OUTPUT-BINDING NAME="OrderReplyBinding">
  <VALUE NAME="orderNumber" TYPE="i4"/>
       doc.orderNumber[0].text</VALUE>
  <VALUE NAME="fortune">doc.fortune[0].text</VALUE>
</OUTPUT-BINDING>
```

This binding applies to the custom-DTD reply message of Example 50-3. Each VALUE element corresponds to a data item that the binding extracts from the message. In this case the binding extracts two strings, but bindings may extract other data types, including records and even XML documents.

Upon receiving the reply message, middleware applies this binding and passes the two strings to the application. Since the application ordered the fortune by issuing a function call on a client stub, the stub returns the strings to the application as output parameters of the function. Middleware completely shields the application from knowledge of XML and from dependence on a specific XML document type.

In this example, the binding only retrieves the order number and the fortune from the reply message, indicating that the application cannot utilize the account balance. The content of each VALUE element is a query, expressed in a document query language, that specifies where to find these items within the message. In this particular case, the query uses the webMethods Object Model, but WIDL is compatible with other query languages as well.

A binding may also define how to translate data into an RPC message. WIDL supports several forms of messages. For request messages, the binding may have the data submitted via the HTTP GET or POST methods, thus providing the data as CGI query parameters. The binding may also have the data submitted as an XML or an HTML message, constructing the message from a particular template. Templates are a straightforward way to generate XML.

Bindings provide a simple way to make applications compatible with a variety of XML message DTDs. Bindings are most useful with custom document types, since it is possible to hard-code document-mapping for generic document types. Generic document types do not require the flexibility that bindings provide, and by hard-coding them middleware can provide more efficient document-mapping.

An integration server puts bindings to work by using them to mask differences in XML document types. By connecting the variable names of bindings to parameter names in interface specifications, an integration server may map any XML document type into any programming language.

To get a feel for the benefits of this capability, take a look at Figure 50-4. Here industries and businesses have defined a variety of DTDs to which different RPC document types conform. The interface defined with WIDL captures a superset of the services and data available through the DTDs. Although different client applications use different XML document types, the integration server is able to bridge these differences to make the application universally accessible.

50.5 | Interoperability attained

WIDL, XML RPC, and integration servers are the pieces that provide application interoperability. With them one can make any application accessible over a network via XML and HTTP.

One can also make a single application available to client applications that use different XML message formats. Or one can upgrade an application, or substitute one application for another, and still allow all previous clients to communicate with the new application.

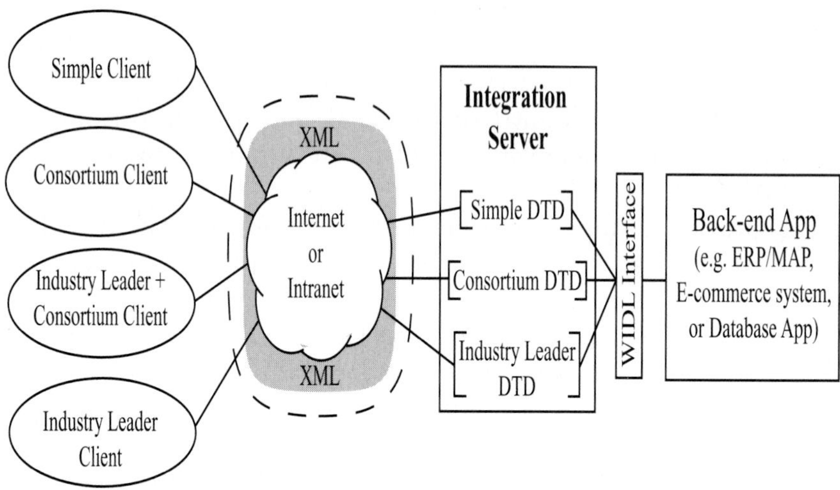

Figure 50-4 Using WIDL to make different XML messages interoperable.

These capabilities should give us second thoughts about hard-coding servers to use specific XML document types. Servers should leave document type decisions to middleware, empowering middleware to make the server widely accessible.

Bean Markup Language (BML)

Application Discussion

- XML active content
- Create, configure, and connect JavaBeans
- Dynamic applications
- Free BML processors on CD-ROM

©2000 The XML Handbook™

Chapter 51

There is a wonderful feeling of empowerment that comes from editing a document and seeing an executing program in the next window instantly change its behavior. IBM alphaWorks, `http://www.alphaworks.ibm.com/`, brings that power to the people in this chapter, which was prepared by David A. Epstein and Sanjiva Weerawarana.

Most applications view XML documents strictly as data to be operated upon. However, there is a steadily growing use of XML to provide active content: descriptions of executable objects. Examples can be found in the use of XML to describe remote procedure calls, the design of wizards and user interfaces, and component programming models. The advantage that XML active content has is that all of the standard XML tools and facilities are now becoming available as part of the infrastructure, a luxury that most other programming systems did not enjoy.

51.1 | BML: The reason why

The development and evolution of BML grew out of a simple challenge: "Create a mechanism in *Java*, using the XML family of standards, that can take a description of a hierarchically structured set of data and automatically synthesize a user interface to collect and display that data."

In retrospect, this direction was close, but not quite correct. A faithful implementation of such a mechanism would only yield an interface for a single instance of the data. The true intention had been to generate an interface for the entire class, supporting all of the potentially allowable data hierarchies. The correct challenge should have been to synthesize interfaces automatically from the DTD describing the data hierarchy class.

It quickly became clear that, given the use of XSLT as a transformation mechanism to generate the executable interface specification, plus the need for extensibility and maintainability, a generic mechanism for describing arbitrary user interface elements would be necessary. What followed was the complete factoring out of any interface-specific requirements. Thus was BML born.

51.1.1 *What is BML?*

The *Bean Markup Language* is really two separate things: a BML document type and a BML processor.

51.1.1.1 BML document type

A BML document is a valid XML document that describes the creation, configuration, and interconnection structure of a set of *JavaBeans*. It is not XMLized *Java* syntax, nor is it a Turing-complete programming language. It does not support conditional or flow of control constructs.

The vocabulary defined by the BML DTD is a language whose functions are to describe how components relate to one another and how each of those components is configured. It is not, however, a modeling language. While it is declarative, it is still directly executable.

51.1.1.2 BML processor

BML also includes the notion of a *BML processor*, a component that is capable of processing documents conforming to the BML DTD. Two instances of BML processors are currently available:

- The BML Player is a very small (approximately 35K jar file) run-time kernel that processes BML documents and document fragments and dynamically creates, accesses, and configures beans. After interpretation of the BML, the Player sits quietly on the side, allowing the configured beans to operate independently with no performance penalties.

- The BML Compiler converts BML into reflection-free *Java* code.

51.1.2 *Objectives of BML*

During BML's design and development, several key goals were conscientiously observed.

1. It was desired that the BML language element types define a minimal set of basic operators necessary to configure any set of *JavaBeans* (in fact, objects).
2. No assumptions were to be made about the type of bean being configured, the types of events that the beans could throw, the datatypes of properties or fields, or the types of containers that could be used for creating hierarchies.
3. BML implementations should be compact and easily embeddable in other software.
4. Objects created and/or configured by BML should interact easily and naturally with objects created and/or configured by other means.

51.2 | BML language elements

The BML language has been carefully designed both for easy generation by machine and for writing by hand. Unlike programming language syntax, which often obscures the semantics of an application's component structure, BML provides a first-class, declarative mechanism for explicitly describing this structure.

In addition, since BML is an XML document type, all of the tools available for use with XML are now available for application and active content development. Specifically, one can now think about using XSLT to style an application based upon a functional description, or on an individual user's needs or abilities.

This list briefly summarizes each of the BML language element types, which will be examined in greater detail below. The BML DTD, which formally defines the relationships between the element types and defines all of the attributes, can be found on the CD-ROM.

bean
: Create a new bean or look one up

args
: Specify constructor arguments

string
: Create a new string bean or look one up

property
: Set or get a bean property

field
: Set or get a bean field

event-binding
: Bind an event from one bean to another, or to a script

call-method
: Call a bean method

cast
: Convert the type of a bean or value

add
: Create a hierarchy of beans by adding one to another

script
: Defines a (BML or other) script to be used somewhere

In addition to the element types, BML processors also support a single processing instruction that can be used to load components into the processor's runtime.

51.2.1 *Bean creation and access*

A `bean` element is used to create new beans, as specified by its *class* attribute, or to look up beans by name. Once a bean has been created or looked up, the children of the bean element are processed, using the parent as the default target of the operations they perform. If there are no child elements, then processing a `bean` element simply results in that bean.

The creation of a bean may result either in its resurrection from a serialized file or in the creation of a new instance of a class. During resurrection or creation, the bean may optionally be registered into BML's object registry via the bean's `id` attribute. Previously registered beans may also be looked up in the BML object registry, a feature used primarily for making an already existing bean the default target object.

By default, the bean's no-args constructor is used when creating class instances. Should a different constructor be required, an `args` element is used to indicate the series of values to be passed to the constructor. After each of these elements is evaluated, the constructor whose signature matches the resulting argument types is located and used to instantiate the bean.

A special feature of the `bean` element type allows one to look up the java.lang.Class object representing a *Java* class so that static methods may be accessed. Special recognition has also been given to the names that represent primitive types, such as “char”, “float”, etc.

Because *Java* string objects (instances of the class java.lang.String) are immutable they need to be treated specially. The only way to create a non-empty string is to specifically use the constructor that takes a literal string (i.e. one enclosed in quotes) as its input.

It first appears straightforward to use an `args` element for this purpose. However, XML's white-space sensitivity in CDATA sections, when coupled with simple formatting, can produce unpredictable results. The solution employed by BML is a special `string` element for which the relationship between the element's markup and its data content is significant.

51.2.2 *Property and field configuration*

A `property` element is used to both get and set the values of a bean's properties. When setting the value of a property, it may either be set to an *imme-*

©2000 THE XML HANDBOOK™

diate value – declared directly in the markup – or to the result of some child element of the property element.

The target object for property operations is the parent bean of the property element, unless otherwise indicated by the property's target attribute. Note that the scoping of this change in target resides solely in the retargeted element and is not propagated to its children.

Properties whose values are primitive types, as opposed to object types, may be set directly via the value attribute. If the type of the supplied value does not match, or is not assignable to, that of the property, then a type conversion is necessary. When this situation is detected, BML dynamically selects an appropriate type convertor from its type convertor registry and applies it to produce a value of an appropriate type.

The value of a property is obtained simply by specifying the property's name in the name attribute and not including a value in either the value attribute or in the element's content. Indexed properties are handled through the specification of the property's index as the value of the index attribute.

When a property element is used to get the value of a property, that value is returned. When it is used to set the value of a property nothing is returned. The latter variation of the element type is only valid as a direct child of a bean element.

Not all objects are "good" beans; that is, they do not conform to the *JavaBean* design patterns for properties but simply use fields instead. BML therefore provides the field element type for getting and setting the values of an object's fields directly. The semantics and attributes associated with this element type are identical to those that can be specified for a property element, with the one exception that a value is always returned.

51.2.3 *Event binding*

The BML event-binding element type supports the binding of events, specified by the name attribute, that are emitted by a bean. The *JavaBeans* event model states that if a bean generates an event of type XEvent, then any listener that implements the XListener interface[1] can be registered and will receive notification of the event whenever it is generated.

1. XListener is a set of methods through which the event is delivered to the event listeners.

In addition to supporting this conventional form of event bindings, the `event-binding` element type also supports an extended form of event binding that allows events to be bound, via a `script` element, to an arbitrary set of actions. This extended form of event bindings allows third party interactions to be initiated when an event occurs.

51.2.4 *Bean method calls*

While BML is primarily a declarative language, it does provide a mechanism, the `call-method` element type, for directly enabling inline method invocations. The method to be invoked is specified in the element's *name* attribute.

Unless otherwise specified by the *target* attribute, the object on which the method is invoked is the one identified by the parent `bean` element. The children of the `call-method` element are used as the arguments to the method.

The specific version of the method that is ultimately called is determined by examining the types of each of the arguments and applying the *Java* language's method resolution algorithm. Static class methods can be invoked by setting the target object to the Class object for the desired class.

51.2.5 *Explicit type conversions*

BML's `property` and `field` elements may implicitly invoke a type convertor that converts one type to another. The `cast` element enables the explicit specification of a type.

Depending on the conversion being performed, the effect of using the `cast` element may be:

- Purely declarative, a simple relabelling of a class to one of its superclasses or interfaces; or
- Actual, in which case an actual type conversion is performed.

If the `cast` element is empty, then a null object of the specified class is returned.

©2000 THE XML HANDBOOK™

51.2.6 *Bean hierarchy creation*

Hierarchies and collections of beans may be constructed by the `add` element. It provides an abstraction for the process of creating bean hierarchies and allows the use of a single element to "add" a contained bean to some container bean without the necessity of knowing the specific types of the beans being operated upon.

The original motivation for the `add` element came from the importance of hierarchy creation in the development of user interfaces, and the desire for easy automatic synthesis of these hierarchies. However, the concept is well-defined for any bean that may serve as a container or collector of other beans, such as vectors, hash tables, and visual containers.

51.2.7 *BML script definition*

The `script` element is used to define an executable sequence of scripting statements in BML or a supported scripting language. BML v2.2 supports the use of BML, *JavaScript*, and *NetRexx* as scripting languages.

The element's *language* attribute is used to identify the particular scripting language. The *src* attribute may be used to specify a URL from which the script should be loaded.

Evaluating a script results in the return of a bean. When the script is written in BML the returned bean is the last element in the script. The return value from other scripting languages is language-dependent, although typically it is the result of evaluating the last script statement.

Arguments to the script can be obtained from the object registry through the use of a set of automatically pre-registered names that are of the form *script:arg***n**. Script elements that are descendants of an `event-binding` element are executed whenever that event is fired; other script elements are executed immediately.

51.3 | The BML processing model

A BML script is an XML document whose document element is a `bean` element. Arbitrary configurations of this and other beans can be expressed within this element using combinations of the element types defined in the BML DTD.

A BML script is evaluated in linear order of the XML document string. More formally, this constitutes a preorder traversal of the DOM tree that represents the conceptual document.

The bean defined by the document element is produced and configured according to the specifications contained within that element. These specifications may include the creation and configuration of other beans.

There are currently two BML processor implementations, the *player* and the *compiler*.

The player uses *Java* reflection to evaluate a BML script from within the context of a larger application. This evaluation often, but not necessarily, occurs during the application's start-up processing.

The compiler is a static tool that generates *Java* code which, at start-up time, will produce a bean configuration equivalent to that described by the script. During compilation, the compiler may temporarily instantiate some beans to learn about their properties, events and methods, but such beans are discarded after the compilation process. Because of this fact, the BML compiler may sometimes require a `bean` element's *class* attribute to be specified even when the bean is used simply for configuration.

According to the *JavaBeans* definitions, a bean's existence is divided into two phases, configuration and run time. During configuration time, a bean has the opportunity to exhibit a configuration user interface. This is typically done within the context of some kind of builder environment. The BML processing model views this configuration time as a process that has already occurred in the environment used to produce BML.

51.4 | A BML example: The Juggler

Example 51-1, which along with several others can be found on the accompanying CD, illustrates how BML can be used to construct and then modify an application. The application is a modification of the now famous *Juggler*, that is often used to demonstrate visual builders. It is shown in Figure 51-1.

In it, a simple animation widget is connected to a set of buttons to start and stop the animation. First, a grey frame that uses border layout is constructed. The animation widget is inserted into the center of the frame and

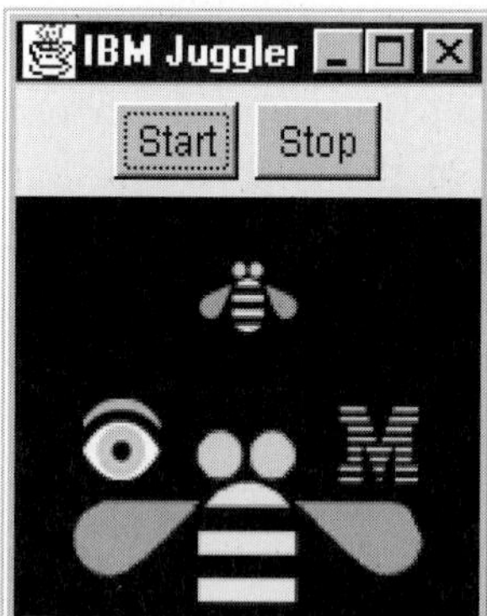

Figure 51-1 The original *Juggler*

started. Finally, two buttons, bound to the *Juggler*'s start and stop methods, respectively, are constructed and put into a panel which is then placed along the top edge of the frame.

In Example 51-2, the *Juggler* application is incrementally modified while it is still running. A slider is added along the right-hand side that controls the speed at which the animation occurs. This is shown in Figure 51-2.

51.5 | The dynamic application spectrum

Application structures form a continuum, the dynamic application spectrum, along which they are increasingly able to take advantage of active content. While Figure 51-3 illustrates only a few of the key positions along the spectrum, it is important to understand that it is a spectrum, as opposed to a series of discrete steps. Consequently, transitions between the levels of functionality can occur smoothly and different portions of an application may be operating simultaneously in different portions of the spectrum. The capability of the BML player to instantiate, configure, and bind objects dynamically enables it to be used over a broad range of this spectrum (see Figure 51-4).

Let's look at the spectrum, starting at the simplest extreme.

Example 51-1. The original *Juggler*

```
<?xml version="1.0"?>
<bean class="java.awt.Frame" id="topFrame">
  <property name="title" value="IBM Juggler"/>
  <property name="background" value="0xeeeeee"/>
  <property name="layout">
    <bean class="java.awt.BorderLayout"/>
  </property>
  <add>
    <bean class="demos.juggler.Juggler" id="Juggler">
      <property name="animationRate" value="110"/>
      <call-method name="start"/>
    </bean>
    <string value="Center"/>
  </add>
  <add>
    <bean class="java.awt.Panel">
      <add>
        <bean class="java.awt.Button">
          <property name="label" value="Start"/>
          <event-binding name="action">
            <script>
              <call-method target="Juggler"
                           name="start"/>
            </script>
          </event-binding>
        </bean>
      </add>
      <add>
        <bean class="java.awt.Button">
          <property name="label" value="Stop"/>
          <event-binding name="action">
            <script>
              <call-method target="Juggler"
                           name="stop"/>
            </script>
          </event-binding>
        </bean>
      </add>
    </bean>
    <string value="North"/>
  </add>
</bean>
```

Example 51-2. Adding a slider to the *Juggler*

```
<?xml version="1.0"?>
<bean source="topFrame">
  <add>
    <bean class="java.awt.Scrollbar" id="scale">
     <property name="minimum" value="0"/>
      <property name="maximum" value="220"/>
      <property name="value">
        <property name="animationRate"
                  target="Juggler"/>
    </property>
      <event-binding name="adjustment">
        <script>
          <property target="Juggler"
                    name="animationRate">
            <property target="event:arg1"
                      name="value"/>
          </property>
        </script>
      </event-binding>
    </bean>
    <string value="East"/>
  </add>
 <call-method name="pack"/>
</bean>
```

Figure 51-2 The augmented *Juggler*

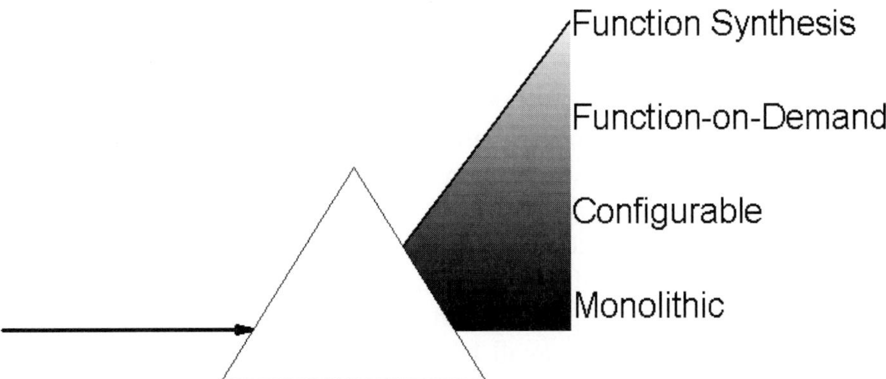

Figure 51-3 The dynamic application spectrum

51.5.1 *Monolithic applications*

Monolithic applications, despite being constructed using object-oriented methodologies, are not configurable at all. They simply execute without the ability to be customized. Applications in this class can be described in a single BML document that is either played or compiled and then run.

51.5.2 *Configurable applications*

While some or even much of a configurable application's functionality is defined in a monolithic manner, some of its components can be configured at runtime from an external source. Such applications can easily take advantage of BML to free themselves of additional parsing and setup functionality that are not key to their core operations.

To do so, the BML player is included and instantiated in the application and objects requiring configuration are registered into the BML object registry. Then the configuration settings – typically just property and field settings – are read in from an external source.

51.5.3 *Function on demand*

Function on demand is often implemented through externalization of functionality. As applications continue to expand and evolve, there has been a growing trend towards modularization. However, even with many of the current object techniques, the entire functionality of the application is effectively bound at compile time.

Because it can dynamically instantiate large functional blocks, BML enables the decoupling and externalization of functionality from an application's core. That allows applications to be restructured to consist of a series of functional blocks and a small kernel that initializes and mediates the interactions among them.

As specific functionality is needed – or even anticipated in a predictive manner to improve performance – it can be instantiated and added into the already running application. This saves application start-up time and memory usage and allows functional blocks to be updated individually, or even supplied after initial application deployment.

51.5.4 *Function synthesis*

Finally, at the far end of the spectrum is the ability to synthesize functionality automatically. While this capability has not yet been employed in practice, it is considered feasible. That is because of the BML player's ability to instantiate function dynamically, coupled with the availability of XML abstractions and XSLT or other generational capabilities. It is a topic of ongoing research.

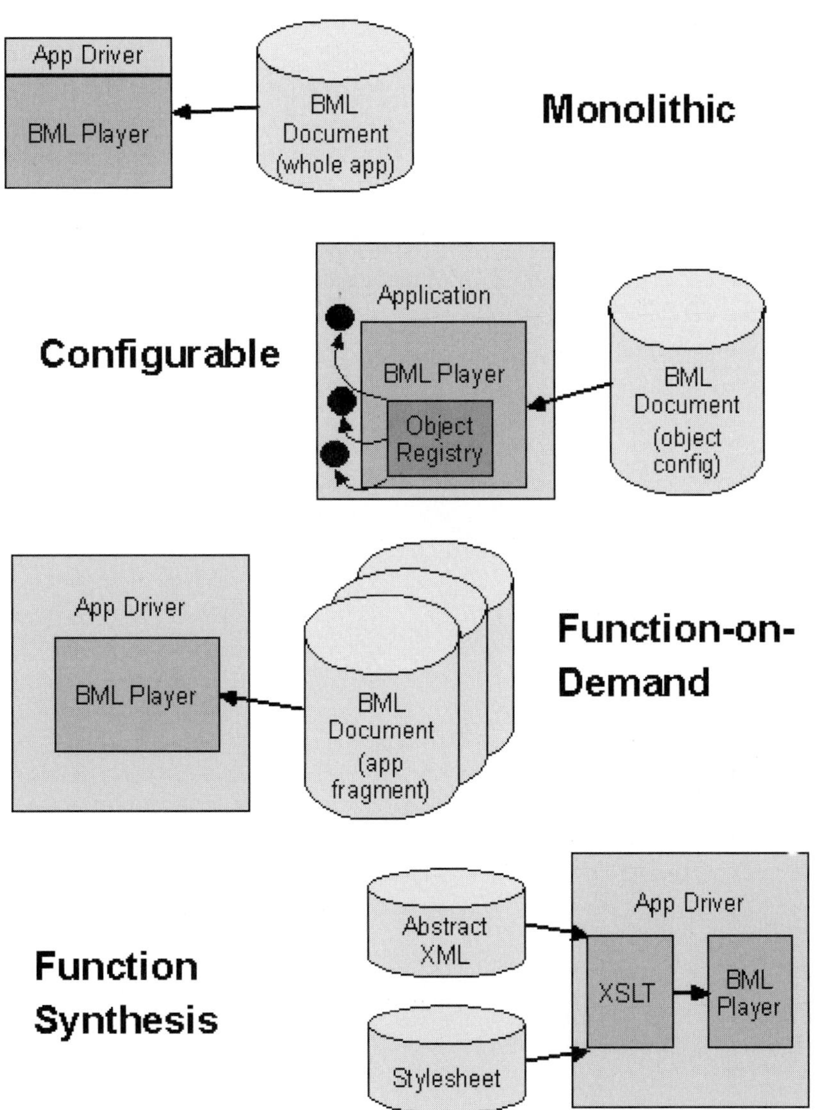

Figure 51-4 BML program structures for points along the dynamic application spectrum

51.6 | Summary

Bean Markup Language from IBM *alphaWorks* provides a mechanism for implementing active content. Through its use, applications can more easily move along the dynamic application spectrum.

Tip *There is lots of other free alphaWorks software where this came from. See 65.2, "IBM alphaWorks", on page 956 and the CD-ROM.*

Luxembourg Police

Case Study

- XML component model and framework
- Automatic code generation
- Uniform interface generation

©2000 THE XML HANDBOOK™

Chapter 52

We've seen that XML can manage content, integrate disparate data sources, and be a model for distributed computing, but why stop at that? Why not let it generate the code as well? So say the envelope pushers at SGML Technologies Group, `http://www.sgmltech.com/`, who sponsor this chapter. It was prepared by Jacques Kasprzak.

INGEPOL is a project of the Gendarmerie Luxembourgeoise, the national police force of Luxembourg. The objective is to deploy a system to automate the creation, administration, and utilization of a centralized database for use by national and local police.

The database includes all facets of police information, including not only case management but also descriptions of people and such objects as firearms, jewelry, driving licenses, stolen vehicles, bank notes, drugs, and art objects.

Distribution of the information, and exchanges with distributed police and administrative systems, are important functions of the system. These functions raise information security issues such as confidentiality, availability, and integrity.

The idea is to improve the effectiveness of all aspects of police work in the field: crime prevention, searches, investigations, and the prosecution of offenders. The method is to give all police throughout Luxembourg the ability to query a complex system of data compiled from many sources, but in a manner that is transparent to the end-user.

The Gendarmerie teamed with SGML Technologies Group to design and develop the system.

52.1 | System architecture

Because the aim of the INGEPOL system is to communicate with distant partner systems, and to centralize and spread information to different units (squads and police stations), a three-tier client/server architecture was chosen (see Figure 52-1).

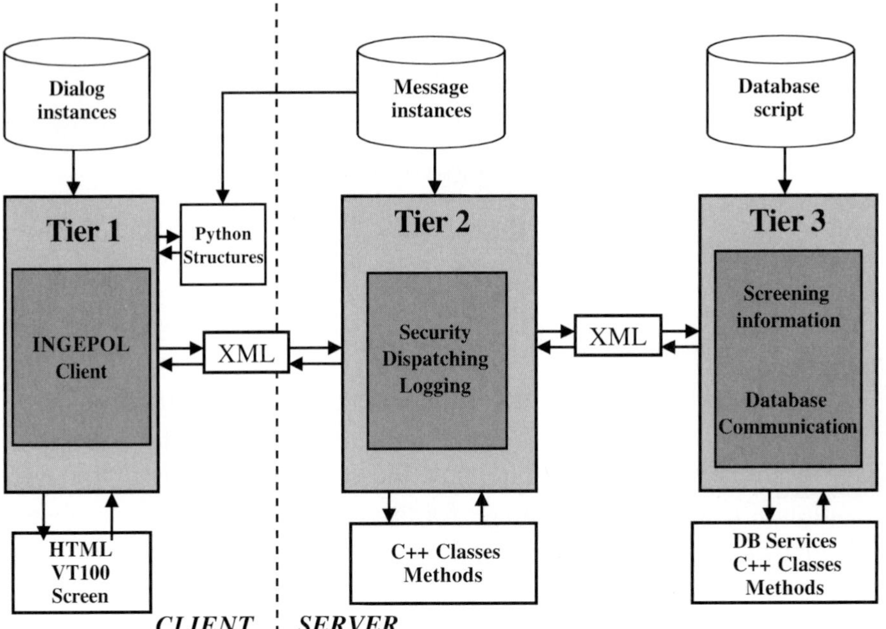

Figure 52-1 Overall architecture of INGEPOL

The three tiers of the system are:

- the client workstations;
- a group of specialized servers that process management rules (security, validation, dispatching, audit, etc.);
- heterogeneous information sources (which give rise to the familiar problems of data integration).

The three tiers communicate by means of XML messages. The messages are structured in three layers:

security
: This layer allows enciphering and deciphering of data transported on the system.

messaging properties
: These include the server addressed, the message family, the expected processing method, the objects affected, etc.

information content
: The content is abstract data that is transformed and/or rendered as required by the target systems.

An XML parser decomposes the message into its elements, each of which will be interpreted by a specialized system service.

52.2 | Strategic considerations

The project team conducted a detailed study that identified a number of demanding criteria:

- The system had to operate with a range of client terminal machines, including PCs, VT100s, and mobile terminals installed in police vehicles.
- Some 250 distinct screens were required for the user interface.
- Over 800 messages were required.
- The external databases that must be accessed by the system were different from one another.
- End-user requests to the system could also generate processing actions that were specific to the client machines.

Given the size of the project and the disparity in both the client systems and data sources, the team concluded that maximum standardization was the best strategy. Code components to drive specific terminal devices and data sources would be generated automatically from standardized descriptions of the system.

©2000 The XML Handbook™

SGML/XML was chosen as the base for the development strategy and INGEPOL was divided into five subsystems:

- Generation of database services;
- Specification of data/message groups;
- Server;
- Specification of dialogs;
- Client terminal.

52.3 | DTD development

DTDs were developed for three of the subsystems:

- Generation of database services (DB DTD);
- Specification of data/message groups (Message DTD);
- Specification of dialogs (Dialog DTD).

52.3.1 *DB DTD*

The team employed modeling tools that generated an SQL database creation file from a physical model. DB DTD allowed the structure of that file to be validated.

They also used DB DTD as input to *Visual SGML*, an SGML parsing system and application language developed by SGML Technologies Group. The tool generates an instance for each identified table or view, and creates an XML description of the object processed.

The grammar describes the tables, columns, and views to be taken into account. The final result is a first version of a message instance.

52.3.2 *Message DTD*

Message DTD allows validation of the message instance.

For each data group, *Visual SGML* was used to generate:

52.4.3 *Server*

It is the server's role to handle incoming messages, to process them appropriately by addressing the necessary services, and to send back a reply to the sending client terminal.

In short, the server must provide the following functionality:

- receive the message and identify the transmitter;
- decipher the message;
- dispatch the message to the specialized service responsible for the necessary operations, depending on the process requested (read or create a new object description, etc.), and the information systems chosen;
- consolidate the return message with information received from the information systems;
- encipher the message;
- dispatch the message to the sending client terminal.

At the server level, the XML message is regarded as a chain of characters that a specialized parser splits into a data group, thus allowing the supply of the C++ structures derived from the classes previously generated. A set of methods or services, generated or specifically developed, allows the appropriate servers to be activated, depending on the nature of the message and the data groups present.

52.4.4 *Specification of dialogs*

The objective of the dialog specification is the generation of a set of HTML templates or VT100 screens. These files represent the user interface and can be interpreted by the client terminal of the target system (see Figure 52-3).

A dialog instance allows the management of screen flows, dynamic management of drop-down menus, the setting of event-driven actions, and inter-area integrity controls. As far as the buttons, drop-down menus, or specific elements are concerned, the associated Python code is simple. It allows manipulation of data groups (creation, deletion, or updating), navigation between the dialog boxes, primary controls that could not be specified at message level, and sending and receiving of messages by means of elementary macro-instructions.

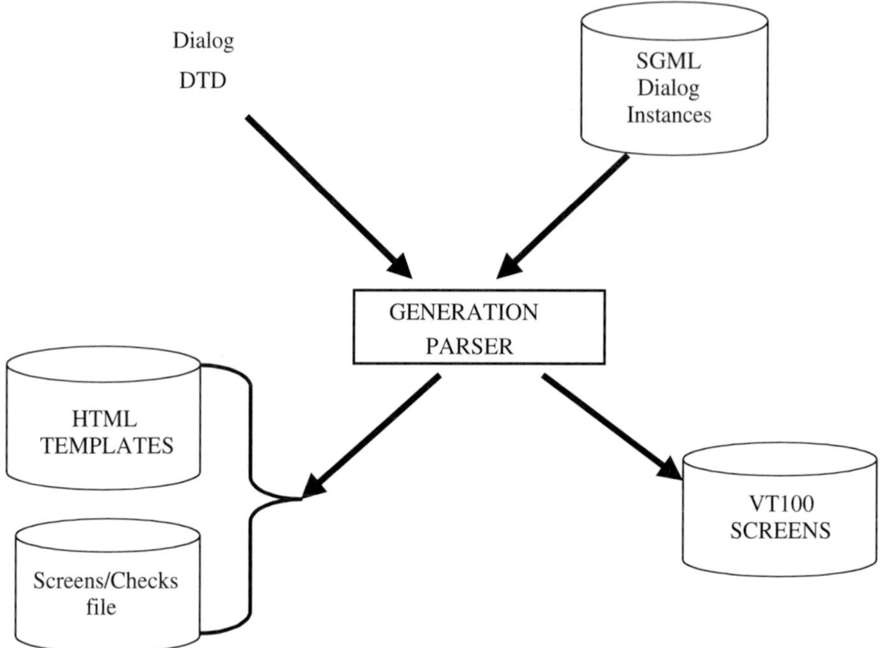

Figure 52-3 Automatic generation of dialogs

The designer of the interface merely describes the management of screen flows and the events to be taken into account, without having to worry about the technical aspects of the client workstation modules.

Example 52-2 illustrates a dialog instance. This dialog is dedicated to a data request after a list response. The element `BUTTON` is named `OK`. When the user pushes it, the code in the content of the `CODE` element is executed. The data group named "REQ_DATA" and the data group "SECURITY" are then created and the message that includes the two data groups is sent to the server.

The response of the server is either a message named "MSG_DATA" if a response is given, or "MSG_ERROR" if an error occurs. Depending on the type of message, the screen "HTML_DATA" or "HTML_ERROR" is displayed with the associated response message.

For workstations in character mode (VT100), the modules generating the user interface process the same dialog instance, but they modify certain classical functions of a graphical interface. For example, the buttons or drop-down menus become function keys and the combo-boxes become

Example 52-2. A dialog instance

```
<DLG NAME="RTLIAR" CLASS="GLISTEOBJET">
   <BOX><DESCR>Arme</DESCR>
      <LSFIELD
       GFIELD="Records" SELVAR="ITEM" SELMODE="MULTIPLE"
       KEYFLD="OBJET.obj_identifiant"><DESCR></DESCR>
         <ROFIELD VFIELD="OBJET.indicateur_signalement"/>
         <ROFIELD VFIELD="ARME.arm_type"/>
         <ROFIELD VFIELD="ARME.arm_modele"/>
         <ROFIELD VFIELD="ARME.arm_serie"/>
         <ROFIELD VFIELD="ARME.arm_calibre"/>
      </LSFIELD>
   </BOX>
   <BUTTON RETCODE="OK" TYPE="DWN" KEEP="CHANGES"><DESCR>OK</DESCR>
      <CODE>
      if ctx().ITEM != None :
         msg = msgdefs.createGroup('REQ_DATA')
         msg.key = grp().Records[ctx().ITEM].OBJET.obj_identifiant
         msg.SECURITY = msgdefs.createGroup('SECURITY')
         msg.SECURITY.usr = user
         msg.SECURITY.terminal = terminal
         msg_ret = request(msg)
         if "MSG_DATA" == msg_ret._classname :
            push(dlgdefs,"HTML_DATA" , msg_ret, ctx())
         elif "MSG_ERROR" == msg_ret._classname :
            push(dlgdefs,"HTML_ERROR", msg_ret, ctx())
      else :
         m = msgdefs.createGroup('ERROR')
         m.msg = "No object selected"
         push(dlgdefs,"HTML_ERROR", m, ctx())
      </CODE>
   </BUTTON>
</DLG>
```

screens that contain a list of all possible values. Scrolling of a screen page is represented by a second screen, and so on. The code inserted into the dialog instance is executed with the help of a Python library.

The objective is to offer the same look-and-feel regardless of the target system.

52.4.5 *Client terminal*

The role of the client terminal is to make a stable, generic tool, that is capable of offering, on the basis of files generated from a formal specification of dialogs, a look-and-feel that is similar to that of a specifically developed client workstation.

The client workstation is a browser-based application that displays HTML pages built from previously generated templates (see Figure 52-4).

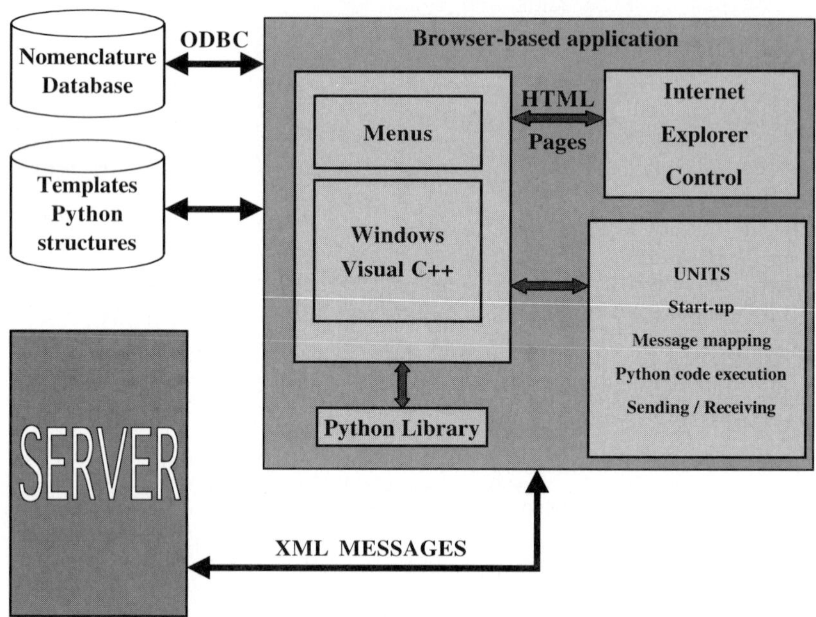

Figure 52-4 Flow at a client terminal

It employs modules for the following functions:

- initialization of the application, connection to the server, and identification of the first screen to be displayed;
- mapping of the message fields onto the associated HTML template in order to build an HTML page;
- display of HTML pages, as shown in Figure 52-5;
- code execution linked to the page related to a user-driven event;
- enciphering and deciphering of messages;
- sending and receiving messages between client and server.

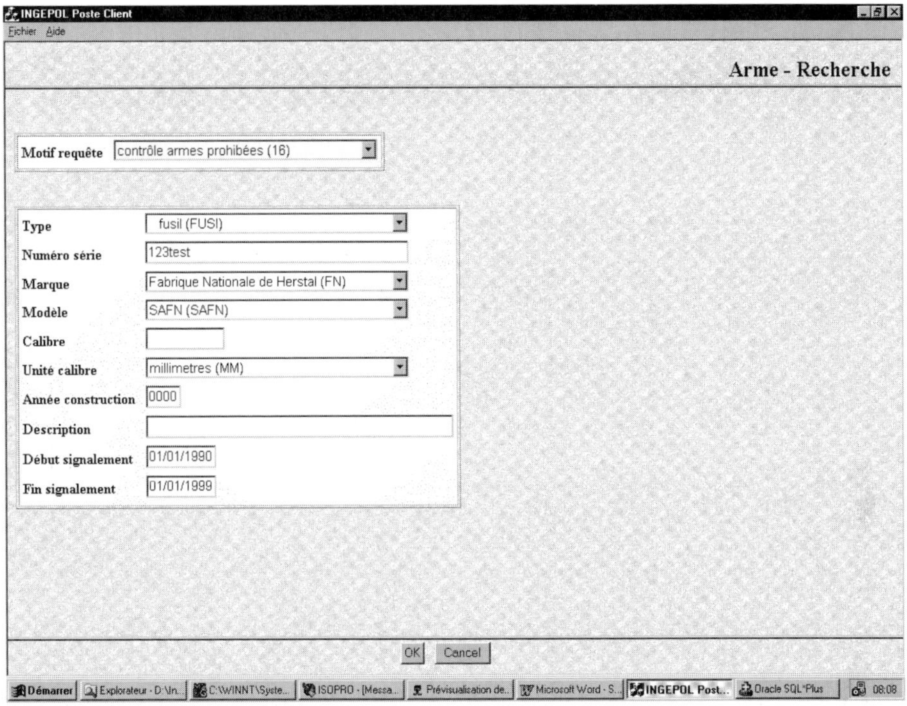

Figure 52-5 A generated HTML page

52.5 | Conclusions

XML was used for validating message instances, generating customized data groups for each database, and generating uniform sets of classes and methods. These uses reduced the risk of programming errors because the generated components were stable, and much code development and testing were eliminated.

SGML and XML also allowed a uniform definition of the user interface despite the different platforms targeted.

Above all, SGML and XML permitted control of the complexity that is inherent in any project that calls for different workstations, distant databases that are conceptually modeled according to their needs, and heterogeneous networks – in short, everything that characterizes large present-day projects.

XML Tutorials

- Basic XML markup
- Document type definitions
- Entities
- Advanced features
- How to read the W3C XML Recommendation
- Full spec on CD-ROM

©2000 THE XML HANDBOOK™

Part Eleven

This part continues the XML tutorial that we began in Part One. If you haven't read Part One in its entirety, please go back and do so, as we introduced some critically important ideas there.

In this part, you'll learn every useful detail of the XML 1.0 language. At the end you'll be able to read the markup of both DTDs and document instances.

The part is intended to be read in order, with one exception. As you read the first four chapters you'll notice that here and there we've included excerpts from the XML 1.0 specification. The tutorials are written so that *you can skip the spec excerpts*. They are not required for continuity; they are there so that the hard-core techies among you can get down with the deepest details.

But they need a little tutorial of their own to be read, which is why we have Chapter 57. Dig into that when – and if – you decide to read the spec excerpts in Chapters 53-56, or to tackle the full spec itself, which is on the CD-ROM.

XML basics

Friendly Tutorial

- Syntactic details
- The prolog and the document instance
- XML declaration
- Elements and attributes

©2000 THE XML HANDBOOK™

Chapter 53

XML's central concepts are quite simple, and this chapter outlines the most important of them. Essentially, it gives you what you need to know to actually create XML documents. In subsequent chapters you will learn how to combine them, share text between them, format them, and validate their structure.

Before looking at actual XML markup (don't worry, we'll get there soon!) we should consider some *syntactic* constructs that will recur throughout our discussion of XML documents. By *syntax* we mean the combination of characters that make up an XML document. This is analogous to the distinction between sounds of words and the things that they mean. Essentially, we are talking about where you can put angle brackets, quote marks, ampersands, and other characters and where you cannot! Later we will talk about what they mean when you put them together.

After that, we will discusses the components that make up an XML document instance[1]. We will look at the distinction between the prolog (information XML processors need to know about your document) and the instance (the representation of the real document itself).

1. Roughly, what the XML spec calls the "root element".

53.1 | Syntactic details

XML documents are composed of characters from the *Unicode* character set. Any such sequence of characters is called a *string*. The characters in this book can be thought of as one long (but interesting) string of text. Each chapter is also a string. So is each word. XML documents are similarly made up of strings within strings.

Natural languages such as English have a particular *syntax*. The syntax allows you to combine words into grammatical sentences. XML also has syntax. It describes how you combine strings into well-formed XML documents. We will describe the basics of XML's syntax in this section.

53.1.1 *Case-sensitivity*

XML is *case-sensitive*. That means that if the XML specification says to insert the word "ELEMENT", it means that you should insert "ELEMENT" and not "element" or "Element" or "ElEmEnT".

For many people, particularly English speaking people, case-insensitive matching is easier than remembering the case of particular constructs. For instance, if a document type has an element type named `img` English speakers will often forget and insert `IMG`. They confuse the two because they are not accustomed to considering case to be significant. This is also why some people new to the Internet tend to TYPE IN ALL UPPER CASE. Most applications of SGML, including HTML, are designed to be case-insensitive. They argue that this eliminates case as a source of errors.

Others argue that the whole concept of case-insensitivity is a throwback to keypunches and other early text-entry devices. They also point out that case-sensitivity is a very complicated concept in an international character set like Unicode for a variety of reasons.

For instance, the rules for case conversion of certain accented characters are different in Quebec from what they are in France. There are also some languages for which the concept of upper-case and lower-case does not exist at all. There is no simple, universal rule for case-insensitive matching. In the end, internationalization won out in XML's design.

So mind your "p's" and "q's" and "P's" and "Q's". Our authoritative laboratory testing by people in white coats indicates that exactly 74.5% of all XML errors are related to case-sensitivity mistakes. Of course XML is also spelling-sensitive and typo-sensitive, so watch out for these and other by-products of human fallibility.

Note that although XML is case-sensitive it is not case-prejudiced. Anywhere that you have the freedom to create your own names or text, you can choose to use upper- or lower-case text, as you prefer. So although you must type XML's keywords exactly as they are described, your own strings can mix and match upper- and lower-case characters however you like.

For instance, when you create your own document types you will be able to choose element type names. A particular name could be all upper-case (SECTION), all lower-case (section) or mixed-case (SeCtION). But because XML is case-sensitive, all references to a particular element type would have to use the same case. It is good practice to create a simple convention such as all lower-case or all upper-case so that you do not have to depend on your memory.

53.1.2 *Markup and data*

The constructs such as tags, entity references, and declarations are called *markup*. These are the parts of your document that are supposed to be understood by the XML processor. The parts that are between the markup are typically supposed to be understood only by other human beings. That is the *character data*. Spec Excerpt 53-1 reports what the XML specification says on this issue.

Spec Excerpt (XML) 53-1. Markup

```
Markup takes the form of start-tags, end-tags, empty-element tags,
entity references, character references, comments, CDATA section
delimiters, document type declarations, and processing instructions.
```

We haven't explained what all of those things are yet, but they are easy to recognize. All of them start with less-than (<) or ampersand (&) characters. Everything else is character data.

53.1.3 *White space*

There is a set of characters called *white space* characters that XML processors treat differently in XML markup. They are the "invisible" characters: space (Unicode/ASCII 32), tab (Unicode/ASCII 9), carriage return (Unicode/ASCII 13) and line feed (Unicode/ASCII 10). These correspond roughly to the `spacebar`, `tab`, and `Enter` keys on your keyboard.

When the XML specification says that white space is allowed at a particular point, you may put as many of these characters as you want in any combination. Just as you might put two lines between paragraphs in a word processor to make a printed document readable, you may put two carriage returns in certain places in an XML document to make your source file more readable and maintainable. When the document is processed, those characters will be ignored.

In other places, white space will be significant. For instance you would not want the processor to strip out the spaces between the words in your document! Thatwouldmakeithardtoread. So white space outside of markup is always preserved in XML and white space within markup may be preserved, ignored, and sometimes combined in weird, and wonderful ways. We will describe the combination rules as we go along.

53.1.4 *Names and name tokens*

When you use XML you will often have to give things names. You will name logical structures with element type names, reusable data with entity names, particular elements with IDs, and so forth. XML names have certain common features. They are not nearly as flexible as character data. See Spec Excerpt 53-2 for more information.

Spec Excerpt (XML) 53-2. Names

A Name [begins] with a letter or one of a few punctuation characters, and [continues] with letters, digits, hyphens, underscores, colons, or full stops, together known as name characters. Names beginning with the string "xml", [matched case-insensitively] are reserved for standardization in this or future versions of this specification.

In other words, you cannot make names that begin with the string "xml" or some case-insensitive variant like "XML" or "XmL". Letters or underscores can be used anywhere in a name. You may include digits, hyphens and full-stop (".") characters in a name, but you may not start the name with one of them. Other characters, like various symbols and white space, cannot be part of a name.

There is another related syntactic construct called a *name token*. Name tokens are just like names except that they *may* start with digits, hyphens, full-stop characters, and the string XML.

Spec Excerpt (XML) 53-3. Name tokens

An Nmtoken (name token) is any mixture of name characters.

In other words every valid name is also a valid name token, but Example 53-1 shows some name tokens that are not valid names.

Example 53-1. Name tokens

```
.1.a.name.token.but.not.a.name
2-a-name-token.but-not.a-name
XML-valid-name-token
```

Like almost everything else in XML, names, and name tokens are matched case-sensitively. Names and name tokens do not allow white space, most punctuation or other "funny" characters. The remaining "ordinary" characters are called *name characters*.

53.1.5 *Literal strings*

The data (text other than markup) can contain almost any characters. Obviously, in the main text of your document you need to be able to use punctuation and white space characters! But sometimes you also need these characters *within* markup. For instance an element might represent a hyperlink and need to contain a URL. The URL would have to go in markup, where characters other than the name characters are not usually allowed.

Literal strings allow users to use funny (non-name) characters within markup, but only in contexts in which it makes sense to specify values that might require those characters. For instance, to specify the URL in the hyperlink, we would need the slash character. Example 53-2 is an example of such an element.

Example 53-2. Literal string in attribute value

```
<REFERENCE URL="http://www.documents.com/document.xml"/>
```

The string that defines the URL is the literal string. This one starts and ends with double quote characters. Literal strings are always surrounded by either single or double quotes. The quotes are not part of the string. See Spec Excerpt 53-4 for more information.

Spec Excerpt (XML) 53-4. Literal data

Literal data is any quoted string not containing the quotation mark used as a delimiter for that string. Literals are used for specifying the content of internal entities, the values of attributes, and external identifiers.

You may use either single (`'`) or double (`"`) quotes to mark (*delimit*) the beginning and end of these strings in your XML document. Whichever type of quote the string starts with, it must end with. The other type may be used within the literal and has no special meaning there. Typically you will use double quotes when you want to put an actual single-quote character in the literal and single quotes when you want to embed an actual double quote. When you do not need to embed either, you can take your pick. For example see Example 53-3.

Example 53-3. Quotes within quotes

```
"This is a double quoted literal."
'This is a single quoted literal.'
"'tis another double quoted literal."
'"And this is single quoted" said the self-referential example.'
```

The ability to have quotes within quotes is quite useful when dealing with human speech or programming language text as in Example 53-4.

©2000 THE XML HANDBOOK™

Example 53-4. Quoted language

```
"To be or not to be"
'"To be or not to be", quoth Hamlet.'
"'BE!', said Jean-Louis Gassee."
'B = "TRUE";'
```

Note that there *are* ways of including a double quote character inside of a double-quoted literal. This is important because a single literal might (rarely) need both types of quotes.

53.1.6 *Grammars*

Natural language syntax is described with a *grammar*. XML's syntax is also. Some readers will want to dig in and learn the complete, intricate details of XML's syntax. We will provide grammar rules for them as we go along. These come right out of the XML specification. If you want to learn how to read them, you should skip ahead to Chapter 57, "Reading the XML specification", on page 820. After you have read it, you can come back and understand the rules as we present them. Another strategy is to read the chapters without worrying about the grammar rules, and then only use them when you need to answer a particular question about XML syntax.

You can recognize grammar rules taken from the specification by their form. They will look like Spec Excerpt 53-5.

Spec Excerpt (XML) 53-5. An example of a grammar rule

```
xhb ::= 'a' 'good' 'read'
```

We will not specifically introduce these rules, because we do not want to interrupt the flow of the text. They will just pop up in the appropriate place to describe the syntax of something.

53.2 | Prolog vs. instance

Most document representations start with a header that contains information about the real document and how to interpret its representation. This is followed by the representation of the real document.

For instance, HTML has a HEAD element that can contain the TITLE and META elements. After the HEAD element comes the BODY. This is where the representation of the real document resides. Similarly, email messages have "header lines" that describe who the message came from, to whom it is addressed, how it is encoded, and other things.

An XML document is similarly broken up into two main parts: a *prolog* and a *document instance*. The prolog provides information about the interpretation of the document instance, such as the version of XML and the document type to which it conforms. The document instance follows the prolog. It contains the actual document data organized as a hierarchy of elements.

Spec Excerpt (XML) 53-6. Document production

```
document ::=  prolog element Misc*
```

53.3 | The logical structure

The actual content of an XML document goes in the document instance. It is called this because if it has a DTD, it is an instance of a class of documents defined by the DTD. Just as a particular person is an instance of the class of "people", a particular memo is an instance of the class of "memo documents". The formal definition of "memo document" is in the memo DTD.

Here is an example of a small XML document.

Example 53-5. Small XML Document

```
<?xml version="1.0"?>
<!DOCTYPE MEMO SYSTEM "memo.dtd">
<memo>
<from>
   <name>Paul Prescod</name>
   <email>papresco@prescod.com</email>
</from>
<to>
   <name>Charles Goldfarb</name>
   <email>charles@sgmlsource.com</email>
</to>
<subject>Another Memo Example</subject>
<body>
<paragraph> Charles, I wanted to suggest that we
<emphasis>not</emphasis> use the  typical memo example in
our book. Memos tend to be used anywhere a small, simple
document type is needed, but they are just
<emphasis>so</emphasis> boring!
</paragraph>
</body>
</memo>
```

Because a computer cannot understand the data of the document, it looks primarily at the *tags*, the markup between the less-than and greater-than symbols. The tags delimit the beginning and end of various elements. The computer thinks of the elements as a sort of tree.

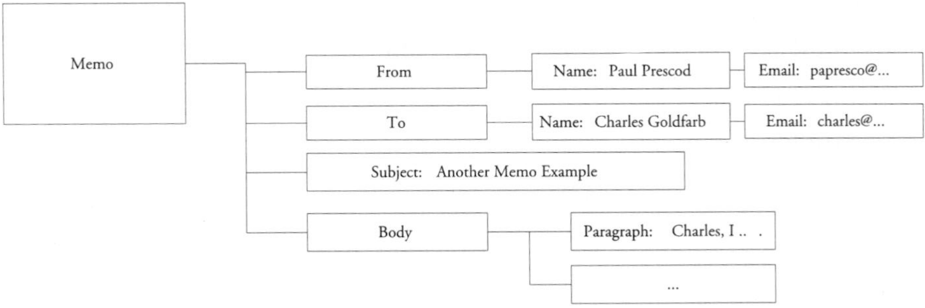

Figure 53-1 The memo XML document viewed as a tree.

Figure 53-1 shows a graphical view of the logical structure of the document. The MEMO element is called either the *document element* or the *root element.*

The document element (`memo`) represents the document as a whole. Every other element represents a component of the document. The `from` and `to` elements are meant to indicate the source and target of the memo. The `name` elements represent people's names. Continuing in this way, the logical structure of the document is apparent from the element-type names.

Experts refer to an element's real-world meaning as its *semantics.* In a particular DTD, the semantics of a `P` element might be "paragraph" and in another it might mean `pence`. If you find yourself reading or writing markup and asking: "But what does that *mean*?" or "What does that look like?" then you are asking about semantics.

Computers do not know anything about semantics. They do not know an HTTP protocol from a supermodel. Document type designers must describe semantics to authors some other way. For instance they could send email, write a book or make a major motion picture (well, maybe some day). What the computer does care about is how an element is supposed to look when it is formatted, or how it is to behave if it is interactive, or what to do with the data once it is extracted. These are specified in *stylesheets* and computer programs.

53.4 | Elements

XML elements break down into two categories. Most have content, which is to say they contain characters, elements or both, and some do not. Those that do not are called *empty elements.*

Example 53-6 is an example of an element with content.

Example 53-6. Simple element

```
<title>This is the title</title>
```

or a single empty-element tag. An element's type is always identified by the generic identifiers in its tags.

The reason we distinguish element types from generic identifiers is because the term "generic identifier" refers to the syntax of the XML document – the characters that represent the real document. The term "element type" refers to a property of a component of the real document.

53.5 | Attributes

In addition to content, elements may have *attributes*. Attributes are a way of attaching characteristics or properties to elements of a document. Attributes have *names*, just as real-world properties do. They also have *values*. For instance, two possible attributes of people are their "shoe size" and "IQ" (the attributes' names), and two possible values are "12" and "12" (respectively).

In a DTD, each attribute is defined for a specific element type and is allowed to exhibit a certain type of value. Multiple element types could provide attributes with the same name and it is sometimes convenient to think of them as the "same attribute" even though they technically are not.

Attributes have semantics also. They always *mean* something. For example, an attribute named `height` might be provided for `person` elements (allowed occurrence), exhibit values that are numbers (allowed values), and represent the person's height in centimeters (semantics).

Here is how attributes of `person` elements might look:

Example 53-8. Elements with attributes

```
<person height="165cm">Dale Wick</person>
<person height="165cm" weight="165lb">Bill Bunn</person>
```

As you can see, the attribute name does not go in quotes, but the attribute value does.

Spec Excerpt (XML) 53-11. Attributes

```
[41]  Attribute ::=  Name Eq AttValue
[25]  Eq ::=  S? '=' S?
```

Like other literals (see 53.1.5, "Literal strings", on page 727), attributes can be surrounded by either single (') or double (") quotes. When you use one type of quote, the other can be used within that attribute value. As we discussed earlier, this makes it convenient to create attribute values that have the quote characters within them. This is shown in Example 53-9

Example 53-9. Attribute values can have quotes in them

```
<PERSON HEIGHT='80"'>
<PERSON QUOTE="'To be or not to be'">
```

There are other ways of getting special characters into attribute values and we will discuss them in 56.2, "Character references", on page 807.

A DTD constrains an attribute's allowed occurrence and values. One possibility is to require an attribute to be specified for all elements. For example, a military document might require `section` elements to have a `security` attribute with the value `unclassified`, `classified`, or `secret`. Example 53-10 demonstrates.

Example 53-10. Security attribute declaration

```
<!ATTLIST SECTION
          SECURITY (unclassified | classified | secret) #REQUIRED >
```

The attribute would need to be specified for each `section` element as shown in Example 53-11.

Example 53-11. Security attribute specification

```
<SECTION SECURITY="unclassified">...</SECTION>
```

It would be a validity error to create a `section` element without a `security` attribute.

Usually empty elements have attributes. Sometimes an element with sub-elements can be modeled just as well with an empty element and attributes. Example 53-12 shows two ways of modeling a `person` element in an email message.

Yet another way to do it would be to let the person's name be data content as shown in Example 53-13

©2000 THE XML HANDBOOK™

Example 53-12. Alternative `person` element

```
<FROM><NAME>Paul Prescod</NAME>
      <EMAIL>"papresco@prescod.com"</EMAIL>
</FROM>
vs.
<FROM NAME="Paul Prescod" EMAIL="papresco@prescod.com"/>
```

Example 53-13. Another alternative `person` element

```
<FROM><PERSON EMAIL="papresco@prescod.com">Paul Prescod
      </PERSON>
</FROM>
```

As you can see, there can be many different ways to represent the same construct. There is no one right way to do so. In the case of `person`, the last version shown is the most typical because the character data of a document generally represents what you would expect to see in a "print-out".

But that is not a hard and fast rule (after all, renditions vary widely). Because there are so many ways to represent the same thing, it is advisable to use a DTD. The constraints in a DTD can maintain consistency across a range of documents, or even within a single large document. There may be many ways to represent a particular concept, but once you choose one, let the DTD help you stick to it.

53.6 | The prolog

XML documents should start with a prolog that describes the XML version ("1.0", for now), document type, and other characteristics of the document.

The prolog is made up of an *XML declaration* and a *document type declaration*, both optional. Though an author may include either, neither, or both, it is best to try to maximize the amount of prolog information provided. This will make later processing more reliable.

The XML declaration must precede the document type declaration if both are provided. Also, comments, processing instructions, and white space can be mixed in among the two declarations. The prolog ends when the first start-tag begins.

Example 53-14 is a sample prolog as a warm-up.

Example 53-14. A simple prolog

```
<?xml version="1.0"?>
<!DOCTYPE DOCBOOK SYSTEM "http://www.davenport.org/docbook">
```

This DTD says that the document conforms to XML version 1.0 and declares adherence to a particular document type, DOCBOOK.

Spec Excerpt (XML) 53-12. Prolog

```
[22]  prolog ::=  XMLDecl? Misc* (doctypedecl Misc*)?
[27]  Misc ::=  Comment | PI |  S
```

53.6.1 *XML declaration*

The XML declaration is fairly simple. It has several parts and they fit together one after another.

Spec Excerpt (XML) 53-13. XML declaration

```
[23]  XMLDecl ::=  '<?xml' VersionInfo EncodingDecl? SDDecl? S? '?>'
```

A minimal XML declaration looks like this:

Example 53-15. Minimal XML declaration

```
<?xml version="1.0"?>
```

Example 53-16 is a more expansive one, using all of its parts.

Example 53-16. More expansive XML declaration

```
<?xml version="1.0" encoding="UTF-8" standalone="yes"?>
```

There is one important thing to note in the last example. It looks like a start-tag with attributes, but it is *not*. The different parts of the XML declaration just happen to look like attributes. Well, not quite "just happen": it could have had a completely different syntax, but that would have been harder to memorize. So the parts were chosen to look like attributes to reduce the complexity of the language. One important difference between XML declaration parts and attributes is that the parts are strictly ordered whereas attributes can be specified in any order.

53.6.1.1 Version info

The *version info* part of the XML declaration declares the version of XML that is in use. It is required in all XML declarations. At the time of writing, the only valid version string is "1.0". But if you always use the version string, you can be confident that future XML processors will not think that your document was meant to conform to XML version 2.0 or 3.0 when and if those languages become available. Since they do not exist yet, you cannot know if your documents will be compatible with them.

In fact, the only reason that the XML declaration is optional is so that some HTML and SGML documents can be used as XML documents without confusing the software that they usually work with. You can imagine that an older browser would not react nicely to an HTML document with an XML declaration. But this "backwards compatibility" consideration is only temporary. Future versions of XML may require the XML declaration.

The XML version information is part of a general trend towards information representations that are *self-identifying*. This means that you can look at an XML document and (if it has the declaration) know immediately both that it is XML and what version of XML it uses. As more and more document representations become self-identifying, we will be able to stop relying on error-prone identification schemes like file extensions.

53.6.1.2 Encoding declaration

An XML declaration may also include an *encoding declaration*. It describes what character encoding is used. This is another aspect of being self-identifying. If your documents are encoded in the traditional 7-bit-ASCII used on most operating systems and with most text editors, then you do not need to worry about the encoding-declaration. 7-bit-ASCII is a subset of a Unicode encoding called *UTF-8* which XML processors can automatically detect and use. If you use 7-bit ASCII and need to encode a character outside of 7-bit-ASCII, such as the trademark sign or a non-English character, you can do so most easily by using a numeric character reference, as described in 56.2, “Character references”, on page 807.

Spec Excerpt (XML) 53-14. Encoding declaration

```
[80]EncodingDecl::= S 'encoding'
                    Eq ('"' EncName '"' | "'" EncName "'" )
[81]EncName::= [A-Za-z] ([A-Za-z0-9._] |'-')*
```

53.6.1.3 Standalone document declaration

An XML declaration can include a *standalone document declaration.* It declares what components of the document type definition are necessary for complete processing of the document. This declaration is described in 56.5, “Standalone document declaration”, on page 815.

53.6.2 *Document type declaration*

Somewhere after the XML declaration (if present) and before the first element, the *document type declaration* declares the document type that is in use in the document. A “book” document type, for example, might be made up of chapters, while a letter document type could be made up of element types such as ADDRESS, SALUTATION, SIGNATURE, and so forth.

The document type declaration is at the heart of the concept of *structural validity*, which makes applications based on XML robust and reliable. It includes the markup declarations that express the *document type definition (DTD).*

The DTD is a formalization of the intuitive idea of a document type. The DTD lists the element types available and can put constraints on the occurrence and content of elements and other details of the document structure. This makes an information system more robust by forcing the documents that are part of it to be consistent.

©2000 THE XML HANDBOOK™

53.7 | Markup miscellany

This section contains information on some more useful markup constructs. They are not as important or as widely used as elements, attributes and the XML declaration, but they are still vital parts of a markup expert's toolbox.

53.7.1 *Predefined entities*

Sometimes when you are creating an XML document, you want to protect certain characters from markup interpretation. Imagine, for example, that you are writing a user's guide to HTML. You would need a way to include an example of markup. Your first attempt might be to create an `example` element and do something like this Example 53-17.

Example 53-17. An invalid approach to HTML examples in XML

```
<p>HTML documents must start with a DOCTYPE, etc. etc. This
is an example of a small HTML document:
<SAMPLE>

  <!DOCTYPE HTML PUBLIC "-//W3C//DTD HTML 3.2 Final//EN">
  <HTML>
  A document's title
  <H1>A document's title</H1>
  </HTML>

</SAMPLE>
```

This will not work, however, because the angle brackets that are supposed to represent HTML markup will be interpreted as if they belonged to the XML document you are creating, not the mythical HTML document in the example. Your XML processor will complain that it is not appropriate to have an HTML DOCTYPE declaration in the middle of an XML document! There are two solutions to this problem: predefined entities and CDATA sections.

Predefined entities are XML markup that authors use to represent characters that would otherwise be interpreted as having a special meaning, such as a start-tag or an entity reference. There are five *predefined* ("built-in") entities in XML. These were included precisely to deal with this problem. They are listed in Table 53-1.

Table 53-1 Predefined entities

Entity reference	Character
&	&
<	<
>	>
'	'
"	"

Why these specific five characters?

Spec Excerpt (XML) 53-15. Predefined entities

The ampersand character (&) and the left angle bracket (<) may appear in their literal form only when used as markup delimiters, or within a comment, a processing instruction, or a CDATA section. [...] If they are needed elsewhere, they must be escaped using either numeric character references or the strings "&" and "<" respectively.

Spec Excerpt (XML) 53-16. Attribute values

To allow attribute values to contain both single and double quotes, the apostrophe or single-quote character (') may be represented as "'", and the double-quote character (") as """.

An entity for the right angle bracket is also provided because it is sometimes useful to avoid putting a special string called *CDEnd* (discussed later) into your document. But you do not have to use this entity in most cases.

We can use references to the predefined entities to insert these characters, instead of typing them directly. Then they will not be interpreted as markup. Example 53-18 demonstrates this.

Example 53-18. Writing about HTML in XML

```
<p>HTML documents must start with a DOCTYPE, etc. etc. This
is an example of a small HTML document:
<SAMPLE>
   &lt;!DOCTYPE HTML PUBLIC "-//W3C//DTD HTML 3.2 Final//EN">
   &lt;HTML>
   &lt;HEAD>
   &lt;TITLE>A document's title
   &lt;/TITLE>
   &lt;/HEAD>
   &lt;/HTML>
</SAMPLE>
```

When your XML processor parses the document, it will replace the entity references with actual characters. It will not interpret the characters it inserts as markup, but as "plain 'ol data characters" (character data).

53.7.2 *CDATA sections*

While predefined entities are convenient, human beings are not as good at decoding them as computers are. Your readers will get the translated version, so they will be fine. But as the author, you will spend hours staring at character entity references while you are editing your XML document. You may also spend hours replacing special characters with character entity references. This can get annoying.[1]

Another construct, called a *CDATA section*, allows you to ask the processor not to interpret a chunk of text as containing markup: "Hands off! This isn't meant to be interpreted." CDATA stands for "character data". You can mark a section as being character data using this special syntax as shown in Example 53-19.

Example 53-19. CDATA section

```
'<![CDATA[' content  ']]>'
```

Example 53-20 and Example 53-21 are other examples.

1. This is especially nasty when you are writing an XML book, where examples tend to contain many angle brackets.

Example 53-20. Writing about HTML in a CDATA section

```
<![CDATA[
<HTML>
This is an example from HTML for Dumbbells!
<p>It may be a pain to write a book about HTML in HTML,
but it is easy in XML!
</HTML>
]]>
```

Example 53-21. Java code in a CDATA section

```
<![CDATA[
if( foo.getContentLength() < 0  && input = foo.getInputStream() )
     open = true;
]]>
```

As you can see, it does not usually matter what you put in CDATA sections because their content is not scanned for markup. There is one obvious exception (and one not-so-obvious corollary). The string that ends the CDATA section, "]]>" (known as *CDEnd*) cannot be used inside the section. Use Example 53-22 as a cautionary tale.

Example 53-22. Illegal CDATA usage

```
<![CDATA[
 JavaScript code: if( a[c[5]]> 7 ) then...
]]>
```

The first occurrence of CDEnd in the middle of the JavaScript expression will terminate the section. You simply cannot use a CDATA section for content that includes CDEnd. You must end the section and insert the character as in Example 53-23.

Example 53-23. Legal CDATA usage

```
<![CDATA[
 JavaScript code: if( a[c[5]]]]>><![CDATA[ 7 ) then...
]]>
```

This is quite painful and can cause a problem for embedding programming languages. But even in those languages, CDEnd is probably a fairly rare character string, so you should just keep an eye out for it.

The non-obvious corollary is:

Caution *CDEnd ("]]>") should only be used to close CDATA sections. It must not occur anywhere else in an XML document.*

This is an absolute requirement, not just a recommendation. Because of it you can easily check that you have closed CDATA sections correctly by comparing the number of CDEnd strings to the number of sections. If you do not close a CDATA section correctly, some of your document's markup may be interpreted as character data. Since ("]]>") is not something that typical documents contain, this restriction is rarely a problem.

With all of these warnings, CDATA sections may sound tricky to use, but they really aren't. This book, for example, has several hundred. Mistakes involving CDATA sections are usually quite blatant, because either markup will show up in your rendered document, or data characters will be interpreted as markup and probably trigger an error message.

Predefined entities and CDATA sections only relate to the interpretation of the markup, not to the properties of the real document that the markup represents.

53.7.3 *Comments*

Sometimes it is useful to embed information about a document or its markup in a manner that will be ignored by computer processes and renditions of the document. For example, you might insert a note to yourself to clean up the wording of a section, a note to a co-author explaining the reason for a particular section of the document, or a note in a DTD describing the semantics of a particular element. This information can be hidden from the application in a *comment*. Comments should never be displayed in a browser, indexed in a search engine, or otherwise processed as part of the data of the real document. They may, however, be treated as metadata.

Example 53-24. A comment

```
<!-- This section is really good! Let's not change it. -->
```

Comments consist of the characters "<!--" followed by almost anything and ended by "-->". The "almost anything" in the middle cannot contain the characters "--". This is a little bit inconvenient, because people often use those two characters as a sort of dash, to separate thoughts. This is another point to be careful of, lest you get bitten.

Spec Excerpt (XML) 53-17. Comment

```
[15] Comment ::= '<!--'((Char - '-')|('-'(Char - '-')))*'-->'
```

Comments can go just about anywhere in the instance or the prolog. However, they cannot go within declarations, tags, or other comments. Example 53-25 is a document using some comments in several correct places.

Example 53-25. Comments all over the place

```
<?xml version="1.0"?>
<!-- There is no other version yet! -->
<!-- Now on to the doctype -->
<!DOCTYPE SAMPLE [
  <!-- This is a comment in the
  doctype declaration internal subset! -->
  <!ELEMENT SAMPLE (#PCDATA)>
  <!-- This is a very simple DTD. -->
]> <!-- Here comes the "root" or "document" element. -->
<SAMPLE>This is some character data.
<!-- That was some character data. -->
</SAMPLE>
<!-- That's all folks -->
```

Markup is not recognized in comments. You can put less-than and ampersand symbols in them, but they will not be recognized as the start of elements or entity references.

Comments are a good place to describe the semantics of element types and attributes. So you might use a comment to tell other DTD maintainers and authors that an element type with a cryptic name like p is actually intended to model paragraphs and not (for example) British currency. Comments are not just about being helpful to other people. After all, even expert document type designers have a limited and imperfect memory. Some day even you will wonder exactly what it was you meant by a particular element-type name. The DTD comments will help. The job that you are saving might be your own!

53.8 | Summary

An XML document is composed of a prolog and a document instance. The prolog is optional, and provides information about how the document is structured both physically (where its parts are) and logically (how its elements fit together). Elements and attributes describe the logical structure. Entities describe the physical structure. To use a rough analogy, the entities are like a robot's body parts, the elements are his thoughts, and stylesheets and software provide his behavior.

©2000 The XML Handbook™

Creating a document type definition

Friendly Tutorial

- Document type declaration
- Element type declarations
- Attribute list declarations

©2000 THE XML HANDBOOK™

Chapter 54

Creating your own document type definition is like creating your own markup language. If you have ever chafed at the limitations of a language with a fixed set of element types, such as HTML, TEI or LaTeX, then you will embrace the opportunity to create your own language.[1]

We should note again that it is possible to keep a document type definition completely in your head rather than writing the declarations for a DTD. Sometimes DTD designers do that while they are testing out ideas. Usually, though, you actually commit your ideas to declarations so that a validating processor can help you to keep your documents consistent.

Note also that, for the present, we are maintaining the distinction, discussed in 5.3, “Document type, DTD, and markup declarations”, on page 72, between a document type, the XML markup rules for it (DTD), and the markup declarations that declare the DTD. Those *DTD declarations* are connected to the big kahuna of markup declarations – the *document type declaration*.

1. With its own set of limitations!

54.1 | Document type declaration

A document type declaration for a particular document might say "This document is a concert poster." The document type definition for the document would say "A concert poster must have the following features." As an analogy: in the world of art, you can *declare* yourself a practitioner of a particular movement, or you can *define* the movement by writing its manifesto.

The XML spec uses the abbreviation DTD to refer to document type definitions because we speak of them much more often than document type declarations. The DTD defines the allowed element types, attributes and entities and can express some constraints on their combination.

A document that conforms to its DTD is said to be *valid*. Just as an English sentence can be ungrammatical, a document can fail to conform to its DTD and thus be *invalid*. That does not necessarily mean, however, that it ceases to be an XML document. The word valid does not have its usual meaning here. An artist can fail to uphold the principles of an artistic movement without ceasing to be an artist, and an XML document can violate its DTD and yet remain a well-formed XML document.

As the document type declaration is optional, a well-formed XML document can choose not to declare conformance to any DTD at all. It cannot then be a valid document, because it cannot be checked for conformance to a DTD. It is not invalid, because it does not violate the constraints of a DTD.

XML has no good word for these merely well-formed documents. Some people call them "well-formed", but that is insufficiently precise. If the document were not well-formed, it would not be XML (by definition). Saying that a document is well-formed does not tell us anything about its conformance to a DTD at all.

For this reason, we prefer the terms used by the ISO for full-SGML: *type-valid*, meaning "valid with respect to a document type", and *non-type-valid*, the converse.

Example 54-1 is an XML document containing a document type declaration and document type definition for mailing labels, followed by an instance of the document type: a single label.

The document type declaration starts on the first line and ends with "]>". The DTD declarations are the lines starting with "<!ELEMENT". Those are *element type declarations*. You can also declare attributes, entities and notations for a DTD.

Example 54-1. XML document with document type declaration

```
<!DOCTYPE label[
    <!ELEMENT label (name, street, city, state, country, code)>
    <!ELEMENT name (#PCDATA)>
    <!ELEMENT street (#PCDATA)>
    <!ELEMENT city (#PCDATA)>
    <!ELEMENT state (#PCDATA)>
    <!ELEMENT country (#PCDATA)>
    <!ELEMENT code (#PCDATA)>
]><label>
<name>Rock N. Robyn</name>
<street>Jay Bird Street</street>
<city>Baltimore</city>
<state>MD</state>
<country>USA</country>
<code>43214</code>
</label>
```

Recall from 2.4, "Entities: The physical structure", on page 28 that an XML document can be broken up into separate objects for storage, called "entities".[1] The document type declaration occurs in the first (or only) entity to be parsed, called the "document entity".

In Example 54-1, all of the DTD declarations that define the label DTD reside within the document entity. However, the DTD could have been partially or completely defined somewhere else. In that case, the document type declaration would contain a reference to another entity containing those declarations.

A document type declaration with only external DTD declarations looks like Example 54-2.

Example 54-2. Document type declaration with external DTD declarations

```
<?xml version="1.0"?>
<!DOCTYPE LABEL SYSTEM "http://www.sgmlsource.com/dtds/label.dtd">
<LABEL>
...
</LABEL>
```

They keyword `SYSTEM` is described more completely in 55.9.1, "System identifiers", on page 800. For now, we will just say that it tells the processor

1. Loosely, an entity is like a file.

©2000 The XML Handbook™

to fetch some resource containing the external information. In this case, the external information is made up of the declarations that define the label DTD. They should be exactly the ones we had in the original label document. The big difference is that now they can be reused in hundreds, thousands, or even millions of label documents. Our simple DTD could be the basis for the largest junk mailing in history!

All document type declarations start with the string "<!DOCTYPE". Next they have the name of an element type that is defined in the DTD. The root element in the instance (described in 53.4, "Elements", on page 732) must be of the type declared in the document type declaration. If any of the DTD declarations are stored externally, the third part of the document type declaration must be either "SYSTEM" or "PUBLIC". We will cover "PUBLIC" later. If it is "SYSTEM", the final part must be a *URI* pointing to the external declarations. A URI is, for all practical purposes, a URL. URIs are discussed in 61.2, "Uniform Resource Identifiers", on page 896.

Spec Excerpt (XML) 54-1. DOCTYPE declaration

```
[28] doctypedecl ::= '<!DOCTYPE' S Name (S ExternalID)? S? ('['
                     (markupdecl | PEReference | S)* ']' S?)? '>'
[75] ExternalID ::=  'SYSTEM' S SystemLiteral
                   | 'PUBLIC' S PubidLiteral S SystemLiteral

[29] markupdecl ::= elementdecl | AttlistDecl | EntityDecl
                     | NotationDecl | PI | Comment
```

54.2 | Internal and external subset

In Example 54-1, the DTD declarations were completely *internal.* They were inside of the document type declaration. In Example 54-2, they were completely external. In many cases, there will be a mix of the two. This section will review these options and show how most XML document type declarations combine an internal part, called the *internal subset* and an external part, called the *external subset.*

From now on, as we'll almost always be writing about DTD declarations, we'll refer to them as "the DTD". We'll resort to the finer distinctions only when necessary for clarity.

We will start with an example of a DTD in Example 54-3.

©2000 THE XML HANDBOOK™

Table 54-1 Content specification types

Content specification type	Allowed content
EMPTY content	May not have content. They are typically used for their attributes.
ANY content	May have any content at all.
Mixed content	May have character data or a mix of character data and subelements specified in mixed content specification.
Element content	May have only subelements specified in element content specification

54.4.1 *Empty content*

Sometimes we want an element type that can never have any content. We would give it a content specification of `EMPTY`. For instance an image element type like HTML's `img` would include a graphic from somewhere else. It would do this through an attribute and would not need any subelements or character data content. A cross-reference element type might not need content because the text for the reference might be generated from the target. A reference to an element type with the title "More about XML" might become "See *More about XML* on page 14".

You can declare an element type to have empty content by using the `EMPTY` keyword as the content specification. See Example 54-9.

Example 54-9. Empty element type

```
<!ELEMENT MY-EMPTY-ELEMENT EMPTY>
```

54.4.2 *ANY content*

Occasionally, you want an element type to be able to hold any element or character data. You can do this if you give it a content spec of `ANY` as in Example 54-10.

Example 54-10. Element type with ANY content.

```
<!ELEMENT LOOSEY-GOOSEY ANY>
```

This is rarely done. Typically we introduce element type declarations to express the structure of our document types. An element type that has an ANY content specification is completely unstructured. It can contain any combination of character data and subelements. Still, ANY content element types are occasionally useful, especially while a DTD is being developed. If you are developing a DTD for existing documents, then you could declare each element type to have ANY content to get the document to validate. Then you could try to figure out more precise content specifications for each element type, one at a time.

54.4.3 *Mixed content*

Element types with *mixed content* are allowed to hold either character data alone or character data with child elements interspersed. A `paragraph` is a good example of a typical mixed content element. It might have character data with some mixed in `emphasis` and `quotation` subelements. The simplest mixed content specifications allow data only and start with a left parenthesis character ("("), followed by the string `#PCDATA` and a final close parenthesis (")"). Example 54-11 demonstrates.

Example 54-11. Data-only mixed content.

```
<!ELEMENT emph (#PCDATA)>
<!ELEMENT foreign-language ( #PCDATA ) >
```

You may put white space between the parenthesis and the string `#PCDATA` if you like. The declarations above create element types that cannot contain subelements. Subelements that are detected will be reported as validity errors.

In other words, these elements do not really have "mixed" content in the usual sense. Like the word "valid", XML has a particular meaning for the word that is not very intuitive. Any content specification that contains `#PCDATA` is called mixed, whether subelements are allowed or not.

We can easily extend the DTD to allow a mix of elements and character data. This is shown in Example 54-12.

Example 54-12. Allow a mix of character data and elements

```
<!ELEMENT paragraph (#PCDATA|emph)*>
<!ELEMENT abstract (#PCDATA|emph|quot)*>
<!ELEMENT title ( #PCDATA | foreign-language | emph )* >
```

Note the trailing asterisks. They are required in content specifications that allow a mix of character data and elements. The reason that they are there will be clear when we study content models. Note also that we can put white space before and after the vertical bar ("|") characters.

These declarations create element types that allow a mix of character data and subelements. The element types listed after the vertical bars ("|"), are the allowed subelements. Example 54-13 would be a valid `title` if we combine the declarations in Example 54-12 with those in Example 54-11.

Example 54-13. Sample data

```
<title>this is a <foreign-language>tres gros</foreign-language>
       title for an <emph>XML</emph> book</title>
```

The `title` has character data ("This is a"), a `foreign-language` subelement, some more character data ("title for an"), an `emph` subelement and some final character data "book". We could have reordered the `emph` and `foreign-language` elements and the character data however we wanted. We could also have introduced as many (or as few) `emph` and `foreign-language` elements as we needed.

54.5 | Content models

The final kind of content specification is a "children" specification. This type of specification says that elements of the type can contain only child elements in its content. You declare an element type as having *element content* by specifying a content model that has only element type names, instead of a mixed content specification or one of the keywords described above.

A content model is a pattern that you set up to declare what subelement types are allowed and in what order they are allowed. A simple model for a `memo` might say that it must contain a `from` followed by a `to` followed by a `subject` followed by a `paragraph`. A more complex model for a `question-and-answer` might require `question` and `answer` elements to alternate.

A model for a `chapter` might require a single `title` element, one or two `author` elements and one or more `paragraphs`. When a document is validated, the processor would check that the element's content matches the model.

A simple content model could have a single subelement type as in Example 54-14.

Example 54-14. A single subelement

```
<!ELEMENT WARNING (PARAGRAPH)>
```

This says that a `WARNING` must have a single `PARAGRAPH` within it. As with mixed content specifications, you may place white space before or after the parentheses. We could also say that a `WARNING` must have a `TITLE` and then a `PARAGRAPH` within it as in Example 54-15.

Example 54-15. Two subelements

```
<!ELEMENT WARNING (TITLE, PARAGRAPH)>
```

The comma (",") between the "TITLE" and "PARAGRAPH" GIs indicates that the "TITLE" must precede the "PARAGRAPH" in the "WARNING" element. This is called a *sequence*. Sequences can be as long as you like (Example 54-16).

Example 54-16. Longer sequence

```
<!ELEMENT MEMO (FROM, TO, SUBJECT, BODY)>
```

You may put white space before or after the comma (",") between two parts of the sequence.

Sometimes you want to have a *choice* rather than a sequence. For instance Example 54-17 shows a declaration for an element type that allows a FIGURE to contain either a GRAPHIC element (inserting an external graphic) or a CODE element (inserting some computer code).

Example 54-17. Allowing choice

```
<!ELEMENT FIGURE (GRAPHIC|CODE)>
```

The vertical bar character ("|") indicates that the author can choose between the elements. You can put white space before or after the vertical bar. You may have as many choices as you want:

Example 54-18. Multiple Choices

```
<!ELEMENT FIGURE (CODE|TABLE | FLOW-CHART| SCREEN-SHOT)>
```

You may also combine choices and sequences using parenthesis. When you wrap parenthesis around a choice or sequence, it becomes a *content particle*. Individual GIs are also content particles. You can use any content particle where ever you would use a GI in a content model:

Example 54-19. Content particles

```
<!ELEMENT FIGURE (CAPTION, (CODE|TABLE|FLOW-CHART|SCREEN-SHOT) )>
<!ELEMENT CREATED ((AUTHOR | CO-AUTHORS), DATE )>
```

The content model for FIGURE is thus made up of a sequence of two content particles. The first content particle is a single element type name. The second is a choice of several element type names. You can break down the content model for CREATED in the same way.

You can make some fairly complex models this way. But when you write a DTD for a book, you do not know in advance how many chapters the book will have, nor how many paragraphs each chapter will contain. You need a way of saying that the part of the content specification that allows captions is *repeatable* – that you can match it many times.

Sometimes you will also want to make an element optional. For instance, some figures may not have captions. You may want to say that part of the specification for figures is optional.

XML allows you to specify that a content particle is optional or repeatable using an *occurrence indicator*. Table 54-2 shows the three occurrence indicators.

Table 54-2 Occurrence indicators

Indicator	Content particle is...
?	Optional (0 or 1 time).
*	Optional and repeatable (0 or more times)
+	Required and repeatable (1 or more times)

Occurrence indicators directly follow a GI, sequence or choice. The occurrence indicator cannot be preceded by white space.

Example 54-20 illustrates how we can make captions optional on figures:

Example 54-20. Captions are optional.

```
<!ELEMENT FIGURE (CAPTION?, (CODE|TABLE|FLOW-CHART|SCREEN-SHOT))>
```

We can allow footnotes to have multiple paragraphs:

Example 54-21. Footnotes have multiple paragraphs

```
<!ELEMENT FOOTNOTE (P+)>
```

Because we used the "+" indicator, footnotes must have at least one paragraph. We could also have expressed this in another way:

Example 54-22. Multiple paragraphs: the sequel

```
<!ELEMENT FOOTNOTE (P, P*)>
```

This would require a leading paragraph and then 0 or more paragraphs following. That would achieve the same effect as requiring 1 or more paragraphs. The "+" operator is just a little more convenient than repeating the preceding content particle.

We can combine occurrence indicators with sequences or choices:

Example 54-23. Occurrence indicators and sequences

```
<!ELEMENT QUESTION-AND-ANSWER (INTRODUCTION,
                               (QUESTION, ANSWER)+,
                               COPYRIGHT?)>
```

It is also possible to make all of the element types in a content model optional:

Example 54-24. Optional content

```
<!ELEMENT IMAGE (CAPTION?)>
```

This allows the `IMAGE` element to be empty sometimes and not other times. The question mark indicates that `CAPTION` is optional. Most likely these `IMAGE` elements would link to an external graphic through an attribute. The author would only provide content if he wanted to provide a caption.

In the document instance, empty `IMAGE` elements look identical to how they would look if `IMAGE` had been declared to be always empty. There is no way to tell from the document instance whether they were declared as empty or are merely empty in a particular case.

54.6 | Attributes

Attributes allow an author to attach extra information to the elements in a document. For instance a `code` element for computer code might have a `lang` attribute declaring the language that the code is in. On the other hand, you could also use a `lang` subelement for the same purpose. It is the DTD designer's responsibility to choose a way and embody that in the DTD. Attributes have strengths and weaknesses that differentiate them

©2000 THE XML HANDBOOK™

from subelements so you can usually make the decision without too much difficulty.

The largest difference between elements and attributes is that attributes cannot contain elements and there is no such thing as a "sub-attribute". Attributes are always either text strings with no explicit structure (at least as far as XML is concerned) or simple lists of strings. That means that a `chapter` should not be an attribute of a `book` element, because there would be no place to put the titles and paragraphs of the chapter. You will typically use attributes for small, simple, unstructured "extra" information.

Another important difference between elements and attributes is that each of an element's attributes may be specified only once, and they may be specified in any order. This is often convenient because memorizing the order of things can be difficult. Elements, on the other hand, must occur in the order specified and may occur as many times as the DTD allows. Thus you must use elements for things that must be repeated, or must follow a certain pattern or order that you want the XML parser to enforce.

These technical concerns are often enough to make the decision for you. But if everything else is equal, there are some usability considerations that can help. One rule of thumb that some people use (with neither perfect success nor constant abject failure) is that elements usually represent data that is the natural content that should appear in every print-out or other rendition, Most formatting systems print out elements by default and do not print out attributes unless you specifically ask for them. Attributes represent data that is of secondary importance and is often information about the information (*"metainformation"*).

Also, attribute names usually represent properties of objects, but element-type names usually represent parts of objects. So given a `person` element, subelements might represent parts of the body and attributes might represent properties like weight, height, and accumulated karma points.

We would advise you not to spend too much of your life trying to figure out exactly what qualifies as a part and what qualifies as a property. Experience shows that the question "what is a property?" ranks with "what is the good life?" and "what is art?". The technical concerns are usually a good indicator of the philosophical category in any event.

54.6.1 *Attribute-list declarations*

Attributes are declared for specific element types. You declare attributes for a particular element type using an *attribute-list declaration.* You will often see an attribute-list declaration right beside an element type declaration:

Example 54-25. My first ATTLIST

```
<!ELEMENT PERSON (#PCDATA)>
<!ATTLIST PERSON EMAIL CDATA #REQUIRED>
```

Attribute declarations start with the string "<!ATTLIST". Immediately after the white space comes an element type's generic identifier. After that comes the attribute's *name*, its *type* and its *default*. In the example above, the attribute is named EMAIL and is valid on PERSON elements. Its value must be *character data* and it is required – there is no default and the author must supply a value for the attribute on every PERSON element.

Spec Excerpt (XML) 54-3. Attribute-list declarations

```
[52]  AttlistDecl ::=  '<!ATTLIST' S Name AttDef* S? '>'
[53]  AttDef ::=  S Name S AttType S DefaultDecl
```

You can declare many attributes in a single attribute-list declaration.[1]

Example 54-26. Declaring multiple attributes

```
<!ATTLIST PERSON EMAIL CDATA #REQUIRED
                 PHONE CDATA #REQUIRED
                 FAX CDATA #REQUIRED>
```

1. That's why it is called a list!

You can also have multiple attribute-list declarations for a single element type:

Example 54-27. Multiple declarations for one element type

```
<!ATTLIST PERSON HONORIFIC CDATA #REQUIRED>
<!ATTLIST PERSON POSITION CDATA #REQUIRED
                 ORGANIZATION CDATA #REQUIRED>
```

This is equivalent to putting the declarations altogether into a single attribute-list declaration.

It is even possible to have multiple declarations for the same attribute of the same element type. When this occurs, the first declaration of the attribute is binding and the rest are ignored. This is analogous to the situation with entity declarations.

Note that two different element types can have attributes with the same name without there being a conflict. Despite the fact that these attributes have the same name, they are in fact different attributes. For instance a SHIRT element could have an attribute SIZE that exhibits values SMALL, MEDIUM and LARGE and a PANTS element in the same DTD could have an attribute also named SIZE that is a measurement in inches:

Example 54-28. Two size attributes

```
      <!-- These are -->
<!ATTLIST SHIRT SIZE (SMALL|MEDIUM|LARGE) #REQUIRED>

      <!-- two different attributes -->
<!ATTLIST PANTS SIZE NMTOKEN #REQUIRED>
```

It is not good practice to allow attributes with the same name to have different semantics or allowed values in the same document. That can be quite confusing for authors.

54.6.2 *Attribute defaults*

Attributes can have *default values*. If the author does not specify an attribute value then the processor supplies the default value if it exists. A DTD designer can also choose not to supply a default.

©2000 THE XML HANDBOOK™

Specifying a default is simple. You merely include the default after the type or list of allowed values in the attribute list declaration:

Example 54-29. Default values

```
<!ATTLIST SHIRT SIZE (SMALL|MEDIUM|LARGE) MEDIUM>
<!ATTLIST SHOES SIZE NMTOKEN "13">
```

Any value that meets the constraints of the attribute list declaration is legal as a default value. You could not, however, use "***" as a default value for an attribute with declared type NMTOKEN any more than you could do so in a start-tag in the document instance.

Sometimes you want to allow the user to omit a value for a particular attribute without forcing a particular default. For instance you could have an element SHIRT which has a SIZE attribute with a declared type of NMTOKEN. But some shirts are "one size fits all". They do not have a size. You want the author to be able to leave this value out and you want the processing system to *imply* that the shirt is "one size fits all". You can do this with an *impliable* attribute:

Example 54-30. Impliable attribute

```
<!ATTLIST SHIRT SIZE NMTOKEN #IMPLIED>
```

The string "#IMPLIED" gives any processing program the right to insert whatever value it feels is appropriate. This may seem like a lot of freedom to give a programmer, but typically implied attributes are simply ignored. In the case of our SHIRT, there is no need to worry about "one size fits all" shirts because anybody can wear them. Authors should only depend upon the implied value when they do not care or where there is a well-defined convention of what the lack of a value "really" means. This is again a case of semantics and would be communicated to the author through some other document, DTD comment or other communication mechanism.

It is easy for an author to not specify a value for an attribute that is not required: just do not mention the attribute. Note that specifying an attribute value that is an empty string is *not* the same as not specifying an attribute value:

Example 54-31. Empty versus non-existent

```
<SHIRT>          <!-- This conforms to the declaration above. -->
<SHIRT SIZE=""> <!-- This does *not* conform to the declaration. -->
```

The opposite situation to providing a default is where a document type designer wants to force the author to choose a value. If a value for an attribute is important and cannot reliably be defaulted, the designer can require authors to specify it with a *required* attribute default:

Example 54-32. Required attribute

```
<!ATTLIST IMAGE URL CDATA #REQUIRED>
```

In this case, the DTD designer has made the `URL` attribute required on all `IMAGE` elements. This makes sense because without a URL to locate the image file, the `image` element is useless.

It may be surprising, but there are even times when it is useful to supply an attribute value that cannot be overridden at all. This is rare, but worth knowing about. Imagine, for instance, that an Internet directory maintainer like *Yahoo*™ decides to write a robot [1] that will automatically extract the first section title of every document indexed by the directory. The difficulty is that different DTDs will have different element-type names for titles. HTML-like DTDs use `H1` etc. DocBook-like DTDs use `title`. TEI-like DTDs use `head`. Even if the robot knows about these DTDs, what about all of the others? There are potentially as many DTDs in existence as there are XML documents! It is not feasible to write a robot that can understand every document type.

The vendor needs to achieve some form of standardization. But it cannot force everyone to conform to the same DTD: that is exactly what XML is supposed to avoid! Instead, they can ask all document creators to label the elements that perform the *role of* section titles. They could do this with an attribute, such as `title-element`. The robot can then use the content of those elements to generate its index.

1. A robot is an automatic Web information gatherer.

Each DTD designer thinks through the list of element types to add the attribute to. They specify what their element types mean in terms of the indexing system understood by the robot. They may not want authors changing the value on an element by element basis. They can prevent this with *fixed* attributes:

Example 54-33. Fixed attributes

```
<!ATTLIST H1 TITLE-ELEMENT CDATA #FIXED "TITLE-ELEMENT">
<!ATTLIST HEAD TITLE-ELEMENT CDATA #FIXED "TITLE-ELEMENT">
<!ATTLIST TITLE TITLE-ELEMENT CDATA #FIXED "TITLE-ELEMENT">
```

Now all of the appropriate elements are marked with the attribute. No matter what else is in the DTD, the robot can find what it is looking for.

54.6.3 *Attribute types*

An important feature of attributes is that attributes have *types* that can enforce certain *lexical* and *semantic* constraints. *Lexical* constraints are constraints like "this attribute must contain only numerals". Semantic constraints are along the lines of "this attribute must contain the name of a declared entity". These constraints tend to be very useful in making robust DTDs and document processing systems.

However, it is vital to remember that **the value of an attribute is not necessarily the exact character string that you enter between the quotation marks**. That string first goes through a process called *attribute-value normalization* on its way to becoming the attribute value. Since attribute types apply to the *normalized value*, we had better digress for a moment to master normalization.

54.6.3.1 Attribute value normalization

XML processors normalize attribute values to make author's lives simpler. If it were not for normalization, you would have to be very careful where you put white space in an attribute value. For instance if you broke an attribute value across a line:

Example 54-34. Normalization

```
<GRAPHIC ALTERNATE-TEXT="This is a picture of a penguin
    doing the ritual mating dance">
```

You might do this merely because the text is too long for a single line in a text editor.

This sort of thing is normalized by the XML processor. The rules for this are a little intricate, but most times they will just do what you want them to. Let's look at them.

All XML attribute values are entered as quoted strings. They start and end with either single-quotes ("'") or double-quotes ("""). If you want to embed a single-quote character into an attribute value delimited by single quotes or a double-quote character into an attribute value delimited by double quotes, then you must use an entity reference as described in 53.7.1, "Predefined entities", on page 741.

The first thing the XML parser does to prepare for normalization is to strip off the surrounding quotes.

Then, character references are replaced by the characters that they reference. As we discussed earlier, character references allow you to easily insert "funny" characters.

Next, general entity references are replaced. This is important to note. While it is true that entity references are not allowed in markup, unnormalized attribute values are *text* – a mixture of markup and data. After normalization, only the data remains.[1].

If the expansion for an entity reference has another entity reference within it, that is expanded also, and so on and so forth. This would be rare in an entity used in an attribute value. After all, attribute values are usually very short and simple. An entity reference in an attribute value cannot be to an external entity.

Newline characters in attribute values are replaced by spaces. *If* the attribute is known to be one of the tokenized types[2] (see below), then the parser must further remove leading and trailing spaces. So "   token   "

---

1. Philosophically, attribute values are metadata, but it is an article of faith in the XML world that metadata is data.

becomes "token". It also collapses multiple spaces between tokens into a single space, so that "space   between" would become "space between". The distinction between *unnormalized attribute value text* and *normalized attribute value data* trips up even the experts. Remember, when reading about attribute types, that they apply to the normalized data, not the unnormalized text.

54.6.3.2 CDATA and name token attributes

The simplest type of attribute is a *CDATA* attribute. The CDATA stands for "character data". The declaration for such an attribute looks like this:

Example 54-35. CDATA Attributes

```
<!DOCTYPE ARTICLE[
<!ELEMENT ARTICLE>
<!ATTLIST ARTICLE DATE CDATA #REQUIRED>
...
]>
<ARTICLE DATE="January 15, 1999">
...
</ARTICLE>
```

Character data attribute values can be any string of characters. Basically anything else is legal in this type of attribute value.

Name token (NMTOKEN) attributes are somewhat like CDATA attributes. The biggest difference is that they are restricted in the characters that name tokens allow. Name tokens were described in 53.1.4, "Names and name tokens", on page 726. To refresh your memory, they are strings made up of

2. If, in other words, attribute-list declarations were provided and the processor is either a validating processor or a non-validating processor that decides to read them.

©2000 THE XML HANDBOOK™

letters, numbers and a select group of special characters: period ("."), dash ("-"), underscore ("_") and colon (":").

Example 54-36. Name token attribute type

```
<!DOCTYPE PARTS-LIST[
...
<!ATTLIST PART DATE NMTOKEN #REQUIRED>
...
]>
<PARTS-LIST>
...
<PART DATE="1998-05-04">...</PART>

</PARTS-LIST>
]>
```

An empty string is not a valid name token, whereas it would be a valid CDATA attribute value.

Name tokens can be used to allow an attribute to contain numbers that need special characters. They allow the dash, which can be used as a minus sign, the period, which can be a decimal point, and numbers. These are useful for fractional and negative numbers. You can also use alphabetic characters to specify units.

Name tokens can also be used for naming things. This is similar to how you might use variable names in a programming language. For instance, if you used XML to describe the structure of a database, you might use name tokens to name and refer to fields and tables. The restrictions on the name token attribute type would prevent most of the characters that would be illegal in field and table names (spaces, most forms of punctuation, etc.). If there is a reason that all fields or record names must be unique, then you would instead use the *ID* attribute type discussed in 54.6.3.4, "ID and IDREF attributes", on page 774.

If it is appropriate to have more than one name token, then you can use the NMTOKENS attribute type which stands for "name tokens". For instance Example 54-37 shows how you might declare a DTD representing a database.

One other difference between CDATA attributes and NMTOKEN attributes is in their *normalization*. This was discussed in 54.6.3.1, "Attribute value normalization", on page 769.

Example 54-37. Name tokens attribute type

```
<!DOCTYPE DATABASE [
...
<!ELEMENT TABLE EMPTY>
<!ATTLIST TABLE NAME NMTOKEN #REQUIRED
                FIELDS NMTOKENS #REQUIRED>
...
]>
<DATABASE>
...
<TABLE NAME="SECURITY" FIELDS="USERID PASSWORD DEPARTMENT">
...
</DATABASE>
```

54.6.3.3 Enumerated and notation attributes

Sometimes as a DTD designer you want to create an attribute that can only exhibit one of a short list of values: "small/medium/large", "fast/slow"; "north/south/east/west". *Enumerated attribute types* allow this. In a sense, they provide a choice or menu of options.

The syntax is reminiscent of choice lists in element type declarations:

Example 54-38. Choice lists

```
<!ATTLIST OPTIONS CHOICE (OPTION1|OPTION2|OPTION3) #REQUIRED>
```

You may provide as many choices as you like. Each choice is an XML *name token* and must meet the syntactic requirements of name tokens described in 53.1.4, "Names and name tokens", on page 726.

There is another related attribute type called a *notation* attribute. This attribute allows the author to declare that the element's content conforms to a declared notation. Here is an example involving several ways of representing dates:

Example 54-39. Different date representations

```
<!ATTLIST DATE TYPE NOTATION (EUDATE|USDATE|ISODATE) #REQUIRED>
```

In a valid document, each notation allowed must also be declared with a notation declaration.

54.6.3.4 ID and IDREF attributes

Sometimes it is important to be able to give a name to a particular occurrence of an element type. For instance, to make a simple hypertext link or cross-reference from one element to another, you can name a particular section or figure. Later, you can refer to it by its name. The target element is labeled with an *ID* attribute. The other element refers to it with an *IDREF* attribute. This is shown in Example 54-40.

Example 54-40. ID and IDREF used for cross-referencing

```
<!DOCTYPE BOOK [
...
<!ELEMENT SECTION (TITLE, P*)>
<!ATTLIST SECTION MY-ID ID #IMPLIED>
<!ELEMENT CROSS-REFERENCE EMPTY>
<!ATTLIST CROSS-REFERENCE TARGET IDREF #REQUIRED>
...
]>
<BOOK>
...
<SECTION MY-ID=Why.XML.Rocks><TITLE>Features of XML</TITLE>
...
</SECTION>

...
If you want to recall why XML is so great, please see
the section titled <CROSS-REFERENCE TARGET="Why.XML.Rocks"/>.
...
</BOOK>
```

The stylesheet would instruct browsers and formatters to replace the cross-reference element with the name of the section. This would probably be italicized and hyperlinked or labeled with a page number if appropriate.

Note that we made the section's `MY-ID` optional. Some sections will not need to be the target of a cross-reference, hypertext link or other reference and will not need to be uniquely identified. The `TARGET` attribute on `CROSS-REFERENCE` is required. It does not make sense to have a cross-reference that does not actually refer to another element.

IDs are XML names, with all of the constraints described in 53.1.4, "Names and name tokens", on page 726. Every element can have at most one ID, and thus only one attribute per element type be an `ID` attribute. All IDs specified in an XML document must be unique. A document with two

ID attributes whose values are the same is invalid. Thus "chapter" would not be a good name for an ID, because it would make sense to use it in many places. "introduction.chapter" would be a logical ID because it would uniquely identify a particular chapter.

IDREF attributes must refer to an element in the document. You may have as many IDREFs referring to a single element as you need. It is also possible to declare an attribute that can potentially exhibit more than one IDREF by declaring it to be of type IDREFS:

Example 54-41. IDREFS attribute

```
<!ATTLIST RELATED-CHAPTERS TARGETS IDREFS #REQUIRED>
```

Now the TARGETS attribute may have one or more IDREFs as its value. There is no way to use XML to require that an attribute take two or more, or three or more, (etc.) IDREFs. You will recall that we could do that sort of thing using content models in element type declarations. There is no such thing as a content model for attributes. You could model this same situation by declaring RELATED-CHAPTERS to have content of one or more or two or more (etc.) CHAPTER-REF elements that each have a single IDREF attribute (named TARGET in Example 54-42).

Example 54-42. IDREF attributes

```
<!DOCTYPE BOOK[
...
<!ELEMENT RELATED-CHAPTERS (CHAPTER-REF+)>
<!ELEMENT CHAPTER-REF EMPTY>
<!ATTLIST CHAPTER-REF TARGET IDREF #REQUIRED>
...
]>
<BOOK>
...
<RELATED-CHAPTERS>
<CHAPTER-REF TARGET="introduction.to.xml">
<CHAPTER-REF TARGET="xml.rocks">
</RELATED-CHAPTERS>
...
</BOOK>
```

©2000 The XML Handbook™

As you can see, element type declarations have the benefit of having content models, which can define complex structures, and attributes have the benefit of attribute types, which can enforce lexical and semantic constraints. You can combine these strengths to make intricate structures when this is appropriate.

54.6.3.5 ENTITY attributes

External unparsed entities are XML's way of referring to objects (files, CGI script output, etc.) on the Web that should not be parsed according to XML's rules. Anything from HTML documents to pictures to word processor files fall into this category. It is possible to refer to unparsed entities using an attribute with declared type *ENTITY*. This is typically done either to hyperlink to, reference or include an external object. This is shown in Example 54-43.

Example 54-43. Entity attribute type

```
<!DOCTYPE ARTICLE[
<!ATTLIST BOOK-REF TARGET ENTITY #REQUIRED>
...
<!ENTITY another-book SYSTEM
        "http://www.buyOurBooks.com/TheOtherBook.html" NDATA HTML>
...
]><BOOK>
...
<BOOK-REF target="another-book">
...
</BOOK>
```

You can also declare an attribute to be of type *ENTITIES*, in which case its value may be the name of more than one entity. It is up to the application or stylesheet to determine whether a reference to the entity should be treated as a hot link, embed link or some other kind of link. The processor merely informs the application of the existence and notation of the entity. You can find information on unparsed entities and notations in Chapter 55, "Entities: Breaking up is easy to do", on page 780 and 54.7, "Notation Declarations", on page 778.

©2000 THE XML HANDBOOK™

54.6.3.6 Summary of attribute types

There are two *enumerated* attribute types: *enumeration* attributes and `NOTATION` attributes.

Seven attribute types are known as *tokenized* types because each value represents either a single token (`ID`, `IDREF`, `ENTITY`, `NMTOKEN`) or a list of tokens (`IDREFS`, `ENTITIES`, and `NMTOKENS`).

The final type is the `CDATA` string type which is the least constrained and can hold any combination of XML characters as long as "special characters" (the quote characters and ampersand) are properly entered. Table 54-3 summarizes.

Table 54-3 Summary of attribute types

Type	Lexical constraint	Semantic constraint
CDATA	None	None
Enumeration	Name Token	Must be in the declared list.
NOTATION	Name	Must be in the declared list and a declared notation name.
ID	Name	Must be unique in document.
IDREF	Name	Must be some element's ID.
IDREFS	Names	Must each be some element's ID.
ENTITY	Name	Must be an unparsed entity's name.
ENTITIES	Names	Must each be unparsed entity's name.
NMTOKEN	Name Token	None
NMTOKENS	Name Tokens	None

54.7 | Notation Declarations

Notations are referred to in various parts of an XML document, for describing the data content notation of different things. A data content notation is the definition of how the bits and bytes of class of object should be interpreted. According to this definition, XML is a data content notation, because it defines how the bits and bytes of XML documents should be interpreted. Your favorite word processor also has a data content notation. The notation declaration gives an internal name to an existing notation so that it can be referred to in attribute list declarations, unparsed entity declarations, and processing instructions.

The most obvious place that an XML document would want to describe the notation of a data object is in a reference to some other resource on the web. It could be an embedded graphic, an MPEG movie that is the target of a hyperlink, or anything else. The XML facility for linking to these data resources is the entity declaration, and as we discussed earlier, they are referred to as *unparsed entities*. Part of the declaration of an unparsed entity is the name of a declared notation that provides some form of pointer to the external definition of the notation. The external definition could be a public or system identifier for documentation on the notation, some formal specification or a helper application that can handle objects represented in the notation.

Example 54-44. Notations for unparsed entities

```
<!NOTATION HTML SYSTEM "http://www.w3.org/Markup">
<!NOTATION GIF SYSTEM "gifmagic.exe">
```

Another place that notations arise are in the notation attribute type. You use this attribute type when you want to express the notation for the data content of an XML element. For instance, if you had a date element that used ISO or EU date formats, you could declare notations for each format:

Example 54-45. Notations for data content

```
<!NOTATION ISODATE SYSTEM "http://www.iso.ch/date_specification">
<!NOTATION EUDATE SYSTEM "http://www.eu.eu/date_specification">
<!ELEMENT TODAY (#PCDATA)>
<!ATTLIST TODAY DATE-FORMAT NOTATION (ISODATE|EUDATE) #REQUIRED>
```

Now the DATE-FORMAT attribute would be restricted to those two values, and would thus signal to the application that the content of the TODAY element conforms to one or the other.

Note *You can specify datatypes more precisely for data content and attribute values by using the facilities described in* *Chapter 63, "Datatypes", on page 918.*

Finally, notations can be used to give XML names to the targets for processing instructions. This is not strictly required by XML, but it is a good practice because it provides a sort of documentation for the PI and could even be used by an application to invoke the target.

This seems like a good way to close this chapter. DTDs are about improving the permanence, longevity, and wide reuse of your data, and the predictability and reliability of its processing. If you use them wisely, they will save you time and money.

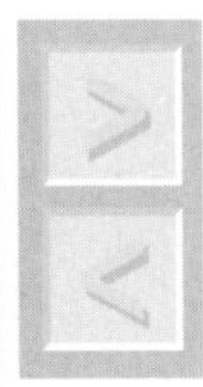

Tip *Learning the syntax of markup declarations so that you can write DTDs is important, but learning how to choose the right element types and attributes for a job is a subtle process that requires a book of its own. We suggest David Megginson's Structuring XML Documents, also in this series (ISBN 0-13-642299-3).*

Entities: Breaking up is easy to do

Tad Tougher Tutorial

- Parameter and general
- Internal and external
- Parsed and unparsed

©2000 The XML Handbook™

Chapter 55

XML allows flexible organization of document text. The XML constructs that provide this flexibility are called entities. They allow a document to be broken up into multiple storage objects and are important tools for reusing and maintaining text.

55.1 | Overview

In simple cases, an entity is like an abbreviation in that it is used as a short form for some text. We call the "abbreviation" the *entity name* and the long form the *entity content*. That content could be as short as a character or as long as a chapter. For instance, in an XML document, the entity `dtd` could have the phrase "document type definition" as its content. Using a reference to that entity is like using the word DTD as an abbreviation for that phrase – the parser replaces the reference with the content.

You create the entity with an *entity declaration*. Example 55-1 is an entity declaration for an abbreviation.

Entities can be much more than just abbreviations. There are several different kinds of entities with different uses. We will first introduce the differ-

Example 55-1. Entity used as an abbreviation

```
<!ENTITY dtd "document type definition">
```

ent variants in this overview and then come back and describe them more precisely in the rest of the chapter. We approach the topic in this way because we cannot discuss the various types of entity entirely linearly. Our first pass will acquaint you with the major types and the second one will tie them together and provide the information you need to actually use them.

Another way to think of an entity is as a box with a label. The label is the entity's name. The content of the box is some sort of text or data. The entity declaration creates the box and sticks on a label with the name. Sometimes the box holds XML text that is going to be *parsed* (interpreted according to the rules of the XML notation), and sometimes it holds data, which should not be.

If the content of an entity is XML text that the processor should parse, the XML spec calls it a *parsed entity*. The name is badly chosen because it is, in fact, unparsed; it will be parsed only if and when it is actually used.

If the content of an entity is data that is not to be parsed, the XML spec calls it an *unparsed entity*. This name isn't so great either because, as we just pointed out, an XML text entity is also unparsed.

We'll try to minimize the confusion and to avoid saying things like "a parsed entity will be parsed by the XML parser". But we sure wish they had named them "text entity" and "data entity".

The abbreviation in Example 55-1 is a parsed entity. Parsed entities, being XML text, can also contain markup. Example 55-2 is a declaration for a parsed entity with some markup in it.

Example 55-2. Parsed entity with markup

```
<!ENTITY dtd "<term>document type definition</term>">
```

The processor can also fetch content from somewhere on the Web and put that into the box. This is an *external* entity. For instance, it could fetch a chapter of a book and put it into an entity. This would allow you to reuse the chapter between books. Another benefit is that you could edit the chapter separately with a sufficiently intelligent editor. This would be very useful if you were working on a team project and wanted different people to work on different parts of a document at once. Example 55-3 demonstrates.

Example 55-3. External entity declaration

```
<!ENTITY intro-chapter SYSTEM "http://www.megacorp.com/intro.xml">
```

Entities also allow you to edit very large documents without running out of memory. Depending on your software and needs, either each volume or even each article in an encyclopedia could be an entity.

An author or DTD designer refers to an entity through an *entity reference*. The XML processor replaces the reference by the content, as if it were an abbreviation and the content was the expanded phrase. This process is called *inclusion*. After the operation we say either that the entity reference has been *replaced* by the entity content or that the entity content has been *included*. Which you would use depends on whether you are talking from the point of view of the entity reference or the entity content. The content of parsed entities is called their *replacement text*.

Example 55-4 is an example of a parsed entity declaration and its associated reference.

Example 55-4. Entity Declaration

```
<!DOCTYPE MAGAZINE[
...
<!ENTITY title "Hacker Life">
...
]>
<MAGAZINE>
<TITLE>&title;</TITLE>
...
<P>Welcome to the introductory issue of &title;. &title; is
geared to today's modern hacker.
...
</MAGAZINE>
```

Anywhere in the document instance that the entity reference "&title;" appears, it is *replaced* by the text "Hacker Life". It is just as valid to say that "Hacker Life" is *included* at each point where the reference occurs. The ampersand character starts all general entity references and the semicolon ends them. The text between is an entity name.

Spec Excerpt (XML) 55-1. General entity reference

```
[68]  EntityRef ::=  '&' Name ';'
```

We have looked at entities that can be used in the creation of XML documents. Others can only be used to create XML DTDs. The ones we have been using all along are called *general* entities. They are called general entities because they can generally be used anywhere in a document. The ones that we use to create DTDs are called *parameter* entities.

We would use parameter entities for most of the same reasons that we use general entities. We want document type definitions to share declarations for element types, attributes and notations, just as we want documents to share chapters and abbreviations. For instance many DTDs in an organization might share the same definition for a paragraph element type named *para*. The declaration for that element type could be bundled up with other common DTD components and used in document type definitions for memos, letters and reports. Each DTD would include the element type declaration by means of a parameter entity reference.

Unparsed entities are for holding data such as images or molecular models in some data object notation. The application does not expect the processor to parse that information because it is not XML text.

Although it is an oversimplification, it may be helpful in your mind to remember that unparsed entities are often used for pictures and parsed entities are usually used for character text. You would include a picture through an unparsed entity, since picture representations do not (usually!) conform to the XML specification. Of course there are many kinds of non-XML data other than graphics, but if you can at least remember that unparsed entities are used for graphics then you will remember the rest also. Example 55-5 demonstrates.

Example 55-5. Unparsed entity declaration

```
<!ENTITY picture SYSTEM "http://www.home.org/mycat.gif" NDATA GIF>
```

We use unparsed entities through an entity attribute. A processor does not expand an entity attribute, but it tells the application that the use occurred. The application can then do something with it. For instance, if the application is a Web browser, and the entity contains a graphic, it could display the graphic. Entity attributes are covered in 54.6.3.5, "ENTITY attributes", on page 776.

55.2 | Entity details

Caution *Like other names in XML, entity names are case-sensitive: &charles; refers to a different entity from &Charles;.*

It is good that XML entity names are case-sensitive because they are often used to name letters. Case is a convenient way of distinguishing the upper-case version of a letter from the lower-case one. "Sigma" would represent the upper-case version of the Greek letter, and "sigma" would be the lower-case version of it. It would be possible to use some other convention to differentiate the upper- and lower-case versions, such as prefixes. That would give us "uc-Sigma" and "lc-Sigma".

Entities may be declared more than once (Example 55-6), but only the first declaration is *binding*. All subsequent ones are ignored as if they did not exist.

Example 55-6. Contradicting entity declarations

```
<!ENTITY abc "abcdefghijklmnopqrst"> <!-- This is binding. -->
<!ENTITY abc "ABCDEFGHIJKLMNOPQRST"> <!-- This is ignored. -->
<!ENTITY abc "AbCdEfGhIjKlMnOpQrSt"> <!-- So is this.      -->
```

Declarations in the internal DTD subset are processed before those in the external subset, as described in Chapter 54, "Creating a document type definition", on page 748. In practice, document authors can override parameter entities in the external subset of the DTD by declaring entities of the same name in the internal subset.

Entities are not difficult to use, but there are several variations and details that you should be aware of. We have already covered the major varieties, but only informally.

There is one special entity, called the *document entity* which is not declared, does not have a name and cannot be referenced. The document entity is the entity in which the processor started the current parse. Imagine you download a Web document called `catalog.xml`. Before a browser can display it, it must start to parse it, which makes it the document entity. It may include other entities, but because parsing started with `catalog.xml`, those others are not the document entity. They are just ordinary external entities.

If you click on a link and go to another XML Web page, then the processor must parse that page before it can display it. That page is the document entity for the new parse. In other words, even the simplest XML document has at least one entity: the document entity. The processor starts parsing the document in the document entity and it also must finish there.[1]

The document entity is also the entity in which the XML declaration and document type declaration can occur.

You may think it is strange for us to call this an entity when it is not declared as such, but if we were talking about files, it would probably not surprise you. It is common in many computer languages to have files that include other files. Even word processors allow this. We will often use the word entity to refer to a concept analogous to what you would think of as a file, although entities are more flexible. Entities are just "bundles of information". They could reside in databases, zip files, or be created on the fly by a computer program.

55.3 | Classifications of entities

There are many interesting things that you can do with entities. Here are some examples:

- You could store every chapter of a book in a separate file and link them together as entities.

---

1. To put it mystically: it is the alpha and the omega of entities.

- You could "factor out" often-reused text, such as a product name, into an entity so that it is consistently spelled and displayed throughout the document.
- You could update the product name entity to reflect a new version. The change would be instantly visible anywhere the entity was used.
- You could create an entity that would represent "legal boilerplate" text (such as a software license) and reuse that entity in many different documents.
- You could integrate pictures and multimedia objects into your document.
- You could develop "document type definition components" that could be used in many document type definitions. These would allow you to reuse the declarations for common element types (such as paragraph and emphasis) across several document types.

Because XML entities can do so many things, there are several different varieties of them. But XML entities do not break down into six or eight different types with simple names. Rather, you could think of each entity as having three properties that define its type. This is analogous to the way that a person could be tall or short and at the same time male or female and blonde or brunette.

Similarly, entities can be *internal* or *external*, *parsed* or *unparsed* and *general* or *parameter*. There is no single word for a short, male, brunette, and there is similarly no single word for an internal, parsed, parameter entity.

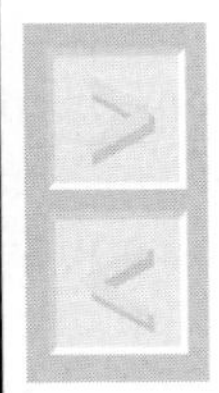

Caution *Some combinations of entity types are impossible. Obviously an entity cannot be both internal and external, just as a person could not be both blonde and brunette. It turns out that due to restrictions on unparsed entities, there are five combinations that are valid and three that are not.*

Most of the rest of this chapter will describe the five types of entities in greater depth. We will use one convention that might be confusing without this note. In a section on, for instance, internal parsed general entities, we may describe a constraint or feature of all general entities. When we do so, we will use the word "general entity" instead of "internal general entity". This convention will allow us to avoid repeating text that is common among entity types. We will refer back to that text from other sections when it becomes relevant.

55.4 | Internal general entities

Internal parsed general entities are the simplest type of entity. They are essentially abbreviations defined completely in the document type declaration section of the XML document.

All internal general entities are parsed entities. This means that the XML processor parses them like any other XML text. Hence we will leave out the redundant word "parsed" and refer to them simply as internal general entities.

The content for an internal general entity is specified by a string literal after the entity's name. The string literal may contain markup, including references to other entities. An example is in Example 55-7.

Example 55-7. Internal general entity

```
<?xml version="1.0"?>
<!DOCTYPE SAMPLE SYSTEM "sample.dtd"[
    <!ENTITY xml "Extensible Markup Language">
]>
<SAMPLE>
    &xml;
</SAMPLE>
```

Internal general entities can be referenced anywhere in the content of an element or attribute value, including an attribute default value (in the DTD). They can also be referenced in the content of another general entity. Because they are general entities, they cannot be used to hold markup declarations for expansion in the DTD. They can only hold element or attribute content. Because of this, Example 55-8 is not well-formed. The only contexts in which general entities can occur in a DTD are entity replacement values and attribute default values.

The grammar rules for internal general entities are described in Spec Excerpt 55-2.

©2000 THE XML HANDBOOK™

Example 55-8. Illegal: General entity cannot contain markup declarations

```
<?xml version="1.0"?>
<!DOCTYPE SAMPLE[
    <!ENTITY xml "Extensible Markup Language">
    &xml;
]>
```

Spec Excerpt (XML) 55-2. Internal general entities

```
[70]  EntityDecl ::=  GEDecl | PEDecl
[71]  GEDecl ::=  '<!ENTITY' S Name S EntityDef S? '>'
[73]  EntityDef ::=  EntityValue | (ExternalID NDataDecl?)
[9]  EntityValue ::=  '"' ([^%&"] | PEReference | Reference)* '"'
                   |  "'" ([^%&'] | PEReference | Reference)* "'"
```

55.5 | External parsed general entities

Every XML entity is either internal or external. The content of internal entities occurs right in the entity declarations. External entities get their content from somewhere else in the system. It might be another file on the hard disk, a Web page or an object in a database. Wherever it is, it is located through an *external identifier*. Usually this is just the word SYSTEM followed by a URI (see 61.2, "Uniform Resource Identifiers", on page 896).

In this section, we are interested specifically in external parsed general entities. Example 55-9 is an example of such an entity.

Example 55-9. External parsed general entity

```
<!ENTITY ent SYSTEM "http://www.house.gov/Constitution.xml">
```

It is the keyword SYSTEM that tells the processor that the next thing in the declaration is a URI. The processor gets the entity's content from that URI. The combination of SYSTEM and the URI is called an external identifier because it identifies an external resource to the processor. There is another kind of external identifier called a PUBLIC identifier. It is denoted by the keyword PUBLIC. External identifiers are described in 55.9, "External identifiers", on page 799

©2000 The XML Handbook™

External parsed general entities can be referenced in the same places that internal general entities can be – the document instance and the replacement text of other general entities – except not in the value of an attribute.

55.5.1 *External parsed entity support is optional*

XML processors are allowed, but not required, to validate an XML document when they parse it. The XML specification allows a processor that is not validating a document to completely ignore declarations of external parsed entities (both parameter and general). There is no way to control this behavior with the standalone document declaration or any other XML markup.

The reason for this is improved Web surfing performance. The XML working group thought that it was important for processors to be able to download the minimum amount of data required to do their job and no more. For instance, a browser could display unresolved external parsed entities as hypertext links that the user could click on to receive. Because the entity would only be downloaded on demand, the original page might display faster.

Unfortunately this is very inconvenient for authors, because it means that external parsed entities are essentially unreliable in systems that you do not completely control (e.g. the Internet vs. an intranet).

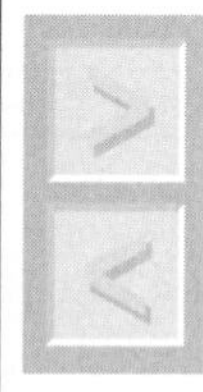

Caution *External parsed entity processing is optional*
XML processors can ignore external parsed entities. If you use them to store parts of your documents, those parts will only show up at the browser vendor's option.

In practice this probably means that you should not put documents that use external entities on the Web until a pattern for browser behavior emerges. In the meantime, tools like James Clark's *sgmlnorm* can read an XML document that uses external entities and expand all of the entities for you.[1] We hope that future versions of the XML specification will make external entity inclusion mandatory.

55.6 | Unparsed entities

Every XML entity is either an *unparsed* entity or a *parsed* entity. Unparsed entities are external entities that the XML processor does not have to parse. For example a graphic, sound, movie or other multimedia object would be included through an unparsed entity. You can imagine the number of error messages you would get if an XML processor tried to interpret a graphic as if it were made up of XML text!

It is occasionally useful to refer to an XML document through an unparsed entity, as if it were in some unparsable representation. You might embed a complete letter document in a magazine document in this way. Rather than extending the magazine DTD to include letter elements, you would refer to it as an unparsed entity. Conceptually, it would be handled in the same way a picture of the letter would be handled. If you refer to it as an unparsed entity, the processor that handles the magazine does not care that the letter is actually XML.

All unparsed entities are external entities because there is no way to express non-XML information in XML entities. They are also all general entities because it is forbidden (and senseless) to embed data in XML DTDs. Hence, the term "unparsed entity" implies the terms "general" and "external".

Syntactically, declarations of unparsed entities are differentiated from those of other external entities by the keyword NDATA followed by a *notation* name.

Spec Excerpt (XML) 55-3. Non-XML data declaration

```
NDataDecl ::=  S 'NDATA' S Name
```

The name at the end is the name of a declared notation. Notation declarations are described in 54.7, "Notation Declarations", on page 778. The

1. sgmlnorm is on the CD-ROM.

processor passes this to the application as a hint about how the application should approach the entity.

If the application knows how to deal with that sort of entity (for instance if it is a common graphics notation) then it could do so directly. A browser might embed a rendition of the entity. It might also make a hyperlink to the entity. If it needs to download or install some other handler such as a Java program or Active-X control, then it could do so. If it needs to ask the user what to do it could do that also. The XML specification does not say what it must do. XML only expects processors to tell applications what the declared notation is and the applications must figure out the rest.

In the rare case that the entity is an XML document, the application might decide to process it, create a rendition of it, and then embed it. Alternatively, it might decide to make a hyperlink to it.

55.7 | Internal and external parameter entities

XML entities are classified according to whether they can be used in the DTD or in the document instance. Entities that can only be used in the DTD are called *parameter* entities. For instance, you might want to wrap up a few declarations for mathematical formulae element types and reuse the declarations from DTD to DTD.

The other entities can be used more generally (throughout the entire document instance), and are called *general* entities. Authors can use general entities as abbreviations, for sharing data among documents, including pictures, and many similar tasks.

There is an important reason why the two types are differentiated. When authors create documents, they want to be able to choose entity names without worrying about accidently choosing a name that was already used by the DTD designer. If there were no distinction between entities specific to the DTD and general to the document instance, according to XML's rules, the first declaration would win. That means that either the author would accidently take the place of ("clobber") a declaration that was meant to be used in the DTD, and thus trigger a cryptic error message, or the DTD designer's entity would clobber the entity that was meant to go in the document instance, and a seemingly random string of DTD-text would appear in the middle of the document! XML prevents this by having two different types of entities with distinct syntaxes for declaration and use.

Parameter entities are distinguished from general entity declarations by a single percent symbol in their declaration, and by a different syntax in their use. Example 55-10 is an example of a parameter entity declaration and use.

Example 55-10. Parameter entity

```
<!DOCTYPE SAMPLE[
    <!-- parameter entity declaration -->
<!ENTITY % sample-entity "<!ELEMENT SAMPLE (#PCDATA)>">
    <!-- parameter entity use -->
%sample-entity;
]>
<SAMPLE>
</SAMPLE>
```

This entity is declared with a syntax similar to that of general entities, but it has a percent sign between the string `<!ENTITY` and the entity's name. This is what differentiates parameter entity declarations from general entity declarations. If you want a general entity you just leave the percent character out.

The entity contains a complete element type declaration. It is referenced on the line after it is declared. Parameter entity references start with the percent-sign and end with the semicolon. The parser replaces the entity reference with the entity's content. In Example 55-10, the processor replaces the reference with the element type declaration "<!ELEMENT SAMPLE (#PCDATA)>". It then parses and interprets the element type declaration as if it had occurred there originally. The element type *is* declared and so the example is valid.

Spec Excerpt (XML) 55-4. Parameter Entity Declaration

```
[72]  PEDecl ::=  '<!ENTITY' S '%' S Name S PEDef S? '>'
[74]  PEDef ::=  EntityValue | ExternalID
[75]  ExternalID ::=  'SYSTEM' S SystemLiteral
              | 'PUBLIC' S PubidLiteral S SystemLiteral
[69]  PEReference ::=  '%' Name ';'
```

Parameter entities can be external, just as general entities can be. But they can never be unparsed. Parameter entities exist to provide building blocks for reusing markup declarations and making DTDs more flexible. It would not make sense to tell the XML processor not to process one! An example of an external parameter entity is in Example 55-11.

Example 55-11. External parameter entity

```
<!DOCTYPE SAMPLE[
    <!-- parameter entity declaration -->
<!ENTITY % sample-entity SYSTEM "pictures.ent">
    <!-- parameter entity use -->
%sample-entity;
]>
<SAMPLE>
</SAMPLE>
```

Parameter entities cannot be referenced in the document instance. In fact, the percent character is not special in the document instance, so if you try to reference a parameter entity in the instance, you will just get the entity reference text in your data, like “%this;”.

Entities can only be referenced after they have been declared. General entities may appear to be referenced before they are declared but that is a mere trick of the light.

Example 55-12. General entity usage

```
<!ENTITY user "This entity uses &usee;.">
<!ENTITY usee "<em>another entity</em>">
```

Example 55-12 is legal because the entity replacement for `&usee;` does not take place until the point where the `user` entity is *referenced.*

With one exception (described below), general entities can only be expanded in the document instance. So the fact that `user` refers to `usee` is recorded, but the replacement is not immediately done. Later, in the document instance, the author will refer to the `user` entity using the general entity reference, `&user;`. At that point, the inclusion of its replacement text will trigger the expansion of the `&usee;` entity reference and the inclusion of its replacement text.

The exception is general entity references in default attribute values. These must be expanded immediately – in the DTD so that they can be checked for validity. These general entities must have been declared before they are used. Whether this exception is important or not depends on how much you use general entities in default attribute values.

Note that the text of a general entity can contain references to other general entities that are declared after it, while the text of a parameter entity cannot reference later-declared parameter entities. That is because parameter entity references are resolved when an entity declaration containing them is *parsed* (i.e., at declaration time). In contrast, general entity references are not resolved until the entity whose declaration contains them is *referenced*, which usually occurs in the document instance, after all DTD declarations have been processed. Referencing can also occur in a default value of an attribute declaration, after all relevant general entity declarations have been processed.

55.8 | Markup may not span entity boundaries

Parsed entities may contain markup as well as character data, but elements and other markup must not span entity boundaries. This means that a particular element may not start in one entity and end in another. If you think of entities as boxes, then an element cannot be half in one box and half in another. Example 55-13 is an example of illegal entity use:

Example 55-13. Elements spanning entity boundaries.

```
<!DOCTYPE SAMPLE[
    <!ENTITY start "<title>This is a">
    <!ENTITY finish "title</title>">
]>

&start;&finish;
```

This document is not well-formed. When the entity references are replaced with their text, they create a title element. This element spans the entities.

Other markup cannot span entities either. Declarations, comments, processing instructions and entity references must all finish in the entity in which they started. This applies to the document entity as much as any other. Markup strings and elements may not start in the document entity and finish in an included entity. This is a subtle but important rule. Documents which fail to conform are not well-formed.

In Example 55-14, entities are used in ways that are illegal. They are all illegal because they start markup without finishing it or finish it without starting it.

Example 55-14. Illegal entities

```
<!DOCTYPE TEST[
    <!ENTITY illegal1 "This will soon be <em>illegal">
    <!ENTITY illegal2 "This will too <em">
    <!ENTITY illegal3 "This will also </em>">
    <!ENTITY illegal4 "And so will <!-- this">
    <!ENTITY illegal5 "And this &too;">
    <!-- note that none of these are illegal yet. -->
...
]><TEST>
<!-- These references are all illegal -->
&illegal1; <!-- Start-tag in entity with no end-tag there. -->
&illegal2; <!-- Start of tag in entity -->
&illegal3; <!-- End-tag in entity with no start-tag there. -->
&illegal4; <!-- Comment start but no end in entity. -->
&illegal5; <!-- Entity reference starts in entity. -->
</TEST>
```

The entities in Example 55-15 can be used legally or illegally. They do not necessarily represent the start or end of elements or markup, because they do not contain the strings that are used to start a tag ("<"), comment ("<!--"), general entity reference ("&") or other markup. Entity content is interpreted as markup if the replacement text would be interpreted as markup in the same context. In other words, the processor expands the entity and then looks for markup. If the markup it finds spans entity boundaries, then it is illegal.

In this case, it is not the declared entities themselves that are causing the problem, but the fact that elements, entities and markup started in the document entity must end there, just as in any other entity. The context of an entity reference is very important. That is what decides whether it is legal or illegal.

This is true even of entities that hold *complete* tags, elements, comments, processing instructions, character references, or entity references. References to those entities are legal anywhere their replacement text would be

Example 55-15. Sometimes legal entities

```
<?xml version="1.0"?>
<!DOCTYPE TEST[
<!ELEMENT TEST (#PCDATA)>
<!ENTITY maybelegal1 "em>"> <!-- May not be part of tag -->
<!ENTITY maybelegal2 "-->"> <!-- May not be comment delimiter -->
<!ENTITY maybelegal3 "ph>"> <!-- May not be part of tag -->
]>
<TEST>
&maybelegal1; <!-- Legal: Interpreted as character data -->
&maybelegal2; <!-- Legal: Interpreted as character data -->
&maybelegal3; <!-- Legal: Interpreted as character data -->

<&maybelegal1; <!-- Illegal: Markup (tag) spans entities -->
<!-- &maybelegal2; Ignored: entity ref ignored in comment -->
<em&maybelegal3;    <!-- Illegal: Markup (tag) spans entities -->
</TEST>
```

legal. The same applies to *validity* (conformance to a document type definition). Example 55-16 is well-formed, but not valid, because the fully expanded document would not be valid. Validity is covered in Chapter 54, "Creating a document type definition", on page 748.

Example 55-16. Well-formed but not valid

```
<?xml version="1.0"?>
<!DOCTYPE TEST[
  <!ELEMENT EVENT (TIME, DESCRIPTION)>
  <!ELEMENT TIME (#PCDATA)>
  <!ELEMENT DESCRIPTION (#PCDATA)>
  <!ENTITY accident "<ERROR>Error</ERROR>">
]>
<EVENT>&accident;</EVENT>
```

The document in the example is well-formed. Both the EVENT and ERROR elements start and end in the same entity. It meets all of the other rules required for it to be well-formed. But it is not valid, because accident's replacement text consists of an ERROR element which is not valid where the entity is referenced. (in the EVENT element).

Conceptually, validation occurs after all entities have been parsed.

Spec Excerpt (XML) 55-5. General entity definition

```
[70]  EntityDecl ::=  GEDecl | PEDecl
[71]  GEDecl ::=  '<!ENTITY' S Name S EntityDef S? '>'
[73]  EntityDef ::=  EntityValue | (ExternalID NDataDecl?)
[72]  PEDecl ::=  '<!ENTITY' S '%' S Name S PEDef S? '>'
[74]  PEDef ::=  EntityValue | ExternalID
```

55.8.1 *Legal parameter entity reference*

Neither general entities nor parameter entities may span markup boundaries, but parameter entities have other restrictions on them. There are precise places that parameter entity references are allowed. Within the internal subset, the rules are simple: parameter entities can only be expanded in places where full markup declarations are allowed. For them to be legal in these contexts they must always contain one or more markup declarations.

Example 55-17. Multiple markup declarations in one parameter entity

```
<!ENTITY % several-declarations
                "<!ELEMENT FOO (#PCDATA)>
                <!ELEMENT BAR (#PCDATA)>
                <!ELEMENT BAZ (#PCDATA)>">
%several-declarations;
```

Because of the way XML handles white space, the replacement text for the entity declaration in Example 55-17 is parsed as it would if the entity declaration had occurred on a single line. In this case we have defined the literal entity value over several lines to make the DTD more readable. When we refer to the parameter entity "several-declarations", the three element types are declared.

The rules for parameter entities in the external subset are much more complex. This is because parameter entities in the external subset are not restricted to complete markup declarations. They can also be parts of a markup declaration. XML restricts parameter entities in the internal subset to full declarations because the internal subset is supposed to be very easy to process quickly by browsers and other processors. The external subset allows more complex, powerful parameter entity references. For instance, in the external subset, Example 55-18 would be a legal series of declarations.

Example 55-18. Entities in the external subset

```
<!ENTITY % ent-name "the-entity">
<!ENTITY % ent-value "This is the entity">
<!ENTITY %ent-name; "%ent-value;">
```

Both the name and the replacement text of the final entity declaration are specified through parameter entity references. Their replacement texts become the entity's name and replacement text.

The tricky part is that there are only particular places that you can use parameter entity references in markup declarations. You might wonder, for instance, if you could replace the string "<!ENTITY" with a parameter entity reference. You might guess that this is impossible because XML does not allow a markup declaration to start in one entity and end in another. You would guess correctly. It would be harder to guess whether you could use an entity reference to fill in the string "ENTITY" which follows the "<!" It turns out that this is illegal as well.

To be safe, we would advise you to stick to using parameter entities only to hold full markup declarations and portions of another entity's replacement text until you are familiar with the text of the XML specification itself. The specification relies on knowledge of grammatical tokens to constrain the places that parameter entity replacement is allowed in the external subset. Those token boundaries are only described in the complete grammar.

55.9 | External identifiers

External identifiers refer to information outside the entity in which they occur. There are two types. System identifiers use URIs to refer to an object based on its location. Public identifiers use a publicly declared name to refer to information.

Spec Excerpt (XML) 55-6. External identifier

```
[75]  ExternalID ::=  'SYSTEM' S SystemLiteral
                      | 'PUBLIC' S PubidLiteral S SystemLiteral
```

55.9.1 *System identifiers*

The *SystemLiteral* that follows the keyword SYSTEM is just a URI. Example 55-19 is another example of that.

Example 55-19. System identifier

```
<!ENTITY ent SYSTEM "http://www.entities.com/ent.xml">
```

You can also use relative URIs to refer to entities on the same machine as the referring entity. A relative URI is one that does not contain a complete machine name and path. The machine name and part of the path are implied from the context. Example 55-20 demonstrates.

Example 55-20. Local external general entity

```
<!ENTITY local SYSTEM "local.xml">
```

If this were declared in a document at the URI `http://www.baz.org/`, then the processor would fetch the replacement text from `http://www.baz.org/local.xml`.

These URIs are relative to the location of the referring entity (such as an external parameter entity or the external subset of the DTD) and not necessarily to the document entity. If your document entity is on one machine, and it includes some markup declarations from another machine, relative URIs in the included declarations are interpreted as being on the second machine.

For example, your document might be at `http://www.myhome.com`. It might include a DTD component with a set of pictures of playing cards from `http://www.poker.com/cards.dtd`. If that DTD component had a

URI, `4Heartss.gif`, it would be interpreted relative to the poker site, not yours.

55.9.2 *Public identifiers*

It is also possible to refer to a DTD component or any entity by a name, in addition to a URI. This name is called a "public identifier". If a few entities become widely used in XML circles then it would be inefficient for everyone to fetch the entities from the same servers. Instead, their software should come with those entities already installed (or else it should know the most efficient site from which to download them, perhaps from a corporate intranet). To enable these smarter lookup mechanisms, you would refer to those DTDs by public identifiers, as shown in Example 55-21.

Example 55-21. Referencing a DTD by public identifier

```
<!DOCTYPE MEMO PUBLIC "-//SGMLSOURCE//DTD MEMO//EN"
                "http://www.sgmlsource.com/dtds/memo.dtd">
<MEMO> </MEMO>
```

The public identifier is a unique name for the entity. It should be unique world-wide. Usually they contain corporate or personal names to make them more likely to be unique. If the software knows how to translate the public identifier into a URI, it will do so. If not, it will use the system identifier.

Right now, the translation from public identifier to URI is typically either hard-wired into a processor or controlled through files called "entity catalogs". Entity catalogs list public identifiers and describe their URIs, in the same way that phone books allow you to look up a name and find a number. Documentation for XML software should mention the format of the catalogs it supports, if any.

In the future there may be intranet- and Internet-wide systems that will look up a public identifier and download the DTD from the site that is closest to you. The Web's designers have been promising this feature for years and XML is ready when they deliver. In the meantime, the system identifier following the public identifier will be used.

55.10 | Conclusion

As you can see, XML separates issues of logical structure from those of the physical storage of the document. This means that document type designers do not have to foresee every possible reasonable way of breaking up a document when they design the document type. This is good, because that sort of decision is best made by those who know their system resource limits, bandwidth limits, editor preferences, and so forth. The document type designer, in contrast, takes responsibility for deciding on a good structure for the document.

Advanced features of XML

Friendly Tutorial

- Conditional sections
- Character references
- Processing instructions
- Standalone declaration

©2000 THE XML HANDBOOK™

Chapter 56

The features in this chapter are advanced in the sense that only advanced users will get around to reading them. They do not require advanced degrees in computer science or rocket science to understand. They are just a little esoteric. Most XML users will get by without ever needing to use them.

56.1 | Conditional sections

Conditional sections can only occur in the external subset of the document type declaration, and in external entities referenced from the internal subset. The internal subset proper is supposed to be quick and easy to process. In contrast, the external subset is supposed to retain some of the full-SGML mechanisms that make complicated DTDs easier to maintain. One of these mechanisms is the conditional section, which allows you to turn on and off a series of markup declarations.

Like the internal and external subsets, conditional sections may contain one or more complete declarations, comments, processing instructions, or nested conditional sections, with optional white space between them.

A conditional section is turned on and off with a keyword. If the keyword is INCLUDE, then the section is processed just as if the conditional section markers did not exist. If the keyword is IGNORE, then the contents are ignored by the processor as if the declarations themselves did not exist, as in Example 56-1

Example 56-1. Conditional sections

```
<![INCLUDE[
 <!ELEMENT magazine (title, article+, comments* )>
 ]]>
 <![IGNORE[
 <!ELEMENT magazine (title, body)>
]]>
```

This is a useful way of turning on and off parts of a DTD during development.

The real power in the feature derives from parameter entity references. These are described in 55.7, "Internal and external parameter entities", on page 792.

If the keyword of the conditional section is a parameter entity reference, the processor replaces the parameter entity by its content before the processor decides whether to include or ignore the conditional section. That means that by changing the parameter entity in the internal subset, you can turn on and off a conditional marked section. In that way, two different documents could reference the same set of external markup declarations, but get slightly (or largely) different DTDs. For instance, we can modify the example above:

Example 56-2. Conditional sections and parameter entities

```
<![%editor[
 <!ELEMENT magazine (title, article+, comments* )>
 ]]>
 <![%author[
 <!ELEMENT magazine (title, body)>
]]>
```

Now editors will have a slightly different DTD from authors. When the parameter entities are set one way, the declaration without comments is chosen:

Example 56-3. Internal subset of a document type declaration

```
<!DOCTYPE MAGAZINE SYSTEM "magazine.dtd"[
   <!ENTITY % editor "IGNORE">
   <!ENTITY % author "INCLUDE">
]>
```

Authors do not have to worry about `comments` elements that they are not supposed to use anyway. When the document moves from the author to the editor, the parameter entity values can be swapped, and the expanded version of the DTD becomes available. Parameter entities can also be used to manage DTDs that go through versions chronologically, as an organization's needs change.

Conditional sections are also sometimes used to make "strict" and "loose" versions of DTDs. The loose DTD can be used for compatibility with old documents, or documents that are somehow out of your control, and the strict DTD can be used to try to encourage a more precise structure for future documents.

56.2 | Character references

It is not usually convenient to type in characters that are not available on the keyboard. With many text editors, it is not even possible to do so. XML allows you to insert such a character with a *character reference*. If, for instance, you wanted to insert a character from the "International Phonetic Alphabet", you could spend a long time looking for a combination of keyboard, operating system and text editor that would make that straightforward. Rather than buying special hardware or software, XML allows you to refer to the character by its *Unicode number*.

Here is an example:

Example 56-4. Decimal character reference

```
<P>Here is a reference to Unicode character 161: &#161;.
```

Unicode is a character set. The character numbered 161 in Unicode happens to be the inverted exclamation mark. Alternatively, you could use the *hex* (hexadecimal) value of the character number to reference it:

Example 56-5. Hex character reference

```
<P>Here is a different reference to Unicode character 161: &#xA1;.
```

Hex is a numbering system often used by computer programmers that translates naturally into the binary codes that computers use. The *Unicode Standard book* uses hex, so those that have that book will probably prefer this type of character reference over the other (whether they are programmers or not).

Here are the specifics on character references from the XML spec:

Spec Excerpt (XML) 56-1. Character reference

```
CharRef ::=  '&#' [0-9]+ ';'
   | '&#x' [0-9a-fA-F]+ ';'
```

Spec Excerpt (XML) 56-2. Interpreting character references

If the character reference begins with "&#x", the digits and letters up to the terminating ; provide a hexadecimal representation of the character's code point in ISO/IEC 10646. If it begins just with "&#", the digits up to the terminating ; provide a decimal representation of the character's code point.

ISO/IEC 10646 is the Borg of character set standards. It seemingly includes every character from every other character set and leaves room for characters not yet created. Unicode is an independently developed industry-standard character set that is identifiable as a subset of ISO/IEC 10646. For XML purposes, there's no real need to distinguish them.

Note that character references are not entity references, though they look similar to them. Entities have names and values, but character references only have character numbers. In an XML document, all entities except the predefined ones must be declared. But a character reference does not require a declaration; it is just a really verbose way to type a character (but often the only way).

Because Unicode numbers are hard to remember, it is often useful to declare entities that stand in for them:

Example 56-6. Entity declaration for a Unicode character

```
<!ENTITY inverted-exclamation "&#161;">
```

Most likely this is how most XML users will refer to obscure characters. There will probably be popular character entity sets that can be included in a DTD through parameter entity references. This technique will free users from learning obscure character numbers and probably even from learning how to use character references.

56.3 | Processing instructions

XML comments are for those occasions where you need to say something to another human being without reference to the DTD, and without changing the way the document looks to readers or applications. Processing instructions are for those occasions where you need to say something to *a computer program* without reference to the DTD and without changing the way that the document is processed by other computer programs. This is only supposed to happen rarely.

Many people argued that the occasions would be so rare that XML should not have processing instructions at all. But as one of us said in *The SGML Handbook*: "In a perfect world, they would not be needed, but, as you may have noticed, the world is not perfect." It turns out that processing instruction use has changed over the years and is not as frowned upon as it was in the early days of SGML.

Processing instructions are intended to reintroduce software-specific markup. You might wonder why you would want to do that. Imagine that you are creating a complex document, and, like a good user of a generalized markup language, you are concentrating on the structure rather than the formatting. Close to the deadline you print the document using the proprietary formatting system that has been foisted on you by your boss. There are many of these systems, some of which are of fantastic quality and others which are not.

©2000 The XML Handbook™

Your document looks reasonable, but you need a way to make the first letter of each paragraph large. However, reading the software's manual, you realize that the formatter does not have a feature that allows you to modify the style for the first letter of a word. The XML Purist in you might want to go out and buy a complete formatting system but the Pragmatist in you knows that is impossible.

Thinking back to the bad-old days of "What You See is All You Get" word processors, you recall that all you really needed to do is to insert a code in the beginning of each paragraph to change the font for the first letter. This is not good "XML Style" because XML Purists do not insert formatting codes and they especially do not insert codes specific to a particular piece of software – that is not in the "spirit" of generalized markup. Still, in this case, with a deadline looming and stubborn software balking, a processing instruction may be your best bet. If the formatter has a "change font" command it may be accessible through a processing instruction:

Example 56-7. Processing instruction

```
<CHAPTER>The Bald and the Dutiful
<P><?DUMB-FORMATTER FONT="16PT"?>N<?DUMB-FORMATTER END-FONT?>ick
took Judy in his arms</P>
```

If you find yourself using many processing instructions to specify formatting you should try to figure out what is wrong with your system. Is your document's markup not rich enough? Is your formatting language not powerful enough? Are you not taking advantage of the tools and markup you have available to you? The danger in using processing instructions is that you can come to rely on them instead of more reusable structural markup. Then when you want to reuse your information in another context, the markup will not be robust enough to allow it.

Processing instructions start with a fixed string "<?". That is followed by a name and, after that, any characters except for the string that ends the PI, "?>".

Here are the relevant rules from the XML specification:

Spec Excerpt (XML) 56-3. Processing Instruction

```
[16]  PI ::=  '<?' PITarget (S (Char* - (Char* '?>' Char*)))? '?>'
[17]  PITarget ::=  Name - (('X' | 'x') ('M' | 'm') ('L' | 'l'))
```

This name at the beginning of the PI is called the *PI target*. This name should be standardized in the documentation for the tool or specification. After the PI target comes white space and then some totally proprietary command. This command is not processed in the traditional sense at all. Characters that would usually indicate markup are totally ignored. The command is passed directly to the application and it does what it wants to with it. The command ends when the processor hits the string "?>". There is absolutely no standard for the "stuff" in the middle. Markup is not recognized there. PIs could use attribute syntax for convenience, but they could also choose not to.

It is possible that more than one application could understand the same instructions. They might come from the same vendor or one vendor might agree to accept another vendor's commands. For instance in the early days of the Web, the popular NCSA (National Center for Supercomputing Activities) Web Server introduced special commands into HTML documents in the form of special HTML comments. Because the NCSA server was dominant in those days, many servers now support those commands.

Under XML we would most likely use processing instructions for the same task. The virtue of XML processing instructions in this case is that they are explicitly instructions to a computer program. In our opinion, one of the central tenets of generalized markup is that it is important to be *explicit* about what is going on in a document. Reusing markup constructs for something other than what they were intended for is not explicit.

For instance, since comments are meant to be instructions to users, an ambitious Web Server administrator might decide to write a small script that would strip them out to save download time and protect internal comments from being read by others. But if instructions to software (like the NCSA server commands) were hidden in comments, they would be stripped out as well. It would be better to use the supplied processing instruction facility, which was designed for the purpose.

Better still (from a purist's point of view) would be a robust XML-smart mechanism for accomplishing the task. For instance, one thing that the NCSA servers do is include the text of one HTML file into another. XML's entity mechanism (see Chapter 55, "Entities: Breaking up is easy to do", on page 780) can handle this, so you do not need processing instructions in that case.

If you want to insert the date into a document, then you could connect the external entity to a CGI[1] that returns the date. If you want to insert

©2000 The XML Handbook™

information from a database then you could have software that generates XML entities with the requested information.

Sometimes, though, the processing instruction solution may be the most expedient. This is especially the case if your application vendor has set it up that way. If your document is heavily dependent on a database or other program, then it is not very "application independent" in any case. If a document is inherently dependent on an application then you may decide that strictly adhering to generalized markup philosophy is just too much work. In the end you must choose between expediency and purity. Most people mix both.

Processing instructions are appropriate when you are specifying information about a document that is unrelated to the actual structure of the document. Consider, for instance, the problem of specifying which stylesheets go with which XML documents on a web site. Given enough money and time you could erect a database that kept track of them. If you already had your XML documents in a text database then this would probably be the most efficient mechanism. If you did not have a text database set up, then you could merely keep the information in a flat text file. But you would have to keep that external information up-to-date and write a program to retrieve it in order to do formatting. It would probably be easier to simply stick the information somewhere in the file where it is easy to find (such as at the beginning).

You could add a `STYLESHEET` element or attribute to each document, but that could cause three problems. First, it would violate the XML Purist principle that elements should represent document components and not formatting or other processing information. Second, if you are using DTDs with your documents then you must add the element or attribute to each DTD that you will be using. This would be a hassle.

The third reason to use processing instructions instead of elements is the most concrete: you may not be able to change those DTDs. After all, DTDs are often industry (or international!) standards. You cannot just go monkeying around with them even if you want to. Instead, you could put a processing instruction at the start of each document. Processing instructions are not associated with particular DTDs and they do not have to be declared. You just use them.

---

1. CGI is the "Common Gateway Interface", a specification for making Web pages that are generated by the server when the user requests them, rather than in advance.

56.5 | Standalone document declaration

We should start by saying that the standalone document declaration is only designed for a small class of problems, and these are not problems that most XML users will run into. We do not advise its use. Nevertheless, it is part of XML and we feel that you should understand it so that you can understand why it is seldom useful.

A DTD is typically broken into two parts, an external part that contains declarations that are typically shared among many documents, and an internal part that occurs within the document and contains declarations that only that document uses (see Chapter 54, "Creating a document type definition", on page 748). The external part includes all external parameter entities, including both the external subset of the document type declaration and any external entities referenced from the internal subset.

The DTD describes the structure of the document, but it can also control the interpretation of some of the markup and declare the existence of some other entities (such as graphics or other XML documents) that are required for proper processing. For instance, a graphic might only be used in a particular document, so the declaration that includes it (an *entity declaration*) would usually go in the internal subset rather than the external one.

Processors that validate a document need the entire DTD to do so. A document is not valid unless it conforms to both the internal and external parts of its DTD. But sometimes a system passes a document from program to program and it does not need to be validated at each stage. For instance, two participants in an electronic data interchange system might agree that the sender will validate the document once, instead of having both participants validate it.

Even though the receiving processor may not be interested in full validation, it may need to know if it understands the document in exactly the same way that the sender did. Some features of the DTD may influence this slightly. Documents with defaulted attributes would be interpreted differently if the attribute declarations are read rather than ignored. Entity declarations would allow the expansion of entity references. Attribute values can only be normalized according to their type when the attribute declarations are read. Some white space in content would also be removed if the DTD would not allow it to be interpreted as text.

If a process can reliably skip a part of the DTD dedicated exclusively to validation, then it would have less data to download and process and could let the application do its work (browsing, searching, etc.) more quickly. But it would be important for some "mission critical" applications to know if they are getting a slightly different understanding of the document than they would if they processed the entire DTD.

The *standalone document declaration* allows you to specify whether a processor needs to fetch the external part of the DTD in order to process the document "exactly right." The Standalone document declaration may take the values (case sensitive) of yes and no.

A value of yes says that the document is *standalone* and thus does not depend on the external part of the DTD for correct interpretation. A value of *no* means that it either depends on the external DTD part or it might, so the application should not trust that it can get the correct information without it. You could always use no as the value for this attribute, but in some cases applications will then download more data than they need to do their jobs. This translates into slower processing, more network usage and so forth.

Example 56-9. A standalone document declaration that forces processing of the internal subset.

```
<?xml version="1.0" standalone="no"?>
<!DOCTYPE MEMO SYSTEM "http://www.sgmlsource.com/memo.dtd" [
<!ENTITY % pics SYSTEM "http://www.sgmlsource.com/pics.ent">
 %pics;
]>
<MEMO></MEMO>
```

Example 56-9 will tell the application that unless the processor fetched the pictures, the application might get a slightly different understanding of the document than it would if it processed the whole document. For instance, the MEMO element might have defaulted attributes.

But if the value is *yes*, the receiving application may choose not to get the external part of the DTD. This implies that it will never know what was in it. Still, it needs to be able to trust the accuracy of the declaration. What if the security level for a document is set in an attribute and the default level is top-secret? It would be very bad if a careless author could obscure that with a misleading standalone document declaration. In the scenario we outlined, the sender has already validated the document. So the sender has enough information to check that the information is correct. The XML

©2000 THE XML HANDBOOK™

specification requires a validating processor to do this (see Spec Excerpt 56-4).

Spec Excerpt (XML) 56-4. Standalone document declaration

The standalone document declaration must have the value "no" if any external markup declarations contain declarations of:

- attributes with default values, if elements to which these attributes apply appear in the document without specifications of values for these attributes, or
- entities (other than amp, lt, gt, apos, quot), if references to those entities appear in the document, or
- attributes with values subject to normalization, where the attribute appears in the document with a value which will change as a result of normalization, or
- element types with element content, if white space occurs directly within any instance of those types.

The last one is very likely to happen. Often people use white space between tags to make the source XML document readable, but that can slightly change the interpretation of the document. Validating processors will tell applications that there are some contexts where character data is not legal, so the white space occurring in those places must be merely formatting white space (see 54.5, "Content models", on page 759). If an application that does not want to validate a document is to get exactly the same information out of the document, it must know whether there are any elements where white space should be interpreted just as source formatting. We say that this sort of white space is *insignificant*.

The standalone document declaration warns the application that this is the case so that mission critical applications may download the DTD just to get the right information out of the document, even when they are not interested in validating it.

The standalone document declaration is fairly obscure and it is doubtful if it will get much use outside of a few mission critical applications. Even there, however, it is safest to just get the external data and do a complete validation before trusting a document. You might find that it had been corrupted in transit.

56.6 | Is that all there is?

We've pretty much covered all the details of XML, certainly all that are likely to see extensive use. There are some things we didn't touch on, such as restrictions that must be observed if you are using older SGML tools to process XML. As the generalized markup industry is retooling rapidly for XML, such restrictions will be short-lived and, we felt, did not warrant complicating our XML tutorial.

In any case, you are now well-prepared – or will be after reading Chapter 57, "Reading the XML specification", on page 820 – to tackle the XML spec yourself. You'll find it in the XML SPECtacular section of the CD-ROM that accompanies this book.

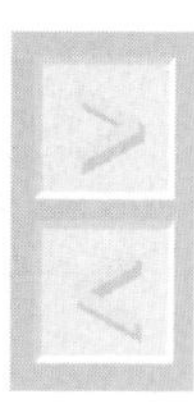

Tip *We can also recommend Bob DuCharme's XML: The Annotated Specification, which is published in this series (ISBN 0-13-082676-6). It is extensively annotated and has over 170 new usage examples.*

Reading the XML specification

Tad Tougher Tutorial

- Grammars
- Rules
- Symbols

©2000 THE XML HANDBOOK™

Chapter 57

The XML specification is a little tricky to read, but with some work you can get through it by reading and understanding the glossary and applying the concepts described so far in this book. One thing you'll need to know is how to interpret the production rules that make up XML's grammar. This chapter teaches how to read those rules.

When discussing a particular string, like a tag or declaration, we often want to discuss the parts of that string individually. We call each part of the string a *token*. Tokens can always be separated by white space as described above. Sometimes the white space between the tokens is required. For instance we can represent the months of the year as tokens:

Example 57-1. Tokens

```
JANUARY FEBRUARY  MARCH    APRIL       MAY            JUNE
```

White space between tokens is *normalized* (combined) so that no matter how much white space you type, the processor treats it as if the tokens were separated by a single space. Thus the example above is equivalent to the following:

Example 57-2. Tokens after normalization

```
JANUARY FEBRUARY MARCH APRIL MAY JUNE
```

Whenever we discuss strings made up of tokens, you will know that you can use as much white space between tokens as you need and the XML processor will normalize it for you.

57.1 | A look at XML's grammar

There are two basic techniques that we could use to discuss XML's syntax precisely. The first is to describe syntactic constructs in long paragraphs of excruciatingly dull prose. The better approach is to develop a simple system for describing syntax. In computer language circles, such systems are called *grammars*. Grammars are more precise and compact. Although they are no less boring (as you may recall from primary school), you can skip them easily until you need to know some specific detail of XML's syntax.

As a bonus, once you know how to read a grammar, you can read the one in the XML specification and thus work your way up to the status of "language lawyer".[1] As XML advances, an ability to read the specification will help you to keep on top of its progress.

The danger in this approach is that you might confuse the grammar with XML markup itself. The grammar is just a definitional tool. It is not used in XML applications. You don't type it in when you create an XML document. You use it to figure out what you *can* type in. Before "the new curriculum", students were taught grammar in primary school. They would be taught parts of speech and how they could combine them. XML's grammar is the same. It will tell you what the parts of an XML document are, and how you can combine them.

Grammars are made up of production *rules* and *symbols*. Rules are simple: they say what is allowed in a particular place in an XML document.

1. You too can nitpick about tiny language details and thus prove your superiority over those who merely use XML rather than obsess over it.

©2000 THE XML HANDBOOK™

Rules have a symbol on the left side, the string "::=" in the middle and a list of symbols on the right side:

Example 57-3. A Rule

```
people ::= 'Melissa, ' 'Tiffany, ' 'Joshua,' 'Johan'
```

If this rule were part of the grammar for XML (which it is not!) it would say that in a particular place in an XML document you could type the names listed.

The symbols on the right (the names, in the last example) define the set of allowed values for the construct described by the rule ("people"). An allowed value is said to *match*. Rules are like definitions in a dictionary. The left side says what is being defined and the right side says what its definition is. Just as words in a dictionary, are defined in terms of other words, symbols are defined in terms of other symbols. Rules in the XML grammar are preceded by a number. You can look the rule up by number. If an XML document does not follow all of the XML production rules, it is not *well-formed.*

57.2 | Constant strings

The most basic type of symbol we will deal with is a *constant string*. These are denoted by a series of characters in between single quote characters. Constant strings are matched case-sensitively (as we discussed earlier). Here are some examples:

Example 57-4. Matching constant strings

```
AlphabetStart ::= 'ABC'
Example1 ::= '<!DOCTYPE'
```

This would match (respectively) the strings

Example 57-5. Matches

```
ABC
<!DOCTYPE
```

When we are discussing a constant string that is an English word or abbreviation, we will refer to it as a *keyword*. In computer languages, a keyword is a word that is interpreted specially by the computer. So your mother's maiden name is not (likely) a keyword, but a word like `#REQUIRED` is.

Symbols in XML's grammar are separated by spaces, which means that you must match the first, and then the second, and so on in order.

Example 57-6. Representing sequence

```
AlphabetStartAndEnd ::= 'ABC' 'XYZ'
NumbersAndLetters ::= '123' 'QPZ'
```

These would match:

Example 57-7. Sequence matches

```
ABCXYZ
123QPZ
```

Note that a space character in the grammar does not equate to white space in the XML document. Wherever white space can occur we will use the symbol “S”. That means that wherever the grammar specifies “S”, you may put in as much white space as you need to make your XML source file maintainable.

Example 57-8. Whitespace

```
SpacedOutAlphabet ::= 'ABC' S 'XYZ'
```

matches:

Example 57-9. Matching whitespace

```
ABC XYZ
ABC      XYZ
ABC                  XYZ
```

This is the first example we have used where a single rule matches multiple strings. This is usually the case. Just as in English grammar there are many possible verbs and nouns, there are many possible strings that match the rule `SpacedOutAlphabet`, depending on how much white space you choose to make your XML source file maintainable.

Obviously XML would not be very useful if you could only insert predefined text and white space. After all, XML users usually like to choose the topic and content of their documents! So they need to have the option of inserting their own content: a *user defined string*. The simplest type of user defined string is *character data*. This is simply the text that isn't markup. You can put almost any character in character data. The exceptions are characters that would be confused with markup, such as less-than and ampersand symbols.

57.3 | Names

The XML specification uses the symbol "Name" to represent names. For example:

Example 57-10. Names

```
PersonNamedSmith :: = Name S 'Smith'
```

When we combine the name, the white space and the constant string, the rule matches strings like these:

Example 57-11. Matching names

```
Christina Smith
Allan        Smith
Michael       Smith
Black           Smith
Bla_ck            Smith
_Black              Smith
```

57.4 | Occurrence indicators

Sometimes a string is *optional.* We will indicate this by putting a question mark after the symbol that represents it in a rule:

Example 57-12. Optional strings

```
Description ::= 'Tall' S? 'dark'? S? 'handsome'? S? 'person'
Tall person
Tallperson
Tall handsomeperson
Tall dark person
Talldarkhandsomeperson
```

Notice that optionality does not affect the order of the tokens. For example, dark can never go before tall. We can also allow a part of a rule to be matched multiple times. If we want to allow a part to be matched one or more times, we can use the plus symbol and make it *repeatable.*

Example 57-13. Repeatable parts

```
VeryTall ::= 'A' S ('very' S)+ 'tall' S 'person.'
A very tall person.
A very very tall person.
A very very very tall person.
```

An asterisk is similar, but it allows a string to be matched zero or more times. In other words it is both repeatable and optional.

Example 57-14. Both repeatable and optional

```
VerySmall ::= 'A' S ('very' S)* 'small' S 'person.'
A small person.
A very small person.
A very very small person.
A very very very small person.
```

Symbols can be grouped with parentheses so that you could, for instance, make a whole series of symbols optional at once. This is different from making them each optional separately because you must either supply strings for all of them or none:

Example 57-15. Grouping with parentheses

```
Description2 ::= 'A' S ('tall' S 'dark' S 'handsome' S)? 'man.'
```

This rule matches these two strings (and no others):

Example 57-16. Matching groups

```
A tall dark handsome man.
A man.
```

We will sometimes have a choice of symbols to use. This is indicated by separating the alternatives by a vertical bar:

Example 57-17. Optional parts

```
Description3 ::= 'A' S ('short'|'tall') S
                   ('fair'|'tan'|'dark') S ('man'|'woman') '.'
A tall dark man.
A short fair woman.
A short tan man.
A tall dark woman.
```

Note that we broke a single long rule over two lines rather than having it run off of the end of the page. This does not in any way affect the meaning of the rule. Line breaks are just treated like space characters between the symbols.

We can combine all of these types of symbols. This allows us to make more complex rules.

Example 57-18. Combining types of symbols

```
Book ::= (('Fascinating'|'Intriguing') S ('XML'|'SGML') S 'Book')
                 | ('Yet another HTML' S 'Book')
Fascinating XML Book
Yet another HTML Book
Intriguing SGML Book
```

So in this case, you should treat the first large parenthesized expression (saying good things about SGML and XML books) as one option, and the second (saying not as good things about HTML books) as another. Inside the first set, you can choose different adjectives and book types, but the ordering is fixed and there must be white space between each part.

57.5 | Combining rules

Finally, rules can refer to other rules. Where one rule refers to another, you just make a valid value for each part and then put the parts together like building blocks.

Example 57-19. Combining rules

```
FunnyDate ::= Month S Day ',' Year
Month ::= 'Jan'|'Feb'|'Mar'|'Apr'|'May'|'Jun'
                 |'Jul'|'Aug'|'Sep'|'Oct'|'Nov'|'Dec'
Day ::= ('1'|'2'|'3')?
                 ('1'|'2'|'3'|'4'|'5'|'6'|'7'|'8'|'9'|'0')
Year ::= '1998'|'1999'|'2000'|'2001'|'2002'
```

This would match strings such as:

Example 57-20. Matching strings

```
Jan 21,1998
May 35,2000
Sep 2,2002
```

As you can see, this is not quite a strict specification for dates, but it gets the overall form or *syntax* of them right.

57.6 | Conclusion

We've explained the bulk of what is needed to understand XML's production rules. There are a few more details that you can find in section 6 of the XML spec itself. It is included in the XML SPECtacular on the CD-ROM.

©2000 The XML Handbook™

Related Tutorials

- Namespaces
- XML Path Language (XPath)
- XML Style Language (XSL and XSLT)
- XML Pointer Language (XPointer)
- XML Linking Language (XLink)
- Datatypes
- XML Schemas
- Full specs on CD-ROM

©2000 THE XML HANDBOOK™

Part Twelve

This part covers seven core XML-related specifications from the World Wide Web Consortium, in varying stages of development. You'll need a pretty firm grasp of the material in Part Eleven before you tackle any of these.

But unlike Part Eleven, it isn't necessary to read these chapters in order unless you are trying to sop up all the good technical stuff that you can. Here's a roadmap in case you are only interested in specific subjects.

Namespaces are an approved Recommendation and are seeing a lot of use. You need to know something about them before reading the other chapters in this part, but you don't need to cover everything.

XPath is a prerequisite for both stylesheets and XPointers, but again you don't need to master all the details before moving on.

XSL and XPointer aren't prerequisites for anything else, although understanding XPointer will add to your appreciation of the power of XLink. XLink isn't a prerequisite either.

Datatypes is a prerequisite for XML Schemas, but here too only the basics are needed.

Namespaces

Friendly Tutorial

- Unique names
- URI-based namespaces
- Namespaces and DTDs

©2000 THE XML HANDBOOK™

Chapter 58

The Namespaces in XML specification is an extension to XML that answers the burning question: Are we talking about the same subject?

Using namespaces it is possible to create elements with the generic identifier `para` in two different documents, with two different document types (or no explicitly-declared document types at all) and write software and queries that recognize that both represent a paragraph. This might not seem like much of a feat, but consider that in a third document an element with that element-type name might represent a paramedic (consider an employment record from the television show "ER"), a paranormal encounter (in a document from the FBI's "X-Files") or a paralegal (court records).

Even a fully spelled-out word can be ambiguous. A `list` can be a list of items or the angle of list (tilt) of a seagoing vessel. Besides, if two different people invented two different document types, they might use the words "list" and "para" to mean the same basic thing but their underlying model of paragraphs and lists might be different. One might expect elements of type "list" to be ordered. The other might want to allow lists to have a header.

Everyone in the world is allowed to invent document types, so we need to be clear about the origin of our element types. If you have a document database containing both ship records and technical manuals, a database-wide query needs to be able to figure out which `list` is which – even if the documents do not have DTDs.

Despite the general agreement on the need for this sort of *disambiguation*, we should mention that the XML namespaces concept is not universally embraced as the best solution. In fact XML namespaces are downright controversial. After reading this chapter you can make up your own mind.

Nevertheless, namespaces are already in widespread use. World Wide Web Consortium specifications already build upon the namespace mechanism and will do so in the future. Microsoft's *Office 2000* document types also use them. Namespaces look like they are here to stay.

58.1 | Problem statement

Namespaces are easiest to understand if we work in the realm of well-formed documents without DTDs. We will address the relationship to DTDs later on.

You may be familiar with email programs that can recognize and visually highlight URLs and email addresses. This works nicely in the program, but when the email is saved to disk or forwarded to a less intelligent email program, that highlighting is lost. It might be better if the program could actually introduce markup representing the highlighting. That way other applications could get the benefit of the email program's analysis and recognition. We could use `web` and `email` element types to capture this information.

Our system would work fine for a while, but the time would come when people would want to send XML documents (remember, well-formed but DTD-less XML documents) through email. We might want to allow our system to continue to work on these documents. The problem is that it is a bad idea for us to presume that any element with an element type name of `web` or `email` was meant to refer to our element types.

Perhaps an XML document will come through the email with a `web` element that is meant to represent spider webs or knowledge webs. Perhaps the `web` elements really do represent URLs, but they use an attribute to hold the address instead of content. Then we have the same meaning but a different internal structure.

What we need to do is clearly separate our names from other people's names. We need to have different so-called `namespaces`. We do this in the real world all of the time.

What would you do if you needed to refer to a particular John Smith without confusing him with any other John Smith. You qualify the name: "John Smith from London." That sets up a namespace that separates Londoners from everyone else.

If that isn't sufficient then you further qualify the namespace: "John Smith from East London". That makes a namespace that separates Easterners from everyone else. You could narrow it down even more: "John Smith from Adelaide Street in East London." The trick is qualifying names in order to separate them from other names. The separate groups of names are known as "namespaces."

58.2 | The namespaces solution

Given that what we want to do is qualify names, the most obvious idea is to have a prefix that does the qualification. `myEmailProgram:web` or `myEmailProgram:email`. This seems to work at first, but eventually two people will make program names that clash. In fact, there will be a strong tendency to use three-letter acronyms. There are only so many of these acronyms!

In the real world people constantly choose names that other people also choose. Even city names can clash: consider how many there are named "Springfield"! If people are allowed to choose names without any central authority then they will eventually choose names that clash.

The World Wide Web Consortium could set up a registry of these acronyms and names. But that would require a great deal of effort both in setting up the registry and in registering individual namespaces.

A better mechanism would be to use a registry that already exists. One such registry is the domain name registry. We could use prefixes like: `mycompany.com:email`. We would call "mycompany.com" the *namespace* and "email" a particular name in that namespace.

This solution is getting much closer but it still is not as democratic as we would like. The problem is that domain names cost $70.00 USD and applying for them is a difficult process. What if an ordinary America

OnLine (AOL) user wants to develop a namespace? Does he have to register a domain name?

Every AOL user has a little bit of space to put files and assign a URL such as `http://www.aol.com/EmailAppGuy`. If we could use that as the basis for a namespace identifier, then we would open up the namespace-creating process to a larger number of people.

This idea also works for organizations other than Internet Service Providers. Consider a big company like General Electric. Various parts of the company may develop XML namespaces. The company probably already has a mechanism for delegating Web URLs. It makes sense to re-use that mechanism for XML namespaces. Example 58-1 shows what URL-based namespace prefixes might look like.

Example 58-1. Mythical (illegal!) URL-based namespace prefix

```
<http://www.aol.com/EmailAppGuy:email>email@machine.com
</http://www.aol.com/EmailAppGuy:email>
```

There are two problems with these prefixes. First, they are not legal XML names because of all of the funny characters such as slashes and dots. Second, they are plug-ugly and incredibly verbose. We need a way to set up a local abbreviation. The XML *Namespaces* specification defines the mechanism for setting up such abbreviations.

58.2.1 *Namespace prefixes*

The *Namespaces* specification defines a rule that attributes that start with the prefix `xmlns:` should be interpreted as prefix-defining attributes. The name immediately following the prefix is a local abbreviation for the namespace.

The attribute value is a URI. You can use any URI (typically a URL) that you would normally have control over. Throughout the element exhibiting that attribute, the prefix stands for the namespace identifier. Example 58-2 demonstrates.

The actual prefix you use is not relevant. It is just a stand-in for the URI. So, for example, when creating an XSL stylesheet you do not need to use the `xsl:` prefix for names defined in the XSL spec. Doing otherwise might be confusing, but it is totally legal.

Example 58-2. Using XML namespaces

```
<eag:email xmlns:eag="http://www.aol.com/EmailAppGuy">
  email@machine.com
</eag:email>
```

Note that the details of the URI are not relevant either. It does not matter whether there is a document at that location or whether the client machine is Internet-connected. There is no need to connect to the Internet to check the contents of the document at that address.

The data (or lack of data) at the other end of the URI is absolutely irrelevant to the namespaces design. Its only goal is to have a long, globally unique string to use in comparisons.

That's an important point! Namespaces work with broken URIs because namespaces only disambiguate names, they don't define names. The URIs therefore don't have to address the definitions of the names in the namespace (although they may).

The only requirement is that you really do control the URI that you use. It is your responsibility to guarantee that nobody else (your spouse?) will accidently but legitimately use the same URI and mean something different by it.

58.2.2 *Scoping*

The prefix scheme is still pretty verbose, but it is some improvement. It looks better when you realize that namespace declarations are *scoped* by their declaring elements. That means that they apply to the element, its children, and the children's children and so forth unless some child has a declaration that specifically overrides the first declaration. Therefore you could declare namespaces in the document (root) element and have them apply throughout the entire document! Example 58-3 demonstrates.[1]

We can minimize the impact even more by removing some of the prefixes. There is a special namespace called the *default namespace*. This namespace is defined without a prefix, so element-type names in the scope of the definition that have no prefix are considered to be in this namespace.[2] If

1. Note that `.con` is the new high-level domain for Internet scams.
2. You can think of the default namespace as having a null prefix, if that helps any.

©2000 THE XML HANDBOOK™

Example 58-3. XML namespace scope

```
<html:html
    xmlns:eag="http://www.aol.com/EmailAppGuy"
    xmlns:html="http://www.w3.org/TR/WD-HTML40"
    xmlns:math="http://www.w3.org/TR/REC-MathML/">
  <html:title>George Soros Personal Wealth Page</html:title>
  <html:h2>Counting My Cash</html:h2>
  <html:p>As you know, my cash rivals the gross national
  product of some small countries. Consider the following
  equation:
  <math:reln>
    <math:eq/>
    <math:ci>wealth</math:ci>
    <math:ci>gnp</math:ci>
  </math:reln>
  If you have any ideas of how I could spend
  this money. Please contact
  <eag:email>georges@aol.con</eag:email>.
</html:p>

</html:html>
```

you expect to use many elements from a particular namespace, you can make it the default namespace for the appropriate scope. In fact, you can even have a document in which the namespaces correspond cleanly to the elements and there are no prefixes at all, as Example 58-4 demonstrates.

Example 58-4. Two default namespaces: HTML and MathML

```
<html
    xmlns="http://www.w3.org/TR/WD-HTML40">
  <title>George Soros Personal Wealth Page</title>
  <h2>Counting My Cash</h2>
  <p>As you know, my cash rivals the gross national
  product of some small countries. Consider the following
  equation:
  <reln xmlns="http://www.w3.org/TR/REC-MathML/">
    <eq/>
    <ci>wealth</ci>
    <ci>gnp</ci>
  </reln>
  If you have any ideas of how I could spend
  this money.</p>
</html>
```

Note that the default namespace is HTML both before and after the reln element. Within the reln element the default namespace is MathML. As you can see, we can eliminate many of the prefixes but still keep the relationship between the element-type names and the namespaces.

We can also establish a scope in which namespaces aren't in use and all names are local, by using an empty URI. In Example 58-5, notes and todo are not in the MathML namespace.

Example 58-5. A scope for local names

```
<reln xmlns="http://www.w3.org/TR/REC-MathML/">
  <eq/>
  <ci>wealth</ci>
  <ci>gnp</ci>
  <notes xmlns="">
    <todo>check the math</todo>
  </notes>
</reln>
```

58.2.3 *Attribute names*

Attribute names can also come from a namespace, which is indicated in the usual way by prefixing them with a namespace prefix. For instance, the current working draft of XLink uses the namespace mechanism to allow XLink attributes to appear on elements that themselves come from some other namespace. Example 58-6 shows such attributes.

Example 58-6. Attributes in XLink namespace

```
<myLink xmlns:xlink="http://www.w3.org/XML/XLink/0.9"
   xlink:type="simple">
...
</myLink>
```

It does not matter what the namespace of the element type is. The XLink attributes are in the XLink namespace even when they are exhibited by an element type that is not in the XLink namespace.

In fact, even attributes without prefixes are not in the same namespace that their element type is in. Nor are they in the default namespace. Attributes without prefixes are in no namespace at all.[1]

©2000 THE XML HANDBOOK™

From a processing standpoint, the lack of a namespace doesn't matter. The attribute name can still be specified in a stylesheet pattern or utilized by the template for the element type's template rule.

In other words, an `html:img` element could have an `href` attribute and that attribute could be processed properly even though it is not formally part of the `html` namespace. Any application that knows how to handle `html:img` will know what to do with an `href` attribute.[1]

From a data modeling standpoint, unprefixed attributes are normal. They are defined by the semantics of their specific element types. In contrast, prefixed attributes have semantics that apply to the class of all element types. XLink is a good example because, in principle, any element can be linked.

58.3 | Namespaces and DTDs

You read about DTDs and type-validation in Chapter 54, "Creating a document type definition", on page 748 and might have wondered why that chapter had no mention of namespaces. That's because namespaces were invented after DTDs.[2] Therefore, type-validation does not behave as you would expect it to behave had it been designed with namespaces in mind.

In fact, the base XML language has no inherent knowledge of namespaces. There is no special part of an element-type name or attribute name called the prefix. The name is all one string that, when name spaces are used, just happens to have a colon in it. The colon could just as easily be an underscore, dot or happy face character from the XML point of view. It is not a special character.

---

1. From the syntactic standpoint of the Namespaces spec, that is. All names have to be in some namespace or they couldn't function as names. An unprefixed attribute is in a (non-syntactic) namespace that is defined by its element type, which, as we said, is not the same as the namespace that its element type itself is in. The `href` attribute of `html:img`, for example, is in the (non-syntactic) `html:img` namespace, while its element type, `img`, is in the (syntactic) `html` namespace.
1. That's because, as we saw in the last footnote, `href` is in the `html:img` namespace.
2. About 30 years after, but who's counting.

You might think, from learning about namespaces, that it would be possible to have two different `list` element types in the same DTD. However, you can only do that if you give them different prefixes. But in DTDs, prefixes must be *hard-wired onto the names.* They are not namespace prefixes and you cannot depend on the default namespace: XML 1.0 allows only one element type declaration for the element type `list`.

Declaring `my:list` and `your:list` would be fine. XML 1.0 sees these as no more the same than `my_list` and `your_list` or `my.list` and `your.list`. But once you define the element types this way, you cannot default them or change the prefix. XML 1.0 would not recognize `list` as a synonym for `my:list`. These are no more related than `list` and `my_list` or `foo` and `bar`.

Therefore, when you create a DTD that uses namespaces, you must declare every `prefix:name` combination individually, exactly as you would if the `:` were just another name character (which it is!).

Example 58-7 illustrates declarations for two different `email` element types. The prefixes disambiguate them, but not in the same way that namespace prefixes would. As far as XML 1.0 is concerned, these are two nine-letter element-type names that differ in their first three letters.

Example 58-7. Disambiguating two `email` element types

```
<!ELEMENT eag:email ...>
<!ATTLIST eag:email
    xmlns:eag CDATA #FIXED "http://www.aol.com/EmailAppGuy">
<!ELEMENT cmp:email ...>
<!ATTLIST cmp:email
    xmlns:cmp CDATA #FIXED "http://www.compuserve.com/email">
```

Note that the `xmlns` attributes are fixed. That is because the prefixes are hard-wired to the names; they can't be changed in a valid document instance regardless of what the *Namespaces* spec says. If authors try to act otherwise, the document will become invalid.

Defining each namespace attribute with a fixed value protects against such mistakes. The parser will issue an error message if an author tries to specify a different namespace value in the document instance.

Fixing namespace attributes enforces markup practices that make a document both type-valid and namespace compatible. It is the sensible thing to do.[1]

A DTD can also simulate scoping and default namespaces, as shown in Example 58-8.

Example 58-8. Scoping and default namespaces in a DTD

```
<!ELEMENT music ...>
<!ATTLIST music
    xmlns CDATA #FIXED "http://www.ihc.org/smdl">
<!ELEMENT math ...>
<!ATTLIST math
    xmlns CDATA #FIXED "http://www.w3.org/TR/REC-MathML/">
```

However, remember that the declared names in a valid document are the *only* names. Example 58-8 works only when the subelement types of `music` and `math` have different names from one another.

One final example to drive home the point: In Example 58-9, the first namespace prefix has no effect. The two element-type names are different in a valid document, even though they are the same according to the *Namespaces* spec.

Example 58-9. `rap:music` isn't `music`

```
<!ELEMENT music ...>
<!ATTLIST music
    xmlns CDATA #FIXED "http://www.rude-noises.go">
<!ELEMENT rap:music ...>
<!ATTLIST rap:music
    xmlns:rap CDATA #FIXED "http://www.rude-noises.go">
```

Remember: The rule is that colons and namespace declarations are not relevant or special to a DTD validator. Always define fixed values for your namespace attributes and your documents should be able to get the best of both worlds.

1. In fact, it makes so much sense that it probably should have been a requirement of the Namespaces spec. The XML implementation in Internet Explorer 5 enforces it as though it were. Maybe some day it will be.

58.4 | Are namespaces a good thing?

We said in the introduction to this chapter that namespaces are controversial. We've seen how namespace prefixes cause clutter and how redefining them causes confusion. Why then were they considered so vital that they were rushed to Recommendation status almost as soon as XML was approved?

And why does the spec allow all that flexibility in their use?

As the application parts of this book show, the predominant use for XML on the Web is data integration. In those applications, a middle-tier server may aggregate XML fragments from many sources into a single well-formed (but not valid) document and send it to a client for processing.

Because only computers ever see those documents, prefix clutter doesn't matter. It adds to the overhead somewhat, but it could also aid in debugging.

And reusing prefixes for different namespaces doesn't matter in those applications either, since the software can base its processing strategy on the full URI, rather than the short nickname.[1]

Furthermore, there are cases where namespace prefixes cause less clutter than alternative approaches might have. In XSL specifications, for example, the prefixes disambiguate the markup that controls the XSL processing from the markup of the generated text in the templates.

But more than that, namespaces provide a mechanism for universal vocabularies of element type names that can be used in all document types. Namespaces provide a way to define element types so that their names are unique throughout the world. As long as everyone adheres to the namespaces convention there can be no confusion about whether element types with identical names belong to one vocabulary or another.

1. In fact, when the W3C schema language is eventually defined, it will probably support validation based on the full URI as well.

XML Path Language (XPath)

Tad Tougher Tutorial

- XPath applications
- XPath data model
- Location expressions

©2000 The XML Handbook™

Chapter 59

This chapter was written using materials prepared by G. Ken Holman of Crane Softwrights Ltd., `http://www.CraneSoftwrights.com`, a member of the ISO *Document Description and Processing Languages* standards committee and author of *Practical Transformation Using XSLT and XPath.*

All XML processing depends upon the idea of addressing. In order to do something with data you must be able to locate it. To start with, you need to be able to actually find the XML document on the Web. Once you have it, you need to be able to find the information that you need within the document.

The Web has a uniform solution for the first part. The XML document is called a *resource* and *Uniform Resource Identifiers* are the Web's way of addressing resources. The most popular form of Uniform Resource Identifier is the ubiquitous Uniform Resource Locator (URL).

The standard way to locate information *within* an XML document is through a language known as the *XML Path Language* or *XPath*. XPath can be used to refer to textual data, elements, attributes and other information in an XML document.

XPath is a sophisticated, complex language. We will cover its most commonly used features, most of which are available using an abbreviated form of its syntax.

59.1 | XPath applications

Over the next few years, XPath is likely to become a basic building block of XML systems. Let's look at just a few possible applications of XPath.

59.1.1 *User scenarios*

Consider the process of stylesheet creation. A paragraph of text in one chapter may refer to another chapter through a cross-reference. During style application it makes sense to fetch the title of the referenced chapter and its chapter number. The stylesheet could then insert those pieces of information into the text of the cross-reference. For example, the marked-up phrase "`Please see <crossref refid="introduction.chapter">.`" might be rendered as "Please see 'Chapter 1, Introduction'." XPath can be used within XSL to find the appropriate chapter, find its title and locate the text of the title.

Now consider an e-commerce application. It might receive a purchase order from another system. In order to do accounting it would need to know the prices of the purchased items. In XPath notation it would locate "`/po/item/price`", meaning all of the prices in all of the items in the current purchase order document.

Finally, imagine an ordinary Web surfer of the near future. He might be reading his favorite recipes Web page. Unbeknownst to him, the page is written in XML (this is the near future, after all!). As he scrolls through, he finds a recipe that he would really love to share with his brother-in-law. He clicks the right mouse button at the beginning of the recipe. One of the choices in the popup menu might be: "email this address."

The menu item would instruct the browser to email a string of characters, termed a *URI reference* to a particular email address. The URI reference would uniquely identify not just the Web page but also the particular `recipe` element. The first part of the string would be an ordinary URI, pointing to the Web page. The last part would be an *XPointer*. XPointers are a customization of XPath for use in URI references.

As you can see, XPath is going to be a valuable tool in all sorts of XML processing.

59.1.2 *Specifications built on XPath*

XPath was developed when the groups responsible for XSLT and XPointer realized that they had to provide many of the same functions and could develop a shared solution.

These two World Wide Web Consortium specifications depend upon XPath today. XPointer uses XPath to build Web addresses (URI references) that reference parts of XML documents. URI references can address individual points and elements, as in our recipe example. They can also address lists of elements, attributes or characters.

The XSL Transformations language (XSLT) uses XPath for transformation and style application. As in our cross-reference example, XPath can be used to retrieve information from somewhere else in the document. XPath can also be used to declare that certain XSLT style rules apply to particular elements in the input document.

XPath's syntax was carefully chosen. XPath is used by XPointer in URI references and by both XPointer and XSLT in attribute values of XML documents. XPath needed to easily fit into attribute values, browser URL fields and other places where XML's element within element syntax would be too verbose. Accordingly, XPath's syntax is very concise and does not depend on an XML parser.

XPath is designed to be extensible. W3C specifications and other XPath applications can create extensions specific to the application's problem domain. XPointer and XSLT already extend XPath.

59.1.2.1 An XLink example

Example 59-1 shows an XLink with an `xlink:href` attribute. The attribute value contains a URI reference. The reference contains an XPointer (starting with the string `xptr`). The characters within the parentheses are an XPath expression.

Example 59-1. XLink use of XPath

```
<A xlink:type="simple"
   xlink:href="infofile.xml#xptr(id('smith')/info[@type='public'])">
   Mr. John Smith
</A>
```

To summarize, Example 59-1 contains an XLink which contains a URI reference which contains an XPointer which in turn contains an XPath expression. Don't worry. We will take you through each part gently!

59.1.2.2 An XSLT example

An example of the XSLT use of the same XPath expression is the `select` attribute of Example 59-2.

Example 59-2. XSLT selecting based on XPath

```
<xsl:apply-templates select="id('smith')/info[@type='public']"/>
```

This `select` attribute finds the element identified `smith` and queries for the `info` subelements with the attribute `type` having the value "`public`". It then processes each of those `info` elements with an XSLT *template rule*. The applicable rule is found by matching each element against an XSLT pattern in the template's match attribute. Example 59-3 demonstrates.

Example 59-3. XSLT use of XPath

```
<xsl:template match="info[@type='public']">
   ...
</xsl:template>
```

59.2 | The XPath data model

It is only possible to construct an address – any address – given a model. For instance the US postal system is composed of a model of states containing cities containing streets with house numbers. To some degree the model falls naturally out of the geography of the country but it is mostly artificial. State and city boundaries are not exactly visible from an airplane. We give new houses street numbers so that they can be addressed within the postal system's model.

Relational databases also have a model that revolves around tables, records, columns, foreign keys and so forth. This "relational model" is the basis for the SQL query language. Just as SQL depends on the relational model, XPath depends on a formal model for the logical structure and data in an XML document.

59.2.1 *Sources of the model*

You may wonder if XML really needs a formal model. It seems so simple: elements within elements, attributes of elements and so forth. It *is* simple but there are details that need to be standardized in order for addresses to behave in a reliable fashion. The tricky part is that there are many ways of representing what might seem to be the "same" information. We can represent a less-than symbol in at least four ways:

- a predefined entity reference: `<`
- a CDATA section: `<![CDATA[<]]>`
- a decimal Unicode character reference: `<`
- a hex Unicode character reference: `<`

We could also reference a text entity that embeds a CDATA section and a text entity that embeds another text entity that embeds a character reference, etc. In a query you would not want to explicitly search for the less-than symbol in all of these variations. It would be easier to have a processor that could magically *normalize* them to a single model. Every XPath-based query engine needs to get exactly the same data model from any particular XML document.

The XML equivalent of the relational model is termed, depending on the context, either a *grove*, an *information set* or a *data model*. The *grove* concept comes from ISO and is thus important when you are working with International Standards like HyTime, Topic Maps and DSSSL.

The XML Information Set is another model of the important information in an XML document. W3C specifications are built on top of the Information Set. Whereas the grove is generalized and can include both XML and non-XML data notations, the information set is specific to XML. XPath is a W3C specification and is only for addressing into XML documents, so its data model is derived from the W3C XML Information Set.[1]

---

1. Perhaps one day a grove-based XPath might be invented. It might allow querying arbitrary information types based on topic metadata.

The XPath specification does not use the Information Set directly. The Information Set takes a more liberal view of what is "important" than XPath does. Therefore XPath has a concept of a *data model*: an Information Set with some XPath-irrelevant parts filtered out.

For instance the Information Set says that it may be important to keep track of what entity each element resides within. The XPath developers chose not to care about that information and it is not, therefore, part of the XPath data model.

59.2.2 *Tree addressing*

The XPath data model views a document as a tree of nodes, or *node tree*. Most nodes correspond to document components, such as elements and attributes.

It is very common to think of XML documents as being either families (elements have child elements, parent elements and so forth) or trees (roots, branches and leaves). This is natural: trees and families are both hierarchical in nature, just as XML documents are. XPath uses both metaphors but tends to lean more heavily on the familial one.[1]

XPath uses genealogical taxonomy to describe the hierarchical makeup of an XML document, referring to children, descendants, parents and ancestors. The parent is the element that contains the element under discussion. The list of ancestors includes the parent, the parent's parent and so forth. A list of descendants includes children, children's children and so forth.

Insofar as there is no culture-independent way to talk about the first ancestor, XPath calls it the "root". The root is not an element. It is a logical construct that holds the document element and any comments and processing instructions that precede and follow it.[2]

Trees in computer science are very rarely (if ever) illustrated as a natural tree is drawn, with the root at the bottom and the branches and leaves growing upward. Far more typically, trees are depicted with the root at the top just as family trees are. This is probably due to the nature of our writing systems and the way we have learned to read.[3] Accordingly, this chapter

---

1. Politicians take note: in this case, family values win out over environmentalism!
2. In the full Information Set, the root is called the document information item and it also contains information about the document's DTD.

refers to stepping "down" the tree towards the leaf-like ends and "up" the tree towards the root as the tree is depicted in Figure 59-1. One day we will genetically engineer trees to grow this way and nature will be in harmony with technology.

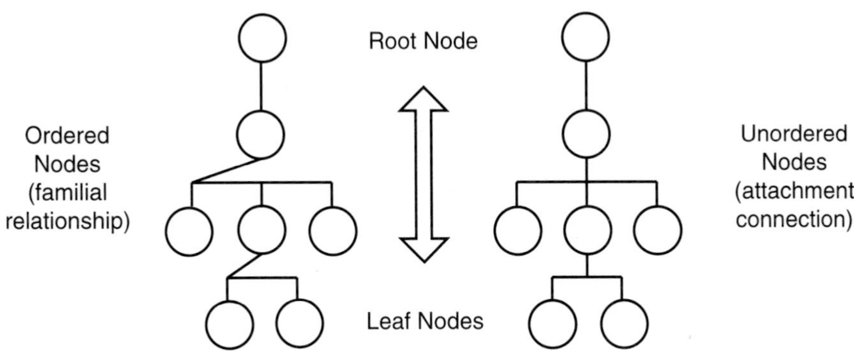

Figure 59-1 Vertical tree depictions

59.2.3 *Node tree construction*

A *node tree* is built by an XPath processor after parsing an XML document like that in Example 59-4.

Example 59-4. Sample document

```
<?xml version="1.0"?>
<!--start-->
<part-list>
  <part-name nbr="A12">bolt</part-name>
  <part-name nbr="B45">washer</part-name>
    <warning type="ignore"/>
  <!--end of list-->
  <?cursor blinking?>
</part-list>
<!--end of file-->
```

3. To do: reverse all tree diagrams for Japanese edition of XML Handbook.

In constructing the node tree, the boundaries and contents of "important" constructs are preserved, while other constructs are discarded. For example, entity references to both internal and external entities are expanded and character references are resolved. The boundaries of CDATA sections are discarded. Characters within the section are treated as character data.

The node tree constructed from the document in Example 59-4 is shown in Figure 59-2. In the following sections, we describe the components of node trees and how they are used in addressing. You may want to refer back to this diagram from time to time as we do so.

59.2.4 *Node types*

The XPath data model describes seven types of nodes used to construct the node tree representing any XML document. We are interested primarily in the root, element, attribute and text node types, but will briefly discuss the others.

For each node type, XPath defines a way to compute a *string-value* (labeled "value" in Figure 59-2). Some node types also have a "name".

59.2.4.1 Root node

The top of the hierarchy that represents the XML document is the root node.

It is important to remember that in the XPath data model the root of the tree representing an XML document is *not the document (or root) element of the document.* A root *node* is different from a root *element.* The root node *contains* the root element.

The nodes that are children of the root node represent the document element and the comments and processing instructions found before and after the document element.

59.2.4.2 Element nodes

Every element in an XML document is represented in the node tree as an element node. Each element has a parent node. Usually an element's parent

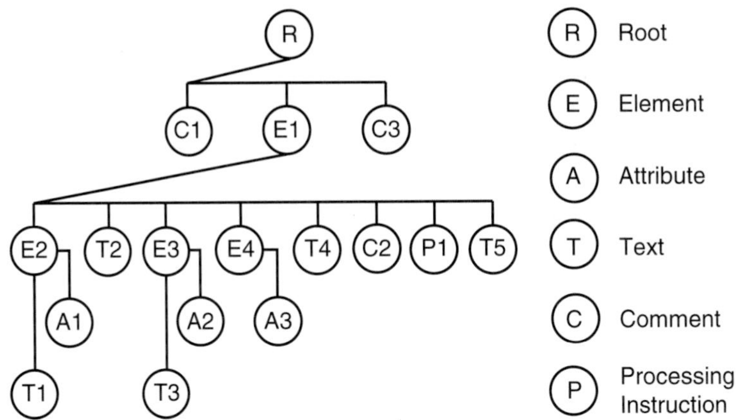

R: value="bolt
washer

"
C1: value="start"
E1: name="part-list" value="bolt
washer

"
E2: name="part-name" value="bolt"
A1: name="nbr" value="A12"
T1: value="bolt"
T2: value="
"
E3: name="part-name" value="washer"
A2: name="nbr" value="b45"
T3: value="washer"
E4: name="warning" value=""
A3: name="type" value="ignore"
T4: value="

C2: value="end of list"
P1: name="cursor" value="blinking"
T5: value="

C3: value="end of file"

Figure 59-2 Node tree for document in Example 59-4

is another element but the document element has as its parent the root node.

Element nodes can have as their children other element nodes, text nodes, comment nodes and processing instruction nodes.

An element node also exhibits properties, such as its name, its attributes and information about its active namespaces.

Element nodes in documents with DTDs may have unique identifiers. These allow us to address element nodes by name. IDs are described in 54.6.3.4, "ID and IDREF attributes", on page 774.

The string-value of an element node is the concatenation of the string-values of all text node descendants of the element node in the document order. You can think of it as all of the data with none of the markup, organized into one long character string.

59.2.4.3 Text nodes

The XML 1.0 Recommendation describes character data as all text that is not markup. In other words it is the textual data content of the document and it does not include data in attribute values, processing instructions and comments.

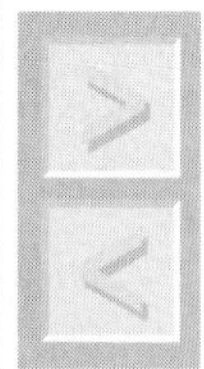

> ***Caution*** *The word "text" means something different in XPath from its meaning in the XML Recommendation (and the rest of this book!). We'll try to minimize the confusion by always saying "text node", even when the context is clear, reserving "text" as a noun for its normal meaning.*

XPath does not care how a character was originally represented. The string "`<>`" in an XML document is simply "<>" from the data model's point of view. The same goes for "`&60;&62;`" and "`<![CDATA[<>]]>`". The characters represented by any of these will be grouped with the data characters that precede and follow them and called a "text node." The individual characters of the text node are not considered its children: they are just part of its value. Text nodes do not have any children.

59.2.4.4 Attribute nodes

If an element has attributes then these are represented as attribute nodes. These nodes are not considered children of the element node. They are more like friends that live in the guest house.

An attribute node exhibits name, string-value, and namespace URI properties. Defaulted attributes are reported as having the default values. The data model does not record whether they were explicitly specified or merely defaulted. No node is created for an unspecified attribute that had an `#IMPLIED` default value declared. Attribute nodes are also not created for attributes used as namespace declarations.

Note that an XML processor is not required to read an external DTD unless it is validating the document. This means that detection of ID attributes and default attribute values is not mandatory.

59.2.4.5 Other node types

Namespace nodes keep track of the set of namespace prefix/URI pairs that are in effect at a particular point in a document. Like attribute nodes, namespace nodes are attached to element nodes and are not in any particular order.

Each comment and processing instruction in the XML document is instantiated as a comment or processing instruction node in the node tree. The string-value property accesses the content of these constructs, as you can see in Figure 59-2.

59.3 | Location paths

An instance of the XPath language is called an *expression*. XPath expressions can involve a variety of operations on different kinds of operands. In this chapter we will focus on two operand types: function calls and location paths.

A *location path* is the most important kind of expression in the XPath notation. Its syntax is similar to the familiar path expressions used in URLs and in Unix and Windows systems to locate directories and files. We covered that syntax with a hands-on tutorial, using free software on the CD-ROM, in Chapter 45, "B2B QueryView: XQL search tool", on page 602, so we won't repeat it here.[1]

1. Yes, that chapter actually deals with XQL, but its path expression syntax and data model are sufficiently similar to XPath to make it usable as an XPath primer.

59.3.1 *Basic concepts*

A location path has a starting point, which XPath calls its *context node*. In a file system path, it might be a computer, a disk drive, or a directory. In an XPath location path it could be, for example, the document element node or some other element node.

The purpose of the location path is to select nodes from the document by locating the desired nodes relative to the initial context node.

Arguably, the simplest location path is "`/`". This selects the root node (not the document element node).

59.3.1.1 Stepping down the hierarchy

We can extend this location path to select the document element node instead of the root node. "`/mydoc`" will select a document element node named "`mydoc`". The name of an element node is the element-type name of the element it represents.

Note *From now on, as long as we are discussing node trees, we'll often just say "element" instead of "element node".*

We have taken a step "down" the tree. We can take another step: "`/mydoc/section`". This will select every `section` element that is a child of the `mydoc` element.

Each slash-separated (`/`) path component is a *step*.

Any amount of whitespace can be present between the parts of a location path. Steps can be written across a number of lines or spaced apart to be more legible to a reader.

59.3.1.2 Predicates

So far we have seen how to build single and multi-level location paths based on element-type names. However, the type name is not the only thing that is interesting about an element. For example, we might want to filter out elements that have (or do not have) particular attributes with particular values. Or we may be interested in the first or seventh element, or just the even-numbered ones.

We can express these constraints with qualifiers called *predicates*. Any step can be qualified. The location path in Example 59-5, for example, selects the seventh paragraph from each `section` with a `security` attribute whose string-value is "`public`".

Example 59-5. Selecting the seventh `para` from each public `section`

```
/mydoc/section[@security="public"]/para[7]
```

59.3.1.3 Selection

Note that we use the word *select* carefully. We could say that the query *returns* certain nodes but that might put a picture in your head of nodes being ripped out of the tree and handed to you: "Here are your nodes!"

Rather, what you get back is a set of locations – pointers to the nodes. Imagine the result of a location path as a set of arrows pointing into the node tree, saying: "Your nodes are here!"

59.3.1.4 Context

The context node keeps changing as we step down the path. As each step is evaluated, the result is a set of nodes – in XPath talk, a *node-set*. The node-set could have one or more nodes, or it could be empty.

The next step is then evaluated for each member of that node-set. That is, each member is used as the context node for one of the evaluations of the next step. The node-sets selected by each of those evaluations are combined (except for any duplicates) to produce the result node-set.

Consider what happens in Example 59-5.

1. The XPath processor first evaluates the "`/`". The root node becomes the initial context node.
2. Next it looks for every child of the context node with the name "`mydoc`". There will be only one member of that node-set because XML allows only a single root element. It becomes the context node for the next step, which is evaluated only once.

3. Next the processor looks for all of the `section` children in the context of the `mydoc` element that have the appropriate attribute value and returns their node-set. The next step will be evaluated once for each selected `section` node, which is the context node for that evaluation.
4. We're almost done. The processor looks for the seventh `para` several times, once for each `section` in the node-set. It puts the selected `para` nodes together into the final node-set and returns a set of pointers to them: "Your nodes are here!".

The initial context does not always have to be the root node of the document. It depends on the environment or application. Whatever application (e.g. database or browser) or specification (e.g. XSLT or XPointer) is using XPath must specify the starting context.

In XSLT there is always a concept of the *current node*. That node is the context node for location paths that appear in XSLT transforms. In XPointer, the starting context is always the root node of the particular document, selected by its URI. In some sort of document database, we might be allowed to do a query across thousands of documents. The root node of each document would become the context node in turn. XPath itself does not have a concept of working with multiple documents but it can be used in a system that does.

In addition to the current node, an application could specify some other details of the context: it could supply some values for variables and functions that can be used in the XPath expression. It could also include namespace information that can be used to interpret prefixed names in a location path.

59.3.1.5 Axes

But wait. That's not all! Up to now we've always stepped down the tree, to a child element. But we can also step *up* the tree instead of down and step many levels instead of one.

We can step in directions that are neither up nor down but more like sideways. For example we can step from elements to attributes and from attributes to elements.

We can also step from an element directly to a child of a child of a child (a descendant).

These different ways of stepping are called *axes*.

For example, the *descendant axis* (abbreviated `//`) can potentially step down all the levels of the tree. The location path "`/mydoc//footnote`" would select all footnotes in the current document, no matter how many levels deep they occur.

The *parent axis* uses an abbreviated syntax (`..`) that is similar to that for going up a directory in a file system. For instance we could select all of the elements *containing* a footnote like this: "`/mydoc//footnote/..`".

The *attribute axis* (abbreviated "`@`") steps into the attribute nodes of an element.

The *namespace axis* is used for namespace information associated with an element node.

59.3.1.6 Node tests

The attribute and namespace axes each have only one type of node, which is (necessarily!) its principal node type.

The other axes, however, have element as the principal node type but have comment, processing instruction, and text node types as well. We'll refer to such an axis as a *content axis* and its nodes as *content nodes*.

A step normally selects nodes of the principal type. In the case of content axes, a node test can be used to select another type. For example, the node test `text()` selects text nodes.

59.3.2 *Anatomy of a step*

We've now seen enough of the basics to take a formal look at the parts of a location step. There are three:

- An axis, which specifies the tree relationship between the context node and the nodes selected by the location step. Our examples so far have used the child axis.
- A node test, which specifies the node type of the nodes selected by the location step. The default type is element, unless the axis is one that can't have element nodes.
- Zero or more predicates, which use arbitrary expressions to further refine the set of nodes selected by the location step.

©2000 THE XML HANDBOOK™

> The expressions are full-blown XPath expressions and can include function calls and location paths. In Example 59-5 the first predicate is a location path and the second uses an abbreviation for the `position()` function.

In this tutorial, we've only been using abbreviated forms of the XPath syntax, in which common constructs can often be omitted or expressed more concisely. Example 59-6 shows the unabbreviated form of Example 59-5. Note the addition of explicit axis names (`child` and `attribute`) and the `position()` function call.

Example 59-6. Unabbreviated form of Example 59-5

```
/child::mydoc/child::section[attribute::security="public"]
             /child::para[position()=7]
```

In the remainder of the chapter, we'll take a closer look at each of the three parts: node tests, axes, and predicates.

59.3.2.1 Node tests

Some node tests are useful in all axes; others only in content axes.

Node tests for all axes are:

`*`
: any node of the principal type; i.e., element, attribute, or namespace.[1]

`node()`
: any node of any type

Node tests solely for content axes are:

`text()`
: any text node

---

1. The asterisk cannot be used as a prefix (`"*ara"`) or suffix (`"ara*"`) as it is in some regular-expression languages.

©2000 THE XML HANDBOOK™

`comment()`
: any comment node

`processing-instruction()`
: any processing-instruction node, regardless of its target name

`processing-instruction(target-name)`
: any processing-instruction node with the specified target name

Here are some examples of node tests used in a *content* axis:

`processing-instruction(cursor)`
: all nodes created from a processing instruction with the target name "`cursor`"

`part-nbr`
: all nodes created from an element with the element-type name `part-nbr`

`text()`
: all text nodes (contrast below)

`text`
: all nodes created from an element with the element type name `text`

`*`
: all nodes created from elements, irrespective of the element-type name

`node()`
: all nodes created from elements (irrespective of the element-type name), contiguous character data, comments or processing instructions (irrespective of the target name)

59.3.2.2 Axes

The most important axes are described here.

59.3.2.2.1 Child

The default axis is the child axis. That means that if you ask for "`/section/para`" you are looking for a `para` in a `section`. If you ask merely for "`para`" you are looking for the `para` element children of the context node, whatever it is.

59.3.2.2.2 Attribute

When using the symbol "`@`" before either an XML name or the node test "`*`", one is referring to the attribute axis of the context node.

The attribute nodes are attached to an element node but the nodes are not ordered. There is no "first" or "third" attribute of an element.

Attribute nodes have a string-value that is the attribute value, and a name that is the attribute name.

Some examples of abbreviated references to attribute nodes attached to the context node are:

`@type`
: an attribute node whose name is "`type`"

`@*`
: all attributes of the context node, irrespective of the attribute name

59.3.2.2.3 Descendant

We can use the double-slash "`//`" abbreviation in a location path to refer to the descendant axis.[1] This axis includes not only children of the context node, but also all other nodes that are descendants of the context node.

This is a very powerful feature. We could combine this with the wildcard node test, for example, to select all elements in a document, other than the document element, no matter how deep they are: "`/doc//*`".

Some examples:

1. You may read in the XPath spec that the axis referred to by the abbreviation is actually the descendant-or-self axis. However, that is merely a technical device to enable the abbreviation to have the desired effect of referencing all descendants. The formal expansion of the abbreviation introduces another step, which would otherwise have caused children of the context node to be excluded. We refer to "`//`" as standing for the descendant axis because that's the way it acts.

`/mydoc//part-nbr`
: all element nodes with the element-type name `part-nbr` that are descendants of the `mydoc` document element; that is, all of the `part-nbr` elements in the document

`/mydoc//@type`
: all attribute nodes named `type` attached to any descendant element of the `mydoc` document element; i.e., all of the `type` attributes in the document

`/mydoc//*`
: all elements that are descendants of the `mydoc` document element; i.e., every element in the document except the `mydoc` element itself

`/mydoc//comment()`
: all comment nodes that are descendants of the `mydoc` document element

`/mydoc//text()`
: all of the text nodes that are descendants of the `mydoc` document element; i.e., all of the character data in the document!

We do not have to start descendant expressions with the document element. If we want to start somewhere farther into the document we can use "//" in any step anywhere in the location path.

We could also begin with "//". A location path that starts with "//" is interpreted as starting at the root and searching all descendants of it, including the document element.

59.3.2.2.4 Self

The self axis is unique in that it has only one node: the context node. This axis can solve an important problem.[1]

1. In fact, we suspect it was invented for that purpose only. It is another ingenious hack, like the one in the previous footnote, for enabling convenient abbreviations to be mapped onto a coherent normalized form.

For instance in an XSLT transformation we might want to search for all descendants of the current node. If we begin with "`//`" the address will start at the root. We need a way to refer specifically to the current node.

A convenient way to do this is with an abbreviation: a period (`.`) stands for the context node. [1]

So "`.//footnote`" would locate all footnote descendants of the context node.

59.3.2.2.5 Parent

The parent axis (`..`) of a content node selects its parent, as the axis name suggests. For a namespace or attribute node, however, it selects the node's attached element.

You could therefore search an entire document for a particular attribute and then find out what element it is attached to: "`//@confidential/..`". You could go on to find out about the element's parent (and the parent's parent, etc.): "`//@confidential/../..`".

59.3.2.2.6 Ancestor

There is also a way of searching for an ancestor by name, but it does not have an abbreviated syntax. For example, "`ancestor::section`" would look for the ancestor(s) of the context node that are named "`section`".

This location path locates the titles of sections that contain images: "`//image/ancestor::section/title`".

59.3.3 *Our story so far*

Here are some examples of location paths using features we have covered so far:

`item`

`item` element nodes that are children of the context node

---

1. This "dot-convention" also comes from the file system metaphor. Unix and windows use "." to mean the current directory.

`item/para`
: `para` element nodes that are children of `item` element nodes that are children of the context node; in other words, those `para` grandchildren of the context node whose parent is an `item`

`//para`
: `para` element nodes that are descendants of the root node; in other words, all the `para` element nodes in the entire document

`//item/para`
: `para` element nodes that are children of all `item` element nodes in the entire document

`//ordered-list//para`
: `para` element nodes that are descendants of all `ordered-list` element nodes in the entire document

`ordered-list//para/@security`
: `security` attribute nodes attached to all `para` element nodes that are descendants of all `ordered-list` element nodes that are children of the context node

`*/@*`
: attribute nodes attached to all element nodes that are children of the context node

`../@*`
: attribute nodes attached to the parent or attached node of the context node

`.//para`
: `para` element nodes that are descendants of the context node

`.//comment()`
comment nodes that are descendants of the context node

Tip *The XPath specification includes numerous other examples of location paths. You can find it on the CD-ROM.*

59.3.4 *Predicates*

It is often important to filter nodes out of a node-set. We might filter out nodes that lack a particular attribute or subelement. We might filter out all but the first node. This sort of filtering is done in XPath through *predicates*. A predicate is an expression that is applied to each node. If it evaluates as false, the tested node is filtered out.

We'll discuss some common types of predicate expressions, then look at some examples.

59.3.4.1 Expression types

59.3.4.1.7 Node-sets

A location path expression can be used as a predicate. It evaluates to `true` if it selects any nodes at all. It is false if it does not select any nodes. So Example 59-7 would select all paragraphs that have a footnote child.

Example 59-7. Using a location path as a predicate

```
//para[footnote]
```

Recall that the evaluation of a step in the path results in a node-set, each member of which is a context node for an evaluation of the next step.[1]

One by one, each member of the result node-set, which in this case is every paragraph in the document, would get a chance to be the context

1. In other words, Example 59-7 is really an abbreviation for "`//para[./footnote]`".

node. It would either be selected or filtered out, depending on whether it contained any footnotes. Every paragraph would get its bright shining moment in the sun when it could be ".".[1]

A number of predicates can be chained together. Only nodes that pass all of the filters are passed on to the next step in the location path. For example, "`//para[footnote][@important]`" selects all paragraphs with `important` attributes and `footnote` children.

Like other location path, those in predicates can have multiple steps with their own predicates. Consider the complex one in Example 59-8. It looks for `sections` with `author` child elements with `qualifications` child elements that have both `professional` and `affordable` attributes.

Example 59-8. A complex location path predicate

```
section[author/qualifications[@professional][@affordable]]
```

59.3.4.1.8 String-values

Not all predicates are location path. Sometimes you do not want to test for the existence of some node. You might instead want to test whether an attribute has some particular value. That is different from testing whether the attribute exists or not.

Testing an attribute's value is simple: "`@type='ordered'`" tests whether the context node has a `type` attribute with value "`ordered`".

In XPath, every node type has a string-value. The value of an element node that is the context node, for example, is the concatenation of the string-values from the expression: "`.//text()`". In other words, it is all of the character data content anywhere within the element and its descendants.

So we can test the data content of a section's `title` child element with "`section[title='Doo-wop']`" and both of the sections in Example 59-9 would match.

1. Unfortunately, the moment is brief and the price of failure is exclusion from the selection set.

Example 59-9. Matching sections

```
<section><title>Doo-wop</title>
...
</section>

<section><title>Doo-<emph>wop</emph></title>
...
</section>
```

59.3.4.1.9 Context position

There is more to the context in which an expression is evaluated than just the context node. Among the other things is the node's *context position*, which is returned by a function call: `position()=number`.

In practice, an abbreviation, consisting of the number alone, is invariably used. A number expression is evaluated as `true` if the number is the same as the context position.

Context position can be a tricky concept to grasp because it is, well, context sensitive. However, it is easy to understand for the most common types of steps.

In a step down the child axis (`a/b`) the context position is the position of the child node in the parent node. So "`doc/section[5]`" is the fifth section in a `doc`. In a step down the descendant axis (`a//b[5]`) it still refers to the position of the child node in its *parent node*, not its numerical order in the list of matching nodes.

XPath also has a function called "`last()`". We can use it to generate the number for the last node in a context: "`a//b[last()]`". We can also combine that with some simple arithmetic to get the next-to-last node: "`a//b[last()-1]`".

59.3.4.2 Predicate examples

Here are some examples, using the predicate types that we've discussed:

`item[3]`
: third `item` element child of the context node

`item[@type]/para`
: `para` element children of `item` elements that exhibit a `type` attribute and are children of the context node

`//list[@type='ordered']/item[1]/para[1]`

first `para` element child of the first `item` element child of any `list` element that exhibits a `type` attribute with the string-value "`ordered`"

`//ordered-list[item[@type]/para[2]]//para`

`para` elements descended from any `ordered-list` element that has an `item` child that exhibits a `type` attribute and has at least two `para` element children (whew!) This last example is illustrated in Figure 59-3.

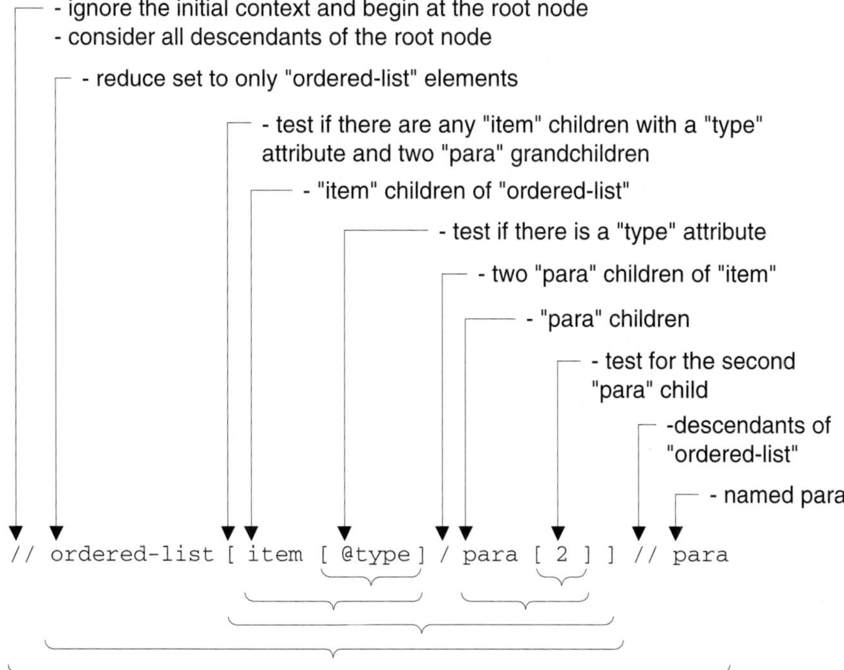
- ignore the initial context and begin at the root node
- consider all descendants of the root node
- reduce set to only "ordered-list" elements
- test if there are any "item" children with a "type" attribute and two "para" grandchildren
- "item" children of "ordered-list"
- test if there is a "type" attribute
- two "para" children of "item"
- "para" children
- test for the second "para" child
-descendants of "ordered-list"
- named para
// ordered-list [item [@type] / para [2]] // para
all "para" element nodes that are descendents of all "ordered-list" element nodes of the entire document node tree that have at least two "para" element node children of an "item" child that has a "type" attribute specified or defaulted

Figure 59-3 Evaluating multiple steps

©2000 THE XML HANDBOOK™

The XPath spec includes numerous other examples of using predicates. XPath is a powerful expression language, including operators and functions that operate on node-sets, numbers, strings, and booleans.

59.4 | ID function

The most common high-level expression in XPath is the location path, which we have explored in some detail. And, as we have seen, a location path can also be used at lower levels – as a predicate expression, for example.

Another form of expression that returns a node-set is a function call to the `id(string)` function. The main use of the function is to select the element node whose ID is the same as the string. For example, "`id('final')`". selects the element node whose unique identifier is "final".

An ID function and a location path can be used in the same expression. One way is to create the union of the two, as in Example 59-10. The result node-set is the element whose ID is "final", plus all `para` elements descended from `ordered-list` elements.

Example 59-10. Union expression

```
id('final') | /ordered-list//para
```

Another way to combine the two is to use the ID function as the initial context node of a location path, to create a path expression like that in Example 59-11. It locates the `title` child of the element whose ID is "A12345".

Example 59-11. Path expression

```
id('A12345')/title
```

Instead of a literal string, the argument could be a node whose string-value would be used, as in "`id(@IDREF)`". This expression locates the element referenced by the IDREF attribute of the context node.

59.5 | Conclusion

XPath is an extremely powerful language and is destined to be as important in the XML world as SQL is in the relational world. Although XPath has depths that we could not address in a friendly tutorial, we have covered all of the most common features.

With all these features one can very powerfully address the nodes of the XML data model. XPath is already in use in both XPointer and XSLT. Microsoft has added XPath support to their DOM through a function called "`selectNodes`". Future versions of the DOM may have XPath support as a standard feature. In short, XPath seems on track to become a central part of many XML systems.

©2000 THE XML HANDBOOK™

Extensible Stylesheet Language (XSL)

Friendly Tutorial

- XSL Transformations (XSLT)
- Template rules
- Patterns
- Templates
- Formatting objects

©2000 THE XML HANDBOOK™

Chapter 60

The Extensible Stylesheet Language (XSL) is a specification under development within the World Wide Web consortium for applying formatting to XML documents in a standard way. Over time a part of XSL called the XSL Transformations (XSLT) has evolved into an independently useful language for transforming one XML document to another. It is now the first part of the standard. The second part defines the semantics of formatting, in the form of a catalog of formatting objects.

Under the covers, XSL borrows from two other specifications: *DSSSL* and *CSS*. DSSSL, Document Style Semantics and Specification Language is a very powerful International Standard from ISO. DSSSL provides the transformational template application paradigm that XSL uses. CSS, the Cascading Stylesheet Language, is a popular World Wide Web Consortium specification. CSS provides much of XSL's formatting model. Although XSL borrows concepts from both of these languages, XSL stylesheets do not look like either DSSSL or CSS. XSL looks like XML! In fact, XSL is an XML vocabulary.

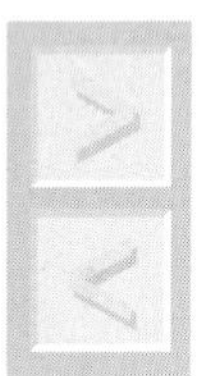

Caution *XSL is still under development, although XSLT is quite stable. Future versions of XSL will include features for animation, interactivity and other very advanced capabilities. However, the central concepts will be the same as those in the current XSL proposal. Those concepts are the focus of this chapter.*

The most important thing to take from this chapter is a feeling for how XML documents are actually processed by XSL. We have seen where XSL is used at a high level in the application chapters, now we'll look at the details of how it works.

XSL's processing model is very similar to that of many XML processing tools. Unlike general purpose programming languages, XML-aware tools can take care of some of the tedious parts of processing so that you can concentrate on your application needs. If you understand XSL then you will be able to use other languages and systems much more effectively.

60.1 | Transformation vs. rendition

XSL is designed to apply style to XML documents. These will usually be marked up entirely according to their abstract structure without (in theory) markup specifically tailored for style application or any other particular kind of processing. Thus XSL is the "missing link" between the abstract data that is intended for computer processing and the formatted rendition required for comfortable reading. In technical terms an XSL processor *transforms* a document from an abstraction to a rendition.

In this context the word "transforms" has a completely general meaning. Simple stylesheet languages such as CSS help documents to put on a little make-up. XSL allows them to get a complete make-over. XSL can reorder duplicate, suppress, sort and add elements. It can move end-notes to the end of a document. It can duplicate the title of a chapter so that appears in the chapter, in the header and in the Table Of Contents. It can suppress a corporation's internal annotations and metadata. It can sort the names in a phone directory. It can also add boilerplate text such as a copyright or corporate logo. In fact, XSL does not so much apply a makeover as a complete Cher-style plastic surgery.

There are many applications where these sorts of *transformations* would be useful. Style processing is a very important one but there are others. Consider an electronic commerce application where many companies must communicate. Each of their internal systems may use similar but different document types. To communicate they need to translate their various document types into a common one. An XSLT transformation provides a sophisticated but simple way to do so.

In fact, XSLT goes even further to support arbitrary processing. The XSLT language has a mechanism that allows you to call into a component written in any programming language. You could refer to a *Java* class file or an ActiveX control. You could even embed a small script from a scripting language such as *Javascript* or *Python*. The function can be defined right in your stylesheet!

In order to allow these general uses, the XSL specification defines style application as a two-part process. The first part is a transformation from XML into some other kind of XML. The result XML could either be a rendition represented as XSL formatting object elements, or something unrelated to rendition, such as an e-commerce document type.

If the result of the first part conforms to the formatting object vocabulary then the XSL processor may display it on a screen, print it out or convert it to some other formatted representation such as PDF, PostScript or Microsoft's RTF. If it conforms to some other document type then the XSL processor can do whatever it thinks is appropriate. Typically it will generate the document so that it may be saved to a file or transmitted over the network.

To summarize: name notwithstanding, XSL is more than just a style language. It has two stages. The first part is a generally useful transformation language called XSLT. The second part is a vocabulary of formatting objects for rendering documents.

Some applications will use only the transformation language. Other applications will use the transformation language to create formatting object elements that can be displayed, printed or saved as renditions in XML or some other representation.

60.2 | Formatting objects

The second part of XSL defines a large and very sophisticated set of formatting objects. If your goal is style application (and not just transformation) then you can use these formatting objects so that the renderer will know what to display.

Imagine taking an XML "manuscript" and typing it into a word processor. You would have to use the constructs provided by the word processor, such as paragraphs, bulleted lists, hypertext links and so on. In XSL terms, those constructs are the formatting objects. XSL stylesheets will typically contain block, display graphic, display rule (for horizontal rules), table formatting objects and so forth. A table formatting object might itself contain blocks. The blocks would contain characters, and also "sequence" formatting objects that would apply formatting like italics and bold to sequences of characters.

Conceptually, these objects form a tree. The page (or Web page) is the root. Paragraphs, tables, sequences and other "container" objects are the branches, and characters, graphics and other indivisible objects are the leaves. The tree of formatting objects is called the "formatting object tree." XML documents also describe a tree so it is logical that the formatting tree should also be an XML document.

Every formatting object has *properties*. The exact set of properties that a formatting object exhibits depends on its *class*. For example, blocks may specify the space before and after the block, clickable links may specify their destinations, characters may specify their font sizes, and pictures may specify their heights and widths.

At the time of writing, the formatting object vocabulary is still changing. Implementing a robust formatting engine is quite difficult so there are very few implementations of the experimental objects. We expect this situation to change once they stabilize.

60.3 | In the meantime

While we wait for the formatting objects to be designed and implemented we still need to get our jobs done.

Many XSLT implementations allow transformations from XML into HTML. This is good for serving to today's mainstream browsers (4.x) and the legacy (2.x, 3.x) browsers that most websites must still support. It also takes advantage of many Web designers' knowledge of HTML. If you format a document using element types from HTML instead of from the formatting object vocabulary it will look to a browser as if it had been created in HTML directly. You can think of this process as a conversion from XML markup to HTML markup. Internet Explorer 5.0 can actually do this conversion right in the browser.

So that you can start using XSL immediately we will use these element types in most of our examples instead of the formatting object element types. We will restrict our usage to only a few of them, namely:

- `h1` and `h2` element types for top-level and second-level headings,
- `p` element type for paragraphs
- `body` element type to contain the document's content; and the
- `em` element type to emphasize a series of characters.

For clarity of the stylesheet itself, we will use XML Namespaces to label these elements with an `html` prefix. (See Chapter 58, "Namespaces", on page 832 for more information.)

There is a subtlety in how this transformation works. The XSL transformation language converts XML to XML. An XML document could look very much like an HTML document if it used HTML element types.[1] However, this is still not quite what a browser understands as HTML.

For instance "legacy HTML" uses a different syntax for empty elements. Most XSL implementations have a special feature to generate real, honest-to-goodness "legacy HTML", suitable for processing with older browsers. They invoke this feature when they recognize that the transformation result namespace is HTML.

60.4 | XSL stylesheets

Most XSL looks more or less like "ordinary" XML. Simple XSL stylesheets are merely a specialized form of XML markup designed for specifying the

1. Recall the discussion of XHTML in Chapter 3, "Where is XML going?", on page 42.

formatting of other XML documents. You can think of XSL as just another document type. The XSL language defines element types and attributes, constrains them to occurring in particular places, and describes what they should look like. However, because of its heavy use of XML namespaces it is not possible in general to use a validating parser to ensure that an XSL document conforms to the XSL specification.

A stylesheet that uses the XSL formatting objects would have a root element that looks like Example 60-1.

Example 60-1. XSL stylesheet using formatting objects

```
<xsl:stylesheet xmlns:xsl="http://www.w3.org/XSL/Transform/1.0"
                xmlns:fo="http://www.w3.org/XSL/Format/1.0"
                result-ns="fo">
   <!-- template rules go here -->
</xsl:stylesheet>
```

The `xsl:stylesheet` element is usually the root element of XSL stylesheets. You can also call this element `xsl:transform`. There is no difference in the processing of the element. `xsl:transform` is merely a synonym.

The `xsl:stylesheet` or `xsl:transform` element must have a namespace declaration for `xsl`. It makes sense to use the same declaration and `xsl:` prefix every time. You can also specify a namespace for the result with the `result-ns` attribute. If you specify such a namespace then all of the result elements in your document must be in that namespace.

The declarations in Example 60-1 are appropriate for XSL formatting object vocabulary output. The declarations for HTML look like Example 60-2.

Example 60-2. XSL stylesheet using HTML elements

```
<xsl:stylesheet xmlns:xsl="http://www.w3.org/Transform/1.0"
                xmlns:html="http://www.w3.org/TR/REC-html40"
                result-ns="html">
   <!-- template rules go here -->
</xsl:stylesheet>
```

The `xsl:stylesheet` element is usually filled with template rules. The template rules describe how to format elements in the source document. Of course almost every element type could be formatted differently from every other element type so there are many rules in an XSL stylesheet. Particular elements could even be formatted differently if they share a type but have different attributes or occur in a different context.

60.5 | Rules, patterns and templates

In the application sections of this book, we looked at many products that mapped parts of a source document into a result document. They did so to convert from a word processor format to XML, to create stylesheets, to convert from XML to a legacy data format, etc. Often, they used a graphical interface to allow the user to define the transformation and generated XSLT or some earlier or variant version of it, or proprietary equivalent.

In this chapter, we look at the actual XSL stylesheet that such products might generate to specify those mappings. Of course, because it is an XML document, it could also be created by means other than application-specific or proprietary product interfaces.

In XSLT, the mapping construct is called a *template rule*. During XSLT processing every element, character, comment and processing instruction in an XML document is processed by some template rule. Some of them will be handled by template rules that the stylesheet writer created. Others are handled by *built-in* template rules that are hard-coded into every XSLT processor.

Template rules consist of two parts, the *pattern* and the *template*. Be careful with the terminology: a template is not a template rule. The pattern describes which source nodes (elements, textual data strings, comments or processing instructions) should be processed by the rule. The template describes the XML structure to generate when nodes are found that match the pattern.

In an XSL stylesheet, a template rule is represented by an `xsl:template` element.[1] The pattern is the value of the `xsl:template` element's `match` attribute, and the template proper is the element's content.

Template rules are simple. You do not have to think about the order in which things will be processed, where data is stored or other housekeeping tasks that programming languages usually require you to look after. You just

1. It would have been clearer had they called it an `xsl:template-rule` element, but they didn't.

declare what you want the result to look like and the XSL implementation figures out how to make that happen. Because everything is done through declarations we say that XSL is a *declarative* language. One important benefit of declarative languages is that they are easy to *optimize*. Implementors can use various tricks and shortcuts in order to make them execute quickly.

60.6 | Creating a stylesheet

XSLT's processing model revolves around the idea of patterns. Patterns allow the XSLT processor to choose which elements to apply which style rules to. XSLT's pattern language is basically XPath with a few extensions.

Patterns can be used in two basic ways: they can be used in the `match` attribute of template rules to specify which elements the rule applies to and they can be used within rules to select other elements (and other nodes) so that the stylesheet can process them also.

60.6.1 *Document-level template rule*

Consider a document with a `book` element type which can contain `title`, `section` and `appendix` element types. `section` and `appendix` elements can contain `title`, `para` and `list` subelements. Titles contain `#PCDATA` and no subelements. Paragraphs and list items contain `emph` and `#PCDATA`. Example 60-3 is a DTD that represents these constraints and Example 60-4 is an example document.

Example 60-3. DTD for book example

```
<!ELEMENT book (title, (section|appendix)+)>
<!ELEMENT section (title, (para|list)+)>
<!ELEMENT appendix (title, (para|list)+)>
<!ELEMENT title (#PCDATA)>
<!ELEMENT para (#PCDATA|emph)*>
<!ELEMENT emph (#PCDATA)>
<!ELEMENT list (item)+>
<!ELEMENT item (#PCDATA|emph)*>
```

Example 60-4. Book document instance

```
<book>
    <title>Chicken Soup for the Chicken's Soul</title>
    <section>
        <title>Introduction</title>
        <para>I've always wanted to write
              this book.</para>
    </section>
</book>
```

First the XSLT processor would examine the root element of the document. The XSLT processor would look for a rule that applied to books (a rule with a *match pattern* that matched a book). This sort of match pattern is very simple. Example 60-5 demonstrates.

Example 60-5. Simple match pattern

```
<xsl:template match="book">
  <!-- describe how books should be formatted -->
</xsl:template>
```

We can choose any basic structure for the generated book. Example 60-6 shows a reasonable one.

Example 60-6. Generated book structure

```
<xsl:template match="book">
  <html:body>
    <html:h1><!-- handle title --></html:h1>
    <!-- handle sections -->
    <html:hr/> <!-- HTML horizontal rule -->
    <html:h2>Appendices</html:h2>
    <!-- handle appendices -->
    <html:hr/>
    <html:p>Copyright 2000, the establishment.</html:p>
  </html:body>
</xsl:template>
```

The template in this template rule generates a body to hold the content of the document. The tags for the body element are usually omitted in HTML but we will want to add some attributes to the element later.The html:body is called a *literal result element.*

60.6.2 *Literal result elements*

The XSLT processor knows to treat `html:body` as a *literal result element* that is copied into the output because it is not an XSLT instruction (formally, it is not in the XSLT namespace). Elements in templates that are not part of the XSLT namespace are treated literally and copied into the output. You can see why these are called templates! They describe the form of the result document both by ordering content and by generating literal result elements. If the XSLT processor supports legacy HTML output then it will know that it should strip off the `html:` namespace prefix.

The `html:h1`, `html:h2` and `html:hr` elements are also literal result elements that will create HTML headings and horizontal rules. The stylesheet is represented in XML so the specification for the horizontal rule can use XML empty-element syntax. If the stylesheet engine supports legacy HTML output then it will create the appropriate syntax in the generated file. Finally the document has a literal result element and literal text representing the copyright. XSLT stylesheets can introduce this sort of *boilerplate* text.

60.6.3 *Extracting data*

The template also has comments describing things we still have to handle: the document's title, its sections and the appendices.

We can get the data content from the `title` element with the `xsl:value-of` instruction. It has a `select` attribute which is a pattern. If this pattern names a simple element type then it will match a subelement of the *current* element.

In this case the current element is the `book` element. That is the element matched by the `match` attribute. Example 60-7 shows what that would look like.

Example 60-7. Extracting data from a subelement

```
<h1><xsl:value-of select="title"/></h1>
```

60.6.4 *The apply templates instruction*

The next step is to handle sections and appendices. We could do it in one of two ways. We could either create a new template rule for handling sections or we could handle sections directly in the book template rule.

The benefit of creating a new rule is that it can be used over and over again. Before we create the new rule we should ensure it will get invoked at the right point. We will use a new instruction, xsl:apply-templates. Example 60-8 shows this instruction.

Example 60-8. The xsl:apply-templates **instruction**

```
<xsl:apply-templates select="section"/>
```

The xsl:apply-templates instruction does two important things.

1. It finds all nodes that match the select attribute pattern.
2. It processes each of these in turn. It does so by finding and applying a template rule that matches each node.

This important principle is at the heart of XSLT's processing model.

In this case, the *select* pattern in the xsl:apply-templates element selects all of the book's subelements of type section. The xsl:apply-templates instruction always searches out the rule that is appropriate for each of the selected nodes. In this case the xsl:apply-templates instruction will search out a rule that applies to sections. The expanded template is in Example 60-9.

Example 60-9. Handling section elements

```
<xsl:template match="book">
  <html:body>
    <html:h1><xsl:value-of select="title"/></html:h1>
    <xsl:apply-templates select="section"/>
    <html:hr/>
    <html:h2>Appendices</html:h2>
    <xsl:apply-templates select="appendix"/>
    <html:hr/>
    <html:p>Copyright 2000, the establishment</html:p>
  </html:body>
</xsl:template>
```

60.6.5 *Handling optional elements*

Our sample document does not have appendices but the stylesheet should support anything that the DTD allows. Documents created in the future may have appendices.

Our stylesheet generates the title element followed by section elements (in the order that they occurred in the document) followed by appendix elements (also in *document order*).

If our DTD allowed more than one title subelement in a book element then this stylesheet would generate them all. There is no way for a stylesheet to require that the document have a single title. These sorts of constraints are specified in the DTD.

Our DTD does permit documents to have no appendices. Our title and horizontal rule separating the appendices from the sections would look fairly silly in that case. XSLT provides an instruction called `xsl:if` that handles this situation. We can wrap it around the relevant parts as shown in Example 60-10.

Example 60-10. Using `xsl:if`

```
<xsl:if select="appendix">
  <html:hr/>
  <html:h2>Appendices</html:h2>
  <xsl:apply-templates test="appendix"/>
</xsl:if>
```

The `xsl:if` instruction goes within a template. We could drop it into our `book` template as a replacement for our current appendix handling.

The instruction also contains another template within it. The contained template is only instantiated (generated) if there is some element that matches the pattern `appendix` exhibited by the `test` attribute.

As with the `select` attribute, the context is the current node. If there is no node that matches the pattern in the `test` attribute then the entire contained template will be skipped.

There is another instruction called `xsl:choose` that allows for multiple alternatives, including a default template for when none of the other alternatives match.

60.6.6 *Reordering the output*

If the DTD had allowed titles, sections and appendices to be mixed together our stylesheet would reorder them so that the title preceded the sections and the sections preceded the appendices.

This ability to reorder is very important. It allows us to use one structure in our abstract representation and another in our rendition. The internal structure is optimized for editing, validating and processing convenience. The external structure is optimized for viewing and navigation.

Reordering is easy when you know exactly the order in which you want elements of various types to be processed. In the case of the body, for example: titles before sections before appendices. But within a section or appendix, reordering is somewhat trickier because we don't know the complete output order.

That is, we need to format titles before any of the paragraphs or lists, but we cannot disturb the relative order of the paragraphs and lists themselves. Those have to be generated in the document order.

We can solve this fairly easily. In DTD syntax the vertical bar (|) character means "or". It means the same in XPath pattern syntax. So we can make a rule like the one in Example 60-11.

Example 60-11. The section rule

```
<xsl:template match="section">
    <html:h2><xsl:value-of select="title"/></html:h2>
    <xsl:apply-templates select="para|list"/>
</xsl:template>
```

This rule forces titles (in our DTD there can be only one) to be handled first and paragraphs and lists to be processed in the order that they are found. The rule that we already defined for paragraphs will automatically be selected when paragraphs appear.

60.6.7 *Sharing a template rule*

Next we can handle appendices. If we wrote out the rule for appendices we would find it to be identical to sections. We could just copy the rule but XSLT has a more elegant way. We can amend our rule for appendices to say

©2000 THE XML HANDBOOK™

that the rule applies to sections *or* appendices. Example 60-12 demonstrates.

Example 60-12. Handling sections and appendices

```
<xsl:template match="section|appendix">
    <html:h2><xsl:value-of select="title"/></html:h2>
    <xsl:apply-templates select="para|list"/>
</xsl:template>
```

60.6.8 *Data content*

Next we can handle paragraphs. We want them each to generate a single HTML element. We also want them to generate their content to populate that element in the order that the content occurs, not in some pre-defined template order.

We need to process all of the paragraph's *subnodes*. That means that we cannot just handle `emph` subelements. We must also handle ordinary character data. Example 60-13 demonstrates this.

Example 60-13. Paragraph rule

```
<xsl:template match="para">
    <html:p><xsl:apply-templates select="node()"/>
    </html:p>
</xsl:template>
```

As you can see, the rule for paragraphs is very simple. The `xsl:apply-templates` instruction handles all of the bookkeeping parts for us. The `select` attribute matches all nodes: element nodes, text nodes, etc. If it encounters a text node it copies it to the result; that is a *default* rule built into XSLT. If it encounters a subelement, it processes it using the appropriate rule.

XSLT handles much of the complexity for us but we should still be clear: transformations will not always be this easy. These rules are so simple because our DTD is very much like HTML. The more alike the source and result DTDs are the simpler the transformation will be. It is especially helpful to have a very loose or flexible result DTD. HTML is perfect in this regard.

©2000 THE XML HANDBOOK™

60.6.9 *Handling inline elements*

emph follows the same basic organization as paragraph. Mixed content (character-containing) elements often use this organization. The HTML element-type name is html:em (Example 60-14). Note that in this case we will use an abbreviated syntax for the xsl:apply-templates element: Because the select attribute defaults to node(), we can leave it out.

Example 60-14. Handling emphasis

```
<xsl:template match="emph">
    <html:em><xsl:apply-templates/></html:em>
</xsl:template>
```

List items also have mixed content, so we should look at the rules for lists and list items next. They are in Example 60-15.

Example 60-15. List and item rules

```
<xsl:template match="list">
    <html:ol>
       <xsl:apply-templates/>
    </html:ol>
</xsl:template>
<xsl:template match="item">
    <html:li><xsl:apply-templates/></html:li>
</xsl:template>
```

The rules in Example 60-14 and Example 60-15 work together. When a list is detected the literal result element is processed and an html:ol element is generated. It will contain a single html:li element for each item. Each html:li will in turn contain text nodes (handled by the default rule) and emph (handled by the emph rule).

60.6.10 *Final touches*

We now have a complete stylesheet but it is rather basic. We might as well add a background color to beautify it a bit. HTML allows this through the bgcolor attribute of the body element. We will not go into the details of

©2000 The XML Handbook™

the HTML color scheme but suffice to say that Example 60-16 gives our document a nice light purple background.

Example 60-16. Adding a background color

```
<xsl:template match="book">
  <html:body bgcolor="#FFDDFF">
    <html:h1><xsl:value-of select="title"/></html:h1>
    <xsl:apply-templates select="section"/>
    <html:hr/>
    <xsl:if select="appendix">
      <html:hr/>
      <html:h2>Appendices</html:h2>
      <xsl:apply-templates test="appendix"/>
    </xsl:if>
    <html:p>Copyright 2000, the establishment</html:p>
  </html:body>
</xsl:template>
```

There is also one more detail we must take care of. We said earlier that the more flexible a document type is the easier it is to transform to. Even though HTML is pretty flexible it does have one unbreakable rule. Every document must have a `title` element. We've handled the `title` element from the source as a heading but HTML has different concepts of heading and title. The title shows up in the window's title bar, in the bookmark list and in search engine result lists. We need the document's title to appear as both the HTML title and as a heading element. Luckily XSLT allows us to duplicate data.

With these additions our stylesheet is complete! It is shown in Example 60-17.

As you can see simple XSLT transformations can be quite simple – evidence of XSLT's good design. XSLT also allows you to do more complex things. It supports all of XPath, sophisticated selections, stylesheet reuse and many other advanced features. XSLT would need a dedicated book to be covered in its entirety.

The important thing for you to recognize is that the basic XSLT processing model is based on template rules, patterns and templates. Flow of control between rules is handled by special instructions. In fact this processing model is ubiquitous in XML processing.

We've covered enough to do interesting things now using HTML for the result document. In the next section we will look into the future. The XSL

Example 60-17. Complete stylesheet

```
<xsl:stylesheet xmlns:xsl="http://www.w3.org/Transform/1.0"
                xmlns:html="http://www.w3.org/TR/REC-html40"
                result-ns="html">
<xsl:template match="book">
  <html:body bgcolor="#FFDDFF">
    <html:title><xsl:value-of select="title"/></html:title>
    <html:h1><xsl:value-of select="title"/></html:h1>
    <xsl:apply-templates select="section"/>
    <html:hr/>
    <xsl:if select="appendix">
      <html:hr/>
      <html:h2>Appendices</html:h2>
      <xsl:apply-templates test="appendix"/>
    </xsl:if>
    <html:p>Copyright 2000, the establishment</html:p>
  </html:body>
</xsl:template>

<xsl:template match="para">
    <html:p><xsl:apply-templates/></html:p>
</xsl:template>

<xsl:template match="section|appendix">
    <xsl:apply-templates select="title"/>
    <xsl:apply-templates select="para|list"/>
</xsl:template>

<xsl:template match="emph">
    <html:em><xsl:apply-templates/></html:em>
</xsl:template>

<xsl:template match="list">
    <html:ol>
       <xsl:apply-templates/>
    </html:ol>
</xsl:template>

<xsl:template match="item">
    <html:li><xsl:apply-templates/></html:li>
</xsl:template>
</xsl:stylesheet>
```

formatting objects will provide us with a rich, extensible formatting model, appropriate to the 21st century.

60.7 | XSL formatting objects

As we described earlier, Part Two of the XSL specification defines a set of formatting objects. Those are based primarily upon CSS. When you use these you use both parts of the XSL specification and you need an implementation that supports both parts of it. That implementation could be a command line utility, a browser or a desktop publishing program. XSL supports both online and print publishing.

Let's start simply and consider a stylesheet that would say that "Paragraphs should use a 12pt font" and "Titles should be 20 point and boldfaced."

Example 60-18 contains a stylesheet with two rules to apply font styles to titles and paragraphs.

Example 60-18. XSLT Example

```
<xsl:stylesheet xmlns:xsl="http://www.w3.org/XSL/Transform/1.0"
                xmlns:fo="http://www.w3.org/XSL/Format/1.0 "
                result-ns="fo">
    <xsl:template match="PARA">
        <fo:block font-size="12pt">
            <xsl:apply-templates/>
        </fo:block>
    </xsl:template>

    <xsl:template match="TITLE">
        <fo:block font-size="20pt" font-weight="bold">
            <xsl:apply-templates/>
        </fo:block>
    </xsl:template>
</xsl:stylesheet>
```

The rules say that whenever the XSLT processor encounters a `PARA` or `TITLE` element in an XML document, it should create a `fo:block` element. Because the result uses the formatting object vocabulary, an XSL processor should proceed to render the document. A renderer could also be a separate software component or program, such as a word processor or Web browser.

The renderer (word processor, browser etc.) generates a block (`fo:block`) of text on the screen which is separated from the text above and below it. This makes sense. Visually a paragraph is just a text block set off from other text. The `fo:block` element has an attribute called `font-size`. This attribute is also defined by the XSL specification and will be properly interpreted by the XSL processor in the rendition stage. Similarly, this stylesheet will look for `title` elements and make them bold and 20pt.

The `fo:root` is the root element and contains everything else. Within the root you can have one or more `fo:page-sequence` elements. Each represents a series of pages – either print pages or Web pages. The main content of the document goes into `fo:flow` elements. There are several different types of "block-level" objects that are allowed to go into the `fo:flow`.

`fo:block`
: The `fo:block` element type holds a block of text. It can be used for paragraphs, titles, block quotations and so forth. Blocks have a huge number of properties for changing the background color, background image, font size, padding (space around block), orphans (handling of page breaks) and so forth.

`fo:inline-graphic`
: The `fo:display-graphic` element type allows you to create a graphic that is formatted inline (between characters). You could use that for icons. The image is specified through a URL.

`fo:display-graphic`
: The `fo:display-graphic` element type allows you to create a graphic the is a block level object with space before and after.

`fo:display-rule`
: The `fo:display-rule` element type creates a horizontal or vertical line. It has properties for changing the color, length, width and style (solid, dotted, dashed).

`fo:display-sequence`
: The `fo:display-sequence` element type allows you to change the formatting of a sequence of blocks. You can specify attributes such as font size, font weight and padding for all of the contained blocks.

©2000 THE XML HANDBOOK™

`fo:table`
: The `fo:table` element type is used for tables. It has a *table model* similar to (but not identical to) that used by HTML.

`fo:list-block`
: The `fo:list-block` element type represents a list. It can contain either a sequence of `fo:list-item-body` elements, representing the list items, or pairs of `fo:list-item-label`, `fo:list-item` elements, representing lists where list items are named. The label/item pairs could be used for a dictionary; the words would be the labels and the definitions would be the items.

`fo:simple-link`
: The `fo:simple-link` element type allows you to create hypertext clickable links to a destination specified by a URL or to another element in the formatting object tree. This element type allows XLinks to be rendered.

`fo:page-number`
: The `fo:page-number` element type generates a page number for printed documents.

60.8 | Referencing XSL stylesheets

There is a W3C Recommendation that specifies how XML documents should refer to their stylesheets. Here is the relevant text:

Spec Excerpt (XML-SS) 60-1. The `xml-stylesheet` processing instruction

The `xml-stylesheet` processing instruction is allowed anywhere in the prolog of an XML document. The processing instruction can have pseudo-attributes `href` (required), `type` (required), `title` (optional), `media` (optional), `charset` (optional).

These are called "pseudo-attributes" instead of attributes. Although they use attribute syntax, they do not describe properties of an element. In real XML terms, only elements can have attributes. The only real syntactic dif-

URN

A new form of URI, *Universal Resource Name (URN)*, isn't location-dependent and perhaps will reduce the number of broken links. However, it has yet to catch on.

URLs are uniform, in that they have the same basic syntax no matter what specific type of resource (e.g. Web page, newsgroup) is being addressed or what mechanism is described to fetch it. They describe the locations of Web resources much as a physical address describes a person's location. URLs are hierarchical, just as most physical addresses are. A land mail address is resolved by sending a letter to a particular country, and from there to a local processing station, and from there to an individual. URLs are similar.

The first part of a URL is the *protocol*. It describes the mechanism that the Web browser or other client should use to get the resource. Think of it as the difference between Federal Express, UPS, and the other courier services. The most common such protocol is `http` which is essentially the "official" protocol of the World Wide Web. The `ftp` file transfer protocol is also widely used, chiefly for large downloads such as new browser versions.

After the protocol, there is a *hostname* and then a *datapath*. The datapath is broken into chunks separated by slash (/) characters, as you have no doubt seen in hundreds of URLs. Technically, a URL ends at that point. Since URLs are just the most common form of URI, it is also safe to say that the URI ends here.

61.3 | URI References

There is another term that is confusingly similar to URI: *URI Reference*. A URI Reference as the combination of a URI (which could be a URL) and an optional *fragment identifier*. For instance you may have seen links into HTML documents that look like Example 61-1.

Example 61-1. Reference into HTML

```
http://www.megabank.com/banking#about
```

In the example, #about is a fragment identifier. It refers to a particular HTML element. XPointers are the form of fragment identifier appropriate for XML documents. They are much more flexible than HTML fragment identifiers. Essentially, XPointers are an extension to URIs (i.e., a fragment identifier syntax) to allow you to point not just *to* an XML document, but into the content of one.

For instance, on today's Web, if you wanted to quote a particular paragraph out of another document, you would go to that document and cut and paste the text into yours. If, in the future, the text on the Web changes, yours does not. If that is what you want, that is fine. But an XPointer and XLink-smart application might allow you to construct a "living document" that quotes and refers to the very latest version of the paragraph.

61.4 | ID references with XPointers

The simplest form of XPointer allows you to refer to a particular element named with an ID. This is also the most robust form of XPointer, because it does not at all depend on the location of the referenced text within its document. Consider the XML document in Example 61-2.

Example 61-2. Example document

```
<?xml version="1.0"?>
<!DOCTYPE HEATWAVE SYSTEM "heatwave.dtd">
<HEATWAVE>
<WAVE ID="summer.92">
    <DURATION>July 22 to August 2</DURATION>
    <TEMPERATURE>101 Degrees</TEMPERATURE>
</WAVE>
<WAVE ID="summer.96">
    <DURATION>June 15 to July 18</DURATION>
    <TEMPERATURE>103 Degrees</TEMPERATURE>
</WAVE>
</HEATWAVE>
```

If this document resides at `http://www.hotdays.com/heatwave.xml`, then we could refer to the second `WAVE` element with the URI in Example 61-3.

Example 61-3. URI with XPointer

```
http://www.hotdays.com/heatwave.xml#xptr( id("summer.96") )
```

The XPointer is the last little bit of the URI, after the pound-sign (#). The text "`xptr`" starts the XPointer. Inside the parentheses we have an XPath. Typically the XPath will be just like those defined in Chapter 59, "XML Path Language (XPath)", on page 844, but sometimes they will use extensions that are defined in the XPointer specification.[1]

We are not restricted to XPath's `id` function. IDs are the most robust way to refer to elements but we can also refer to elements that do not have IDs. This is especially important if we do not control the document that we are referencing. Any XPath can be used.

61.5 | The role of XPointers

You could say that an XPointer is mostly just a shell for an XPath, but the shell is very important. The XPointer is the glue between the URI that precedes the pound-sign and the XPath in the parentheses. If you think in terms of software components, the XPointer component parses the XML document and hands the document node to the XPath component. "Here's a document node. Here's an XPath. Do your thing."

An important thing to note is that an XPointer does not *do* anything. It refers to something. Whether the object is included, hyperlinked, or downloaded is completely a function of the context of the reference.

It is just like referring to a person by name. The act of referring to him doesn't really accomplish anything. You have to refer to someone before you can tell somebody to do something to him (hopefully something nice), but the reference is not the action.

For instance, you could use the XPointer in an XLink to create a hyperlink to something, or in a browser address window to download and display

1. These extensions are not yet concrete enough to discuss here.

a particular element. It is also up to the software to decide whether the referenced element is returned alone, or in the context of its document.

For instance, if you use an XPointer in a browser window, it would probably present the whole document and highlight the referenced element. But if you use it in an inclusion link to include a paragraph, it would probably take that paragraph out of its context and present it alone in the new context. The specific behavior depends on your link processor and stylesheet.

61.6 | Conclusion

XPointer is an extension and customization of XPath. XPointer allows XPath expressions to be used as parts of URIs (including URLs). Using the XPointer extension it is possible to make references deep into an XML document. This will allow new forms of commentary, annotation and information reuse.

©2000 THE XML HANDBOOK™

XML Linking Language (XLink)

Friendly Tutorial

- Linking and addressing
- Simple links
- Extended links

©2000 THE XML HANDBOOK™

Chapter 62

Hypertext links are the backbone of the World Wide Web. Documents were shuffled around the Internet long before today's Web existed, but it was the ease of moving from page to page with hypertext links that made the Web into the mass market phenomenon it is today.

However, despite their centrality, Web links have many weaknesses. The linking system that we use today is essentially unchanged from the earliest version of the Web. Unfortunately, market inertia has prevented anything more powerful from coming along ... until now.

The XML-family hyperlinking specification is called XLink. It allows links that go far beyond those provided by HTML. XLinks can have multiple end points, be traversed in multiple directions, and be stored in databases and groups independently of the documents they refer to.

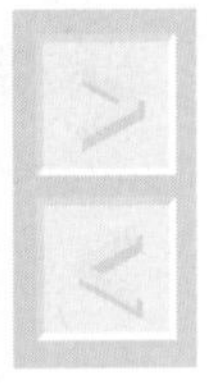

Caution *XLink is still not quite there yet. Although there are partial implementations in several products, they are not mainstream. The current version of XLink is a working draft and will change before it is completed. The basic concepts are well understood and will not change, but the specifics may change between now and then. However, the parts we cover here are those that appear to be relatively stable.*

62.1 | Basic concepts

The most important (and sometimes subtle) distinction in any discussion of hyperlinking is that of *linking* versus *addressing*. Linking is simply declaring a relationship between two (or more) things. If we say "George Washington and Booker T. Washington share a last name" then we have linked those two people in some way.

Addressing, on the other hand, is about describing how to find the two things being linked. There are many kinds of addresses, such as mail addresses, email addresses and URLs. When you create a link in XML, you declare a relationship between two objects referred to by their addresses (URI References). We refer to these objects as *resources*. We discuss the addresses more in 61.2, "Uniform Resource Identifiers", on page 896.

If you have created Web pages before, you are probably familiar with HTML's simple `A` element. Whether or not you are familiar with HTML, that link is a good starting point for understanding hyperlinking in general.

The `A` stands for *anchor*. Anchor is the hyperlinking community's term for what the XLink spec calls a *participating resource*. An HTML link has two ends, termed the *source* and *destination*. When you click on the source end, (designated with an `A` element and `HREF` attribute), the Web browser transports you to the other end. Example 62-1 shows how this works.

Example 62-1. An HTML (not XML) link

```
<A HREF="http://www.mysite.com">Go to my site!</A>
```

In this case, the A element itself describes a link, and its HREF attribute points to one of the resources (the destination). As we know, links connect resources, so there must be at least one more resource involved. The other resource, the source, is actually the content of the A element itself! The XLink spec calls this a *local resource*. As we will see, XML *simple* links also use the content of the linking element as one of the resources.

There is another pervasive type of link in HTML documents. Consider the HTML markup to embed an image (Example 62-2).

Example 62-2. HTML (not XML) image-embedding link

```
<IMG SRC="http://www.hotpics.com/jalapeno.gif">
```

That may not seem like a link but it is.[1] It declares a relationship between the containing document and the embedded image: "that picture goes in this document." HTML element types that use href attributes to address Java applets and plug-in objects are also forms of link.

Note that the destination of a link does not necessarily know that it is a destination. If you want to link to the Disney home page, you do not need to inform Disney. If a particular document has fifty A elements with HREF attributes, then you know that it has fifty links out. But the Web provides no way to know how many links into it there are.

In the more general *extended* link case, we will link two things such that *neither* end will "know" that the two are being linked. The link exists in some third location. This is intuitive if you go back to the definition of linking as defining a relationship. In a real-world sense, I can "link" Jenny Jones and Oprah Winfrey just by speaking of them in the same sentence. Unless they are interested in careers as XML experts, they will probably never know. XLink provides a standardized way to express this relationship in markup.

We might even want to link something that is not explicitly labeled. For instance, we might want to link the third paragraph of the fourth sub-point of the second section of a legal document to the transcript of a relevant court case.

1. What it isn't is a navigational link. You don't click on it to go somewhere else. Instead, its traversal is actuated automatically, as we'll see later in this chapter.

This is analogous to the real world situation where you can either send something to a labeled location ("Please take this to the White House.") or you can give directions to the destination. In hyperlinking terms, we would consider either one of these to be an "address." Obviously there must be some way of locating a resource from a link, but it could be either an address, a label or a combination of the two: "The building is 5 blocks down the street from the White House."

62.1.1 *Simple links*

Although XLink allows more flexible links than does HTML, it also offers simple links that are not much more complicated than HTML's links are. This sort of link is referred to as a *simple link*. A simple link has two ends, a source and a destination, just like an HTML link. One end represents a resource (usually the source) and it refers to the other end through a URI as in Example 62-3.

Example 62-3. XLink simple link

```
. . . for more information, consult
<citation xlink:type="simple"
          xlink:href="http://www.uw.ca/paper.xml">
Biemans(1997)
</citation>
```

The biggest difference between this link and the HTML link is that this element is not designated a link by its element-type name. It is not called `A` or any special element-type name specified in the XML specification. You can call your linking elements whatever you want to. This is an important feature, because it allows you to have many different types of linking elements in a document, perhaps with different declarations, attributes and behaviors. Just as XML allows you to use any element-type name for paragraphs or figures, it allows you flexibility in your linking element-type names.

The link is actually designated an XML link by its `xlink:type` attribute. The `xlink:type` attribute describes what kind of link is being described. In this case, it is a *simple* link. The `xlink:` prefix indicates that this attribute's allowed values and semantics are defined by the XLink specification.

Formally speaking, the attribute lives in the xlink: namespace. Namespaces are discussed in Chapter 58, "Namespaces", on page 832. This namespace should be declared in your document: probably in the document (i.e., root) element as shown in Example 62-4.[1]

Example 62-4. Namespace declaration in root element

```
<yourdoc xmlns:xlink="http://www.w3.org/XML/XLink/0.9">
...
</yourdoc>
```

For type-valid documents, it is best to declare the xmlns:xlink attribute in the DTD as a fixed attribute of the root element type, as shown in Example 62-5.

Example 62-5. Namespace declaration in DTD

```
<!ATTLIST yourdoc xmlns:xlink CDATA
                  #FIXED "http://www.w3.org/XML/XLink/0.9">
```

Note *All of the examples in this chapter assume that the linking element is in the scope of a declaration of the* xlink *namespace.*

62.1.2 *Link roles*

In HTML, link resources are either sources or destinations. The linking element is always the source. The resource referred to is always the destination. In XML, this rigid distinction is not hard-wired. An application can make either or both resources into sources or destinations.

Consider, for instance, if a Web browser made it possible to create notes about someone else's Web site and "stick" them on to it like Post-It notes.

1. At the time of writing the XLink namespace had a version number of "0.9", but when the XLink recommendation is finalized the version will likely be "1.0".

These *annotations* might be represented as XLink *extended* links as in Example 62-6.

Example 62-6. XLink annotations.

```
<annotation xlink:type="extended"
       xlink:href="http://www.mynewspaper.com">
As usual, your editorial is filled with the kind of claptrap and
willywag that gives me the heebie-jeebies!
</annotation>
```

In this case, we actually want the application to make some form of clickable "hotspot" at the *other* end, on the newspaper's Web page. Of course we don't want them to have control of the actual linking element, or else they might just choose not to show our link. So we want the link to exist in one spot and create a "hotspot" at another. This is the opposite of traditional HTML links.

In order to reverse linking roles, we must somehow tell the application that we want it to do so. One way would be to use an element-type name that the application is hard-coded to understand as having that semantic. For instance an "annotation server" might only deal with `annotation` elements, or perhaps a few different variants, and would thus know exactly how to handle it.

Another way would be to use some form of stylesheet. But you would still need to have something special in the document that would differentiate annotations from other links (perhaps the annotation element-type name). The stylesheet would provide an extra level of translation to allow your private element-type names to be interpreted as annotations by software.

Yet another way to solve this problem would be to provide an attribute that describes the role of the link in the document and hypertext system. Any of these are valid approaches, and the XLink specification provides a special `role` attribute to handle the last case. Example 62-7 is an example of that attribute in action.

In this case, the role designation has moved from the element-type name (now `hlink` instead of `annotation`) to the role attribute. Which is more appropriate will depend on your DTD, your software and your taste. XLink could perhaps dictate one style or the other, but real world usage is not that simple. For instance you might need to use an industry standard DTD and

Example 62-7. Role attribute

```
<hlink role="annotation"
    xlink:type="extended"
    xlink:href="http://www.mynewspaper.com">
As usual, your editorial is filled with the kind of claptrap and
willywag that gives me the heebie-jeebies!
</hlink>
```

thus have no control over element-type names. In another application, you might need to constrain the occurrence of certain kinds of linking elements, and thus need to use element-type names and content models.

62.1.3 *Is this for real?*

You might well ask whether all of this annotation stuff is likely to happen. After all, there are all sorts of social, technical and financial difficulties related to being able to annotate someone else's Web page. Imagine annotation spam: "Tired of reading this boring technical Web page? Click here for HOT PICS!!!"

It turns out that early versions of the pre-Netscape Mosaic browser allowed remote annotations (using a proprietary linking scheme), and you could share your annotations with friends or co-workers, but not with everybody on the Web. There are various other experimental services and products that provide the same ability for the modern-day Web. However, each uses a distinct link description notation so that they cannot share.

We may or may not get to the point where everybody can publish annotations to the whole world, but we already have the technology to create annotations that can be shared by other people we know. Unfortunately, this technology has never been widely deployed.[1] Perhaps when XLink is finalized and third-party annotation products are able to interoperate, Web pages will become generally annotatable and even more linkable than they are today.

So what can you do without a world-wide link database? Well let's say that your organization was considering buying a very expensive software product. You and your co-workers might agree to submit your opinions of

1. One product that has recently taken another run at the problem is called Third Voice™.

©2000 The XML Handbook™

the product specifications published on the vendor's Website. You could make a bunch of external links from the vendor's text to your comments on it and submit that to your organizational link database. When your co-workers go to see the page, their browsers can fetch your links and actually display them as if they were part of the original document. When your co-workers click on them, the browser will take them to your annotations.

In fact, with a reasonably large link database, you could annotate any Web page you came upon in this manner. When others from your organization came upon the page, they would see your annotations. In one sense, you are editing the entire Web! Of course, the bigger your organization is, the more points of view you can see on each page. On the other hand, sometimes you might not want to share all of your comments with the entire company, so you might have a smaller departmental database which is separate, and only shared by your direct co-workers. And of course at the opposite end of the spectrum, there might be a database for everyone on the Web (if we can make link database software that scales appropriately and find someone to run it).

External links can be useful even without a link database. Without such a database, there is no easy way to distribute your links to other people, so you must communicate the links' existence in some other way. For instance, you could include a critique of a Web page as an attachment to an email. You could also build a document full of links that annotated one of your own Web pages with links to glossary and bibliographic information. We might term each collection a *link sheet*. Depending on which link sheet the reader used, he would get either the glossary links or the bibliographic links or both sets of links overlapping.

If it makes sense to "project" a link from your home computer onto an existing website, then surely it makes just as much sense to link two existing websites. For instance, we could make a link that is targeted towards members of the SGML newsgroup that links the World Wide Web consortium's XML Web page to a related page we know about on the Web. This link would still have two ends, but both could be sources and destinations at the same time. If so, we would term that link *bidirectional*, because you could *traverse* it from either end. Because the link would exist on your Web site, but link two other pages, we would call it *out-of-line*. And if it makes sense to link two pages, then why not three, or four, or five? Extended links allow this.

62.1.4 *Link behaviors*

XML authors usually go out of their way to avoid putting information about formatting and other types of document behavior into XML documents. We've already been through all of the benefits of keeping your information "pure". As we have said, if you just mark up your documents according to their abstractions, you can apply formatting and other behavior through stylesheets.[1]

Even though it is usually best to put behavioral information in a stylesheet, XLink provides a more direct mechanism. There are some link behaviors that are so common – almost universal – that the XML working group decided that it should provide some attributes so that users could easily specify them. This facility removes a level of indirection and thereby makes hyperlinking a little bit easier. Still, one should think thrice about adding rendition attributes to abstract documents. The stylesheet is usually the best place to describe behavior and other presentational issues.

The most interesting type of link behavior is *traversal.* When you click on a hyperlink, you are *traversing* it. If a link is intended to embed information from one resource in another, then the process of actually accomplishing the embedding is a traversal.

The behavioral descriptions are still abstract enough to allow a variety of specific behaviors, depending on the situation. For example, a printer might interpret them differently from a Web browser. Although a printer might not seem like a machine that would care about hyperlinks, it might be useful to have one that could directly print Web pages and their annotations, and that could access the images to print by traversing XLinks in the Web pages.

62.1.4.1 Show

As the name implies, the `show` attribute describes how the results of a link traversal should be shown. When you click on a Web link, that is a link traversal – one initiated by your click. On the other hand, if you have ever

1. That is the theory, anyhow. At the time of writing, however, mainstream stylesheet languages did not support the recognition of XLinks or the execution of link behaviors. As we said in the introduction, XLinks are not quite there.

been to a site where a Web page comes up and says: "You will be forwarded to another page in just a few seconds", then that is a link traversal that is automatic. Typically on the Web, when a link is traversed (manually or automatically) it replaces the previous document in the Web browser window. XLink allows an author to request this behavior with the `replace` value of the `show` attribute:

Spec Excerpt (XLINK) 62-1. Replace

The `replace` option is the one most commonly seen on the World Wide Web, where the document being linked from is entirely replaced by the object being linked to.

For example see Example 62-8.

Example 62-8. A `replace` link

```
<A  xlink:type="simple"
    xlink:show="replace"
    xlink:href="http://www.gop.org/">
Click here to visit the GOP</A>
```

Occasionally you will also come across a link that actually opens a new window, so that after traversal there is a window for the new page in front of the window for the old page. XLink allows this through the `new` value of the `show` attribute.

Spec Excerpt (XLINK) 62-2. New

The `new` option indicates that the remote resource should be shown in a new window (or other device context) without replacing the previous content.

Example 62-9 shows a link where the remote resource is launched into a new window.

Example 62-9. A new link

```
<A xlink:type="simple"
    xlink:show="new"
    xlink:href="http://www.democrats.org/">
Click here to launch a new window and visit the the Dems.</A>
```

As we have seen, a link can represent *any* relationship. We discussed the relationship between a document and an embedded graphic, and the same thing applies to embedded text. It can be represented as an XLink also.

Of course, you can embed text using what XML calls a "parsed entity", but XLink provides another way of doing the same thing, which can be used in situations where the entity mechanism is not expressive enough by itself.

In this case, you can use the `parsed` value described in Spec Excerpt 62-3.

Spec Excerpt (XLINK) 62-3. Parsed

The `parsed` option, relating directly to the XML concept of a parsed entity, indicates that the content should be integrated into the document from which the link was actuated.

Example 62-10 demonstrates.

Example 62-10. A `parsed` link

```
<MyEmbed xlink:type="simple"
    xlink:show="parsed"
    xlink:href="http://www.democrats.org/platform.xml"/>
```

62.1.5 *Actuate*

The `actuate` attribute allows the author to describe when the link traversal should occur. For instance it could be user-triggered, such as by a mouse click or a voice command. Or else it could be automatic, such as the automatic embedding of a graphic, or an automatic forward to another Web page (e.g. "This page has moved. You will be directed to the new page momentarily.")

The `user` value indicates that the traversal should be user-triggered. When it is combined with a a `show` attribute of `replace`, it is a typical, click-here-to-go-there link, at least in a graphical browser. On a text-based browser, it might be a type-this-number-to-go-there link. On a spoken-word browser it might be a say-this-number-to-go-there link.

When it is combined with a value of `new` it opens a new "context" (usually a browser window) at user command and leaves the old one open. When it is combined with a value of `parsed`, the target resource is displayed embedded in the source, replacing the linking element.[1]

The `auto` value of the `actuate` attribute is used to specify that traversal should be automatic. For instance, most `show="parsed"` links would specify automatic traversal. If you combine `show="new"` with `actuate="auto"`, then you can create a Web page that immediately opens another Web page. Perhaps with a stylesheet or other attribute, you could make them appear side by side. The final combination is `show="replace"` with `actuate="auto"`. You would use this to set up a "forwarding" link, such as the one we have described, and thus forward users from one page to another.

62.2 | Extended links

In this section, we will discuss more features of *extended links*. One that we have already discussed is the ability to specify them out-of-line. Extended links also allow for more link ends, more advanced link roles, and other good stuff. We will also be able to re-describe the simple links that we have already seen in the terminology of the more general extended link system.

62.2.1 *Locator elements*

The first extension we will undertake is links with more than two link ends. Consider, for example, that you are redirecting users to several different

1. In hypertext terms, this is called a transclusion.

interpretations of a text. For instance if there were two competitive schools of thought on a topic, each hotspot in the document might allow traversal to a different interpretation of the topic. Now you have three link ends, one for the source and one for each of the interpretations of it. Just as in real life, XLink allows you to make logical links among two or more concepts.

The first big difference between simple links and extended links is that we need to figure out how to specify the address of more than one destination link. We do this by putting *locator* subelements into the extended linking element. Example 62-11 demonstrates.

Example 62-11. Multi-ended link

```
<commentary xlink:type="extended">
    <locator xlink:type="locator"
             xlink:href="roberts.xml"
             xlink:role="analysis"/>
    <locator xlink:type="locator"
             xlink:href="beam.xml"
             xlink:role="rebuttal"/>
    <locator xlink:type="locator"
             xlink:href="goodwin.xml"
             xlink:role="precis"/>
<P>My fellow Americans, this speech will go down in history...</P>
</commentary>
```

In this case, the three locators each address a resource. A sufficiently sophisticated browser displaying this document might represent each with an icon or supply a popup menu that allows access to each of the resources. It could even open a small window for each interpretation when the hotspot is selected. This could be controlled by a stylesheet or a behavior attribute. As you can see, each locator can have a different role, but they could also share roles. The role just specifies a semantic for processing the resource when processing the link, not some sort of unique identifier.

Locators can also have some other associated attributes. They can have titles, specified through a `title` attribute. These provide information for human consumption. The browser does not act on them. It merely passes them on to the human in some way, such as a popup menu, or text on the status bar. Locators can also have `show` and `actuate` behavior attributes with the same semantics as for a simple link. Locators seem very similar to

©2000 The XML Handbook™

simple links because a simple link is a combination of a link and a locator. In fact, this is how they are defined in the XML spec:

Spec Excerpt (XLINK) 62-4. Simple links

Simple links can be used for purposes that approximate the functionality of a basic HTML `A` link, but they can also support a limited amount of additional functionality. Simple links have only one locator and thus, for convenience, combine the functions of a linking element and a locator into a single element. As a result of this combination, the simple linking element offers both a locator attribute and all of the behavior and semantic attributes.

It is both useful and convenient that simple links combine these two things, but it means that we must be careful to keep the ideas separate in our heads. The link describes a relationship. The locators say what resources are being related. A simple link uses the linking element itself as one resource and the target of its `href` as the other.

62.2.2 *Link groups*

It is often useful to be able to process a group of hyperlinked documents all together. For instance, if one document contains some text and another contains a rebuttal of the text, the browser might want to show them "side by side". It could also allow link traversals in one window to trigger the correct portion of the rebuttal in the other.

Such processing can only work if the browser knows about both documents at the same time. Extended link groups allow you to tell the browser about all of the nodes that should be processed together.

An *extended link group* element is a special kind of extended link. It describes a list of other documents that should be seen to be in this *link group*. Example 62-12 is an example of such a link.

In one sense, a link group is a small database of hyperlinks. A browser, editor or other application could look in the link group to see which elements are hyperlink resources and what their behaviors and roles are.

©2000 THE XML HANDBOOK™

Example 62-12. Extended link group

```
<xlink:group>
<xlink:document href="annotation.html"/>
<xlink:document href="rebuttal.html"/>
<xlink:document href="support.html"/>
</xlink:group>
```

62.3 | Conclusion

XLink has the power to change the Web, and our lives, in unforseeable ways. For more of the vision, see Chapter 44, "Extended linking", on page 588. For the current version of the spec, see the *XML SPECtacular* on the CD-ROM.

Datatypes

Friendly Tutorial

- Datatype requirements
- Built-in datatypes
- User-generated datatypes
- Using datatypes in DTDs

©2000 The XML Handbook™

Chapter 63

This chapter was written using materials prepared by Bob DuCharme, http://www.snee.com/bob/xmlann, author of *XML: The Annotated Specification*.

Perhaps the most eagerly-awaited aspect of the W3C XML Schema project is the datatype work. It has been made a separate Part 2 of the XML Schema spec, with the intention "that it be usable outside of the context of XML Schemas for a wide range of other XML-related activities".

In this chapter, we describe the basic concepts of XML datatypes and show how they can be used both in XML Schema Structures (Part 1 of the spec) and in one of those "other XML-related activities": XML 1.0 DTDs.

> ***Caution*** *XML Schema Datatypes are in an early stage of development. We present only the most basic and stable aspects in this chapter.*

63.1 | Datatype requirements

Datatypes answer important questions about the description and validation of character data in element content or attribute values.

How do you say that a `date` element should contain content that conforms to the syntax `YYYY-MM-DD` or that an email address must be of the form `name@machine.domain.code`? How would you even say that a `description` element must not be empty?

A system to support datatypes must meet three requirements:

- First, you need a way for an application to know that an element type's content or an attribute's value is always supposed to be of a particular type. Ideally a programmer would not need to specially program knowledge about the datatypes into each application. Dates would just appear to the application code as date objects, integers as integer objects and so forth.
- Second, you need a way to validate that the data really conforms to the restrictions of the datatype. There should be no February 30 in a date, every email address needs an "`@`" symbol and so forth.
- Finally you need a way to define new datatypes. Just as XML allows you to define new element types, you would want to be able to define datatypes that are specific to your domain. A geographer might define a latitude/longitude notation. A mathematician might define a notation for matrices.

A datatype name is usually applied to both the conceptual object (the "abstract datatype") and its representation as a character string. That is, in markup language terms, datatypes are notations and XML's notation attribute type can be used to describe the datatype of an element's content.

However, there is no registry for data content notations so the full notation identifier for (e.g.) "real number" is not universally defined. Without that standardization, there is no way to create common software for validating real numbers in XML documents.[1]

1. Although techniques similar to mimetype and file extension associations are frequently used.

©2000 THE XML HANDBOOK™

Furthermore, XML does not provide a language for defining new datatypes. You can refer to datatypes if you have a name for them but for all XML cares the "definition language" could be a regular expression, C++ code or Swahili. We need a standard for the definition language.

XML Schema Datatypes address these issues.

63.2 | XML Schema Datatypes

The DTD fragment in Example 63-1 shows the declaration for an attribute whose value is intended to be a year.

Example 63-1. Attribute declaration in a DTD

```
<!ATTLIST poem pubyear CDATA #IMPLIED>
<!-- Publication year should be four-digits -->
```

Although the pubyear value is supposed to represent a year, XML's set of attribute types cannot say that directly. All of the pubyear values in the start-tags shown in Example 63-2 would be valid.

Example 63-2. Legal pubyear CDATA values

```
<poem publisher="B and L" pubyear="1922">
<poem publisher="B and L" pubyear="0">
<poem publisher="B and L" pubyear="99999999999999999999999">
<poem publisher="B and L" pubyear="-3">
<poem publisher="B and L" pubyear="3.14159265">
<poem publisher="B and L" pubyear="1.0e+6">
<poem publisher="B and L" pubyear="Hello_World">
<poem publisher="B and L" pubyear=":">
<poem publisher="B and L" pubyear="----">
```

Wouldn't it be nice if the declaration for a pubyear attribute – or even for a pubyear element type –could specify that its value (or content) must be a four-digit number between 1000 and 2100?

This would make it easier to write robust applications that use that data. If your application must check whether this poem is in the public domain yet, it might add 75 to that pubyear value and compare the result with the current year to see if the poem is more than 75 years old.

You can only do this calculation reliably if you know that the value is an integer. You could do this by writing error-checking code, but one major goal of all schemas (including DTDs) is to reduce the need for custom error-checking code.

Programmers want to plug in an off-the-shelf, validating XML processor and have it check the mundane details of datatype conformance. When they get a weekly salary value out of a document they don't want to write code to make sure that it's a usable decimal floating point number before they subtract it from another number.

More importantly: end users want to be able to do the checks with off-the-shelf processors also. It is very common for programmers to forget or purposely leave out some checks. For instance you can make hundreds of mistakes in an HTML document and most browsers will load the HTML without a complaint! You can only find your mistakes by using an HTML validator.

Let's look at the datatypes the spec makes available so we can choose an appropriate one for the `pubyear` attribute.

63.2.1 *Built-in datatypes*

The XML Schema Datatypes spec defines two categories of datatypes: primitive and generated. All of the former and several of the latter must be supported by every implementation of the spec; they are called *built-in datatypes* and are described in this section.

63.2.1.1 Primitive datatypes

The *primitive datatypes* are the building blocks of all others, as well as being useful themselves. The first eight, which are shown in all upper-case letters below, all come from XML. Note that XML's `CDATA` type is missing, because the `string` primitive type (listed later) can do `CDATA`'s job.

- ID
- IDREF
- IDREFS
- ENTITY
- ENTITIES

- NMTOKEN
- NMTOKENS
- NOTATION

The remaining datatypes in the list are common datatypes in most programming languages and database management systems.

`string`
: Equivalent to CDATA in a DTD.

`boolean`
: `true` and `false` values.

`number`
: A basis for specialized numeric types such as real numbers and integers.

`dateTime`
: Based on the SQL and ISO 8601 date format standards. All lexical representation formats conforming to those standards are acceptable, so 1:32 PM on November 24, 1999 could be represented as 1999-11-24T13:32Z.

`binary`
: For non-textual data that has been encoded for representation in XML. You could use a binary-containing element to embed a bitmap image in an XML parsed (i.e., textual) entity.

`uri`
: Uniform Resource Identifiers. These are a generalization of the concept of URLs. See 61.2, "Uniform Resource Identifiers", on page 896 for more information.

63.2.1.2 Generated datatypes

The *generated datatypes* are built from the primitive ones. The XML Schema Datatypes spec defines some generated datatypes and provides facilities for users to define their own.

The ones defined in the spec are listed below. They are either numeric types more specific than number, or types based on components of the `dateTime` primitive type:

- `integer`
- `decimal`
- `real`
- `date`
- `time`
- `timePeriod`

`timePeriod` is based on the ISO 8601 and SQL standards. This datatype can be represented as specific start- and end-times or as a duration.

63.2.2 *User-generated datatypes*

In addition to the built-in datatypes, the spec provides a means of creating *user-generated datatypes.*

Users generate a datatype by defining it in a `datatype` element in an XML Schemas Structures document. Usually they do so by adding constraints to an existing datatype. For example, we can define a user-generated datatype to solve our `pubyear` problem, as shown in Example 63-3. The `datatype` element defines a `pubYearDate` datatype as an integer that must fall between 1000 and 2100.

Example 63-3. Defining a restricted range integer datatype

```
<datatype name="pubYearDate">
  <basetype name="integer"/>
  <minInclusive>1000</minInclusive>
  <maxInclusive>2100</maxInclusive>
</datatype>
```

You can also define a datatype as a named list of allowable values by using an `enumeration` element. In Example 63-4, we define a `daysOfWeek` datatype.

Note that in a datatype definition, the `datatype` element's first child is `basetype`. Here, the base type is a primitive datatype (`string`), but it

Example 63-4. Defining an enumerated datatype

```
<datatype name="daysOfWeek">
  <basetype name="string"/>
  <enumeration>
    <literal>Monday</literal>
    <literal>Tuesday</literal>
    <literal>Wednesday</literal>
    <literal>Thursday</literal>
    <literal>Friday</literal>
    <literal>Saturday</literal>
    <literal>Sunday</literal>
  </enumeration>
</datatype>
```

doesn't have to be – a user-generated type can be based on any built-in datatype, whether primitive or generated.

63.3 | Using datatypes

Although XML Schema Datatypes were originally designed for use with XML Schema Structures, they can also be used with DTDs.

63.3.1 *XML Schema Structures*

XML Schema Structures is described in some detail in Chapter 64, "XML Schemas", on page 928. It is sufficient for our purposes here to say that the spec defines how to represent a document type schema using another XML document.

In Example 63-5, the pubYearDate datatype is defined as it was in Example 63-3. A pubyear attribute is declared that uses that datatype.

Example 63-5. Defining and using a user-generated datatype

```
<datatype name="pubYearDate">
  <basetype name="integer"/>
  <minInclusive>1000</minInclusive>
  <maxInclusive>2100</maxInclusive>
</datatype>

<attrDecl name="pubyear" required="false">
  <datatypeRef name="pubYearDate"/>
</attrDecl>
```

63.3.2 *XML DTDs*

Since XML Schema Datatypes were designed after DTDs[1], there is no built-in provision in DTD declarations for declaring the use of datatypes. Instead, users and software developers have adopted a convention for making the association.

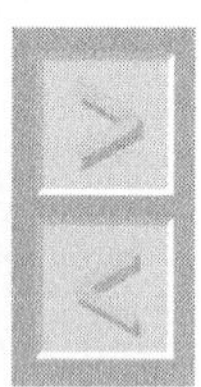

Tip *This convention is supported by open source software available on the CD-ROM, and by the XML Authority schema editor described in Chapter 16, "Building a schema for a product catalog", on page 214, a trial version of which is also available on the CD-ROM.*

The convention uses two reserved attribute names:

e-dtype
: The value of this attribute is the name of the datatype for the element's data content. The attribute is only declared if the element type has a datatype for its data content. In a valid document, it should be declared as a fixed attribute.

1. About 30 years after, but who's counting.

`a-dtype`

The value of this attribute is the names of the datatypes for all the attributes that have datatypes. In order to link each attribute with its datatype, the `a-dtype` attribute value is a list of pairs, each attribute name being followed by its datatype name. The attribute is only declared if the element type has a datatype for one or more of its attributes. In a valid document, it should be declared as a fixed attribute.

If a datatype is not a built-in datatype, you can optionally declare a notation of the same name to reference its definition. An implementation can use that information to invoke the software program that checks and/or processes the data.

In Example 63-6, the `a-dtype` attribute declares the datatypes for the `pubyear` and `linecount` attributes. The datatype of `linecount` is built-in, but the datatype of `pubyear` is user-generated so there is a `NOTATION` declaration that references its definition.

Example 63-6. Declaring datatypes for attributes

```
<!NOTATION pubYearDate   SYSTEM "datatypeDefs.xml\pubYearDate">
<!ATTLIST poem a-dtype   CDATA #FIXED (pubyear   pubYearDate
                                        linecount integer      )>
<!ATTLIST poem pubyear   CDATA #IMPLIED -- dtype: pubYearDate --
               linecount CDATA #IMPLIED -- dtype: integer     -->
```

XML Schemas

Tad Tougher Tutorial

- Syntax and element types
- Archetypes
- Other new capabilities

©2000 THE XML HANDBOOK™

Chapter 64

This chapter was written using materials prepared by Bob DuCharme, `http://www.snee.com/bob/xmlann`, author of *XML: The Annotated Specification*.

XML's Document Type Definition mechanism serves many important purposes in real XML systems. DTDs allow us to check XML documents for conformance to strict rules.

The DTD is a specific case of a more general concept called a schema definition. The dictionary defines schema as a "general conception of what is common to all members of a class."

Schemas are used in a variety of domains in the computer industry; interface definitions and databases are two that immediately come to mind. However, DTDs are unique in that they declare what must be common to all members of a class of XML/SGML documents. This chapter will review the role of DTDs and then discuss a new schema definition language being developed in the World Wide Web Consortium: XML Schemas

> **Caution** *The XML Schemas spec is in an early stage of development and is subject to change. This chapter only covers the high level concepts and not the details. It should be considered a preview of the main concepts and not a definitive reference.*

64.1 | DTDs and schemas

In the early days of computing, application programs completely controlled the format of the data they processed. There was very little interchange of data between programs. For document processing today, applications still tend to control their own data formats; interchange is possible (after a fashion) only because each program tries to understand the data representation of its major competitors.

Markup languages and DTDs are changing all that.

DTDs allow mere mortals (as opposed to program developers) to define the rules for representing conceptual documents of various types as XML documents. Those rules – programmers sometimes characterize them as "languages" – define a vocabulary of element type and attribute names and constraints on their combination. Using DTDs, mortals can check XML documents for conformance to those languages.

Were it not for DTDs, you would have to trust a particular piece of application software to tell you whether the data you created is conforming. For example only *MS Word* can say for sure whether a file is a legal *Word* document.

With DTDs ordinary users can consult a "neutral third party", a validating XML parser. The validating parser could be used on its own or as a component embedded in a software application.

It is common for the code for a single validating parser to be embedded in hundreds of different software products. This means that these parsers are usually very well tested. Even in the unlikely event that a parser has a bug, XML 1.0 and XML DTDs are so simple that you could easily check your data by hand.

We admit, it would be tedious. The important thing is that you could do it without special tools or a degree in rocket science. In a very real sense, you own your XML application's document types because you do not need to depend on a black box to validate for you. A document either conforms to a DTD or it does not, and DTDs are simple enough that we humans can check for ourselves.

64.1.1 *Next generation schemas*

But simplicity isn't the only virtue, especially among those who are trained to deal with complexity. The popularity of XML has brought SGML and

DTDs to entirely new constituencies. The database experts and programmers who are taking to XML in droves are examining it from the standpoint of their own areas of expertise and familiar paradigms.

All of these creative folks have ideas about what could be done differently. Not everyone will agree what should be different but everyone has ideas. The World Wide Web Consortium is trying to incorporate these ideas into a design for an enhanced schema definition facility called *XML Schemas*.

XML Schemas addresses four major areas of potential improvement:

Datatypes
: Datatypes are now the subject of a separate Part 2 of the XML Schemas spec and were discussed in Chapter 63, "Datatypes", on page 918.

Namespaces
: Namespaces were invented after DTDs[1] and are not fully supported by them. This subject was discussed in Chapter 58, "Namespaces", on page 832.

Syntax
: XML DTDs are represented in a dedicated notation that is a subset of SGML's DTD declarations. As XML documents are such an excellent vehicle for representing structured abstractions, many feel that schema definitions should be XML documents as well.

New capabilities
: Capabilities for schema definition have been proposed that are not supported by existing DTD declarations.

In this chapter we will discuss the two items not addressed elsewhere – syntax and new capabilities – in the context of Part 1 of the XML Schemas spec: Structures. The new capabilities are by far the more interesting of the two, so let's get the syntax issue out of the way.

---

1. About 30 years after, but as we said, who's counting.

©2000 The XML Handbook™

64.1.2 *XML Schemas syntax*

Many consider the DTD syntax to be too different from the rest of XML. People ask: "If XML elements and attributes can be used to represent any kind of information, why not use XML to represent XML schemas?" In other words, why not represent DTDs in an element-based syntax? You could have element types for element type declarations, element types for attribute declarations and so forth. Computer programmers really like this sort of recursion.

One virtue of this approach is that tools for manipulating XML elements automatically become tools for manipulating DTD declarations. One downside is that the schemas typically become much larger and (arguably) harder to read. There are other arguments both for and against this idea but for the time being they are moot. The recursionists have won and XML Schemas uses XML element syntax.

64.2 | A simple sample schema

We will explain schemas by introducing a sample DTD to use as a baseline, then developing an equivalent schema and comparing the two.

64.2.1 *Baseline DTD*

The sample DTD in Example 64-1 demonstrates how some of XML 1.0's most important features are used in a DTD. Comparing this DTD with the W3C Schema equivalent will give us a baseline to work from.

Example 64-1. Poem DTD

```
<!ELEMENT    poem       (title, picture, verse+)>
<!ATTLIST    poem       publisher CDATA     #IMPLIED
                        pubyear   NMTOKEN   #IMPLIED>
<!ELEMENT    title      (#PCDATA)>
<!ELEMENT    verse      (#PCDATA)>
<!ELEMENT    picture    EMPTY>
<!ATTLIST    picture    picent    ENTITY    #REQUIRED>
<!ENTITY     pic1       SYSTEM    "img/tse.jpg" NDATA JPEG>
<!NOTATION   JPEG       PUBLIC    "Joint Photographic Experts Group">
```

The DTD defines a poem element type that consists of a title element followed by a picture and one or more verse elements. The poem element type has two optional attributes: publisher and pubyear.

The picture element type's required picent attribute is declared as an ENTITY attribute, so any values for it must be declared as entities. The entity declarations must include a notation name, and the notation name itself must be declared.

There is an entity declaration for pic1. Its NDATA parameter names JPEG as the entity's notation. A NOTATION declaration officially declares JPEG as a notation that the document can use.

Example 64-2. Poem document

```
<poem publisher="Boni and Liveright" pubyear="1922">
<title>The Waste Land</title>
<picture picent="pic1"/>
<verse>April is the cruellest month, breeding</verse>
<verse>Lilacs out of the dead land</verse>
</poem>
```

Example 64-2 shows a document that conforms to the DTD in Example 64-1. Its one picture element has a picent value of pic1.

64.2.1 *Declaring an element type*

Example 64-3 is an XML Schema definition for the poem document type.

The most noticeable thing about the example is that instead of using the syntax of XML 1.0 DTD declarations, it represents a schema definition as a well-formed XML document.

The root element type is named schema. This element's name attribute is optional, but it comes in handy when referring to the schema definition from elsewhere.

Just as our DTD example had four element type declarations, the schema definition has four elementType elements, which perform the same task: they declare the element types that can be used in documents conforming to this schema.

They also perform an additional task: while DTDs use separate declarations for attributes, schemas include them as part of the element type declaration.

Example 64-3. XML Schema definition for the poem document type

```
<schema name="http://www.snee.com/xml/poem.xsd">
  <elementType name="poem">
    <sequence minOccur="1">
      <elementTypeRef name="title"/>
      <elementTypeRef name="picture"/>
      <elementTypeRef name="verse" minOccur="1" maxOccur="*"/>
    </sequence>
    <attrDecl name="publisher" required="false">
      <datatypeRef name="string"/>
    </attrDecl>
    <attrDecl name="pubyear" required="false">
      <datatypeRef name="NMTOKEN"/>
    </attrDecl>
  </elementType>

  <elementType name="title">
    <datatypeRef name="string"/>
  </elementType>

  <elementType name="verse">
    <datatypeRef name="string"/>
  </elementType>

  <elementType name="picture">
    <empty/>
    <attrDecl name="picent" required="true">
      <datatypeRef name="ENTITY"/>
    </attrDecl>
  </elementType>

  <unparsedEntity
           name="pic1" system="img/tse.jpg" notation="JPEG"/>
  <notation name="JPEG"
           public="Joint Photographic Experts Group"/>
</schema>
```

More precisely, a schema element type declaration associates an element type name with an *archetype*, consisting of a content type definition and optional attribute declarations. The *archetype* is the content of the `elementType` element.

For example, the archetypes in the `title` and `verse` declarations tell us that the content of elements of these types must conform to the `string` datatype (i.e., character data). We saw the range of possibilities offered by the `datatypeRef` element type in Chapter 63, "Datatypes", on page 918.

64.2.2.1 Content models

Consider the poem element type declaration in Example 64-3. Its archetype represents the content model with a `sequence` element, which defines a `poem` element to contain a `title`, a `picture`, and one or more `verse` elements, in that order. The `sequence` element identifies these content element types by using `elementTypeRef` elements, which refer to element types declared elsewhere in the schema.

There are other element types that can be used to define a content model. Here is the full list, together with the indicators used in DTDs for the same constructs:

- `sequence` (“`,`”)
- `choice` (“`|`”)
- `mixed` (“`(#PCDATA|..)`”)
- `all` (SGML “`&`”)
- `any` (“`ANY`”)
- `empty` (“`EMPTY`”)

The `all` element type has no equivalent in an XML content model. It is one of the SGML facilities that was not included in the XML 1.0 design. It is similar to `sequence` in that all of the parts must be matched. The difference is that they may be matched in any order.

Like `sequence`, a `choice`, `mixed` or `all` model can use `elementTypeRef` elements to refer to element types declared elsewhere in the schema. A content model can even be defined in a stand-alone `modelGroup` element, and archetypes can then refer to this named model group when defining their content models.

For more complex content models, content model groupings can be nested. For example, we can duplicate the XML 1.0 content model `(title,picture,verse+, (footnotes|bibliography))` with a `choice` element within a `sequence` element as shown in Example 64-4.

64.2.2.2 Empty element types

The `picture` element type declared in Example 64-5 uses the `empty` element to declare that picture elements should all be empty.[1]

1. Note that the `empty` element is itself empty.

Example 64-4. Sequence with nested choice

```
<sequence minOccur="1">
  <elementTypeRef name="title"/>
  <elementTypeRef name="picture"/>
  <elementTypeRef name="verse" minOccur="1" maxOccur="*"/>
  <choice minOccur="1">
    <elementTypeRef name="footnotes" minOccur="1"/>
    <elementTypeRef name="bibliography" minOccur="1"/>
  </choice>
</sequence>
```

Example 64-5. Picture declaration

```
  <elementType name="picture">
    <empty/>
    <attrDecl name="picent" required="true">
      <datatypeRef name="ENTITY"/>
    </attrDecl>
  </elementType>
```

64.2.3 *Declaring attributes*

The poem and picture element type declarations both contain attribute declarations equivalent to those in our original DTD. Example 64-6 shows a declaration for the poem element type's optional publisher and pubyear attributes.

Example 64-6. Attribute declarations

```
    <attrDecl name="publisher" required="false">
      <datatypeRef name="string"/>
    </attrDecl>
    <attrDecl name="pubyear" required="false">
      <datatypeRef name="NMTOKEN"/>
    </attrDecl>
```

They are optional because the required attribute in their definitions is false. As we saw in Chapter 63, "Datatypes", on page 918, available datatypes include not just the usual XML attribute types like NMTOKEN, ID, IDREF, ENTITY, and ENTITIES, but also traditional programming datatypes such as integer, real, date, boolean and string.

ment of a refinement, and so on). A conforming element must have all the non-optional declared elements and attributes of the archetype. It may also have the optional ones, and may have others, depending on the value of the archetype's `model` attribute.

The `model` attribute can have three possible values. They indicate two things:

- Whether the archetype can be refined.
- Whether a conforming element can have what we will call *non-archetypical* elements and attributes: those declared outside the archetype definition.

The possible values are:

closed
This archetype cannot be refined. A conforming element may not have non-archetypical elements or attributes.

open
This archetype may be refined. A conforming element may have non-archetypical elements or attributes, regardless of whether they are declared in a refinement.

refinable
This archetype may be refined. A conforming element may have non-archetypical elements or attributes, but only if they are declared in a refinement.

64.3.3 *Sharing schema components*

XML Schemas offer two techniques for composing schemas from parts of other schemas: schema inclusion and schema import. There are also means for restricting the export of parts of a schema.

64.3.3.1 Schema inclusion

XML 1.0 DTDs can share text by means of external parameter entities. For example, the `common` parameter entity declared and referenced in Example

©2000 THE XML HANDBOOK™

64-16 tells an XML processor to treat the DTD as if the two lines of Example 64-17 had been inserted at the fourth line.

Example 64-16. DTD with an external parameter entity reference

```
<!ELEMENT  book     (title,chapter+)>
<!ELEMENT  chapter  (title,par+)>
<!ENTITY % common   SYSTEM "common.dtd">
%common;
```

Example 64-17. `common.dtd` file referenced in Example 64-16

```
<!ELEMENT title (#PCDATA)>
<!ELEMENT par   (#PCDATA)>
```

The *schema inclusion* facility works similarly. It allows a schema to treat some or all of another schema's contents as part of its own. Example 64-18 uses the `include` element to incorporate the element type declarations for `title` and `par` from the schema in Example 64-19. The `title` and `par` declarations are thenceforth treated as part of the `book.xsd` schema.

Example 64-18. `book.xsd` schema including declarations from `common.xsd`

```
<schema name="book.xsd">
  <include schemaName="common.xsd">
    <elementTypeRef name="title"/>
    <elementTypeRef name="par"/>
  </include>

  <elementType name="book">
    <sequence minOccur="1">
      <elementTypeRef name="title" minOccur="1"/>
      <elementTypeRef name="chapter" minOccur="1" maxOccur="*"/>
    </sequence>
  </elementType>

  <elementType name="chapter">
    <sequence minOccur="1">
      <elementTypeRef name="title" minOccur="1"/>
      <elementTypeRef name="par" minOccur="1" maxOccur="*"/>
    </sequence>
  </elementType>
</schema>
```

Example 64-19. *common.xsd* schema

```
<schema name="common.xsd">
  <elementType name="title">
    <datatypeRef name="string"/>
  </elementType>

  <elementType name="par">
    <datatypeRef name="string"/>
  </elementType>
</schema>
```

64.3.3.2 Schema import

XML schemas can also import from other schemas. *Schema import* is subtly different from inclusion. With inclusion, the other declarations are treated exactly as if they had been in the including schema all along.

In contrast, when declarations are imported, they keep their formal ties to the exporting schema. Every time the main schema refers to them, it does so in the context of the exporting schema.

Example 64-20 shows how the book.xsd schema would look if it imported the declarations from the common.xsd schema instead of including them.

Example 64-20. book.xsd **schema importing declarations from** common.xsd

```
<schema name="book.xsd">
  <import schemaAbbrev="common"
          schemaName="http://.../common.xsd"
          datatypes="true" archetypes="true">
    <elementTypeRef name="title"/>
    <elementTypeRef name="par"/>
  </import>

  <elementType name="book" export="true">
    <sequence minOccur="1">
      <elementTypeRef name="title" schemaAbbrev="common"
                      minOccur="1"/>
      <elementTypeRef name="chapter" schemaAbbrev="common"
                      minOccur="1" maxOccur="*"/>
    </sequence>
  </elementType>
</schema>
```

The import element looks similar to the include element in the previous example. It names the external schema and uses elementTypeRef elements to name the individual element type declarations that it needs from that schema.

In addition to element types, you could name individual datatypes, entities, archetypes, and other named schema constructs. You could also import entire categories of schema constructs by means of attributes, as illustrated by datatypes and archetypes in Example 64-20.

The way that imported declarations are used, however, is different from included ones, because they aren't treated as part of the importing schema. Each time book.xsd refers to an imported common.xsd construct, it must specify the schema where it came from.

It might do this with the elementTypeRef's schemaName attribute, which refers to the schema by a URI, as shown in Example 64-21. Alternatively, the clutter of a long schema name could be avoided by using the schemaAbbrev attribute, as was done in Example 64-20.

Example 64-21. Using the schemaName attribute

```
<sequence minOccur="1">
  <elementTypeRef name="title"
       schemaName="http://.../common.xsd"
       minOccur="1"/>
  <elementTypeRef name="chapter"
       schemaName="http://.../common.xsd"
       minOccur="1" maxOccur="*"/>
</sequence>
```

64.3.3.3 Export controls

Can you import any schema you have access to? Or, to put it another way, when you make a schema publicly available on the Web, can anyone import any part of it they want?

Not necessarily; you can use the optional export element to control which parts of your schema may be imported by other schema. By putting the empty export element at the beginning of your schema, you can prevent various categories of schema components from being imported by other schema.

In Example 64-22 you can see that the export element has seven attributes, one for each category of named construct that can be exported.

The default value for all of these categories is "true," so omitting all of these attributes means that your whole schema can be imported. Example 64-22, however, prevents all named constructs in `http://www.snee.com/xml/poem.xsd` from being imported by another schema.

Example 64-22. Using the `export` element

```
<schema name="http://www.snee.com/xml/poem.xsd">
<export datatypes="false" archetypes="false"
        elementTypes="false" attrGroups="false"
        modelGroups="false" entities="else" notations="false"/>

  <elementType name="poem">
    <sequence minOccur="1">
      <elementTypeRef name="title"/>
      <elementTypeRef name="picture"/>
      <elementTypeRef name="verse" minOccur="1" maxOccur="*"/>
<!-- schema continues... -->
```

64.3.4 *Other capabilities*

Several other capabilities are planned for XSL Schema Structures but are not presently well-defined.

64.3.4.1 Documentation

Schemas currently offer the same kind of commenting that you can put in DTDs: anything you put inside of `<!-- -->` is ignored by the processor. To publish external documentation for the schema, an automated process using the DOM or SAX interface (or even scanning the unparsed text) could find these comments easily enough. However, in the absence of an agreed convention, it would have no clue as to their purpose.

Schemas should provide the opportunity to add structured documentation. This will probably come in the form of specialized element types, to be used within the various schema declaration elements, that describe supplemental information about the declarations. These might include their purpose, author, last date updated, and so forth. These documentation elements will allow an automated process similar to the *javadoc* program, to generate usable, formatted documentation from a schema.

64.3.4.2 Schema evolution

Once a schema – any kind of schema, whether for XML documents, a relational database, or an object-oriented database – is written and put into production, making efficient, backward-compatible changes to that schema can be difficult.

How difficult? Computer science researchers do thesis work on it.

Addressing the potential problems of schema evolution in the W3C spec is an ambitious but eminently worthwhile objective.

64.3.4.3 Conformance

The conformance clause of the spec is where details are provided about the means of determining whether a schema conforms to the schema specification and whether a document conforms to a given schema. Among the issues are distinguishing fatal errors from non-fatal errors, the responsibilities of schema-aware processors, and the exact information that we can count on a schema to represent.

These are gory details to be sure, but crucial to a spec that hopes to provide a reliable basis for a range of software applications that plan on being compatible with one another.

Part Thirteen

On the back cover of the first edition of this book, an inspired copywriter wrote: "The accompanying CD-ROM brings together an amazing set of XML resources."

As authors, we of course don't engage in such hyperbole, except on behalf of technologies that excite us. However, we feel obligated to make the purely factual observation that the CD-ROM for this edition is far superior to the first.

There are over 125 free XML software packages, compared to 55 in the first edition. Please note that we use the word "free" very precisely. We mean genuinely free use, XML-centric, no time limit, uncrippled software, that is usable with your own documents.

In addition, there are 27 contributors to the Sponsor Showcase, compared to 14 last edition. Their materials include more free software, plus trial versions of major commercial products for your evaluation, and white papers, live demos, and examples.

Plus there are XML-related standards and specs and clickable directories of Web sources for free software and more specifications.

And if you like to read actual books, this part includes a reader's guide to other books in this series.

Free resources on the CD-ROM

Resource Description

- Over 125 free software packages
- IBM alphaWorks XML software suite
- XML SPECtacular

©2000 THE XML HANDBOOK™

Chapter 65

Do you really need 125 XML software packages? Not likely, but our CD-ROM will save a lot of download time while you decide which you do need. Most are described in this chapter, along with the specifications that are on the CD, in sections prepared by Lars Marius Garshol. The section on IBM alphaWorks, `http://www.alphaWorks.IBM.com`, is sponsored by them and was prepared by David A. Epstein and Daniel Jue.

The CD-ROM supplement of The XML Handbook contains a wide variety of resources. There is free trial software, genuine freeware with no time limit, demos, white papers, markup and code samples, product information from our sponsors, and the full text of the most important standards and specifications.

We describe most of the free software and specs in this chapter, but not all of it; you'll need to dig into the disc for the rest.

Enjoy!

65.1 | Software featured on the covers

In this section, we briefly describe the free software and trialware that our sponsors feature on the covers of the book. We specify the platforms supported and, if it is trialware, the time limit or other usage description.

65.1.1 *XMLSolutions ExeterXML Server*

The *ExeterXML Server* is an XML-capable Web server that can serve XML documents to any client software, regardless of whether or not the client understands XML. The product is the centerpiece of XMLSolutions' *ExeterXML* e-commerce software suite, where it is used to serve XML documents in business-to-business e-commerce transactions. However, it can also operate independently and owners of *The XML Handbook* may use it freely.

The CD contains a free binary distribution, ready to install on any *Solaris*™ 2.5.1, 2.6, or 2.7 platform.

There is further information on the inside front cover of the book.

65.1.2 *IBM alphaWorks XML software suite*

This suite of free software contains a wide variety of programs, most of which will run on any Java platform.

The programs are described in the next section of this chapter.

65.1.3 *webMethods B2B QueryView XML/XQL viewer*

This free product supports XQL queries into XML documents. It is described in Chapter 45, "B2B QueryView: XQL search tool", on page 602, which includes detailed operating instructions.

The product runs on all Java platforms.

65.1.4 *Object Design eXcelon e-business information server*

eXcelon is a development environment and deployment platform for building e-business applications. It includes a suite of graphical development tools, connectivity tools to leverage legacy systems, and a data server for storing, managing, querying, and delivering XML information. There is further information in Chapter 8, "eXcelon: Serving information", on page 110.

The trial version on the CD-ROM runs on Windows NT. The trial period is 45 days from installation.

65.1.5 *Enigma INSIGHT XML publishing software*

INSIGHT is software for automating the electronic publishing process. It turns large-document collections into intelligent cross-indexed and hyperlinked publications that can be distributed on the Internet, on intranets, and on CD-ROM. You can learn more about *INSIGHT* in Chapter 41, "INSIGHT: The role of stylesheets", on page 550.

The trial version on the CD-ROM runs on Windows 95/98 and Windows NT. It has no time limit, but publications can be viewed only with the product; they cannot be distributed for viewing with Web browsers or on CD.

65.1.6 *Excosoft Documentor hyperlinked XML editor*

Documentor is a standards-based XML editor that lets you create and edit highly-structured documents. Its hyperlinking facilities let you navigate large and complex documents and document collections, and collaborate either over a local area network or the Web. There is more information in Chapter 47, "The universal collaborative Web", on page 636.

The trial version on the CD-ROM runs on Windows 95/98 and Windows NT. The trial period is 60 days from installation.

65.1.7 *Extensibility XML Authority schema editor*

XML Authority is a graphical development tool for creating and modifying XML schemas, and for converting other data structures to XML schemas. The product can support DTDs, and can export DTDs and such other

©2000 The XML Handbook™

schema notations as XML-Data, XDR, DCD, SOX, and DDML. There is more information in Chapter 16, "Building a schema for a product catalog", on page 214.

The trial version on the CD-ROM runs on Windows 95/98 and Windows NT. There is no time limit, but the trial is limited to ten uses of the product.

65.2 | IBM alphaWorks

IBM *alphaWorks* is a team dedicated to speeding emerging IBM technology to the marketplace, from fields as diverse as management and transaction functions, networking, security, and power management.

Its website operates on a unique premise.

65.2.1 *The alphaWorks idea*

The *alphaWorks* website is a focal point for bidirectional communication with early adopters of strategic emerging technologies. At the site, users can download "alpha-code" implementations of those technologies. More importantly, they can also access and provide feedback to IBM's top researchers and developers, through the site's technology discussion forums.

alphaWorks serves as one of IBM's primary channels for the distribution of XML technology. You can find several different categories of XML technology at the site.

1. One of the main categories, which fulfills one of *alphaWorks*' primary goals, is implementations that track the important W3C Recommendations and other related XML specifications. One of the objectives in providing these implementations is to have them available in a timely manner, often the same day that Recommendations (proposed and final, and early Notes) become public.
2. In addition to these implementations of the important XML specifications, the site also serves as a distribution point for example applications that make use of these specifications.

3. *alphaWorks* also serves as a proving ground in which experimental new XML technologies are introduced and evaluated. User feedback is monitored directly by the research and development staff, and updated according to the comments supplied by users.
4. Finally, the site offers a variety of tools and components that provide a bridge between the XML and Java spaces.

65.2.1 *XML at alphaWorks*

The list of emerging XML technologies on *alphaWorks* is already quite long and growing almost daily. Rather than try to list all of them, we'll briefly describe a representative selection. Those marked [On CD] are included on the accompanying CD, along with others that aren't discussed here.

DataCraft [On CD]
A set of components that enable a user to visually navigate XML and RDF schemas, generate a set of query skeletons from the schemas, and apply them in a variety of ways (including via a Web browser interface) to a relational database server.

Data Descriptors by Example [On CD]
A Java component library for inferring a DTD or Schema from a set of XML instances. The components support several control parameters that allow users to direct the derivation of the generated content models and attribute definitions.

LotusXSL [On CD]
A Java implementation of an XSLT processor that tracks the W3C specification. It is designed to be used either as a stand-alone application, as a submodule of a larger application, or within an applet or servlet. In addition to supporting the standard DOM 1.0 API, it can also be configured to generate streaming SAX output.

P3P Parser [On CD]
A Java implementation of a Platform for Privacy Preferences (P3P) protocol parser and constructor. It contains the classes necessary

to parse, generate, manipulate, and evaluate P3P proposals and responses. A specific implementation of a parser and evaluator for APPEL (A P3P Preference Exchange Language) is also included.

PatML [On CD]
An experimental XML document pattern matching and replacement processing engine. While similar to XSLT in its usage of rule-based specifications, it also allows for the specification of conditional predicates in *Java*.

RDF for XML [On CD]
A *Java* implementation of an RDF processor that enables the creation, query, and manipulation of RDF structures. The package also supports the ability to read and write the RDF structures in XML.

Speech Markup Language
A selection of components for processing Speech Markup Language, an XML language for building network-based conversational (using spoken input and output) applications. A conversationally enhanced browser is included among the several demonstration applications that are provided.

techexplorer Hypermedia Browser
An application for the interactive publication and exploration of scientific and technical documents. Available as both a browser plug-in and a standalone application, techexplorer enables the display of TeX documents and the MathML Mathematical Markup Language.

TexML [On CD]
A package containing a DTD for describing a document in the TeX format and a processor, TeXMLatte, that converts a TeXML document into TeX for the generation of high-quality print output. Intended to be used with XSLT, the TeXML system provides a simple and convenient method for completing the path from XML data to high-quality printed output.

Xeena [On CD]

A DTD-driven XML editor. Using a visual, tree-oriented editing paradigm coupled with a context-sensitive palette of elements, Xeena provides an intuitive, self-validating, mechanism for viewing and editing XML documents.

XML BeanMaker [On CD]

A tool that simplifies *Java* access to XML documents by building upon the generic DOM interface. The XML BeanMaker automatically generates get, set, and notification methods for a set of *Java* classes that correspond to the set of XML element types and attributes defined in a DTD.

XML Parser for C++ (XML4C) [On CD]

A validating XML parser written in a portable subset of C++. Implemented as a single shared library, it provides classes for parsing, generating, manipulating, validating, and emitting XML documents.

XML Parser for Java (XML4J) [On CD]

A configurable XML parser written in *Java*. The package contains classes for parsing, generating, manipulating, validating, and emitting XML documents. The package is designed in a modular fashion so that a variety of specially configured parsers can be constructed.

XML Security Suite [On CD]

A collection of XML security capabilities that provide, or can be used to build, additional protection to XML documents beyond that afforded by SSL. The current version of the suite also includes a reference implementation of the DOMHASH canonical digest value for XML documents, as well as sample applications that illustrate its use for digital signatures, element-wise encryption, and access control.

XML Translator Generator [On CD]

A tool that automatically generates specialized translators capable of converting XML documents from one DTD to another. The

©2000 The XML Handbook™

translators are generated from instances of documents conforming to each of the DTDs.

XML Treediff [On CD]

A package of *JavaBeans* that can efficiently compute the structural differences in DOM trees, generate an XML representation of the differences, and apply those differences to update a copy of the source DOM to that of the target.

XML Bean Suite

A set of more than three dozen documented *JavaBeans* that provide a comprehensive set of functionality for manipulating XML content. These beans can be readily integrated into applications directly or via inclusion in visual builder environments.

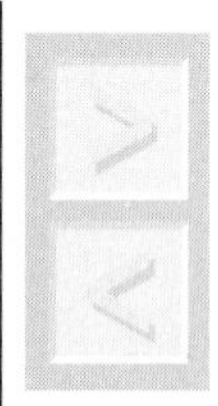

Tip *You can visit the alphaWorks site,* `http://www.alphaWorks.IBM.com`*, to engage IBM researchers and developers at the earliest stages of development and to download the latest software.*

65.3 | An eXtravagance of free XML software

To make this list, software has to be genuinely free, worthwhile XML software. That means:

- It must have substantial XML-oriented functionality; no graphics packages, file utilities, or other general-purpose filler.
- It must let you do useful processing of your own documents. If you are taking the trouble to install and learn it, you should get some benefit from it.
- It can't have a time limit on its use. As above: you should be the one to decide when it's no longer interesting.

- Most of all, it's got to be pretty good stuff! Some of it is proven code that rivals the best ever written for speed and stability. Other packages are promising newcomers.

You'll find fuller descriptions of everything on the CD-ROM, along with hyperlinks to the vendor's website for the latest versions of the programs that you like. The descriptions here are just to give you the flavor and, of course, they apply only to the version on the CD.

65.3.1 *Parsers and engines*

This category includes XML parsers, parsing toolkits, HyTime engines and DSSSL engines.

65.3.1.1 Architectural forms engines

XAF

XAF is an architectural forms engine which offers a SAX 1.0 interface to the transformed document. XAF can be used with any SAX 1.0 parser. Only a subset of architectural forms is supported and this release is at beta level.

xmlarch.py

xmlarch.py is an architectural forms engine written in Python that works with any SAX 1.0 parser and offers a SAX 1.0 interface to the processed documents. It is also possible to receive architectural document events for several architectures in one parse pass.

65.3.1.2 XLink/XPointer engines

Parser for XPointer

Is is an XPointer parser developed with the JavaCC parser generator. So far it does no more than just parse XPointers, and does not attempt to actually locate any nodes in a document.

PyPointers

PyPointers is a Python implementation of the XPointer locator language. It contains a general XPointer parser and an implementation that locates DOM nodes using PyDOM.

XPointers for PSGML/Emacs

This is a small Elisp package that adds support for automatically creating XPointers in the PSGML editing package for Emacs.

XLink SAX Parser Filter

The XLink SAX Parser Filter is based on John Cowan's Parser Filters and provides a simple way to extract XLinks from a SAX event stream for later use.

65.3.1.3 XSL engines

SAXON

See under XML middleware.

XT

xt is an XSL engine that implements the tree construction and transformation half of the XSL 19990421 draft. It is at beta level, but coming from James Clark that means it's probably rather stable and reliable. It can be used with any SAX 1.0 parser.

Koala XSL Processor

This is an XSL processor written in Java, that uses the SAX 1.0 and DOM standard APIs. Any SAX parser and DOM implementation can be used, and a SAX parser and the Docuverse DOM SDK come with the processor. It is unclear which Working Draft of XSL the processor implements.

FOP

FOP is a Java application that takes an XML document conforming to the formatting half of the XSL 19990421 Working Draft and produces PDF output. This way it can be used with any SAX 1.0 parser to produce PDF from XML + XSL. FOP can be invoked from the command line and read from a file, or it can be given a DOM document or a SAX DocumentHandler at run-time.

xsl:p

XSLP is a free Java XSL processor that implements the tree construction half of the 19981216 XSL WD.

4XSL

4XSL is an XSL processor implemented in Python on top of 4DOM. It is currently an alpha release. A version of 4DOM comes with the engine.

Xport

Xport is an XSL engine provided as a COM object, and thus accessible from most programming languages under Windows.

65.3.1.4 DSSSL engines

Jade

Jade is James Clark's excellent DSSSL engine, which is really a general SGML tool for conversion from SGML to other SGML DTDs or to output formats like RTF and TeX. Jade can process XML documents and can also output XML. Jade uses SP to parse the SGML/XML input.

65.3.1.5 SGML/XML parsers

SP

SP is an SGML/XML parser, and is fast, complete, highly conformant and very stable. SP has been the parser of choice for most of the SGML community for many years and has been embedded in lots of other applications. SP supports architectural forms as well as SGML Open catalogs.

SGMLSpm

SGMLSpm is a Perl script that reads ESIS output (from parsers like SP) and offers an event-based interface to the parser. As long as the parser can parse XML this also works for XML.

SPIN_py

SPIN is a C module that can be compiled into the Python interpreter to provide an interface to the SP SGML parser.

SPIN_tcl

SPIN is a C module that can be compiled into the tcl interpreter to provide an interface to the SP SGML parser.

65.3.1.6 XML parsers

expat

expat is a non-validating parser written in C, and is the parser previously known as XMLTok. It is used in Mozilla 5.0 and in parser modules for several different scripting languages.

TclXML

This is a validating XML parser written entirely in tcl. The parser offers both event-based and tree-based interfaces, and with Tcl 8.1 it supports Unicode.

XP

XP is written to be fully-conforming and as fast as possible, with an emphasis is on server-side production use. There is no validation, only well-formedness checking. Even though 0.5 is a beta release it is very stable and extremely fast. A SAX 1.0 driver is included. XP supports several Unicode encodings.

XML::Parser

This is James Clark's expat C parser wrapped as a Perl module that can be compiled into the Perl interpreter. This version adds support for XML namespaces.

Pyexpat

This is James Clark's expat C parser module wrapped up as a Python module. This means that by compiling this into the Python interpreter (which is much easier than it sounds) one can have a fast C parser available from within Python. The interface is non-standard, but a SAX 1.0 driver is available.

Lark

Lark was one of the two first XML parsers to appear, written by XML spec co-editor Tim Bray, but was non-validating for a long time. Tim Bray has now added Larval, a validating parser, to the package.

Ælfred

Ælfred is designed to be small and fast, especially intended for use in Java applets (uses only two .class files). It has a non-standard interface, but comes with a SAX 1.0 driver. Ælfred also handles a large number of different Unicode encodings.

sgmlop

sgmlop is a C replacement module for the sgmllib and xmllib parsers that come with the standard Python distribution. The author claims that sgmlop is 6 times faster than the Python originals.

xmlproc

xmlproc is a validating parser written in Python. It implements nearly all of the XML Recommendation, including XML namespaces. (The home page lists the deviations.) xmlproc provides access to DTD information and also offers a DTD parsing module. xmlproc supports SGML Open catalogs and XCatalog. xmlproc can report errors in Norwegian and English and can easily support other languages as well.

xmllib

The xmllib parser is part of the Python 1.5 distribution. The version included here is a newer version than the one in the standard distribution. xmllib is non-validating, but a fairly

©2000 The XML Handbook™

complete well-formedness parser with a simple and intuitive interface. A SAX 1.0 driver is available in saxlib.

RXP

RXP is a thread-safe validating parser written in C. It is distributed as C source and must be compiled before use. It supports Unicode and XML namespaces and comes with a command-line application that prints out the parsed document. RXP is also available as part of the LTXML package. RXP also supports the ISO 8859-1 to ISO 8859-9 character encodings.

Windows Foundation Classes

WFC is a collection of C++ classes for Windows programming. Included are a non-validating XML parser as well as other tools for working with XML documents. The parser has been tested on Unix too.

TclExpat

TclExpat is the expat C XML parser wrapped as a Tcl module. Version 1.1 uses the final 1.0 version of expat.

SXP

SXP is a validating Java XML parser developed as part of the Silfide project. SXP supports XML namespaces (REC 14.Jan.99) DOM 1.0 level 1 (REC 01.Oct.98), XPointer (WD 03.Mar.98) and XLink (WD 03.Mar.98). SXP has both non-standard and SAX 1.0 interfaces.

Expat Module for Ruby

This module wraps up James Clark's expat parser for access from within the Ruby interpreter. (Ruby is an object-oriented scripting language.) It also has a DOM 1.0 implementation and XPointer support.

XML Parser Component for Delphi

This is an XML parser written in Delphi that parses XML documents into an element tree that can then be modified and traversed. The component also allows programs to build XML tree structures and write them out as an XML document. There is also a package for Borland C++ Builder users.

libxml

libxml is an XML parser written in C that builds an in-memory DOM 1.0 tree of the parsed document. It is used by the GNOME project, among others.

fxp

fxp is a validating XML parser written in Standard ML, a functional programming language in the ML family. fxp has a programming interface, and comes with some example command-line applications. It has only been tested with the Standard ML of New Jersey compiler under Unix, but might well work elsewhere as well. fxp supports XCatalog.

OpenXML

OpenXML is a validating XML parser written in Java, with both SAX 1.0 and DOM 1.0 support. OpenXML also supports XCatalog. It can also parse HTML and supports the HTML parts of the DOM.

Whisper

Whisper is a general-purpose application framework written in C++, Whisper contains (among many other things) a validating XML parser with support for Unicode.

eXML

eXML is James Clark's expat parser wrapped into the Eiffel programming language. (Eiffel is an industrial-strength object-oriented language with many features beyond what Java and C++ offer.) eXML also implements a tree-building package on top of the wrapped expat parser.

Microsoft XML Parser Redistributable

The Microsoft XML Parser is a COM component that can be accessed from any COM-aware application in any programming language. The parser is validating and supports the DOM 1.0,

XML namespaces, XSL, querying and XML schemas. The parser requires Microsoft Internet Explorer.

Perl libxml

The Perl libxml includes the Perl version of SAX 1.0, PerlSAX (a special Perl version of SAX), a SAX driver for XML::Parser, a SAX driver that can read ESIS output from SP and XML::Grove integration code.

Tony

Tony is a lightweight XML parser written in the functional programming language Objective CAML. It claims to be much smaller than most other XML parsers, but is not complete. Tony comes with an advanced configurable pretty-printer.

HaXml

HaXml is a collection of libraries for using XML in Haskell. This includes a non-validating XML parser, an HTML parser, a library for transforming XML documents (and generating HTML) and special modules for building Haskell data structures from XML documents and dumping them back out as XML. HaXml supports Unicode if the Haskell compiler does.

65.3.1.7 DOM implementations

Docuverse DOM SDK

The Docuverse DOM SDK is a Java implementation of the Document Object Model (DOM 1.0) that uses any SAX 1.0 client (just use the SAX package and any of the parsers you like) to build the DOM document tree. The DOM builder part of the implementation is very general, so one can extend it to use other kinds of builders as well. The DOM SDK also supports the DOM HTML API.

TclDOM

TclDOM is a 100% Tcl implementation of the DOM 1.0. The aim is to create a standard Tcl version of the DOM to be used with any DOM implementation/parser.

4DOM

4DOM is a Python implementation of the final DOM 1.0 specification that supports CORBA (but does not require you to use an ORB). 4DOM uses saxlib to parse XML files.

XML::DOM

XML::DOM is an object-oriented Perl module that implements the DOM 1.0 recommendation. It uses Clark Cooper's XML::Parser to parse documents, and is also available through CPAN.

InDelv Java DOM

The InDelv Java DOM is a DOM 1.0 implementation written in Java. It can use any SAX 1.0 parser to build a DOM.

InDelv Smalltalk DOM

The InDelv Smalltalk DOM is a DOM 1.0 implementation written in Smalltalk, and comes with a non-validating Smalltalk XML parser with a SAX-like interface.

65.3.1.8 XML middleware

These are general software packages for making XML-aware applications of some form.

saxlib

saxlib is a Python translation of the SAX 1.0 parser interface. It has drivers for xmllib, xmlproc, Pyexpat, sgmlop and for the XML-Toolkit parser. There are also two demo applications: saxdemo.py, which produces canonical XML output and saxtimer.py, which measures the time used to parse a document with an empty document handler.

SAX

SAX is a simple event-based API for XML parsers. It is not an official standard, since it was developed by the participants of the xml-dev mailing list instead of a standards body. However, SAX is very much a de facto standard, since it is supported by at least 13 parsers, has been translated to Python and is used by at least 3 other applications.

SAX drivers for Lark and MSXML

This is a package consisting of two SAX 1.0 drivers for two Java parsers that do not support SAX natively, namely Lark and the now obsoleted Microsoft parser.

XML::Grove

XML::Grove uses XML::Parse to build a tree structure from the parsed document that programs can access and change. Similar to DOM, that is, but non-standard.

SAXON

SAXON is a Java interface for processing XML documents optimized for XML->XML/SGML/HTML conversions. SAXON is built on top of SAX 1.0 and DOM 1.0, and should work with any compliant implementation of these. SAXON gives you a nice interface to element handlers and some element handlers for the most common tasks. In addition SAXON supports most of the 21.Apr.99 XSL WD (with some extensions) and allows for the integration of XSL and Java code to perform specific tasks.

Docuverse HTML SDK

The Docuverse HTML SDK is an SDK for working with HTML using standard XML interfaces. There is a SAX 1.0 driver for the Swing HTML parser and a DOMReader that can be used to read HTML documents into the Docuverse DOM SDK.

ExCost

ExCost is an extension to the SGML Cost system that allows XML documents to be loaded into Cost directly using the expat parser, without having to parse them into ESIS files first.

Parser Filters

The ParserFilters are classes that wrap SAX 1.0 parsers in classes that provide SAX 1.0 parser interfaces. This allows for the development of extra services layered on top of ordinary parsers.

DOMParser

The DOM Parser is a SAX 1.0-compliant parser that turns a DOM Document into a SAX event stream, instead of parsing an XML document.

XSL-Pattern

XSL-Pattern is a pure Python implementation of the XSL pattern language that can be used to locate nodes in a DOM tree. It is built on top of PyDOM.

MDSAX

MDSAX is a toolkit built on SAX that makes it easier to work with parser filters. MDSAX should work with any SAX 1.0 parser. It comes with several filters, including John Cowan's Parser Filters and XAF.

XML::XQL

This is Enno Derksen's implementation of the XML Query Language (XQL) proposal. (Note: XQL is not XML-QL) XML::XQL is an object oriented Perl module that uses XML::DOM and XML::Parser underneath. The module is still beta code. See the Web page for links to the XQL proposal, tutorials etc.

Cocoon

Cocoon is a Java servlet that can be used to publish XML on the Web as HTML. It tries to establish a three-layer framework for this, with the three layers being content (i.e. XML source documents), style (i.e. XSL style sheets) and a so-called logic sheet.

tmproc

tmproc is a Python implementation of Topic Maps (ISO 13250), a standard for creating navigational indexes on large sets of documents. tmproc requires saxlib and can also be used with xmlarch if architectural processing is wanted.

MDServlet

MDServlet is a Java servlet that wraps the MDSAX framework, making it easy to use this for Web publishing of XML documents. MDServlet is highly configurable, with a large number of parameters.

GMD-IPSI XQL Engine

The GMD-IPSI XQL engine is a Java implementation of the W3C-QL'98 workshop paper syntax of XQL, based on a persistent thread-safe DOM implementation. The PDOM can be built from XML documents using a SAX 1.0 parser.

XML::Writer

XML::Writer is a Perl module which makes it easier to generate correct XML output from Perl. It has intelligent support for XML namespaces and will automatically generate prefixes (although this can be controlled, if desired).

XML::QL

XML::QL is a Perl implementation of the proposed XML-QL XML query language (note: this is not XQL), built directly on top of XML::Parser.

CGI::XMLForm

CGI::XMLForm is a Perl module that extends CGI.pm to create custom XML from HTML form input and can also create HTML form values based on XQL-like queries of XML data. CGI::XMLForm uses XML::Parser.

Python XML package

The Python XML package is a package of various Python XML tools that has been put together by the Python XML Special Interest Group, a group of volunteers led by Andrew M. Kuchling, for the convenience of Python XML developers. The package contains saxlib, a HOWTO document, Pyexpat, a Python implementation of the DOM 1.0 and xmlarch.py. A module for serializing and deserializing Python objects into XML is also included, as well as a number of demos.

Xml2Beans

Xml2Beans reads XML DTDs and generates a JavaBean for each element that can process XML according to the DTD. With specialized bean editors (not yet available) it will be possible to make application-specific editors for any DTD.

65.3.2 *Editing and composition*

These are tools for interactive creation, modification and composition of XML documents.

65.3.2.1 XML editors

JUMBO2

JUMBO is an XML browser/editor which displays documents in several different ways without using a style sheet. It is meant to be a core which can be extended to support new XML-related standards. JUMBO is built on SAX 1.0 and can use any SAX-compliant parser.

PSGML

Emacs is easily one of the most powerful (if not the most powerful) text editors in the world. It has an internal Lisp programming language, which means that new modes are easy to write, and as a consequence Emacs has modes for most programming languages ever invented, as well as a Web browser with CSS (and budding DSSSL) support and a world-class news reader.

Visual XML

Visual XML is an XML editor written in Java with JFC (Swing). It lets you edit a tree view of the XML document.

XED

XED is a simple XML editor written in C, Python and Tk. It tries to ensure that the author cannot write a document that is not well-formed and reads the DTD in order to be able to suggest valid elements to be inserted at any point in the document.

Amaya

Amaya is the W3C testbed browser, and is an HTML and XHTML browser (and editing tool) with CSS support. It also supports the MathML XML DTD and can edit and display presentational MathML graphically.

XML Notepad

XML Notepad is an XML editor that lets you work with a tree-based view of your XML document. XML Notepad ensures that documents produced with it are well-formed, and if MSIE 5 is installed it will also validate the document when it is loaded into the editor. No validation is performed during editing.

sxml-mode

sxml-mode is a simple extension to the Emacs PSGML mode that adapts it for XML editing. sxml-mode comes with an XML parser and a SAX 1.0 application for validating XML documents from within Emacs. sxml-mode can be used with any validating XML parser (in Java) that has a SAX driver.

EXml

EXml is a non-validating editor which provides both a source view and a tree view of the document being edited. In the tree view, the data content of elements is displayed beside the tree, making the editor easier to use.

Emilé

Emilé is an XML editor that reads the DTD to provide short-cuts for the user during editing. Emilé can export documents as HTML.

65.3.3 *Control information development*

These tools are for creating, modifying and documenting DTDs, XSL style sheets etc.

65.3.3.1 DTD editors

ezDTD

ezDTD is a DTD editor that tries to make DTD editing a bit simpler. It stores DTDs in its own format (with metadata), but can import arbitrary DTDs. It can export DTDs into HTML and save them as either SGML (with minimization info) or XML (without).

tdtd

This is an Emacs major mode for editing DTDs. It does syntax coloring, has some convenience macros for inserting commonly-typed constructs as well as ETAGS integration. It is a stand-alone mode, but works well together with PSGML.

65.3.3.2 DTD generators

xml2ddml

These are two OmniMark scripts that convert XML DTDs to DDML schema documents.

FirstSTEP EXML

FirstSTEP EXML is a tool that can convert from product data declarations in the EXPRESS language (part of the STEP standard for product data) into XML DTDs. STEP data can then be represented in XML using this DTD.

65.3.3.3 DTD documenters

perlSGML

perlSGML is a collection of Perl tools for working with SGML, but they also work with XML. Included are DTD documentation tools, a DTD diff tool and several useful related libraries.

DTDParse

See under DTD parsers.

©2000 The XML Handbook™

65.3.3.4 DTD parsers

xmlproc
See under XML parsers

DTDParse
DTDParse is a Perl module that can parse a DTD into an in-memory structure. This structure can then be used in various kinds of programs that need DTD information. It comes with several scripts that can produce DTD documentation using this module.

65.3.4 *Document Storage and Management*

These are tools for supporting document management, such as document databases and search engines.

65.3.4.1 XML document management utilities

Xtract
Xtract is a document search tool with a query language loosely based on XQL. Xtract can handle both HTML and XML documents. It is currently at beta level.

65.3.5 *Conversion*

These tools are for scripted (i.e., automated and non-interactive) creation and modification of XML documents.

65.3.5.1 General S-converters

XML converters (or "S-converters") are tools for automated processing of XML documents.

Ace

Ace is a scripting language for processing SGML and XML documents. It's a full strongly-typed programming language, with garbage collection and user-defined types. Source code is not available.

xtr2any

xtr2any is a general-purpose XML down-conversion tool that can be used to convert to (in theory) any format. It uses a configuration file that describes the mappings that are to take place and runs as a command-line application. The free version has a limit on the number of elements it can process, but no other limits.

TransformXML

TransformXML is a simple tool for doing XML transformations, either in batch mode or using a GUI. It's written in Visual Basic and interprets a very simple script language which can do simple transformations.

XTAL

XTAL is a general Java package for XML conversions, and has a general architecture consisting of frontends (which read data in) and backends that produce output. Currently there is only an XML frontend and XML and TeX backends. More will probably be developed. XTAL uses a declarative language for specifying transformations, but can also be extended using Java.

65.3.5.2 Specific N-converters

These are tools whose purpose is to generate XML according to a specific document type from non-XML source documents.

RTF2XML

RTF2XML (formerly known as RTF2SGML) reads RTF files and converts them to an XML document corresponding to an XML DTD that comes with RTF2XML. RTF2XML supports Unicode RTF. RTF2XML is written in OmniMark and so requires OmniMark to run.

SiRPAC

SiRPAC is the W3C RDF reference implementation that parses the XML representations of RDF into the triple data model, to be used in applications. SiRPAC can be run as a command-line tool or embedded in Java applications. SiRPAC uses SAX 1.0 to parse documents, which means that it can work with nearly any Java XML parser.

XML Convert

XML Convert is a general tool for converting from flat files (sequences of records) into XML. It uses a flat file schema language called XFlat schemas to describe the structure of the flat files. The converted files will use the XFlat DTD (which is not the same as an XFlat schema).

65.3.5.3 General N-converters

Non-XML converters (or "N-converters") are designed for converting from non-XML representations (typically word-processing formats) to XML.

Majix

Majix is an RTF-to-XML converter written entirely in Java. It can handle RTF styles and also lets you customize it to fit your own XML DTDs.

Tidy

Tidy is a tool that can read your XML and HTML markup and detect and to some extent also fix errors in it. This can be used to clean up bad HTML and XML and also to convert from poor HTML to XML. Tidy can also pretty-print your markup.

DB2XML

DB2XML is a tool for generating XML from database queries. It is a GUI-driven application written in Java, but can also be used as a servlet and as a command-line application. The XML generated is configurable, and metadata (types etc.) can optionally be included, dates can be customized and currency representation can be localized. DB2XML can generate external and internal DTDs for the XML produced, and can also handle binary data (either included in the generated XML file or externally). It can also handle different character encodings and primary keys.

Some2XML

Some2XML is a Perl script that can convert text files (with some internal structure) into XML, given a set of conversion rules. The conversion rules can contain Perl code.

XML::DT

XML::DT is a Perl package for simplifying down-translation from XML into some other format, for example LaTeX or HTML. XML::DT uses mapping rules that map element type names to Perl handler functions.

65.3.6 *Electronic delivery*

These are tools for electronic delivery and display of XML documents.

65.3.6.1 XML browsers

Amaya

See under XML editors.

Mozilla

This is version 5 of Netscape Navigator, which can display XML documents with CSS style. Please note that this is not even an alpha release, and so is relatively unstable.

Jumbo

Jumbo was the first XML browser to appear, but does not support stylesheets, so documents are currently shown in a tree view. (There is built-in support for some DTDs, notably CML.) Jumbo is not delivered with a parser, but installing a parser with a SAX (not 1.0) driver in your class path will automatically enable Jumbo to parse XML documents.

Plume

Plume is a Web browser written in tcl using Tk for the user interface. Plume has an experimental XML parser extension, which allows it to display a tree view of XML documents. Plume already supports CSS stylesheets, but so far only with HTML.

HyBrick

HyBrick is a general SGML/XML browser that uses James Clark's SP parser to display SGML/XML documents with DSSSL style sheets. Jade is used for the DSSSL processing, but it has been extended to handle the scroll flow objects as well. HyBrick supports subsets of both XLink and XPointer, both on the local file system and over the network.

InDelv XML Browser

The InDelv XML Browser is an XML browser written in Java that uses XSL stylesheets to display the documents.

65.4 | The XML SPECtacular

The CD includes a collection of the relevant standards and specifications that you can browse, search, and print. There is a brief description of each.

For each document, we've included a link to a website where you can learn more about the underlying project and obtain the latest version of the spec. Where copyright and production considerations allowed, we've also included a browseable copy on the CD-ROM.

In this listing, we've only included brief summaries of specs for which the full text exists on the CD.

65.4.1 *W3C base standards*

The following standards are either approved W3C Recommendations or are in development.

XML: Extensible Markup Language

Here it is: the XML standard itself. For a standard it is mercifully short and readable, and nicely unambiguous. This is definitely recommended reading!

Namespaces in XML

This standard enables XML element-type names to be globally unique. This can be used in many ways, such as to mix elements from different vocabularies in a single document, as RDF and XSL do.

DOM1: Document Object Model - level 1

The DOM is an important XML standard that is often used to implement many of the others. It describes a standardized API for accessing, manipulating and building XML and HTML document structures in memory, and is often the basis for implementations of XSL, XPointer, XQL and many other standards. It is also intended to be used by browsers and editors.

DOM2: Document Object Model - level 2

This DOM specification extends the DOM level 1 with constructs for handling namespaces, style sheets, events, filters and iterators and ranges.

RDF: Resource Description Framework - Model and Syntax Specification

RDF promises to become an important part of the infrastructure of the Web in the future. It provides a framework for describing resources on the Web and as such holds great promise of providing new means of navigation on the Web and better guidance for Web robots.

RDF: Resource Description Framework Schemas

This RDF specification builds on the RDF syntax and data model specification and provides a schema syntax for RDF models.

XPath: XML Path Language

XPath is a language for addressing and querying the content of XML documents. XPath is used in both XSLT and XPointer. It is a very important standard.

©2000 THE XML HANDBOOK™

XLink: XML Linking Language

XLink is a crucial part of the XML standards family as it describes hyperlinking in XML documents and takes major steps beyond the hyperlinking provided by HTML.

XPointer: XML Pointer Language

XPointer is a companion standard to XLink that describes mechanisms for addressing a particular part of a document.

XML Fragment Interchange

This standard describes how to exchange fragments of XML documents while retaining interesting parts of the context of the fragment, such as the DTD reference, ancestor information for the fragment, etc.

XML Information Set

This standard is much more important than it may seem at first glance. The XML recommendation itself only describes a syntax for representing the data in XML documents, but an actual data model for XML documents is not provided there. And, when you think about it, the only reason we have the syntax is to enable us to exchange documents and then recreate the data described by the document inside our systems and programs. And this is what the XML Information Set provides: a formal data model for XML documents.

XML Schema Part 1: Structures

This is perhaps one of the most important standards in the set of XML-related standards. XML 1.0 already has DTDs, which can be used to define what particular types of XML documents can and cannot contain. Schemas go beyond the features offered by DTDs in order to offer functionality required in the many new areas where XML is currently being used.

XML Schema Part 2: Datatypes

This specification provides the features used to define the datatypes of element content and attribute values. This can be used to declare that an element contains dates or URLs, and similarly for attributes. Although datatypes are part of the work on schemas, they can also be used in DTDs. (There is open source software on the CD-ROM that supports such use.)

XSL: Extensible Stylesheet Language

This is another important standard which provides a means of rendering XML documents in a way that is optimized for end-users of the information. This can be as visually formatted documents or as aurally formatted documents destined for text-to-speech synthesis.

XSLT: XSL Transformations

XSLT is an XML-based language for describing transformations on XML documents. This can be used to convert between XML document types, to HTML or to XSL flow objects as described in the XSL standard.

Associating stylesheets with XML documents

This very simple standard describes how to reference a style sheet from an XML document in a stylesheet-language- and application-independent way. A necessary reference.

CSS2: Cascading Style Sheets - level 2

CSS is the style sheet standard that is implemented in browsers today and can be used right now. It is simple, but effective and elegant. Software that can support CSS-based display of XML is already here and more should be just round the corner.

65.4.2 *W3C XML applications*

These application standards are either approved W3C Recommendations or are in development.

SMIL: Synchronized Multimedia Integration Language

SMIL is an XML application that can be used to integrate a set of multimedia objects into a coherent presentation, complete with hyperlinks and synchronization.

MathML: Mathematical Markup Language

MathML is the long-awaited solution to a problem many scientists and teachers have struggled with: how to publish mathematical formulae on the Web. It also provides a solution for exchanging formulae between programs.

XHTML: The Extensible HyperText Markup Language

XHTML is a reformulation of HTML 4.0 in XML syntax, and is intended to be the basis for further work on HTML. This work is likely to consist of both a modularization of XHTML as well as extensions to it.

SVG: Scalable Vector Graphics

SVG is an XML application that can be used to describe two-dimensional vector graphics, text and raster images. This allows for styling images with style sheets, and hyperlinking into (and out of) images.

65.4.3 *Other specifications*

These standards are developed by industry consortia, collaborations of several vendors, or informal user groups.

SAX1: Simple API for XML 1.0

SAX is a general event-based API for XML parsers. Using SAX enables application programmers to write applications that are parser-independent.

XMLNews

XMLNews is a set of specifications for exchanging news items, and allows optional richness of markup. There are two specifications: XMLNews-Story which is a document type for news stories, and XMLNews-Meta which is a document type for news story metadata records.

XSA: XML Software Autoupdate

XSA is an XML-based system for automatically discovering new releases of software products. Software developers publish an XSA document which describes all their software products, and list maintainers and other interested parties poll these documents to discover new releases and address changes.

©2000 The XML Handbook™

Other XML-related books

Resource Description

- Program development with XML
- DTDs and schemas
- XML reference
- An awesomely unique XML/SGML application
- Knowledge management
- Learning the foundations of XML

©2000 THE XML HANDBOOK™

Chapter 66

This chapter was written by Charles, based on material from his website, All the XML Books in Print™, `http://www.xmlbooks.com`.

Ed Mosher, Ray Lorie, and I invented the first structured markup language in 1969, IBM's Generalized Markup Language (GML). It led to SGML, HTML, XML, and countless applications and variations on the theme.

But strangely, considering that markup is for documents, for the first two decades in which the markup language concept was gaining its now universal acceptance, hardly any books were published on the subject. (Amazingly, a few survivors of that period are in Amazon.com's current retail database, including a few ancient IBM product manuals. I never tried to find out what would happen if someone actually attempted to order one.)

Well, the last two years have more than made up for the first two decades. When we went to press, my website, All the XML Books in Print, listed more than 65 titles. I won't repeat them all here, but I will describe the ones I recommend most highly.

These are the books from the Open Information Management series that I edit for Prentice-Hall PTR, and its Definitive XML sub-series, in which The XML Handbook appears.

XML isn't HTML with a capital X. It requires new ways of thinking about Web content. The authors of these books have gotten the message and know how to share it with you. I recruited them personally for my book series because I know they are genuine experts. We worked together to make their books accurate and clear, which is why I am able to recommend the books from personal knowledge.

Of course, the book you are now reading is my recommendation for an introduction to XML. It focuses on what XML is and what it can do for you, but it doesn't purport to tell you how to go about doing it. For that, there are more specialized books.

66.1 | Program development with XML

Contrary to misuse in the popular press, and by some experts who ought to know better, XML isn't a programming language. It is a markup language, of course, and that means it's a data description language. You use normal programming languages, including scripting languages, to develop XML applications. These books show you how.

XML by Example: Building E-Commerce Applications

Sean McGrath / 1998

Also published in Japanese and Portuguese.

This book will teach you XML application programming from the ground up, all the while developing a full-blown e-commerce application. Programmers can learn the XML language from this book as well.

Designing XML Internet Applications

Michael Leventhal, David Lewis, Matthew Fuchs / 1998

On the other hand, if you need to put an internet app together in a hurry – and the word "hack" doesn't offend you – here's your book.

66.2 | DTDs and schemas

Nature abhors a schema-less database equally as much as she abhors a vacuum. Create a data table in a spreadsheet and the program will immediately search for field names, and supply them even if you fail to. Although XML will let you create a document without an explicit formally-written schema (also known as a "document type definition", or DTD), the benefits of having one are enormous. These books make the job easy, whether you write out the DTD using XML markup declarations, or one of the proposed new schema languages.

Structuring XML Documents
David Megginson / 1998
Also published in Japanese.
This book covers the fundamentals of good DTD design, illustrated by popular industry DTDs. It also has full coverage of architectural forms, which allow object-oriented development of XML DTDs.

The XML and SGML Cookbook: Recipes for Structured Information
Rick Jelliffe / 1998
On the other hand, if you're looking for specific proven techniques for an enormous variety of DTD challenges, plus a definitive exposition on dealing with Asian languages, you'll want this book.

66.3 | XML reference

XML: The Annotated Specification
Robert Ducharme / 1999
Japanese translation in preparation.
After you've gotten a working knowledge of XML from our other books, you'll want this one on your shelf for referencing the details. It is an annotated edition of the official XML spec, with over 170 new usage examples.

66.4 | An awesomely unique XML/ SGML application

TOP SECRET Intranet: How U.S. Intelligence Built Intelink – The World's Largest, Most Secure Network

Frederick Thomas Martin / 1998

If you've wondered how spies would use XML, how they could share information securely on a vast international network – and how you could apply their techniques to your own – now you can find out. This is the first book ever to describe an ongoing U.S. Intelligence operation.

66.5 | Knowledge management

Knowledge is more than information or data, it exists only in the minds of the knowledgeable and in properly-designed computer files. While most knowledge management books concentrate on the management of the knowledge acquisition and dissemination processes, the books listed here focus on the overlooked but vital task of knowledge retention: How do you keep the enterprise from forgetting what it has learned?

SGML Buyer's Guide:? A Unique Guide to Determining Your Requirements and Choosing the Right SGML and XML Products and Services

Charles F. Goldfarb, Steve Pepper, Chet Ensign / 1998

Don't let the title of this book put you off. There are at least three books packed into these 1200 pages, and the first of them is about knowledge retention. Specifically, it shows how you can manage documents and other persistent information to minimize information loss, optimize reuse, and reduce costs. (The second "book" shows how to evaluate XML and SGML products and services, while the third is a directory of the XML and SGML industry.)

SGML: The Billion Dollar Secret

Chet Ensign / 1997

If your enterprise, like most, has an enormous investment in unmanaged knowledge – such as word processing files and desktop publishing data – you'll want this book. It contains fascinating case studies of household-name companies who've applied SGML to knowledge retention, and saved billions in the process.

66.6 | Learning the foundations of XML

XML is a proper subset of SGML and the XML Recommendation is much shorter than the SGML International Standard. But the subsetting isn't the only reason for the shorter document. The XML spec is written for parser implementors and deliberately doesn't discuss applications, philosophy, style, alternatives, and other usage issues. I don't claim that you need to learn SGML in order to use XML, but I think it would help you use it better.

SGML on the Web: Small Steps Beyond HTML
Yuri Rubinsky, Murray Maloney / 1997
Here is an engaging, friendly, rich, yet simple hands-on guide to SGML. All the exercises are on the CD-ROM, along with a fully-licensed, fully-functional, commercial-quality browser to view them with.

The SGML Handbook
Charles F. Goldfarb / 1991 / Oxford University Press
On the other hand, if you really must know every detail of SGML, here is the official ISO Standard, annotated by yours truly (who is also the Project Editor of the Standard). I've added a structured overview of the complete language that introduces every term and concept in context. This book has been in print for nine years and was the essential reference used by the W3C Working Group when designing XML.

Tip *You can find Charles' up-to-date list of* All the XML Books in Print *at* `http://www.xmlbooks.com`.

Index

A

B

C

E

I

J

N

U

V

Y

LICENSE AGREEMENT AND LIMITED WARRANTY

READ THE FOLLOWING TERMS AND CONDITIONS CAREFULLY BEFORE OPENING THIS SOFTWARE MEDIA PACKAGE. THIS LEGAL DOCUMENT IS AN AGREEMENT BETWEEN YOU AND PRENTICE-HALL, INC. (THE "COMPANY"). BY OPENING THIS SEALED SOFTWARE MEDIA PACKAGE, YOU ARE AGREEING TO BE BOUND BY THESE TERMS AND CONDITIONS. IF YOU DO NOT AGREE WITH THESE TERMS AND CONDITIONS, DO NOT OPEN THE SOFTWARE MEDIA PACKAGE. PROMPTLY RETURN THE UNOPENED PACKAGE AND ALL ACCOMPANYING ITEMS TO THE PLACE YOU OBTAINED THEM FOR A FULL REFUND OF ANY SUMS YOU HAVE PAID.

1. GRANT OF LICENSE: In consideration of your payment of the license fee, which is part of the price you paid for this product, and your agreement to abide by the terms and conditions of this Agreement, the Company grants to you a nonexclusive right to use and display the copy of the enclosed software program (hereinafter the "SOFTWARE") on a single computer (i.e., with a single CPU) at a single location so long as you comply with the terms of this Agreement. The Company reserves all rights not expressly granted to you under this Agreement.

2. OWNERSHIP OF SOFTWARE: You own only the magnetic or physical media (the enclosed CD-ROM) on which the SOFTWARE is recorded or fixed, but the Company retains all the rights, title, and ownership to the SOFTWARE recorded on the original CD-ROM copy(ies) and all subsequent copies of the SOFTWARE, regardless of the form or media on which the original or other copies may exist. This license is not a sale of the original SOFTWARE or any copy to you.

3. COPY RESTRICTIONS: This SOFTWARE and the accompanying printed materials and user manual (the "Documentation") are the subject of copyright. You may not copy the Documentation or the SOFTWARE, except that you may make a single copy of the SOFTWARE for backup or archival purposes only. You may be held legally responsible for any copying or copyright infringement which is caused or encouraged by your failure to abide by the terms of this restriction.

4. USE RESTRICTIONS: You may not network the SOFTWARE or otherwise use it on more than one computer or computer terminal at the same time. You may physically transfer the SOFTWARE from one computer to another provided that the SOFTWARE is used on only one computer at a time. You may not distribute copies of the SOFTWARE or Documentation to others. You may not reverse engineer, disassemble, decompile, modify, adapt, translate, or create derivative works based on the SOFTWARE or the Documentation without the prior written consent of the Company.

5. TRANSFER RESTRICTIONS: The enclosed SOFTWARE is licensed only to you and may not be transferred to any one else without the prior written consent of the Company. Any unauthorized transfer of the SOFTWARE shall result in the immediate termination of this Agreement.

6. TERMINATION: This license is effective until terminated. This license will terminate automatically without notice from the Company and become null and void if you fail to comply with any provisions or limitations of this license. Upon termination, you shall destroy the Documentation and all copies of the SOFTWARE. All provisions of this Agreement as to warranties, limitation of liability, remedies or damages, and our ownership rights shall survive termination.

7. MISCELLANEOUS: This Agreement shall be construed in accordance with the laws of the United States of America and the State of New York and shall benefit the Company, its affiliates, and assignees.

8. LIMITED WARRANTY AND DISCLAIMER OF WARRANTY: The Company warrants that the SOFTWARE, when properly used in accordance with the Documentation, will operate in substantial conformity with the description of the SOFTWARE set forth in the Documentation. The Company does not warrant that the SOFTWARE will meet your requirements or that the operation of the SOFTWARE will be uninterrupted or error-free. The Company warrants that the media on which the SOFTWARE is delivered shall be free from defects in materials and workmanship under normal use for a period of thirty (30) days from the date of your purchase. Your only remedy and the Company's only obligation under these limited warranties is, at the Company's option, return of the warranted item for a refund of any amounts paid by you or replacement of the item. Any replacement of SOFTWARE or media under the warranties shall not extend the original warranty period. The limited warranty set forth above shall not apply to any SOFTWARE which the Company determines in good faith has been subject to misuse, neglect, improper installation, repair, alteration, or damage by you. EXCEPT FOR THE EXPRESSED WARRANTIES SET FORTH ABOVE, THE COMPANY DISCLAIMS ALL WARRANTIES, EXPRESS OR IMPLIED, INCLUDING WITHOUT LIMITATION, THE IMPLIED WARRANTIES OF MERCHANTABILITY AND FITNESS FOR A PARTICULAR PURPOSE, EXCEPT FOR THE EXPRESS WARRANTY SET FORTH ABOVE, THE COMPANY DOES NOT WARRANT, GUARANTEE, OR MAKE ANY REPRESENTATION REGARDING THE USE OR THE RESULTS OF THE USE OF THE SOFTWARE IN TERMS OF ITS CORRECTNESS, ACCURACY, RELIABILITY, CURRENTNESS, OR OTHERWISE.

IN NO EVENT, SHALL THE COMPANY OR ITS EMPLOYEES, AGENTS, SUPPLIERS, OR CONTRACTORS BE LIABLE FOR ANY INCIDENTAL, INDIRECT, SPECIAL, OR CONSEQUENTIAL DAMAGES ARISING OUT OF OR IN

CONNECTION WITH THE LICENSE GRANTED UNDER THIS AGREEMENT, OR FOR LOSS OF USE, LOSS OF DATA, LOSS OF INCOME OR PROFIT, OR OTHER LOSSES, SUSTAINED AS A RESULT OF INJURY TO ANY PERSON, OR LOSS OF OR DAMAGE TO PROPERTY, OR CLAIMS OF THIRD PARTIES, EVEN IF THE COMPANY OR AN AUTHORIZED REPRESENTATIVE OF THE COMPANY HAS BEEN ADVISED OF THE POSSIBILITY OF SUCH DAMAGES. IN NO EVENT SHALL LIABILITY OF THE COMPANY FOR DAMAGES WITH RESPECT TO THE SOFTWARE EXCEED THE AMOUNTS ACTUALLY PAID BY YOU, IF ANY, FOR THE SOFTWARE.

SOME JURISDICTIONS DO NOT ALLOW THE LIMITATION OF IMPLIED WARRANTIES OR LIABILITY FOR INCIDENTAL, INDIRECT, SPECIAL, OR CONSEQUENTIAL DAMAGES, SO THE ABOVE LIMITATIONS MAY NOT ALWAYS APPLY. THE WARRANTIES IN THIS AGREEMENT GIVE YOU SPECIFIC LEGAL RIGHTS AND YOU MAY ALSO HAVE OTHER RIGHTS WHICH VARY IN ACCORDANCE WITH LOCAL LAW.

ACKNOWLEDGMENT

YOU ACKNOWLEDGE THAT YOU HAVE READ THIS AGREEMENT, UNDERSTAND IT, AND AGREE TO BE BOUND BY ITS TERMS AND CONDITIONS. YOU ALSO AGREE THAT THIS AGREEMENT IS THE COMPLETE AND EXCLUSIVE STATEMENT OF THE AGREEMENT BETWEEN YOU AND THE COMPANY AND SUPERSEDES ALL PROPOSALS OR PRIOR AGREEMENTS, ORAL, OR WRITTEN, AND ANY OTHER COMMUNICATIONS BETWEEN YOU AND THE COMPANY OR ANY REPRESENTATIVE OF THE COMPANY RELATING TO THE SUBJECT MATTER OF THIS AGREEMENT.

Should you have any questions concerning this Agreement or if you wish to contact the Company for any reason, please contact in writing at the address below. Robin Short Prentice Hall PTR One Lake Street Upper Saddle River, New Jersey 07458 USA

About the CD-ROM

The CD-ROM is packed with useful XML tools and information. A full description can be found in "Resources" on pages 950-985.

There are three main areas:

- A hand-picked collection of genuine, productive, no-time-limit XML-centric free software. There are over 125 titles.
- A showcase for leading XML software and service providers. It features in-depth product and service information, white papers, XML samples, live demos, and trialware.
- The XML SPECtacular, a collection of the relevant specifications that you can browse, search, and print.

How to use the CD-ROM

The CD-ROM is just another drive on your Windows 95/98 or Windows NT computer. No special installation is necessary. Just do this:

1. Start your Web browser.
2. Select "Open File" from the File menu.
3. Type "d:\index.htm" as the file name, where "d" is your CD-ROM drive.

License Agreement

Use of the The XML Handbook CD-ROM is subject to the terms of the License Agreement and Limited Warranty on the preceding pages.